www.wadsworth.com

wadsworth.com is the World Wide Web site for Wadsworth and is your direct source to dozens of online resources.

At *wadsworth.com* you can find out about supplements, demonstration software, and student resources. You can also send email to many of our authors and preview new publications and exciting new technologies.

wadsworth.com
Changing the way the world learns®

Human Relations in Business

DEVELOPING INTERPERSONAL AND LEADERSHIP SKILLS

Michael G. Aamodt
Radford University

Bobbie L. Raynes
New River Community College

WADSWORTH

™

THOMSON LEARNING

Australia • Canada • Mexico • Spain • United Kingdom • United States

WADSWORTH

THOMSON LEARNING ™

Psychology Editor: Marianne Taflinger
Assistant Editor: Annie Berterretche
Marketing Manager: Jenna Opp
Signing Representative: Jody Hornick
Project Editor: Trudy Brown
Print Buyer: Karen Hunt
Permissions Editor: Joohee Lee
Production Service: The Book Company

Text Designer: Carolyn Deacy Design
Copy Editor: Pat Brewer Editorial Service
Illustrator: EmSpace Artwork
Cover Designer: Carolyn Deacy Design
Cover Image: Nicholas Wilton
Cover Printer: Von Hoffmann Graphics
Compositor: Thompson Type
Printer: Von Hoffmann Graphics

For permission to use material from this text, contact us by
Web: http://www.thomsonrights.com
Fax: 1-800-730-2215
Phone: 1-800-730-2214

ExamView® and *ExamView Pro®* are registered trademarks of
FSCreations, Inc. Windows is a registered trademark of the
Microsoft Corporation used herein under license. Macintosh and
Power Macintosh are registered trademarks of Apple Computer,
Inc. Used herein under license.

Library of Congress Cataloging-in-Publication Data

Aamodt, Michael G.
    Human relations in business: developing interpersonal and
leadership skills / Michael G. Aamodt, Bobbie L. Raynes.
        p. cm
    Includes index.
    ISBN 0-534-35508-0
        1. Communication in management. 2. Interpersonal commun-
    ication. 3. Supervision of employees. 4. Customer relations.
    5. Self-management (Psychology) I. Raynes, Bobbie.
    II. Title.

HD30.3 .A225 2001
658.3'145—dc21
                                    00-036339

Wadsworth/Thomson Learning
10 Davis Drive
Belmont, CA 94002-3098
USA

For more information about our products, contact us:
Thomson Learning Academic Resource Center
1-800-423-0563
http://www.wadsworth.com

International Headquarters
Thomson Learning
International Division
290 Harbor Drive, 2nd Floor
Stamford, CT 06902-7477
USA

UK/Europe/Middle East/South Africa
Thomson Learning
Berkshire House
168-173 High Holborn
London WC1V 7AA
United Kingdom

Asia
Thomson Learning
60 Albert Street, #15-01
Albert Complex
Singapore 189969

Canada
Nelson Thomson Learning
1120 Birchmount Road
Toronto, Ontario M1K 5G4
Canada

This edition is dedicated to the memory of John M. Mann, our dear friend and a role model for effective human relations at work

Brief Contents

Contents

SECTION II
Keys to Working With Others

CHAPTER 8
■ UNDERSTANDING GROUP INTERACTION 253

CHAPTER 9
■ GETTING OTHER PEOPLE TO LIKE US 275

Keys to Leading and Managing Others

CHAPTER 13

■ DEVELOPING OTHERS: ORGANIZATION DEVELOPMENT 403

CHAPTER 14

■ PERSUADING AND INFLUENCING OTHERS 437

CHAPTER 15

■ COMMUNICATING EXPECTATIONS 457

Preface

Interpersonal effectiveness is about understanding and managing behavior—primarily your own. Through the management of your own behavior, you may be able to change or coach others into more effective behavior. Why is this important? Because the most important activity that will remain constant in your life is the development of new relationships or the preservation of current important relationships. Whether these relationships are personal (e.g., between a parent and child) or professional (e.g., between supervisors and employees), to ensure success, you need two major ingredients:

- Knowledge about people in general: how they perceive the world in which they live, how they perceive you, and how their experiences affect who they are, what they think, and how they behave.

- The skills to take that knowledge and apply it to your own behavior so that the interactions between you and others is as effective and appropriate as possible.

Our purpose in writing this text is to ensure that you have both of these key ingredients to be successful in your everyday interactions with coworkers, employers, friends, and family members. The skill-building information in this textbook is especially important in today's world, as organizations become increasingly more diverse. You cannot be successful in life without the support and help of other humans. We hope that as you read this book you will become stronger in your interactions with others.

■ FEATURES OF THE TEXT

To maximize your ability to learn about human relations and to apply what you have learned, this book contains several features:

- Each chapter begins with a list of **Chapter Objectives** so that you can see what you will be able to do by the end of each chapter.

- Each chapter contains **projects** to help you apply what you have learned. Some of these projects are free-writes that allow you to think about how a topic relates to your life. Other projects contain psychological measures such as personality tests, career interest inventories, and leadership style tests. After you have completed and scored these tests, you will have gained insight into your personality, interests, behavior, strengths, and weaknesses. All of the projects are on perforated paper so it will be easy to tear them out—either to turn in to your instructor or to keep as a personal profile.

- **Quick Projects** ask you for a short answer regarding upcoming material and are meant to stimulate your thinking on the topic.

- Each chapter concludes with a **Chapter Recap** that provides an overview of what you have just read and **Critical Thinking Questions** to test your knowledge.

- At the end of each chapter, **Key Terms** and a **Practice Exam** should be useful in studying and reviewing the main concepts in the chapter.

- **Web Sites** give you URLs for exploring specific topics further.

We have done our best to make this book enjoyable to read by including humor, anecdotes, stories, and examples. To make reading easier, when using singular examples we used masculine pronouns (e.g., he, his, him) in the even-numbered chapters and feminine pronouns (e.g., she, her, hers) in the odd-numbered chapters.

Human Relations in Business includes the text, workbook, and study guide under one cover with a large, soft-cover format. The price for this integrated text, workbook, and study guide is less than the price of a new hard-cover text by itself. And the text is perforated to make it easier for you to turn in assignments.

■ STRUCTURE AND OBJECTIVES OF THE TEXT

To help you master human relations, this book is divided into three sections: managing yourself, working with others, and managing others. The chapters in Section I will help you be a more effective person and employee. By the end of Section I, you will:

- better understand your own behavior as well as the behavior of others
- be more able to manage stress, change, and personal problems
- be better able to effectively manage your time
- understand the importance of ethics and professionalism

The chapters in Section II will help you work better with the people you encounter daily in your life and in your job. By the end of Section II, you will:

- be better able to understand and work with diverse groups of people
- be more able to deal with the inevitable conflicts that occur when working with others
- have a better understanding of how to communicate effectively with others
- have a better understanding of group dynamics
- have increased skills in getting others to like you (impression management)

The chapters in Section III can help you in two ways. One, if you currently manage or lead others (e.g., as a supervisor at work, an officer in a civic club, a little league coach) or plan to manage or lead others later in your career, the chapters in Section III will teach you how to be a more effective leader. If you never plan on becoming a manager or a leader, the chapters in Section III will provide you with insight into your manager's thinking. By the end of Section III, you will:

- understand what makes an effective leader
- know how to make a job more satisfying
- know how to motivate, develop, and persuade others
- know how to communicate expectations so that others will know what you want of them

■ RESEARCH CITATIONS AND RESEARCH TERMS

We have been careful to ensure that what we wrote is supported by research. Throughout the book, you will see research citations with the author's name and the year of the study. The citations are there to support what we wrote and to provide you with a reference should you desire further reading on a topic. When a citation appears dated (e.g., Asch, 1958), it is because we are listing either a classic study on a topic or the first researchers to study a topic. Rest assured that recent studies have been conducted that still support the original research.

Two research terms will be used throughout the book: correlation and meta-analysis. We will discuss these terms briefly, to ensure that when you come across them, you will know what we are talking about.

Correlation

Throughout this text, you will see the term *correlation*. For example, in Chapter 11 we will discuss the correlation between job satisfaction and performance, and in Chapter 2 we will discuss the correlation between stress and work performance.

Correlation is a statistical procedure that allows a researcher to determine the *relationship* between two variables: for example, the relationships found between an employment test and future employee performance, or job satisfaction and job attendance, or performance ratings made by workers and supervisors. It is important to understand that correlational analysis does not necessarily say anything about causality.

The result of correlational analysis is a number called a **correlation coefficient** (usually denoted r). The values of this coefficient range from 0 to $+1$ and from 0 to -1. The further the coefficient is from zero, the greater the relationship between two variables. That is, a correlation of .40 shows a stronger relationship between two variables than a correlation of .20. Likewise, a correlation of $-.39$ shows a stronger relationship than a correlation of $+.30$. The $+$ and $-$ signs indicate the *direction* of the correlation. A positive $(+)$

correlation means that as the values of one variable increase, so do the values of a second variable. For example, we might find a positive correlation between intelligence and scores on a classroom exam. This would mean that the more intelligent the student, the higher her score on the exam.

A negative ($-$) correlation means that as the values of one variable increase, the values of a second variable decrease. For example, we would probably find a negative correlation between the number of beers that you drink the night before a test and your score on that test. In human relations research, we find negative correlations between job satisfaction and absenteeism, age and reaction time, and nervousness and interview success.

Why does a correlation coefficient not indicate a cause and effect relationship? Because a third variable, an **intervening variable,** often accounts for the relationship between two variables. Take the example often used by psychologist David Schroeder. Suppose there is a correlation of $+.80$ between the number of ice cream cones sold in New York during August and the number of babies that die during August in India. Does eating ice cream kill babies in another nation? No, that would not make sense. Instead, we look for that third variable that would explain our high correlation. In this case, the answer is clearly the summer heat.

Another interesting example was provided by psychologist Wayman Mullins in a presentation about the incorrect interpretation of correlation coefficients. Mullins pointed out that data show a strong negative correlation between the number of cows per square mile and the crime rate. With his tongue firmly planted in his cheek, Mullins suggested that New York City could rid itself of crime by importing millions of head of cattle. Of course, the real interpretation for the negative correlation is that crime is greater in urban areas than in rural areas.

As demonstrated above, a good researcher should always be cautious about variables that seem related. A few years ago, *People* magazine reported on a minister who conducted a "study" of 500 pregnant teenaged girls and found that rock music was being played when 450 of them become pregnant. The minister concluded that because the two are related (that is, they occurred at the same time), rock music must cause pregnancy. His solution? Outlaw rock music and teenage pregnancy would disappear. However, suppose that we conducted our own study and found that in all 500 cases of teenage pregnancy, a pillow also was present. To use the same logic as that used by the minister, the real solution would be to outlaw pillows, not rock music. Although both "solutions" are certainly strange, the point should be clear: Just because two events occur at the same time or seem to be related does not mean that one event or variable causes another.

Meta-Analysis

Another term you will encounter throughout the text is meta-analysis. A meta-analysis is a statistical method for combining the results of several studies into one overall result. That is, instead of separately discussing 20 different studies on a topic, the results of the 20 studies can be combined into one number. For example, suppose that we report that a meta-analysis shows that the correlation between job satisfaction and performance is .19. What this means is that even though some studies might have shown a small relationship between job satisfaction and performance and some might have shown a big relationship between the two variables, when we combine all of the studies ever conducted on the topic, the correlation between the two is .19—a relatively small relationship. The beauty of meta-analysis is that it provides a "final word" on a topic. That is, instead of arguing that five studies show one thing and five studies show another thing, a meta-analysis combines all studies and gives us one overall number. This overall number is depicted either as a correlation coeffient (r) or an effect size (d).

■ ACKNOWLEDGMENTS

We are grateful to the excellent staff at Wadsworth/ Thomson Learning including Marianne Taflinger, Annie Berterretche, Suzanne Wood, Jenna Opp, Trudy Brown, copyeditor Pat Brewer and at the production service, Dustine Friedman. The quality of the text was greatly enhanced by the thoughtful responses of reviewers, including Steve Brown, DeVry Institute of Technology; Kathryn Cid, Lincoln Technical Institute; David Cooper, University of Tennessee at Marin; Nicholas DiMartina, Bryant & Stratton College; Jay Hollowell, Bryant & Stratton College; W. George Jones, Danville Community College; Melodye Lembo, Education America-Fort Worth Campus; Raul Martinez, South Texas Community College; James Pickens, Tulsa Community College; Karen Rosa, Education America-Little Rock Campus; Jan Sesser, High-Tech Institute Inc.; Carol Walters, Quest Education Corporation; Jim Watkins, Concorde Career Colleges, Inc.; Blaine Weller, Baker College.

We would also like to thank our family, friends, and students for accommodating our time spent writing and for all their ideas and support. We appreciate our colleagues Mark Nagy, Nora Reilly, Bruce Brown, and Michael Surrette who patiently allowed us to bounce ideas off them, vent, and ask dumb questions. Thanks also to our APA, SIOP, IPMA, IPMAAC, and SHRM colleagues for their insight and stories.

Michael G. Aamodt
Bobbie L. Raynes

About the Authors

Since 1983, **Michael G. Aamodt** has been a professor of Industrial/Organizational Psychology at Radford University in Radford, Virgina. He received his B.A. in Psychology from Pepperdine University in Malibu, California and both his M.A. and Ph.D. from the University of Arkansas.

As a teacher, Mike teaches courses in employee selection, psychology of work behavior, job analysis, employee training and development, social psychology, forensic psychology, organizational psychology, and introductory psychology. Mike has received teaching awards at both the University of Arkansas and Radford University.

As a researcher, Mike has published 37 articles in professional journals and presented more than 75 papers at professional conferences. In addition to coauthoring this text, he is the author of *Applied Industrial/Organizational Psychology,* now in its third edition, and also published by Wadsworth. Mike is the associate editor for the *Assessment Council News,* the associate editor for the *Journal of Police and Criminal Psychology,* and the editor of *Applied H.R.M. Research.*

As a trainer and consultant, Mike has helped a wide variety of organizations deal with such issues as employee selection, performance evaluation, downsizing, organizational change, compensation, and motivation.

Mike is active in a variety of professional organizations. He is the past president of the Society for Police and Criminal Psychology, a board member for the International Personnel Management Association Assessment Council (IPMAAC) and for the New River Valley SHRM chapter, and a member of SHRM, IPMA, SIOP, APA, and the Academy of Management.

In his spare time, Mike likes to make lame attempts at being athletic, cook what at times turn out to be edible meals, travel, and SCUBA dive. He lives in Pulaski, Virginia with his wife Bobbie, son Josh, three neurotic dogs (Astrud, Ally, and Sydney),and a three-legged cat named Ilean.

Bobbie L. Raynes received her B.G.S. in Organizational Communication and her M.S. in Corporate and Professional Communication from Radford University.

After spending 8 years as an administrator in the public sector, Bobbie became the Director of Training and Development for Personnel Research Associates, Inc.. Bobbie's main responsibilities include:

- Conducting conflict mediation sessions and teaching mediation skills
- Conducting career assessments and career advising for employees
- Delivering training workshops on a wide variety of topics including conflict management, dealing with angry and difficult people, stress management, time management, diversity issues, and job search skills
- Working with law enforcement agencies to select the best employees

Bobbie serves as an adjunct instructor for New River Community College in Dublin, Virginia and for Radford University. As an instructor, Bobbie teaches courses in Organizational Behavior, Human Resource Management, Continuous Quality Improvement, and Supervision at New River. At Radford, she teaches Psychology of the Work Place. In addition to teaching, Bobbie has published four research articles and presented eight research papers at professional conferences.

In her leisure time, Bobbie likes to read, compete with her neighbors to see who can grow the best flowers, SCUBA dive, and travel. Bobbie's community activities include serving as a rape crisis companion for the Women's Resource Center in the New River Valley, as a mediator for the Conflict Resolution Center in Roanoke, VA, and as a member of the Virginia Mediation Network.

CHAPTER ONE

Understanding Yourself and Others

■ UNDERSTANDING HUMAN RELATIONS

There are few aspects of life that do not involve interacting with other people. The extent to which you are skilled in handling these interactions, often called *human relations,* will greatly influence your success in life. Successful human relations have never been easy, but four recent changes to the workplace promise to make human relations more challenging.

1. As you will see in Chapters 8 and 13, *an increasing number of organizations require employees to work as teams, rather than as individuals.* This change has greatly increased the amount of human interaction and skill required of an employee.

2. As you will see in Chapter 5, *the workforce is becoming more diverse.* Whereas the American workplace of 50 years ago was overwhelmingly White and male, White males will have become the minority by the year 2000. This increase in workforce diversity demands that successful people understand how to relate to a wide variety of people and cultures.

3. *The workforce is becoming more dynamic.* Fifty years ago, the norm was for people to stay in one geographic area their entire lives and work for just one organization during their entire careers. However, in the workplace of the 21st century, the norm is to change jobs every 5 years. These changes often involve establishing new interpersonal relationships both at work and at home.

4. *Jobs are becoming more complex.* Rather than being expected to perform one task at a high level, employees are now expected to be proficient in a variety of areas including basic business skills, core job skills, and human relations skills. As a result of these new expectations, there are few jobs in which human relations are not an important factor.

What could possibly have caused serial killer Arthur Shawcross to murder 2 children and 14 prostitutes? Why is Jesse Jackson so energetic? Where did David Letterman get his sense of humor? Why is Elizabeth Dole such a good leader? Why is Dennis Rodman so . . . different? When you are able to understand why people act they way they do, it makes it easier to interact with them. For example, you are less likely to think someone is "impossible" if you know how the environment in which a person is raised can affect behavior. You will be less likely to label a person from the North *rude* when you learn that what would be considered rude in the South is appropriate behavior for other regions. Having this knowledge about behavior will help you work better with your coworkers and peers, as well as better understand your friends and family.

This chapter will answer *some* of the questions posed above by discussing where people get the personalities, attitudes, and values that, ultimately, explain some of their behavior—behavior that you might find "different." By the end of this chapter, you will:

> Understand the factors that influence our predispositions toward certain behaviors
>
> Understand the importance of learning on our behavior
>
> Understand the importance of situational factors affecting behavior
>
> Better understand why people behave the way they do

When asked why people behave the way they do, life would be simple if we could provide one answer that covers every person and every behavior; for example, if we could say such things as "Serial killers murder because they were abused as children" or "People are extroverts because their parents were extroverts." Unfortunately, humans are very complex and no one variable completely explains all behavior.

As shown in Exhibit 1-1, people's behavior is a function of three main influences: the genetic, physiological, and learning factors that predispose them to behave in certain ways; the situational factors that encourage or discourage behavior; and the reasoning process, including the factors that affect our ability

■ EXHIBIT 1-1

Factors Influencing Behavior

| Predisposing factors | + | Situational factors | + | Reasoning process | = | Behavior |

EXHIBIT 1-2

Factors Affecting Our Personality, Values, and Attitudes

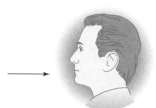

Physiological factors
Gender
Birth order
Childhood trauma
Developmental era
Illness and disability
Rewards and punishments
Significant emotional events
Culture
Hometown
Genetics
Physical appearance
Race

Personality, values, and attitudes

---

to think and decide how we will behave in a given situation.

> **Focused Free-Write**
> To get you thinking about who you are and why you are that way, complete the Focused Free-Write at the end of this chapter.

It is important to understand that people can do the same things for different reasons. For example, one person might become a serial killer primarily because she was sexually abused as a child whereas another person might become a serial killer primarily because she had several head injuries. It is also important to understand that most people who were sexually abused do not become serial killers nor do most people with head injuries. Each of the many factors discussed in the following pages is a potential contributor to certain types of behaviors.

■ PREDISPOSING FACTORS

In any given situation, people bring with them a predisposition to behave in a certain way. This predisposition arises from an individual's personality, temperament, values, or attitudes. For example, Bob might be an introvert who goes into every social situation with the predisposition to being quiet. Sue, a natural leader, goes into every meeting with the inclination for taking charge. Although in some situations Bob might become very talkative and Sue might become

a follower, each has certain traits that predispose them to act a particular way in most situations. As shown in Exhibit 1-2, many factors influence our personalities, values, and attitudes. Though there are probably hundreds of reasons for these predispositions, the following pages will focus on some of the most important and interesting.

Genetic Influences

Several decades ago, psychologists believed that people were born with a blank slate and that their personalities, values, and attitudes were determined solely by their environment. Psychologists now acknowledge the important effect of **genetics** on human behavior. That is, to some extent, we are born with a predisposition to be a certain type of person. For example, research indicates that about 60% of intelligence, 30% of personality, 40% of the tendency to be satisfied and happy in life, 50% of criminality, 70% of severe depression, and 45% of schizophrenia are genetic. Notice that none of these percentages is 100—no behavior is entirely genetic. However, as shown in Exhibit 1-3, the range from 30% to 90% indicates that we can thank (or curse) our parents for a considerable portion of who we are.

How do scientists determine what percentage of human behavior is genetic? The answer lies in twin studies. In twin studies, scientists compare the similarity of identical twins on some variable (e.g., intelligence, personality) with the similarity of fraternal twins on the same variable. The reasoning behind this is that **identical twins** emerge from one **zygote** (a fertilized egg) and thus have a 100% genetic overlap

EXHIBIT 1-3

How Much of Our Behavior Is Due to Genetics?

Characteristic	% that is genetic
Height (Plomin, 1994)	90
Major depression and affective disorders	70
Intelligence (Snyderman & Rothman, 1987)	60
Divorce (Jockin et al., 1996)	55
Smoking (Azar, 1999)	50
Criminality (Raine, 1993)	50
Aggression (D. R. Miles & Carey, 1997)	50
Schizophrenia (Gottesman, 1991)	45
Personality (Bouchard, 1994)	30
Job satisfaction	40
Anxiety disorders (Torgersen, 1983)	30

whereas **fraternal twins** emerge from two separate zygotes and only have a 50% genetic overlap. Twin studies can be enhanced when we can compare identical and fraternal twins who were separated at birth and lived apart with identical and fraternal twins who lived together. To be technically correct, it is important to understand that 99% of the genetic makeup of any two individuals is identical. When we talk about how much of something is genetic, we are talking about the percentage of the remaining 1% of genetic makeup that is common between twins. Thus, identical twins share 100% of their genes, fraternal twins share 99.5% of their genes, unrelated siblings share 99%+ of their genes, and any two human beings share 99% of their genes.

> **PROJECT A** *Genetics*
> Are you like your parents? Complete Project A to determine the potential genetic influence in your own life.

Physiological Influences

HEAD INJURIES AND BRAIN ABNORMALITIES

The brain is a very sensitive structure, with various parts each playing important roles in human behavior. When a segment of the brain is damaged, it is not surprising that behavior can be affected. For example, research on aggression (cited in Raine, 1993) has shown that more than 80% of death row inmates had serious head injuries, 52% of wife batterers suffered a head injury, 61% of males with violent dating/marital behavior had head injuries, and 80% of violent inmates had some type of neurological impairment compared to 25% of nonviolent inmates.

The brain contains billions of small structures called **neurons,** which control behavior. These neurons communicate with one another through chemicals called **neurotransmitters.** Problems with neurotransmitters can affect a wide variety of behaviors. For example, shortages of the neurotransmitter acetylcholine is a contributing factor in memory loss and Alzheimer's disease, low levels of the neurotransmitter serotonin is related to aggression, and shortages of the neurotransmitter norepinephrine are associated with depression, whereas an overabundance of norepinephrine activity is associated with schizophrenia.

HORMONES

Hormones are chemicals released by the endocrine glands and are an important physiological factor affecting human behavior. For example, aggression increases after injections of male hormones (e.g., steroids). After the age of 25, both androgen levels (a male hormone) and rates of violent crime decrease. Not surprisingly, auto accident rates and consequently insurance rates drop at the age of 25.

AROUSAL LEVELS

An interesting theory proposed by psychologist Hans Eysenck (1964) is that humans strive to keep an optimal level of arousal. If we fall below our optimal level of arousal, we seek stimulation; if we rise above our optimal level, we avoid stimulation. According to Eysenck, our typical levels of arousal are related to our personality. Extroverts are people whose natural body state is one of underarousal. Thus, they seek social activities, conversation, parties, and events that will increase stimulation and raise their arousal to the optimal level. Introverts, however, are people whose natural body state is one of overarousal. Thus, to maintain the optimal level of arousal, they avoid the types of social stimulation that extroverts seek. This theory on the optimal level of arousal has been used to explain some aspects of criminal behavior.

DIET

The old expression "you are what you eat" actually has some validity. For example, although 90% of a person's height is genetically determined, the remainder is affected by diet. Diet is also related to a person's ability to maximize her intellectual functioning. That is, a healthy diet has been shown to increase memory, alertness, and decision making. According to Blaun (1996), for peak mental efficiency:

- Eat fish and eggs to increase levels of choline.
- Use canola, soy, and walnut oils to cook.
- Reduce cholesterol (triglyceride) levels.
- Eat fruits and vegetables.
- Use moderate levels of caffeine and sugar.
- Get a good supply of carbohydrates.
- Take vitamin E supplements.

Children and adults who have diets consistent with these suggestions think more clearly, have better memories, and make better decisions than their counterparts with diets that are not nutritionally balanced (Huijbregts et al., 1998; Walling, 1997). Such research argues strongly for the importance of school breakfast programs for nutritionally at-risk children (Pollitt, 1995).

Diet seems also to be related to violence. For example, aggressive behavior increases when blood sugar levels are low. Think about the last time you missed breakfast or lunch. What was your mood as you approached your next meal? Did you get a bit grouchy? Perhaps lose your patience or snap at someone? Interestingly, the symptoms for hypoglycemia (low blood sugar) peak from 11:00 a.m. to 11:30 a.m., as do assaults on inmates and prison staff.

Though low blood sugar levels are related to violence, so are high blood sugar levels. For example, one research study (Schoenthaler, 1982) reported a 48% reduction in discipline problems after switching delinquents to a diet of reduced sugar consump-

tion. In the 1970s, a person shot and killed the mayor of San Francisco and a city supervisor and then successfully claimed that his diet was responsible for his aggressive behavior. Using what was called the "Twinkie defense," Dan White argued in court that because of his passion for junk food, his body chemistry did not allow him to think clearly. The jury put enough stock in his defense that they found him guilty of voluntary manslaughter rather than first-degree murder.

Understanding the effects of diet is important. For example, we might see an employee increase her mistakes and attribute the reason to sloppy work, we might think a child is not very intelligent because she doesn't do well in school, or we might think a customer is a difficult person because she snapped at an employee. Though our attributions might be correct, it may be that the behavior of each of these individuals is partially affected by poor diet.

QUICK PROJECT

Compared to the proper diet discussed in this section, how would you evaluate what you eat?

_____

_____

_____

_____

Nutritionally balanced diets help reduce the effects of stress. As you will see in more detail in Chapter 2, the effects of stress can be reduced by eating fruits and vegetables and reducing caffeine and alcohol.

Physical Appearance

PHYSICAL ATTRACTIVENESS

Part of who we are is based on our physical attractiveness as research indicates that attractive people are more self-confident, have better social skills, and are lower in social anxiety than their less attractive counterparts (Feldman, 1998). Why is this so? Apparently, our level of physical attractiveness affects how we are treated by others. In infancy, attractive babies are held, cuddled, and kissed more than are unattractive babies. In childhood, attractive children have more friends; unattractive children are ridiculed more often; teachers rate attractive children as being smarter and more popular than unattractive kids with identical academic records; and attractive children who act out are not disciplined as often as unattractive children who act out. In adolescence, attractive teens have more dates.

In adulthood, attractiveness affects behavior in a variety of settings. In the workplace, attractive adults receive higher job interview scores and higher performance appraisal scores. In the legal system, attractive adults are sent to jail less often, are less likely to be detected and reported when they shoplift (Davis, 1991), receive more lenient sentences, and are committed to mental health facilities less often than are unattractive adults. In everyday life, attractive adults receive more help in emergencies than do unattractive adults.

When studying the effect of attractiveness on crime, Masters and Graves (1967) found that 60% of criminals had facial defects compared to 20% of controls. Furthermore, K. M. Thompson (1990) reviewed nine studies and found that in six, recidivism decreased after plastic surgery.

BODY TYPE

An interesting theory related to physical appearance was postulated by William Sheldon in the 1940s. Sheldon stated that there are three major body types—mesomorphs, ectomorphs, and endomorphs—and that each body type was associated with particular personality traits. **Mesomorphs** have an athletic, muscular build and are considered to be assertive, energetic, strong, brave, and confident individuals. **Ectomorphs** are thin and are thought to be shy, lonely, pensive, and introverted. **Endomorphs** are obese and are associated with the traits of being happy, sociable, lazy, affectionate, and jolly.

The key to properly understanding Sheldon's theory is to see that body type itself does not cause certain personality traits, but instead, that the way each of the body types is treated by others affects self-image, and consequently personality. For example, in junior high school, who is most likely to be picked on—the strong, athletic child or the skinny one? To gain the attention of the opposite sex, who would need to try hardest to develop an interesting personality, the person with an athletic build or the person who is obese?

Some research supports Sheldon's theory that people are treated differently based on their body type and that this differential treatment is related to personality. For example, research indicates that obese individuals are treated differently in employment interviews than are nonobese individuals (Pingitore, Dugoni, Tindale, & Spring, 1994; Volker, 1993); thin people are rated as being worse leaders than their larger counterparts (Young & French, 1998); and body type affects the way we perceive ourselves and the way we dress (Chowdhary, 1993).

Furthermore, studies have shown that, consistent with Sheldon's theory, athletes are more confident and dominant than nonathletes (Aamodt, Alexander, & Kimbrough, 1983; McWhirter, 1998).

Illness and Disability

People's personality, attitudes, and values can be influenced by illness or disability. However, as with much of what we have discussed in this chapter, illness and disability do not affect people in the same way. For example, a person who has had to overcome a serious childhood health problem might become an adult who is very sensitive toward others with serious health problems. Or the same illness might result in another person becoming intolerant as an adult, reasoning that "If I can overcome such a serious problem, so should everyone else." Thus, illness and disability unquestionably affect who we are, but research has not found a consistent way in which most people emotionally develop as the result of the illness or disability.

Though the effects of illness are not consistent, knowing that a person had a physical problem can help us gain insight into current behavior. For example, we have a friend who is very quiet, hates sports, and doesn't like to socialize in groups. But when we go out to dance, he never turns down an invitation. Why the contradiction? As it turns out, he had a serious leg injury when he was young, so serious that he was bedridden for almost 3 years. Instead of playing with other children, he read books. As his leg improved, he still wasn't able to play sports, so the doctors told him to take dance lessons to strengthen his legs and increase his coordination. So, with this piece of knowledge, a guy we thought was kind of odd turns out to be not so odd after all.

Learning Influences

DEVELOPMENTAL ERA

Psychologist Morris Massey developed an interesting theory that our values, attitudes, and personalities are partially determined by the decade in which we grew up. In Massey's theory (1975), each decade is marked by several important events that influence behavior—see Exhibit 1.4. For example, people who lived in the 1930s had to survive the Great Depression, a time of high unemployment, great poverty, and no unemployment insurance, no social security, and little public assistance. Many banks crashed, causing people to lose their life savings (bank deposits were not guaranteed then). Thus, many people struggled merely to survive!

Did such an event affect the values of this generation? To answer this question, think about the be-

EXHIBIT 1-4

Major Events Affecting Each Generation

Decade		Major events
1980s and 90s		Advent of chip technology End of the Cold War Movement to suburbs Race relations (Rodney King, O.J. Simpson trials) Conflicts with Iran and Iraq
1960s and 70s		Watergate Civil rights movement Vietnam conflict Shift from blue-collar to white-collar occupations Space exploration Decrease in family size
1950s		Advent of television Korean conflict Great economic boom Cold War begins
1930s and 40s		World War II Great Depression President Franklin D. Roosevelt and the New Deal Rise of labor unions
1910s and 20s		World War I Prohibition Advent of the automobile Population shift from rural to urban Typical work week dropped from 60 hours to 45 hours

haviors of your grandparents or great-grandparents who lived in the 1930s. Do they do strange things such as hide all their money under a mattress rather than put it in a bank? Do they save margarine containers, pieces of string, and jars? Do they refuse to use credit cards and ATM cards? If you answered yes, you have seen for yourself the effects of the Depression on the values of that generation.

Contrast those values with those of people raised in the 1980s and 1990s. These individuals can best be described as independent and easily bored. Why? Think about the independence aspect. Members of Generation X can order food (e.g., Domino's), shop (Internet), watch movies (e.g., cable, pay-per-view), play (video games, Internet), go to school (distance education programs), and go to work (telecommuting) without ever leaving the house. Thus, this generation is not unfriendly but prefers to work alone rather than in groups. This preference is important because, as you will see in later chapters, the increased use of teams in organizations is in direct contrast to the values of young employees.

In terms of being easily bored, think about how fast the world moves now. We used to be amazed that a letter could be sent from coast-to-coast in a week. Then came next-day delivery. Today, we can fax or e-mail information and have it across the world in seconds. When we were in sixth grade, we heard a rumor that they were about to market this thing you could put in your hand and solve math problems. This "thing" turned out to be a calculator and was an amazing advance. Compare our generation's excitement about a calculator with the current generation's knowledge and expectations about computer speed and use, and it is easy to see differences in generations.

Though Massey's ideas are generalities, they do make the case that the reason each generation thinks that the other generations are "strange" is because each generation experiences very different events. Thus, behavior that makes perfect sense to a person who experienced the Depression or World War II would seem odd to a person who has been surfing the net since childhood.

HOMETOWN

Another major contributor to our personality, attitudes, and values is the place where we grew up. Hometown influences include population size, geographic region (e.g., east versus west), and location (urban versus rural). For example, who would you predict would be more friendly, a person from the country or a person from the city? Most people respond that "country folk" are the most trusting and friendly. For example, when we ask our students if they lock their doors at night, not surprisingly, most of those who do not are from rural environments. Likewise, when asked who would pull over and help a stranded motorist, country folk are more likely to help. If these differences in behavior are true, could the traffic jams, high crime rates, noise, and crowding associated with urban life be the culprits?

What stereotypes do we associate with people from the Northeast? The South? California? Our guess is that it didn't take you long to think of such words as aggressive, slow, and laid-back. What adjustments do you think someone who grew up in a big city in California would have to make if she moved to a college town in the South?

Family

BIRTH ORDER

Another factor affecting personality is birth order. Though birth order does not account for a lot of our personality, research does indicate that it is a small, but consistent, contributor. For example, only children are high in intelligence and independent; firstborns (the oldest) are achievement oriented, perfectionist, conservative, conscientious, conforming, inclined toward leadership, competitive, and determined; middleborns are outgoing, have good social skills, and are good mediators; and lastborns are the most creative, are flexible, enjoy the limelight, have a good sense of humor, are risk takers, and are most likely to be rebels.

Why the personality differences based on birth order? The answer is most likely an interaction between sibling rivalry and parental behavior. Only children have no siblings with whom to compete and thus can be the sole focus of their parents' attention

and financial resources. Firstborns initially had that attention but then are forced to share it with new siblings. To maintain their share of attention, firstborns overachieve. At the same time, they realize the importance of being a role model and thus behave in a more conservative, conscientious manner. Middleborns must negotiate with their older siblings to not beat them up and with their younger siblings to not tattle on them! Thus, they learn better social and mediation skills. Younger-borns must compete with their older siblings for parental attention, and they receive the benefits of their parents' experience in raising children. That is, parents are still learning how to be good parents with their first few children, but by the time they reach their final children, they are not only worn out, but have also learned the "tricks of the trade."

QUICK PROJECT

Think about your own birth order. Are your personality and birth order consistent with the research?

_____

_____

_____

_____

CHILDHOOD TRAUMA

There is little question that such traumatic events in childhood as divorce, physical abuse, and psychological abuse can greatly impact one's personality, attitudes, and values. For example, an abundance of research has linked abuse in childhood to later criminal behavior (Widom, 1989) and psychological problems (Lang, 1997). As with most things in life, childhood trauma affects people in vastly different ways. For example, many children from broken homes grow up to be perfectly normal whereas others suffer from psychological problems or get into trouble with the law.

Operant Conditioning

As we go through life, our personality and behavior are shaped by **operant conditioning**—the rewards and punishments we receive. The basic idea behind operant conditioning is that we will continue to behave in ways that bring rewards and stop behaving in ways that are punished. If our jokes and stories are rewarded through attention, laughter, or social acceptance, we will be more likely to exhibit an outgoing personality than we would if the same behaviors were received by silence or inattention. Likewise, if we are rewarded for being late to class, meetings, or work (e.g., an increase in attention by teachers, parents, employers), we are not likely to develop the personality trait of being timely.

For example, Mike is not a person who likes to plan in advance. He packs for trips the morning his plane leaves, seldom makes hotel reservations in advance, and almost never makes "to do" lists. These behaviors drives his wife crazy! Why does he do them? Because he has yet to experience a negative consequence as a result of this lack of planning: He always finds a hotel, always gets packed on time, and usually gets his work done. If he starts missing planes or sleeping on the street, his behavior would quickly change.

Operant conditioning is an essential concept in understanding people. For behaviorists (people who strongly believe in the power of operant conditioning), if people behave in a certain way, they are somehow being rewarded for that behavior. If they are not behaving a particular way, they either are not being rewarded or they are being punished for that behavior. Thus, one of the keys to understanding people is to understand their reinforcement history. Were they punished or encouraged when they were talkative? Were they punished or rewarded when they took chances? Behaviorists believe that by properly using reward and punishment, even the most shy people can be turned into extroverts.

One of the difficult aspects of operant conditioning is that the same consequence can be a reward for one person and a punisher for another. For example, suppose that a student makes a comment in class that shows extraordinary insight. The professor is so excited that she compliments the student for several minutes. For many people, this attention would be rewarding and would result in continued comments in the future. However, for some people, such attention might be embarrassing as the student might be very shy or might be worried about being considered a teacher's pet.

An excellent example of this difference in what is rewarding comes from two friends of ours. One friend is short in stature and never received the acceptance he desired from his father. As a consequence, he values awards, certificates, and plaques. His walls at home are covered with every award and gold star he received since grade school! When he was asked to join a professional society, his first question was "Do I get a certificate?" The other friend has always been successful in life and places little value on rewards. His plaques and certificates, at least the few he has kept, are stuffed in a box in his closet, and he never

attends the annual company banquet in which service awards are given. For the one friend, we can get him to do anything by printing a certificate on the computer. For the other friend, we would need to provide cash!

Gender, Race, and Culture

As shown in Exhibit 1-5, peoples' personalities, attitudes, and behaviors are affected by their gender and race. Whether these effects are due to genetics, physiological factors, learning history, cultural differences, or discrimination is much debated. However, what isn't debated is the significant role that gender and race play in determining who we are. For example, census data indicate that compared to Whites, African Americans have lower incomes, graduate less often from college, and are less likely to own their own home. Compared to American males, females in the United States have lower incomes, live 6 years longer, and are less likely to smoke.

Racial differences can be found in many aspects of life. For example, racial differences are found not only in the sports we play (compare professional basketball and professional hockey) but in positions within the same sport (compare the race of most quarterbacks and running backs). Racial differences occur in the music we listen to (e.g., rap versus country), the television shows we watch (e.g., in 1998 the sitcom *Friends* was the 2nd highest rated show for White audiences but only the 125th most popular show for Black audiences), the food we eat, and the political candidates for whom we vote.

Likewise, gender differences are common in many aspects of life. A quick look at everyday life finds differences in the way we communicate (e.g., *Men Are From Mars, Women Are From Venus*), the television networks we watch (*ESPN* versus *Lifetime*), and the careers we choose (engineering versus nursing).

Cultural differences in human behavior are common as well. Two examples: the murder rate in the United States is much higher than in any of the European nations or Japan; conformity is higher in collectivist countries than in individualistic ones (e.g., United States, England).

Significant Emotional Events

Psychologists agree that events occurring in our early years have the greatest influence on personalities, values, and attitudes. In fact, Sigmund Freud theorized that our personality is pretty much set by the age of 7, and psychologist Morris Massey hypothesized that the age of 10 is key for learning values. Though psychologists don't agree on a specific age as being the

EXHIBIT 1-5

Influence of Race—Percentage Differences in Five Areas

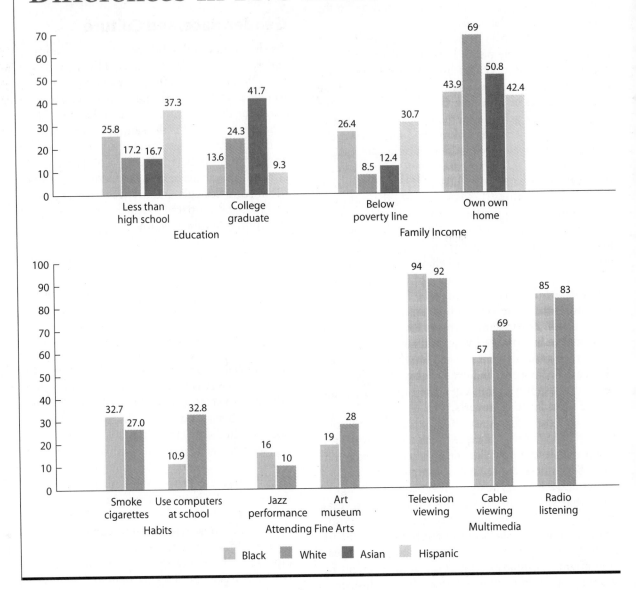

most important, they do agree that the early years are the most important and that our personality becomes fairly stable by the time we reach the age of 25. Does that mean that as we grow older we don't change? Not at all. It just means that for adults to change, a significant emotional event will probably have to occur. A significant emotional event is something that stops us in our tracks and makes us think about our lives. Such events can be unpleasant such as a divorce, a death in the family, an illness, or a near-death experience, or they can be pleasant such as a marriage or a birth of a child.

That adults seldom change their personalities or attitudes without a significant emotional event is important to understand because as employers, we often think that we can change a poor employee, or as spouses, we are convinced that we can change our partner's personality flaws. Such thinking is likely to result in frustration. Through the use of techniques discussed throughout this text, we can change the way a person *behaves* in a particular situation (e.g., attendance record at work), but short of a significant emotional event, we are not likely to change the person's *personality* or *values*.

QUICK PROJECT

Have you had a significant emotional event that changed your personality, values, or attitudes? What was it and how did it change you?

_____

_____

_____

_____

■ SITUATIONAL FACTORS

In the previous section of this chapter, we discussed the factors that predispose individuals to behave in certain ways. Though personality and temperament are good predictors of behavior across a lifetime, in any given situation people often act in ways that might be contrary to their personalities, attitudes, and values. That is, in many circumstances, the environment plays a more important role than personality. For example, suppose that an employee has the personality of being irresponsible and never showing up on time. However, her current employer has a strict attendance policy in which being late or missing work more than twice in an evaluation period results in termination. If the employee needs the job, the situational aspects (the attendance policy) will have a greater effect on her attendance than will her predisposition to be irresponsible.

Another example of situational importance: A friend of ours is an extrovert who loves to socialize on weekends but always eats lunch alone during the week. What could explain this contradiction in behavior? He is a professor, a consultant, and a person active in the community. His entire days during the week are spent talking to people, lecturing in classes, and attending meetings. Thus, each day he has an overdose of contact with people and uses the lunch hour to reduce the amount of stimulation.

Though there are too many situational factors to list in this chapter, examples include the behavior of others, time and resource limitations, competing values, and availability of alternatives.

Behavior of Others

Though conformity will be discussed in great detail in Chapter 14, it is important to mention it here. Regardless of our predisposition to behave a certain way, it is the rare person who does not conform his or her behavior to be consistent with the expectations of others. Our pace of work, the extent to which we volunteer to talk in class, the way we dress, and thousands of other behaviors are affected by the way in which the people around us behave.

Time and Resource Limitations

Often, the way we want to behave and the way we actually behave is a function of time and resource limitations. Take for example, a person whose personality and values are to help others. However, in the past year, this individual has not contributed any money to worthy causes nor has she volunteered her time to help others. Why the inconsistency? It may be that during this period of her life, she lacks the time and financial resources to engage in altruistic endeavors. Thus, this individual may still have a very caring and helpful personality but is not currently engaging in caring and helpful behavior. Does this sound familiar?

Competing Values

Our values and personality may not be consistent with our behavior because of the presence of competing values. For example, suppose that you are an outgoing person and enjoy socializing on weekends. You also are a serious student and want to make an A in this class. You have been invited to a party the night before your final exam. What do you do? If you choose to attend the party, your behavior will be consistent with your outgoing personality but inconsistent with your desire to be a serious student. If you stay home and study, your behavior will be consistent with your desire to be a serious student but not with your outgoing personality.

In life, we are often confronted with competing values and must make choices—quality versus quantity, career versus family, ethics versus profit. In some cases, the stronger value wins out. In others, the situational demands or expectations of others take precedence. Chapter 4 on ethics will discuss such dilemmas in more detail.

Availability of Alternatives

Another reason people behave in a manner inconsistent with their personalities, attitudes, or values is the lack of alternatives. That is, we might work at a job we dislike because no other jobs are available; we might go to the movies with a person because nobody else is around; or we might not attend religious services because no church of our faith is in the area. The small town we live in provides an excellent example of behavior inconsistent with values. A particular restaurant in our town is known for poor service, insensitivity to nonsmokers, and sexual harassment of its workers. For years, our colleagues and we refused to eat at this restaurant—our version of a 90s social protest. However, all of the competing restaurants have closed, so if we want to be able to walk to lunch, we only have one choice (as hard as we tried, the school cafeteria is just not a realistic alternative). Thus, we engage in a behavior (eating at the restaurant) that is inconsistent with our values and beliefs because we have no reasonable alternative.

■ THE REASONING PROCESS

Though our personality, attitudes, and values predispose us to behave a certain way in any given situation, we may behave in ways very different from that predisposition. One of the reasons for this difference is our reasoning process. Humans normally use logic to draw conclusions and to make decisions. How we use logic and the weights we give to alternatives may be influenced by predisposing factors, but an active thinking process usually precedes behavior. That is, in normal situations, people think about the consequences of their behavior before acting. For example, a driver balances the likelihood and cost of a speeding ticket against the value of arriving home a few minutes early, or an employee balances the likelihood and value of a potential raise with the effort needed to complete a job. Our personalities and values normally affect this decision process in that certain personalities might not think they will ever get caught speeding whereas other personalities are convinced that if they speed, they will always get caught.

Drugs, alcohol, and strong emotions affect our reasoning process. Under these influences, we might act inconsistently with what is normal for us or what might be the most logical way to behave.

Drugs and Alcohol

Drugs and alcohol are certainly factors that can affect our ability to reason. Have you or someone you know ever been drunk and said things or done something that would never have been said or done in a sober state? Drugs and alcohol are such powerful influences on our decision making that they are associated with many criminal behaviors such as domestic violence, assault, and homicide (Chong, 1998) as well as risky dating behavior (S. T. Murphy, Monahan, & Miller, 1998).

Emotion (Stress, Anger, Love)

Intense emotion (e.g., stress, anger, love) can also affect our decision making. Think of the last time you were in an argument. Did your argument make any sense? How about the last time you were madly in love. Did you do some stupid things? Take chances? Ignore behaviors that your friends told you were important signs? If you answered yes to any of these questions, you understand firsthand how emotion can cause us to behave in ways in which we would not normally behave. In fact, such behaviors as workplace violence and handgun carrying by adolescents has been associated with stress and emotion (Simon, Richardson, Dent, Chou, & Flay, 1998).

Cognitive Ability and Experience

Cognitive ability and experience are two other factors that affect our decision making. For example, imagine that you are confronted by an angry customer. Would you react the same way now as you did when you were 16 and had your first job? Probably not. The knowledge and experience we gain over the years help provide us with more options for most of life's dilemmas as well as insight into how well each of these options will work in a particular situation.

■ MEASURING PERSONALITY

Now that we have discussed some of the reasons *why* people are different, it is time to discuss *how* people differ from one another. Though there are many theories of personality and many tests that measure personality, the current thinking is that personality has five main dimensions—often called the **Big 5**. These five personality dimensions, which can be remembered with the acronym OCEAN, are openness to experience (bright, smart, adaptable, curious), conscientiousness (reliable, dependable, prompt), extroversion (outgoing, talkative, assured), agreeableness (loyal, conforming, trusting), and neuroticism (anxious, nervous, manic).

These five dimensions are called **central traits** by psychologist Gordon Allport (1961). Central traits are the major characteristics that form the core of an individual's personality. When one of these central traits dominates the way a person behaves, it is called a **cardinal trait.** Within each central trait are a series of **secondary traits,** the traits that make each individual unique. For example, extroversion is a central trait and might be composed of such secondary traits as being talkative, liking to dance, and having an active social life. That is, not all extroverts are alike. By definition, all extroverts enjoy being with other people, but not all extroverts enjoy dancing, drinking, gossiping, or playing sports.

An individual's central and secondary traits are often measured through paper-and-pencil personality tests. Typically, these tests use one of two formats: rating scales or forced-choice. Tests using a rating scale format might have a list of statements such as "I am always happy" or "I am very quiet" to which respondents answer on such scales as true/false, agree/disagree, like me/not like me. Tests using a forced-choice format usually have pairs of traits (e.g., introverted–extroverted, calm–anxious), and respondents are asked to choose which of the two traits is most like them. Commonly used paper-and-pencil personality tests include the California Personality Inventory (CPI), NEO-PI, Hogan Personality Inventory (HPI), and Sixteen Personality Factor Questionnaire (16-PF).

Another personality test that you might be familiar with is the Minnesota Multiphasic Personality Inventory (MMPI). This test is used to measure psychopathology (e.g., depression, schizophrenia); that is, personality disorders. Other such measures include the Millon Clinical Multiaxial Inventory (MCMI-III) and the Clinical Assessment Questionnaire (CAQ).

> **PROJECT B** *Your Own Personality*
> To discover your own personality, take the Employee Personality Inventory in Project B.

In addition to paper-and-pencil measures of personality, there are projective personality tests such as the Thematic Apperception Test (TAT) and Rorschach Inkblot Test. With the TAT, respondents are shown a series of cards and asked to tell a story about each card. The content of the stories is then analyzed to determine such needs as achievement, affiliation, and power. With the Rorschach, respondents are shown a series of inkblots and asked to indicate what they see in the inkblot.

Personality tests are especially useful in classroom and training situations in which people are trying to learn about themselves and others. However, because personality tests are easy to fake, especially ones using a rating scale format, they have not been particularly useful in selecting new employees. That is, it would be obvious to most applicants applying for sales positions that they should choose words demonstrating extroversion such as outgoing, friendly, and assertive, whereas applicants applying for an accounting position would probably want to choose words showing conscientiousness such as detailed, careful, and accurate. For this reason personality tests used in employment or clinical settings often contain scales to help determine whether a person is completing the test in a forthright manner.

As stated in the beginning of this chapter, understanding why people behave in the manner in which they do can greatly increase your interpersonal effectiveness. By learning not to make impulsive assessments about people, you can have more successful personal and professional relationships.

> **PROJECT C** *Applying What You Have Learned*
> To apply what you have learned complete Project C.

CHAPTER SUMMARY

In this chapter you learned:

- Genetics are responsible for 30–70% of who we are.
- Physiological factors (e.g., brain abnormalities, hormones, diet) play an important role in our behavior.
- Physical attractiveness, race, and gender play a role in how we are treated by others and thus influence our personality.
- A significant emotional event is needed to change someone's personality during adulthood.
- Our decision making and behavior is affected by drugs, alcohol, emotion, and cognitive ability.

Critical Thinking Questions

1. What is the relative importance of genetic and environmental factors?
2. What events have greatly influenced your life?
3. How real are the stereotypes involving gender, race, and geographic region?
4. Why is it important to understand the factors that cause a person to be the way they are?

WEB SITES

For further information, log on to the following web sites.

www.queendom.com/tests/
An excellent web site that has lots of free personality tests that you can take and score online.
www.quincyweb.net/quincy/psychology.html
Another web site with personality tests.

KEY TERMS

Big 5 The five main personality dimensions: openness to experience, conscientiousness, extroversion, agreeableness, and neuroticism.

Cardinal trait The main trait that forms the core of an individual's personality.

Central traits The major characteristics (thought to be 5) that form a person's personality.

Ectomorph From Sheldon's theory, a person with a thin body type.

Endomorph From Sheldon's theory, a person with an obese body type.

Fraternal twins Siblings born at the same time that emerge from two separate zygotes and have a 50% genetic overlap.

Genetics Characteristics, independent of the environment, that are passed from parents to offspring.

Hormones Chemicals that circulate throughout the blood and affect behavior.

Identical twins Siblings born at the same time that emerge from one zygote and have a 100% genetic overlap.

Mesomorph From Sheldon's theory, a person with an athletic body type.

Neurons Specialized message-carrying cells that form the core of the nervous system.

Neurotransmitters The chemicals in the brain that are responsible for communication among neurons.

Operant conditioning The theory that people behave in ways to be reinforced and avoid behaviors that result in punishment.

Secondary traits Lesser personality traits that form a central trait and that help to make each individual unique.

Zygote A fertilized egg.

PRACTICE EXAM

1. Identical twins emerge from one ____.
   a. egg
   b. zygote
   c. axon
   d. neuron

2. Fraternal twins have a ____ genetic overlap.
   a. 100%
   b. 25%
   c. 75%
   d. 50%

3. Genetics seems to account for about ____ of our behavior.
   a. 0%
   b. 15%
   c. 50%
   d. 90%

4. About what percentage of violent inmates have some type of neurological impairment?
   a. 0%
   b. 20%
   c. 40%
   d. 80%

5. Hormones are chemicals released by the ____.
   a. endocrine glands
   b. nervous system
   c. brain
   d. none of the above are true

6. Chemicals that communicate between neurons are called:
   a. neurotransmitters
   b. hormones
   c. peptides
   d. endomorphs

7. According to Eysenck, extroverts:
   a. are underaroused
   b. are overaroused
   c. have no arousal levels
   d. are at the optimal level of arousal

8. Which of the following would not increase mental efficiency?
   a. eating fish and eggs
   b. using olive oil to cook
   c. eating fruit and vegetables
   d. taking vitamin E supplements

9. Violence is related to ____ blood sugar levels.
   a. high
   b. low
   c. both high and low
   d. moderate

10. Physical attractiveness is related to:
    a. crime
    b. interview scores
    c. how we are perceived by teachers
    d. attractiveness is related to all three

11. A person who is strong and athletic would be said by Sheldon to have a(n) ____ body type.
    a. endomorphic
    b. mesomorphic
    c. ectomorphic
    d. plasamorphic

12. Compared to people raised in the 1990s, people raised in the 1930s are:
    a. more frugal
    b. more independent
    c. more impatient
    d. all of the above are differences

13. A person who is achievement oriented and conscientious was probably:
    a. an only child
    b. a secondborn
    c. a firstborn
    d. the youngest child in the family

14. Psychologists typically agree that unless a significant emotional event occurs, our personality is pretty much set by the age of:
    a. 5
    b. 10
    c. 25
    d. birth

15. The dominant trait that forms an individual's personality is called a ____ trait.
    a. central
    b. secondary
    c. core
    d. cardinal

ANSWERS 1 b, 2 d, 3 c, 4 d, 5 a, 6 a, 7 a, 8 b, 9 c, 10 d, 11 b, 12 a, 13 c, 14 c, 15 d

Focused Free-Write

To get you thinking about what causes people to be the way they are, write a brief description of your personality, attitudes, and values. Who are you? After describing yourself, write why you think you are that way.

_____

_____

_____

_____

_____

_____

_____

_____

_____

_____

_____

_____

_____

_____

_____

_____

_____

_____

_____

_____

Now, think about a person you find difficult to understand or to get along with. Why do you think the person behaves the way he or she does?

_____

_____

_____

_____

_____

_____

_____

_____

_____

_____

_____

_____

_____

_____

_____

_____

_____

_____

_____

_____

PROJECT A

Genetics

How similar are you to your parents? Complete the chart below to see what role genetics might have played in determining who you are.

	Your Mother	Your Father	You
Physical Attributes			
Hair color	_____	_____	_____
Eye color	_____	_____	_____
Facial features	_____	_____	_____
	_____	_____	_____
	_____	_____	_____
Height	_____	_____	_____
Build	_____	_____	_____
Personality			
Outgoing or shy	_____	_____	_____
On time or late	_____	_____	_____
Funny or serious	_____	_____	_____
Conservative or liberal	_____	_____	_____
Energetic or calm	_____	_____	_____

How similar are you and your parents? How much of this similarity do you think is due to genetics? How much to the environment? How much might be due to the situation?

_____

_____

_____

_____

_____

_____

Employee Personality Inventory

The Employee Personality Inventory (EPI) is a short personality test that is used mostly for seminars about understanding people but has also been fairly successful in predicting performance in several jobs.

Instructions Choose the word in each pair that is most like you. Even if both words are like you, you must choose only one word. If neither word is like you, you must still choose one of the words. After completing the test, your instructor will show you how to score the test and then you can read about your personality type on the following pages. Please note that the EPI may not be reproduced in any format without the written permission of the author of this text.

Thinking _____ Communicating _____ Organizing _____

Directing _____ Soothing _____

1. ____ Calm	____ Efficient	21. ____ Loyal	____ Chatty
2. ____ Accurate	____ Energetic	22. ____ Outspoken	____ Soft-spoken
3. ____ Original	____ Competitive	23. ____ Clever	____ Socializer
4. ____ Introverted	____ Extroverted	24. ____ Powerful	____ Insightful
5. ____ Careful	____ Bold	25. ____ Dependable	____ Self-assured
6. ____ Resourceful	____ Trusting	26. ____ Frisky	____ Intense
7. ____ Empathic	____ Inquiring	27. ____ Peaceful	____ Smart
8. ____ Assertive	____ Exact	28. ____ Spontaneous	____ Cautious
9. ____ Playful	____ Dominant	29. ____ Innovative	____ Systematic
10. ____ Curious	____ Detailed	30. ____ Orderly	____ Cooperative
11. ____ Precise	____ Tolerant	31. ____ Daring	____ Sincere
12. ____ Ambitious	____ Helpful	32. ____ Methodical	____ Outgoing
13. ____ Outgoing	____ Imaginative	33. ____ Sharp	____ Fun
14. ____ Talkative	____ Agreeable	34. ____ Rebellious	____ Punctual
15. ____ Enterprising	____ Friendly	35. ____ Fun-loving	____ Fearless
16. ____ Persuasive	____ Sociable	36. ____ Bright	____ Dynamic
17. ____ Patient	____ Convincing	37. ____ Modest	____ Perceptive
18. ____ Organized	____ Inventive	38. ____ Detailed	____ Ingenious
19. ____ Conversational	____ Self-disciplined	39. ____ Mingler	____ Courteous
20. ____ Confident	____ Creative	40. ____ Supportive	____ Logical

Thinkers

General Personality

Often called rebels or mavericks by others, Thinkers are creative, unconventional, insightful, inventive individuals who love the process of thinking, analyzing, and creating. They challenge the status quo, create new products and ideas, and provide new ways to think of things. Though they create new products and ideas, Thinkers consider the idea the end result, and seldom get excited about the process of carrying through on a project. Thinkers hate schedules, dislike rules and policy, and have little need for authority. They are free spirits and independent thinkers who value freedom and require the latitude to do things "their way." Thinkers can often be identified by the notion that they always seem to be preoccupied with thought. They can walk right by a person without even seeing them.

Of the five personality types, Thinkers are the most difficult to predict. They are complex people who are not easily understood or categorized. However, they do make excellent artists, writers, computer programmers, troubleshooters, engineers, and marketing analysts.

Communication Style

Thinkers communicate with others by discussing ideas, being sarcastic, creating puns, and dreaming. Their communication style is a combination of the other four styles in that they tend to be friendly like the Communicator, adventurous like the Director, and introverted like the Soother. The best way to communicate with a Thinker is to discuss the "big picture." Do not get caught up in detail. Rather than being provided with solutions to problems up front, Thinkers should be asked what they think a good solution might be.

Leadership Style

Thinkers do not seek leadership positions but can become leaders because they are often the people with the best ideas. When they do become leaders, they lead through motivation and inspiration. Others get carried away by their ideas.

Strengths

- Have ability to develop new ideas and systems
- Are not afraid of change
- Can see the big picture
- Are good problem solvers

Weaknesses Associated With Very High Scores or Stressful Situations

- May not carry through on their ideas
- Often have problems with rules and structure
- May not always be realistic
- Are easily bored and distracted

Directors

General Personality

Directors are fast-paced, efficient, confident, assertive individuals who are more interested in quantity than quality. Directors set high goals for themselves and for others. They are highly competitive: Doing well is not enough for Directors; they want to do better than everyone else. Directors are fearless and are willing to take chances—"play it safe" is a phrase seldom uttered by a Director. They tend to be independent and are much happier working alone than with others. Their greatest strength to an organization is that when given a job to do, they will always get the job done ahead of schedule.

More than anything, Directors fear being taken advantage of and thus are not very trusting of others. Directors also tend to be impatient and easily agitated. As a result of this impatience and lack of trust, Directors are often considered to have poor interpersonal skills.

Communication Style

Directors communicate with others in a very direct fashion. They tend to dislike small talk, prefer to get right to the point, and prefer executive summaries rather than pages of detail. Directors communicate best if they are told the purpose of the meeting before it occurs. Directors use eye contact when they speak and like to be given more than an average amount of personal communication space. Directors are not good at picking up subtle hints or nonverbal cues so the best way to communicate with them is to look them in the eye and tell them exactly what you want. Directors should never be told they "must" do something, as their automatic reaction is to resist threats to their freedom.

Leadership Style

Directors enjoy being in charge but are not always good at leadership. They tend to use a very directive style of leadership and rarely ask for the advice or approval of others. They set goals, provide direction, and expect a high level of performance from everyone. As leaders, Directors are good at quickly making tough decisions, exuding a can-do attitude, and cutting through red tape.

Strengths

- Have ability to get things done
- Are willing to take charge
- Are able to quickly make tough decisions
- Use time efficiently, resulting in a high volume of work

Weaknesses Associated With Very High Scores or Stressful Situations

- Often are perceived as being too competitive
- Can be abrasive, impatient, and short with people
- Are often not good followers or team players
- Have a tendency to break rules and regulations

Communicators

General Personality

Communicators are outgoing, friendly, talkative individuals who are much more interested in people than they are in projects or paperwork. They get along well with other people and tend to mingle well in social situations. Because Communicators like fun and excitement, they are easily bored. As a result of their people skills, Communicators make excellent supervisors, teachers, and customer service representatives.

More than anything, Communicators fear not being liked and thus, are not as direct with others as they at times need to be. Communicators need a lot of attention and often dislike sharing the limelight. Because of their preference for people as opposed to things, Communicators often delay work that involves data or reports.

Communication Style

Communicators talk with others in a very friendly, animated fashion. They tend to dislike business or serious discussions and would prefer to talk about fun things, exchange stories, and tell jokes. Thus, the best way to talk to a communicator is to start the conversation with an interesting topic and then slowly move toward the actual topic. Communicators are very expressive when they speak.

Leadership Style

Communicators do not necessarily seek leadership positions but often find themselves being chosen as a leader because they are well liked by others. When placed in charge, Communicators will usually adopt a participative leadership style in which they will probably call a meeting and ask for feedback from the people that are involved with the problem or decision.

Strengths

- Can talk with anyone about anything (good mingling skills)
- Have good sense of humor
- Are well liked
- Can increase the morale of a group
- Are best at dealing with angry or difficult people

Weaknesses Associated With Very High Scores or Stressful Situations

- Often are late to appointments or miss work and deadlines
- Are easily bored and distracted
- Have trouble getting to the point (ramble)
- Have a tendency to gossip

Soothers

General Personality

Soothers are individuals who are calm and steady and whose greatest strength is their ability to get along with a variety of people. Soothers tend to be warm, caring people who are very loyal to their friends and their organization. Soothers enjoy stability and thus tend to keep the same friends and jobs for long periods of time. Interestingly, some evidence provided by counseling psychologists suggests that Soothers are the least likely personality type to get a divorce. Soothers tend to make excellent counselors, and if they have a high score on Thinking, also tend to be excellent computer programmers.

Soothers most fear conflict and will do almost anything to avoid it. Thus, they are inclined to allow others to take advantage of them because they will not confront others. Soothers are the most likely personality type to develop ulcers, especially if they are working with a Director. Soothers tend to set low goals for themselves, are responsive to praise, and are easily hurt by criticism.

Communication Style

Soothers communicate in a positive fashion with just about everyone. They seldom criticize others and don't want to hear others criticize them. Soothers are the most sensitive about picking up nonverbal cues and emotional states in others. They tend to listen more for the way in which things are said than for what is actually said. Soothers seldom yell, and they react poorly to those who yell at others.

Leadership Style

Soothers seldom seek leadership positions but do occasionally find themselves in leadership roles because they are good compromise candidates. That is, because they seldom have enemies, it is difficult to find a person who dislikes a Soother. When they are thrust in leadership roles, they lead by delegating work to others and then providing the emotional support necessary to complete the project. Soothers utilize a participatory leadership style in which they solicit the opinions of others before making decisions.

Strengths

- Are loyal and trusted
- Are good listeners
- Are well liked and seldom have enemies
- Are good followers, team players, and group members

Weaknesses Associated With Very High Scores or Stressful Situations

- Have difficulty making tough decisions involving people
- Tend to avoid confrontation
- Often deny that problems exist
- Are often walked on

Organizers

General Personality

Organizers are detailed, organized individuals who are more concerned with quality than with quantity. Because Organizers are perfectionists who want everything done perfectly or not done at all, they produce high-quality work. As their name implies, Organizers' greatest strength is their ability to organize people and things; they have a system for everything. Because Organizers are so compulsive, they tend to be critical of others. Due also to their love of detail, Organizers usually would rather work with data than with people.

Organizers believe in the system and in authority. They follow rules, create new regulations and policies, and expect others to also believe in and follow the system. Organizers are hard workers who do what it takes to get a job done properly. Organizers are on time to appointments and expect others to be as well. Unlike Thinkers and Communicators, Organizers enjoy carrying out the details of ideas; they are doers rather than talkers or thinkers.

Communication Style

Organizers communicate with others in a detailed, factual manner. They don't want to chitchat, and they don't want general ideas. They prefer "just the facts." Organizers are poor at noticing nonverbal cues and can be even worse at understanding the real meaning behind what is being said. They pay attention only to the details of the conversation.

Leadership Style

Organizers lead by organization and strategy. They have an uncanny ability to take the knowledge and resources of others and organize them so that a task can be accomplished. Like Soothers, Organizers tend to delegate authority but demand that things be done by the book.

Strengths

- Have strong organizational skills
- Are good risk managers
- Understand the process
- Produce high-quality work

Weaknesses Associated With Very High Scores or Stressful Situations

- Have difficulty seeing the big picture
- Are resistant to change
- Are overly critical
- Are often inflexible

Applying What You Have Learned

In the Focused Free-Write, you were asked to describe who you are and why you are that way. After reading this chapter, what would you change about your answer?

_____

_____

_____

_____

_____

_____

_____

_____

_____

_____

_____

_____

_____

_____

_____

_____

_____

_____

_____

_____

_____

_____

In the second part of the Focused Free-Write, you were asked to describe a person you found difficult to understand. After reading this chapter, why do you think the person is the way he or she is?

_____

_____

_____

_____

_____

_____

_____

_____

_____

_____

_____

_____

_____

_____

_____

_____

_____

_____

_____

_____

_____

_____

CHAPTER TWO

Managing Stress to Meet the Demands of Life and Work

Stress Defined

Predisposition to Stress

Sources of Stress

Consequences of Stress

Organizational Responses to Stress

Managing Stress

Workplace Violence

Chapter Recap

Key Terms

Practice Exam

Projects
Focused Free-Write
Project A: Type A Behavior
Project B: Optimism
Project C: Lifestyle Questionnaire
Project D: Empowering and Motivating Yourself:
Gaining Control Over Your Life

A major factor that influences your behavior and thus your relations with others at work is stress. Not only does stress affect your interpersonal style, it can also have serious health implications if ignored and not properly managed. To properly manage stress you must first identify and understand what causes your stress and then learn ways to handle that stress. The purpose of this chapter is to identify some of the sources of stress (known as **stressors**) and to suggest successful ways for dealing with it. By the end of this chapter you will:

- Learn the definition of stress
- Be able to name common stressors
- Learn the common consequences of stress (strains)
- Understand the effects of stress on behavior
- Learn ways to reduce stress

■ STRESS DEFINED

Though psychologists cannot agree on one definition for the word *stress* (Beehr, 1996), for the purpose of this chapter, **stress** will be defined as the psychological and physical *reaction* to certain events or situations (called stressors) in your life. Here the emphasis is on how we respond to the stressor, as opposed to the stressor itself. **Strain** will be defined as the physical and psychological *consequences* of stress.

Focused Free-Write
To get you thinking about stress, complete the Focused Free-Write at the end of this chapter.

As you may have already discovered, what might be considered a stressor to you may not be stressful to another person. For example, if you have ever been in a minor car accident in which no one was hurt, you may or may not have experienced stress depending on how your body and mind responded to the incident. Maybe you and the other party, while exchanging phone numbers and insurance information, had a good laugh over what happened. Others of you may have experienced extreme fear and suffered from nightmares and body aches for several days or weeks (strain from your reaction to the event).

Eustress

Believe it or not, some stress is good. **Eustress** occurs when stress is converted to positive energy and becomes motivating. You might say it is a desirable outcome of stress. An example of positive stress is the anx-iety you feel before taking a test or meeting with your boss for your annual performance evaluation. If you feel no anxiety at all, you might not have the motivation to spend the necessary time studying for the exam or preparing for the evaluation. Thus, some stress in this particular situation might be useful because it could motivate you to perform better; this amount of stress is known as the optimal level of arousal. As shown in Exhibit 2-1, in general, having no or too much arousal results in poor performance, while moderate levels of arousal (or stress) generally result in the highest levels of performance. Of course, the **optimal level of arousal** is different for each person.

Distress

Bad or negative stress, known as **distress,** happens when there is too much stress and when nothing is done to eliminate, reduce, or counteract its effects. It usually occurs in situations or events on which you place great importance, that put great demands on you and your time, and over which you might perceive you have little or no control. For example, having to wait in line to cash a check or buy groceries may be irritating, but it's usually not important enough to cause distress. But interviewing for a new job or promotion that you really need for financial reasons can be a big source of stress, particularly if you feel you have little control over whether you get the job or promotion. Quite simply, negative stress occurs when we perceive an imbalance between the demands (stressors) placed on us and our ability to meet those demands in a certain amount of time (Davidson, 1997).

■ PREDISPOSITION TO STRESS

Individuals appear to differ in the extent to which they are susceptible or tolerant to stress. For example, rates of coronary heart disease, exacerbated by stress, are higher for divorced persons than married people. Married people report higher satisfaction and less stress than unmarried people; top corporation executives have lower mortality rates than second-level executives; and people who live in suburban environments have more stress-related illness than people who live in rural environments. Some individual differences can be explained by the following factors.

Stress Personalities

Some personalities are more inclined to respond negatively to stressors. These include individuals with Type A personalities and pessimists. Others, such as

EXHIBIT 2-1

Optimal Level of Arousal

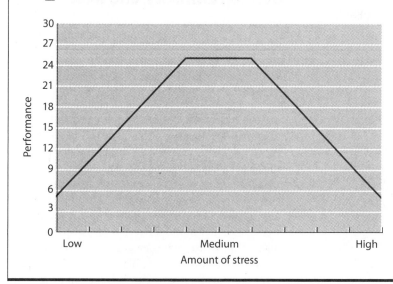

Type B personalities and optimists, seem to respond more positively toward stressors.

TYPE A

Do you, or does someone you know, talk and walk fast, get impatient easily, and always seem to be in a hurry? Chances are you or the person who has these characteristics is a Type A personality. **Type A** individuals have three main characteristics: competitiveness, impatience from time urgency, and hostility from anger. Type A individuals tend to do many things at one time (called multitasking). For example, a Type A individual would read the paper while eating lunch, type on the computer while talking to someone on the phone, and eat breakfast while driving to work. Type A personalities always seem to be on the go. They are achievement-oriented, competitive individuals who tend to place work before pleasure. These characteristics become exaggerated when the Type A personality experiences stress (Schaubroeck, Ganster, & Kemmerer, 1994). Type A individuals under stress are more likely than others to exhibit high blood pressure and high levels of stress-related hormones. In addition, Type A individuals recover more slowly after the stressor is removed (Schaubroeck et al., 1994).

TYPE B

Type B individuals seem to be more relaxed and easygoing. When a potentially stress-producing event occurs, they are better able to keep it in perspective and use more positive ways to deal with it. They are more relaxed and more agreeable. An example of a Type B individual would be someone who, while stuck for hours in a traffic jam, would look upon it as a challenge or an opportunity. He would most likely get out of his car to talk to other drivers, read a book or newspaper (if there happens to be one in the car), or take a quick nap.

> **PROJECT A**   *Type A Behavior*
> To determine if you are a Type A personality, complete Project A at the end of this chapter.

PESSIMISTS AND OPTIMISTS

Pessimists are negative people who don't respond appropriately to stress. They tend to ignore the problem or source of the stress, often give up on goals blocked by stress, and do not attempt to develop positive ways to deal with the problem. A pessimist in a traffic jam might think of all the negative consequences that are going to happen (e.g., "I'm going to be late so I'll have to work late tonight to finish the report on time, which means my spouse is going to yell at me and probably kick me out of the house!") **Optimists,** on the other hand, deal with stress head on. In fact, they are more likely to seek proactive means of dealing with stress, such as obtaining advice from others or planning for such stressors as traffic jams by always having something to do or read in the car. They seem to recognize that it's not the end of the world if they are late for work!

PROJECT B *Optimism*
To determine if you are an optimist or a pessimist, complete Project B at the end of this chapter.

Exhibit 2-2 summarizes these stress personalities and methods for managing stress for each.

DEMPCY AND TIHISTA'S SEVEN TYPES

Dempcy and Tihista (1996) believe there are actually seven types of stress personalities. You may see yourself in one or all of them because most of us have a blend of personalities that influence our behavior. These personalities can actually be a *source* of stress as you can see by their descriptions. The advantage to understanding and recognizing your stress personality is being able to modify your behavior in future stress-producing situations.

Pleasers want to make everyone happy and are usually cooperative and helpful. They tend to take on many demands and responsibilities. Under stress, which occurs when they are no longer able to meet their needs or those of others, they display resentment and perhaps anger.

Internal timekeepers also seem desirous of taking on a lot of responsibility, perhaps to please others or just because of their varied interests in many areas. Under normal situations, they are energized, efficient, and competent. Under stress, which is often caused by taking on too much, they become inefficient and anxious.

Strivers are ambitious and competitive and are usually their own source of stress. Why? Because they often place demands on themselves that they cannot meet. Their goal is to be successful at everything, even if it means to work, work, work until they burn out.

Inner con artists convince themselves not to work too hard, to avoid conflict (which usually means avoiding responsibility), and to ignore potentially stress-producing situations. This self-defeating behavior ultimately leads to even more stress in the long run as these types of people, also known as *procrastinators,* fall behind in both personal and work responsibilities.

Critical judges, when under stress, focus on the negative about themselves and their situation. This type of personality focuses on mistakes, not on *learning* from mistakes.

Worriers are as negative as critical judges and are highly influenced by unpredictability and unclear situations. If they don't know what is going to happen next, they predict the worst! In that sense, they are pessimists. Their constant obsessing over the future increases their stress levels. Worriers need others to tell them what they can expect from situation to situation.

Finally, **Sabertooths** respond to stress with a great deal of anger, often expressed through sarcasm or humorous insults. This type of stress personality can also be the source of stress and conflict to others.

Gender, Ethnicity, and Race

Much of the research on gender and stress is conflicting. Many studies suggest that women have more stress than men and that depression is twice as common among women than men. Other studies claim that gender does not influence how stress affects you (e.g., Guppy & Rick, 1996). The conflicting information about gender may be due to the fact that reports on stress and depression come from mental health institutions in which women are more likely than men to report their depression and seek help.

Only minor differences in reactions to stress have been found among racial and ethnic groups. These few differences mostly concern physical reactions to stress. For example, since the physiological mechanisms that cause hypertension are sensitive to the effects of emotional stress, Black men have more physical reactions to stress than White men because Black men experience higher rates of hypertension, in general (Ornish, 1984).

Stress Sensitization

The amount of stress we have experienced throughout our life seems to affect how we handle immediate or future stress. For instance, if we are exposed to high levels of stress (such as abuse) over a long duration, studies suggest that we are likely to react more quickly and more negatively to situations that are potentially stress-producing because, in a sense, we have become "trained" to respond in such a way (Carpi, 1996). That is, if we are used to being jumpy because of the stress we experienced earlier in our lives, we are more likely to react that way with future stress. This, of course, has implications for our future health and our stress behaviors. Desensitization can occur through learning new behaviors to handle stress and working through feelings about past stress.

■ SOURCES OF STRESS

Many events and factors could be considered stressors, and, as previously stated, what is stressful for one person may not be for another. What determines whether something will be a stressor depends a great deal on its importance and the amount of perceived controllability. Stressors can be grouped under two broad categories: personal and occupational. Exhibit 2-3 lists common personal and occupational sources of stress.

EXHIBIT 2-2

Profile of Individual's Various Stress Personalities

Type	Personality Behavior Causing Stess	Managing Stress
Pleaser	You desire to accommodate, help, and be cooperative; stress occurs when you no longer can meet both your needs and the needs of others.	Learn to say no when you are at a point where you can't help out without the risk of becoming stressed. Engage in goal setting and time management that will help you better balance your demands and the demands of others.
Internal Timekeeper	When you take on more than you can handle, your internal timekeeper breaks and causes feelings of being overwhelmed.	Learn to be assertive and say no. Engage in goal setting and learn time management techniques.
Striver	Your ambitiousness and achievement-oriented personality cause stress when you won't accept that you can't or don't have to be perfect in everything.	Focus on what you do well; learn your strengths and, if possible, take steps to improve your weaknesses.
Inner Con Artist	That part of your personality that rationalizes bad behavior (e.g., You can't work all the time so don't work at all!) keeps you from taking responsibility for your actions.	Accept responsibility for your actions. Engage in goal setting that will help you meet your responsibilities and stay on track.
Critical Judge	Stress causes you to focus only on your mistakes and the negatives in your life.	Write down your recent achievements. Engage in positive problem solving. Focus on what you learned from your mistakes and how you will handle things in the future.
Worrier	Stress is caused from the constant fear of failure, uncertainty, and the unknown.	Concentrate on the successes in your life. Learn those areas that you can control (empower yourself) and stop worrying over what you can't control.
Sabertooth	When you have taken as much as you can of life's daily stressors, you overreact with anger, and fits of yelling and rage.	Find a positive outlet for your anger and frustration: exercise, talk to someone, recognize how your negative behavior affects others.

Personal Stressors

Personal sources of stress arise from such nonwork issues as family and intimate relationships, marriage, divorce, health issues, financial problems, returning to college after a long absence, sexual orientation, and raising children. Angry people or people with difficult personalities are also sources of stress because of the conflict they cause in our personal and work life. In addition, having to deal with life's changes can be enormously stressful. In fact, change is a big stressor for most people, whether the change is moving to a new home, ending or beginning a new relationship, or attempting to change ourselves.

Exhibit 2-3 shows how teenagers and adults are stressed by the demands of school, college, and making the transition from the security of childhood to student to adult. Change is a major contributor to

stress and affects our professional life as well as our personal life. Why do you think that is? For most of us, change gives rise to at least one, if not all, of the following three responses—fear, resistance, and resentment—all of which ultimately lead to stress.

FEAR

When we voluntarily or involuntarily leave a stage of our lives that has become comfortable and predictable, we enter another stage in which we don't know what will happen. The challenge and potential excitement from the change can produce eustress in some people who thrive on unpredictability. But to many of us, fear of the unknown produces negative stress. For example, some students in your class may have returned to school after being out for many years. This substantial life change holds many unknowns such as, "Can I do

EXHIBIT 2-3

Common Stressors

Young Adults (Age 17-21)	Older, Working Adults
Graduation from high school	Organizational change
Starting college	Job insecurity
Moving away from home	Balancing family and work demands
Starting a new job	Job relocation
Nagging parents	Paying bills
Peer pressure	Increasing job demands
Taking exams	Boring or unchallenging work
Fear of the future	Pay inequity
Graduating from college	Going to school while working full-time
Interviewing for jobs	Planning for retirement

it?" "What happens if I can't pass the test?" or "How will I juggle school with work or family obligations?" Some people may love the challenge and unpredictablity of returning to school, but most initially start out frightened. You have probably learned that the key to handling fear of the unknown is seeing that the monsters you thought would be there aren't there. In other words, handling your fears of the future means realizing that most change does not end up being as bad as you first predicted.

RESISTANCE

Let's face it—some of us just don't want to leave the security and structure of our known universe. We resist change because we like the predictability in our lives, no matter how boring! We like knowing what is going to happen from day to day, and telling us that we have to change our routine can throw us into a tailspin. Something as minor as having to change brands of toothpaste can be too much for some people to handle and send them into a determined stubbornness not to change!

A good illustration of resistance to change is holding on to old traditions that are no longer feasible. For example, we met a man at a conference who said that for many years after his divorce he still expected to spend Christmases with his former in-laws! This had been a tradition for him for over 15 years, and he didn't understand why that tradition should stop just because he was no longer legally part of the family. He called his ex-wife for several Christmases after the divorce, asking to join in the festivities. He was turned down, and the continued stress from this rejection and his refusal to change eventually led him to seek coun-

seling. He seems to be doing better now and has even begun trying to start his own holiday traditions with the new woman in his life. Resisting change doesn't allow people to cope with inevitable changes that come from living. This resistance leads to stress.

RESENTMENT

Changes that are forced upon us, particularly those that we feel we had no control over, can cause resentment. If we don't want the change, don't understand why we have to make the change, and don't like how the change makes us feel (e.g., scared and confused), it raises feelings of resentment. Later in this chapter, we will discuss more about how to deal with life's changes.

Occupational Stressors

Exhibit 2-3 shows how experience and age contribute to what individuals consider sources of stress. Individuals who have been on their own and in the workforce full time seem preoccupied with the stress that work brings. Organizational stressors can be grouped under two broad categories: job characteristics and organizational characteristics (Cordes & Dougherty, 1993).

JOB CHARACTERISTICS

Three main job characteristics cause stress: role conflict, role ambiguity, and role overload.

Role conflict occurs when our work expectations and what we think we should be doing don't match up with the work we actually have to do. For example, a woman who was hired as assistant to the chief executive officer (CEO) of one particular organization was informed, upon hire, that she would be handling such administrative duties as policy development, participating in and contributing to management meetings, and serving as a liaison between the CEO and the public. However, after she was on the job, she heard herself referred to by the CEO and by other department heads as *secretary*. In fact, the only "contribution to and participation in" committee meetings consisted of taking minutes and ensuring there was food at those meetings. Her other duties included routine clerical work such as answering the phone and routing interoffice mail. There was role conflict because her expectations of the position were incompatible with what she was actually required to do. This role conflict caused her a great deal of stress, and, consistent with the research literature on the effects of role conflict (e.g., Rahim & Psenicka, 1996), she eventually quit her job.

Role ambiguity occurs when an individual's job duties and performance expectations are not clearly defined. In the preceding example, the woman experienced not only role conflict but also role ambiguity because what her boss expected her to do was different than what the other staff expected her to do. Although her boss referred to her as *secretary,* a job title that clearly denotes certain duties, he felt that she should have an equal say in certain decisions affecting the organization. The department heads, however, did not consider her their peer and did not feel she should have the same power or authority that they had. Because the CEO never settled the issue, she was never sure just how she was supposed to act at meetings, with coworkers, or with department heads. Each day brought more stress as she struggled to find out, on her own, just what her job responsibilities should be. Consistent with the research of Frone, Russell, and Cooper (1995), the stress of this role ambiguity caused her to become depressed, and consistent with the meta-analysis by Abramis (1994), her job satisfaction decreased.

QUICK PROJECT

Think of a time when role ambiguity happened to you or to someone you know. List the emotional and behavioral effects caused by the ambiguity.

_____

_____

_____

_____

Role overload develops when individuals either feel they lack the skills or workplace resources to complete a task or perceive that the task cannot be done in the required amount of time (Cordes & Dougherty, 1993). Role overload has been cited as one of the primary reasons for job stress. Research indicates that role overload can cause anxiety, depression, and anger (Rahim & Psenicka, 1996).

The key to minimizing the stress that comes from role conflict, role ambiguity, and role overload is to get clarification about your job duties. When you are given a job description upon hire (hopefully), make sure you sit down with your boss to ensure that you know just what he expects from you. It is wise to discuss the particulars of the job description prior to hire so that you are clear about work expectations. If you have been assigned a project you don't fully understand or feel you can't complete, let your employer know. Further, if possible, suggest that you be allowed to participate in training to help you complete the project. Finally, it is sometimes beneficial if your boss explains your job responsibilities to other staff. This explanation should reduce any misunderstanding about your role in the organization.

ORGANIZATIONAL CHARACTERISTICS

Organizational characteristics that are likely to cause stress include such factors as person-organization fit, management philosophy, supervisory relationships, work environment, organizational change, and relationships with other workers.

Person-organization fit The term **person-organization fit** refers to how well such factors as skills, knowledge, abilities, expectations, personality, values, and attitudes match those of the organization. At one time, organizations were primarily concerned that applicants had the necessary skills and knowledge to perform certain jobs. Now organizations, as well as workers, realize that compatibility in other areas is critical for an employee to fit into an organization and perform well. For example, a pro-life individual may not work well in an organization such as Planned Parenthood, a nonsmoker may not feel comfortable working for Phillip Morris, and an environmentally conscious person may be unhappy working for Exxon because the philosophies of the individual and the organization are not the same. This incompatibility in philosophies and values can cause stress (Lovelace & Rosen, 1996), lower job satisfaction, and increase turnover (Bretz & Judge, 1994).

Management philosophy The management philosophy of an organization may not meet the expectations of some individuals. For example, a person who works best in a very structured environment where everyone must follow a chain of command and specific rules (e.g., the military) may not work well in a team-oriented environment where workers are encouraged to make and enforce policy.

Supervisory relationships If an employee's expectation of that relationship differs from the supervisor's, not only will stress result, but conflict between the parties will inevitably arise. For example, if you expect your direct supervisor to be an empowering one and he isn't, stress can arise.

Work environment The environment in which you work can produce stress. For example, noise in the workplace can be stressful to some people, thereby affecting their performance. Research indicates that continued exposure to high levels of noise can raise blood pressure (Evans, Hygge, & Bullinger, 1995), increase cases of worker illness (Cohen, 1972), and produce more aggressive and irritable behavior in response to the stress noise causes (Donnerstein & Wilson, 1976).

Shift work can also have stressful consequences on individuals. Research shows that working evening and late night shifts has many physical, mental, and work-related effects. These include fatigue (Nicholson, Jackson, & Howes, 1978), deterioration in physical health (Frese & Semmer, 1986), and mental health (Jamal, 1981).

Organizational change As will be discussed in Chapter 13, a major contributor to organizational stress is change, which occurs most often from downsizing and restructuring, trends that are expected to continue into the 21st century (Offerman & Gowing, 1990). Realizing the amount of stress accompanying change, organizations are placing increasing emphasis on workplace wellness by offering programs that teach employees how to cope with change and manage stress.

Relations with others Coworkers and customers can be a major source of workplace stress. For example, an employee we met worked at a job she enjoyed, and her personal life was more fulfilling than it had been in years. Despite these positive aspects, she had trouble sleeping, lacked energy, and was depressed. The source of this strain was a difficult coworker who constantly yelled, used sarcasm, and belittled everyone. Such examples are not unusual and demonstrate the role that interpersonal relationships play in causing stress. In fact, a study of over 15,000 employees over a 4-year period found that stress from interpersonal conflict at work resulted in a number of severe psychiatric problems (Romanov, Appelberg, Honkasalo, & Koskenvuo, 1996).

Other Sources

MINOR FRUSTRATION

Minor frustration is the typical stress in our daily lives and might include irritations such as waiting in traffic or not being able to get some information from the library. Minor frustrations may try our patience, but in and of themselves, these daily frustrations may not be a problem and usually last for only a short duration, such as a few hours. But over time, if we do not have a healthy outlet for our frustrations, they build up until they control us. These short-term frustrations may then carry over to the next day and then the next, until finally they become long-term stressors.

Minor frustrations can be managed through perspective taking. **Perspective taking** means rating the frustration on a scale of 1 to 10 with 10 meaning the situation is worthy of high levels of irritation. An acquaintance of ours rates everything on a scale of life and death. He says that during potential stress-producing situations he asks himself the following question: "How bad is this in relation to death?" Because he served in Vietnam, faced death often, and saw many of his friends killed, most of the situations he confronts get a very low rating! Most of us can't relate to life's situations on that basis because we have never come close to experiencing death. But we can still ask ourselves: "In the scheme of things, just how important was that incident? Is it important enough for me to have a bad day, increase my chances of a heart attack, or die for?" See how perspective taking works? Making sure we don't make mountains out of molehills can keep us from having to deal with the long-term effects of stress.

FORECASTING

The stress from **forecasting** develops from our constant worrying about the future and wasting time and energy on *what ifs*? This continuous fretting about things over which we may have no control or that may never even happen can become emotionally and physically draining, even debilitating. Forecasting very quickly becomes long-term stress if we continue to keep our minds and bodies in a fearful and anxious state. Learning how to recognize those areas we can't control and ceasing to worry about them is the key to eliminating stress from forecasting.

RESIDUAL STRESS

Residual stress is stress carried over from previous stressful situations that we refuse to let go. Minor frustrations can become residual stress if we don't handle those daily problems effectively and then rehash them over and over again. Many people con-

EXHIBIT 2-4

The Stress Process

Stressors		Strains	Behaviors
Personal	Relations with others	**Psychological**	**Health**
Marital problems	Coworker problems	Depression	Smoking
Family problems	Supervisor problems	Anxiety	Drinking
Health problems	Difficult and angry customers	Anger	Drug abuse
Financial problems	Lack of empowerment	Sleep problems	
Daily hassles	**Personality/Habits**		**Work Related**
Residual stress	Type A	**Physical**	Absenteeism
Occupational	Pessimism	Illness	Turnover
Job Characteristics	Tendency to forecast	Cardiovascular problems	Lower productivity
Role conflict		Headaches, body aches	Workplace violence
Role ambiguity		Joint pain, arthritis	
Role overload		Immune system problems	
Organizational Characteristics		Ulcers	
Person-organization fit		Hair loss	
Work environment		Sweating	
Change			

tinue to carry grudges, hurt, or anger from past situations that keeps them in a constant state of stress. For example, have you ever been in a relationship that ended unexpectedly? If you didn't want the relationship to end, you may have been very hurt and then became angry. Now every time you think of that situation, you get angry and hurt all over again. Many people continue to dredge up those bad feelings long after the relationship is over. All these actions recycle the stress process. Residual stress is almost always long term: If not dealt with, it chips away at our physical and emotional well-being until we become prisoners to its effects. This type of stress eventually leads individuals to therapy and counseling to learn positive ways, such as learning to forgive, to cope with past negative experiences.

■ CONSEQUENCES OF STRESS

Personal Consequences

How we respond to stress can have devastating consequences. For instance, responding with anger or rage can lead to family members being hurt, the loss of jobs, and perhaps trouble with the law. Responding with the use of alcohol and drugs can lead to addiction, broken relationships, and even death. Financially, the impaired decisions that we make while

under stress can have negative consequences. In an interesting study, Repetti and Wood (1997) examined the effects of work stress on the relationships between 30 working mothers and their preschool children. The results of the study indicated that on highly stressful workdays, mothers spoke less often to their children and had fewer expressions of affection.

Exhibit 2-4 shows some of the numerous physical responses to stress. For example, many people report that interviewing for a job is very stressful and causes them to sweat. Headaches and body aches are also symptoms of stress. If you are prone to migraines, you may find that they occur more often during stressful situations. Body aches often are the result of tensing up during stressful times. Many people report that when they awake in the morning, their backs, necks, shoulders, and legs are very sore, which can be attributed to tensing during sleep. Extreme physical responses to stress include hair loss. Although we typically lose several strands of hair a day, hair that falls out in clumps is one of the body's ways of signaling high amounts of stress.

Stress has been labeled the *silent killer* because it can quietly chip away at your immune system, thereby weakening the body's ability to prevent or fight off illnesses and diseases. It is often the source of debilitating ulcers, escalating blood pressure, heart attacks, strokes, or worse: death. Stress may also increase the symptoms of rheumatoid arthritis because the hormones that are released in response to stress can cause swelling in the joints (Carpi, 1996).

EXHIBIT 2-5

Signs of Burnout

Signs of Burnout

Less energy	Apathy
Lower productivity	Dread of coming to work
Consistently late for work	Feelings of little impact on co-workers or the organization
Complaining and negativity	Feeling overwhelmed
Decreased concentration	Tense and frustrated
Forgetfulness	

Research suggests that 50 to 70% of all illnesses, such as coronary heart disease, can be attributed to stress. Even minor ailments such as recurring colds can be attributed to recent stressful events.

Depression is another health problem associated with stress. Most of us experience some form of depression from time to time. Usually, a good night's sleep or being with friends and family will lift that depression. Sometimes a few visits to a counselor who can help us sort out our feelings and put things in perspective will be helpful. Long-term stress, however, can eventually lead to clinical depression, which often requires medical treatment. In addition, prolonged depression has effects on the body such as stroke-triggering clots, hypertension, and high heart rates (Elias, 1997). Early diagnosis and treatment of depression is the key to managing it. If you feel you are suffering from depression, you may want to consult the counseling center at your college. Or if your town has a public mental health agency, contact someone there. Any visit you make to a counselor is confidential.

Organizational Consequences

JOB PERFORMANCE

Studies show a curvilinear relationship between stress and job performance (Robbins, 1998). That is, moderate levels of eustress can actually improve productivity, increase energy levels, and heighten creativity. However, when stress levels exceed that energizing level, job performance declines.

BURNOUT

Burnout, the state of being overwhelmed by stress, is usually experienced by professionals who are highly motivated and are faced with high work demands. Initial studies on burnout targeted people in the health care field as employees most likely to experience burnout. But over the years the definition has expanded to include other types of workers who become emotionally exhausted and no longer feel they have a positive impact on other people or their job. People who feel burned out have a lack of energy and are filled with frustration and tension. Emotional symptoms of burnout include dreading coming to work each day (Cordes & Dougherty, 1993). As shown in Exhibit 2-5, behavioral signs may include cynicism toward coworkers, clients, and the organization. People who are burned out display detachment toward the people (e.g., clients) with whom they work. Eventually, burned-out people may become depressed and respond to burnout through absenteeism, turnover, and lower performance (Parker & Kulik, 1995).

ABSENTEEISM AND TURNOVER

Absenteeism and turnover, resulting in loss of productivity and subsequently revenues, are highest during times of burnout and increased stress as employees struggle to deal with physical and emotional ailments. Two percent of the workforce is absent each day, and many of those absences can be attributed to stress. For example, a study by Neubauer (1992) indicated that as stress increases, so does absenteeism. With this in mind, the question then becomes: Is this absenteeism due to illness brought about by stress or does it represent "mental health days" in which employees miss work to take a break from stress? From a study by Heaney and Clemans (1995), it appears that the stress-illness relationship best explains absenteeism. Such absenteeism costs employers billions of dollars a year in lost productivity and is thought to be a warning sign of intended turnover (Mitra, Jenkins, & Gupta, 1992).

Interestingly, even if employees took a mental health day, the strategy would apparently not be highly effective. In a study of hospital nurses, Hackett and Bycio (1996) found that although stress was lowered immediately following a day of absence, taking a day off had no longer-term effects.

DRUG AND ALCOHOL ABUSE

Unfortunately, as stress levels rise and anger increases, so often does the abuse of drugs and alcohol. Most incidents of domestic violence and other types of violence occur after an individual has been drinking and/or using drugs. This doesn't excuse the violator's behavior, but it does indicate the relationship between drugs, alcohol, and anger and rage. The number of news reports of violence occurring in the workplace is high. Of those violent events that are carried out by employees, many are by employees who have abused drugs and alcohol.

■ ORGANIZATIONAL RESPONSES TO STRESS

Because of the increasing problems of drug and alcohol abuse in organizations, many companies have set up employee assistance programs (EAPs) to which they refer employees suspected of drug or alcohol abuse, as well as those who are depressed and experiencing other problems. EAPs use professional counselors to deal with employee problems. Some large companies have their own EAP counselors, but most use private agencies, which are often run through local hospitals.

Many organizations also offer stress management programs that help people learn how to cope with stress. Having such organizational programs that can be used as a positive outlet for stress and the problems that come from it can often be beneficial in employees' regaining control over their lives.

As organizations recognize the consequences of stress, they are beginning to take better precautions against it. For example, free voluntary counseling is made available by many organizations to all employees exhibiting emotional or discipline problems and particularly to those who have been terminated or laid off (Mantell & Albrecht, 1994).

One other organizational, as well as personal, consequence of stress is an increase in health insurance premiums. Because of the high use of medical facilities and options by employees suffering from illnesses caused by stress, organizations that at one time paid the full cost for health insurance benefits are passing the increases on to the employees. This additional financial burden can be a new source of

stress for some employees. The answer is reducing the number of ailments caused by stress, thereby decreasing the need to seek medical attention.

■ MANAGING STRESS

Because many of our behavioral responses to stress are learned, the negative ones can be unlearned. Stress management teaches us positive and healthy behavioral responses. The key is acknowledging when you use destructive methods and taking measures to correct those negative behaviors.

Managing stress or changing your behavior to healthfully respond to stress, should occur before, during, and after stress. Managing stress before it happens means incorporating daily practices (e.g., exercise) that will prepare your mind and body to handle the effects of stress. During stress you should continue with your pre-stress management techniques (such as reducing caffeine), as well as incorporate some others. Finally, after the stressor is eliminated (if that's possible), you should continue to proactively manage stress.

Pre-stress Actions

Pre-stress actions and techniques help your mind and body counteract stress. Some of these techniques to proactively reduce stress can also be used during the time you are actually engaged in stress.

EXERCISE

Exercise keeps your heart strong and resistant to the effects of stress, and it can also help reduce your stress levels during particular stressful moments. Incorporating some kind of exercise program into your life at least three or four times a week for 20 minutes is recommended by all health care professionals. Any activity from walking to swimming, running, playing sports, or climbing stairs will reap great benefits to you because these strengthen your cardiovascular system, thereby making you more resistant to the effects of stress. Even such household chores as mowing, vacuuming, or washing your car can help your cardiovascular system. The good news is that not all exercise has to be strenuous. Certain relaxation techniques (explained later in this section) are good pre-stress techniques that can be used during and after stress.

To begin an exercise program, start simple. For instance, instead of taking the elevator at work or school, walk the stairs. Or consider this: Stop driving around the mall parking lot 20 times looking for the perfect parking spot! Instead, make a conscious effort to park farther away and walk the distance. From these first steps, make the transition into a

EXHIBIT 2-6

Psychological and Physiological Effects of Humor and Laughter

Psychological		**Physiological**
Decreases anxiety		Relaxes muscles
Decreases stress		Stimulates circulation
Improves self-esteem		Exercises lungs and chest muscles
Increases motivation and perceived quality of life		Decreases stress-producing chemicals and hormones

Source: Berk, R. (1997, September). *The 7 humourous habits of highly effective professors (plus 3 bonus habits)*. Invited address presented to the Mid-Atlantic Personnel Assessment Consortium Fall Conference, Baltimore, MD.

more serious exercise routine. Just remember to pick a program that works for you, which might not be the one your friends use. If you don't like running, don't do it. There is no need to add to your stress by choosing exercises that you absolutely can't tolerate. As a good example, many of our graduate students lift weights to reduce stress. They have repeatedly asked us to join them, but we decline because we know that their plan of "We're going to work on abs for an hour this morning and then shoulders for an hour this evening" involves more time than is practical for our Type A personalities.

Organizations realize how important exercise is in managing the effects of stress, as evidenced by the increase of worksite fitness and health programs over the last 15 years. Research shows exercise can reduce coronary heart disease by reducing blood pressure and lowering cholesterol (Gebhardt & Crump, 1990). In addition, absenteeism and turnover are reduced, and morale and job performance improve (Daley & Parfitt, 1996; Gebhardt & Crump, 1990; Heaney & Clemans, 1995).

LAUGHTER

As shown in Exhibit 2-6, humor has been shown to buffer stress (Berk, 1997; Chubb, 1995) in several ways. First, humor can help you put a new perspective on a stressful situation. You have probably heard many jokes about death—many of which are told by police officers, doctors, and morticians. The purpose of such jokes is not to hurt feelings or show callousness but to better deal with an uncomfortable topic. It is better to laugh at it than to dwell over what we can't control. But be careful when telling such jokes:

Not everyone will appreciate the humor, and a little sensitivity and common sense should be exercised before sharing the joke. Second, when you are upset and in what seems to be a difficult situation, going to a funny movie, listening to a comedian, or watching a funny television show can help distance you from the situation until you have calmed down enough to begin thinking rationally again.

Physically, laughter can reduce your blood pressure. Studies show that laughing through a funny movie has the same effect on your heart as 10 minutes on a rowing machine (Stanten, 1997). So next time you have the opportunity to go to a funny movie, go! Or if you have a favorite comedy show that comes on more than once a week, watch as many episodes as possible.

DIET

Foods that have been shown to counteract the effects of stress include fresh fruits and vegetables, whole grains, and nonfat yogurt (which contains the B vitamin considered to be lost during high-stress periods of time [Ornish, 1984]). A daily dose of one or more of these can help you meet stress head on! Decrease your intake of fat because your body has to work overtime to digest fatty foods, adding to your level of stress (Carpi, 1996). To help reduce the effects of stress, many organizations are including healthier items in their vending machines.

Water (at least eight glasses a day) helps keep your body hydrated and able to cope with daily stressors. Caffeine should be gradually eliminated from your diet altogether. But before your stress level elevates from thinking about going without your daily caffeine boost, notice we said "should be." If you can't eliminate caffeine, at least reduce your daily intake; be aware of the amount of caffeine you are getting: You may be getting more than you think. It's not just cola and coffee products that contain caffeine: Chocolate, green tea, and many types of medicines and other foods have caffeine. If you do decide to eliminate caffeine from your diet, do it gradually. Most people who are used to large amounts of daily caffeine experience withdrawal symptoms such as nausea, severe headaches, and fatigue if they quit cold turkey.

SMOKING REDUCTION

Although many smokers say smoking decreases their feelings of stress, research indicates that smoking cessation leads to reduced levels of stress (Parrott, 1995). This is an important finding because research also indicates that smokers increase their smoking when they feel stressed (McCann & Lester, 1996). Thus, smoking and stress become a vicious cycle in which people smoke because they are stressed and then become more stressed because they smoke.

SLEEP

No one study says absolutely just how much individuals need to sleep. What studies show is that sleep deprivation or lack of sleep can cause negative behavior such as irritability, fatigue, lack of concentration, and even depression. Alcohol can severely affect sleep, although it may seem to people that it helps them go to sleep. But studies show that the sleep of people who have had as little as two drinks before bed is interrupted several times a night (Davidson, 1997). In addition, stay away from caffeine at least 6 hours before going to bed.

> **PROJECT C** *Lifestyle Questionnaire*
> To examine how your own lifestyle prevents or contributes to stress, complete Project C at the end of this chapter.

SUPPORT GROUPS

Studies show that people who have someone to talk to, like a family member or friend, are better able to manage their stress. You may have already experienced this. When you feel you aren't doing well in your job or in class, do you talk to someone about your feelings? Do you feel better afterward? Sometimes talking to someone we trust helps put things in perspective. So if you don't have a good support system, seek one out. For extreme situations, familiarize yourself with the type of professional help that is available on or off campus that can give you the support you need during stressful times.

SELF-EMPOWERMENT

In Chapter 13 you will learn about empowerment— the process of gaining control over one's life. Most of the literature on empowerment is approached from an organizational, managerial perspective. That is, the literature explains how management can empower employees by giving employees more control over important decisions that affect their lives. This has become important to organizations because research suggests that not having input into matters that affect us can be a significant source of stress.

What most of the literature doesn't discuss is how employees can and need to learn to empower themselves. Ninety percent of workers think employers must act to reduce stress. But because employees cannot control what organizations do, it is more important for employees to find their own ways to reduce stress, which is another form of self-empowerment. In addition, instead of complaining about not participating in organizational decision making, employees need to take the initiative to volunteer to participate on committees or on group projects; this is one way to take back some control they perceive they have lost.

Individuals can also empower themselves in their personal lives. Instead of feeling like a victim, someone who believes life has singled him out to play dirty tricks on, individuals can learn to find ways to gain control over those situations they can control. This means taking an active role in finding out why something didn't turn out the way they wanted and making changes to prevent the event from occurring again. Chronic complaining about being mistreated by everyone is, to most people, a behavioral response to what is perceived as lack of control in life. Most victimization is learned behavior that we see modeled by family members, friends, coworkers, and even people we don't know, such as those in the news. To break that behavior, attending workshops such as assertiveness training and decision making can be beneficial. These types of workshops are often offered through colleges, community groups, and religious organizations. If you are interested in attending such training, check with your school to see what may be available.

> **PROJECT D** *Self-Empowerment*
> To apply the concept of self-empowerment, complete Project D at the end of this chapter.

COPING SKILLS

Improving your coping skills often means learning how to deal with conflict. It also means learning how to accept what you can't change. Workers can't change the fact that their organizations are downsizing or that mergers and restructuring are trends for today's companies. Spending energy and time on worrying about it or being angry is a waste of time. The best solution is finding areas that they can control to meet organizational change, which includes returning to school or taking technical or computer training to make themselves marketable should they be laid off.

For students, worrying about whether you will graduate with a 4.0 GPA is both emotionally and physically stressful. Though setting a goal of high achievement is admirable, worrying about it for the entire duration of your program is unproductive.

During and After Stress

Much of the stress you will have to deal with comes from that experienced during changes in either your personal or your work life. Consequently, this section focuses on managing change.

According to Pritchett and Pound (1995), people make several mistakes when dealing with change. Three of the most glaring mistakes are (1) expecting somebody else to reduce their stress, (2) deciding not to change, and (3) trying to control the uncontrollable. We already talked above about empowering yourself so that you take responsibility for these areas of your life. Change is going to happen no matter how you resist. To help you better cope with these changes, try the following strategies:

- Determine why the change is necessary. At work, ask why your job duties are changing. In your personal life, recognize that you have no choice but to make the change (e.g., graduating from high school or ending a relationship).

- Find out how the change is going to be made. For example, many of you who knew you were going to college sat down and planned some goals. Those goals helped organize how your life would change over the next few years. Setting goals can reduce the anxiety that comes from fear of the unknown.

- Make a list of positive consequences that will result from the change. There may be some negatives, but focusing on the positives will help keep your spirits up and may even challenge you into action.

- Finally, if you are still having trouble with the change and seeing any positive consequences, ask someone you trust to talk you through it. Sometimes when we are too close to a situation that we don't like, we are unable to be objective or positive. Turning to others can help us with our perspective taking.

All of these steps give you some amount of control. Also, when you feel out of control in one area, try to find control in others, even in minor areas. People find a measure of control when they clean out their closets or tidy up the living room. They say they may not have control over such things as their jobs, but they can at least control how their room looks!

RELAXATION TECHNIQUES

Another stress-reducing technique is relaxation. The American Red Cross considers these relaxation techniques beneficial: abdominal breathing, muscle relaxation, and meditation.

Abdominal breathing is especially helpful for emotional calming. Get into a comfortable position, either sitting or lying on your back. Close your eyes and place your left hand on your abdomen and your right hand on your chest. Breathe normally, mentally counting from one to four as you inhale through your nose. Pause for two counts. Then open your mouth and mentally count from one to six as you exhale through your mouth. After several minutes of slow, rhythmic breathing, let your hands slowly move to your sides as your abdomen continues to move freely in and out with each breath. When you are finished, open your eyes and sit quietly.

Progressive muscle relaxation is used to relax the body. In a sitting or prone position, close your eyes and tense the following muscle groups: hands and arms; face, neck and shoulders; stomach and abdomen; buttocks and thighs; calves; and feet. Tense and relax each group separately for a few seconds each, while breathing normally. Slowly release the tension as you focus on the pleasant contrast between tight and relaxed muscles.

Meditation is helpful for quieting a chaotic mind. Sit in a comfortable position and close your eyes. Breathe slowly from the abdomen. Focus your mind on a single word (e.g., *calm*), phrase (*peace, love, joy*), or sound (*ooommm*). Mentally repeat the chosen sound over and over. Adopt a passive attitude toward the process. When intruding thoughts occur, as they will, slowly and gently redirect your mind back to your repetitive sound. After 15 to 20 minutes, slowly open your eyes.

Your local library or hospital will have information on other relaxation techniques if you are interested in finding out more.

TIME MANAGEMENT

Because a general feeling of "being out of time" can be a big source of stress, we devote an entire chapter to it. Using several time management techniques before and during stress can be very useful, and we discuss those in more detail in Chapter 3.

■ WORKPLACE VIOLENCE

In the past few years, the issue of workplace violence has received considerable interest. This interest stems from research indicating that 19% of workplace deaths are homicides (Slage, 1997). Homicide represents 12% of fatal workplace injuries among men and 42% of the fatal workplace injuries among women. Furthermore, 10% of employees in a given year are threatened with or victimized by workplace violence. The gender differences in workplace violence can be explained by the fact that men traditionally work in higher risk occupations such as mining, which have high levels of fatalities caused by other means such as driving and construction accidents (Thornburg, 1993).

Though these figures are certainly attention getting, from a human resource perspective they can be misleading. Though the exact numbers are not available, a relatively small portion of the homicides were committed by current or former employees. Incidents of workplace violence can be placed into one of three categories. The first category, representing 75% of job-related homicides, is violence against an employee occurring as a result of a *crime* being committed. The most common examples are employees assaulted during the commission of a robbery. Taxi drivers and convenience store clerks are the two occupations most susceptible to workplace violence.

The second category, representing 11% of job-related homicides, is violence against law enforcement officers (e.g., police officers, sheriffs, FBI agents) or security guards in the *line of duty*. Law enforcement officers have a homicide rate of 9.3 per 100,000 employees, and the rate for security guards is 3.6 per 100,000. The average for all workers is 0.7 per 100,000.

The third category, representing 14% of job-related homicides, is violence against an employee or supervisor as an act of *anger or vengeance* by another employee, a customer, or a jilted lover. It is this category of violence that most involves human resource professionals and has captured the imagination of the public. The majority of these acts of violence are committed by employees against other employees. However, annually 13,000 acts of violence and 31 homicides are committed by husbands and lovers against women in the workplace (Reynolds, 1997).

Employee violence against other employees is usually the result of interpersonal disagreements. For example, on April 6, 1999 a bus mechanic in Ottawa, Canada killed four coworkers and then himself because he was upset that he was being harassed by his coworkers.

However, employees can be assaulted when coworkers take out their anger on a supervisor. For example:

- In 1998, an employee at the Connecticut State Lottery who was upset with his supervisors for not listening to him killed four employees before killing himself (36% of employees committing workplace violence then commit suicide).

- In 1994, a Tulsa, Oklahoma, Wendy's employee, angry because his boss asked him to start work early, fired 12 shots from a .380-caliber handgun, wounding his supervisor and five other employees.

Thirteen percent of workplace violence incidents involve employees seeking revenge against a supervisor as a result of being fired, laid off, or subject to some form of negative personnel action. For example:

- In 1999, an employee at Watkins Motor Lines in North Carolina killed his supervisor with whom he was having problems.

- A former employee of the California Department of Transportation killed four former coworkers because he was angry about being fired.

- After being fired, an employee at Firemen's Fund Insurance killed three supervisors before shooting himself.

- An employee shot his supervisor at Dahn's Fresh Herbs in Houston after his boss threatened to fire him.

Perpetrators of Workplace Violence

Research on workplace violence by employees reveals a fairly consistent pattern. Perpetrators tend to be male (80%), be between the ages of 20 and 50 (usually in their 40s), have their self-esteem tied to their job, be fond of violent films and TV shows, be fascinated by guns, have ready access to guns, often subscribe to *Soldier of Fortune,* and are usually described as loners (Dietz, 1994). Psychologically, they are often classified as suffering from paranoid disorders. About 15% are suffering severe stress due to family problems; 8% are suffering from other severe sources of stress; and another 10% have severe substance abuse problems (Trenn, 1993).

Reducing Workplace Violence

Acts of workplace violence cannot completely be eliminated, but they can be reduced through security measures, employee screening, and management awareness (Dietz, 1994).

SECURITY MEASURES

Increased security measures can decrease the probability of workplace violence. These measures include such physical changes as adding surveillance cameras, silent alarms, bright external lighting, bulletproof barriers, sophisticated lock systems, and security guards; making high-risk areas more visible; and using drop safes and posting signs stating that only limited cash is kept on the premises. Staffing changes can include increasing the number of staff on duty; closing during the higher risk late-night and early morning hours; and training employees how to deal with robberies, conflicts, and angry customers.

EMPLOYEE SCREENING

Though the security measures mentioned above are primarily aimed at reducing workplace violence resulting from other crimes such as robbery, they can also aid in reducing violence caused by current and former employees. Another method of reducing violence committed by current and former employees is to use psychological tests, reference checks, and background checks to screen applicants for violence potential.

Background and reference checks can provide information about an applicant's history of violence (Tonowski, 1993). These checks are important because employees who engage in workplace violence are chronically disgruntled, have a history of causing trouble, and frequently change jobs. Dietz (1994) provided two interesting examples. An applicant at a California maintenance company was hired in spite of a history of domestic violence and burglary convictions. He later set fire to a bookkeeper who wouldn't give him his paycheck. Another organization was sued because an employee who had killed a coworker was rehired by the same company in an effort to employ ex-convicts. After a short period on the job, the employee killed another coworker.

It is important to say that ex-convicts cannot categorically be denied employment. An organization must take into account the length of time that has passed since the crime was committed, the seriousness of the crime, and the relevance of the crime to the job in question.

Psychological tests such as the MMPI and a variety of integrity tests can potentially predict violence in people without histories of violence. However, an empirical link between scores on these tests and workplace violence has yet to be made (Tonowski, 1993). Care must also be taken, as the Americans with Disabilities Act (ADA) provides limitations to the use of tests designed to determine psychological problems.

MANAGEMENT AWARENESS

Workplace violence can be greatly reduced by making managers aware of high-risk situations and then empowering them to take immediate action. Most experts on workplace violence (e.g., Dietz, 1994; Turner, 1994) believe that **berserkers**—employees who "go crazy" and shoot people—give indications that they are going to commit future violence. Such indications include threats, acts of violence, comments about wanting to get even, excessive talk of guns, and comments about famous serial and mass murderers. In one survey, 50% of human resource practitioners who had incidents of workplace violence in their organizations observed warning signs prior to the incident (Trenn, 1993).

Take, for example, Thomas McIlvane, a fired postal worker who shot eight postal employees, killing four. Prior to a union hearing appealing his termination, he stated that if he lost his grievance he would make a shooting incident in Oklahoma that took the lives of 14 postal workers "look like a tea party." As another example, prior to being fired and then killing his supervisors, Larry Hansel was reprimanded for excessively talking about a postal worker who killed two coworkers in Escondido, California (Graham, 1991).

Janik and Hagness (1994) advised zero tolerance for threats and violence; that is, one act and the employee is fired. Dietz (1994) suggested that anyone who makes others feel uncomfortable is potential trouble. Turner (1994) suggested that employees whose behavior makes others feel scared should be screened for violence potential. This screening includes interviews with coworkers and supervisors as well as meetings with a clinical psychologist. From these interviews and meetings, Turner and his associates place the employee into one of five risk categories:

1. High violence potential, qualifies for arrest/ hospitalization
2. High violence potential, does not qualify for arrest/hospitalization
3. Insufficient evidence for violence potential but sufficient evidence for *intentional* infliction of emotional distress upon coworkers
4. Insufficient evidence for violence potential but sufficient evidence for *unintentional* infliction of emotional distress upon coworkers
5. Insufficient evidence for violence potential and insufficient evidence for infliction of emotional distress upon coworkers

The potential for workplace violence can also be reduced through careful handling of terminations and layoffs. In Chapter 15 we will discuss specific ways to fairly evaluate and terminate employees. In addition to these techniques, free voluntary counseling is available to many employees, especially those exhibiting emotional, interpersonal, or discipline problems (Mantell & Albrecht, 1994).

CHAPTER RECAP

In this chapter you learned:

- Stress is the psychological and physical reaction to certain life events or situations.

- Common sources of stress include personal stressors; such occupational stressors as job characteristics (role conflict, role ambiguity, role overload), organizational characteristics, work environment, and change; and relationships with others (e.g., conflict, difficult people, angry customers).

- At a personal level, stress can affect marriages and relationships with others. And stress results in a number of health problems: psychological (e.g., anxiety, depression) and physical (e.g., joint pain, cardiovascular problems). At an organizational level, stress results in burnout, increased drug and alcohol use, lower job satisfaction, increased absenteeism, and increased turnover.

- Type A individuals and pessimists are more prone to stress than Type B individuals and optimists.

- Such techniques as exercise, laughter, a healthy diet, not smoking, getting plenty of sleep, joining support groups, self-empowerment, and time management are ways to reduce stress.

- Workplace violence can result from employee stress.

Critical Thinking Questions

1. Why are some people more affected by stress than others?
2. What job characteristics are most likely to result in high levels of stress?
3. Why should organizations be concerned about employee stress?
4. Do stress management techniques actually work?
5. Why does workplace violence occur?

WEB SITES

For further information, log on to the following web sites.

www.psychwww.com/mtsite/smpage.html
www.virtualpsych.com
Both sites provide useful information about stress and stress management.
www.mnsi.net/~wohis/violence.htm
www.nvc.org/ddir/info54.htm
These sites provide information about workplace violence.

KEY TERMS

Burnout The psychological state of being overwhelmed with stress.

Critical judge A person who, when under stress, focuses on negative aspects of him- or herself and the situation.

Distress Stress that results in negative energy and decreases in performance and health.

Eustress Stress that results in positive energy and improvements in performance and health.

Forecasting Constant worrying about the future.

Inner con artist A person who convinces him- or herself not to work too hard.

Internal timekeeper A person who becomes stressed because he or she takes on too many activities.

Optimal level of arousal The balance at which a moderate amount of stress results in the highest levels of performance.

Optimist A person who looks at the positive aspects of every situation.

Person-organization fit The extent to which an employee's personality, values, attitudes, philosophy, and skills match those of the organization.

Perspective taking Rating potential stressors by asking "All things considered, in reality, how bad is this situation?"

Pessimist A person who looks at the negative aspects of every situation.

Pleaser A person who wants to make everyone happy and is usually cooperative and helpful.

Residual stress Stress that is carried over from previous stressful situations.

Role ambiguity The extent to which an employee's roles and expectations are clear.

Role conflict The extent to which an employee's actual role and expected role are the same.

Role overload The extent to which an employee is able to psychologically handle the number of roles and tasks assigned.

Sabertooth A person who responds to stress by using sarcasm or humorous insults.

Strain The physical and psychological consequences of stress.

Stress The psychological and physical reaction to stressors.

Stressors Sources of stress (events, feelings, people).

Striver An ambitious and competitive person whose source of stress is often self-placed demands.

Type A personality A stress-prone person who is competitive, impatient, and hurried.

Type B personality A non-stress-prone person who is relaxed and agreeable.

Worrier A person who always thinks the worst is going to happen.

PRACTICE EXAM

1. Eustress is _____ and occurs when stress _____.
   a. bad / is converted into positive energy
   b. good / overwhelms individuals
   c. good / is converted into positive energy
   d. bad / overwhelms individuals

2. Distress is _____ and occurs when stress _____.
   a. bad / is converted into positive energy
   b. good / overwhelms individuals
   c. good / is converted into positive energy
   d. bad / overwhelms individuals

3. Factors that turn potential stress into actual stress include all except the following:
   a. importance
   b. constraints
   c. frustrations
   d. demands

4. Four factors that turn potential stress into actual stress are:
   a. importance, constraints, demands, perception
   b. constraints, demands, perception, frustrations
   c. demands, perception, constraints, perspective taking
   d. importance, constraints, frustrations, burnout

5. A contributing factor to negative reactions to change is _____.
   a. denial
   b. fear of unknown
   c. bargaining
   d. eustress

6. Which of the following react negatively to stress?
   a. Type A personality
   b. Type B personality
   c. optimists
   d. both b and c

7. Role conflict results:
   a. from the uncertainty and unpredictability that individuals have in their jobs
   b. when work expectations don't match the work individuals actually do
   c. when individual values and expectations do not match that of an organization's
   d. when individuals perceive they cannot do their assigned task

8. Role ambiguity results:
   a. from the uncertainty and unpredictability that individuals have in their jobs
   b. when work expectations don't match the work individuals actually do
   c. when individual values and expectations do not match that of an organization's
   d. when individuals perceive they cannot do their assigned task

9. Role overload results:
   a. from the uncertainty and unpredictability that individuals have in their jobs
   b. when work expectations don't match the work individuals actually do
   c. when individual values and expectations do not match that of an organization's
   d. when individuals perceive they cannot do their assigned task

10. _____ refers to how well such factors as your skills, needs, and values match those of the organization.
    a. Person-organization fit
    b. Role ambiguity
    c. Role conflict
    d. Role overload

11. Forecasting is stress from:
    a. constant worrying
    b. daily irritations
    c. unresolved issues
    d. perspective taking

12. Residual stress is from:
    a. constant worrying
    b. daily irritations
    c. unresolved issues
    d. perspective taking

13. Stress that develops from worrying about the future is called:
    a. forecasting
    b. residual stress
    c. frustration
    d. Type B stress

14. Burnout is an organizational consequence of stress characterized by all of these except:
    a. depression
    b. absenteeism
    c. rage
    d. detachment

15. How an individual responds to certain stressors may depend on the individual's
    a. gender
    b. personality
    c. optimism
    d. all of the above

16. On the basis of research, you absolutely need to do all the following except _____ to reduce stress:
    a. eliminate or reduce caffeine
    b. get plenty of rest
    c. vigorously exercise every day
    d. quit or reduce smoking

17. When under stress, _____ focus on negative aspects about themselves.
    a. worriers
    b. strivers
    c. inner con artists
    d. critical judges

18. About what percentage of workplace deaths are due to homicide?
    a. 5
    b. 20
    c. 50
    d. 75

19. The greatest number of work-related homicides is due to:
    a. violence against police
    b. revenge
    c. anger
    d. violence during the commission of a crime

20. The typical perpetrator of workplace violence is in his or her:
    a. 20s
    b. 30s
    c. 40s
    d. 50s

Focused Free-Write

To get you thinking about how this chapter applies to your own life, write down a recent event that you thought was stressful. Think about and write down how that event made you feel and behave. What did you do to handle the effects of that stress?

_____

_____

_____

_____

_____

_____

_____

_____

_____

_____

_____

_____

_____

_____

_____

_____

_____

_____

_____

_____

_____

_____

_____

Type A Behavior

To determine if you are a Type A personality, complete the Gardner Personality Test below. Circle the number that corresponds to the extent to which you never, rarely, sometimes, usually, or always engage in the behaviors below.

N = Never   R = Rarely   S = Sometimes   U = Usually   A = Always

Questions

	SD	D	N	A	SA
1. I walk fast even when I have plenty of time to get where I am going.	1	2	3	4	5
2. I am on time for appointments.	1	2	3	4	5
3. I daydream.	5	4	3	2	1
4. I eat a meal while I am doing other things such as studying or watching TV.	1	2	3	4	5
5. Close friends or relatives tell me to slow down and take it easier when we participate in activities together.	1	2	3	4	5
6. I complete school assignments in as little time as possible.	1	2	3	4	5
7. I must attain all my goals in the time frame I set.	1	2	3	4	5
8. People who speak slowly irritate me.	1	2	3	4	5
9. When I have my mind set on certain tasks, I am easily distracted.	5	4	3	2	1
10. When having a conversation about a topic I am interested in, I let others dominate the conversation.	5	4	3	2	1
11. I keep all of my school notes as orderly as possible.	1	2	3	4	5
12. I relax when others are in control of a situation I am in.	5	4	3	2	1
13. I expect the highest grade in my class on any given project.	1	2	3	4	5
14. On days when I have completed my homework, I have a difficult time relaxing.	1	2	3	4	5
15. When I make a mistake and correct it, I view the experience as a learning experience and don't get upset.	5	4	3	2	1

To get your Type A score, add the numbers you circled for each item. Your score is _____.
The higher your score, the more likely you are to be a Type A personality.

Your Type A Score	Percentile
69 – 75	99
62 – 68	95
60 – 61	90
55 – 59	80
53 – 54	70
50 – 52	60
48 – 49	50
46 – 47	40
44 – 45	30
42 – 43	20
37 – 41	10
00 – 36	5

What does your score say about your personality?

_____

_____

_____

_____

_____

_____

_____

_____

_____

_____

_____

_____

Optimism

For each of the questions below, indicate the extent to which you agree or disagree with the statement.

SD = Strongly disagree   D = Disagree   N = Neutral   A = Agree   SA = Strongly agree

Questions

		SD	D	N	A	SA
1.	I try to learn from my failures.	1	2	3	4	5
2.	Most people are good.	1	2	3	4	5
3.	If something can go wrong, it will.	5	4	3	2	1
4.	I can handle most of life's difficulties.	1	2	3	4	5
5.	It is difficult to trust people.	5	4	3	2	1
6.	I enjoy life.	1	2	3	4	5
7.	One can find something positive in most bad situations.	1	2	3	4	5
8.	I have a great life ahead of me.	1	2	3	4	5
9.	I find it hard to find things I enjoy doing.	5	4	3	2	1
10.	Life is hard.	5	4	3	2	1
11.	I will be very successful in my career.	1	2	3	4	5
12.	Most people who meet me will like me.	1	2	3	4	5
13.	Most politicians are crooks and liars.	5	4	3	2	1
14.	Most people will help you if they can.	1	2	3	4	5
15.	Most people would say I have a good attitude.	1	2	3	4	5
16.	I am usually happy.	1	2	3	4	5
17.	I feel that I control my own destiny.	1	2	3	4	5
18.	I make other people happy.	1	2	3	4	5
19.	I seldom complain.	1	2	3	4	5
20.	I often seem to focus too much on the negative aspects of life.	5	4	3	2	1
21.	There are few problems that can't be solved.	1	2	3	4	5
22.	Life just seems so boring.	5	4	3	2	1
23.	People who want to be successful can be successful.	1	2	3	4	5
24.	I can smile in even the worst of situations.	1	2	3	4	5

To get your Optimism score, add the numbers you circled for each item. Your score is_____.
High scores indicate you are an optimist, whereas lower scores indicate you are a pessimist.
Pessimists are more likely to be affected by stress.

Your Optimism Score	Percentile
107 – 120	99
105 – 106	95
102 – 104	90
99 – 101	80
95 – 98	70
93 – 94	60
90 – 92	50
87 – 89	40
84 – 86	30
81 – 83	20
79 – 80	10
24 – 78	5

What does this score say about your stress-related personality?

_____

_____

_____

_____

_____

_____

_____

_____

_____

_____

_____

_____

Lifestyle Questionnaire

Circle the number on the right that best corresponds to your answer for each of the ten questions below.

1. How many cigarettes do you smoke each day?   1 2 3 4 5
    1=none, 2=a few cigarettes, 3=half a pack,
    4=one pack, 5=more than one pack

2. How often do you drink alcohol?   1 2 3 4 5
    1=never, 2=once a month 3=once a week,
    4=2 to 3 times a week, 5=more than 3 times a week

3. How often do you drink beverages with caffeine?   1 2 3 4 5
    1=never, 2=once a month, 3=once or twice a week,
    4=3 to 5 times a week, 5=more than five times a week

4. How often do you eat fruit?   1 2 3 4 5
    5=never, 4=once a month, 3=once a week,
    2=several times a week, 1=daily

5. How often do you eat vegetables?   1 2 3 4 5
    5=never, 4=once a month, 3=once a week,
    2=several times a week, 1=daily

6. How often do you exercise or play sports?   1 2 3 4 5
    5=never, 4=once a month, 3=once a week,
    2=several times a week, 1=daily

7. How many glasses of water do you drink on a normal day?   1 2 3 4 5
    5=none, 4=one, 3=two, 2=three or four, 1= five or more

8. How many hours of sleep do you normally get each night?   1 2 3 4 5
    1=more than eight, 2=eight, 3=seven, 4=six, 5=less than six

9. How many times in a week do you take a short nap?   1 2 3 4 5
    1=five or more, 2=four, 3=three, 4=one or two, 5=none

10. How cluttered is the room, house, or office where you spend   1 2 3 4 5
    most of your time?
    1=very neat, 2=neat, 3=average, 4=cluttered, 5=very cluttered

To get your Lifestyle score, add the numbers you circled for each item. Your score is _____.
The higher the score, the more your lifestyle makes you susceptible to the effects of stress.

Your Lifestyle Score	Percentile
35 – 50	99
33 – 34	95
32	90
30 – 31	80
29	70
27 – 28	60
26	50
25	40
24	30
23	20
21 – 22	10
10 – 20	5

Based on your score, what lifestyle changes can you make to make you less susceptible
to the effects of stress?

_____

_____

_____

_____

_____

_____

_____

_____

_____

_____

_____

_____

Empowering and Motivating Yourself: Gaining Control Over Your Life

1. List those areas in your life over which you want to gain more control. These areas could be in your working situation, personal life, or both. Be sure to write down only those areas you believe you can control *(e.g., "More control over where my money goes and how much money I have").*

_____

_____

_____

_____

_____

_____

_____

2. Now, for each area you listed above, write down specific steps you are going to take to get better control. If you aren't sure of how to do it, talk with a classmate, friend, or family member for suggestions and ideas. Be specific about how you will empower yourself *(e.g., Write down a daily budget; stay within that budget; get a job or ask for a raise; put money into savings account).*

_____

_____

_____

_____

_____

_____

_____

_____

3. Finally, write down those items you want to control but feel you can't. Look at them and discuss them with someone you trust. Can you think of ways to take more control (if not complete control) in those areas? If so, using these new items, answer Question 2 again.

_____

_____

_____

_____

_____

_____

_____

CHAPTER THREE

Managing Time and Demands

Time Management and Interpersonal Effectiveness

Time Management vs. Behavior Management

Time Management Strategies

Chapter Recap

Key Terms

Practice Exam

Projects

In today's busy world, you probably have to juggle numerous daily responsibilities. Somewhere in between those responsibilities, you attempt to include some entertainment—going to a ballgame, movie, or party. Whether you are a student, full-time employee, or a little of both, trying to meet your own needs while attempting to meet the demands of others (e.g., professors, bosses, partners) can be a big stressor in your life. Thus, learning how to manage your time to minimize stress becomes a critical interpersonal skill. The purpose of this chapter is to help you identify ways to balance your life using effective time management techniques. After reading and working through the projects, you will:

- Be able to identify your time-wasters and how to deal with them
- Learn the importance of goal setting in managing your time
- Learn appropriate problem-solving skills to make timely decisions
- Know when and how to delegate your responsibilities

■ TIME MANAGEMENT AND INTERPERSONAL EFFECTIVENESS

What does time management have to do with interpersonal effectiveness and relating to other people? How you handle *your* time both at home and work can significantly affect *other* people. Read the cases in Exhibits 3-1 and 3-2 to see how poorly managed time can have negative consequences for you and others.

You can see from these examples how your organizational skills, or lack of them, can affect others.

Tom's disorganization financially affected individuals who trusted him, and he subsequently failed to be promoted. Tammy chose to prioritize her life so that her social life came first and everything else came last. This affected her grades, her behavior, and ultimately her relationships with friends, family, and an instructor. Preventing similar problems from happening to you means understanding the concept of time management and behavior management.

> *Focused Free-Write*
> Before reading further, complete the Focused Free-Write at the end of this chapter. This exercise will help you understand the consequences of poor time management skills and the importance of being a good time manager.

■ TIME MANAGEMENT VS. BEHAVIOR MANAGEMENT

Although we talk about "managing time," in reality time can neither be managed nor controlled. Like the Energizer Bunny, those 24 hours in a day keep on going and going. Ultimately, then, when we talk about managing time, we are actually referring to managing *behavior* (Ambraziejus, 1992). In other words, **time management** can best be defined as an adjustment in your attitude and behaviors toward meeting daily demands, thereby decreasing stress (Macan, 1994). The advantage to that adjustment and engaging in time-management behavior is gaining control over your life and over decisions that affect you (Branch, 1997).

The first step in becoming a better time manager is evaluating your time management behaviors and determining your time-wasters.

■ EXHIBIT 3-1

Case of the Disorganized Paralegal

Tom was a legal assistant with a caseload of 21 clients. These clients had been denied various types of public assistance benefits (e.g., food stamps, aid to dependent children, Social Security disability). There are strict deadlines for appealing denial of such benefits, and Tom's clients risked losing their appeals if they did not file proper papers on time. Unfortunately, because of Tom's disorganization and poor management skills, he missed three appeal deadlines. Consequently, at least three clients, all under the poverty line, became ineligible for any public assistance. In addition, these clients could have sued the law firm and Tom. The consequence for Tom was that his reputation and his career with that firm was hurt. No other legal assistant would agree to work with Tom on any cases, and it was several years before Tom finally received any promotion.

Case of the Busy College Student

Tammy was a full-time student whose weeks were filled with attending class, studying, and hanging out with friends. One week, she had two tests on Friday. Because Tammy's priorities for the week included going to the movies on Monday and Wednesday, attending a party on Tuesday, and going to the mall to shop on Thursday afternoon, she had only a few hours Thursday night to study for two exams, one of which was scheduled for 8:00 a.m. Because she had to pull an "all-nighter," she did poorly on both exams. This just added to the stress Tammy had been feeling for sometime. She reacted to her stress by snapping at her friends and yelling at her professor.

PROJECT A *Evaluating Your Time Management Behaviors*
Before reading further, evaluate your time management behaviors by completing Project A at the end of this chapter.

People engage in three types of time-wasters: attitudinal, behavioral, and situational.

Attitudinal Time-Wasters

The **attitudinal time-waster** arises from how you think about or judge time. If your attitude is "put off today what I can do tomorrow," you are misjudging time, and this attitude causes you to engage in behavioral time-wasters. Many people have the attitude that they have 24 hours in a day in which to complete their responsibilities, and their behavior reflects that attitude. But somewhere in that 24-hour period you must sleep and allow for unanticipated factors such as illness that keep you from your responsibilities.

Consider that the average person sleeps approximately 6 to 8 hours a day. Subtract that number from 24, and only 16 hours remain in the day for you to handle your responsibilities. Subtract the hours you spend getting ready for the day, commuting to work or school, and eating meals, and you now have maybe 10 hours for work and handling personal matters such as exercising or visiting with friends and family. Factor in a number of sick days and you can see how practicing poor time management and engaging in time-wasting behaviors leads to chaos. How do you spend your hours in a day?

PROJECT B *Where Does Time Go?*
To help you become more aware of your time-wasters and how you use your time, complete Project B at the end of this chapter. The remainder of this section will identify several time-wasters. Are any of them yours?

The following section explains how your attitude about time affects your behavior.

Behavioral Time-Wasters

Behavioral time-wasters are time-wasters you create for yourself. These include staying with familiar habits, procrastinating, avoiding responsibilities, engaging in perfectionism, unassertiveness, and work addiction.

FAMILIAR HABITS

The behavior Has anyone ever asked you why you always do a task a certain way—particularly when that way doesn't make sense? For example, do you make a shopping list before going to the grocery store? If you said yes, congratulations! Most people confess they never use shopping lists. For them, it has become a familiar habit to rush to the grocery store without a list even though lists can save time by eliminating an extra trip to the store for an item you forgot on the first trip.

Why won't people break old habits and begin new ones such as making grocery lists? Because, as Steven Covey (1989, p. 47), in *The Seven Habits of Highly Effective People*, explains: "A **habit** is the intersection of knowledge, skill, and desire. **Knowledge** is the what to do and the why. **Skill** is the how to do. And **desire** is the motivation or the want to do. In order to make something a habit in our lives, we have to have all three." In other words, you have to *want* to break a habit, have a *desire* to learn a new way of doing something, and have the *ability* to do the task the new way. All of this, of course, takes time and energy because you must engage in a particular behavior 30 consecutive days before it becomes a habit.

People may also continue bad habits or refuse to learn new ones because they fear the unknown. Familiarity is easy, less risky, and becomes very comfortable. Routine actually provides some much needed structure to our otherwise busy and chaotic lives. The fact is, you will never know if another way of doing something is better until you try it.

Finally, people may be unwilling to try new behaviors because of low self-esteem, fear of failing in the new behavior, or simply because they just don't like any kind of change. As explained in Chapter 2, change can often lead to increased stress.

Whatever the reason you might refuse to give up old habits or acquire more effective ones, one thing is clear. Becoming a better time manager means incorporating new habits into your daily life.

Changing the behavior Some suggestions for breaking old habits and learning new ones are:

- Acknowledge that there may be a better way of doing what you are doing.
- Brainstorm, either on your own or with someone else, other ways to do the task that may be more efficient and effective.
- If necessary, ask for and get training on how to do the task a better way.
- Be willing to learn a new way.
- Work on the new habit each day until it becomes a life or work style.

QUICK PROJECT

List a habit that you have been trying to break. Why do you think it's so difficult to break?

_____

_____

_____

_____

PROCRASTINATION

The behavior Procrastination is the tendency to postpone action toward a goal we recognize needs to be accomplished now (Ambraziejus, 1992). As you have probably already discovered, the more you procrastinate, the more you run into time conflicts. For example, say you have a report due in 3 weeks, but you put off working on it until the day before it's due because you think it will only take half a day to complete. Between the time you could be working on the project and when you actually start, you take a short vacation, work on another project that's not due for 2 months (you like that project better), and go to a day and a half workshop on stress. What happens if you get sick, are unexpectedly called out of town, or some other unforeseen situation arises that keeps you from working on the report on your designated day? Your disorganization and lack of self-discipline, which are common to procrastinators (J. L. Johnson & Bloom, 1995), can lead to time problems. The solution is to structure your days so that you have plenty of time to complete your required work, allow for emergencies, and still have time to do enjoyable activities.

People typically decide when to perform tasks based on whether the task is easy, routine, and likeable.

Easy vs. complex tasks People generally will do an easy task before starting a complex one for three reasons: ability, fear of failure, and time factors. In other words, they may not know how to do the complicated one due to lack of training or knowledge and ability; they fear failure, which may be due to low self-esteem (Ferrari, 1991); or the complex one takes too long to do.

Routine vs. new tasks Routine tasks are easier and can be done faster than new tasks, which take time to learn. Plus, people risk failing when they try a new task, and most people do not like to fail. The disadvantage of performing only routine tasks is that people become bored, stagnated, and subsequently unmotivated, which affects overall productivity and organizational goals (Knowdell, 1996).

An underlying process influencing this area is **instant gratification**, a force that pulls us toward the activity that will have the best result in the shortest amount of time (Ferrari, 1991). An example of instant gratification occurs when your instructor lets you choose between writing an extra credit research paper of at least ten pages (worth ten points) or writing a one-page summary of what you have read thus far (worth five extra credit points). Which extra credit project would you choose? You would probably learn the most from writing the ten-page research paper and would receive more points, but it would be harder and take more time, whereas the one-page summary will still gain you some points, but for half the effort!

Likeable vs. distasteful tasks It only makes sense that we do tasks we like to do before those we dislike. For example, which do you prefer: washing dishes or taking out the trash? Maybe you don't like to do either, but of the two, you probably have a preference, and that preference will no doubt be completed sooner than the other.

These factors not only play a role in how people choose what tasks to do first but impact when and how decisions are made. For example, when individuals make decisions about issues with which they are unfamiliar, they often procrastinate in making that decision. In addition, the more conflict that might arise from that decision, the more likely people are to postpone making that decision. An example of procrastination in decision making can be seen in the following true situation, which occurred in an organization going through restructuring.

A new manager was faced with deciding whether or not to lay off or transfer staff. Because he was new and still on probation, he was not very knowledgeable about certain procedures and policies and did not want to cause too much conflict that might reflect poorly on him. As a result, he delayed many decisions that could have been made sooner in the process. Ultimately, many of those delays caused even more stress for employees, and subsequently, problems in the organization.

Changing the behavior You can choose from several strategies for changing procrastination.

- When procrastination is caused by fear of failure, confusion about a complex task, or inexperience, learn more about the task and seek training.

- Ask for assistance from a more experienced person.

- If you need to make a decision in matters with which you are not familiar, do some research. How have other people handled such a situation? What are the disadvantages and advantages to the decisions? We talk more about decision making later in this chapter.

- If the task seems overwhelming or it appears too much time is involved, divide the task into smaller individual steps that can be accomplished and managed easier.

- At first, schedule a certain amount of time (e.g., 15 minutes) to work on the project. You may find that once you actually get started on the project, you won't want to stop and will get more done than anticipated.

- When procrastination is due to dislike of the task, change how you view an unpleasant task. Instead of thinking about the negatives of the task, consider the positives (e.g., "If I get it done before noon, I will be able to go to the beach the rest of the day!")

- Structure your time by setting goals and determining how to handle tasks in a more motivating manner to you. According to research, through better structuring of time, the tendency toward procrastination may be reduced (Vodanovich & Seib, 1997).

- To address procrastination at work, managers should clarify expectations and tasks, ensure that workers have the training they need to feel comfortable doing the more complicated tasks, and build self-esteem by providing accurate and constructive feedback (Vodanovich & Seib, 1997). Instead of saying "You really messed up this time," a manager might say "It looks as if I didn't explain the task to you well enough—what don't you understand?"

- Employees should be allowed input regarding how to complete a particular task. This may reduce some of the negative feelings employees have about doing the task, thus reducing the likelihood of procrastination.

QUICK PROJECT

Think about the last time you put off doing a task. Why? How do you determine what tasks get done first?

_____

_____

_____

_____

AVOIDANCE

The behavior Avoidance is the intentional act of ignoring your responsibilities with the hope you won't have to do them or someone else will do them for you. For example, if one of your daily chores is to take out the trash, you may avoid doing it because you know someone else in your home will eventually do it for you. Avoidance is not conducive to a healthy relationship, but it does get you out of doing distasteful jobs!

Avoidance is not the same as procrastination. Procrastinators are usually responsible and competent individuals who eventually complete their responsibilities (particularly if they have been given the knowledge and training to perform well). Avoiders are less responsible and more self-centered. That is, the reason they are not performing a task is because either they simply don't want to or it's not beneficial to them. What avoiders might soon discover is they are probably going to end up doing the task anyway, particularly if it's work-related and assigned by a supervisor.

By postponing the inevitable, avoiders often find themselves in a painful time crunch.

Changing the behavior Following are several ways you can change the avoiding behavior.

- Become aware of the negative consequences of avoiding your responsibilities, such as loss of a job or negative impact on a friend or family member. Knowing the consequences may be enough to break that destructive behavior.

- If you are avoiding a task out of resentment (e.g., you don't think it's fair you have to do it), talk to the person who assigned the task. Ask that person the purpose of the task and why it was assigned to you. Sometimes understanding why you have to do something can break any resentment you have in doing it.

- Use the strategies discussed under Procrastination to get started on your next task.

PERFECTIONISM

The behavior Perfectionism is the desire to perform every task and behavior with top precision and accuracy. Mediocrity is definitely not in the perfectionist's vocabulary. This goal is admirable and one worth aiming for; however, when perfectionists allow their desire for, perfection to delay the completion of the job, perfectionism becomes a time-wasting behavior. For example, individuals who continually rewrite a routine report or memo because it doesn't look quite right are wasting considerable time.

Perfectionists often set unrealistic goals for themselves and usually expect too much from other people as well. As supervisors, they may force their employee to rewrite a report three or four times until it is perfect. Perfectionists may have learned their behavior because of past treatment when they made mistakes. If past mistakes were met with unfair and destructive criticism, then perfectionists fear the negative consequences of performing imperfectly.

Changing the behavior Try some of these strategies for managing perfectionism.

- First and foremost, allow yourself to make mistakes. Ask yourself: "What's the worst that will happen to me if this isn't perfect?"

- Make a list of *other* goals you need to get done in a day. Using a list to keep you on track, time-wise, may force you to spend less time on perfecting something else.

- Before beginning a project, set a time for how long you think it should take to complete it. For example, let's say that the Focused Free-Write

should take about 20 minutes. If you find 30 minutes have passed and you are still working on it, you might be trying too hard to be perfect. Setting timelines can help you break your perfectionist behavior.

- Some tasks don't require 100% effort; 90 to 95% accuracy is acceptable in most organizations. Reworking a project that is considered correct enough until it is perfect would take at least another hour (Davidson, 1997). If you try for perfection on everything, those hours add up until you eventually run out of time.

- For people who work or live with perfectionists, you can help them by analyzing how you treat them. Have you criticized them in the past? Have they been disciplined for their mistakes or have they been allowed to learn from them? It may take a behavior change on your part to help the procrastinator break her behavior.

UNASSERTIVENESS

The behavior Unassertiveness generally involves an individual's inability to say no to requests for help by others on tasks that are not the responsibility of the unassertive person. An example of this behavior can be seen in a bookkeeper in a public mental health organization who continually asks her coworkers if they need help with anything. When she isn't asking, her coworkers will ask her for help and she rarely says no to their requests. The bookkeeper has her own work that keeps her very busy, and when she takes on the tasks of others, she quickly becomes overwhelmed, often missing deadlines for her own work. This behavior has been linked to low self-esteem and a need to be liked, gain approval, and be accepted.

Although we all want to be well thought of, when individuals carry this need to an extreme they get themselves into a time bind. This type of behavior has been reported by many organizations as problematic, and people using it are often defined as "difficult." We talk more about difficult people and their behaviors in Chapter 6.

Changing the behavior The following strategies may help you say no:

- First, it's important to understand *why* you are unable to say no to people. It may be due to a need to be liked or to low self-esteem. But if it's because you just like being involved in many projects because you like everything, using some of the other time management techniques discussed later in this chapter may be useful.

- Try saying no to a minor request. See what happens. Do your friends stop talking to you? Do coworkers walk away from you at work as if you have the plague? The answer to both of these questions is probably no. If people do get angry at you for taking the responsibility to turn down their requests because of your own demanding schedule, those people have problems of their own and really aren't your friends.

- Set specific goals and timelines for yourself. When you are asked for help on another project, refer to your goals and timelines. If you find that you won't have the time to meet your goals and help the other person, focus on reaching your goals first.

- When you do say no, explain why. Tell people your schedule and the timelines you are under. This will reduce any chance that they may be offended by your refusal. Most people are understanding of individual time constraints and pressures.

- If you have low self-esteem and fear saying no, attend an assertiveness training. Many day-long or week-long trainings are offered in various locations every year. In addition, many good self-help books on the topic can be purchased in bookstores or checked out from your local library.

- Managers can help build employees' self-esteem by providing positive reinforcement for jobs well done and letting the individual know it is acceptable to say no.

WORK ADDICTION

The behavior You have probably heard about *Murphy's Law,* which is espoused most often by negative people: "If something can possibly go wrong, it probably will." There is another popular "law" by which workaholics subscribe to called *Parkinson's Law.* According to C. Northcote Parkinson, whenever there is a free minute of unexpected time, workaholics fill it with more work (Lakein, 1973). Instead of using a cancellation to catch up on old work, workaholics might use that extra time to generate new work for themselves. Many people seem to engage in **work addiction**. In fact, the amount of time Americans spend at their jobs has been steadily rising in the last 20 years (Schor, 1991).

Changing the behavior Some of these strategies may help you control your desire to work so much.

- Keep a list of projects and work that must be done and by when.

- The next time you have a few extra minutes due to a canceled appointment, look at your list to see what projects still need to be done. Keep strictly to the list.

- Don't engage in any new projects until you have completed all (or most) of the projects on your to-do list.

- If you have no other projects, don't immediately add new ones. Force yourself to go for a walk, watch a movie, or read a book. This break from any work will help to increase your productivity on new projects.

- Set a goal each day to be finished at work (or with projects) by a reasonable hour. Keep to that goal.

Situational Time-Wasters

Situational time-wasters often result from behaviors or activities of *other* people who are seemingly unaware of the demands they place on your time. The most demanding situational time-wasters others generate for you are paperwork (including reading material), telephone calls, and ineffective meetings. Since you can't often *change* other people's behaviors, we will provide you with suggestions for *managing* other people's behaviors.

PAPERWORK AND READING MATERIAL

At work and at home, we are often besieged with catalogs, informational brochures, memos, reports, and letters. To stay informed, many of us attempt to read everything, particularly at work. The time involved in reading material and then doing the work that the material may generate is astounding.

Suggestions The following advice can help you better manage the time demands of reading and paperwork.

- If something has been lying on your desk or in your house, such as an article, magazine, or some other correspondence, for more than a week, you probably aren't going to read it or get to it at all. So, after a week, throw it away! A CEO for a major company is infamous for his policy of throwing away every piece of correspondence he receives. His rationale? "If it is really important, the person will get back in touch with me." This is a perfect example of taking good advice to the extreme.

- Divide the material into separate piles: That to which you must respond fairly quickly (put notes on the material indicating the due date), that which you would like to read for your own personal or professional improvement, and that which is not important and which you will probably see again or could find elsewhere if necessary.

- Focus on the pile that requires quick action.

- Throw away the pile marked "not important"— you will probably see it again in the future.

TELEPHONE CALLS

As with paperwork and reading, most people spend a lot of time on the phone, either answering it or returning messages. At work, this might involve looking up information for customers, determining which department to refer them, and frequently calling customers to let them know the status of their request.

Suggestions

- Screen your telephone messages. At home, you can use an answering machine. We conduct our business out of a home office, and we get at least three or four telemarketing calls a day. Each one of those calls could take up to 10 minutes while we listen to what the person is selling (we probably need to be more assertive and just hang up on them!). Screening the messages has saved us countless hours on the phone each week. At work, training the receptionist to try to help telephone callers would provide an initial screening process.

- If you don't have the luxury of another individual screening your calls at work, identify frequently asked questions, put them in a booklet format, and place the information by your telephone to be available when people call. Include a directory that lists various departments and the issues they handle.

- Set a specific time each day to return phone calls that are not considered urgent. Maybe late morning and early afternoon would be good times.

MEETINGS

One of the issues you may have already confronted at work is attending inefficient and unproductive meetings that steal precious time. Ever increasing amounts of time are devoted by managers to meetings and interacting with others (Branch, 1997). Most organizations have at least two meetings a week; some have even more. As managers or supervisors, you may be required to attend most if not all of these meetings. In fact, you may be responsible for calling and leading a meeting. When you factor in how long it takes to get to the meeting, you may lose an entire day. The more disorganized and farther away the meetings are, the more time you waste.

Suggestions As a participant in the meeting or as the future chair of such meetings, there are things you can do and suggestions you can make to ensure

future meetings are more effective. These include steps you should take before, during, and after each meeting:

Before the meeting

1. *Develop an agenda* Prepare and distribute to every person attending the meeting a well-structured agenda so that people will be prepared with questions (or answers to issues). The agenda should, at the minimum include:
   - The information or material that should be brought to the meeting. A great deal of time is wasted when people have to return to their offices to get information they should have brought with them. And, of course, once they are in their office, many people can't help but return a few telephone calls! Exhibit 3-3 shows an example of an effective agenda.
   - Place, date, and time of the meeting.
   - Follow-up: summarizing actions taken from the last meeting.
   - Topics for discussion with time limits. Decide how much time you will devote to each agenda item. Keep to that time limit. If you haven't reached a decision in the allotted amount of time, either wrap up the discussion or schedule the item for the next meeting.

2. *Decide the Location* Your meeting can be enhanced or detracted from based on the location site. Most meetings are held in a conference room or meeting room. Be sure the room meets these criteria:
   - Provides adequate space to work, with enough table space to spread out papers.
   - Has an area to set up coffee and some snacks.
   - Is not too cold or too warm.
   - Is located near a restroom.
   - Provides little distraction.

   There may also be times when you hold a meeting at a restaurant. The advantages of meeting in a restaurant include fewer interruptions, possibly more space, readily available food, and a more relaxed atmosphere. The disadvantages are that it works best with short meetings with less than three agenda items, may lack adequate space, and, depending on the time of your meeting, may actually be noisier with more distractions than a conference room.

3. *Decide the meeting time* Deciding whether to schedule a morning or afternoon meeting can impact its effectiveness, with advantages and disadvantages to both times. In the morning, many people feel more creative and alert, but the disadvantages are that members may feel rushed

EXHIBIT 3-3

Effective Agenda

Team: Diversity Team
Place: Admin Bldg, Room 206
Meeting date: March 3, 2001
Time: 4:30 p.m.–6:00 p.m.

Please bring Last month's meeting minutes and your copy of the list of possible activities for this spring.

Goal of this meeting To select three activities that we can implement before the end of the semester that will help raise diversity awareness.

Agenda Items	Time Allotted for Discussion
Follow-up from last meeting	15 minutes
Select minute-taker for this meeting	2 minutes
Discuss and put in order of interest the current suggested list of activities	45 minutes
Select three activities	15 minutes
Decide who will be on planning team for each activity	10 minutes
Summarize meeting and set next meeting	5 minutes

to get back to work or to their next meeting. Afternoon meetings may get higher attendance because many people like the idea of combining lunch with a meeting, but the disadvantages are that it may not work for long meetings, people may become sluggish or sleepy after eating a big meal, and people may still feel rushed to get back to work.

During the meeting

- *Keep to the set time limits* Decide that no new agenda items will be added or discussed at the current meeting unless it's an emergency. If, at the end of the meeting, someone wants to discuss something not on the agenda, schedule it for the next meeting.

- *Deal with tardiness* Don't wait for last minute stragglers. One individual we know locks the meeting door promptly at the time the meeting is to start. Although this may seem extreme, late arrivers learn fast not to be tardy again. If this is too extreme, schedule an agenda item for the next meeting where you and your group discuss promptness and consequences of lateness.

- *Keep minutes* People often can't remember from meeting to meeting what they discussed or what they decided. Minutes are a detailed write-up of the meeting, including all votes taken or motions made. Minutes from past meetings should be brought to each new meeting to keep people on track and refresh memories. Assign someone to take minutes for each meeting. Participants can still take their own notes—and then check the minutes for accuracy.

- *Stay focused* Ask "How does this discussion pertain to our goal?"

- *Distribute a meeting summary* Assign someone to distribute a summary of each meeting indicating who is responsible for handling the action steps developed at the meeting and the deadlines for the action steps. Exhibit 3-4 shows an example of a meeting summary.

- *Have visible goals* If there are specific goals you are trying to meet, write those goals down, bring them to the meeting, and put them where everyone can see them. For example, if your goal is to make a certain decision by a certain date, bring that goal and how you plan to meet it to all the meetings. Meetings often get off track, and you can get them back on track by saying: "That's a good question, but how does it pertain to our goal? Let's try to stick to our original goal at this time, and if we need to schedule a new agenda item for some other meeting, we can do that later."

EXHIBIT 3-4

Meeting Summary

Diversity Team Meeting Summary
Date of Meeting: March 3, 2001

Action to be taken	By Whom	When
1. Type and distribute March 3 minutes	Terry	Out by March 5
2. Begin planning action steps for activities		
– Staff Picnic	Cindy	March 15
– Golf tournament	Terry	March 15
– Whitewater rafting event	Carlos and Lisa	March 15

- *Decide the next meeting date and time* Set the next meeting date before ending your current meeting, which gives individuals time to prepare and reduces unanticipated meetings. Additionally, everyone can coordinate their calendars at once, which reduces the likelihood of having to call people several times with possible meeting dates.

After the meeting

- *Send minutes* Minutes that include the date and time of the next meeting should be sent out within 48 hours.

- *Write a meeting summary* A meeting summary with actions to be taken and by whom should be sent to the appropriate people within 24 hours of the meeting.

Exhibit 3-5 summarizes the time-wasters and solutions for handling them. The remainder of this chapter discusses additional time management strategies.

■ TIME MANAGEMENT STRATEGIES

There has been some debate in recent years about whether time management training, and the behaviors it teaches, actually works. But to the extent that the training teaches goal setting and prioritizing, it is generally agreed that time management training can be effective (Macan, 1994). Some argue that time management skills such as goal setting should be taught during adolescence to receive the most effect (Bruno, 1996). The thinking is that early time management training can carry over into adulthood to ensure that time management becomes a lifestyle. Time management techniques include planning and goal setting, action-step planning, using a prioritized to-do list, determining peak energy periods, finding hidden time, using effective decision-making skills, and delegating.

Planning and Goal Setting

As you can see from the recommendations made in our discussion of time-wasters, goal setting plays a major role in effective time management. Goal setting has been recognized by many organizations as an effective motivational strategy in job performance. One reason may be that people have a sense of having control over their lives when they can see goals being met (Macan, 1994). Another advantage of goal setting is that it can reduce stress by reducing the uncertainty involved with doing an assigned task (Robbins, 1998).

Setting goals begins with two questions:

- What are the things you *need* to do? (e.g., find a different/new job, get a college degree)
- What are the things you *want* to do? (e.g., buy a Miata, go to Europe, become a millionaire).

If you haven't asked yourself these two questions, you will probably have difficulty getting things done. Goals help you organize your life and your time. Goals should follow these five rules, which you can remember with one word: **SMART:**

- *Specific* Often our attempts at setting goals are ambiguous or vague. For example "I want to get a new job" is vague. "I want to get a job in the Human Resources Department by the end of the year" is more specific and concrete.
- *Measurable* You should have some way of determining if you are meeting, or have met, your

EXHIBIT 3-5

Summary of Time-Wasters and Solutions

Time-Waster	How to Handle
Attitudinal Time-Waster	
Misjudging time	Set daily goals and set specific timelines to complete each goal. Use daily calendars to write down important dates. Place calendars where you can easily see them.
Behavioral Time-Wasters	
Familiar habits	Identify habits that are ineffective. Consider more effective habits. Engage in that habit daily (or when feasible). Reward yourself each time you use that behavior. Write down the positive consequences of using the new behavior. Seek training if necessary. Ask a friend to positively reinforce your new behavior.
Procrastination	Make a to-do list with timelines. Reward yourself for beginning the task early. Seek clarification/training on how to do tasks. Break tasks into smaller steps. Seek help when necessary.
Avoidance	Become more aware of the negative consequences of your behavior. Find positives in a distasteful task. Ask for purpose/clarification of task.
Perfectionism	Set a time to be done with your task. Check your time every 30 minutes. If you go over your time limit, move on to the next task.
Unassertiveness	Seek assertiveness training. Learn to say no to people. Find ways to build your self-esteem by successfully completing projects. Set goals, and when asked to do other things, refer to existing goals and timelines.
Work addiction	Set goals and timelines. Don't add any new goals or tasks until at least three of your other projects and goals have been met. Use extra time to catch up on existing projects and goals.
Situational Time-Wasters	
Paperwork and reading material	Throw away magazines, information, and other reading materials that have been on your desk or in your house for more than 2 weeks. Prioritize paperwork on the basis of when things need to be done. Use the computer to save time retyping forms you use daily. Cancel subscriptions.
Telephone calls	Set aside a certain time each day to return calls. Use an answering machine to screen unwanted calls. Use e-mail to send messages.
Ineffective meetings	Ensure that a well-prepared agenda is distributed prior to each meeting, stick to the agenda and allotted time frame for discussion, clarify who needs to do what by the next meeting, and send minutes and meeting summary.

goals. For example, the way to measure whether you are successful in your classes is by the grades you get; the way to measure how you are doing at work is by the rating you get on your performance evaluation.

- *Achievable* You should not set a goal that you know you will be unable to achieve. If you are musically challenged, setting a goal to become a famous singer is unlikely to be achievable. However, this does not mean that goals should be easy. Challenging goals will keep you more interested and motivated than trying to meet easy ones.

- *Realistic* Having a goal that is not realistic to your life is not a worthy goal. For example, setting a goal to win the lottery is not realistic. It may be achievable, but the odds of you winning are a million to one; waiting for that money to come rolling in does not make much sense.

- *Timed* For each goal you set, you should have a deadline in which to meet it. Setting a specific time frame in which to meet a goal can serve as a motivator and can help keep you focused.

In addition to SMART, goals should be written down and visible so that you can refer to them on a daily basis in order to see your progress. How will you know if you have achieved your goal if you have forgotten what it is or don't know your next step? Once you have identified and written down your goals, an effective way to ensure you meet them is to use an action-step planning strategy.

Action-Step Planning

Action-step planning is a step-by-step process of identifying everything you need to do and by when in order to meet your overall goals. For example, let's

EXHIBIT 3-6

Goal Setting and Action-Step Planning

Goal: Getting an A in Human Relations Class

Action Steps:

1. Do writing assignment
   a. go to library to do literature review
   b. write draft
   c. have professor review and make suggestions

2. Study for Test 1 (test date: October 2)
   a. read book *How to Study for College Tests*
   b. rewrite classnotes
   c. review text and take notes from book
   d. review classnotes and book notes

Timeline: End of semester

Timeline:

begin: September 1
by: September 2
by: October 1
by: November 1

begin: September 25
by: September 25
by: September 28
by: September 30
by: October 1

say your goal for this class is to get an A. How will you meet that goal? You would have to be successful on all tests and do well on the written assignments. In your action-step planning, list when you plan to begin writing your paper, when and how you will study for tests, and what materials or instruments you might need to help you do well in class (e.g., reading a book on how to ace a test). Exhibit 3-6 is an example of how this goal might look using action-step planning.

> **PROJECT C** *Goal Setting and Action-Step Planning*
> Use the form in Project C at the end of this chapter to identify at least three goals you want to accomplish and how you will accomplish them.

TO-DO LISTS

Theoretically, some tasks will need to be accomplished each day to help you meet your goals. Because you will probably have several goals from month to month or week to week, you will have several activities you need to accomplish during any one day in addition to your daily responsibilities. **To-do lists** are written statements that serve as reminders of the tasks you need to accomplish on a particular day. Exhibit 3-7 is an example of a to-do list that includes actions for a particular day to meet the goal of getting an A in class. Research suggests that lists provide people with concrete evidence of reaching certain goals and gives them a sense of control over their time (Macan, 1994). To the extent that you feel like you have control, you are more likely to continue to engage in time management behaviors.

An important rule to remember with goal setting and list making is *flexibility*. If you can't meet all of your obligations on your to-do list due to unexpected circumstances, try to meet them the next day. Sometimes something happens, and you may never reach a goal. Your goals should allow for crises or changes (Branch, 1997). People who are too structured and inflexible will experience stress and depression from what they consider to be a failure. For example, we know a 40-year-old woman who realized she had gained more than 20 pounds since her 30s. She set a goal of losing that 20 pounds in 2 months. She began strenuously exercising every day and reduced her caloric and fat intake. Unfortunately, she did not meet her goal. But instead of changing her goal to one that may have been more realistic for her age and body structure, she gave herself 1 more month and exercised even more. She still did not meet her goal, became frustrated and depressed, stopped exercising, and is now even heavier than she was when she set her original goal.

PRIORITIZING

Prioritizing means assigning importance to each activity you have to do and determining which activity must be worked on first. Exhibit 3-7 is an example of a prioritized list. Again, you should allow flexibility. Make the activities that need to be done today the top priority and rank the other activities in order of importance. If you can't get everything done today, reprioritize the remaining activities for the next day.

> **PROJECT D** *Creating Prioritized To-Do Lists*
> To help you start a new habit, complete the To-do List in Project D at the end of this chapter.

EXHIBIT 3-7

Prioritized To-Do List

To do	When	Done?
1. Pay bills	9:30 a.m.	_____
2. Go to library and get book on how to take test	10:30	_____
3. Look up literature on research topic	10:45	_____
4. Lunch with Chris	12:00 p.m.	_____
5. Go to cleaners—drop off and pick-up	1:30	_____
6. Pick up food for twins' birthday party tonight Need: chips, soda, dip, ice, cake, candy	2:00	_____
7. Study for test on Monday	3:30–6:00	_____
8. Get ready for twins' party	6:00	_____

Determining "Peak Energy" Period

Often we fall behind schedule when we try to work on projects or tasks at times when our energy levels are the lowest. For example, some individuals may do their best work early in the day, from 8:00 a.m. until about 2:00 p.m. After that, those people may lose some of their energy and not perform as well. If they tried to handle a major task in the late afternoon, they may be unable to accomplish as much work due to low energy. On the other hand, some people are most effective later in the day and late at night. The issue is to identify the time of day you have the most energy, and if possible, save your most demanding tasks until that time. This will ensure that you perform at optimal levels, accomplishing more work than if you had done the task at your low-energy time.

QUICK PROJECT

Think about when you do your best work. Is it in the morning or afternoon? List what happens when you save complex tasks for low-energy periods.

_____

_____

_____

Finding Hidden Time

Most people actually have more time in a day than they think—particularly if they incorporate some of the time management strategies we have been discussing. Finding this hidden time just takes a matter of analyzing how you spend your day. You already did some of this in Project B. While you compiled your Time Log, you may have determined some free time you didn't know you had. If not, consider these hidden time areas when you can be doing some work:

- *Commuting to work or school* If you are a passenger in a car, you can use that time to catch up on your reading or studying. Some people use a tape recorder to dictate work or organize their thoughts.

- *Coffee breaks* Most people take several breaks during the day—they chat for a few minutes with friends, coworkers, or just go on their own. Although these breaks are important in keeping your productivity high, eliminating a couple will add valuable time to your day. A friend of ours is a very social person who loves to talk. However, she has come to realize that her daily routine of talking to her colleagues is the main reason she must work several hours of overtime each day.

- *Lunch time* Using lunch breaks to handle such tasks as going to the grocery store for a few items, catching up on reading material, or planning your next day can save you time. Some people combine meetings with lunch.

- *Waiting time* While waiting in daily traffic, catch up on your reading material and other paperwork in the car, or make notes or lists while waiting in line at the post office, lunch line, or bank. It's amazing what can be done during these short free-time spots.

- *Bath time* Many people get their best studying or reading done while taking a bath or doing other "bathroom stuff!"

Once you analyze your days, you may find other hidden time. Adding an hour or two to your day goes a long way in helping you achieve your goals and carry out your responsibilities.

Making Effective Decisions

Some people have difficulty making decisions in a timely manner. They often agonize over the simplest of decisions: Should I buy *Cheer* or *Tide* laundry detergent? Should I handle the project this way or the other way? Should I take the shortcut or the highway? People get "stuck" for four main reasons: fear of the unknown, fear of conflict, lack of knowledge or inexperience, and/or poor decision-making skills.

FEAR OF THE UNKNOWN

Many people are afraid of what might happen when they make a particular decision. Yet making no decision at all may be worse than making the wrong decision—it is just postponing the inevitable.

FEAR OF CONFLICT

Many decisions result in conflict. Most people don't like conflict and do everything they can to avoid it. We talk more about conflict and how to deal with it in Chapter 6.

LACK OF KNOWLEDGE

Some people don't have enough information to make a good, effective decision. The key here is obtaining as much information as possible, either by getting feedback from other people or by talking to more experienced people who have been in similar situations.

POOR DECISION-MAKING SKILLS

Finally, many people simply lack the skills to make effective decisions. Making quality decisions is a skill that can be improved with training. Making effective decisions begins by identifying and defining your issue or problem. Let's say your issue is whether you will stay in your current apartment or move to one closer to work that is also close to the police department.

- *Write down your goal* Why are you even considering the move? Is it to save money or to feel safer? You can't even begin to make a decision unless you know your goal.

- *Write down all the possible solutions to your question or problem* If your goal is to feel safe, maybe an alternative to moving is to put additional locks on your windows and doors or install a security system.

- *Evaluate each alternative solution and consider the advantages and disadvantages* Next to each

alternative, consider and write down the advantage of choosing it and how well it meets your goal, then write down its disadvantages. Let's say your goal is to feel secure and save money. Perhaps finding a roommate and installing a security system will be cheaper than moving to an apartment closer to the police department.

- *Identify the solution or answer that is going to meet your goal the best*

- *Carry out your decision* Agonizing over whether it is right or wrong is just a waste of time. Every decision has a negative consequence, but with your evaluation you will know what they are. Staying in your current apartment may mean that you don't have access to some of the amenities (e.g., shopping) that moving can offer you. That's not a huge disadvantage, but one nevertheless.

- *Monitor and test your decision* Many decisions can be reversed or at least changed if your original decision does not work. Although you may have to sign a year's lease, if staying in your current apartment doesn't work out, the next year you can determine whether you need to look for another apartment.

Remember, the keys to making effective decisions are writing down goals, brainstorming possible answers (sometimes asking for input from others can help), and evaluating and changing goals when necessary.

PROJECT E *Effective Decision-Making*
To help you practice the decision-making strategies discussed in this section, complete Project E at the end of this chapter.

Delegating

How many times have you done something either at work or at home that was the responsibility of someone else or could have been done by another coworker, friend, or employee? For example, one of the biggest problems in mismanaged time in organizations is that a supervisor will do a routine task, such as filing correspondence, that could be assigned to nonmanagerial staff. **Delegation** is the process of assigning to other people specific tasks that do not need your expertise. Delegation frees up your time to handle responsibilities that only you or a small group of experts can handle. Three factors are involved in successful delegation: the delegatee, the delegator, and the situation (MacKenzie, 1972).

THE DELEGATEE

Delegation requires you have someone to whom to delegate! At a recent time management workshop, a supervisor complained that her office did not have its own secretary and so people had to do their own filing. This example raises a good point that some strategies won't be appropriate because of barriers such as organizational constraints. However, by concentrating on those time management techniques you can use, you will still free up some extra time to handle other responsibilities if you are unable to delegate.

Another common complaint is that "by the time that person does the job I delegate, I could have done it myself in less time." This is a legitimate complaint. Perhaps the delegatee needs training in certain tasks—initially, this training may take up additional time of yours, but in the long term, you will benefit. At the end of this section, we list some strategies you can use to overcome this barrier.

THE DELEGATOR

The previous comment about it taking less time for you to do the work than for someone else raises another barrier: The inability of the delegator to *stop* managing and *start* empowering the delagatees. Sharing control and giving up small amounts of it in certain circumstances is absolutely critical in effective time management.

THE SITUATION

If you work in an environment where only the managers are rewarded or disciplined for the success or failure of a project, delegation probably won't work. Everyone must take responsibility for the ultimate results of a project. If a project fails, instead of focusing on the failure and negative consequences, the failure should be used as a learning process and additional training should occur. After all, no one will want to be a delegatee if she thinks she will be punished for failing.

QUICK PROJECT

Briefly write down the last time you delegated something to someone. What was it? Did you stand over their shoulder?

_____

_____

_____

_____

STEPS FOR SUCCESSFUL DELEGATION

These steps for successful delegation in the workplace should be followed whenever you plan to delegate projects to other people.

1. Determine if your delegatees are ready for the amount of responsibility that comes from working more on their own than with direct supervision from you. If they don't seem ready, determine how to get them ready (e.g., do they need training?).

2. Clarify the goal—that is, be able to explain to your delegatees the exact results you are looking for.

3. Break the task into smaller parts with deadlines for each part. This will help keep delegatees from feeling overwhelmed at what they might consider time-consuming projects.

4. Each time one step is completed, compliment the delegatees on a job well done.

5. Define responsibility and authority levels. Be specific about whether you want employees to have decision-making authority or whether you want them to check with you on certain areas before a decision is made. We encourage managers to share their decision-making authority whenever possible. Delegation depends on delegatees being able to do their work without constantly interrupting you and your work schedule.

6. Coach, don't lead. If you trust your staff enough to ask them to do the task, then that trust should carry over to the final product. In other words, don't "stand over your delegatee's shoulder" waiting for the work to be done. Tell delegatees that you will be available if they need help.

7. Require completed work. Initially, you may have to remind the delegatee several times about timelines and that you need to see completed projects on time.

8. Provide training: Ask the delegatee if she feels comfortable doing the project. If she says no, ask her what kind of information or training she feels she needs to be comfortable with doing the job. Ensure she gets that training.

Exhibit 3-8 summarizes the barriers to effective delegation and how to overcome them.

CHAPTER RECAP

The key points from this chapter are:

- Mismanaged time can impact other people, not just you.

- Time management means managing your behavior, not time.

EXHIBIT 3-8

Overcoming Barriers to Effective Delegation

Barriers for Delegator	Overcoming Barriers
Preference for doing instead of managing	Learn through workshops how to be a teacher and coach.
Demanding that you know all the details	After explaining the task, brainstorm possible ways to handle task. Let delegatee choose or suggest some alternatives that you both can agree on.
Believing you can do it better yourself	Choose a delegatee whose work you have observed and whom you trust.
Lack of job knowledge	Seek training so you can clarify the task.
Fear of being disliked	To decrease resentment from the delegatee for asking her to do a task, assure delegatee that you are asking her help because of her competence. Be sure she feels comfortable coming to you if she runs into trouble.
Perfectionism that leads to overcontrol	Use the behavioral change techniques in this chapter.
Lack of organizational skills in balancing workload	Practice time management techniques listed in this chapter. Begin by setting goals for yourself and your delegatee.
Failure to delegate corresponding authority with level of responsibility	Explain whether you want your delegatee to generate new ideas or carry out specific duties.

Barriers for Delegatee	
Lack of experience, competence	Obtain training to increase knowledge, self-esteem, and confidence.
Overdependence on the boss	Before asking the delegator "How would you do this?" first think of the ways you think it should be handled. Then, if you feel more comfortable with feedback, seek out the delegator and say "This is how I was planning to do this. What do you think?"
Avoidance of responsibility	Ask yourself why the task isn't done. If lack of experience, ask for training. If resentment for having to do the task, have the delegator explain why the task is important and why you were asked to do it. Set goals and specific deadlines.

Barriers in the Situation	
"One-man show" policy	Organizational culture should be one that supports team effort where all involved in a project are rewarded similarly.
No toleration of mistakes	Mistakes should be opportunities for learning, not disciplinary action.
Confusion in responsibilities and authority	Roles and expectations should be clearly defined through job descriptions, performance feedback, and team meetings.

- The three types of time-wasters are attitudinal, behavioral (which includes bad habits, procrastination, avoidance, perfectionism, unassertiveness, and work addiction), and situational (which includes paperwork and reading, telephone calls, and unproductive meetings).

- Meeting preparation includes consideration of the steps needed before, during, and after the meeting.

- The most important step before meetings is preparation and distribution of a one-page, well-structured agenda that includes the day, time, and place of the meeting; items to bring to the meeting, follow-up from the last meeting, and agenda items with the amount of time allotted for each item.

- Other time management strategies include goal setting, action-step planning, prioritized to-do lists, determining peak energy periods, finding hidden times, learning effective decision-making skills, and delegating.

- Goal setting is effective in time management because it gives people a sense of control over their lives and reduces stress from uncertainty involved with doing assigned tasks.

- Setting goals begins with two main questions: What are the things I need to do? and What are the things I want to do?"
- Goals should be specific, measurable, achievable, realistic, and timely (SMART).
- People don't make timely, effective decisions for one or all of the following reasons: fear of the unknown, fear of conflict, lack of knowledge, and poor decision-making ability.
- Effective decision making requires that you identify and write down your goal, identify all the possible solutions to a problem or alternatives to a decision, consider the advantages and disadvantages of each alternative, identify the alternative that best meets your goal, carry out your decision, and evaluate, monitor, and change your decision when necessary.
- Delegation involves three factors: the delegatee, the delegator, and the situation.
- Steps for successful delegation include clarifying the goal to the delegatee, breaking tasks into smaller parts with deadlines for each part, complimenting the delegatee on good work, defining responsibility and authority levels, coaching, requiring completed work, and providing training to delegatees on complex tasks of which they are unsure.

Critical Thinking Questions

1. Think about the one person at work who has the most negative effect on your time. What does he or she do? What are some things you could do so that person's behavior doesn't waste your time? What could you say?

2. What kind of calendar do you keep? Is it a pocket calendar, a desk blotter that covers most of your desk, or one in a stand that sits in the corner of your desk? Is it a daily, weekly, or monthly calendar? How visible is it? That is, if your calendar also serves as a desk blotter, can you easily see it to check important dates and appointments? What kind of calendar do you think might work best?

3. The next time you are assigned an office or class project with another person, what are some of the things you can do ahead of time that can help both of you work better together on the project to ensure it is completed in a timely manner?

WEB SITES

For further information, log on to the following web sites.

www.daytimer.com
Provides a great link to time management articles and tips. To use this site, click the resource center tab, choose library, and then choose articles and tips.
www.GetMoreDone.Com
Provides time management tips and time management trivia.

KEY TERMS

Action-step planning A step-by-step process identifying everything you need to do and the time when it needs to be done.

Attitudinal time-waster A time-waster based on how individuals think about or judge time.

Avoidance The intentional act of ignoring your responsibilities with the hope you won't have to do them.

Behavioral time-waster A time-waster that individuals create for themselves such as sticking to familiar habits, procrastination, and unassertiveness.

Delegation The process of assigning tasks to other people.

Desire The motivation or want to do of a habit.

Habit The intersection of knowledge, skill, and desire.

Instant gratification A force that pulls people toward the activity that will have the best results in the shortest amount of time.

Knowledge The what to do of a habit and the why.

Perfectionism The desire to perform every task and behavior with top precision and accuracy.

Prioritization Assigning importance to each activity you have to do and determining which activity must be worked on first.

Procrastination The tendency to postpone action toward a goal that individuals recognize needs to be done now.

Skill The how to do of a habit.

Situational time-wasters Time-wasters that are created by other people such as the generation of paperwork, telephone calls, and ineffective meetings.

SMART The criteria for goals: specific, measurable, attainable, realistic, and timely.

Time management An adjustment in your attitude and behavior toward meeting daily demands.

To-do list Written statements of the tasks you need to accomplish on any particular day.

Unassertiveness An individual's inability to say no to requests by others for help on tasks that are not the responsibility of the unassertive person.

Work addiction An individual's inability to stop working or use unanticipated time to catch up with current workloads.

PRACTICE EXAM

1. Time management means
   a. controlling your time
   b. managing your time
   c. managing your behavior
   d. controlling others' behaviors

2. "I have plenty of time to do this report—why bother doing it today?" is an example of a(n) _____ time-waster.
   a. attitudinal
   b. behavioral
   c. situational
   d. management

3. Joe has no time to go to lunch today because he has to catch up on reading all the mail and other correspondence that has crossed his desk over the last few weeks. This reading material is an example of a(n) _____ time-waster.
   a. attitudinal
   b. behavioral
   c. situational
   d. management

4. Judith never seems pleased with the work her team does. Every time they complete a report, she gives it back to them two or three times with revisions. This is an example of a(n) _____ time-waster known as _____.
   a. attitudinal; procrastination
   b. situational; ineffectiveness
   c. behavioral; unassertiveness
   d. behavioral; perfectionism

5. A habit involves all of the following except:
   a. knowledge
   b. attitude
   c. skill
   d. desire

6. Instant gratification is one reason why people pick _____ tasks over _____ tasks.
   a. routine; new
   b. complex; easy
   c. likeable; distasteful
   d. new; routine

7. Maya has a problem with her roommate Donna. On the weeks that Donna has dish-washing duty, she lets the dishes pile up and stay in the sink until Maya can't take it anymore. Maya usually ends up doing the dishes. Donna's time-wasting behavior is
   a. procrastination
   b. unassertiveness
   c. perfectionism
   d. avoidance

8. Doug is going crazy. He has two reports due this week; his girlfriend asked him to go over to her house and feed her dog three times a day while she's on vacation; he told his sick room-mate that he would go to his class to get his roommate's notes; and he has agreed to help his instructor enter some data for a research project due at the end of the week. Doug doesn't feel he has enough time to do everything. His time-wasting behavior is probably due to:
   a. avoidance
   b. unassertiveness
   c. perfectionism
   d. procrastination

9. Goals should be:
   a. smart, easy, realistic, attainable, timely
   b. simple, monumental, attainable, realistic
   c. specific, measurable, attainable, realistic, timely
   d. simple, measurable, attainable, realistic, timely

10. Which is the *best* definition of an effective agenda? An agenda:
    a. includes time, date, location of meeting and is sent out several days before a meeting
    b. includes time and date of a meeting and is given out at the beginning of the meeting.
    c. includes the goals of each meeting.
    d. allows time for team members to follow up their actions from their last meeting.

11. Delegation involves these three factors:
    a. delegator, situation, time
    b. situation, to-do lists, action-steps
    c. delegator, flexibility, control
    d. delegatee, situation, delegator

12. The Quality Team was pleased to be asked by the Administrative Team to address the issue of improving the computer system. They came up with what they considered an excellent plan for improvement. When they gave the recommendation to the Administrative Team, the Team said they didn't like the idea and would use their own idea. The Quality Team was upset with the way the Administrative Team had delegated this project. Of the eight steps to effective delegation, which step did the Administrative Team forget to do?
    a. require completed work
    b. define responsibility and authority level
    c. explain the task
    d. give feedback

13. Which is *not* a step for effective decision making?
    a. selecting the first alternative to a solution
    b. writing down your goal
    c. rating negative and positive consequences
    d. monitoring your decision

14. The benefits of managing your time include all *except*:
    a. reduced stress
    b. control over time
    c. organization
    d. better results

15. It takes _____ consecutive days for a behavior to become a habit.
    a. 15
    b. 25
    c. 30
    d. 5

ANSWERS 1 c, 2 a, 3 c, 4 d, 5 b, 6 a, 7 d, 8 b, 9 c, 10 a, 11 d, 12 b, 13 a, 14 b, 15 c

Focused Free-Write

Think about an incident in which you feel you did not manage your time well. This incident could have happened at work, home, or school. Write down the impact "running out of time" had on both you and others. How did you and others react to your running out of time?

_____

_____

_____

_____

_____

_____

_____

_____

_____

_____

_____

_____

_____

_____

_____

_____

_____

_____

_____

Evaluating Your Time Management Behaviors

Read each behavior statement carefully. Circle whether or not you generally engage in such behavior. There is no overall score on this exercise. However, a minus (−) represents ineffective behavior and a plus (+) represents good behavior. Reflect on how your behaviors might have affected you in the past and how they will affect you in the future. After reading the remainder of Chapter 3, you will learn how to turn your minuses into pluses.

	Yes	No
1. I make a daily to-do list that is always visible.	+	−
2. I put off today what I can do tomorrow.	−	+
3. I mark down important dates on my calendar and look at them daily.	+	−
4. I prioritize my daily activities in the order they should be done.	+	−
5. I ask for help when I am busy with other things.	+	−
6. I keep working on a task or project until I think it is perfect.	−	+
7. I have written down weekly, monthly, and yearly goals.	+	−
8. When I get busy, I tell people I cannot talk to them right now.	+	−
9. I can make minor and routine decisions fairly quickly.	+	−
10. I solicit feedback from others on decisions that I am considering.	+	−
11. I use spare moments such as riding in the car or listening to commercials to catch up on work or studying.	+	−
12. I rarely say no when people ask for my help, even when I'm busy.	−	+
13. I set clear and realistic deadlines for meeting obligations.	+	−
14. I carry index cards in my wallet, purse, or briefcase so I can jot down ideas or things I need to do.	+	−
15. I do what I like to do first, then anything I dislike or don't understand I put off until another day.	−	+
16. In the last 6 months, I have met my responsibilities and still had time to do the things I wanted to do such as spend time with family and friends.	+	−
17. When I am assigned work, I immediately organize how I am going to do it and when it will be completed.	+	−
18. I get very stressed if I cannot meet all of my daily goals.	−	+
19. I rarely change the way I do a task once I have learned it a certain way.	−	+

On the basis of how you answered the 19 questions, how would you evaluate your current time management skills?

_____

_____

_____

_____

_____

_____

_____

_____

_____

_____

_____

_____

_____

_____

_____

_____

_____

_____

_____

_____

_____

Where Does Time Go?

Use this Time Log to help identify potential time-wasters in your life. For one complete week, write down every activity you do and how long it takes you to do it. Begin with the time you got up in the morning and end with the time you went to bed. To help you get started, we have listed some activities most people do each day. Don't forget to include activities such as lunch and dinner, exercising, spending time with friends or on the phone. At the end of the week, review your Time Log, and consider how you might have made better use of your time.

Day 1	Time to complete activity
Time I woke up in morning	_____
Got ready for work, class, etc.	_____
Ate breakfast	_____
Commuted to work (or class)	_____
Cleaned house/room	_____
_____	_____
_____	_____
_____	_____
_____	_____
_____	_____
_____	_____
_____	_____
_____	_____
_____	_____
_____	_____
_____	_____

Goal Setting and Action-Step Planning

List three goals you want to accomplish this week. After each goal, determine the action steps you need to take to meet those goals.

Goal   **Timeline**

1. _____   By: _____

    Action Steps:_____   by: _____

    _____   by: _____

    _____   by: _____

    _____   by: _____

    _____   by: _____

2. _____   By: _____

    Action Steps:_____   by: _____

    _____   by: _____

    _____   by: _____

    _____   by: _____

    _____   by: _____

3. _____   By: _____

    Action Steps:_____   by: _____

    _____   by: _____

    _____   by: _____

    _____   by: _____

    _____   by: _____

Making Prioritized To-Do Lists

Refer to your goals and action steps. Write down things you want or have to do TOMORROW in order to stay on track with your action steps and goal timelines. Be sure to write down other daily tasks you need to do. **Prioritize these in order of importance and how critical it is for them to be done tomorrow.**

Tasks To Do   **Done?**

_____   _____

_____   _____

_____   _____

_____   _____

_____   _____

_____   _____

_____   _____

_____   _____

_____   _____

_____   _____

_____   _____

_____   _____

_____   _____

_____   _____

_____   _____

_____   _____

Improving Your Decision-Making Skills

Read the following case study that presents you with a decision-making dilemma. In Section A, list all of the possible choices you could make. Don't just list the obvious ones because most decisions aren't that simple: Usually more is involved when accepting a job. Beside each possible choice, list the positive and negative consequences of that decision. Each choice might have both positive and negative consequences, so be sure to list them all. Use another sheet of paper if you have to. When you are finished, complete Sections B and C.

Case Study: Currently, you are attending school in Perfect Town, Iowa, where you have always lived. You will be graduating in less than a month. You have received two job offers: One in your hometown of Perfect Town, the other in California. Both jobs sound good. The job in California pays more with great benefits, but your work schedule will be 10 hours a day, five days a week. You will be managing four other people. The one in Perfect Town pays less but has better health insurance, including dental and eye care (you wear glasses). In the job in California, you have an opportunity to become a top manager within 2 years. You aren't sure of the opportunities with the job in Perfect Town. But California seems so far away from your family. Both companies need to have your answer day after tomorrow, so you don't have a lot of time to think about it. You have to decide between the job in Perfect Town and the one in California. You are "stuck" in your decision. Use this form to help you make your decision.

Section A

Choice	Consequences of Choice	Negative	Positive
1.			
2.			
3.			

Section B

Count and write the number of positive and negative consequences for each choice

Choice	Number of positive consequences	Number of negative consequences
1. _____	_____	_____
2. _____	_____	_____
3. _____	_____	_____

Section C

Just based on the number of positive consequences, which choice (or decision) would you make? If you don't have a decision that has more positive consequences than the other choices, re-evaluate your consequences until you can get to a decision that is clearly better than the others. The decision you make won't necessarily be the same as your friends because of your goals, personality, and perspective on the advantages and disadvantages.

_____

_____

_____

_____

_____

_____

_____

_____

_____

_____

_____

_____

_____

_____

_____

_____

CHAPTER FOUR

Developing a Sense of Ethical Professionalism

In the last three chapters, you learned how such interpersonal skills as managing stress, using time management strategies, and understanding individual differences can help make you a more effective and competent worker. In fact, the purpose of this entire book is to ensure your professionalism when you enter the workforce.

But professionalism means more than just improving your interpersonal skills and knowing how to interact with others. Although some people may think they are professionals merely because of their college degrees, professional certifications, licenses, and/or job experiences, professionalism has as much to do with the *image* you project as it does with what you know and how you behave toward others. Additionally, professionalism is defined by your workplace ethics. The purpose of this chapter is to identify factors that can improve your professionalism and how professionalism is important in ethical decision making. In this chapter you will:

Learn what it means to be a professional

Understand the importance of matching your career preferences with job choices

Learn how to dress for success

Understand how to maintain positive customer service

Be able to define workplace ethics

Understand why people make unethical decisions

Learn how to influence ethical behavior

■ PROFESSIONALISM

Professionalism is the continuous process of developing competence in the following areas: career planning, knowledge, presentation of self, empathy, job performance, customer service, and ethical decision making. Therefore, a **professional** is an individual who is continuously motivated to seek, learn, and apply, in a fair and ethical manner, the knowledge and skills needed to do his particular job.

> *Focused Free-Write*
> To get you thinking about professionalism and appropriate work behaviors, complete the Focused Free-Write at the end of this chapter.

Career Planning and Development

Compare a job you liked with one you disliked. Did you perform your duties well in the job you disliked? Did you have the right skills and knowledge to perform the job? Were you absent more on the job you disliked than on the job you liked? Some research suggests that dissatisfied workers are more likely to be absent than satisfied workers—behavior that is often perceived as unprofessional. Also, if you accept a position in which you really aren't interested and for which you know you don't have the skills, you may be perceived as unethical (Lowman, 1998). Therefore, to decrease the likelihood of your dissatisfaction and increase your chances of an appropriate fit between you, the job, and the organization in which you take the job, you should engage in career development prior to and after entering your chosen field.

Career development is a lifelong process of understanding your career preferences; identifying, obtaining, and developing appropriate skills and training for that career; and continually evaluating your career preferences and skills over your working life to determine if they continue to meet your needs and those of the organization (Zunker, 1990).

In the past, large organizations such as AT&T have taken on the task of developing their employees' careers. AT&T offers employees an opportunity, with the assistance of a career advisor, to identify future careers in which they are interested and help them find needed training for those careers. However, because of downsizing and attempts to reduce costs, fewer organizations are providing such a benefit to their employees. Consequently, most organizations consider employees responsible for developing their own careers and acquiring the appropriate skills needed to keep a job and do it well (Hammond, 1996).

The three stages to career planning and development include assessment, exploration, and goal setting and action-step planning (Knowdell, 1996).

STAGE 1: ASSESSMENT

During this stage, you should ask yourself:

1. *What are my occupational interests?* Some people have difficulty determining what they want to do in life. For example, many college students don't declare their majors until their sophomore or junior year because they are unsure of what they want to do. This stage is important even if you are an adult student who already has a job.

   One way to narrow your career preference is by completing a vocational interest survey. The purpose of such a survey is to determine in what career areas you are most and least interested. Why is this important? Research suggests that there is a positive correlation between matching your career interests, the job you choose, and work satisfaction. That is, you are more likely to stay in a job and to go to work if you like the work and it keeps you interested.

EXHIBIT 4-1

Essential Skills for the 21st Century

Basic Skills
 Reading
 Writing
 Analysis
 Problem solving
 Grammar

Computer Skills
 Keyboarding (minimum of 35 words per minute)
 Word processing
 Spreadsheets

Interpersonal Skills
 Speaking and listening
 Customer service

Analytical Skills

Flexibility

PROJECT A *What Is the Best Career for You: Aamodt Vocational Interest Survey*
Complete the vocational interest survey in Project A at the end of this chapter to determine the careers in which you are most and least interested.

On a vocational survey, scoring high in a particular area doesn't necessarily mean you should pursue that particular career (Knowdell, 1996). For example, let's say you score high in the vocational interest category of agriculture. Does that mean you should be a farmer, rancher, or cattleman? Probably not! What it might indicate is that you have a strong interest in being outside, working with your hands, or doing some type of environmental work. Understanding these strong interests can help guide you toward a career that offers those opportunities.

2. *What education, training, and skills do I need to do the job?* To answer this question, seek the advice of your advisor or instructors who can inform you of the *minimum* skills and education employers in your chosen career expect, or interview individuals in your chosen career field. For example, if you are interested in the Protective vocational area, you could interview an EMT, police officer, or park ranger. Many colleges hold an annual Career Fair for just this purpose, inviting professionals to set up booths and meet with students to discuss the skills and education needed

for specific careers. If a Career Fair is available, you should make every attempt to attend.

Another alternative for finding out the skills and educational training you need is to refer to the *Occupational Outlook Handbook* issued by the U.S. Department of Labor every 2 years, which lists hundreds of jobs. Your local or college libraries may actually have such information on the computer, making it easier to access.

In addition to specific skills, an increasing number of employers are requiring certain minimum skills, regardless of job choice. Exhibit 4-1 lists some of the essential skills for the 21st century. Of particular interest is flexibility. Because of mergers, downsizing, globalization, job sharing, and reorganization, companies are constantly changing, and workers need to be flexible in their way of thinking and in the jobs they do. We can almost guarantee that the job you are hired for when you graduate will look different within a year after you start. A true professional is able to adjust to changing circumstances.

PROJECT B *The Right Skills for the Right Job*
Complete Project B at the end of this chapter to help you identify the skills and education you need for your chosen career.

3. *What skills and education do I currently have?* At this point, you need to consider your education

and determine any discrepancy in that area based on the minimum required in your chosen career. Next, look at the skills and training you currently have and any discrepancies based on those needed for an entry-level position.

PROJECT C *The Skills and Education I Have*
Complete Project C at the end of this chapter to identify the skills you currently have that meet your chosen career.

After completing Stage 1 and Projects A, B, and C, you can go on to Stage 2 in the career development process.

STAGE 2: EXPLORATION

The vocational interest survey you completed lists several jobs under each vocational interest or career category. Exploration involves three steps. The first is to explore which specific jobs under the vocational interest area in which you scored highest appeal to you the most. Because we provide only a partial listing of jobs, there may be another job that you have already been considering. Remember, this inventory doesn't necessarily tell you which field you should enter but does indicate certain work interests that are important to you in a career (e.g., being able to work outside, interacting with a lot of people, working on your own as opposed to working in a team environment). You can make this exploration simultaneously with Step 1, prior to determining the skills you need to do a job.

The next step in the exploration stage is determining if your chosen career is realistic and obtainable. That is, your dream may be to become the next Denzel Washington or Helen Hunt. Realistically, that may need to remain a dream. The fact that you like acting, however, may mean you would be interested in a job where you give training or presentations to other people. For example, one of our colleagues took drama in college and did very well at it; she has an outgoing personality and is extremely talented. However, she realized that her first goal of becoming an actress wasn't realistic and instead received her master's degree in organizational psychology and is the director of a human resource department in a large hospital. One of her duties includes setting up training and morale building workshops where she puts her love of acting to work. She's funny, creative, and her staff usually leaves those meetings in high spirits!

Finally, the third step in exploration is researching the extended outlook for the career in which you are interested. This information can be obtained through your school, the U.S. Department of Labor, or your local employment commission. You probably don't want to go into an occupation that is expected to de-

cline or be nonexistent in the next decade. For example, the employment of court reporters is expected to decline. On the other hand, according to the U.S. Department of Labor (1995), the job outlook for health services managers is expected to grow faster than the average for all occupations through the year 2005. This growth increases your chances of obtaining and retaining employment in this area. Exhibit 4-2 lists the hot careers for the 21st century.

After exploring your options, you enter the final stage in career development: goal setting and action-step planning.

STAGE 3: GOAL SETTING AND ACTION-STEP PLANNING

Now that you have narrowed your career interest to a specific career and know the education and skills you need, the next step is developing a strategy for reaching your destination. You need to ask such questions as:

- How and where will I get the education and training I need?
- What can I financially afford for education and training?
- How long will it take me to get that education and training?
- Where are the jobs in my chosen career (e.g., are the best jobs in big cities, on the east coast or west coast?)
- What type of advancement or salary am I looking for?
- Am I willing to relocate to where the best jobs are?

The answer to each one of these questions may raise other questions. The more questions you ask yourself, the more likely you will get into the college or training program that will best meet your needs.

PROJECT D *Goal Setting and Planning*
Complete Project D at the end of this chapter to help you set goals and timelines to meet your career objectives.

Once you have completed Projects A through D, you will have developed a Career Profile to which you can refer, change, and update from this point on. Exhibit 4-3 shows what your completed Career Profile might look like.

Knowledge

To be a true professional, you should have knowledge about your job (skill knowledge), your organization, and how to interact well with other people

EXHIBIT 4-2

Hot Careers for the 21st Century

Health care field

nursing assistant

technicians (lab, pharmacy)

dental assistants

physical therapy

Business

computer and data processing

temporary employment agencies

legal (paralegal, legal assistant)

engineering

management services

Education

teachers

teacher aides

Social services

residential care facilities for older people

day care centers for both young and older individuals

(emotional intelligence). In addition, most employers require basic business and communication skills.

SKILL KNOWLEDGE

Usually you will enter your job with some of the required skills. You are learning new skills as you take this class. However, it will undoubtedly be necessary to obtain additional training after you begin your job. You will have a better understanding of what those skills are after completing your career profile. A true professional continues to attend workshops and trainings annually to upgrade his current skills.

ORGANIZATION KNOWLEDGE

How well you know your organization (e.g., the products it sells, how well it is doing, its long-term goals, and mission) reflects on your credibility and professionalism (Alessandra & Hunsaker, 1993). Therefore, it is important that you read annual reports and keep abreast of other events or changes occurring within your company. The Internet is one source you can use to research companies, their purpose, products they make, and services they provide.

EMOTIONAL INTELLIGENCE

Emotional intelligence refers to your ability to interact well with others and your competency in the following areas (Goleman, 1998):

- Recognizing your feelings and the feelings and needs of others with whom you interact. For example, when others are upset, angry, or happy, do you pick up on those feelings? Do you acknowledge or ignore them?

- Being able to motivate yourself instead of waiting for your supervisors or employers to offer some type of motivating incentive. That is, rather than meeting expectations, do you exceed them?

- Managing your emotions instead of letting your emotions manage you. This competency refers to how you deal with anger, frustration, and disappointment.

According to Goleman, emotional intelligence is just as important as job-specific skills. He suggests that any job field requires different emotional competencies. For example, bankers must have the ability to respect the confidentiality of customers while nurses must have a sense of humor. These emotional competencies are more difficult to teach, and perhaps learn, because they require individuals to be willing to admit to their shortcomings and change, accordingly.

BASIC KNOWLEDGE

Exhibit 4-4 lists the minimum basic knowledge that organizations look for in their professionals (Crane, 1994). As you can see, many of these correspond

EXHIBIT 4-3

Completed Career Profile

Stage 1: Assessment

A. **Career Interest**: Management/leadership position in Top 500 Company

B. **Education I need**	**Education I have**	**Discrepancy**
Bachelor's degree in Business Management	Associate's degree in business	Need 2 more years

C. **Skills I need**	**Skills I have**	**Discrepancy**
problem solving	problem solving	analytical skills
human relations	human relations	conflict management
presentation skills	presentation skills	coaching/leadership
analytical skills		
conflict management		
coaching others		

D. **Work Experience I should have**	**Experience I have**	**Discrepancy**
supervising others	none in management	supervising

Stage 2: Exploration

A. Is this a realistic goal?	Yes
B. Can I reach it in a realistic time frame?	Yes

Stage 3: Goal Setting and Action-Step Planning

A. **Education**		
Get bachelor's degree in business	By: June 2002	At Sunnybrook College
Complete application to college	By: Sept. 2000	
Get master's in business	By: 2005	Go to Sunnybrook part-time after graduating from bachelor's program and obtaining full-time work

B. **Training/Skills**		
Take course in leadership	By: Spring 2001	At Sunnybrook College
Enroll in conflict management or mediation	By: Summer 2001	County Conflict Center
Join club where I have to make professional presentations	By: Fall 2000	Sunnybrook College

C. **Work Experience**		
Get job at fast food restaurant	By: Fall 2000	
Try to get assistant management position	By: Fall 2001	

with the minimum skills needed for the 21st century listed in Exhibit 4-1. You have already gained much of this knowledge, either in other jobs you have held or through classes you have taken. For other basic skills, you may need to enroll in additional training either through college or by attending workshops.

PROJECT E *Self-Assessment of Basic Knowledge*
Complete Project E at the end of this chapter to rate your basic knowledge.

Obtaining the knowledge in all of these areas will make you multi-competent and highly marketable (Timm, 1992). Most important, your organizational value, credibility, and professionalism increases as you become more versatile.

Presentation of Self

Presentation of self involves knowing how to dress and groom appropriately for your particular job,

EXHIBIT 4-4

Minimum Basic Knowledge

- Basic writing, math, analytical, logic, and computer skills
- Ability to interpret data
- Decision making
- Flexibility and adaptability to constant changes that might occur in the organization
- Communication skills
- Ability to work in teams (Crane, 1994)
- Leadership

using proper business etiquette, and dealing with office politics.

DRESSING FOR THE JOB

How you dress communicates something about yourself, as does your grooming (Alessandra & Hunsaker, 1993; Eggert, 1992; Fowler, 1991). The clothes, cologne, perfume, shoes, or makeup you choose can make a difference in how you are treated by others. For example, what would you think if you went to a doctor's office and the doctor you spoke to was in torn jeans, had food all over his shirt and tie, and had an offensive odor? Most people would run to the nearest exit! You would probably even go to a different doctor. Even though the first doctor may be the best in his field, most people will generally judge an individual's competence based on his or her appearance. Whether that is right or wrong is irrelevant. Your appearance is so important that many books and articles have been written on the subject—particularly on how to dress for an interview. It is so important that some organizations define appropriate ways to dress in the initial training of their communication officers.

An increasing number of organizations are recognizing diverse cultural differences in dress in the United States and have relaxed their dress codes to accommodate that diversity. But courts have previously ruled that organizations *do* have the right to set a certain standard of dress and level of grooming unless it discriminates against employees on the basis of their race, religion, ethnic background, or gender (Rothstein, Craver, Schroeder, Shoben & VanderVelde, 1994; Wolkinson & Block, 1996). Consequently, many organizations subscribe to a "traditional" way of dressing. Therefore, it is important and practical that you know what's in and what's out. The exception to these rules on what's in and what's out has to

do with your company's organizational culture. We talk more about organizational culture later in this chapter, but with regard to dress, the point is that if you work in a job where everyone, including the CEO and top management, wears jeans and/or no ties, that is the way you should probably dress.

What's in? Biegeleisen (1994) gives several tips on clothing and grooming practices that are still consistently acceptable and considered professional for many jobs. These tips are listed in Exhibit 4-5. Of particular interest is that conservatism is still "in." Professional colors still remain the traditional off-white, navy blue, gray, and tan. Consider this: The last time you were in a bank or other business, how were people dressed? Most of them were probably in these traditional colors, unless the company was having a casual-dress day ("dress-down Friday"). Then, you might have seen employees dressed more informally. The traditional way of dressing doesn't necessarily mean you can't vary somewhat and wear more colorful apparel, as many employees do. The point is that true professionals are aware of what is considered professional in their particular position and career field and adjust their behavior and clothing accordingly.

What's out? Employers continue to weed out applicants who violate dress expectations (USA Today, 1997). Whether you are an applicant or an employee, the following grooming and clothing choices are still considered unprofessional.

Visible tattoos and nose rings are definitely out for men and women. Many companies won't let men wear earrings. For example, employees at Disneyland are required to present a wholesome look, which doesn't include earrings or long hair on men, or lots of jewelry or revealing clothes on women.

EXHIBIT 4-5

Dressing for the Job

Men

- **Grooming**

  Hair is neat, well-trimmed, clean, free from dandruff.

  Face should be well shaved, no nicks or blood, beard should be trimmed and neat.

  Hands are clean and nails are properly trimmed, no ragged cuticles.

- **Basic Wardrobe**

  Dress conservatively in colors of dark blue or gray made of blend of wool and silk (no polyester)

  Executive should wear three-piece suits, lower level positions, two-piece.

  Shirts should be well pressed and show no signs of fraying around collar or cuffs.

  Ties should be clean and free from wrinkles and be color coordinated with your suit.

  Shoes should be well shined and in good condition; slip-on shoes are okay; shoestrings should be tied.

- **Miscellaneous**

  Jewelry such as watches should be conservative and not goofy, such as a Mickey Mouse watch.

- **Personal Hygiene**

  Shower or bathe every day.

  Use nonfragrant deodorant.

  Brush teeth daily and use mouthwash.

Women

- **Grooming**

  Hairstyle coiffures are not appropriate; trim long hair to moderate length.

  Makeup should be light, use eyeshadow to accentuate, not hide, eyes.

  Hands should be meticulously clean, nail polish should be appropriate color, not neon.

- **Basic Wardrobe**

  Dress conservatively in a well-fitted tailored suit, dress, or coordinated skirt/trousers and blouses; zippers should lie flat, seams should have no raw edges,

  Buttonholes should line up, and there should be no loose threads.

  Avoid skin-tight sweaters, see-through blouses, and low necklines.

  Shoes should have medium heels and coordinate with your conservative outfit.

  Neutral-toned pantyhose are more appropriate than colored ones.

- **Miscellaneous**

  No big rings or large necklaces; no more than 2 rings on each hand (not finger!); no ankle bracelets, earrings should be of moderate size.

  Eyeglasses should enhance your appearance not detract from it; new designer styles are smarter looking than traditional eyewear; consider contact lenses.

  No visible body piercing or tattoos.

- **Personal Hygiene**

  Perfume should be minimal, if any at all.

  Shower or bathe every day.

  Brush teeth daily and use mouthwash.

Many experts also advise against cologne for men or perfume for women (Biegeleisen, 1994) for two primary reasons. First, other people may actually be allergic to colognes and perfumes and can become ill around someone wearing them. Second, some people don't realize how much they are putting on and can overwhelm an entire office with their strong scent. The example we like to give concerns our son who, at seventeen, was preparing for a date one evening. As we bid him farewell at the door, we were almost knocked over by his cologne. Although the cologne was a nice scent, too much of it was sickening! We were able to convince him to tone it down by washing some of it off.

Jeans, too, are usually not acceptable in most organizations, but some individual companies allow them. For example, most high-tech companies allow their employees to wear jeans, and jeans are allowed on casual-dress days in many organizations.

BUSINESS ETIQUETTE

Business etiquette pertains to using good social skills in business situations. The emphasis is on how you treat others and how you behave in social situations.

Your treatment of others is important to whether others perceive you as being professional. For example, how often do you say *thank you* for a job well done or when you receive help from others? Do you preface or end a request with *please*? Are you free with your apologies when you forget to call someone, are late for a meeting, or make a mistake? Dr. Shirley Willey of Etiquette and Company states that one out of three men and women sabotage their success when they appear rude or arrogant, are not courteous, fail to return phone calls promptly, or use profanity. The more frequently you ignore these social skills, the less professional you are perceived to be.

Business etiquette also means acquiring the skill to interact and dine in business situations. Have you ever gone out with a work colleague who embarrassed you by belching or loudly munching on their food? If it embarrassed you, how do you think *your* skills in this area affect others? Not only can such behavior end good working relationships, but with individuals with the authority to promote you, chances are you will not look like the true professional they are seeking. Exhibit 4-6 lists some business etiquette rules that you may want to follow at your next social setting.

The importance of teaching business etiquette has been recognized, and training is available. The training might entail a full-course meal and lessons on how to eat properly, ordering appropriate videos on hotel television when attending overnight conferences, and lessons on appropriate topics to discuss with groups of other professionals. Even if you are already in a professional position, we highly recommend such training if your college or training institution offers it.

OFFICE POLITICS

Office politics are those activities people engage in to influence who gets or doesn't get certain organizational advantages (e.g., promotions, coveted offices). Office politics has to do with power: who has it, who wants it, and who uses it to get their way. Although power is not inherently bad, the abuse of it is considered unprofessional, as well as unethical. There are two types of office politics: acceptable and unacceptable.

Acceptable office politics include such behavior as legitimately complaining to a boss about how one worker is mistreating another or how one employee isn't pulling his share of the load. The complainer might be a supervisor who uses his position to influence what happens to the person about whom he is complaining. In an instance like this, the use of power is acceptable and functional because the person using it is trying to make positive changes for the good of the organization and its employees.

Unacceptable office politics include unprofessional behaviors such as organizational sabotage, lying, consistently breaking company policies, and personal verbal attacks on others. For example, think about two employees who are applying for the same position. In an attempt to influence the promotion decision, Worker A attempts to make Worker B look bad by spreading a rumor that Worker B has been using sick leave instead of vacation days. Although this trick may work, the consequence of using unacceptable office politics is to your credibility and professionalism. The more unacceptable behaviors you are perceived as using, the less professional you are considered.

Kirkwood (1993) lists several rules for dealing with office politics.

Rules for office politics

1. Never repeat anything you have been told. People love knowing what no one else knows. It can be fun, prestigious, and powerful to be the first with information. But it isn't fun unless you can tell someone else, right? However, some things are told to you in strict confidence. People trust you. If you repeat what you are told, particularly when you know you shouldn't, that trust will be reduced, as will your credibility.

2. Don't say anything you would be embarrassed to have repeated on the news or written on the front page of the newspaper. Have you ever gone to a party where you had a really good time but the next morning you woke up hating yourself for saying the wrong thing to someone? Imagine

EXHIBIT 4-6

Mastering Business Etiquette

Men

- **Before the Social Situation**

  Always respond (with acceptance or regrets) to an invitation.

  Arrive on time.

- **During the Social Situation**

  Seek out your host and thank him or her for inviting you.

  Stand and sit up straight.

  Make eye contact with people who are talking to you. Ask open-ended questions.

  Wait until everyone has been served before eating.

  Wait until host begins eating.

  Eat with utensils from outside in.

  Always pass dishes to your right. Do not serve yourself first.

  Cut one piece of food at a time. Lay knife across top of plate with blade toward you.

  Break off bite-sized pieces of bread or rolls.

- **After the Social Situation**

  When finished eating, put your fork on either the right or left side, depending upon which hand you are. Knife should be laid across the top of the plate.

  Place napkin on right side of place setting.

  Send thank you note.

---

that happening at work or a professional function, and imagine that getting into the newspaper or on the radio! The rule here is: Think before you speak or act.

3. Show the same amount of support and respect to everyone. Don't treat coworkers with higher level positions better than those with less position. A true professional believes that individuals are equal and should be treated with the same amount of respect.

4. Deal appropriately with the other gender. Sexual harassment is a significant organizational issue, and make no mistake—men, as well as women, can be sexually harassed. Research shows that as many as 40% of women and 15% of men have been sexually harassed in organizations (Moulton, 1994).

Sexual harassment involves being treated differently from others because of your gender. In the legal sense, this treatment must be of an unwelcome verbal or physical nature that intentionally or unintentionally interferes with your performance on the job, makes you feel threatened or intimidated, makes you

feel you are the target of someone else's hostility, or makes your working environment feel uncomfortable. The courts consider sexual harassment as discrimination, and most companies have policies that provide sanctions for such behavior (Lowman, 1998). The problem is defining what constitutes harassing behavior.

As you learned in Chapter 1, people have different perspectives on behavior that makes them feel uncomfortable. For example, your coworker next to you may not mind being pinched or listening to your off-color jokes, but the worker down the hall may take offense, be humiliated by your actions, intimidated, and yes, even scared. Because of these different perspectives, your goal isn't to determine which behaviors you can use with one person and which behaviors you can use with another. Your goal is to treat everyone with the same professional attitude as you would want to be treated.

Our objective in bringing up this topic is to identify general behaviors that every professional, male or female, should or should not engage in at work, which will take the guesswork out of whether your actions could be perceived as sexual harassment.

EXHIBIT 4-7

Professionalism: Interacting with the Other Gender

General Rules

- Recognize that sexual harassment happens to both men and women.

- Understand that what's acceptable behavior to one person may not be acceptable to another.

- Pay close attention to the nonverbals of people with whom you are interacting. Do they seem offended by something you said or did? If you put an arm around them or a hand on their shoulder, do they tense up or move away? These important nonverbal signals should be noted and respected.

- Be professional enough to ask the individual: "Did I say or do something that offended you?"

- Apologize for the perceived offensive behavior and stop doing the behavior.

- If you are the one offended, communicate that discomfort to the offender. Describe your reaction to the offense.

- Discuss the situation in private.

- Focus on the offender's behavior, not the person's personality.

Responding to Harassment at Work

- Consider talking to the person who is engaging in the inappropriate behavior. Simply telling him or her you do not like something he or she is doing to you may be enough to stop the behavior.

- If you are unsure about how to handle the situation, discuss it with a friend or coworker.

- If you are uncomfortable telling the other person to stop his or her behavior, you may want to talk to your supervisor. However, most policies require that supervisors report suspected harassment to the Human Resources Department. The HR director then determines whether to address the issue through a formal in-house investigation or through other avenues, such as mediation (discussed further in Chapter 6).

- If your harasser is your supervisor, you may need to talk to the Human Resources Department. Usually, most organizations have policies that specify how employees should handle harassment situations when the harasser is the supervisor.

- Sexual harassment can make you feel bad—about the job, yourself, and toward others. You may want to talk to a professional such as a counselor. Many organizations provide employees the opportunity to see counselors that are provided through the company's Employee Assistance Program (EAP).

- Remember, if you are being harassed, it is not your fault and the results of your actions (e.g., reporting the behavior) are not responsible for how the harasser is ultimately treated (e.g., terminated). The harasser is responsible for the outcome, even if it includes his or her termination from work.

Harassment Workplace Policy

- To reduce liability, all organizations should have a written policy against workplace harassment advising employees that harassment will not be tolerated.

- Annual training on the company's harassment policy should take place.

- The policy should include a procedure for resolving harassment charges and should encourage victims to come forward without fear of reprisal.

- Employees should have several people to whom they can take their complaint—supervisor, department head, Human Resources Department, or company president.

These behaviors are listed in Exhibit 4-7. Since human relations deals with response to behavior, we have also included in Exhibit 4-7 suggestions on how to deal with another person's harassing behavior toward you.

Empathy

Empathy means psychologically and emotionally putting yourself in another person's shoes to understand what they are felling (Timm, 1992). Empathy includes showing concern for others, which is a very important skill for professionals and leaders to have. You could also say that empathy is part of emotional intelligence (discussed earlier in this chapter). Some people seem to be inherently good at this; for others, it takes training. Chapter 7 on interpersonal communication and listening skills explains several strategies that can help you understand others and show your concern.

Job Performance

Every organization has the right to expect the highest quality performance from its employees. The organization's responsibility to you is to ensure you get the training and materials you need to perform at top quality. Your responsibility to the organization is to seek that training and continue to strive for quality performance. Your professional goal should be to *exceed*, not just meet, what is expected of you to improve the organization and people with whom you work, including those you manage.

Customer Service

Providing quality customer service is essential in today's service-focused market. Where once the focus was on *making* products, it is now on *selling* products. This means certain skills are necessary to deal with those to whom we are selling! When customers are treated unprofessionally, they show it by taking their business elsewhere. Losing one customer a day can cost hundreds of thousands of dollars. Consequently, professionals should understand the importance of customer service skills.

PROFESSIONAL CUSTOMER SERVICE SKILLS

According to Finch (1987), a true professional:

- Accepts responsibility for providing courteous and helpful service to customers.
- Understands that an organization's success is measured by and depends upon maintaining and fostering positive relationships with customers.
- Continues to upgrade and use effective interpersonal skills to deal with customers.

The skills you need in this area include all of the ones you have learned thus far in this textbook and those you will learn in later chapters. Those skills include knowing and responding to the following four basic needs of customers: to be understood, to feel welcome, to feel important, and to feel comfortable (Martin, 1989).

The need to be understood Customers need to have their concerns and their feelings validated. That is,

they want to know their concern isn't wrong or just *their* problem. Consequently, it is important that you let customers know you appreciate their bringing their concerns to you and that their comments are important to your organization. For example, when a customer tells you that all the buttons fell off her new blouse, you might say: "That must have been frustrating for you. I'm glad you brought it back to let us know. We'll make sure to check the other merchandise for the same problem."

The need to feel welcome When customers walk into an organization, they don't want to be treated as if they are interrupting a salesperson's lunch. Have you ever walked into a store where two salespeople are standing at the register, and as you approach them, they just look at each other? They seem to be saying: "I don't want to deal with this customer. It's your turn." How does that make you feel when that happens? The solution for this situation is to acknowledge a customer's arrival with a smile and nod of your head and say: "Let me know if you need any help with anything. I'll be standing by the cash register. Take your time."

The need to feel important No matter who the customer is, you should make him feel as if every question is a good one and that he is special. This need to feel important is a basic human need. For example, when a customer comes out of the waiting room and asks if what he has on looks good, you might reply: "You look like you have long legs and those type of pants are perfect for someone with your build." Or "let me show you what would be perfect for you!" The customer took a risk asking a perfect stranger for an opinion. Your job, then, is to show customers how glad you are that they asked your opinion.

The need for comfort This need pertains to both physical and emotional comfort. No one wants to stand for long periods of time while waiting to see you or someone else—provide a place to sit and rest. Clothing stores often provide chairs by the dressing rooms so that people can comfortably wait for a friend or partner who is trying on clothes. In addition, customers become very uncomfortable when they think you are treating them with anger, impatience, or indifference. Therefore, you need to ensure their emotional comfort as well.

When these four basic needs are met, customers will perceive you as being a true professional and will think more highly of the customer service provided by your organization. Exhibit 4-8 shows how you can address each one of these customer needs.

EXHIBIT 4-8

Connecting with Customers' Needs

Need	Meeting needs with respect and empathy
to be **Understood** (validated)	What you are telling me is important. I m sorry that happened. I would be upset, too. You re right!
	Paraphrase: What I think I heard you say is: Did I hear/understand you correctly? I m sorry: I m not sure I heard everything you said. I m sorry to make you repeat yourself, but I want to make sure I fully understand what happened so I can help you in the most appropriate way.
to feel **Welcome** (guest vs. intruder)	Thank you for bringing this to my attention. I know how some people feel uncomfortable pointing out mistakes, but it helps us improve when you do. Thank you for calling. If there is anything else I can do, don t hesitate to call me back.
to **Feel Important** (valued vs. unappreciated)	How are you today? I m going to check on this right away. I promise to call you right back and let you know the answer.
for **Comfort** (reassured vs. distressed)	Physical: I ll keep checking back with you while you are on hold. Emotional: Do you feel comfortable with this plan and the monthly cost or would something else work better?

PROJECT F *Customer Satisfaction Rating*
Complete Project F at the end of this chapter to help you think about the difference between poor and good customer service skills.

■ ETHICAL BEHAVIOR

Professionalism also pertains to your workplace ethics and how to make ethical decisions. According to Washington and Lee's University professor Louis Hodges, "every business decision has an ethical dimension" (D. Smith, 1998). **Ethical dilemmas** are situations that often require a personal judgment of what is right and wrong and for which there are no rules, policies, or legal statutes guiding such decisions. For example, most people agree that lying and cheating are unethical. But the definition of those terms may be somewhat ambiguous in a given business situation. Consequently, individuals must often rely on their own personal interpretation of a situation that can lead to what others might consider unethical behavior.

Dr. Jack Kevorkian, called "Dr. Death," has assisted many terminally ill people to commit suicide.

Many people believe that a person has the right to ask assistance to terminate his own life and feel it is unethical to let people suffer if they choose not to. However, others call Dr. Kevorkian emotionally unstable, highly unethical, and a murderer. After Michigan passed a law banning assisted suicide, Dr. Kevorkian was convicted of murder and sentenced to prison.

Further muddying the waters is that personal judgments are often based on the specific situation. For example, consider the following ethical dilemmas:

- Naomi is a psychology major and has to perform research on lab animals, which includes dissecting frogs, rabbits, and rats. If she doesn't, she can't pass her classes and, consequently, can't graduate. So she does what she has to do for the grade.

- Sam is trying to sell his car and tells the prospective buyer that his car, which overheats regularly on long trips, is very reliable.

- John sees his best friend cheat on a test. He chooses not to say anything to either his friend or their professor.

Which of these situations would you classify as unethical? No laws have been broken, right? So who

EXHIBIT 4-9

Unethical Workplace Behaviors

Using company computers to shop the Internet during working hours

Copying company software for personal use

Using a sick leave day instead of vacation day when you aren t sick

Viewing pornographic material on web sites

Doing personal work on company time

Supervisors dating subordinates

Taking longer lunch hours than allowed by the organization

Using company vehicles to run personal errands

Sexual harassment

Lying

Conflict of interests

is to say what is right or wrong? Is animal research that can potentially lead to elimination of a terrible and painful disease worth the suffering and death of animals? At first, you might answer no. However, if your parent or other loved one had cancer, you might think it was morally right to do everything possible to find a cure that could end your family member's suffering. Exhibit 4-9 lists some workplace behaviors that are generally considered unethical (Robbins, 1998). How you perceive a situation is also affected by the type of ethical dilemma you think it is.

Types of Ethical Dilemmas

TYPE A DILEMMAS

Type A Dilemmas are situations with a high level of uncertainty about what is right or wrong and where there appears to be no best solution (Nash, 1993). There are both negative and positive consequences to the Type A decision. For example, many people would say that using animals to test potentially life-saving drugs is a Type A dilemma because it has both advantages and disadvantages.

An organizational example of a Type A dilemma includes policies that allow managers to access employees' e-mail. Some employees perceive such a policy as an invasion of privacy and therefore unethical. On the other hand, this policy can protect an organization's interest by reducing organizational espionage and reducing the organization's liability to charges of allowing inappropriate material to circulate in the workplace environment. Generally, decision makers considering a Type A dilemma try to do what's best while attempting to minimize the negative consequences to as many people as possible.

TYPE B DILEMMAS

Type B dilemmas are situations where right and wrong are clear and (1) individuals know what is right but choose another solution based on what's most advantageous to themselves or (2) they convince themselves that what they are doing is right because everyone else does it. Type B dilemmas are often called *rationalizing dilemmas* because individuals are able to justify to themselves the appropriateness of a particular situation (Nash, 1993). In the example above, Sam may be able to rationalize his decision about his car by convincing himself that "that's the way everyone does business" or "she won't drive it very much anyway, so that information is irrelevant to her."

> **PROJECT G** *The Case of the Barbie MasterCard*
> Complete Project G at the end of this chapter to better understand the difficulty of determining ethical and unethical behavior.

Reasons for Unethical Behavior

Individual, situational, and organizational factors are involved in unethical behavior and decision making.

INDIVIDUAL FACTORS

Individual factors that can lead to unethical workplace behavior include an individual's moral development, maturity level, mental stability, ignorance, and willingness to accept personal responsibility.

Moral development Moral development concerns an individual's ability to make his or her own decision about what is right and wrong without being influenced by others' behavior, opinions, or rules (Robbins, 1998). For example, Sam's justification for excluding negative information about his car is that "everybody else does it." We would say that his moral development is low to moderate: He appears to be influenced by how other people act. Should he enter an organization where people are highly unethical, he is more likely to be influenced to behave that way. However, in organizations that have specific rules about ethical behavior, he will most likely conform to that ethical behavior (as long as others are conforming).

On the other hand, individuals at the high end of moral development are less likely to be influenced by others and more likely to act ethically. Their emphasis is on the rights of others. For example, if you think withholding information from customers is wrong because it is the same as cheating, you will be more likely to admit that information to the buyer regardless of what anyone else might do.

Maturity level and mental stability In Chapter 3 on Time Management, we talked about a concept called instant gratification and the fact that many people make choices depending on how quickly they can get some kind of advantageous result for themselves. The concept of gratification is a factor in making ethical decisions. High gratifiers are immature and unstable in that they consider only themselves and not the impact their decision may have on others (Ferrell & Gardiner, 1991).

Ignorance level We aren't referring to an individual's intelligence when we say that ignorance can lead individuals to make unethical decisions. Ignorance pertains to a lack of skills to make sound decisions (Ferrell & Gardiner, 1991). Ignorance also includes not having all of the information needed to make the most appropriate decision. Organizations must ensure that employees are trained in ethical decision making and that they have access to information they need to make the decisions necessary to do the job, correctly *and* ethically.

Personal responsibility Personal responsibility refers to the willingness to be accountable for your decisions and actions without blaming others (Bird, 1996). Individuals high in personal responsibility will generally be more ethical. People who are low in responsibility are more likely to make unethical decisions because of how easy it is for them to blame others if something goes wrong. For people to accept personal responsibility, they must believe they have control of their decisions, have the skill to make good decisions, and be shown that they will not be punished for making legitimate decisions that may turn out wrong

(Ford & Richardson, 1994). Organizations can increase employees' willingness to accept personal responsibility by positively acknowledging people who admit when they are wrong and through training on decision-making skills and on their assigned tasks.

SITUATIONAL FACTORS

Situational factors that cause unethical behavior include economic need, special circumstances, and pressure.

Economic need Individuals who are highly ethical may make an unethical decision based on their financial situation. Most embezzlers begin their criminal career to help pay for mounting bills. Banks and police departments conduct credit checks of their applicants for this reason. Economic need may also have to do with greed (Ferrell & Gardiner, 1991). Drug pushers are an example of how greed leads to unethical, as well as illegal, behavior, although their behavior is also driven by individual factors.

Special circumstances Individuals who wouldn't ordinarily choose a decision they think is unethical sometimes *do* choose an unethical one because of a particular situation or special circumstance. It is a "just this once" situation. For example, someone may cheat one time on his taxes when he is faced with a high tax payment (Ferrell & Gardiner, 1991).

Pressure People face life and job pressures every day: Unrealistic timelines and monthly quotas are two examples of job pressures. When the pressure gets too high, people may take shortcuts—for instance, an apartment complex construction company may use inferior building supplies if faced with financial pressures and timelines such as meeting this month's payroll. Or an employee may not use accurate data for his financial summary because the information is due immediately and it will take several more days to get the right information. Students may plagiarize their research papers because of not enough time to do their own research.

ORGANIZATIONAL FACTORS

Organizational factors influencing unethical behavior include employee relationships and organizational culture.

Employee relationships Employee relationships include the interactions between coworkers, coworkers and managers, and the relationships workers have, or don't have, with the organizations in which they work. Research suggests that unethical behavior is most likely to occur when organizational relationships are weak, singular, and unbalanced (Brass, Butterfield, & Skaggs, 1998).

Weak relationships exist between employees who don't know each other well and who are geographically isolated from each other. This type of relationship can encourage such unethical behaviors as cheating and lying because no bond or trust exists between the parties.

Singular relationships are those in which employees primarily have only a working relationship, that is, they don't socialize or interact outside of their working environment. Therefore, it is easier to rationalize unethical behavior because there is no personal bond. A multiple relationship, on the other hand, can prevent unethical behavior. An example of a multiple relationship: Students and instructors become friends and socialize outside of the classroom. For instance, many instructors will join students in ballgames or go out to dinner with them. This multiple relationship may constrain unethical classroom behavior such as cheating on a test because students know they risk jeopardizing a friendship as well as the instructor-student relationship.

Although a student's potential for unethical behavior may be reduced with this multiple relationship, some instructors suggest such a relationship could lead to favoritism by instructors and is therefore actually unethical. In fact, the reviewers of this textbook, which mainly consisted of college professors, were divided on whether we should leave this example in or not. Once we saw the reaction to the example, we chose to leave it in because it demonstrated the complexity of defining unethical behavior. What do you think about multiple relationships?

Unbalanced relationships are those in which one party is more emotionally involved in the relationship than the other party. Emotional involvement constrains unethical behavior for the trusting individual and presents opportunities for the uninvolved party to take advantage of the other person.

Organizational relationships can be strengthened by providing opportunities for employees to interact outside of the business day and by assigning people to work in teams so that individuals will have fewer chances to engage in unethical behavior. However, the extent to which organizational relationships can be strong, multiple, and balanced depends on the organizational culture and how conducive it is to such relationships.

Organizational culture Often referred to as corporate climate or corporate culture, **organizational culture** is the shared values, beliefs, and traditions that exist among individuals in organizations (A. Y. Chen, Sawyers, & Williams, 1997; Nwachukwu & Vitell, 1997). This culture establishes workplace norms of ethical behavior by defining the roles and expectations that employees and management have of each other. Organizational culture has a strong control over individual behavior and can aid employees in behaving optimally. However, organizational culture can also be a contributing factor in unethical behavior.

For example, think of your classroom as an organization. From the first day of class, norms such as good attendance and class participation may have been established, either orally by your instructor or through your class syllabus. If you know that the classroom culture is one where you are expected to discuss your reading material, you are more likely to read your text each week prior to class. Your instructor may use certain rewards to maintain the culture, such as giving points for classroom participation and attendance. Eventually, this culture gets communicated to other students, who decide whether they want to be members of that culture. In other words, if the class expectations are considered too strenuous, students may enroll in a different class.

Employees learn unethical behavior through organizational culture in two ways: the socialization process and modeling.

Organizational socialization is the process whereby new employees learn the behaviors and attitudes they need to be successful in the organization. It also helps newcomers define their roles and what is expected of them in their positions (Gundry & Rousseau, 1994). Organizations can influence the socialization process, and thereby their cultures, by:

- Communicating the culture through mission statements, value statements, personnel policies, and language used in day-to-day correspondence such as employee newsletters, and rituals or traditions such as annual staff retreats, picnics, or monthly staff meetings. For example, an organization that establishes an on-site wellness center is communicating a culture of concern for its employees' well-being.

- Allowing open dialogue that permits disagreement to selected solutions (Gottlieb & Sanzgiri, 1996). Employees will be less likely to conform to unethical behavior if the culture is one in which they are allowed to and feel comfortable disagreeing with other coworkers and supervisors.

- Involving new employees immediately in an orientation training that defines the culture, including the responsibilities and roles of employees. This orientation positively influences the socialization process and should incorporate the company's Code of Ethics, if there is one.

Modeling is the process of learning behavior by watching the behaviors of others, such as supervisors and top management (Nwachukwu & Vitell, 1997; Weber, 1996). Going back to the classroom example, if your instructor comes in late every class or several of your classmates consistently arrive late without negative consequences, a culture of irresponsibility or unaccountability may be created. It also creates an unethical culture because you could say that your instructor is getting paid for hours he isn't really working. You may eventually become one of those students with poor attendance because tardiness has become the norm.

Similarly, if top management in an organization consistently engages in unethical behaviors and decision making, it is likely that their employees will learn such norms and incorporate them into their own professional value system. To change that behavior, the cultural norms that hinder change must be eliminated (Van Slyke, 1996). Unfortunately, in a recent survey of 500 corporations, 70% stated that they did not think culture was important when considering ethics or did not know how to change their cultures (Sherriton & Stern, 1997). Without such knowledge, changes in the way a company operates and employees behave cannot be achieved.

Supporting Ethical Behavior

The two factors involved in managing workplace ethics are the organization and you. Supervisors and managers should model ethical behavior and verbally explain, train on, and evaluate what is acceptable behavior. For example, a telecommunication center at a county sheriff's department is evaluated on such ethical behaviors as the ability to describe the departmental procedures for reporting unethical and/or illegal conduct on the part of another officer, acting in a manner that develops and maintains respect from others, striving to strengthen personal weaknesses, and demonstrating responsibility and timeliness in work assignments.

Strategies that can help teach ethical behavior include training on appropriate behaviors, sanctions for unethical behaviors, ensuring that employees know how to make sound decisions when faced with ethical dilemmas, and adopting a Code of Ethics.

TRAINING

An increasing number of schools are requiring classes in ethics. A large number of U.S. corporations have formal ethics programs and provide training on recognizing ethical dilemmas, developing problem-solving skills, and learning how to reduce ambiguity in one's job and in expectations of other workers. Role plays that present actual ethical dilemmas that have occurred in other organizations have proven to be an effective

strategy to get employees to recognize ethical dilemmas and the impact their decisions have on others.

SANCTIONS FOR UNETHICAL BEHAVIOR

Individuals engaged in unethical behavior should not be ignored—their behaviors should be sanctioned. In fact, other people who suspect unethical behavior are obligated to pursue it and bring it to the attention of the appropriate person. Otherwise, they too are considered unethical (Lowman, 1998). Sanctions might include, but not be limited to, formal reprimand, unpaid suspension from work, probation, or termination.

ETHICAL DECISION MAKING

Ethical decision making is the process of identifying an ethical dilemma, generating solutions to that dilemma, and selecting the best solution to meet the goal (Guy, 1990). The decision-making steps used to make this type of decision are no different than those explained in Chapter 3. That is, you need to identify the problem, write down all the possible solutions, evaluate each alternative solution and consider the advantages and disadvantages of each, identify the solution that is going to be best for all concerned, carry out your decision, and monitor your decision. However, a final step is added in ethical decision making: determining if the decision at which you arrive actually is ethical. Answering the following three basic questions after your decision can help you with that step:

- *Have you minimized the disadvantages or risks to the most number of people who will be affected by this decision?* If not, reconsider your decision. You may not be considering all the available options.

- *Does the decision have more positive advantages for you than it has for others who will be affected by the decision?* If yes, your decision might be unethical. Reconsider it.

- *How would a majority of other people consider the decision?* Ethics is defined by the perceptions others have of your decisions. Consequently, we suggest that whenever you are faced with an ethical dilemma, you run your decision by several people you trust, such as family members, close friends, or peers, before implementing it. If the consensus is that the decision is unethical, it probably is. Reconsider it.

> **PROJECT H** *Recognizing Ethical Dilemmas*
> Complete Project H at the end of this chapter to learn more about ethical dilemmas.

Finally, one other strategy that supports ethical behavior is the adoption of a Code of Ethics.

EXHIBIT 4-10

Spotsylvania County Telecommunicator's Code of Ethics

- As a telecommunicator, I regard myself as a member of an important and honorable profession.
- I will keep myself in the best possible physical condition at all times.
- I will perform my duty with efficiency at all times.
- I will be exemplary in my conduct, edifying in my conversation, honest in my dealings, and obedient to the laws of the city, state, and country.
- I will not, in the performance of my duty, work for personal advantage or profit.
- I will at all times recognize that I am a public servant.
- I will give the most efficient and impartial service of which I am capable at all times.
- I will be courteous in my contacts at all times.
- I will regard my fellow telecommunicators with the same standards as I maintain myself.
- I will be loyal to my fellow telecommunicators, my superiors, and my agency.
- I will accept responsibility for my actions.
- I will do only those things that will reflect honor on my fellow telecommunicators, my agency, and myself.

CODE OF ETHICS

A **Code of Ethics** is a statement of goals and commitment to employees, customers, and the organization (Guy, 1990). Codes include statements of responsibility of the organization to employees and customers, employee responsibilities to the organization and customers, relationships with vendors, and social responsibilities the organization might have to the community such as commitment to refrain from polluting the lakes and rivers. Employees state they are more likely to stay with an organization in which they feel a strong ethical bond (IPMA News, 1998). Codes can strengthen that bond.

In particular, Codes should encourage employees to do the following (F. B. Bird, 1996):

- Speak out regarding their concerns about issues they regard as wrong.
- Question activities that appear unethical.
- Respond to moral issues raised by others.
- Recognize and acknowledge their personal biases in order to keep them from affecting their decision making.

An example of a Code of Ethics adopted by Spotsylvania County Communication Officers in Spotsylvania, Virginia, is in Exhibit 4-10.

According to Ford and Richardson (1994), Codes of Ethics can only influence ethical behavior if they list the rewards for ethical behavior and sanctions for violations. Many companies choose to deal with the rewards for ethical behavior in their Codes and address sanctions for violations in actual personnel policy. The thinking is that Codes should focus on the positive, which includes the types of positive behaviors people should maintain in the organization.

CHAPTER RECAP

In this chapter, you learned:

- Professionalism and workplace ethics are essential to success at work.
- Professionalism means continuous improvement in career planning, knowledge, presentation of self, empathy, job performance, customer service, and ethical decision making.

- Customers have a need to be understood, to feel welcome, to feel important, and to be comfortable.
- Dressing for the job is important in communicating your professionalism.
- Business etiquette means knowing what social skills to use in business situations.
- Workplace ethics involve ethical dilemmas, which are situations that require a personal judgment of what is right and wrong behavior.
- Organizational culture can be a contributing factor in ethical or unethical behavior.
- Ethical behavior can be influenced with training, sanctions for unethical behavior, ethical decision-making skills, and a Code of Ethics.

Critical Thinking Questions

1. What can you do to improve your professional image?
2. How would you professionally respond to a customer's complaint?
3. Why might you consider an action of your supervisor unethical while others consider it ethical?

WEB SITES

For further information, log on to the following web sites.
www.ethics.ubc.ca/resources/business
Site provides copies of codes of ethics as well as links to a variety of ethics-related articles and web sites.
www.dsmo.com/laborres.htm
Contains excellent links to many employment law issues.

KEY TERMS

Acceptable office politics Legitimate use of power to influence organizational situations.

Career development A lifelong process of understanding career preferences; identifying, obtaining, and developing appropriate skills and training for that career; and evaluating career preferences and skills over your working life.

Code of Ethics A statement of goals and commitment to employees, customers, and the organization.

Emotional intelligence Refers to the ability to interact well with others and the following competencies: recognizing the feelings and needs of others, being able to motivate yourself, and managing your emotions.

Empathy The process of putting oneself in another person's shoes to look at the situation from his or her eyes.

Ethical decision making The process of identifying a dilemma, generating solutions to that dilemma, and selecting the best solution that meets the goal.

Ethical dilemma Situation that requires a personal judgment of what's right and wrong behavior and for which there are no rules, policies, or legal statutes guiding such decisions or behaviors.

Moral development The degree to which individuals are able to make their own decisions about what is right and wrong without being influenced by others' behavior, opinions, or rules.

Office politics Activities people engage in to influence who gets or doesn't get certain organizational advantages.

Organizational culture The shared values, beliefs, and traditions of an organization, which establish its workplace norms of ethical behavior.

Organizational socialization The process whereby new employees learn behaviors and attitudes they need to be successful in the organization.

Personal responsibility The willingness to be accountable for your decisions and actions without blaming others.

Professional An individual who is continuously motivated to seek, learn, and apply, in a fair and honest manner, the skills to do his or her job.

Professionalism The continuous process of developing competence in career planning, knowledge, presentation of self, empathy, job performance, customer service, and ethical decision making.

Sexual harassment Unwelcome treatment of a verbal or physical nature because of an individual's gender, which intentionally or unintentionally interferes with the harassed person's performance on the job, makes the person feel threatened or intimidated, makes the person feel like the target of someone's hostility, or makes the working environment feel uncomfortable.

Singular relationships Organizational relationships in which employees do not interact outside of work.

Type A dilemma Situations with a high level of uncertainty about what is right or wrong and where there appears to be no best solution.

Type B dilemma Situations where individuals know what is right but fail to do it because the wrong solution has the most advantages to them.

Unacceptable office politics Abusing power to influence organizational situations.

Unbalanced relationships Organizational relationships in which one individual is more emotionally involved than the other party.

Weak relationships Organizational relationships that exist between employees who don't know each other well and who are geographically isolated from each other.

PRACTICE EXAM

1. Professionalism is the process of developing competence in all but one of the following areas:
   a. empathy   b. knowledge
   c. acceptable office politics   d. customer service

2. Career planning and development begins with _____ and ends with _____.
   a. exploration; assessment
   b. assessment; goal setting
   c. action-step planning; goal setting
   d. goal setting; exploration

3. Determining if your chosen career is realistic and obtainable is part of the career development process known as _____.
   a. assessment   b. exploration
   c. action-step planning   d. goal setting

4. Skill knowledge involves _____.
   a. having the minimum skills specific to the job you choose
   b. having expertise outside of your chosen career
   c. knowing the ins and outs of the company
   d. those minimum skills necessary for the 21st century

5. Tom Jones, an applicant for the position of sales manager, came to his interview in a navy blue suit, a white shirt, tie, and a small diamond earring in one ear. His appearance, in general, would probably be considered _____ because _____.
   a. unprofessional because navy blue suits are no longer considered professional.
   b. unprofessional because traditionally earrings for men are considered inappropriate.
   c. professional because he is dressed in a navy blue suit and tie.
   d. professional because he looks the part of a sales manager in a traditional organization.

6. Barbara Harper really wants to be promoted to team leader. The decision is being left up to Mrs. Banks in the personnel office. Barbara keeps having lunch with Mrs. Banks, has told her of the office romance occurring between a manger and a subordinate, and even told Mrs. Banks of a negative comment another potential team leader said about Mrs. Banks. Barbara is engaging in the practice of _____.
   a. ethical behavior
   b. acceptable office politics
   c. career advancement
   d. unacceptable office politics

7. Empathy means:
   a. determining the rightness or wrongness of a decision
   b. being able to exceed performance expectations
   c. walking a mile in another person's shoes
   d. focusing on selling products, not just making them

8. Professional customer service skills include all but the following:
   a. accepting responsibility for providing courteous service
   b. maintaining positive relationships
   c. upgrading interpersonal skills
   d. engaging in office politics to get ahead

9. Customers have four primary needs, which include the need to:
   a. be understood, told they are right, be comfortable, feel important
   b. be understood, feel welcomed, be comfortable, and feel important
   c. feel comfortable, be understood, feel important, speak to the supervisor
   d. feel important, be understood, feel welcomed, be compensated for their trouble

10. Judy knows that Allen did not tell the truth when the boss asked him why the monthly report was not completed on time. Judy is afraid the boss might think it was Brenda's fault for the late report. But if she tells what really happened, Allen, her friend, might be fired. This could be considered _____.
    a. an ethical dilemma
    b. unacceptable office politics
    c. sexual harassment
    d. acceptable politics

11. Type B ethical dilemmas are when ___while Type A are when _____.
    a. uncertainty is high about what's right an there is no best solution; decision makers know the right solution but choose the wrong one.
    b. decision makers make the right decision based on their values; decision makers make the wrong decision because of their values.
    c. decision makers know the right solution but choose the wrong one; uncertainty is high about what's right and there is no best solution.
    d. decision makers rationalize their decisions; decision makers focus on decisions that will bring the most advantage to themselves.

12. Individual factors explaining why people use unethical behavior include all but the following:

a. moral development
b. organizational relationships
c. maturity level
d. lack of personal responsibility

13. Situational factors explaining why people are unethical include all but the following:
    a. pressure
    b. economic need
    c. special circumstances
    d. lack of personal responsibility

14. Bobby thinks highly of his coworker, Debbie. He feels Debbie does a good job. He is always supportive of Debbie and has a great deal of trust in her. Debbie, on the other hand, doesn't know Bobby very well and can't even remember his name. She doesn't feel any special bond with him so doesn't feel obligated to keep his secrets. This relationship between Debbie and Bobby is _____ and is often a reason for _____ behavior.
    a. unbalanced; unethical
    b. weak; ethical
    c. multiple; unethical
    d. multiple; ethical

15. Every time a group of new employees begin work at the XYZ company, the first 3 hours of the day is spent on training them on their job responsibilities and Code of Ethics. This process is called:
    a. culture   b. moral development
    c. socialization   d. modeling

ANSWERS 1 c, 2 b, 3 b, 4 a, 5 b, 6 d, 7 c, 8 d, 9 b, 10 a, 11 a, 12 b, 13 d, 14 a, 15 c

Focused Free-Write

Think about individuals you know or have seen in a business such as a bank, school, department store, or auto dealership. Answer the following questions:

- What did they do to make you think they were professional or unprofessional?
- How were they dressed?
- What kind of behavior did they use that made them professional or unprofessional?
- What do you think defines a true professional?

_____

_____

_____

_____

_____

_____

_____

_____

_____

_____

_____

_____

_____

_____

_____

_____

_____

_____

What Is the Best Career for You: Aamodt Vocational Interest Survey

In this exercise, you will take a shortened version of the Aamodt Vocational Interest Survey (AVIS). The AVIS is used for adult employees who are thinking about changing careers.

Instructions For each of the following activities, rate the extent to which you might enjoy performing the activity often or for long periods of time. On the AVIS answer sheet, rate each statement using the following scale:

1   I would absolutely hate doing this activity.
2   I would dislike doing this activity.
3   I would neither dislike nor like doing this activity (I'm neutral).
4   I would enjoy doing this activity.
5   I would very much enjoy doing this activity.

Questions

1. Filing patients' charts in alphabetical order
2. Calming an angry customer
3. Testing blood samples for the presence of disease
4. Appraising the value of real estate
5. Calling people to determine their interest in a product
6. Raising livestock
7. Driving a bus
8. Overhauling an engine
9. Arresting a drug dealer
10. Caring for patients in a hospital
11. Evaluating the performance of an employee
12. Baking bread at a deli
13. Creating an advertising campaign

14. Entering information into a computer
15. Helping customers make travel arrangements
16. Taking X rays of an injured foot
17. Predicting the success of stocks and bonds
18. Selling automobiles at a car lot
19. Planting vegetables
20. Picking up passengers in a cab
21. Repairing a broken VCR
22. Giving first aid and CPR in an emergency situation
23. Teaching young people a topic in your favorite area
24. Making tough decisions

25. Sewing clothing

26. Writing a computer program

27. Typing letters and reports

28. Answering questions about products or services

29. Cleaning teeth

30. Appraising the value of a damaged car

31. Asking people to donate money to charity

32. Baling hay

33. Delivering packages to stores

34. Fixing leaks in household plumbing

35. Driving an ambulance through the streets at a high speed

36. Helping people with marital problems

37. Setting production goals

38. Cleaning hotel rooms

39. Designing a floral arrangement

40. Sorting mail

41. Ringing up merchandise on a cash register

42. Testing urine samples for the presence of drugs

43. Determining ways to reduce a client's taxes

44. Calling people to determine their interest in selling their home

45. Plowing a field

46. Driving through heavy traffic

47. Building a house

48. Explaining crime prevention techniques to citizens

49. Working with a physically disabled person

50. Organizing daily work activities

51. Cooking meals at a nice restaurant

52. Playing a musical instrument

53. Scheduling appointments for a business executive

54. Solving customers' problems

55. Filling prescriptions at a pharmacy

56. Forecasting the economy

57. Selling products at a department store

58. Spreading fertilizer over a field

59. Parking cars in a parking garage

60. Assembling electronic components

61. Writing a ticket for a speeding motorist

62. Taking care of young children

63. Setting up employee work schedules

64. Shortening the length of a skirt

65. Coming up with ideas for a new product

AVIS Answer Sheet

(1) absolutely hate (2) dislike (3) neutral (4) enjoy (5) very much enjoy

1. _____	14. _____	27. _____	40. _____	53. _____	_____
2. _____	15. _____	28. _____	41. _____	54. _____	_____
3. _____	16. _____	29. _____	42. _____	55. _____	_____
4. _____	17. _____	30. _____	43. _____	56. _____	_____
5. _____	18. _____	31. _____	44. _____	57. _____	_____
6. _____	19. _____	32. _____	45. _____	58. _____	_____
7. _____	20. _____	33. _____	46. _____	59. _____	_____
8. _____	21. _____	34. _____	47. _____	60. _____	_____
9. _____	22. _____	35. _____	48. _____	61. _____	_____
10. _____	23. _____	36. _____	49. _____	62. _____	_____
11. _____	24. _____	37. _____	50. _____	63. _____	_____
12. _____	25. _____	38. _____	51. _____	64. _____	_____
13. _____	26. _____	39. _____	52. _____	65. _____	_____

After you have rated each activity, add the numbers across each row and enter the sum on the blank line farthest to the right of each row. Now circle the corresponding number in the AVIS Profile Sheet for each of the vocational interest areas. Look at the career areas corresponding to your highest circled scores. Which careers best match your interests?

AVIS Profile Sheet

Vocational Interest Area	Low Interest																				High Interest
1. Clerical	5	6	7	8	9	10	11	12	13	14	15	16	17	18	19	20	21	22	23	24	25
2. Customer Service	5	6	7	8	9	10	11	12	13	14	15	16	17	18	19	20	21	22	23	24	25
3. Science	5	6	7	8	9	10	11	12	13	14	15	16	17	18	19	20	21	22	23	24	25
4. Analysis	5	6	7	8	9	10	11	12	13	14	15	16	17	18	19	20	21	22	23	24	25
5. Sales	5	6	7	8	9	10	11	12	13	14	15	16	17	18	19	20	21	22	23	24	25
6. Agriculture	5	6	7	8	9	10	11	12	13	14	15	16	17	18	19	20	21	22	23	24	25
7. Transportation	5	6	7	8	9	10	11	12	13	14	15	16	17	18	19	20	21	22	23	24	25
8. Trades	5	6	7	8	9	10	11	12	13	14	15	16	17	18	19	20	21	22	23	24	25
9. Protective	5	6	7	8	9	10	11	12	13	14	15	16	17	18	19	20	21	22	23	24	25
10. Helping/Caring	5	6	7	8	9	10	11	12	13	14	15	16	17	18	19	20	21	22	23	24	25
11. Leadership/Management	5	6	7	8	9	10	11	12	13	14	15	16	17	18	19	20	21	22	23	24	25
12. Consumer Economics	5	6	7	8	9	10	11	12	13	14	15	16	17	18	19	20	21	22	23	24	25
13. Creative	5	6	7	8	9	10	11	12	13	14	15	16	17	18	19	20	21	22	23	24	25

Career Areas

Clerical

Health Care	medical insurance clerk, medical records clerk, medical secretary, medical transcriptionist, admissions clerk
Banking	credit clerk, mortgage clerk, loan interviewer, teller
Hospitality	hotel clerk, ticket agent, reservation clerk
Legal	court reporter, legal secretary, paralegal
Office	administrative assistant, clerk, mail clerk, payroll clerk, secretary
Manufacturing	stock clerk, shipping and receiving clerk
Transportation	toll collector, dispatcher

Customer Service

Health Care	dental assistant, collections, hospital insurance representative
Banking	teller, loan officer, collections, customer service representative
Hospitality	server, caterer, bartender, dietitian, dietitian's assistant
Office	operator, switchboard, receptionist, personnel assistant
Cosmetology	hair stylist, manicurist, barber
Retail	cashier, sales representative, customer service representative
Travel	travel agent, flight attendant

Science

Dental	dental technician, dental hygienist
Medical	medical technologist, radiographer, sonographer
Optical	optician, optical lab technician, lens grinder
Pharmacy	pharmacist, pharmacy assistant
Science	lab technician
Veterinary	veterinarian, veterinary assistant

Analysis

Accounting	accountant, bookkeeper, financial analyst, economist
Insurance	insurance appraiser, claims adjuster, underwriter
Investments	financial planner, stock broker
Law	lawyer, paralegal
Real estate	real estate appraiser

Sales

Aggressive	insurance, fundraiser, manufacturer's representative
Real Estate	real estate agent, real estate broker
Retail	sales representative, demonstrator
Telemarketing	telemarketer

Agriculture

Farming

Ranching

Transportation

Public	bus driver, cab driver, chauffeur, car lot attendant
Delivery	delivery truck driver
Long Haul	truck driver, escort driver

Trades

Construction	painter, mason, asphalt paver, heavy equipment operator, carpet layer
Electrical	electrician, electronic repairer, appliance repairer, cable installer, office machine repairer, vending machine repairer
Mechanical	automotive, truck, maintenance, and aircraft mechanics
Metal	welder, sheet metal worker
Physical Labor	logger, miner, jackhammer operator
Plumbing	plumber
Production	assembler, solderer, machinist, foundry worker
Wood	cabinetmaker, carpenter, woodworker, furniture assembler
Other	locksmith

Protective

Dispatch	police dispatcher, 911 operator
Emergency	EMT, paramedic
Fire Science	firefighter
Outdoor	lifeguard, park ranger, fish and game warden
Police Science	police officer, security guard

Helping/Caring

Day Care	babysitter, child care, home companion
Health Care	nurse, nurse's aide, physician's assistant
Banking/Finance	loan counselor, financial counselor
Education	teacher, teacher's aide, special education teacher
Law	parole officer
Outdoor	camp counselor
Social Services	social worker, psychologist, counselor

Management

Education	principal
Hospitality	hotel manager, restaurant manager
Office	office manager, personnel director
Production	supervisor
Retail	store manager, assistant manager

Consumer Economics

Cooking	baker, caterer, cook, chef, dietitian, nutritionist
Housekeeping	janitor, maid
Textiles	tailor, sewing machine operator, weaver, dry cleaner

Creative

Art	painter, sculptor
Business	advertising, marketing
Computers	computer programmer, graphic artist
Fashion	fashion design, fashion buyer
Floral	floral design
Oral	actor/actress, trainer, teacher, disc jockey, broadcaster
Outdoor	landscaper
Photography	photographer
Retail	jeweller
Writing	writer, poet, technical writer, reporter

The Right Skills for the Right Job

This exercise is the second step in the assessment stage of career planning and development. To determine the skills you need for the job you want, answer the following questions.

1. *I am interested in the following career(s):*

   _____   _____

   _____   _____

2. *To find out the skills I need, I will talk to:*

   _____ college advisor/counseling center   _____ instructors in the career area

   _____ professionals in the career area

3. *I need the following education (check all that apply to your career choices):*

   _____ High school degree   _____ Associate degree
   – focus should be in:_____   – major should be:_____

   _____ Four-year degree (B.S., B.A.)   _____ Master's degree
   – major should be:_____   – major should be:_____

   _____ Postgraduate work
   – doctorate
   – other_____

4. *I should have the following training/skills prior to entering the career:*

   _____ management/leadership   _____ training/presentation skills

   _____ computer literate   _____ strong basic skills
   – word processing   – math
   – spreadsheets   – grammar
   – graphics   – logic
   – other   – analysis

   _____ customer service   _____ written/oral communication

   _____ conflict management   _____ problem solving/decision making

   _____ data entry   _____ team management

5. *I need the following prior work and/or internship experience to obtain an entry level position:*

   _____ no experience necessary   _____ 1-5 years experience   _____ more than 5 years

The Skills and Education I Have

This exercise provides a place to compile the education and skills you already have.

Education

_____ Associate degree   _____ Four-year degree
      – major:_____   – major:_____

Work Experience (include volunteer, unpaid, and internship positions)

Position	Months/Years in Position	Job Duties
_____	_____	_____
_____	_____	_____
_____	_____	_____
_____	_____	_____

Special Training/Skills I Have

_____ management/leadership   _____ training/presentation skills

_____ computer literate   _____ strong basic skills
     – word processing _____   – math   _____
     – spreadsheets   _____   – grammar _____
     – graphics   _____   – logic   _____
     – other   _____   – analysis _____

_____ customer service   _____ written/oral communication

_____ conflict management   _____ problem solving/decision making

_____ data entry   _____ team management

_____ other (list)

_____

_____

_____

Goal Setting and Planning

After assessing the skills you need and those you have, you need to determine any discrepancy between the two so that you can set goals on how to obtain what you need in order to get the job you want. The purpose of this exercise is to help you develop goals that will ensure you identify the education and training you need to meet your career goal.

A. Discrepancy Between What You Have and What You Need

Education: I need the following education:

____ Associate degree   ____ Four-year degree   ____ Master's degree
____ Postgraduate

Skills/Training: I need:

_____

_____

_____

Work Experience: I need:

_____

_____

_____

B. Goals and Action-Step Career Planning

You know what you need. Now set your goals and guidelines for getting there.

Educational Goal How will you do it?	By (date)	Where (what school) or
Degree: _____	_____	_____
_____	_____	_____
Apply for Financial Assistance	_____	_____

Other steps I need to take to meet Education Goal

_____	_____	_____
_____	_____	_____

Educational Goal   **By (date)**   **Where (what school) or**
How will you do it?

Training/Skill Goals

_____   _____   _____

_____   _____   _____

_____   _____   _____

Work Experience

Internship   _____   _____

Volunteer Work   _____   _____

Paid Experience   _____   _____

PROJECT E

Self-Assessment of Basic Knowledge

Use this exercise to assess your basic knowledge. Place a check next to the areas you think are strong enough to brag to an employer about. Using the following scale, rate how well you think you do in these basic knowledge areas:

1 = very poor   2 = poor   3 = satisfactory   4 = good   5 = very good

Basic Skills

_____ Math

_____ Advanced math (algebra, geometry)

_____ Grammar (punctuation, sentence structure)

_____ Logic

_____ Verbal (spelling and correct word usage)

Interpersonal Skills

_____ Customer Relations

_____ Handling difficult customers/employees

_____ Mingle and talk easily with strangers

_____ Sense of humor

_____ Working in teams

_____ Ability to convey empathy/
_____ sensitive to others' feelings

_____ Understanding group process

Management/Leadership Skills

_____ Mediation

_____ Conflict management

_____ Decision making

_____ Persuasion

_____ Planning/scheduling activities

_____ Problem solving

_____ Time management

_____ Stress management

_____ Proficient about training technique

_____ Discipline

_____ Running/chairing a meeting

_____ Chairing a committee

_____ Delegating work to others

_____ Dealing with change and helping others deal with change

Communication Skills

_____ Giving speeches

_____ Training groups of people

_____ Conveying expectations

_____ Listening

Written Communication

_____ Editing work

_____ Proofreading work

_____ Reading numbers

_____ Reading words

_____ Writing reports

Computer Skills

_____ Database management

_____ Desktop publishing

_____ Operating mainframe

_____ Graphics (e.g., PowerPoint)

_____ Spreadsheets (e.g., Excel)

_____ Using operating systems (e.g., Windows, UNIX)

_____ Word Processing

_____ Programming

Customer Satisfaction Rating

Providing quality customer service is essential in today's service-focused market. The best way to understand customer satisfaction is by thinking about situations that caused you to walk away satisfied or dissatisfied. That is the purpose of this exercise.

Instructions Read each situation and rate what your level of satisfaction would be if the situations happened to you. For each "1" or "4" that you give the examples, explain what made you satisfied or dissatisfied. Use the following scale:

1 = poor   2 = neutral   3 = okay   4 = satisfied

1. You walk up to the cash register to pay for your merchandise. Two employees are standing behind the cash register talking about the company picnic they attended on Saturday. They acknowledge you by briefly glancing your way but continue talking for at least 2 minutes before one finally turns to you and says: "Will this be all?"

Rating: _____

Explanation: _____

_____

_____

2. You call your long-distance phone company complaining about a long-distance charge on your bill for a call you didn't make. The representative asks you to hold while he pulls up your account on the screen. He asks you how the weather is in your state. He needs to put you on hold again. Thirty seconds later he comes back and tells you he is still checking on the status. He asks if you have time to hold another minute or should he call you back? After another minute, he returns to the phone, apologizes for taking so long, and tells you he will take that charge off your account. "Is there anything else I can do for you today?" he asks. "Other than this mistake, how are you satisfied with our service in general?"

Rating: _____

Explanation: _____

_____

_____

3. You call a company, for the third time, about a problem you are having. The representative says: "I really don't know why our service person didn't return your call. Did you try and call them back?"

Rating: _____

Explanation: _____

_____

_____

4. You order a fantastic appliance through the mail, and for 2 months, it works great. Then it breaks. You call the company for a replacement. The representative says: "No problem, we will ship you a replacement part at no cost to you." Two months later, you still haven't received it. You call again to check on the status. The representative says: "I'm really sorry about that. We have a backlog. But let me make sure we have your order. Yes, we do. Let me verify your mailing address." Three weeks later, you finally get your replacement part. In addition, you get three extra attachments, free of charge, to go with your appliance. The letter reads: "For your patience, we want to give you these three attachments free of charge. We apologize for the delay. If we can be of further service, please don't hesitate to call, fax, or write."

Rating: _____

Explanation: _____

_____

_____

5. You go to a clothing store to get a new outfit to wear to a friend's evening wedding. Men: You try on a pair of khakis and a jacket, but aren't sure how it looks. Women: You try on a pair of nice slacks and dressy blouse. You ask the clerk for an opinion and he or she says: "Oh, you look perfect."

Rating: _____

Explanation: _____

_____

_____

Same situation, except the clerk asks: "Where do you plan to wear the outfit? What time of day is the wedding? The outfit itself looks great on you. But if I can make a suggestion, since it's an evening wedding, you might want to wear something a little more formal. We have some nice suits/formal dresses on sale that might be more appropriate. Or, if you really aren't a suit/formal dress type of person and don't want to waste money on an outfit you will never wear again, how about this idea?"

Rating: _____

Explanation: _____

_____

_____

The Case of the Barbie MasterCard

Decision making often requires a personal judgment of what is right and wrong and for which there are no rules, policies, or legal statutes guiding such decisions. This case study is an actual situation. As you read it, think about how ethics has been defined in this chapter, then answer the questions after the case.

MasterCard is using Barbie to advertise its services. The "Cool Shopping Barbie" comes with a Barbie-sized credit card with the MasterCard logo, a battery-powered cash register, and a card scanner that says "Credit Approved" when the credit card is run through it. A MasterCard spokesman says that the doll "empowers children to play out a realistic shopping adventure." Some parents and consumer advocates say the doll makes children think credit cards are toys and sends a wrong message to children. Proponents of the marketing idea say it could help to teach kids financial literacy, although the box with all of this equipment shows Barbie with several shopping bags in hand.

What MasterCard and Mattel are doing is not illegal, but some people say it is unethical. What do you think? Incorporate what you learned in Chapter 4 into your answer. Explain your support or opposition of the advertising campaign. What is your opinion based on?

_____

_____

_____

_____

_____

_____

_____

_____

_____

_____

_____

_____

_____

_____

_____

Recognizing Ethical Dilemmas

These case studies have actually occurred in various organizations. Use the ethical decision-making model outlined in Chapter 4 to determine if the situations could be considered ethical. Write down why you think the situation is ethical or unethical. How would you have handled the situation?

1. Shannon was a clerk in the Accounting Department. She and her boss, Jim, started dating. Because he was her supervisor, they agreed that they shouldn't tell anyone. Eventually, the relationship ended. Jim felt uncomfortable working with Shannon so he had her transferred to another department, against her objections. Did Jim do the right thing?

_____

_____

_____

_____

_____

_____

_____

2. Sally was an administrator in a local hospital. She was also part of the management team responsible for deciding which employees to downsize. Based on recent action, she was privy to which 10 employees might be laid off by the end of the year, one of whom was Ben. Ben came to her one day excited because he and his wife had found the perfect house. It was their first house, and they were anxious to make an offer on it. Fearing for Ben's financial situation, Sally asked her boss if she could tell Ben that he might be laid off. She was told she could not tell anyone anything because the organization had not made any final decisions, and they did not want to start a panic. Consequently, she did not tell Ben that he was on the cut list. Did Sally do the right thing?

_____

_____

_____

_____

_____

_____

_____

_____

3. Beale asked Pam her opinion of Dawn, whom he was considering promoting to Human Resources Manager. Beale had a great deal of respect for Pam's opinion and ability to judge other people. Unbeknownst to Beale, Pam and Dawn were best friends. Pam gave Dawn an outstanding recommendation—even though she knew that Dawn had a problem with keeping confidentiality. Dawn was offered, and accepted, the position. Should Pam have given Dawn such a good recommendation?

_____

_____

_____

_____

_____

_____

_____

Answers for Ethical Dilemmas. These answers are based on critiques of similar situations by Robert Lowman (1998).

Ethical Dilemma 1: Probably unethical. The supervisor should not have engaged in a romantic relationship. Because he was the individual in authority, it was his responsibility to avoid the potential harm that could occur from such a relationship, even if the relationship was consensual. The decision he made to transfer Shannon was best for himself and did not offer any advantages to Shannon.

Ethical Dilemma 2: Probably ethical. The information Sally had was confidential, and she was obligated to keep it so. However, the organization itself, may have been unethical for withholding potentially harmful information. One solution may have been to tell Ben: "Have you considered whether that is the best thing to do at this time?" However, this solution borders on unethical because she is coming dangerously close to giving Ben information he shouldn't have. The best Sally could do was encourage the management team to reconsider letting people know that there may be a layoff.

Ethical Dilemma 3: Probably unethical. Regardless of the friendship between Dawn and Pam, Pam had a responsibility to Beale and to the organization to give an unbiased reference on Dawn. Pam's reference should have been based on actual behaviors that she had personally witnessed in Dawn. Because Pam's reference was governed by self-interest (that of keeping her relationship with Dawn), Pam's behavior was highly questionable.

Understanding the Diverse Nature of Others

Throughout history, prejudicial attitudes and stereotyping have been contributing influences to human behavior and interaction. Discrimination against those perceived as different or inferior from the dominant group continues to be pervasive and harmful.

Understanding diversity is an important issue in human relations in the United States because the number of people belonging to groups historically discriminated against (e.g., Hispanics, Asians, African Americans, women, and older workers) is increasing, making the workforce more diverse than ever. Consequently, it is imperative that people learn more about each other and how this diversity among groups and individuals can be used to strengthen working as well as personal relationships.

The purpose of this chapter is to build an awareness of how prejudice and discrimination affect personal and working relationships and how diversity in the workplace can strengthen, rather than break down, the organization. Our goal is to demonstrate how some of the stereotypes or biases you hold can cause you to unfairly discriminate against certain groups of people. The projects in this chapter are specifically geared to provoke critical thinking about real life situations that have occurred or are still occurring because of prejudicial attitudes. The implication of acknowledging prejudices and discriminatory practices is that you can become more successful and effective in your future relationships.

In this chapter you will:

Learn the difference between prejudice and discrimination

Define the sources of prejudice

Understand the types of discrimination that occur in the workplace

Know the legislation protecting minorities and other protected classes against discrimination

Learn organizational strategies for reducing prejudice and celebrating diversity

■ PREJUDICE VERSUS DISCRIMINATION

Prejudice

Traditionally, **prejudice** has been defined as a negative attitude toward individuals who belong to groups considered to be different than the **dominant group**—the group that has the most advantages in society and who is most likely to cause unequal treatment (Healey, 1998). For example, in both the United States and South Africa, the dominant group is Whites. Though Whites are a statistical minority

in South Africa, they control most of the finances and property, consequently making them the dominant group. However, it is also true that members of a nondominant group can and do harbor prejudices against members of the dominant group or even other minority groups. In other words, no one is immune from holding prejudicial attitudes. We talk more about this later in the chapter.

> *Focused Free-Write*
> To get you thinking about the concepts of prejudice, stereotyping, and discrimination, complete the Focused Free-Write at the end of this chapter.

Attitudes, in general, are affective and cognitive evaluations of people, ideas, and situations. That is, attitudes are people's *emotions* or feelings (affect) toward some idea or someone based on what they *think* (cognition), which is obtained from the information they have about the idea or person. For example, you may love this textbook (affective evaluation) because you think (cognitive evaluation) it does a good job of presenting all of the pertinent issues involved with human relations, based on what you already know about human relations. Someone else may dislike it because she thinks it has left out some important topics relating to human relations. Often, attitudes have little scientific support. That is, you may hold a particular attitude not because it is factually based and supported by research, but because you are misinformed, lack information, or jump to conclusions. For instance, do you think a four-day, 10-hour a day work week makes people more or less productive? Most people think it makes workers less productive because it increases fatigue. However, research shows that productivity actually *increases* with such a schedule, with only a *moderate* increase in fatigue (Williamson, Gower, & Clarke, 1994; Moores, 1990).

Attitudes usually direct behavior. The behavior that often results from prejudicial attitudes is discrimination. Using the example above, because of your positive attitude toward this textbook, you may read the entire book, front to back, with enthusiastic fervor! The Quick Project on the next page will give you firsthand experience, and consequently, maybe a better understanding, of how attitudes can influence your behavior.

MINORITY GROUPS

Generally, when we speak about prejudice and the groups against which others are prejudiced, we think about minorities. Wagley and Harris (1958) were the first to define minority—a definition that still stands today. A **minority group** shares the following characteristics:

1. They experience a pattern of disadvantage or inequality in such areas as financial security, housing, political power, health care, or schooling.

2. They have visible identifying traits. Such physical characteristics as skin color, facial structure, or hair color are three of the most evident identifying traits.

3. They are aware of their disadvantages and that they have not had equal access to power or status like members of the dominant group.

4. They are born into their minority classification.

5. They usually marry within their own group.

QUICK PROJECT

This weekend, eat at a restaurant that serves ethnic food (e.g., Chinese, Indian, Mexican) and where the servers are of that cultural background. Write down your opinion of the service. What do you base your opinion on? Do you think your opinion is based on your attitude about the culture? Would you be comfortable returning to that restaurant? Why or why not?

_____

_____

_____

_____

Contrary to what the term suggests, minority groups can be large and can actually *outnumber* the dominant group. For example, women have traditionally been thought of as a minority group (although they don't exactly fit the sociological definition). Statistically, women are actually in the majority in the United States, as they comprise 51% of the population.

But when we talk about diversity, individual differences, and prejudice, we aren't just referring to attitudes of the dominant group toward minority groups. Again, prejudicial attitudes reflect how people feel about others they perceive as different from themselves or the dominant norm. For instance, people with disabilities are often thought of as less competent workers. Overweight people are blamed for their obesity and often treated unkindly. Churches with an all-Black congregation may make it uncomfortable for non-Blacks to join. Men small in stature are often considered "effeminate" and bullied. Women will "bash" men by making derogatory remarks about their be-

havior or certain body parts. These groups don't meet the legal or sociological definition of *minority,* but their negative treatment is discrimination, nevertheless, based on prejudicial attitudes.

An excellent example of nonminority prejudice was illustrated in the 1998 blockbuster *Lethal Weapon 4* with Mel Gibson, Danny Glover, and Joe Pesci. In the first three *Lethal Weapons,* Joe Pesci's character, Leo, is a small-time crook who becomes friends with Gibson's and Glover's characters. Leo is short, not too bright, and was raised in a poor home environment. In *Lethal Weapon 4* he has rehabilitated himself and is now a private investigator. In a moving moment, Leo tells Gibson's character how he grew up without friends because he was poor and dressed and acted differently. Although this was only a movie, Leo's story clearly depicts reality and how people who are considered different are treated by others. You can probably think of several other groups who don't meet the definition of minority but who have been treated unfairly.

QUICK PROJECT

List all the groups of people who can't be classified as minorities but who you think are typically treated differently than other people.

_____

_____

_____

_____

SOURCES OF PREJUDICE

There are three primary sources of prejudice (Healey, 1998): personality, learned behavior, and intergroup competition.

Innate personality Consistent with the discussion regarding genetics in Chapter 1, many people would say that some people are *born* prejudiced. The rationale behind this theory is that some people have an unhealthy personality and are unable to accept and cope with their shortcomings. Subsequently, they blame others for problems. An example of this might be lazy and irresponsible employees who are continually terminated from one job after another. Their irrational reaction to their terminations is that "the government is making the organization make room for all those Blacks, so they fired me first." Instead of being accountable for their own failings, these prejudiced people point the fingers elsewhere—either at minorities or people whom the prejudiced person feels are different or inferior to them.

Learned behavior As adults, have you ever caught yourself in the middle of doing something and thought: "Oh my gosh, I'm doing exactly what my mom (or dad) used to do!" Even though it's behavior you swore you would *never* do when you got older, you end up doing it anyway! As discussed in Chapter 1, much of who you are and what you do you learned from those significant others with whom you associated—your parents, siblings, close friends, and religious or spiritual acquaintances. The culture in which you were raised has great influence on you. If you grew up in a racist household, you are more likely to hold prejudicial attitudes. Unlike the innate personality theory, the learned behavior theory suggests that people aren't born prejudiced. Their behaviors toward certain groups are influenced by their upbringing and by those with whom they associated in their lives.

Prejudicial attitudes are then perpetuated by the following factors: similarity and proximity (or exposure) to different groups and ideas.

Similarity and prejudice Contrary to the popular saying "opposites attract," research shows that people are more likely to associate and be attracted to others who are most like themselves. That is, the people who you are more likely to hang out with are those with similar personality characteristics, values, attitudes, and behaviors as yours (Griffin & Sparks, 1990). Think about the neighborhood in which you grew up. Who lived in that neighborhood? Research suggests that your parents, when considering where to make their home, sought out neighborhoods with people more like themselves.

How does this "similarity attracts" theory produce prejudice and discrimination? People are less likely to voluntarily seek out others who look or act differently from them. So, the fact that you have no friends of another race or income class may have absolutely nothing to do with prejudicial attitudes (as some sociologists might suggest), but more to do with the fact that you just feel more comfortable with people like yourself. Unfortunately, the effect of low attraction to dissimilar people increases and carries over into the workplace. The disadvantage of choosing only similar people with whom to associate is that you are unable to understand the ideas, feelings, and attitudes of other groups.

Proximity and prejudice Physical proximity can also play a key role in producing prejudice. In addition to similarity, people are more likely to become friends with others who live or work closest to them. Be-cause neighborhoods are generally segregated and because neighbors, because of their proximity, are more likely to become friends with each other rather than with people across town, we start out having less exposure to others from different races or ethnic backgrounds. This, too, eventually carries over into the workplace.

Intergroup competition Finally, a third theory about the source of prejudicial attitudes is that they derive from competition between groups contending for the same rewards or limited resources. In a famous study known as *Robbers Cave* conducted in the 1950s (Sherif, 1961), this theory was put to the test. In his study, Sherif grouped 11- and 12-year-old boys at a summer camp into two teams, based on their ages: the Rattlers versus the Eagles. The two groups lived in different cabins and competed with each other in various activities for prizes. Eventually, negative attitudes developed between the two competing groups, culminating in name-calling and arguments. Interestingly, when Sherif developed activities in which both groups could work cooperatively, prejudicial attitudes began to decline. Eventually, some friendships developed among members of the two groups.

When we generalize Sherif's research to society as a whole, we might hypothesize that from the beginning of time, people have naturally grouped into similar groups and have competed against other groups for different benefits. These benefits are typically resources such as land; money in the form of salaries, wages, and funding for special activities; housing; and, ultimately, power or control. Groups don't have to be racially, culturally, or gender different, as evidenced by Sherif's study of age groups. The mere fact that two "teams" are competing against each other can cause negative attitudes. Exhibit 5-1 summarizes these theories about the sources of prejudicial attitudes.

QUICK PROJECT

Which theory, or source, of prejudice would you agree with the most? What are some of the limitations of each theory?

_____

_____

_____

_____

_____

EXHIBIT 5-1

Sources of Prejudicial Attitudes

Theory	Description
Innate Personality	People are born prejudiced. They have an unhealthy personality and are unable to accept their shortcomings. They are more likely to blame others instead of taking responsibility for their own problems. Minority groups become the scapegoats for their prejudice.
Learned Behavior	People are not born prejudiced. They learn prejudicial attitudes and discriminatory behavior from those with whom they associate. Prejudicial attitudes from learned behavior are perpetuated by the concepts of similarity and proximity.
Intergroup competition	Prejudicial attitudes arise between groups contending for the same rewards or limited resources. Racial, culture, or gender differences play a minor role. Competition between two groups is enough to cause negative attitudes.

STEREOTYPING

Prejudice generally begins with **stereotyping,** which is the process of generalizing about individual people on the basis of the common characteristics shared by the group to which that individual belongs. Most often, these generalizations are exaggerated and negative and are applied to all individuals who belong in that group. For example, would you choose an Eastern Indian as your doctor? Many people would say no because they feel that Eastern Indian physicians don't speak English well enough to be understood by their patients. As you are probably aware, this is not true for *all* Eastern Indians. Negative stereotypes come from the belief that only the particular group we belong to is competent, intelligent, and likeable, whereas other groups are not (Fiske, 1998).

> **PROJECT A** *Stereotyping*
> Before reading more about stereotyping, complete Project A at the end of this chapter.

Although stereotyping has received a bad rap as the United States strives to become more united with its diverse cultures, stereotyping actually has its benefits. For example, if we know that, *generally, based on sound research*, women continue to be the primary caretakers of children and are consequently absent from work more often than men to care for children, organizations can use that research to develop options that might increase attendance, such as an on-site day care facility.

Notice our emphasis on the words "generally" and "based on sound research." When we make unsubstantiated and unscientific generalizations about people, it is unfair and more likely to lead to negative stereotyping. There are two implications of negative stereotyping. One is that certain minorities are denied the same financial, educational, professional, and power advantages afforded to other groups. The other is that negative stereotyping allows people to rationalize the mistreatment of other individuals. In other words, negative stereotyping leads to discrimination. Police use of "racial profiling" to randomly stop Black drivers is an excellent example of the dangers of improperly using stereotypes and statistics.

QUICK PROJECT

List the attitudinal and behavioral characteristics of the following groups: African American, Asian American, and traditional college students. Compare your answers with your classmates. How do they compare? Do you think those characteristics apply to *all* individuals in those groups?

_____

_____

_____

_____

_____

_____

Discrimination

Discrimination is behavior that *usually* results from a prejudicial attitude toward certain groups and that interferes in the equal distribution of power and privileges to minorities and other groups. For example,

EXHIBIT 5-2

Types of Discriminators

		Level of Discrimination	
		low	*high*
Level of Prejudicial Attitude	*low*	Tolerator	Conformist
	high	Law Abider	Violator

your *attitude* might be that divorced men are not good caretakers or custodial parents of their children. If you were a judge, your *discriminatory behavior*, then, might be to always grant custody of minor children to the mother. Without substantiated proof that this particular mother would be a better caretaker than the father, your behavior would interfere with the equal rights of individuals in the male group. In the workplace, discriminatory behaviors might include hiring Whites in preference to Blacks, promoting men over equally qualified women, refusing to hire people over 40, or terminating the employment of people who practice certain religious beliefs unrelated to job performance.

We say discrimination *usually* follows prejudicial attitudes because many prejudiced people don't discriminate, either because they believe discrimination is wrong or because legislation has forbidden it. Conversely, people who aren't prejudiced can be highly discriminatory. As shown in Exhibit 5-2, people can generally be classified into four types of discriminators, based on the level of their prejudicial attitudes and the level of discriminatory behavior they demonstrate.

TYPES OF DISCRIMINATORS

Tolerators Tolerators hold low levels of prejudice against some groups but demonstrate few to no discriminatory behaviors. That is, they don't deny certain groups the same rights afforded to others. They usually recognize their own prejudices and work to overcome them. For example, Tolerators might actually believe that women are the weaker sex, but Tolerators may refuse to support current legislation that forbids women from combat. Tolerators might believe certain minority groups need special advantages to make up for past discrimination, so Tolerators may support affirmative action. Or they may join certain organizations to show their support of a minority group. At work, Tolerators can work well with diverse groups.

Conformists Like Tolerators, **Conformists** actually have few prejudices against any particular groups. Unlike Tolerators, however, Conformists may be highly discriminatory because of the expectations of the group in which they themselves belong. For example, let's say you hold no negative attitudes toward people with alternative lifestyles. Yet, you may choose not to socialize with them (e.g., sit with them in the lunchroom) because your coworkers do not like people with alternative lifestyles. Because it's important that you are accepted and liked by these coworkers, you *conform* to their expectations. In this example, that conformity results in your treating some groups of people in a manner you might not otherwise do if it weren't for your colleagues. You might even laugh at or tell racist jokes because that's the norm in your group. Peer pressure may cause you to conform to the norms of your group. At work, Conformist managers may not hire certain individuals (even though it's illegal) because they "know" that "these people wouldn't work well" in the organization.

Law Abiders **Law Abiders** are highly prejudiced against most minority or other groups of people but don't exhibit discriminatory behavior because the law doesn't allow it. They may keep their negative attitudes to themselves, at least while they are at work. In the workplace, Law Abiders may even work zealously to ensure equal opportunity for everyone—but only because they want to reduce the chances of lawsuits not because they believe everyone deserves an equal opportunity. For example, we know of a public high school teacher who is a bigot but is able to hide his attitude while teaching 6 hours in a predominantly Black high school. However, outside of the workplace, he becomes a Violator. Law Abiders strictly conform to the letter of the law.

Violators Violators publicly acknowledge their prejudices and often overtly violate the rights of those groups of people they consider different. For example, some Violators may sincerely believe that homosexuality is morally wrong. Consequently, Violators may refuse to associate with people with alternative lifestyles and may join an organization that publicly announces it will not accept homosexuals. In the extreme, the KKK and skinheads are good examples of Violators. In the workplace, Violators may refuse to hire certain people and may blatantly participate in other discriminatory practices, regardless of the law, until they are stopped by someone filing a lawsuit.

> **PROJECT B** *Prejudice and Discriminatory Behavior*
> Complete Project B at the end of this chapter to better understand types of discriminatory behavior.

Relatively speaking, discrimination is easier to control or change than prejudice because discrimination is a *behavior* whereas prejudice is an attitude. Behavior can be managed, even if it has to be done through legislation. Over the years, federal, state, and local governments have been able to enact legislation to stop certain discriminatory behaviors. Probably the most famous recent example of this is the federal government's order to two public all-male military schools—the Virginia Military Institute and The Citadel—to admit women. Unfortunately, attitudes still haven't changed significantly about whether women should be allowed in such schools.

Another recent case in which the government has intervened involves sports. For many years, one criterion for eligibility to play in NCAA games as freshmen was to pass 13 core high school classes. Unfortunately, because learning-disabled students often take courses not deemed core courses, they were unfairly prevented from playing and earning athletic scholarships. In 1998, the Justice Department held that the NCAA was in violation of Title III of the Americans with Disabilities Act, pointing out that many special courses for learning-disabled students have been devised to cover the same material that nondisabled students take. The NCAA revised its policies and agreed to certify classes designed for students with learning disabilities if the classes provide the same types of skills and knowledge as those designated core high school classes.

In 1997, President Clinton recognized that the nation still has a way to go to end prejudice and racism and organized the Presidential Advisory Board on Race Relations, which held its first meeting on July 14, 1997. As of the writing of this textbook, the committee is still sitting. The mission of the committee is to ensure that one day society becomes more than just tolerators of differences. Their goal is that people learn to be acceptors and even celebrators of diversity, thereby ending all types of discrimination.

TYPES OF DISCRIMINATION

Federally protected classes Federal courts over the years have formally recognized nine groups that need protection from discrimination: race, color, national origin, religion, sex, age, disability, pregnancy, and Vietnam veteran status. These groups are referred to as **federally protected classes,** and people who fall under one or more of these classes have legal recourse through the federal courts if they believe they have been discriminated against.

Individuals who fall under the race, color, sex, national origin, and religion categories are protected by the **Civil Rights Acts of 1866, 1964,** and **1991,** which make it illegal for employers with more than 15 employees to:

1. Fail, refuse to hire, discharge any individual, or otherwise discriminate against any individual with respect to his compensation, terms, conditions, or privileges of employment because of the individual's race, color, religion, sex, or national origin.

2. Limit, segregate, or classify employees or applicants for employment in any way that would deprive, or tend to deprive, any individual of employment opportunities or otherwise adversely affect his or her stature as an employee because of an individual's race, color, sex, religion, or national origin.

The four other federally protected classes are covered by different legislation, which we will explain as we proceed through this chapter. We will look at the federally protected classes first and then at other groups who have traditionally been discriminated against and who may be recognized by state legislation as protected classes, but not by federal legislation.

Race Although behaviorial scientists (Rushton, 1995) find little evidence of "race" based on other than superficial cosmetic differences, according to Congress, there are four races: African American (Black), Asian American/Pacific Islander, Native American Indian, and European American (White). A few years ago, a group of mixed-race Americans belonging to Project RACE (Reclassify All Children Equally) attempted to get Congress to add a fifth category: multiracial. However, in 1997, a federal task force recommended that this new category not be added, reasoning that such a category would increase racial tension and further fragment the country. They did say, however, that people should be able to check more than one race, if applicable. The Federal Office of Management and Budget adopted the task force's recommendation in October 1997, and 2000 Census Forms allowed multiple checkoffs for race.

Typically, when people talk about discrimination in the United States based on race, they are generally referring to discrimination against African Americans, Asian Americans/Pacific Islanders, and Native American Indians. But, as we stated earlier in the chapter, European Americans (the dominant group in the U.S.) can also be discriminated against in what has been called *reverse discrimination*. The most famous case illustrating reverse discrimination is *Bakke v. University of California* (1978). In this case, courts ruled that the university had discriminated against Bakke, who is White, when they rejected his application in favor of a minority applicant who had similar qualifications as Bakke's.

Color Though commonly used as a synonym for race, the reference to color protects individuals within one race against discrimination based on variations in skin color. For example, in the 1989 case of *Walker v. Secretary of the Treasury*, a district court found that a darker skinned African American supervisor at the Internal Revenue Service illegally fired a lighter skinned African American employee.

National origin National origin means the continent on which we or our ancestors were born. Claims of discrimination based on national origin have increased greatly over the past few years, due primarily to "unprecedented" immigration (Barton, 1993). One of the most common complaints is "English only" or "understandable English" speaking requirements. The courts have generally ruled that language requirements are legal if they are job related (Quinn & Petrick, 1993) and limited to communication during "company time" rather than on breaks. Organizations that close their eyes to prejudice and discrimination toward individuals based on national origin will grow ineffective, because significant increases in Hispanics and Asians are expected through the 21st century. According to the United States Department of Labor (1998) they will account for approximately 35% of the workforce by the year 2005.

Religion Prejudice and discrimination against people with differing religious backgrounds is common throughout the world. Catholics and Protestants continue to fight in Ireland, Serbs fight Bosnians (who are half Muslim and half Christian), and many Americans continue to hold anti-Semitic opinions. In the workforce, it is illegal to use an individual's religion in an employment decision unless the nature of the job is religious. For example, the Catholic Church can require its priests to be Catholic but not its clerical staff. Courts have extended this reasoning to allow wearing of religious garments to work, to forbid an employer from requiring its employees to

say "Merry Christmas" to customers, and to prohibit organizations from requiring individuals of a particular religion to work on certain days (e.g., Seventh-Day Adventists and Jews generally cannot work from sundown Friday to sundown Saturday).

Gender Women are expected to comprise 48% of the workforce by the year 2005. Past discriminatory practices have included firing females who become pregnant and request time off, reassigning returning mothers to lesser positions because of the length of time they took off, giving women lower pay, and reducing their promotion opportunities. Often overlooked is the fact that men, too, are discriminated against. As discussed in Chapter 4 on ethics and professionalism, 15% of men are also discriminated against in the workforce. Both the Civil Rights Act and the **Equal Pay Act of 1963** prevent intentional discrimination against either females or males. In addition to employment decisions such as selection and promotion, the Civil Rights Acts of 1964 and 1991 also have been interpreted by the courts to cover the "atmosphere" of the organization, which includes such behavior as sexual harassment (discussed in Chapter 4). In 1998 the U.S. Supreme Court ruled that federal law barring sexual discrimination in the workplace applies to harassment between workers of the same sex. That is, individuals who create a hostile environment by making lewd comments, groping, or otherwise mistreating individuals of the same sex can be held liable for sexual harassment.

Age The traditional attitude about older workers has typically been that they are ineffective, slower to learn, and more likely to get sick and be absent from work. Little significant research supports this opinion, yet many people over 40 will tell you that they believe they weren't hired for a job or were not promoted because of their age. It's not unusual for courts to agree that older workers have been discriminated against. In July 1998, the Courts found the University of Notre Dame guilty of age discrimination and awarded former assistant coach Joe Moore, age 64 at the time, $86,000 in damages. The Court determined that the university knowingly disregarded the law. Moore claimed he was fired because of his age and that his replacement, Bob Davie, age 45, was hired instead.

This type of discriminatory attitude and behavior can have negative effects on organizations. The overall population distribution in America is getting older, partly because of declining birth rates and improvements in medical technology that allow people to live longer. The median age of all workers by the year 2005 will be 40.5 years. Consequently, as the labor pool gets older, employers must overcome their negative attitudes.

The **Age Discrimination in Employment Act (ADEA)** forbids employers or unions from discriminating against individuals over the age of 40. In part, this act was designed to protect older workers from employment practices aimed at reducing costs by firing older workers. Though mandatory retirement ages are allowed in certain circumstances (e.g., for pilots and college professors), they are generally illegal because, as research indicates, work performance does not necessarily decline as one gets older.

QUICK PROJECT

Think about and write down how you would feel if you were told you could not hold a certain job because of your age.

_____

_____

_____

_____

_____

Disability Discrimination against people with disabilities who work in the federal government is forbidden by the **Vocational Rehabilitation Act of 1974**, and discrimination against people with disabilities by any other employer (e.g., private employers, and state and local government employers) with 15 or more employees is forbidden by the **Americans with Disabilities Act (ADA) of 1990**. The ADA requires organizations with 25 or more employees to make reasonable accommodation for people with physical and mental disabilities unless to do so "would impose an undue hardship." Though Congress did not provide a complete *list* of disabilities, it defined disability as:

1. *A physical or mental impairment that substantially limits one or more of the major life activities of an individual* Major life activities include such things as walking, hearing, and speaking. Examples of conditions considered disabilities by case law or the Department of Labor are blindness, paralysis, asthma, muscular dystrophy, and various learning disabilities such as dyslexia. Conditions not considered disabilities include fear of heights and sprained ankles.

2. *A record of such impairment* This part of the definition was designed to protect people who were once disabled but no longer are. Examples include recovering alcoholics, cancer patients in remission, people who spent time in a mental health facility, and drug addicts who have successfully completed treatment and are no longer using drugs.

3. *Being regarded as having such an impairment* This protects individuals who don't have a disability but are treated as if they do. Examples of people protected under this clause are those with facial scarring or severe burns who have been discriminated against throughout their lives.

Case law over the next several years will continue to better define *disability*. The most recent clarification by the Supreme Court of what constitutes a disability is HIV status. AIDS was already covered by ADA, but in 1998, the Court decided that individuals did not need to have AIDS to be disabled: Those with the HIV virus are also covered by the legislation because they are limited in what they can do.

Pregnancy The **Pregnancy Discrimination Act** states that "women affected by pregnancy, childbirth, or related medical conditions shall be treated the same for all employment-related purposes, including receipt of benefit programs, as other persons not so affected but similar in their ability or inability to work." Simply put, this act requires pregnancy to be treated as any other disability. The **Family Medical Leave Act of 1993** also protects pregnant women by allowing eligible male and female employees a minimum of 12 weeks of unpaid leave to deal with the birth or adoption of a child, as well as with the serious illness of a child, parent, or the employee him- or herself.

Vietnam-era veteran status At one time, returning veterans from the Vietnam War were discriminated against in the workplace because of the attitudes and feelings about the war itself. Because of such attitudes, Congress passed the **Vietnam Era Veterans Readjustment Act** in 1974. This act mandates any contractor or subcontractor with more than $10,000 in federal government contracts to take affirmative action to employ and promote Vietnam-era veterans. This law is one reason that veterans applying for civil service jobs receive credit for their military service as well as for their qualifications. A list of the federally protected classes is shown in Exhibit 5-3.

State and Locally Protected Classes Some groups who do not have federal protection have been provided state or local protection from discriminatory practices. For example, as of this writing, discrimination against gays is illegal under state statute in California, Connecticut, Hawaii, Massachusetts, Minnesota, Maine, New Jersey, Rhode Island, Ver-

EXHIBIT 5-3

Federally Protected Groups

Protected Group	Federal Law
Race	Civil Rights Act of 1964, 1991
Color	Civil Rights Act of 1964, 1991
Ethnic origin	Civil Rights Act of 1964, 1991
Gender	Civil Rights Act of 1964, 1991; Equal Pay Act of 1963
Religion	Civil Rights Act of 1964, 1991
Age (over 40)	Age Discrimination in Employment Act (ADEA) of 1967
Disability	Americans with Disabilities Act Vocational Rehabilitation Act of 1974
Pregnancy	Pregnancy Discrimination Act of 1978
Vietnam veterans status	Vietnam-Era Veterans Readjustment Act of 1974

mont, Wisconsin, New Hampshire, and the District of Columbia. Virginia prevents discrimination based on marital status, and the City of Cincinnati prevents discrimination based on Appalachian Heritage.

The newest fear is genetic discrimination, and numerous agencies and politicians are calling for legislation to protect employees from genetic discrimination. Workers fear employers will use information from routine medical exams to weed out people with inherited medical conditions that can run up insurance costs (Armour, 1998). In February 2000 President Clinton prohibited genetic discrimination against federal employees.

PROJECT C *Protected Classes*
Test your understanding of what you read about protected classes by completing Project C at the end of this chapter.

■ PREJUDICE, DISCRIMINATION, AND RACISM IN THE 21ST CENTURY

Many people insist that prejudicial attitudes and discrimination no longer exist in the United States or have been significantly reduced, mainly because of the integration of diverse populations in neighborhoods, churches, and organizations. In fact, interracial marriages are on the rise and the number of teens who are dating or have dated someone of a different race or ethnicity have increased in the last several years (Peterson, 1997). Exhibit 5-4 shows a letter to the editor in the July 14, 1998 edition of *USA Today* from a government official who holds the belief that America is not a racist society.

QUICK PROJECT
Briefly write your reaction to the letter printed in Exhibit 5-4.

_____

_____

_____

_____

_____

Symbolic Racism

This contemporary view that prejudice no longer exists has been called symbolic racism (Sears, 1988). Traditionally, **racism** has been defined as a belief system that asserts the inferiority of a group and rationalizes unequal treatment of them (Healey, 1998). It assumes that certain groups of people are biologically or genetically inferior. **Symbolic racism** rejects this

EXHIBIT 5-4

The U.S. Not a Racist Society

In replying to Camille Cosby's comments that America taught her son's killer, a Ukrainian immigrant, to hate Blacks, a public official wrote the following letter to the editor:

> *My heart goes out to Camille Cosby on the death of her son, but her July 8 [1998] comments . . . must be dismissed for what they are: irresponsible and inaccurate. America is not a racist society. That does not mean there are no racists in America, but it is unfair to blame all non-black Americans for her son's death. . . . I challenge [Mrs. Cosby] to name a single American institution now that is racist. It is socially and politically unacceptable to be a racist in 1998 America, and our laws make it illegal to discriminate in almost any public activity.*

Printed in part, published in *USA Today*, July 14, 1998

biological or genetically based belief. However, it holds the following assumptions, which is why some people call it "symbolic" racism (Healey, 1998):

- There is no longer any serious discrimination in American society.

- Any residual inequality that may exist is the fault of the minority group.

- Demands for preferential treatment or affirmative action for minority groups is unfair and, in fact, is discriminatory toward those considered the dominant group.

People considered to be symbolic racists believe that focus on diversity and celebrations of various ethnic or racial differences is no longer necessary, nor positive, for continuous harmony between groups. This belief is illustrated in the newspaper commentary in Exhibit 5-5.

QUICK PROJECT

After reading Exhibit 5-5, discuss in class with your classmates and instructor whether you agree with the commentary. Why or why not?

_____

_____

_____

_____

_____

Symbolic racism is considered prejudice because it continues (albeit indirectly) to uphold a system that does not acknowledge that prejudice and discrimination continue. As you can see from the examples in Exhibit 5-6 on page 141, prejudicial attitudes and discrimination are still very real in our society.

PROJECT D *Prejudice and Discrimination Continue*
Complete Project D at the end of this chapter to understand how prejudicial attitudes are still prevalent.

Affirmative Action

Many people feel that the elimination of affirmative action is a form of symbolic racism. In the workplace, **affirmative action** is a process of ensuring proportional representation of employees based on variables such as race and sex. It is a broad term encompassing a number of employment strategies that can be placed into three categories, including the following:

1. *Intentional recruitment of minority applicants* For instance, to increase the number of minority employees, an organization might make such efforts as recruiting at historically Black and female colleges and working with local NAACP chapters.

2. *Removal of discriminatory workplace practices* The concept is to remove practices that discourage minorities from applying for or accepting jobs with an organization. Such practices might involve organizational policy, supervisor attitudes, or the way in which a workplace is decorated. For example, an African American employee in a southern city filed a lawsuit alleging

EXHIBIT 5-5

Constant Racial Comparisons Perpetuate Stereotypes (Letter to the Editor)

Recently, there have been a number of references in [the newspapers] about African Americans based on opinion polls. . . . I continue to ask myself what useful purpose these polls serve. . .

. . . the media's constant comparisons of blacks and whites do little more than perpetuate greater polarization and stereotypes. . . Here's something to consider: While Americans still have issues to work through, most of us have more in common than differences across racial lines. But we constantly choose to point out so-called differences. Let's face it, most of us, regardless of race, drive similar cars, wear similar clothes, eat very similar foods and do similar stuff. . . I hope one day soon we'll get over the obsession we have about race and really find a way to make a difference in this great country.

Printed, in part, in *USA Today*, September, 1998

---

race as the reason he wasn't promoted. As evidence, he cited the embroidered Confederate flag hanging in his supervisor's office. The city's Affirmative Action officer suggested the flag be removed because, even though the supervisor was a Civil War enthusiast rather than a racist, a Confederate Flag in a supervisor's office might give the perception of institutional acceptance of racism.

PROJECT E *Workplace Practices*
Complete Project E at the end of this chapter to better understand how workplace practices might be perceived as intolerant to certain groups.

3. *Preferential hiring and promotion of minority applicants* This strategy has been most referred to in recent cases, and some states (e.g., California) have abolished it altogether. The most recent case focusing attention on the legality of preferential hiring and promotion of minorities is *Taxman v. the School Board of Piscataway, NJ*, which was scheduled to be heard by the U.S. Supreme Court in January 1998 but was settled out of court in 1997.

In this case, a White teacher (Taxman) and a Black teacher (Williams) were hired by the Piscataway school system in 1980. They both worked in the same department and received similar performance ratings. In 1989 budget problems forced the school board to lay off one teacher. The board terminated Taxman,

stating that keeping Williams would increase the school's diversity. In 1993, the federal court ruled that the school system was wrong in using race as a factor in its employment decisions and awarded Taxman $144,000 in back pay. The court in this case, as have other courts in the past, asked three primary questions to determine the legality of using race, gender, or national origin in employment decisions:

1. *Was there a history of discrimination in the organization?* Typically this history is determined by a large disparity between the percentage of minority employees in various positions within the organization and the percentage of qualified minorities in the relevant geographic area.

2. *Were goals based on the qualified workforce rather than the area population?* This question concerns which of two types of populations were used to statistically determine disparities and to set affirmative action goals. In establishing numerical disparity, the percentage of qualified minorities in the relevant geographic area, as opposed to the percentage of minorities, must be used.

3. *Did the affirmative action plan trammel the rights of nonminorities?* To determine the legality of an affirmative action program, the courts examine the extent to which the program "unnecessarily trammels" the rights of nonminorities. That is, a plan that helps females cannot deny the rights of males. Preference can be given to a qualified minority over an equally qualified nonmi-

EXHIBIT 5-6

Prejudice and Discrimination Continue

May 1999	A New York police officer pleads guilty to torturing with a broom handle a Haitian immigrant taken into the police station bathroom after arrest.
October 1998	The U.S. Supreme Court rejected a challenge to the military's "don't ask, don't tell" policy. This was the fourth time in recent years the court has refused to hear the appeals of former service members ousted for discussing their homosexuality.
September 1998	Two men in Laramie, Wyoming beat, burned, and tied to a fence a young University of Wyoming student because he was gay.
July 1998	Three white men in Jasper, Texas were indicted on capital murder charges in the hate-slaying of a Black man whom they chained to the back of a pickup and dragged to his death. The men were subsequently convicted of murder.
July 1998	A "football-field-sized" swastika was cut in a cornfield in a rural area in New Jersey.
1998	The California State Supreme Court ruled that, under the state's civil rights laws, the Boy Scouts of America is free to exclude homosexuals and religious nonbelievers from membership.
February 1998	The PGA Tour was sued by a young disabled professional golfer, Casey Martin, for refusing to allow him to ride a cart in competition. The PGA contended that using the cart would give Martin an unfair advantage over others. The courts agreed with Martin, who is now allowed to play on the PGA Tour.
June 1997	The Southern Baptist Convention boycotted the Walt Disney Company for "promoting homosexuality" by offering health benefits to the domestic partners of gay employees and allow Gay Days at its theme parks. They also attempted to get their members not to watch the television sitcom "Ellen" because of its lesbian lead character.

nority, but a lesser qualified minority can never be hired over a more qualified nonminority. For an affirmative action plan to be narrowly tailored and not trammel the rights of nonminorities:

- The magnitude of the goal must be reasonable.
- All people hired and/or promoted must be qualified.
- Race and gender can be used if several people are equally qualified.

In *Taxman,* the court ruled that Piscataway could not show a history of discrimination as the percentage of African American teachers in both the high school and the school system was in line with the percentage of African Americans in the local community. Because there was no history of discrimination, the court ruled that the desire for diversity did not outweigh Taxman's right to keep her job.

This ruling and others like it, contrary to what the media reports and the general public believes, does not eliminate affirmative action in general nor will it eliminate the potential for considering race,

gender, or national origin as a factor when the percentage of minorities in an organization falls well below the percentage of minorities in the qualified workforce. Affirmative action can still be a part of a company's plan to increase and celebrate diversity. Exhibit 5-7 shows how to determine the legality of a preferential hiring plan.

■ DISCRIMINATION IN THE WORKPLACE

How can prejudice and discrimination affect relationships in the workplace? First and foremost, it can affect the fair selection, evaluation, and promotion of workers. Think back to what we discussed about sources of prejudice and similarity. Who supervisors hire or promote can be influenced by how similar that person is to them.

As you have learned, employment decisions based on membership in a protected class are illegal *unless*

EXHIBIT 5-7

Determining the Legality of a Preferential Hiring Plan

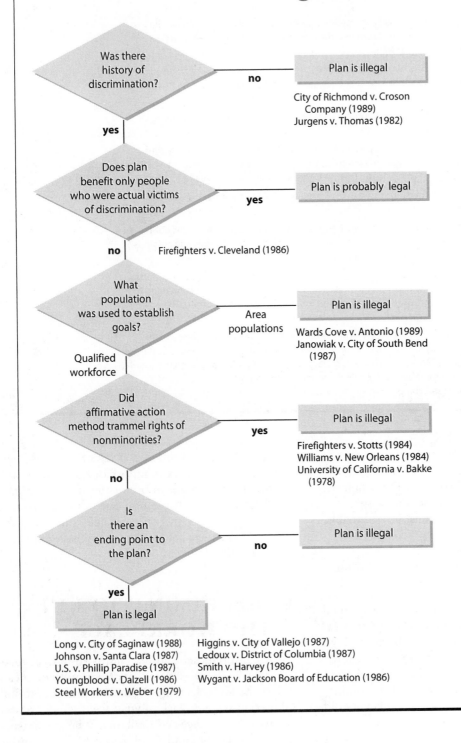

Was there history of discrimination?

no → Plan is illegal

City of Richmond v. Croson Company (1989)
Jurgens v. Thomas (1982)

yes ↓

Does plan benefit only people who were actual victims of discrimination?

yes → Plan is probably legal

no ↓ Firefighters v. Cleveland (1986)

What population was used to establish goals?

Area populations → Plan is illegal

Wards Cove v. Antonio (1989)
Janowiak v. City of South Bend (1987)

Qualified workforce ↓

Did affirmative action method trammel rights of nonminorities?

yes → Plan is illegal

Firefighters v. Stotts (1984)
Williams v. New Orleans (1984)
University of California v. Bakke (1978)

no ↓

Is there an ending point to the plan?

no → Plan is illegal

yes ↓

Plan is legal

Long v. City of Saginaw (1988)   Higgins v. City of Vallejo (1987)
Johnson v. Santa Clara (1987)   Ledoux v. District of Columbia (1987)
U.S. v. Phillip Paradise (1987)   Smith v. Harvey (1986)
Youngblood v. Dalzell (1986)   Wygant v. Jackson Board of Education (1986)
Steel Workers v. Weber (1979)

the employer can demonstrate that the requirement is a bona fide occupational qualification (**BFOQ**). That is, if a job can only be performed by a person in a particular class, the requirement is considered a BFOQ. For example, only a woman can be a wet nurse; only a Catholic can be a Catholic priest. Overall, very few jobs in our society can *only* be performed by a particular race, gender, or national origin. For example, let's say a job involves lifting 150 pounds a day. A company could not set a "male-only" job requirement just because, in *general,* men are stronger than women. The real BFOQ in this example is *strength*, not gender. There are many women who can lift more than 150 pounds and some men who can't lift that much.

However, basing employment decisions on strength and the ability to lift at least 150 pounds, even though job related, can still be discriminatory. There are two types of discriminatory employment decisions: **disparate treatment** (intentional discrimination) and **disparate impact** (also known as **adverse impact,** which is unintentional discrimination.) We have already explained disparate treatment, which is fairly clear. However, adverse impact isn't as clear.

Adverse Impact

Adverse impact occurs when a particular employment decision that is based on job relatedness results in negative consequences more often for members of one protected group than for members of the non-protected group. For example, requiring applicants to be able to lift at least 150 pounds because it's part of the daily job, may *unintentionally* have negative consequences for women. An employee-selection requirement of a college degree generally leads to a lower percentage of Black applicants being hired when compared to White applicants because 22% of Whites have a bachelor's degree compared to 11% of Blacks. Employee selection methods that require applicants to take a cognitive ability test can also cause adverse impact because minorities typically score lower on such tests. National aptitude tests given in public schools and college-entrance tests like the SAT, ACT, or GRE have been considered as having adverse impact for years.

Procter and Gamble (P&G) ran into adverse impact several years ago with a hiring requirement to have a driver's license. When P&G was hiring in Russia, most of the applications they received were from men, because Russian women rarely have driver's licenses. Consequently, P&G's requirement was *adversely impacting* women. That is, it was not P&G's intention to exclude women from this particular position. P&G resolved the problem simply by changing their job requirements. Exhibit 5-8 is a flowchart

outlining the criteria organizations follow and to which courts refer to determine whether an employment practice is legal.

> **PROJECT F**   *Interview Questions*
> Using the flowchart in Exhibit 5-8, check your knowledge of legal interview questions by completing Project F at the end of this chapter.

Managing a Diverse Workforce

Federal, state, and local legislation can limit people's behaviors toward minority groups, but it can't mandate attitudes. In fact, the greatest barrier to managing diversity is individual attitudes (Goldhirsh, 1993). The ultimate goal of society, of course, is to change negative attitudes, not just behavior, toward various groups. Since research shows that behavior is often guided by attitudes, it is important to focus on attitudes. Denny's and Shoney's, two national restaurants who were sued several years ago for discriminatory practices, are now two of the best 50 companies for Asians, African Americans, and Hispanics, because they were able to change employee attitudes, thereby reducing discriminatory behaviors. According to Denny's and Shoney's, companies can take the following action to ensure more positive attitudes toward diversity (Digh, 1998):

- Encourage conversations among employees about racial issues.

- Set up minority employee groups as business resources to better understand race issues.

- Hold people accountable for how they deal with diverse populations. Base bonuses and rewards on diversity competence (how well teams, supervisors, and employees address diversity).

- Increase the number of minorities on boards and management teams.

Additionally, because similarity and proximity play a key role in employee interactions, diverse groups of people should be strategically placed, either individually or as teams, close together when possible and where appropriate. Because so often conflict between different groups grows from misunderstanding the differences and needs of each other, allowing diverse groups to work together, communicate better, and discuss their issues can help promote successful diversity.

There are a variety of other ways organizations attempt to change prejudicial attitudes. Many organizations develop formal diversity programs, which include training, diversity celebrations, and diversity teams.

EXHIBIT 5-8

Determining Whether an Employment Practice Is Legal

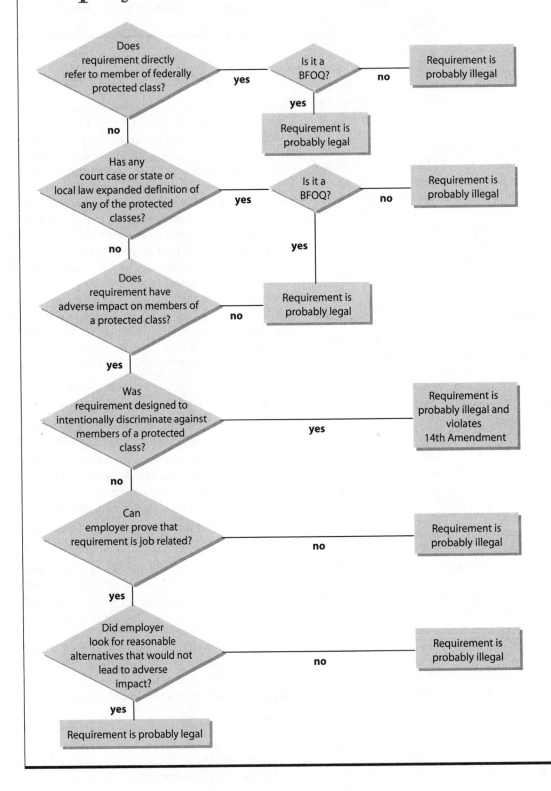

TRAINING

Diversity training should focus on two areas: awareness and skill building (Sherman, Bohlander, & Snell, 1998). At Sara Lee, management builds awareness of diversity by asking divisions with the best diversity performance and the one with the worst to meet and discuss improvements. Sara Lee CEO John Bryan is committed to drawing on the wealth of experience that comes from diverse populations. Procter and Gamble builds awareness by assigning mentors to promising employees as well as by discussing poor diversity performance with managers during performance appraisals. Many companies have on-site training where consultants are brought to the organization and employees are encouraged to attend the consultant's diversity training. Other organizations provide funding for employees to attend off-site week-long diversity training.

Unfortunately, a concern with diversity training is that many people often leave the training with bad feelings. In a large telecommunications organization that periodically requires employees to attend diversity training, a majority of the employees leave the meetings feeling as if they had been "attacked" by the workshop trainers. "They made me feel like I should be ashamed that I'm a White person" is a common remark we hear. When this is the consequence of such training, companies must then hire another consultant to "fix" the damage that diversity training programs have presented. Although the mission behind diversity training is good, the focus too often is just on Black-White, male-female adversarial issues and how nonminorities should be more sensitive rather than on how individuals can learn from each other's differences. Remember what we said earlier: Minority groups also harbor prejudicial attitudes toward the dominant groups and other minorities, and consequently, will discriminate against those groups.

QUICK PROJECT

Think of the last diversity training you attended. What was its content? Did it focus mostly on race and age? Or did it add some of the newer diversity dimensions?

_____

_____

_____

_____

_____

Conversely, however, Digh (1998) reports that some people speculate that the new diversity programs that are enlarging the definition of diversity beyond race and gender and now focus on other diversity dimensions such as personality types, educational levels, and discriminatory practices by minorities against nonminorities, make it appear that racism has ended.

DIVERSITY CELEBRATIONS AND CULTURAL TEAMS

An increasing number of organizations are proactively addressing diversity by holding diversity awareness workshops and designating special days for diversity celebrations. In most instances, diversity committees or teams have been appointed to lead the organization in such celebrations. For example, a local mental health agency has a Diversity Committee that meets regularly to discuss problems that may be occurring in the workplace and to plan yearly diversity programs.

Unfortunately, one of the biggest challenges to such a team is the time involved in meetings and development of workshops and yearly programs—this perceived overwhelming time can diminish productivity, energy, and eventually interest in and commitment to the team. Gardenswartz and Rowe (1998) suggest the following steps for reenergizing a diversity team, all of which pertain to setting goals, defining action steps, and creating timelines.

1. Keep the team's purpose front and center.
2. Articulate and define specific tasks and goals the team has or would like to meet.
3. Make separate, smaller goals (action steps) within the team's overall goal that will reduce feelings of being overwhelmed.
4. Create accountability deadlines through the process. That is, determine who is responsible for doing what task and by when. This can motivate individual team members to carry through on projects.
5. Stay connected. When not meeting in a group, find some way to talk to each other throughout the week, if only to check in on how things are going.
6. Do some training. Members need to be knowledgeable about and stay abreast of racial and diversity information. Consequently, opportunities should be created for additional training in this area for members of the team.

AFFIRMATIVE ACTION PROGRAMS

As stated earlier, affirmative action programs are *not* illegal. However, preferential hiring and promotion of minorities can be illegal if the questions in Exhibit 5-7 are violated. An increasing number of companies voluntarily develop affirmative action programs from a desire to be good citizens and to ensure that their employment practices are fair to all groups of people.

MANAGING PREJUDICED EMPLOYEES

What can you do about an employee or coworker who continuously harasses or makes racial, gender, ethnic, or sexual orientation slurs on the job? If the violator is breaking the law, you are legally obligated to report it. However, what if the behavior hasn't crossed over into discrimination? According to Gardenswartz and Rowe (1999), you are ethically obligated to confront the behavior by letting the person know that such behavior is offensive and degrading. Additionally, people should walk away from the person making the remarks and should not laugh at such jokes.

Glass (1995) recommends the use of "The Calm Questioning Technique" to better manage prejudiced coworkers. This technique shows outspokenly prejudiced people how unfair or unsubstantiated their prejudicial ideas or comments are by having them answer yes or no to statements you ask. For example, let's say your coworker stated that she is not going to work with another employee on a project because that person's disability makes him incompetent. You might say:

> So, you're saying you dislike him because of his disability?
>
> Have you ever worked with a disabled person?
>
> Have you ever worked with this person?
>
> Do you think Casey Martin (a disabled professional golfer) is stupid?
>
> Has a disabled person done something to you in the past to hurt you?

According to Glass, this line of questioning causes most rational people to stop and think about the statements they are making. In other words, it holds them accountable for their behavior and what they say. Now, it may not change their prejudicial attitudes, but it may at least cause them to think twice about making their comments out loud, thereby, reducing poor relationships.

Supervisors and managers need to let employees know that violations of diversity policies will not be tolerated. Employees should be held accountable for their behavior, and rules against this type of behavior should be as vigorously enforced as those on sexual harassment. In most cases, simply meeting with the offending party to point out how such behavior is affecting others can be enough to stop that behavior.

CHAPTER RECAP

In this chapter, you learned:

- Prejudiced attitudes toward individuals who belong to the nondominant group contribute to discriminatory behavior, causing the unequal distribution of power and privileges to certain groups.

- Prejudice has three primary sources: a person's personality, learned behavior, intergroup competition, or a combination of these.

- Proximity, similarity, and unsubstantiated stereotyping play key roles in perpetuating prejudice and discriminatory behavior.

- People can generally be classified into four types of discriminators: tolerators, conformists, law abiders, and violators.

- Federal legislation has helped address discriminatory behavior toward certain groups of people, classified as protected classes, who fall under one or more of the following categories: race, color, sex, national origin, religion, age, disability, pregnancy, and Vietnam veteran status.

- Symbolic racism is prevalent in today's society.

- Prejudice can affect relationships in the workplace by affecting the selection, interviewing, and promotion of employees.

- An employment requirement based on membership in a protected class is illegal unless the employer can demonstrate the requirement is a bona fide occupational qualification (BFOQ).

- There are two types of discriminatory employment decisions: intentional (known as disparate treatment) and unintentional (adverse or disparate impact).

- Managing a diverse workforce requires a diversity program that is composed of training, diversity celebrations, diversity work teams, and an affirmative action plan that ensures that employment practices are fair to all groups of people.

Critical Thinking Questions

1. Based on all that you have read in this chapter, what are the factors that contribute to prejudicial attitudes and discriminatory behavior?

2. If you were appointed to a Diversity Committee, what are some of the programs or activities you would have to help people change their attitudes?

3. Some people comment that prejudice and discrimination will never really go away, no matter

what others do. Do you agree with this thought? Why or why not?

4. When someone tells a racist or other type of joke at the expense of other classes of people, do you participate in the joke, walk away, or express your opinion about that type of joke? If you keep quiet, why do you think that is? If you don't condone it, what are some of the actions that you take to minimize this type of behavior?

WEB SITES

For further information, log on to the following web sites.

www.mapnp.org/library/emp_well/diversty/diversty.htm
Provides links to hundreds of diversity sites.
www.socialpsychology.org/social.htm#prejudice
Provides links to a variety of sites with information on diversity and prejudice.

KEY TERMS

Adverse impact Unintentional discrimination resulting from an employment decision that results in negative consequences more often for members of one protected group than for members of non-protected groups.

Affirmative action A process of ensuring proportional representation of employees based on variables such as race and sex.

Age Discrimination in Employment Act (ADEA) Federal legislation that forbids employers or unions from discrimination against individuals over the age of 40.

Americans with Disabilities Act (ADA) Federal legislation that prevents organizations from discrimination against people with disabilities and that requires organizations with 25 or more employees to make "reasonable accommodation" for people with physical and mental disabilities.

Attitude Affective and cognitive evaluations of people, ideas, and situations.

Bona Fide Occupational Qualification (BFOQ) A requirement such as an ability or skill that is related to the duties to be performed by employees.

Civil Rights Act of 1964 and 1991 Federal legislation that prevents organizations from discrimination against people based on their race, color, gender, ethnic origin, or religious beliefs.

Conformist One type of discriminator who has few or no prejudices against any group but who is highly discriminatory.

Discrimination Behavior, usually resulting from prejudicial attitudes, that interferes in the equal distribution of power and privileges to minorities and other groups.

Disparate impact See Adverse Impact.

Disparate treatment Intentional discrimination.

Dominant group The group who has the most benefit in society and who often causes inequality.

Equal Pay Act of 1963 Federal legislation that prevents intentional discrimination against males and females in the workplace.

Family Medical Leave Act (FMLA) Federal legislation protecting pregnant women by allowing them and their spouses a minimum of 12 weeks of unpaid leave to deal with birth, adoption, or illness of a child, parent, or the employee him- or herself.

Federally protected classes Groups of people who are protected by federal legislation from discrimination—these groups are race, color, sex, religion, age, Vietnam veteran status, disability, pregnancy, and national origin.

Law abider One type of discriminator who is highly prejudiced but does not engage in discriminatory behavior.

Minority group Individuals who share the following characteristics: they experience a pattern of disadvantage or inequality, they have visible identifying physical traits, they are aware of their disadvantages, they are born into their minority classification, and they usually marry within their own group.

Pregnancy Discrimination Act Federal legislation that requires that women affected by pregnancy, childbirth, or related medical conditions be treated the same for all employment-related purposes as others not affected by such conditions.

Prejudice A negative attitude toward individuals who belong to groups considered to be different than the dominant group.

Racism A belief system that asserts the inferiority of a group and rationalizes unequal treatment of that group.

Stereotyping The process of generalizing about people based on the group to which they belong.

Symbolic racism Contemporary view of prejudice that assumes that there is no longer any serious discrimination in American society, any residual inequality that exists is the fault of the minority group, and the demand for preferential treatment is unfair and discriminatory toward the dominant group.

Tolerator One type of discriminator who has few or no prejudicial attitudes toward others and who does not discriminate against groups.

Vietnam Veterans Readjustment Act Federal legislation that mandates that any contractor or subcontractor with more than $10,000 in federal government contracts take affirmative action to employ and promote Vietnam-era veterans.

Violator One type of discriminator who is highly prejudicial and overtly discriminates against other groups.

Vocational Rehabilitation Act of 1974 Federal legislation preventing the federal government from discriminating against employees with disabilities.

PRACTICE EXAM

1. Gloria didn't think her new roommate, Joanne, would last very long in college. Joanne was visually impaired, so Gloria felt Joanne wouldn't be able to keep up with the work. Another name for Gloria's attitude about Joanne's disability is:
   a. discrimination
   b. stereotyping
   c. prejudice
   d. domination

2. When Peter's friends found out he was gay, they no longer wanted to remain his friends. In fact, they went out of their way to exclude Peter from activities such as going to their church or their country club. Peter's friends' behavior is called:
   a. discrimination
   b. stereotyping
   c. prejudice
   d. domination

3. Minorities share all but one of the following characteristics:
   a. They have visible identifying traits
   b. They are aware of their disadvantage
   c. They are all numerically in the majority
   d. They marry within their group.

4. In this chapter you learned there are three theories about the sources of prejudice. The innate personality theory suggests that people:
   a. learn how to be prejudiced
   b. are born prejudiced
   c. are seldom prejudiced
   d. quit being prejudiced when they get old

5. In the learned behavior theory of prejudice, it is suggested that:
   a. The closer diverse groups of people geographically live, the more likely they are to become prejudiced.
   b. People are born prejudiced.
   c. Similarities between people may cause prejudice.
   d. Dissimilarities between people may cause prejudice.

6. Sam couldn't believe that Tom hired a retired Marine officer who had served in the Vietnam War for the position of human resources manager. "Don't you know that all ex-vets are too directive and authoritarian? That type of personality will just cause low morale!" Sam is
   _____.
   a. stereotyping
   b. discriminating
   c. prejudiced
   d. correct

7. After Sam complained about Tom's choice for a human resources manager, he made the following comment: "If it was me, I would never have hired a retired Marine officer regardless of the law." Based on the types of discriminators you read about in this chapter, you could say that Sam is a _____.
   a. Tolerator
   b. Conformist
   c. Law abider
   d. Violator

8. All of the following are federally protected classes *except* _____.
   a. African Americans
   b. Caucasians
   c. People over 30
   d. Hispanics

9. Refer again to the section in your text regarding the type of discriminators. Tolerators _____ while Conformists _____.
   a. hold low levels of prejudice and demonstrate few or no discriminatory behaviors; have few or no prejudices but are highly discriminatory.
   b. are highly prejudiced but have low discriminatory behavior; have few or no prejudices but are highly discriminatory.
   c. have few or no prejudices but are highly discriminatory; hold low levels of prejudice and demonstrate few or no discriminatory behaviors.
   d. are highly prejudiced and highly discriminatory; are highly prejudiced but have low discriminatory behavior.

10. The Violator discriminator:
    a. is highly prejudiced and highly discriminatory
    b. has few or no prejudices but is highly discriminatory.
    c. is highly prejudiced but has low discriminatory behavior.
    d. holds low levels of prejudice and demonstrates few or no discriminatory behaviors.

11. Bon Air Company's policies are to hire only men to work in their hardware department. This is an example of _____.
    a. disparate treatment
    b. sexual harassment
    c. adverse impact
    d. disparate impact

12. As the HR director, one of your responsibilities is to perform a yearly audit on promotion policies. Recently, you noticed that mostly

white men were being promoted to higher level managerial jobs. Your policy states that anyone is allowed to enter the managerial training program, so you know there is no intentional discrimination going on. But once that managerial training program is completed, everyone must pass a cognitive ability test to be eligible for certain managerial positions. You think that you need to look at the cognitive ability test to make sure it does not have _____.

a. adverse impact   b. disparate treatment
c. a BFOQ   d. symbolic treatment

13. Symbolic racism assumes all but the following:
    a. There is no longer any serious discrimination in America.
    b. Any residual inequality is the fault of the minority group.
    c. Some groups are genetically inferior.
    d. Affirmative action is discriminatory.

14. All but one of the following statements is true about affirmative action plans:
    a. There must be a history of discrimination or a plan to be legal.
    b. Any plan cannot deny the rights of nonminorities.
    c. Affirmative action goals must be based on the qualified workforce.
    d. Preferential hiring should be mandatory.

15. People over 40 _____
    a. are protected by the ADEA
    b. are not a protected class
    c. are protected by the ADA
    d. are not as effective as 20-year-olds

ANSWERS 1 c, 2 a, 3 c, 4 b, 5 d, 6 a, 7 d, 8 c, 9 a, 10 a, 11 a, 12 a, 13 c, 14 d, 15 a

Focused Free-Write

1. Think about a time when you may have intentionally or unintentionally discriminated against someone because of your prejudicial attitude toward them. Describe that situation and the group to which the person belonged. What stereotype did you hold about the person based on the group he or she belonged to? What discriminatory behavior did you use? What would you do differently now?

2. Think about a situation where you think you were discriminated against. Describe the situation. On what basis do you feel you were discriminated? How did it make you feel? Think of some of the stereotypes people have about your group: Do you feel you share some of those characteristics?

_____

_____

_____

_____

_____

_____

_____

_____

_____

_____

_____

_____

_____

Stereotyping

For the following statements, check how much you agree or disagree with the statement.

CD = completely disagree   SA = somewhat agree   TA = totally agree

	CD	SA	TA
1. Women make the worst drivers.	_____	_____	_____
2. Alcoholics and drug addicts are less likely to have or hold down a job.	_____	_____	_____
3. Disabled people can't drive.	_____	_____	_____
4. Older people drive too slowly.	_____	_____	_____
5. White males are controlling and power hungry.	_____	_____	_____
6. Men never ask for directions.	_____	_____	_____
7. Criminals of any type cannot be rehabilitated.	_____	_____	_____
8. Native Americans are more likely to have drinking problems than Caucasians.	_____	_____	_____
9. African Americans are more likely to commit crimes than Caucasians.	_____	_____	_____
10. Overweight people can lose weight if they want.	_____	_____	_____
11. Women are more emotional than men.	_____	_____	_____
12. Italians have hot tempers.	_____	_____	_____
13. Men are more logical than women.	_____	_____	_____
14. People who fly the Confederate flag are racists.	_____	_____	_____
15. Most African Americans can dance well.	_____	_____	_____
16. All men prefer to watch sports; women prefer shopping.	_____	_____	_____
17. Spousal abuse happens mostly in poor families.	_____	_____	_____
18. Child abuse usually occurs the most in poor families.	_____	_____	_____
19. Jewish people make good financial experts.	_____	_____	_____
20. Asian Americans make the best computer experts.	_____	_____	_____

For each statement that you marked "somewhat agree" or "totally agree," write down why you think that. Particularly, specify if you know of some research that backs up each of the statements. Also, write down if something happened to you or with someone you know that reinforces the statement.

_____

_____

_____

CHAPTER FIVE *Understanding the Diverse Nature of Others*

PROJECT B

Discriminatory Behavior

Part A

Based on each of the following four situations, can you identify what type of discriminator is involved in each case? Explain your reasoning for classifying that person as you did.

1. A friend at the gym with what you think is a great sense of humor, always tells disparaging jokes about overweight people. Yet, his wife and two children are slightly overweight.

   Tolerator_____   Conformist_____   Law abider_____   Violator_____

   Reasoning:_____

   _____

   _____

2. Your minister finds out that Joe, a deacon, is gay. The minister talks to Joe and asks him to resign his position saying that "we can't have gays as church leaders."

   Tolerator_____   Conformist_____   Law abider_____   Violator_____

   Reasoning:_____

   _____

   _____

3. One of your coworkers remarks to you that "Blacks were born at a disadvantage and, consequently, need additional help to get certain jobs and gain admittance into college." Your coworker is on the diversity team and supports affirmative action.

   Tolerator_____   Conformist_____   Law abider_____   Violator_____

   Reasoning:_____

   _____

   _____

4. Your supervisor consistently refers to women as "bimbos with nothing between their ears but their heads." Yet, his hiring and promoting decisions always seem fair.

   Tolerator_____   Conformist_____   Law abider_____   Violator_____

   Reasoning:_____

   _____

   _____

Part B

Think of someone you know who fits into one of the discriminatory categories. Describe his or her behavior. What are some of the implications of the behavior?

_____

_____

_____

_____

_____

_____

_____

_____

_____

_____

_____

_____

_____

_____

_____

_____

_____

_____

_____

_____

_____

_____

Part C

To help you identify the category you might fall under, consider the following true-life situation and answer the questions that follow.

> In late 1999, it was determined through genetic testing that one of Thomas Jefferson's slaves, Sally Hemings, had borne a son by Jefferson. Now, descendants of Jefferson and Sally Hemings want to be buried at the Jefferson family graveyard at Jefferson's Monticello estate. Jefferson's legitimate offspring are unsure how they feel about allowing slave descendants into the grave. Currently, 185 legitimate family members are buried there, and there is room for 200 more.

Do you think the slave descendants have the right to be buried in the cemetery? Explain why or why not. How might you act toward someone who has the opposite opinion of you? Can you tell by the rationale of your answer which type of discriminator you might be? Is your answer based on how you feel or do you have facts supporting your opinion?

Protected Classes

Several groups are protected by federal legislation. In the questions below, indicate by circling Yes or No whether the person is a member of a **federally** protected class or not. In making your decision, do not take into account whom you think would win the case—base your answer only on whether or not the person making the complaint is in a federally protected class. For each *yes* answer, indicate the protected class and the federal legislation protecting that class.

Protected?

1. A World War II veteran claims he was discriminated against because he was in the war.   Yes   No

   _____
   _____
   _____

2. A Mormon says his religion forbids him to work on certain days.   Yes   No

   _____
   _____
   _____

3. A person wearing glasses claims she is disabled.   Yes   No

   _____
   _____
   _____

4. A gay applicant wasn't hired for a sales position because of his sexual orientation.   Yes   No

   _____
   _____
   _____

5. A 24-year-old wasn't hired for a sales position in a retail store specializing in female athletic shoes.   Yes   No

   _____
   _____
   _____

6. A Norwegian applicant claimed he wasn't hired because a Chinese restaurant only hired Asians.　　　　Yes　　No

_____

_____

_____

7. A store wouldn't hire anyone with a college degree because college graduates have no common sense.　　　　Yes　　No

_____

_____

_____

8. A fast-food chain refused to hire people with long hair.　　　　Yes　　No

_____

_____

_____

9. An applicant with an Appalachian accent feels he was discriminated against because of his accent.　　　　Yes　　No

_____

_____

_____

10. An individual who stated that he/she occasionally uses marijuana was not hired for a job.　　　　Yes　　No

_____

_____

_____

PROJECT D

Prejudice and Discrimination Continue

Pull an article from a newspaper or magazine that you think describes a situation in which discrimination is occurring. Summarize the article and identify the discriminatory behavior. What group is being discriminated against? What is your opinion?

_____

_____

_____

_____

_____

_____

_____

_____

_____

_____

_____

_____

_____

_____

_____

_____

_____

_____

_____

_____

Workplace Practices

Consider some of the following workplace practices that occur in many organizations. They may even occur where you work. Write your opinion of each practice. Explain what group, if any, the practices might offend.

Annual Christmas Party

_____

_____

_____

_____

_____

_____

Office Birthday Celebrations

_____

_____

_____

_____

_____

_____

Mother-Daughter Work Day

_____

_____

_____

_____

_____

_____

Putting up an office Christmas tree or other Christmas decorations

_____

_____

_____

_____

_____

_____

Office Halloween Party

_____

_____

_____

_____

_____

Starting an office sports team like baseball, basketball, or volleyball

_____

_____

_____

_____

_____

Other (List other practices your office/school might engage in and explain
how you feel about those activities.)

_____

_____

_____

_____

_____

Interview Questions

One employment practice that courts have stopped is asking certain interview questions because of their potential adverse impact. Based on what you read about adverse impact, job relatedness, and protected classes, determine if the following interview questions would be legal, illegal, or it depends. If you mark *illegal*, explain why. If you mark *depends*, explain on what it depends.

	Legal	Illegal	Depends

1. Do you have any health problems?

_____

_____

_____

2. Have you ever been arrested?

_____

_____

_____

3. Have you ever been convicted?

_____

_____

_____

4. To what clubs or societies do you belong?

_____

_____

_____

5. Where were you born?

_____

_____

_____

	Legal	Illegal	Depends

6. You have an unusual last name. What nationality are you?

_____

_____

_____

7. I see that you are using a cane. Is that temporary or do you have to use it every day?

_____

_____

_____

8. Are you fluent in any foreign language?

_____

_____

_____

9. You may have to work on Saturdays and Sundays. Is that a problem?

_____

_____

_____

10. How often were you sick last year?

_____

_____

_____

CHAPTER SIX

Working With Difficult People in Difficult Situations

Conflict from "people problems" arising both at work and in your personal life is inevitable and a natural outgrowth of interactions with others. Learning how to handle such problems is a key component of human relations. At the minimum, conflict can cause feelings of anger and distrust when ignored or improperly managed. At the extreme, it can seriously impair or end relationships between family members, friends, coworkers, and peers.

This chapter's goal is to give you the necessary tools to better manage conflict arising not only from difficult people, but from other sources as well. After reading the chapter, you will:

- Understand what constitutes a conflict
- Be able to identify the major sources of conflict
- Know the difference between hidden and surface sources of conflict
- Know when conflict is most likely to occur
- Learn your preferred way of dealing with conflict
- Learn effective ways of managing conflict, including mediation
- Identify difficult people and learn how to deal with them

■ DEFINING CONFLICT

Generally, **conflict** is the consequence of one person's response to what he perceives about a situation or behavior of another. For example, let's say you forgot to tell your best friend some really juicy gossip. Your friend responds to your forgetfulness by yelling at you and not answering the telephone for several days when you try to call. Maybe your friend perceives that you were trying to hide that information. In response to that behavior, you get angry and stop talking to him. Because of your friend's *initial* response to his perception of your forgetfulness, the situation may escalate into hot conflict.

Focused Free-Write
Before reading further, complete the Focused Free-Write to understand how you perceive conflict.

Conflict is either hot or cold (Lawson & Shen, 1998). **Cold conflict** is functional and provides an opportunity to share contrasting ideas, seek information, evaluate options, and negotiate goals and alternatives—it involves little emotion. **Hot conflict,** on the other hand, is dysfunctional and involves a great deal of emotion, including anger and frustration.

Factors Influencing Conflict

Four factors influence conflict: attitudes, perceptions, control imbalance, and outcome importance.

ATTITUDES

Many people view conflict only as bad and destructive, so they may avoid any attempts to confront a conflict situation. Unfortunately, conflict cannot be resolved unless it is acknowledged by *all* parties engaged in it. Consequently, if you are in conflict with someone with a negative attitude about conflict, your challenge is getting the other person to acknowledge the conflict and be willing to talk about it so that it can ultimately be resolved or, at least, tensions can be reduced.

PERCEPTIONS

Perception, the process of assigning meaning to what we see or hear, is central to defining and influencing conflict (Lulofs, 1994). One of the best definitions of conflict is that it is the "verbalization of our perceptions" (Sessa, 1994). Perceptions are important because people respond to one another in terms of how they evaluate a situation. Misperceptions can escalate a rather innocuous situation to conflict or interfere in the resolution of it. The degree to which parties perceive the following factors will increase the likelihood of conflict.

Interdependence If the general perception is that the parties are highly dependent on each other for a particular outcome, hot conflict is more likely to occur. For example, let's say your boss requires you to work with another employee to complete a project. To be successful, both you and your partner must complete your assigned tasks. Completing the project, and subsequently receiving a good performance evaluation, is dependent on both people fulfilling their responsibilities.

Different goals If parties perceive that their goals don't match, there is likely to be conflict. For example, if your goal is to complete that project at least 1 week ahead of time and you perceive that your partner's goal is to complete it on the due date, there will likely be some conflict. In many conflict situations most people have the same goals—what differs is how they think they should reach those goals. To resolve a conflict based on misperceptions about goal, people must be helped to recognize that they do have similar goals so that they can work together on finding the best steps toward meeting those goals. The hardest part of the conflict is over once they understand that their goals are actually similar.

EXHIBIT 6-1

Conditions for Conflict

Condition	Potential for Conflict
Perceptions	
High interdependency	High
Different goals	High
Many barriers to goals	High
Violation of relationship expectations	High
Control	
Shared levels of control and responsibility	Low
Control imbalance	High
Outcome importance	
High importance on situational outcome	High
Situation has little importance to parties	Low

One party is keeping the other from reaching goals
If you perceive that your partner's lack of effort is keeping you from meeting the deadline at all, there will be conflict because you are being prevented from meeting your goal.

Violation of relationship expectations An example of violated expectations is your best friend sharing your secret with another person. In an organization, if employees feel they are not being heard or have been lied to by management, the employee's response to their perception of their expectations being violated might be to reduce their productivity.

Understanding perceptions is critical to understanding the conflict. And changing perceptions is a goal of conflict management, one that can help move conflict to resolution.

CONTROL OR POWER IMBALANCE

Another factor influencing conflict is the degree to which individuals feel they have lost control over a situation, thereby causing a power imbalance. For example, if you suddenly find one day that you have been transferred to another office, you will most likely experience a loss of control: You had no input in a decision that will ultimately affect your working life. Additionally, if that decision was made by a peer, or maybe just a coworker who happens to be on a team making such decisions, you will probably feel a power imbalance: That person making the decision has more rights and authority than you do in making decisions that affect you.

QUICK PROJECT

Write down three areas in which you feel conflict would occur based on your perception that your control has been diluted. How would you react to someone taking control of these areas?

_____

_____

_____

_____

OUTCOME IMPORTANCE

The degree to which we feel we have lost control over issues that are *important* to us determines whether conflict will arise. In the example above, if being moved to another office without prior notice is unimportant to you, conflict may not arise. However, if that decision causes you problems, the situation will most likely give rise to conflict because you no longer have control over a situation that was important. Exhibit 6-1 summarizes the factors under which hot conflict may occur.

The Conflict Process

Conflict can be viewed as a process—what occurs each time we interact with others. Thomas (1970)

EXHIBIT 6-2

Ways to Approach a Conflict Situation

Wrong:	"We need to *fight* this out."
Right:	"We need to *discuss* this."
Wrong:	"I want to find out the *other side of the argument*."
Right:	"I'm willing to hear *another side to the argument*."
Wrong:	"We need to *debate* this."
Right:	"We need to *discuss* this."
Wrong:	"We need to *focus on our differences*."
Right:	"We need to *search for common ground*."
Wrong:	"You're the *opposite* party."
Right:	"You're the *other* party.
Wrong:	"The most *controversial* thing you did was …"
Right:	"The most *important* thing you did was …"

developed a five-stage process model for conflict: frustration, conceptualization, behavior, others' reaction, and outcome. We have added one other stage—analysis—which occurs before the other stages.

ANALYSIS

First, we analyze a situation, which is influenced by our perceptions of that situation. Let's say you receive what you consider an unfair performance evaluation score. Your analysis of the situation might be that your boss is treating you differently than his other employees and, therefore, must not like you. If this is important to you, you move into the next stage: frustration.

FRUSTRATION

Frustration occurs when we perceive that another party has hindered our goals. In the above example, your boss may be frustrating your goal to get a promotion or pay raise. Based on your frustration, you move into the conceptualization stage.

CONCEPTUALIZATION

In the **conceptualization** stage, you attempt to define the problem and articulate your concern. In the example above, you would talk to your boss and share your concerns about your score. Your boss, in turn,

might share with you the criteria he used to give that score.

BEHAVIOR

The *behavior* you use is critical in the conflict process, and your behavior will most likely affect that of the other party. If you first approach your boss yelling and arguing, the conflict will likely escalate.

In discussing behaviors that people choose to use when confronting a situation, Tannen (1998) suggests that there is an "argument culture" in our society that places more emphasis on combative, argumentative, and litigious behavior than on problem solving. She calls this emphasis "America's war of words" and explains that approaching a situation ready to fight rather than listen, discuss, and problem-solve is an impulsive approach to conflict. To end the argument culture, Tannen suggests ways to communicate during a conflict, emphasizing dialogue and understanding rather than war. Exhibit 6-2 lists some of those communication techniques. We talk about other communication techniques to help reduce conflict later in this chapter.

OTHERS' REACTIONS

If your boss responds in kind to your anger, the conflict may escalate. If, however, he agrees with your

EXHIBIT 6-3

Conflict Model

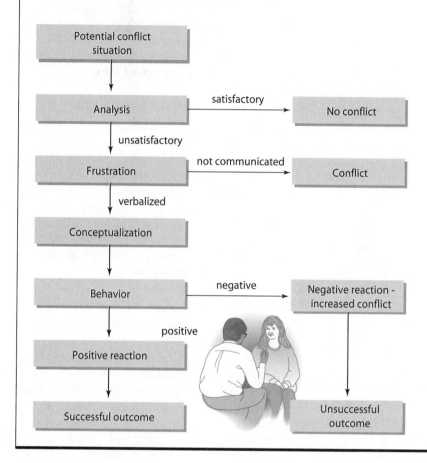

argument or works with you to develop ways to improve your future performance evaluation ratings, the conflict will most likely de-escalate.

OUTCOME

In this stage we decide how we will respond to the way the conflict has been handled or responded to up to this point. For example, if you are not pleased with your boss's response to your concerns about your evaluation ratings, you may choose to further pursue, ignore, or escalate the conflict. Managing conflict assumes people are able to rationally control their behavior. Good conflict managers will use the strategies outlined later in this chapter to deal with what they perceive as hot conflict. Poor conflict managers will choose such dysfunctional behaviors as yelling, anger, withdrawal, or avoidance from the situation. The outcome of a situation depends on the behaviors you choose. Exhibit 6-3 summarizes the conflict process.

PROJECT A *Analyzing a Conflict Situation*
Complete Project A to determine how you went through the conflict process on a recent conflict.

■ ANALYZING CONFLICT

Consequences of Conflict

The consequences of conflict can be destructive or productive. In fact, there is a curvilinear relationship between conflict and optimal behavior (Scholtes, Joiner, & Streibel, 1996). That is, if there is too little conflict, individuals and organizations become stagnant, apathetic, and willing to accept the status quo (Rahim, Garrett, & Buntzman, 1992). Too much conflict can cause the breakup of relationships, distrust, and poor performance.

Productive consequences occur when people work cooperatively to achieve their goals and realize satisfactory outcomes (Scholtes, Joiner, & Streibel, 1996). Conflict can serve three desirable functions: learning, consensus building, and enhancement of individual and organizational effectiveness (Franz & Jin, 1995).

LEARNING

Conflict facilitates the learning process because individuals have to identify problems, determine conflicting goals, and learn about each other's various viewpoints. In addition, during conflict, individuals are forced to identify how they may have violated others' expectations. Defining violations leads to clarification of future expectations. Conflict is also the time to clarify behaviors that are not acceptable to each other.

CONSENSUS BUILDING

Moderate amounts of conflict help in building consensus. That is, when conflict is recognized, individuals collaboratively determine how to solve problems to the satisfaction of all parties involved in the conflict.

ENHANCEMENT OF ORGANIZATIONAL EFFECTIVENESS

Conflict can actually increase organizational effectiveness, particularly in teams. In addition, control can become more balanced. By working together to identify mutual and conflicting goals, work and personal roles, and expectations of each other, parties learn how to share their control and power.

QUICK PROJECT

Can you think of other benefits from conflict? Write them down in this space.

_____

_____

_____

_____

_____

Types of Conflict

INTERPERSONAL CONFLICT

Interpersonal conflict occurs between two individuals. It can develop between coworkers, friends, family members, or between supervisor and employee. For example, conflict may arise when one individual does not agree with the lifestyle of another individual. In this example, the goal in resolving this conflict is not to change each other's opinions or philosophy about which lifestyle is right. Changing another person's philosophy may not happen. The goal is to focus on what *behaviors* someone is using that *directly affects* another person's goals or life.

INDIVIDUAL-GROUP CONFLICT

Individual-group conflict occurs when an individual's needs, goals, and expectations are different from that of the group's. For example, a Marine might want more independence than the Marine Corps will give him; a basketball player may want to shoot when the team needs him to set picks; a faculty member might be more interested in teaching when the university wants him to publish; and a store employee might be more interested in customer relations when the store wants him to concentrate on sales.

GROUP-GROUP CONFLICT

Group-group conflict occurs between two or more groups. It is frequently seen in organizations that use team goal-setting. One team may decide the goal of the organization should be to expand into other markets and sell other products, while another team believes the company should market only its current products. Often, the conflict is between teams and management, another type of group. Teams frequently come up with suggestions to issues that conflict with what managements believes the answer should be. This type of conflict may also be seen during the annual budget process when one department competes with another for dwindling resources such as personnel or salary increases.

Sources of Conflict

There are many causes of conflict, and they are either hidden or surface conflicts. **Hidden conflicts** are causes that may not be easy to identify and are usually emotional such as hurt, anger, embarrassment, distrust, or jealousy. Think of conflict as an iceberg where hidden conflicts are those below the water's surface. If you only address the surface conflicts (the ice above the water) and not the hidden ones, conflict will continue to escalate. Many surface conflicts have a certain amount of hidden conflicts simply because of the duration of the dispute. For example, one way to resolve the dispute between a cheating spouse (surface conflict) and partner is to have the guilty party promise not to repeat the behavior.

However, conflict may continue to arise because the hidden conflicts have not been addressed.

QUICK PROJECT

Referring to the example above, what do you think would be the hidden sources of conflicts of the party who had been cheated on?

_____

_____

_____

_____

_____

Surface conflicts are easier to recognize and deal with. The most common of the surface conflicts include competition for resources, task interdependence, jurisdictional ambiguity, communication barriers, incompatible personalities, and cultural and value differences.

COMPETITION FOR RESOURCES

On the personal level, **resources** can be defined as intangibles such as attention, love, recognition, and even acceptance. For example, when we are competing for someone else's love or attention, conflict can arise in personal relationships, such as sibling rivalry.

In organizations, resources have traditionally been defined as such tangible items as salaries, promotions, office funding, office space, equipment, and even personnel. Conflict occurs when there are not enough resources to satisfy the needs of every person or every group (E. R. Smith & Mackie, 1995). A good example of this occurs annually when Congress decides the nation's budget; with only limited tax revenues and many worthy programs, tough choices must be made.

TASK INTERDEPENDENCE

Task interdependence is the dependence of people or groups of people on each other to get a job done. When one or more individuals perceive that someone is not doing his portion of the task, conflict can arise. For instance, in a small community-based day care center, teachers depended on one another to carry out the organization's educational curriculum. The children's understanding of one section of the curriculum depended on another section being taught first. In that situation, one of the instructors decided not to teach a certain area. This caused other teachers to rearrange their lesson plans. Eventually, conflict escalated to the extent that the executive director had to ask for help to resolve it. It was resolved when the teachers met, identified organizational goals, developed action steps for meeting those goals, and defined how each person could help the organization meet those goals.

JURISDICTIONAL AMBIGUITY

Jurisdictional ambiguity occurs when geographical boundaries or lines of authority are unclear. The term includes role ambiguity, which, as discussed in Chapter 2 , occurs when people do not know or are confused about what is expected of them. Jurisdictional ambiguity occurs most often with new situations and new relationships that result from organizational change. A good example occurred several years ago when a small organization changed from typewriters to computers. Before the change, the head of the secretarial department was in charge of selecting and purchasing all the secretarial equipment, and the head of the data-processing department was responsible for selecting and purchasing all of the organization's computer equipment. Conflict developed when the new equipment being used by the secretaries was considered computer equipment and thus came under the purview of the data-processing department. The two department heads waged a "turf battle" to determine who would have authority for the word-processing equipment and programs.

COMMUNICATION BARRIERS

Communication barriers are another source of conflict. The barriers to interpersonal communication can be physical, such as separate office locations of the same business or a long-distance romance with a significant other; cultural, such as different languages, hard-to-understand accents, or different customs; or psychological, such as personalities. An in-depth discussion of the communication process can be found in Chapter 7.

PERSONALITY

In Chapter 1 you took a personality test that gave you some idea of your interpersonal, leadership, and communication styles. Your styles may be different from your classmates', and incompatibility in these styles may cause conflict. Thrust into a working relationship, it is highly likely that conflict would arise between two people with significant personality differences. For example, a person who is very quality oriented will probably have conflicts with a person who is very quantity oriented. Likewise, a "big picture" person is likely to have conflicts with a "nuts and bolts" person. In addition, people with difficult personalities also increase the likelihood of conflict.

Difficult people It is important to distinguish the difficult personality type from others because difficult people are considered to be locked into patterns of unreasonableness and irrationality (R. Fisher & Ury, 1981; Rifkind & Harper, 1994). Difficult personalities maintain constant difficult patterns of behavior, and their way of dealing with conflict makes it harder to manage conflict situations (Monroe, Borzi, & DiSalvo, 1989). Consequently, how conflict situations are handled with them differs, as you will see later in this chapter.

Difficult people chronically use such problematic interpersonal behaviors as yelling, complaining, or sarcasm to express themselves, to manipulate others' behaviors, and/or to make others feel inferior. The consequence of their behavior is alienation of others, that is, no one wants to be around them or to work with them. Additionally, they can be a big source of low morale and job satisfaction. In fact, they can potentially be a cause of long-term employees leaving the organization in response to the conflict caused by the difficult person.

Although there has been little research investigating difficult people, a fair amount has been written about the topic in the popular press. Bramson (1981) was the first to define difficult people and their problematic interpersonal styles. Since Bramson, other books have classified difficult people as *jerks* (Meier, 1993), *Neanderthals* (Bernstein & Rozen, 1992), and *toxic* (Glass, 1995). Difficult people usually display one of two types of behaviors: verbally aggressive or passive and/or nonverbal (Raynes, 1997b). Both types of behaviors are attempts to control the situation to yield a result most favorable for the difficult person. Brinkman and Kirschner (1994) believe it is the individual's abnormally high need for control, perfection, approval, and affection that forms the basis for the difficult personality.

Verbally aggressive behaviors Verbally aggressive behavior is used by those whose main goal is to look superior by making others look inferior. For example, the *Tank* personality is usually very pushy, does a lot of yelling, and is very authoritarian. *Snipers* choose sarcasm, embarrassment, and humiliation to control the situation. *Grenades* like to throw temper tantrums. Just like Tanks, they yell, swear, rant, and rave to control the situation and get attention. *Know-It-Alls* dominate conversations and reject arguments counter to their positions. *Think-They-Know-It-Alls* exaggerate, lie, and give unwanted advice to control

the situation. *Whiners* constantly complain about the situation but rarely try to change it; the main goal of *Whiners* appears to be gaining attention. And the *No Person* believes that nothing will ever work and thus disagrees with every suggestion or idea that someone presents.

Passive behaviors According to research, the primary goal of people who choose passive behaviors is to gain approval and affection. Passive people may have low self-esteem, a high need to be liked, and a high fear of failure, which cause them to overuse such otherwise positive behaviors as helping others and postponing decisions until they can seek feedback from others. They act that way to reduce the likelihood of conflict and rejection. For instance, *Nothing Persons* respond to difficult situations by doing and saying nothing; they simply give up or retreat from the situation. *Yes Persons* agree to everything and as a result, often overextend themselves and thereby are unable to keep their obligations. Finally, *Maybe Persons* avoid conflicts by never taking a stand on any issue—they delay making decisions, seldom offer opinions, and rarely commit to any course of action. In organizations, *Maybe Persons* are deadly because they can be responsible for late or missed deadlines, and consequently, lost money and customers.

A summary of Difficult People and their behaviors can be found in Exhibit 6-4. Do you recognize any of these people?

Self-esteem and difficult personalities Regardless of a difficult person's goal in using his behavior, research suggests both types of behaviors are due to deficiencies in interpersonal skills and low self-esteem (Monroe, Borzi, & DiSalvo, 1989). Some research suggests that people with low self-esteem do not feel they measure up to others so they resort to three types of behavior to feel less inferior: bringing others down, avoidance of risk taking, and ingratiation. An example of bringing others down is the schoolyard bully who constantly berates and picks on children who are often smaller and weaker. The bully is emphasizing his superiority by making others look inferior. Also, low self-esteem people avoid risk taking or doing anything that they perceive may emphasize their inferiority by failing. Ingratiation includes doing or saying whatever others want you to do or say in order to be liked.

There is some dispute about whether these behaviors are due to low self-esteem or high self-esteem. In a recent study, some behaviors such as those associated with the Know-It-All and No Person were shown to actually be a result of *high* self-esteem (Raynes, 1997a).

EXHIBIT 6-4

Difficult People

Type	Behavior	Interpersonal Style
Tank	Aggressive	Pushes, yells, gives orders, intimidates
Sniper	Aggressive	Uses sarcasm, criticizes, and humiliates
Grenade	Aggressive	Throws tantrums; yells
Whiner	Aggressive	Constantly complains
No Person	Aggressive	Disagrees with everything
Know-It-All	Aggressive	Dominates conversations, doesn't listen to others
Think-They Know-It-All	Aggressive	Exaggerates, lies, gives advice
Nothing Person	Passive	Doesn't say or do anything
Yes Person	Passive	Agrees to everything; takes on more than they can handle
Maybe Person	Passive	Unable to make a decision

Angry customers Similar to Difficult People, angry customers are also potential sources of conflict. **Customers** are people to whom we provide a service or product. **Internal customers** consist of our peers, coworkers, and supervisors. **External customers** are consumers not affiliated with the organization who buy or use the organization's services and products. Unlike difficult people who are chronically problematic, **angry customers** are basically rational individuals who have momentary lapses of unreasonableness when they are upset. Also unlike difficult people, the behaviors of angry customers are relatively short-lived and can be dealt with fairly quickly, thereby making it easier to defuse further conflict.

The behaviors of angry customers are usually a result of poor customer service. Their goal is to be listened to and understood, to be respected and have their feelings validated, to know that someone cares about how they feel, and to have their concerns appropriately addressed.

Like Difficult People, there are several types of angry customers and behaviors. They too choose between aggressive or passive behaviors.

Aggressive behaviors *Warriors* know only one way to solve problems: yell, rant, and rave. Why do they continually choose aggressive behavior? Because it almost always works! For example, many banks react quickly to *Warriors* because they don't want other customers to hear another customer yelling and making a scene. *Unloaders* unload their anger on a safe source: you! They may be angry at someone else within or outside of the organization, but you are the person on whom they have decided to take out their

anger. The *Child* throws tantrums when he is angry. Much like the Warrior, he yells a lot and may even use name-calling. *Blamers* are more interested in finding fault than solving problems; they too are yellers. No matter how hard you try to resolve their complaint, they are never going to be satisfied. They are the ones who will most likely ask "to speak to your supervisor."

The worst type of aggressive angry customers are *Gunnysackers*, who store up their anger until their "anger bag" is full. If their complaints are never resolved or are handled poorly each time they contact a particular company, they will eventually blow up. The most extreme example of a *Gunnysacker* is the person who gets fed up with life's problems and goes on a shooting rampage.

Passive behaviors The more passive behaviors are used by *Survivalists* who whine and complain because they fear the consequences if their problem doesn't get resolved. For example, if the information you need for a class report never arrives because the post office lost it, you may get a little whiny with the post office. Why? Because you fear the wrath of your professor when you tell him your paper will be late. *Guiltmakers* use guilt to get their problem resolved, telling you how something catastrophic and earth shattering will befall them if their complaints aren't handled satisfactorily. They may even end up crying. *Parents* patronize others and talk down to them, using sarcasm and even insults. This type of customer is likely to tell you, while smiling and patting your hand, that it must be difficult to deal with complaints and help customers when it is obvious you are so poorly trained.

EXHIBIT 6-5

Angry Customers

Type	Behavioral Description
The Warrior	Knows only one way to solve problems: by yelling and being aggressive.
The Unloader	Unloads anger on a safe source. Might be angry at something else but vents anger on the person being talked to at the moment.
The Guiltmaker	Uses guilt to get his or her own way. Often tells a sad story about what will happen if the situation doesn't end the way the Guiltmaker thinks it should. May resort to crying.
The Child	Throws tantrums; yells.
The Blamer	Is more interested in finding fault than solving the problem. Most likely to ask to speak to a supervisor even after the employee has tried to solve the problem the way the Blamer wants.
The Survivalist	Is scared of what will happen if the problem isn't solved. May whine and have difficulty shifting into a problem-solving mode.
The Parent	Patronizes, talks down to others, and uses insults. May use sarcasm.
The Pretender	Pretends not to be upset but will most likely tell friends and other potential customers about the company's "bad" service. Uses silence to express anger.
The Gunnysacker	Stores up anger until his "bag" is full. This person is the most likely to vent anger in a destructive way.

Finally, *Pretenders*, just as their name implies, pretend not to be upset, thank you for your time, and quietly leave the situation, but they stew all the way home and tell their friends about how badly they were treated. This type of angry customer is very harmful to an organization because they use silence to show their anger. Instead of sharing their concerns with an employee so that the employee can try to resolve the problem, they choose to stop using that organization's services instead. Exhibit 6-5 summarizes angry customers and their behaviors.

Handling angry customers, as you will see later in this chapter, often takes different strategies than dealing with difficult people. Learning to deal with angry customers is very important because the loss of one customer a day costs organizations thousands of dollars. And remember, without customers, there is no company. And without that company, there will be no need for you, the employee!

VALUES AND CULTURAL DIFFERENCES

In Chapter 5, we discussed how prejudicial attitudes toward cultural differences can lead to discrimination in the workplace. Discrimination is a source of conflict. Often, institutional discrimination is the real source of conflict. For example, there is continuous conflict between the U.S. Supreme Court, minority bar groups, and the NAACP regarding the low num-

ber of minority law clerks that are hired each year by the Justices. The Justices, who pick their applicants from such law schools as Yale and Harvard, blame the law schools' underrepresentation of minorities for this lack of diversity in the Supreme Court's hiring. However, critics believe the Justices are too passive and should be proactive in expanding their search for law clerks to more minority universities. Overall, it may not really matter who is to blame. Feelings of injustice by minorities and nonminorities in the workplace can cause conflict between coworkers and supervisors and must not be ignored. Although the Justices eventually released a letter in 1998 justifying their selection process, they have declined invitations to meet with minority bar groups or NAACP to discuss the issue further and look for resolution. This is an example of how ignoring conflict can escalate it.

Another big source of conflict is diverse values. **Values** are ideals of how we believe we should behave and think and how others should act. Values are generally based on our culture and the environment in which we grew up. For example, if an individual grows up in a military family, the culture might be one of rules and structure. Consequently, the individual may believe that rules are important and in general should be followed. Another individual may have grown up in a more permissive environment where rules were few and creative thinking was encouraged. When these two individuals work together, conflict may arise from the differences in values that affect their individual behaviors. Another example involves eye contact: American culture values strong eye contact. People who do not maintain eye contact are considered lying. However, in other cultures, direct eye contact is considered rude. How do you think someone who values eye contact (e.g., Americans) might react to someone who will not keep, or is uncomfortable with, eye contact (e.g., Asians)?

When interacting in an organizational setting, differences in culture and values can interfere with effective interactions between employees (Conrad & Sinclair-James, 1995; Deutsch, 1994). Lawson and Shen (1998) suggest that to manage conflict arising from cultural differences, both sides need to understand each other's perspective and how conflict is viewed and approached. For example, the Japanese culture approaches conflict from a win-win approach, so using a win-lose conflict style would probably cause a situation to escalate. On the other hand, the French like conflict; they take a long time to manage conflicts and focus more on winning than on preserving the relationship.

QUICK PROJECT

What are some other sources of personal or workplace conflict that you have witnessed or been directly involved with and which are not listed above?

_____

_____

_____

_____

_____

Donnellon and Kolb (1994) suggest four approaches to handling diversity disputes in organizations:

- Increase the scope of diagnosis: That is, treating the complaint as a possible symptom of broader concerns rather than as an individual complaint will lead to an alternative set of solutions.

- Validate the other's culture and viewpoint: Each culture must recognize and give credence to diversity issues and demonstrate that it values a diversified perspective.

- Encourage workplace diversity: Diversity should be encouraged in organizations through such

workgroups as a cultural diversity committee, which will allow airing of diversity issues.

- Identify and redistribute, if necessary, control and power: Constructive handling of diversity issues may involve some redistribution of power. If minorities are elevated in power, they may be more adept at handling sensitive issues of diversity conflicts.

Differences in Dealing With Conflict

Have you ever wondered why one friend lets conflict roll off his shoulders while another goes ballistic over the most minor issue? People deal with conflict the way they do for several reasons: personality traits, learned behavior, relationship between parties, gender differences, past conflict experiences, and conflict style.

PERSONALITY TRAITS VS. LEARNED BEHAVIOR

Some portion of how we respond to conflict can be traced to our personality traits, or rather our predisposition to behave in a certain manner in our everyday lives (see Chapter 1). What isn't due to this predisposition, however, can be attributed to learned behavior, or a combination of both. Learned behavior is that which we model from watching how others deal with conflict. Most specifically, we tend to use the same type of behaviors we see people significant to us use (e.g., parents and siblings). Learned behavior can be unlearned—which is one of the goals of conflict management workshops.

RELATIONSHIP OF DISPUTING PARTIES

The relationship between the individuals involved in a conflict influences how people deal with it. For example, we handle a conflict involving an acquaintance such as a grocery clerk differently from how we handle a conflict with our boss, coworker, or partner. One study showed that employees involved in a conflict with their supervisor were more likely to ignore, joke about, or accept the conflict (G. E. Martin & Bergmann, 1996). Other employees choose to discuss the conflict with other coworkers rather than go to the supervisor. Relationship factors that influence our response to conflict include how much the parties trust each other, how long they have known each other, and how they have handled conflict in the past with each other.

GENDER DIFFERENCES

Research is mixed on whether females and males handle conflict differently (G. E. Martin & Bergmann, 1996). Some research reports small, but significant, results that females avoid direct confrontation and are more accommodating than men

(Korabik, Barel, & Watson, 1993). Other studies show females as more competitive than men, less accommodating, and not significantly different in their use of collaborative or compromising modes of conflict management (Duane, 1989). However, in a meta-analysis on conflict and gender, Watson (1994) found that the empirical data does not provide *consistent* support that conflict management differences exist between males and females.

PAST CONFLICT EXPERIENCES

Our past experiences with conflict also influence how we handle future conflict. If conflict situations have always turned out negative, with no "happy endings," we will be much more likely to avoid conflict in the future. Individuals who have been victims of violence, such as battered women or abused children, may be less willing than others to deal with conflict because of how they were treated in former relationships.

CONFLICT STYLE

Finally, research suggests that we all have a preferred method for dealing with conflict. (Cohen, 1997)

PROJECT B *Identifying Your Conflict Style*
Before reading further, take the Cohen Conflict Response Inventory in Project B at the end of this chapter. When you are finished, resume reading the rest of this chapter.

Individuals' conflict styles are based on two dimensions: concern for meeting their own goals and concern for the goals of others and preserving the relationship (Rahim & Bonoma, 1979). People usually use one of five conflict styles (Thomas, 1970). An individual with a **collaborative style,** such as the *Sage,* is interested in a win-win result. The focus is on meeting the individual's goals, ensuring that others meet their goals, and on preserving the relationship between the conflicting parties. This style of dealing with conflict works best when both parties are willing to resolve the dispute and have the capacity to empathize with each other (Wisinski, 1993).

The **compromising style** used by the *Diplomat* is a give-and-take technique that allows each side to get some of what it wants, but not everything. Although this approach focuses on meeting everyone's goals, it acknowledges that this may not be possible. This approach to conflict is best when both parties have competing goals, when time constraints prevent parties from considering all alternatives, and when the collaboration style is not successful.

People such as the *Ostrich* use an **avoiding style,** which places so much emphasis on preserving the relationship that they choose to ignore the conflict in hopes that the conflict will resolve itself. Or they ignore the conflict out of fear of the other's reaction. Unfortunately, over time, the relationship is usually harmed because the conflict continues to spiral out of control. Although it may temporarily go away, it will continue to surface. There are times when the avoiding style is the best style to use, however—when additional time is needed to gather information, when both parties need to cool off and gain a new perspective on the situation, or when the negative consequences of confronting the conflict and the other person is physically dangerous.

When individuals like the *Philanthropist* are so intent on settling a conflict that they give in and risk hurting themselves, they have adopted an **accommodating conflict style**. A person who uses this style usually has a high concern for satisfying the needs of others. This style is more successful at times when the issue is more important to the other person than it is to you, when you determine that you are wrong, or when, as a supervisor, you want others to learn from their decision making.

Finally, *Warriors* use a **forcing style** and handle conflict in a win-lose fashion. Their focus is to win at any cost, regardless of the feelings or goals of the other person. This style can be effective in winning, but it also can damage relations so badly that other conflicts will result. However, this style may be necessary in situations where a quick decisive action is needed, others lack expertise to make a decision, and when other methods of handling conflict have been tried and been unsuccessful.

Knowing your conflict style has two basic benefits. First, knowing how you might tend to react to conflict can help you learn in what areas you need to change to become a more effective conflict manager. Second, seeing how other individuals might react to conflict will help you know how you should adapt your style. For example, if you know that you are about to deal with someone who has a dominating, forcing conflict style, using a passive conflict style, like the Philanthropist, would be ineffective in getting your needs met. The Warrior would walk all over you! On the other hand, if you are approaching a timid Ostrich and you really care about that person and preserving the relationship, you would want to stay away from using a Warrior's strategy. This could cause fear in the Ostrich and eventually destroy the relationship.

■ MANAGING CONFLICT

After defining and analyzing conflict, we are ready to learn to manage it. Effective conflict management depends on handling the three stages of conflict properly, identifying the correct conflict management

EXHIBIT 6-6

Strategies for Conflict Management

Style	Situation	Individual(s)
		Works best when:
Dictation	Conflicting parties are irrational and unwilling or unable to reach an agreement and when a quick resolution is necessary.	Disputants are unwilling to compromise or work together to solve their issues and are unwilling to accept responsibility for their part in the conflict.
Arbitration	Conflicting parties are willing to work out their differences but are unable or unwilling to reach an agreement; when there are not time constraints and no mental health issues.	Disputants are rational and willing to accept responsibility for their part in the conflict but can't agree on a mutually satisfactory solution.
Mediation	Disputants are willing to work out their differences, are able to brainstorm alternatives to reach a mutually satisfactory agreement, maintain at least a small amount of trust in each other and the mediator, and there are no time constraints for resolving the conflict.	Disputants are rational, capable of reaching an agreement on their own, and trustful of each other and the process. Both have good communication skills.
Negotiation	When there are goals that can be negotiated and parties are willing to give up less important points.	Both parties are willing to give and take. Both parties must have good communication skills and approach the situation from a win/win perspective.

strategy, and learning proper communication techniques for dealing with your own or other's conflict.

Stages of Conflict Management

Conflict management has three stages: analysis, confrontation, and resolution (R. Fisher, 1994).

ANALYSIS STAGE

The first step in the Analysis Stage is determining which conflict management strategy is appropriate for the particular situation. There are four strategies: dictation, arbitration, mediation, and negotiation (see Exhibit 6-6).

Dictation Sometimes, the best strategy for handling conflict is dictation. For example, if one child is fighting with another over who gets a teddy bear, it may be best (and easiest) for you to make that decision, particularly if the children are young and unable to work it out among themselves. If you are a supervisor of two individuals in a very small office who are in conflict because they both want to vacation during the same week, you may dictate the decision by telling one of them to pick another week. You might first try to have them work it out among themselves; however,

sometimes that's not possible. If you do have to dictate, try to address and reduce perceptions of preferential treatment. In this example, you might preface your decisions by saying: "This year, Employee A can have the first pick of which week to take off, and next year, Employee B will have the first choice."

Dictation is the best, and actually only, solution under the following circumstances:

- Parties are irrational (threatening, drunk, under drug influences).
- Parties are too angry to be realistic.
- One or all parties are under great stress.
- One or all parties do not have the skills to communicate and work out their difference on their own.

Arbitration In **arbitration**, an arbitrator, whether a supervisor, another employee, or an outside consultant, listens to both sides of the conflict and, based on the facts, dictates or imposes a solution on the parties. For example, in the situation above, the arbitrator will ask both parties why each should have the particular week off instead of the other. The decision is then based on what they tell the arbitrator (or how persuasive they are!). The advantage of arbitration is that it can end a particular conflict quickly and both parties have the opportunity to be heard. The downside is that neither party had control over the outcome of the conflict so they have less buy-in to the solution. The less control or input individuals have into a decision, the easier it is for the parties to continue to engage in the same kind of behavior they were engaged in prior to the current conflict. Some research even suggests performance may drop and turnover increase as a result of an arbitrator's decision (Bretz & Thomas, 1992).

Mediation Mediation is a nonthreatening process involving a neutral third party who helps individuals engaged in conflict defuse their conflict and create a voluntary agreement (Ross & Wieland, 1996). That is, mediators are facilitators of a communication process in which employees can listen to each other and decide their own resolution to the problem. The advantage to mediation, then, is that both parties are allowed to vent and be heard and they get to decide how best to solve the problem. Unlike arbitration, a mediator does not make a decision. A second advantage is that, unlike court, mediation is not a public forum—all proceedings are confidential. In addition, mediation, in the long term, takes less time so consequently is less cost prohibitive to both the organization and disputing parties.

Often, supervisors serve as mediators between disputing employees, peers, or coworkers. When this is the case, the supervisor's objective should be to create an environment of trust between himself and the employees engaged in conflict and between parties (Flores, 1992). The most important criterion for an internal mediator is to remain neutral throughout the entire mediation process. If you plan to use a mediation strategy, there are certain rules—Exhibit 6-7 describes the rules and how to set the environment for a successful mediation process.

Because of the trust issue organizations may choose an external mediator. Even though a supervisor or another employee (e.g., Human Resources Director) may claim to be neutral, disputing parties still may not feel comfortable. Regardless of whether an internal or external mediator is used, mediation works best when:

- Conflicting parties are rational and want to reach a solution, rather than take their complaint to court.

- Some sort of trust still exists between conflicting parties and with the mediator.

- There are no time demands and the mediator can take several hours or days to help disputants work out a mutually agreeable solution.

- Both parties have a certain level of communication skills.

- Parties would prefer making their own decisions instead of having one imposed upon them.

Exhibit 6-8 lists other factors that should be considered when individuals contemplate mediation (Lovenheim, 1996).

An increasing number of organizations are implementing policies mandating that employees use mediation or arbitration to resolve their workplace conflicts. Both mediation and arbitration have been recognized by the courts as an enforceable alternative to resolving workplace disputes in court, as long as the following conditions are met (Coleman, 1998):

1. If arbitration, the arbitrator must have the authority to award the employee the same relief available had the employee gone to court.

2. A procedure must be in place that will allow for the selection of a neutral mediator or arbitrator.

3. Procedural fairness must allow for some prehearing discovery rights.

4. Allow parties to have representation of their own choosing.

5. Do not impose an undue financial burden on the employee for pursuing arbitration or mediation. That is, if an outside party is used, the organization should pick up the costs. Considering what it would cost if the case went to court, not to mention the cost to an organization's public image, the organization should be more than willing to pay for this process rather than court.

Research has found that problem-solving styles of handling conflict (such as mediation) produce more tangible and enduring agreements than arbitration (Kressel, Frontera, Forlenza, Butler, & Fish, 1994). In fact, 90% of employee cases that have been referred to mediation are successfully resolved without litigation. In the workplace, mediation has been used in such areas as discrimination issues, and an increasing number of organizations are using mediation to handle sexual harassment cases. When supervisors determine that an employee is leaning toward filing a harassment case with the Equal Employment Opportunity Commission (EEOC), the federal agency handling such claims, their initial response is to ask if parties would be willing to settle the issue through mediation. Many times, during the mediation process, it is determined that there was a misunderstanding about another person's behavior. In that instance, the party using the inappropriate behavior hears how the behavior has offended another party and agrees to stop such behavior. In instances where the situation has already gone to the EEOC, been investigated, and probable cause has been found, organizations can still mediate resolutions instead of resolving the issue in court.

EXHIBIT 6-7

Setting the Stage for Mediation

Step 1: Stabilize the Setting

- Get commitment from all parties to mediate
- Confirm your neutrality and confidentiality
- Explain your role
    - If you are the parties' supervisor, explain that today you are serving only as a neutral party, nothing will go in the personnel file, and that your goal is to help parties be able to better communicate their needs to each other.
    - If you think there may be a chance parties may not be able to develop a solution and that it will be necessary for you to change from mediator to dictator, you should make this clear to them.
- Define Ground Rules (get parties to agree on the following)
    - No name calling
    - Both parties must treat each other with respect
    - Don't say *never* or *always*
    - Don't interrupt the other party
    - Be truthful and completely expose all facts

Step 2: Help Parties Communicate

- Allow all parties to tell their side of the story uninterrupted by you or the other party
- After each party finishes, paraphrase and clarify what the party said
- Identify and define the surface and hidden sources of conflict
- Focus on areas on which parties might already agree, even if it's only that they agree they have a conflict!
- Prioritize what needs to be settled (often, parties will have more than one conflict that needs to be resolved; address each conflict one at a time before moving on to the next conflict)
- Identify what each party wants out of the process (goal setting)

Step 3: Help Parties Negotiate

- Seek cooperation
- Help parties explore alternative solutions for their conflict (brainstorm)
- Allow them to vent but with no accusations
- Keep focusing on similar goals
- Allow them as much control over the process as possible. (There will be times, however, when you may need to step in; for example, if they are name calling, you must regain control by saying "Remember, we agreed there would be no name-calling.")

Step 4: Clarify the Agreement

- Summarize their agreement
- Put the agreement in writing (research suggests that parties are more likely to honor agreements that are in writing)
- Identify and clarify who is responsible for doing what, where, when, and how
- Offer them the opportunity to return to mediation if their original agreement isn't working or if another conflict arises; however, the goal with mediation is to give them the skills they need to handle future conflicts on their own.

Negotiation Another conflict management strategy is negotiation, which is a form of compromise that can benefit both sides (Forsythe, 1999). The most important points are negotiated and less important points are given up. This process usually begins with each side making an offer that asks for much more than it really wants. For example, union leaders might demand $10 an hour while management offers

EXHIBIT 6-8

Conditions of Mediation

Favorable

- When the law cannot provide the remedy you want
- When you want to end a problem, not a relationship
- When your dispute is no one else's problem and you want to keep it that way
- When you want to minimize costs: Mediation is cheaper than going to court
- When you want to settle your dispute promptly: Mediation is faster than litigation
- When you are having trouble initiating negotiations or lack negotiating skills

Unfavorable

- When you want to prove the truth or set a legal precedent
- When you want to go for the jackpot
- When one party refuses to mediate, is absent, or incompetent
- When the dispute involves a serious crime
- When you need a court order to prevent immediate harm
- When your case would be better off in small claims court
- When the other party's position is so weak that you can easily win in regular court or arbitration

---

$6 an hour. Each side understands what the other is doing, so the union might lower its demand to $9 and management might raise its offer to $7. This process continues until an acceptable compromise has been reached.

Whether you are the negotiator in your own dispute or one involving other parties, Ury (1993) developed a five-stage *negotiation model,* to which many seasoned negotiators adhere:

1. **Don't react** Ury warns not to control the other person's behavior but, rather, concentrate on your own behavior. Instead of reacting to the other's anger or attack, take a mental time-out and focus on your goals and keeping the situation under control.

2. **Don't argue** For any negotiation to take place, the climate must be conducive for it: That is, anger must be defused and trust must be built. To do this, listen and validate or acknowledge the other person's side. Focus on similar goals and where you agree rather than on where you differ.

3. **Don't reject** Instead of immediately refusing their suggestions, ask them how that suggestion might meet mutual goals. Questions such as "Why do you think that would work?" can help the other party rethink their ideas. This is called *reframing.*

4. **Don't push** This is when negotiations really begin. Don't say no—make it easy for the parties to say yes by outlining mutual goals. Find a way for them to save face. It's often difficult for people to admit they are wrong. Find a way for them to think they were right.

5. **Minimize escalation** If resistance is still occurring, make it harder for them to say no. Don't use threats, however. Instead, try to help the other party see what their solution may involve: the costs and the consequences.

The next step in the Analysis stage is determining the sources of conflict. This step focuses on people's perceptions of the conflict and their goals. That is, disputing parties clarify what they think is causing the problem and possible solutions. This step is important because how the conflict is managed depends on its source. Here, it is important to focus on each other's behaviors, not personality. The use of the following dialogue may be useful in sharing information:

> *"When you don't arrive to meetings on time with me, it makes me feel like you don't think what I have to share is important. That hurts my feelings because I feel I can't do my job properly without your input."*

Notice how the last sentence explains how one person's behavior affects another. We think you would agree that the above example is a more productive way of sharing information than the following:

"I think you are a lazy jerk because you never show up in time for class meetings."

See the difference! In this example, the focus is more on personality than behavior.

Also, refrain from using words such as *never* and *always*. In fact, this is one of the ground rules conflict mediators tell disputants because very rarely are those words accurate. To say someone "never" listens to you would not be true in every situation. Saying that your friend is "always" late probably wouldn't be accurate, either. In addition, *never* and *always* are considered "fighting words" and they just increase the anger or resistance of the other party.

CONFRONTATION STAGE

In the confrontation stage, both parties agree to engage in dialogue that may help move the conflict into the resolution stage. This stage can also be called a mutual problem-description stage (Nicotera, 1995) because you attempt to change the perspective from "this is *my* problem and my goal" to "this is *our* problem and our goals." Clarification statements such as "Could I ask you a few questions to see whether my facts are right?" "Let me see if I understand what you are saying," and "Let me show you where I have trouble following some of your reasoning," are nonconfrontational and nonintimidating ways to get at the heart of the matter (R. Fisher & Ury, 1991).

RESOLUTION STAGE

Although it's true that not all conflicts can be resolved, productive problem solving is a way to increase the likelihood of resolution. There are six steps in cooperative problem solving:

1. Parties recognize there is a problem. This step is usually done in the analysis stage and involves both parties being open and honest about their perceptions.

2. The cause of the problem is determined. The confrontation stage provides an opportunity for this to occur.

3. Alternatives to solving the problem are brainstormed and discussed. **Brainstorming** is a process in which everyone involved in the conflict talks, uninterrupted, about all possible solutions to the conflict. While they are talking, the other parties listen, without judging. When one party is finished, another individual shares his ideas. After everyone is finished talking and sharing their ideas, the parties discuss those alternatives, refuse the ones they absolutely can't live with, and revise the ones they believe might work.

4. The parties eventually choose the best solution that is mutually satisfactory.

5. They then use that mutually agreed upon solution to solve the problem.

6. Finally, the parties monitor the situation to make sure the chosen solution actually solves the problem. If it doesn't, they will have to select and try another solution. This step continues until they finally arrive at the best possible solution for their conflict.

> **PROJECT C** *Case Study*
> To practice analyzing a conflict situation and determining its sources, complete Project C at the end of this chapter.

Whether you use dictation, arbitration, mediation, or negotiation, the most important ingredient to resolving conflicts, whether your own or others, is excellent communication skills.

Communication Techniques in Conflict Management

Communication skills, in general, are discussed more in Chapter 7. But it is important to understand what specific techniques can be used to more effectively deal with conflict. Each of the following techniques are useful in all four conflict management strategies.

ACTIVE LISTENING

Has anyone ever told you that you might be hearing but you were not listening? One way to let another individual know you are listening and understanding what they say is through active listening. **Active listening** is communicated through such nonverbal gestures as nodding and eye contact to show that you are listening. Then you use your verbal skills such as reflecting and paraphrasing.

REFLECTING

Reflecting provides clarification to what another individual has just said. Unlike quoting where you repeat word for word, you *paraphrase* and summarize what you think you heard. Reflecting is a way of showing *immediacy* or how attentive you are to what the other person is saying. The following example demonstrates how reflecting is used.

"What it sounds like you are saying is that I hurt your feelings when I show up late." Or "What I think I'm hearing you say is that you don't like it when I'm always late because it hurts your feelings." Reflecting and paraphrasing give you the opportunity to learn if you are understanding the problem as it is being defined by the other person. It also allows the other person to know if they have said what they meant to say. If not, they have the opportunity for further clarification: "Yes, that's what I said (or mean)." Or "No, that's not what I'm talking about . . . that's not what I meant." You may have to do this several times until the issues are clarified to mutual understanding.

PROJECT D *Paraphrasing and Clarifying*
Complete Project D at the end of this chapter to learn more about how to paraphrase and clarify information that you are given.

In addition, using open-ended rather than closed-ended questions can clarify the other party's issues. Closed-ended questions are those that can be answered yes or no or with a two- or three-word sentence. For example, look at the following question:

"Is that all you have to say about it?" This is a closed question because the other party is most likely to say yes or no. This type of question typically closes off further discussion and will not provide clarification. On the other hand, the following open-ended questions can help flush out more details than the above closed question:

"Tell me more about what you are saying."

"Help me understand how you are feeling or why you feel that way."

PROJECT E *Open-Ended vs. Closed-Ended Questions*
Complete Project E at the end of this chapter to practice the difference between open-ended and closed-ended questions.

EMPATHY

Empathy (discussed in Chapter 4) is the process of putting yourself in the other person's shoes, so to speak, and trying to look at the situation from his or her eyes. Phrases such as "I can understand how what I did could have hurt your feelings" encourages the other party to share concerns and lets them know you truly are listening and willing to resolve the conflict.

QUESTIONING

Questioning is a good technique to use, particularly in the problem-solving stage (Brody, 1982). *Leading questions* suggest an idea with the question: "I was wondering whether we should consider this solution first before trying something else?" *Stimulating questions* encourage new ideas: "Are there other ways to solve this problem?" *Participation questions* encour-

age the participation of all those involved in the conflict: "Who else has some ideas?" *Alternative questions* compare two or more alternative solutions that have been posed: "Which of the two solutions seems best to you?" *Closure questions* encourage parties to make the decision: "It sounds as if we have agreed to do the following, right?" And finally, *evaluation questions* help ensure that you and the party with whom you're in conflict assess your solutions and how they might work in the future: "What will happen if we handle the situation this way instead of the other way?"

HIGHLIGHTING COMMON GOALS

Often when we are in conflict with another individual we focus on the negative. Effective conflict management skills include being able to highlight similarities in goals, opinions, and solutions. From there, you can define other goals that may be in conflict and how to resolve them.

CREATING TRUST

Trust has been defined as "a person's capacity to depend on or place confidence in the truthfulness or accuracy of another's statements or behavior" (Moore, 1987, p. 140). Trust has been identified as the variable that has the greatest effect on other conditions of conflict (Lulofs, 1994). How much people trust each other influences whether they will be willing to work toward resolution (Ross & Wieland, 1996). In fact, trust-building is so important, Ury (1993) made it stage 2 in his five-stage negotiation model. Showing the other party they will be listened to and not laughed at leads toward a more successful process.

In creating trust, you must attempt to save the other person from embarrassment. There are many times when one party recognizes the conflict was his fault or that the conflict could be resolved if he would only compromise. But that party can't or won't back down for fear of embarrassment. Therefore, the goal here is to develop a way that parties can save face without admitting guilt.

INQUIRING SILENCE

Finally, using silence to promote discussion is a useful nonverbal technique. Many people are uncomfortable with silence. So, when one or both parties appear to be resistant to talking or sharing their feelings, just a moment of silence may be enough to open dialogue.

PROJECT F *Dealing with a Conflict Situation*
Complete Project F at the end of this chapter to better recognize the strategies you used to deal with your last conflict situation.

EXHIBIT 6-9

Handling Angry Customers

- Assume the customer has a legitimate complaint.
- Put things in perspective.
- Acknowledge their anger.
- Allow them to vent.
- Listen to their story.
- Empathize with their situation.
- Probe for additional details if necessary.
- Give a sincere, personal, and timely apology.
- Determine what the customer wants and do it.
- Fix the problem quickly and fairly.
- Keep all promises made.
- Follow-up: Don't assume the problem is fixed.

Dealing With Angry and Difficult People

In addition to the above techniques, some additional ones can be used with angry customers—see Exhibit 6-9. Difficult people are a different matter, however. Many conflict management strategies may not be effective in situations that involve interactions with the difficult personality because rational conduct does not usually apply to them. Consequently, dictation may be the best conflict management strategy. Hollwitz, Churchhill, and Hollwitz (1995) developed an approach to dealing with conflict with difficult people that includes direct intervention, indirect intervention, direct coping, or indirect coping.

DIRECT INTERVENTION

Overt attempts should be made to change behavior. That is, someone should address the behavior. A supervisor should let a difficult employee know that his behavior is bothering other people and if the behavior doesn't stop, it may result in disciplinary action.

INDIRECT INTERVENTION

The use of more subtle approaches may be more successful in changing some behaviors. For example, complimenting Tanks about how well they handled a particular situation could reinforce positive behavior that they will be more willing to try in the future.

DIRECT COPING

With this strategy, you minimize the impact of difficult people's behavior by insulating them from other employees. Unfortunately, in today's team-oriented organizations, it is not always feasible to isolate team members from each other.

INDIRECT COPING

This strategy is the one most often exercised in organizations. That is, *other* employees are sent to training and workshops that teach them how to cope with the difficult behaviors of their coworkers.

Exhibit 6-10 describes other techniques that can be used specifically with difficult people.

Effectiveness of Conflict Management Techniques

The effectiveness of the conflict management techniques discussed in this chapter depends on several factors, including disputants' skills, conflict perspective, power distribution, and personal responsibility.

DISPUTANTS' SKILLS

We aren't born knowing how to solve problems. Problem solving requires being able to explain how we feel and what we want, takes skill in negotiating our demands and knowing when and how to compromise, and requires the ability to understand the other person's concerns and why he is behaving in a particular manner. Finally, it requires a willingness to engage in productive problem solving.

CONFLICT PERSPECTIVE

What people focus on during conflict can determine the success of conflict management techniques. Pinkley

EXHIBIT 6-10

Dealing With Difficult People

Type	Best Way to Handle
Tank	Don't counterattack or offer excuses, let them vent, hold your ground, demand respect
Sniper	Call them on their sarcasm and have them explain what was really behind their comment; be honest and tell them their comment was rude and unkind
Grenade	Don't show anger, let them vent, tell them you take their concerns seriously, give them a chance to cool down
Whiner	Listen but don't get drawn into their complaining; focus them on specific solutions; shift to problem-solving mode
No Person	Don't rush them or try to persuade them they are wrong; acknowledge their concerns and input
Know-It-All	Acknowledge their expertise and competence, make your statements appear as if they are in agreement
Think-They Know-It-All	Give them attention; be patient; don't embarrass them
Nothing Person	Try to draw them out; ask them specific questions without making them feel they are being attacked
Yes Person	Encourage the person to be honest; make it safe for them to say no
Maybe Person	Help them learn decision-making skills; reassure them about the decisions they make; let them know it's OK to take risks

and Northcraft (1994) suggest that people focus on one of four areas when they are engaged in conflict:

Preservation of the relationship It may be more important for you to maintain your relationship with the other party than to achieve what you actually want. You may be more likely to ignore or give into the conflict in order to "keep the peace." Too much focus on preserving the relationship may actually cause the conflict to spiral down and never be resolved.

Emotions Many people focus on the emotions involved in the conflict (e.g., jealousy) instead of the behaviors. For example, your coworker may be very jealous of your new position. You may focus more on that jealousy than on the behaviors caused by the jealousy. It is easier to manage behaviors than feelings.

Sharing responsibility Sharing responsibility is a *cooperative orientation* toward conflict (Deutsch, 1973). Individuals who focus on shared responsibilities for conflict are interested in meeting their own goals as well as those of others. People who approach conflict from this perspective use smoothing and conciliation tactics that express a desire for cooperation—offering compliments, avoiding negative interaction,

emphasizing the similarities of the two parties, and pointing out common philosophies. A conflict is more likely to be managed or resolved successfully if both parties have this orientation toward conflict.

Blaming the other An individual with this *competitive orientation* toward conflict is not concerned with the goals of the other party (Deutsch, 1973). People who view conflict from this perspective take a "win-at-all-costs" strategy. This orientation causes a conflict to very rarely be solved. In fact, people with this orientation toward conflict can actually be the *source* of continued conflict.

POWER DISTRIBUTION

Power is not inherently good or bad, but it creates an environment for how conflict will be handled. The power that people have influences the way they analyze issues of the conflict and set goals. Power can come from a person's position, such as a boss or parent, or it can come from a person's expertise or experience in a certain area. If one party uses their power to get the conflict resolved their way, the other party might see that as manipulative. It's important to know in what way people choose to use their power in a conflict situation.

ACCOUNTABILITY

People must be willing to take responsibility if their actions or perceptions were wrong. Accountability means owning up to your part in any negative situation. In today's world, it seems victimization is in and responsibility is out. That is, people guilty of inappropriate behavior present themselves as victims, blaming other people, their parents, the situation, even their dogs for something they chose to do. An extreme example of this is when domestic abusers blame their victims for the victim's abuse. Conflicts can't be resolved if you don't accept responsibility for the behaviors you choose to use. Saying "I was wrong" or "I'm sorry" is a strong statement not a weak one. Lack of accountability is a major barrier to successful conflict management.

Preventing Workplace Conflict

Although we started this chapter by saying that conflict is inevitable, particularly in the workplace, several strategies can be used to prevent workplace conflict before it starts. These strategies also work on a more personal, individual-to-individual level:

- Provide clear expectations to all employees. If employees understand what is expected of them, they are less likely to misunderstand or misperceive. Organizations can provide expectations by developing and distributing to employees up-to-date and well-written job descriptions, conducting biannual performance evaluation meetings, providing timely and helpful feedback, and holding well-planned staff meetings with minutes disseminated after each meeting.
- Company goals and timelines for meeting those goals should be well understood, published, and placed in an area where all employees can review them easily and quickly review them as often as possible.
- All personnel and other policies should be well written. New policies or any changes to existing policies should be accompanied by a memorandum to each employee explaining the purpose of the policy, how it was developed, and how it will be enforced. When possible, staff meetings should be held to encourage questions and discussions on new and revised policies.

You may find that one day you will have to do some informal mediation between friends, coworkers, and maybe even your own children. It is highly likely that you will be in a class group one day that gets stuck in conflict. Someone is going to have to take the first step to get them out. That could be you,

and the use of the communication techniques as well as other suggestions in this chapter can help you be successful in that mediation. The goal of improving your conflict management skills is to create better personal and working relationships and to promote a healthy work environment.

> **PROJECT G** *Mediating a Workplace Conflict*
> View the roleplays in the video your instructor will show. Using the form provided in Project G, rate how well the mediators handled their conflict situations.

CHAPTER RECAP

Key points you should have learned from this chapter are:

- Conflict is the consequence of one person's response to what he or she perceives about a situation or behavior of another.
- Conflict can be cold (functional) or hot (dysfunctional).
- To turn hot conflict into cold, four factors influencing conflict must be addressed: conflict attitudes, individual perceptions, control and power imbalances, and outcome importance.
- The perceptions under which hot conflict is most likely to occur include interdependency, different goals, one party keeping the other from reaching those goals, and violation of relationship expectations.
- The six stages of the conflict process are analysis, frustration, conceptualization, behavior, others' reaction, and the outcome.
- The benefits of conflict include facilitating the learning process, building consensus, and enhancing team effectiveness.
- There are three types of conflict: interpersonal conflict between two individuals, individual-group between one individual and a group, and group-group between two or more groups such as work teams.
- The sources or causes of conflict are either hidden, which include emotional factors such as fear, embarrassment, anger, or hurt, or surface which include competition over resources, task interdependence, jurisdictional ambiguity, personality incompatibilities, difficult and angry people, communication barriers, and values and cultural differences.
- How people handle conflict is influenced by their personality traits and learned behavior, the relationship of the disputing parties, past conflict experiences, and individual conflict styles.

- The five types of conflict styles are collaborative, compromising, avoiding, accommodating, and forcing.
- There are four primary conflict management styles: dictation, arbitration, mediation, and negotiation.
- The three stages of conflict management are analysis, confrontation stage, and resolution.
- Ury's (1993) five-stage model for negotiation includes don't react, don't argue, don't reject, don't push, and minimize escalation.
- Communication techniques in conflict management include active listening, reflecting, empathy, questioning, highlighting common goals, creating trust, and inquiring silence.
- The Hollwitz, Churchhill, and Hollwitz model for dealing with difficult people includes direct intervention, indirect intervention, direct coping, or indirect coping.
- The success of conflict management techniques depends on the communication skills of the parties, their conflict perspective (focusing on behaviors rather than personality, sharing responsibility for the conflict), power distribution, and accountability.

Critical Thinking Questions

1. If third-party intervention such as arbitration and mediation is so successful, why do you think some organizations are hesitant to use it?

2. Would you consider an argument in which you disagreed with someone on which movie to go to a *conflict*? Use the conflict model to explain why or why not.

3. It has been suggested that organizations going through restructuring develop a conflict management plan. Why do you think this is important?

WEB SITES

For further information, log on to the following web sites.

www.work911.com/conflict/index.htm
Provides links to a variety of sources on conflict and dealing with difficult people.

www.mindconnection.com/library/business/conflict.htm
Lists several tips on dealing with angry people and provides links to conflict mediation sites.

KEY TERMS

Accommodating conflict style A conflict style that focuses on satisfying the needs of others at the risk of hurting the individual.

Active listening Communication through the use of nonverbal gestures such as nodding or eye contact.

Angry customers Rational individuals who have momentary lapses of unreasonableness when they are upset.

Arbitration A third-party conflict intervention technique where a neutral party listens to all parties' arguments and makes a decision on the solution.

Avoiding conflict style A conflict style that emphasizes preserving the relationship to the extent that conflict is ignored and not addressed.

Brainstorming A conflict management technique in which everyone involved in the conflict talks, uninterrupted, about all possible solutions to the conflict.

Cold conflict Functional conflict that provides an opportunity to share contrasting ideas, seek information, evaluate options, and negotiate goals and alternatives.

Collaborative conflict style A conflict style that is interested in a win-win result with an emphasis on meeting the goals of both parties and preserving the relationship.

Compromising conflict style A give-and-take style of managing conflict where each side gets some of what it wants but not everything it wants.

Conceptualization That part of the conflict process where parties attempt to define and articulate their concerns.

Conflict The consequence of one person's response to what he or she perceives about a situation or behavior of another.

Customers People to whom we provide a service or product.

Difficult people People who are locked into unreasonable behavioral patterns such as yelling, complaining, or sarcasm and who are a source of conflict.

External customers Consumers not affiliated with the organization who buy the company's services and products.

Forcing conflict style A style that addresses conflict in a win-lose fashion.

Frustration Part of the conflict process that occurs when individuals perceive that another party has hindered their goals.

Group-group conflict Conflict between two or more groups such as teams.

Hidden conflict Source of conflict that is below the surface, more difficult to determine than surface conflict, and is usually emotional such as anger or embarrassment.

Hot conflict Dysfunctional conflict that involves emotion such as anger, frustration, and sadness, which is viewed as threatening and harmful to all situations.

Individual-group conflict Conflict that occurs when an individual's needs, goals, and expectations are different from the group's.

Internal customers Other employees, coworkers, supervisors, and peers to whom employees provide a service.

Interpersonal conflict Conflict occurring between two individuals.

Jurisdictional ambiguity Source of conflict that occurs when geographical boundaries or lines of authority are unclear.

Mediation A nonthreatening conflict management process involving a third party who helps individuals in a conflict situation defuse their conflict and create a voluntary agreement.

Perception Process of assigning meaning to what we see and hear.

Reflecting A listening technique that provides clarification to what another individual has said.

Resources Source of conflict that includes tangible resources such as office funding, office space, equipment, promotions, and personnel or such intangible resources as promotions, attention, love, and recognition.

Surface conflict Source of conflict that is easily identifiable, the most common being competition for resources, task interdependence, jurisdictional ambiguity, personality, communication barriers, and cultural and value differences.

Task interdependence The dependence of people or groups of people on each other to get a job done.

Trust The capacity to depend on or place confidence in the truthfulness or accuracy of another's statements or behavior.

Values Ideals of how we believe we should behave and think and how others should act.

PRACTICE EXAM

1. Hot conflict is _____ whereas cold conflict _____ is.
   a. dysfunctional; functional
   b. functional; dysfunctional
   c. good; functional
   d. bad; dysfunctional

2. Sally and Tom have been engaged in conflict that continues to escalate downward and that has seen an extreme amount of anger. Their conflict is:
   a. cold   b. functional
   c. hot   d. pseudoconflict

3. Conflict is most likely to occur under all of these perceptions except when:
   a. conflicting parties have different goals.
   b. conflicting parties have a high amount of trust.

   c. one party is keeping another party from a goal.
   d. relationship expectations have been violated.

4. According to your text, four elements play a key role in turning potential conflict into real conflict. These are:
   a. individual perceptions; control; goals; other's behavior
   b. control; goals; conceptualization; frustration
   c. gender; individual perceptions; outcome; control
   d. individual perceptions, importance of outcome; attitudes; control

5. When we enter into an interaction with another individual, according to the conflict process model, the first thing we do is:
   a. conceptualize the situation
   b. become frustrated
   c. analyze the situation
   d. judge the other person's behavior

6. Frustration occurs when
   a. we perceive that another party has hindered our goals
   b. we define a problem and articulate our concern
   c. we decide whether to manage or ignore a conflict
   d. conflict becomes pseudoconflict

7. Jane and Betty have been arguing a great deal over the last week. Jane knows their strained relationship has to do with something Betty did a few days ago. Jane decides to talk to Betty and articulate her concerns and what she feels the problem is. According to the process model for conflict, Jane has entered the _____ stage.
   a. frustration   b. conceptualization
   c. pseudoconflict   d. analysis

8. There are four ways to manage conflict. The following is *not* one of those ways:
   a. mediation   b. arbitration
   c. disagreeing   d. dictation

9. The conflict occurring between Betty and Jane in question 7 is:
   a. interpersonal   b. group-group
   c. productive   d. group-individual

10. Steve Jones, manager of the marketing department, consistently yells in meetings, bullies his staff, and complains about both his personal and professional job. His employees and co-workers have a hard time getting along with him. Steve could be called a(n) _____ person.
    a. angry   b. compromising
    c. difficult   d. forcing

11. Indira has noticed that her team seems unchallenged and uncreative so she decides to introduce

a moderate amount of conflict into the next team meeting. Indira is doing this because:
a. she is a poor team leader
b. research suggests there is a curvilinear relationship between conflict and productivity
c. research suggests there is positive relationship between conflict and productivity
d. she knows conflict is always good

12. On the basis of the research on conflict style, a person who uses a win-win approach to conflict is:
a. accommodating   b. compromising
c. collaborative   d. forcing

13. Mike is shy and very rarely confronts people during times of conflict. His conflict style is:
a. compromising   b. avoiding
c. accommodating   d. forcing

14. The confrontation stage of conflict management is when disputing parties:
a. agree to engage in dialogue to see how a conflict can be managed
b. engage in cooperative problem solving
c. seek and share information
d. engage in brainstorming

15. The analysis stage of conflict management is when disputing parties:
a. agree to engage in dialogue to see how their conflict can be managed
b. engage in cooperative problem solving
c. identify the source of their conflict
d. engage in brainstorming

ANSWERS 1 a, 2 c, 3 b, 4 d, 5 c, 6 a, 7 b, 8 c, 9 a, 10 c, 11 b, 12 c, 13 b, 14 a, 15 c

Focused Free-Write

Write down how you feel about conflict. In particular, ask yourself these questions:

- Do I believe conflict is valuable?
- Am I energized when I feel I am in a conflict situation?
- Do I believe that conflict can help individuals develop and reach mutual goals?
- Do I believe conflict management skills are necessary to properly handle conflict?

_____

_____

_____

_____

_____

_____

_____

_____

_____

_____

_____

_____

_____

_____

_____

_____

_____

_____

_____

_____

_____

_____

_____

Analyzing a Conflict Situation

Think of a recent situation in which you have been involved that you considered a conflict. It could have been with a friend, classmate, instructor, or an individual with whom you work. Using the model in Exhibit 6-3, describe what happened during each of the stages in the conflict process.

Analysis

_____

_____

_____

_____

_____

_____

Frustration

_____

_____

_____

_____

_____

_____

_____

Conceptualization

_____

_____

_____

_____

_____

_____

_____

Behavior

_____

_____

_____

_____

_____

_____

Other's Reaction

_____

_____

_____

_____

_____

_____

Outcome

_____

_____

_____

_____

_____

_____

Cohen Conflict Response Inventory (short version)

Read the items below and after each one, circle the number under the category that indicates how much the item is like you. Answer the questions in terms of how you handle conflict situations. There are no wrong answers to these questions.

	very unlike me	unlike me	neutral	like me	very like me
1. I try to find the best solution to a problem that is acceptable to both parties.	1	2	3	4	5
2. I try to find a middle of the road solution to conflicts.	1	2	3	4	5
3. I try to keep myself out of disagreements.	1	2	3	4	5
4. I usually give in to other people's needs.	1	2	3	4	5
5. I tend to use my power or authority to get my way in a conflict situation.	1	2	3	4	5
6. I share ideas with others so that we may collaborate and come up with a final solution.	1	2	3	4	5
7. I try to find a middle ground solution to a problem.	1	2	3	4	5
8. I try to avoid argument situations.	1	2	3	4	5
9. I try to make other people happy.	1	2	3	4	5
10. I will use threats if I have to in order to get people to see it my way.	1	2	3	4	5
11. I share resources with others so that we may come up with the best possible solution.	1	2	3	4	5
12. I try to negotiate with people to find an acceptable solution.	1	2	3	4	5
13. I tend to avoid engaging in conversations about differences.	1	2	3	4	5
14. I usually go along with the solutions offered by the other party.	1	2	3	4	5
15. I often get very angry and hostile when others do not agree to my solution to a problem.	1	2	3	4	5
16. I try to investigate problems with others so we can get to the root of the problem.	1	2	3	4	5
17. I try to put all other things aside so that a solution can be reached that is acceptable to all.	1	2	3	4	5
18. I pretend or deny the fact that a conflict situation exists between myself and another.	1	2	3	4	5
	1	2	3	4	5
19. I try to satisfy the needs of others.	1	2	3	4	5

		very unlike me	unlike me	neutral	like me	very like me
20.	I sometimes bully my way to get others to agree with me.	1	2	3	4	5
21.	I try to meet the needs and goals of both parties to come up with a final solution.	1	2	3	4	5
22.	I tend to give up some of my own needs to come up with a mutually acceptable decision.	1	2	3	4	5
23.	I usually withdraw from a disagreement.	1	2	3	4	5
24.	I feel it is important to satisfy others' needs.					
25.	I try to show my expertise and knowledge to get others to agree with me.	1	2	3	4	5

Scoring

For each statement, write down the number you circled. Add up the total for each combination of statements as instructed below. Record that total in the blank under Conflict Response Style.

Statement Number and Score	Conflict Response Style
1, 6, 11, 16, and 21	_____ Sage
2, 7, 12, 17, and 22	_____ Diplomat
3, 8, 13, 18, and 23	_____ Ostrich
4, 9, 14, 19, and 24	_____ Philanthropist
5, 10, 15, 20, and 25	_____ Warrior

The style under which you recorded your highest score is your preferred way of dealing with conflict. The description of each style follows.

Descriptions of Conflict Response Styles

Sage

Sages have a high concern for both themselves and the other party involved in a conflict situation. They use an integrating, cooperative conflict style and view conflict in a positive light. This style is solution oriented where an open exchange of information is used. It is associated with problem solving and brainstorming with others, which leads to the best possible solution to a conflict, one that is mutually beneficial to all parties. Overall, this is the best way to effectively resolve conflict.

Diplomat

The Diplomat uses a compromising conflict style. This style involves give and take to derive a mutually acceptable solution to all parties. Solutions are reached that involve the least amount of personal loss, with both parties negotiating, splitting the differences, or seeking a middle-ground solution to a conflict. Most likely, the end result is not the best solution, but a solution that both parties can live with. Diplomats are concerned with getting their own needs met first.

Ostrich

The Ostrich tends to avoid conflict situations at all costs. They view conflict in a negative fashion, using this style to steer clear of conflict situations or to remove themselves from an existing conflict. Ostriches tend to ignore the needs of themselves and others. Sometimes Ostriches will procrastinate when they have to deal with a conflict situation and generally won't deal with it if possible. Most likely they do so because they don't like the stress and tension that conflict creates and feel intimidated by it.

Philanthropist

The Philanthropist uses an obliging or peaceful coexistence conflict style. This involves giving up one's own needs in order to satisfy the needs of others. This style attempts to play down differences and emphasize commonalities to satisfy the concerns of the other party. Philanthropists try to keep other people complacent and will sacrifice their own needs to achieve this. Using this style may send messages to others that you are a pushover and that you can be easily persuaded.

Warrior

Warriors view conflict as a win-lose situation and will use a dominating, forcing style to get what they want. They view conflict as a positive challenge and opportunity to win something for themselves. They commonly use threats, aggression, and anger to win. If you use this style, the other party may view you negatively and have resentment and hostility toward you. This is generally because your focus is so much on yourself that you totally negate the feelings of others.

Do you think this inventory accurately portrays how you handle conflict? Explain. Which style would you feel least comfortable with?

_____

_____

_____

_____

_____

_____

_____

_____

_____

Analyzing a Conflict Situation: A Case Study

Analyze the following conflict situation. Explain how you would handle the conflict based on what you read about the three stages of conflict management. In particular, answer the following questions:

1. What is the source of the conflict(s)?

2. Is this a case for mediation, arbitration, dictation, or negotiation?

3. What do you think are some of the feelings all parties might be having?

> *In a small university, the English department was in conflict with Administration because, unbeknownst to the English department, Administration had changed some of the core courses the English department was required to offer to students. Administration claimed the English department knew about the changes; the English department denied that they had been communicated with. In fact, the English department alleged they had no input into any of the changes and that the changes would cause hardship not only to the professors but to the students enrolled in the English program. Over the last 2 years, the English department has had various disagreements with Administration over how policy was being carried out. In particular, the English department had several run-ins with one particular administrator and his clerical staff who consistently made errors in the English department's purchase requisitions. Numerous complaints were made about this staff person to the administrator but the staff continued to make mistakes. Administration recently heard that the English department had hired a lawyer to assist them in a grievance against the university for changing the rules in mid-semester. Administration requested a meeting with the department chair and key faculty but faculty refused to meet with them. The question is, is there an alternative to resolving this situation outside of court?*

_____

_____

_____

_____

_____

_____

_____

_____

_____

_____

Paraphrasing and Clarifying

As a supervisor who is receiving these complaints from your employees, how would you praphrase each of the statements below? Concentrate only on paraphrasing and not on how you and/or the employee would solve the situation.

1. "Bob consistently reports to work late which causes us to start our day later than I would like. This is totally unacceptable. Because of his tardiness, we often have to work through lunch or have a shorter lunch break. This is driving me crazy, and I've come close to just punching him out! I've talked to him on numerous occasions and he's not taking me, or his responsibilities, seriously. I just can't take it any more."

_____

_____

_____

_____

_____

_____

_____

2. "You know, I don't mind Sally telling her sexist jokes around other people. But when she seeks me out to tell me in person, I don't like it. The jokes are demeaning to men and make me feel uncomfortable. It's getting to the point that I don't want to come into work anymore. If it doesn't stop soon, I may ask for a transfer to another department or just quit. I'm afraid to talk to her myself because she'll probably go ballistic and tell everyone I'm treating her differently than my male buddies."

_____

_____

_____

_____

_____

_____

_____

3. "The people in my department work just as hard, if not harder, than the people in Accounting, yet, once again, the Accounting people are getting a 10% budget increase for the next fiscal year. We are only getting 3.5%. Morale is getting lower and lower, as well as productivity, in my department. People are threatening to look for other work. If I lose some of these people, I don't know what I'm going to do. I'm already carrying a heavy workload. I can't afford to lose staff. It's just not fair. If we understood why Accounting keeps getting more monies than our department, maybe we would feel better. But we are clueless."

_____

_____

_____

_____

_____

_____

4. "What do you mean I have to go to another diversity training? I've gone to three already since I've been here and they are all the same. I feel like I'm being attacked when I go. And they don't do any good. Plus that, we don't have any race problems here. Making me and the other employees go to these types of yearly trainings makes us feel like management thinks all of us white people are racists."

_____

_____

_____

_____

_____

_____

Open-Ended vs. Closed-Ended Questions

Identify which statements are open and which are closed by placing either an "O" (open) or "C" (closed) in the blanks. Next to each closed statement, write how you would make it open.

1. _____ Did you get the project in on time?

   _____

   _____

2. _____ Were you mad about what happened today?

   _____

   _____

3. _____ And then what happened?

   _____

   _____

4. _____ Are you having problems understanding the system?

   _____

   _____

5. _____ What can we do to improve customers' perceptions of our store?

   _____

   _____

6. _____ Your coworkers say you consistently report to work late. Is that correct?

   _____

   _____

7. _____ Was the suspect wearing jeans?

_____

_____

8. _____ Is that all you have to say about what happened?

_____

_____

9. _____ What do you think would be a good solution?

_____

_____

10. _____ Did the complaint come in on Friday?

_____

_____

11. _____ What are some of the rumors you have been hearing?

_____

_____

12. _____ You know that isn't policy, don't you?

_____

_____

PROJECT F

Dealing with a Conflict Situation

Use the conflict situation in Project A or think of another conflict situation in which you were involved. Check those techniques below that you used to deal with it. If necessary, reread the section on *Conflict Management Strategies* to understand the definition of each technique.

Your Conflict Style

_____ Collaboration

_____ Compromise

_____ Avoidance

_____ Accommodation

_____ Forcing

Your Conflict Strategy

_____ Dictation

_____ Arbitration

_____ Mediation

_____ Negotation

_____ Combination (explain) _____

_____

_____

Communication Techniques You Used

_____ Active listening

_____ Reflecting

_____ Empathy

_____ Questioning

_____ Highlighting common goals

_____ Creating trust

_____ Inquiring silence

Was the conflict resolved to your satisfaction? Why or why not?

_____

_____

_____

_____

_____

_____

_____

_____

Based on your reading, what would you have done differently?

_____

_____

_____

_____

_____

_____

_____

_____

Mediating a Workplace Conflict

Video 1

After watching the first role-play on the video, mark each one of the behaviors you see modeled by the mediator. Under Comments, explain what you think the mediator should have done differently.

Stage 1: Stabilize the Setting

_____ Table prepared with pens/paper   _____ Greeted the parties

_____ Explained the mediation process   _____ Defined the ground rules

_____ Confirmed neutrality   _____ Ensured confidentiality

Comments _____

_____

_____

_____

_____

Stage 2: Help Parties Communicate

_____ Allowed uninterrupted "storytelling"   _____ Identified all sources of conflict

_____ Clarified unclear issues   _____ Summarized main concerns

_____ Focused on areas of agreement   _____ Maintained impartiality

_____ Put/kept control in parties' hands   _____ Acknowledged emotions

_____ Prioritized what needed to be settled

Comments _____

_____

_____

_____

_____

Stage 3: Help Parties Negotiate

_____ Sought cooperation   _____ Allowed venting

_____ Explored alternative solutions   _____ Set realistic goals and timelines

_____ Acknowledged feelings   _____ Focused on behaviors, not personality

Comments _____

_____

_____

_____

_____

_____

Stage 4: Develop/Clarify Agreement

_____ Focused on areas of agreement   _____ Summarized terms of agreement

_____ Staged each party's role in agreement   _____ Explained follow-up procedure

Comments _____

_____

_____

_____

_____

Do you think the disputing parties were happy with this mediation?
Why or why not?

_____

_____

_____

_____

_____

_____

_____

_____

_____

Video 2

After watching the second role-play on the video, mark each one of the behaviors you see modeled by the mediator. Under Comments, explain what you think the mediator should have done differently.

Stage 1: Stabilize the Setting

_____ Table prepared with pens/paper   _____ Greeted the parties

_____ Explained the mediation process   _____ Defined the ground rules

_____ Confirmed neutrality   _____ Ensured confidentiality

Comments _____

_____

_____

_____

_____

_____

Stage 2: Help Parties Communicate

_____ Allowed uninterrupted "storytelling"   _____ Identified all sources of conflict

_____ Clarified unclear issues   _____ Summarized main concerns

_____ Focused on areas of agreement   _____ Maintained impartiality

_____ Put/kept control in parties' hands   _____ Acknowledged emotions

_____ Prioritized what needed to be settled

Comments _____

_____

_____

_____

_____

_____

Stage 3: Help Parties Negotiate

_____ Sought cooperation   _____ Allowed venting

_____ Explored alternative solutions   _____ Set realistic goals and timelines

_____ Acknowledged feelings   _____ Focused on behaviors, not personality

Comments _____

_____

_____

_____

_____

_____

Stage 4: Develop/Clarify Agreement

_____ Focused on areas of agreement   _____ Summarized terms of agreement

_____ Staged each party's role in agreement   _____ Explained follow-up procedure

Comments _____

_____

_____

_____

_____

_____

Do you think the disputing parties were happy with this mediation?
Why or why not?

_____

_____

_____

_____

_____

_____

_____

CHAPTER SEVEN

Understanding Interpersonal and Organizational Communication

Picture the following situations:

- A male employee cannot understand why he was reprimanded for referring to female employees as the "girls in the office."

- A supervisor has tried everything to communicate with her employees, but they still seem lost.

- Customers don't like Sheila because she appears cold and aloof, though she is actually a very caring person.

- A supervisor is frustrated because her employees never read the notices posted on the bulletin board in the break room.

All four situations represent common communication problems. This chapter looks at ways in which employees communicate within an organization, problems in the communication process, and ways in which communication can be improved. By the end of this chapter, you will:

> Know the types of organizational communication
>
> Understand why interpersonal communication often is not effective
>
> Learn how to increase your listening effectiveness
>
> Learn ways to improve your communication skills

■ TYPES OF ORGANIZATIONAL COMMUNICATION

Upward Communication

Upward communication is communication of subordinates to supervisors or of employees to managers. Of course, in ideal upward communication, employees speak directly to management in an "open door" policy environment. In fact, the quality of upward communication is a significant factor in employee job satisfaction (E. W. Miles, Patrick, & King, 1996). Such a policy, however, is often not practical for several reasons. Perhaps the most important reason involves the potential volume of communication if every employee communicated with a specific manager. Direct upward communication also may not be workable because employees often feel threatened by managers and may not be willing to openly communicate bad news or complaints. This is especially true of employees who have strong aspirations for promotion and for organizations that have distinct status levels.

To minimize the number of different people communicating with the top executive, many organizations use **serial communication**. With serial commu-nication, the message is relayed from an employee to her supervisor, who relays it to her supervisor, who relays it to her supervisor, and so on until the message reaches the top. Although this type of upward communication relieves the top executive of excessive demands, it suffers several serious drawbacks.

> *Focused Free-Write*
> To get you thinking about communication, complete the Focused Free-Write at the end of this chapter.

The first is that the message's content and tone changes as it moves from person to person. As we will discuss later, messages are seldom received the way they were sent—especially if the message is being passed verbally from person to person.

The second drawback to serial communication is that bad news and complaints are seldom relayed. S. Rosen and Tesser (1970) have labeled this tendency the **MUM (minimize unpleasant messages) effect**. The MUM effect negatively affects the organization by keeping important information from reaching the upper levels. But for an employee, the MUM effect is an excellent survival strategy—no one wants to be the bearer of bad news. Interestingly, people have no problem passing on bad news to peers, especially when the climate is generally negative (Heath, 1996).

> **PROJECT A**   *The MUM Effect*
> To apply the MUM effect to your own life, complete Project A at the end of the chapter.

Serial communication's third drawback, especially with informal communication channels, is that it is less effective the farther away two people are from one another. That is, a supervisor is more likely to pass along a message to another supervisor if the two are in close physical proximity. It is unlikely, therefore, that an informal message originating with an employee at a plant in Atlanta will reach another employee at the corporate office in Phoenix. The importance of physical proximity cannot be overstated. In fact, a major source of power often comes from being physically near an executive. Seasoned executives have been known to place rising executives in distant offices to reduce their potential power. And going to lunch "with the big guys" has long been recognized as a means of obtaining new information and increased power.

As you would imagine, proximity does not play a role when messages are communicated electronically using e-mail (Valacich, Parantia, George, & Nunamaker, 1993). Thus, e-mail may reduce the power of proximity when communication is formal.

Because of these problems with serial communication, organizations use several other methods to facilitate upward communication. One method, the **attitude survey**, is usually conducted annually by an outside consultant who administers a questionnaire asking employees to rate their opinions on factors such as satisfaction with pay, working conditions, and supervisors. Employees are also given the opportunity to list complaints or suggestions to management. The consultant then tabulates the responses and reports the findings to management.

Although attitude surveys are commonly used, they are useful only if an organization takes the results seriously. If an organization finds that its employees are unhappy and does nothing to address the problem areas, the survey results will not be beneficial. Furthermore, to increase trust, an organization should share survey results with employees (Sahl, 1996).

If survey results are to be shared, then management must share *all* of them. While proposing a project to a local police department, I encountered a great deal of hostility from many of the senior officers. After a little probing, the officers revealed that several years earlier they had completed an attitude survey for the city. A few months later, the results were made public. The city cited five main complaints by the officers and promised that action would be taken to solve these problems. The officers were happy until they realized that none of their complaints about pay and working conditions were included in the report—the city was ignoring them. The officers became so resentful and mistrustful of consultants and management that they vowed to never again participate in a project.

Another method for facilitating upward communication is a **suggestion box** or a **complaint box**. Theoretically, these two boxes should be the same, but a box asking for suggestions is not as likely to get complaints as a box specifically labeled *complaints* and vice versa. The biggest advantage of these boxes is that they allow employees to immediately communicate their feelings.

For these boxes to be beneficial, management must respond to the suggestions and complaints in a timely manner. Management can respond to every suggestion or complaint by placing it on a bulletin board along with management's response. In this way, employees receive feedback about their ideas, which further encourages other employees to use the boxes to communicate.

Some organizations take employee suggestions quite seriously and reward employees who provide useful ideas. Hercules, Inc., for example, provides cash awards up to $10,000 for employees who suggest money-saving ideas, and Ingersoll-Rand gives plaques to employees who submit cost-saving ideas that are ultimately adopted by the company.

The use of a **liaison** or an **ombudsperson** can increase upward communication. Both are responsible for taking employee complaints and suggestions and personally working with management to find solutions. The advantage of this system is that the ombudsperson is neutral and works for a solution that is acceptable to both employees and management. Furthermore, the ombudsperson is typically supervised at the vice-presidential level, so she is not concerned about being fired if she steps on a few toes while looking for a solution.

As good as it is, the ombudsperson method is often not used because organizations do not want the expense of an employee who "does not produce." To overcome this problem, Moore Tool Company in Springdale, Arkansas, started its "Red Shirt" program in which selected senior employees wear red shirts that identify them as informal ombudspeople. If employees have a problem, they can seek help from a Red Shirt who has authority to help find a solution. This system not only opens communication channels but also provides job enrichment for senior employees.

In organizations that have their employees represented by unions, the job of the ombudsperson is typically handled by the **union steward**. But management-union relationships are often adversarial, so union stewards have a difficult time solving problems because they are not perceived by management or union members as being neutral.

Downward Communication

Downward communication is that of supervisor to subordinate or management to employees. The downward communication process in organizations has changed greatly over the years (Brandon, 1997). Originally, downward communication involved newsletters designed to bolster employee morale by discussing happy events such as the "3 B's"—babies, birthdays, and ballgame scores. Now, however, downward communication is considered a key method not only of keeping employees informed, but of communicating vital information needed by employees to perform their jobs.

Such communication can be accomplished in many ways. You have probably received one of the most common—the memorandum or *memo*. Memos have the advantage of providing detailed information to a large number of people in a short period of time. With the widespread use of photocopy machines, however, employees (especially office workers) now receive so many memos that they often do not read them. Remember the executive in Chapter 3 who never read a memo when it first came to him. Instead, he believed that if the message was really important, the person would talk to him about it later. Although such an attitude probably is not a good one, it does underscore the excessive use of memos and their diminishing effectiveness in communication.

Another method of downward communication is the *telephone call*. In the past, this method was appropriate only when the message was short and when only a few people needed to receive the communication. With the advent of conference calls, the number of people who can be reached by this method has certainly increased. Furthermore, telephone calls were previously appropriate only for messages that did not involve detail. But the facsimile, or fax, machine now allows detailed sketches or numbers to be sent to people in different locations in a matter of seconds, and these can then be discussed by telephone. Phone calls, even when long distance, have been shown to be less expensive in communicating a message than most memos or letters (Fulger, 1977).

One limitation of phone calls, of course, is that nonverbal cues are not available. Thus, a major portion of the message is often not communicated. For important calls, however, video-enhanced teleconferencing (videoconferencing) can now be used. Many organizations save interview expenses by having job applicants across the country participate in such teleconferences, which allow both parties to see one another. A second limitation to phone calls is that conversations are not documented. For example, our department recently had a problem with an administrator who continually provided incorrect information over the phone or at meetings, denied that she had done so, and then blamed our department for errors that resulted from the use of the information. To correct this problem, we quit talking to the administrator over the phone and stuck to e-mail where every "conversation" was documented.

Today many memos and telephone calls have been replaced with *e-mail* and *voice mail* (sophisticated phone-answering systems). Voice mail and e-mail are primarily used to exchange general information, ask questions, and exchange *timely* information (R. E. Rice, 1993). The ability to easily document the sending and receiving of e-mail gives it an advantage over voice mail in many situations. The advantages to e-mail and voice mail include a reduction in the use and filing of paper and time saved by avoiding small talk when communicating a short message by phone. A survey of human resource managers found that 80% thought that e-mail increased productivity (R. W. Thompson, 1997).

On the downside, voice mail often results in phone tag, and both e-mail and voice mail reduce opportunities for personal contact. In fact, Carillon Health Care Systems recently got rid of its voice mail system because employees and customers were tired of getting answering machines and wanted to talk to "a real person." Voice mail systems should probably be limited to simple tasks (Pospisil, 1997). Well-designed voice mail systems have short menus and

allow a caller to talk to a real person at any time during the call (Packard, 1997).

PROJECT B   *Voice Mail Problems*
Complete Project B at the end of the chapter to discuss problems you have had with voice mail.

The **bulletin board** is yet another method of downward communication. The next time you visit a company, look around for bulletin boards. You will see them everywhere. Their main use, however, is to communicate non-work-related opportunities such as scholarships, optional meetings, and items for sale. Important information is seldom seen because the bulletin board is not the appropriate place to post a change of policy or procedure. Still, bulletin boards have the advantage of low cost and wide exposure to both employees and visitors, especially if the boards are placed in high-traffic areas such as outside restrooms and cafeterias or near time clocks. Electronic bulletin boards, also called *in-house message networks*, allow the display of even more current information (Ladio, 1996).

Instead of the bulletin board, the **company manual** is the place for posting important changes in policy or procedure. This manual contains all the rules under which employees must operate. Most manuals are written in highly technical language, although they *should* be written in a less technical style to encourage employees to read them as well as to make them easier to understand. Furthermore, the contents of these manuals are considered binding contracts by courts, so the manuals must be updated each time a policy changes. This usually is done by sending updated pages to employees: To make this process easier, many organizations punch binder holes in the pages to facilitate the replacement of older material with newer.

The typical company manual is hundreds of pages long, so it is not surprising that many employees do not want to read it. To reduce length problems, most organizations have two types of company manuals. The first, called a *policy manual*, is very specific and lengthy, containing all of the rules and policies under which the organization operates. The second type, usually known as the *employee handbook*, is much shorter and contains only the most essential policies and rules, as well as general summaries of less important rules.

An example that supports the need for two manuals involved security guards at a manufacturing plant. The security guards were paid minimum wage and had an average tenure of about 3 months before quitting. The company became concerned for two reasons. First, 3 months was not enough time for the guards to learn all of the policies in the 300-page

EXHIBIT 7-1

Tips for Effective Writing

Rather Than	Try
Trying to impress someone with your vocabulary	Using a more conversational style
personnel	employees
utilize	use
urban mass-transit vehicle	bus
cognizant	aware
Writing in generalities	Writing what you mean
I wasn't gone long	I was gone for 5 minutes
A survey said that most of our employees …	A survey said that 54% of our employees …
Using an entire phrase	Using a single word
Enclosed please find …	Enclosed is …
Motivation is the idea that …	Motivation is …
Should it come to pass that you …	If you …

emergency procedures manual. Second, the manual was written by an engineer, and none of the security guards were able to understand the writing. The organization thus had student interns develop a short, easy-to-read procedure manual that could be read and understood in a day or two. Tips for effective manual writing are shown in Exhibit 7-1.

To replace bulletin boards, newsletters, and company manuals, an increasing number of organizations are turning to **intranets**—organization-wide versions of the Internet. For example, Fletcher Challenge, a Canadian paper and pulp company, designed "FletcherNet" to improve employee communication. One of the most useful aspects of an intranet is the speed at which the company can survey employees about new ideas (S. Cohen, 1998). Other advantages include employee self-service, convenience, 24-hour support, and reduced paper, printing, and postage costs (Gray, 1997).

Management must communicate with employees to train and motivate them effectively. Thus, the effectiveness of company policy and the attainment of company goals are to a large extent determined by the way in which policy and goals are communicated. For downward communication to be effective, management must demonstrate a receptive attitude that includes respect, honesty, and openness (B. House, 1997).

Horizontal Communication

The third direction of organizational communication is **horizontal communication**. As you might guess, this is communication among employees at the same level and can involve job-related information as well as informal information. Often, informal information is transmitted through the **grapevine**, a term that can be traced back to the Civil War, when loosely hung telegraph wires resembled grapevines. The communication across these lines was often distorted. Because unofficial employee communication is also thought to be distorted, the term has become synonymous with an informal communication network. Grapevines are common because they provide employees with information, power, and entertainment (Laing, 1993).

K. Davis (1953) studied the grapevine and established the existence of four grapevine patterns: single strand, gossip, probability, and cluster. As Exhibit 7-2 shows, in the **single strand** grapevine, Jones passes a message to Smith, who passes the message to Brown, and so on until either the message is received by everyone or someone "breaks the chain." This pattern is similar to the children's game of telephone. In the **gossip** grapevine, Jones passes the message only to a select group of people. Notice that with this pattern, only one person passes the message along and not everyone has a chance to receive, or will receive, the message. In the **probability** grapevine, Jones tells the message to a few other employees, and they in turn randomly pass the message along to other employees. In the **cluster** grapevine, Jones tells only a few select employees who in turn tell a few select others.

Research on the grapevine has supported several of Davis's (1953) findings. Sutton and Porter (1968)

EXHIBIT 7-2

Grapevine Patterns

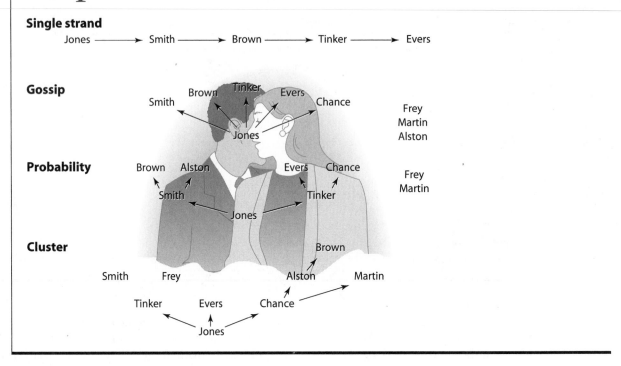

Single strand

Jones ⟶ Smith ⟶ Brown ⟶ Tinker ⟶ Evers

Gossip

Brown   Tinker   Evers
Smith   Chance   Frey
          Jones   Martin
                                 Alston

Probability

Brown   Alston   Evers   Chance
   Smith   Tinker   Frey
          Jones   Martin

Cluster

                                        Brown
Smith   Frey   Alston   Martin
Tinker   Evers   Chance
          Jones

studied 79 employees in a state tax office and reached several interesting conclusions. They found that employees could be placed into one of three categories. **Isolates** were employees who received less than half of the information; **liaisons** were employees who both received most of the information and passed it to others; and **dead-enders** were those who heard most of the information but seldom passed it on to other employees.

Managers tended to be liaisons because they had heard 97% of the grapevine information and most of the time passed this information on. Nonmanagerial employees heard 56% of the grapevine information but seldom passed it on. Only 10% of nonmanagerial employees were liaisons; 57% were dead-enders and 33% were isolates.

Although most people consider the grapevine to be inaccurate, research has shown that information in the grapevine often contains a great deal of truth (Zaremba, 1988). Walton (1961) found that 82% of the information transmitted across the grapevine in one company was accurate. Such a statistic, however, can be misleading. Consider the following hypothetical example: A message travels through the grapevine that "the personnel director will fire 25 people on Monday morning at 9 o'clock." The truth, however, is that the personnel director will *hire* 25 people on

Monday morning at 9:00 a.m. Thus, even though four out of five parts of the message, 80%, are correct, the grapevine message paints a picture quite different from reality.

QUICK PROJECT

On the basis of the above discussion, are you a dead-ender, isolate, or liaison?

_____

_____

_____

_____

_____

Not to be confused with the grapevine, **rumor** is poorly substantiated information that is transmitted across the grapevine. Usually, rumor occurs when the available information is both interesting and ambigu-

EXHIBIT 7-3

The Interpersonal Communication Process

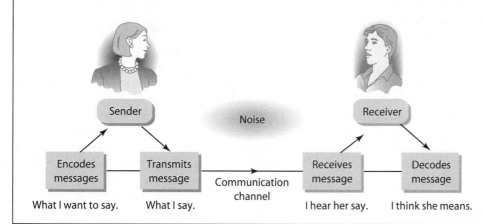

ous. Rumor and gossip are often ways in which employees can relieve stress (Mishra, 1990), respond to perceived organizational wrongs in a nonaggressive way (Tucker, 1993), and maintain a sense of control (Waddell, 1996).

Certainly, not all horizontal communication is informal. Employees at the same level often exchange job-related information on such topics as customers and clients, the status of projects, and information necessary to complete a particular task. To increase the amount of job-related horizontal communication, many organizations have adopted the practice of self-managed work groups (Overman, 1994).

For example, at Columbia Gas Development in Houston, 12-person drilling teams were formed. The team approach greatly increased communication between geologists, engineers, and other staff members who had previously been located in separate departments. As another example, the use of teams at Meridian Insurance in Indianapolis increased communication and efficiency so much that a 29-step process for handling paperwork was reduced to 4 steps.

■ INTERPERSONAL COMMUNICATION

Interpersonal communication involves the exchange of a message across a communication channel from one person to another. As shown in Exhibit 7-3, the interpersonal communication process begins with a sender encoding and transmitting a message across a communication channel (*e.g.,* memo, orally, nonverbally) and ends with another person (the receiver) receiving and decoding the message. Although this seems like a simple process, there are three main problem areas where things can go wrong and interfere with the message's accurate transmission or reception.

Problem Area 1: Intended Message vs. Message Sent

For effective communication, the sender must know what she wants to say and how she wants to say it. Interpersonal communication problems can occur when the message a person sends is not the message she intended to say. This problem has three solutions: thinking about what you want to communicate, practicing what you want to communicate, and learning better communication skills.

THINK ABOUT WHAT YOU WANT TO COMMUNICATE

Often the reason we don't say what we mean is that we are not really sure what we want to say. For example, think of using the drive-through window at a fast-food restaurant. As soon as you stop, but before you have a chance to read the menu board, a voice booms "Can I take your order?" You intelligently reply something such as "Uhhhhhhh, could you hang on a minute?" and then quickly try to place an order as the pressure builds. As you drive off, you realize that you did not really order what you wanted.

Does this scenario sound familiar? If so, you are not alone. Foster and his colleagues (1988) found that many fast-food restaurant customers have so little time to think about their order that they make ordering mistakes. Foster et al. (1988) found that placing a menu sign *before* the ordering station gave customers more time to think about their orders and that this decreased average ordering times from 28 seconds to 6 seconds and ordering errors from 29% to 4%.

As another example, think about calling a friend and unexpectedly getting an answering machine. Have you ever left a message in which the first few sentences sounded reasonably intelligent? Did the first sentence again begin with "Uhhhhhhhhh?" Or have you ever made a call expecting to get an answering machine and instead had an actual person answer the phone? These examples show the importance of thinking about what you want to communicate.

> **PROJECT C** *Problem Area 1*
> To apply what you have just learned, complete Project C at the end of the chapter.

PRACTICE WHAT YOU WANT TO COMMUNICATE

Even though you may know what you want to say, communication errors can occur if you do not actually say what you mean. Thus, when communication is important, it should be practiced. Just as consultants practice before giving a training talk and actors rehearse before a performance, you too need to practice what you want to say in important situations. Perhaps you can remember practicing how you were going to ask a person out on a date: changing the tone of your voice, altering your first line, or thinking of topics to discuss so that you would appear spontaneous.

LEARN BETTER COMMUNICATION SKILLS

Even if you know what you want to say and how you want to say it, communication errors can still occur if you do not have the proper communication skills. It is essential to take courses in public speaking, writing, and interpersonal communication so that you will be better prepared to communicate effectively. Reading this chapter is a good start toward better communication. However, many courses are offered at your school that can improve your communication skills. Ask your instructor to provide you with a list of recommended courses. Because of the importance of communication skills, many organizations also offer a wide range of communication training programs for their employees.

Problem Area 2: Message Sent vs. Message Received

Even though an individual knows what she wants to say and says it exactly as she planned, as shown in Exhibit 7-4, many factors affect how that message is received.

THE ACTUAL WORDS USED

A particular word may mean one thing in one situation but something else in another. Take the word *fine* as an example. If I told you that you had *fine jewelry*, you would probably take the statement as a compliment. If the word were used to describe the weather—"The weather here in Virginia is just fine"—it would still have a positive connotation. However, if a spouse asked "How was the dinner I cooked?" or "How did you like our evening of romance?" an answer of "Fine" would probably result in a very lonely evening.

A particular word may also mean one thing to one person and something different to another. For example, a 60-year-old man with a rural background may use the word *girl* as a synonym for *female*. He may not understand why the women at work get upset when he refers to them as the "girls in the office." When we conduct training sessions for police officers, we discuss how such words as *boy, son*, and *pretty little lady* can be emotionally charged and should thus be avoided.

Words or phrases that are vague can also cause problems. For example, you need a set of data by the end of the day, so you tell your assistant that you need the data immediately. At the end of the day, however, the data are not there. The next morning, the employee proudly brings you the data compiled in "less than a day" and is confused about why you are angry. In this example, you encoded the message as "I need it by five o'clock," you transmitted the message as "I need it immediately," and the employee decoded it as "She needs it tomorrow."

If someone told you, "I won't be gone long," when would you expect her back? When we ask this question of our classes or seminar audiences, the answers usually range from 10 minutes to 3 hours. Interestingly, at one seminar we conducted, a woman responded that her husband said that very phrase and came back 4 days later.

These examples demonstrate the importance of being more concrete in the words that we use. Why, then, are we often vague in the way we communicate? One reason is that we want to avoid confrontations. If a husband tells his spouse that he will be gone for 4 hours, he may know that she will object. By being vague, he avoids the initial confrontation

EXHIBIT 7-4

Factors Affecting the Message Sent vs. the Message Received

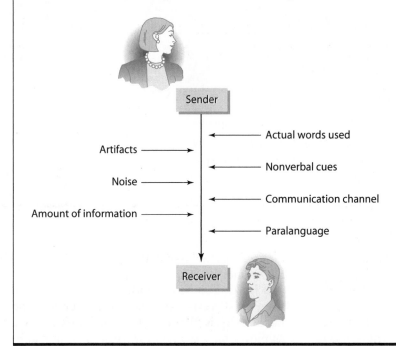

and hopes that she will not notice how long he has actually been gone—a common ploy used by us males but one that never seems to work.

Another reason for vagueness is that it gives us a chance to "test the water" and see what a person's initial reaction might be before we say what we really want. Asking someone out on a date is a perfect example. Instead of being direct and saying, "Do you want to go out this Friday?" we often say something such as "So, what are you up to this weekend?" If the response is positive, we become a bit more bold.

Gender is another factor that influences our use of words. As shown in Exhibit 7-5, Deborah Tannen (1986; 1990; 1994) believes that men and women speak very different languages and have different communication styles. By understanding these differences, we can drastically improve communication in the workplace as well as at home.

On the basis of our discussion, communication can be improved by choosing our words carefully and asking, "How might the other person interpret what I am about to say?" If I use the word *girl* will anyone be upset? If so, what word could I use that would be better?

PROJECT D *Gender Differences in Communication*
Complete Project D to discuss gender differences in communication that you have seen.

COMMUNICATION CHANNEL

Problems in communication can occur as a result of the **channel** through which the message is transmitted. Information can be communicated a variety of ways such as orally, nonverbally, through a second party, or through a written medium such as a letter or memo. The same message can be interpreted in different ways based on the channel that was used to communicate it. For example, an employee being reprimanded will receive the message very differently if it is communicated in a memo rather than face to face. A employee who gives the cold shoulder to another employee will receive a different response than if she yelled at the employee or discussed her anger.

Another example of the channel's importance is that of a supervisor criticizing an employee in front of other employees. The employee might be so embarrassed and angered that the criticism was made in

EXHIBIT 7-5

Gender Differences in Communication

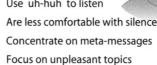

Men	Women
Talk about major events	Talk about daily life
Tell the main point	Provide details
Are more direct	Are more indirect
Use *uh-huh* to agree	Use *uh-huh* to listen
Are comfortable with silence	Are less comfortable with silence
Concentrate on the words spoken	Concentrate on meta-messages
Sidetrack unpleasant topics	Focus on unpleasant topics

Source: Adapted from Tannen (1986, 1990).

front of others that she would not hear the message's content. Again, the transmission of a message through an inappropriate channel interferes with the message's meaning and accurate interpretation.

Often, the communication channel is the message itself. For example, if top management sends a "gofer" to deliver a message, it is essentially communicating that either the message or the receiver is not important. A colleague at another university tells about a former boss who always personally delivered good news (e.g., promotions, raises), as well as donuts on Friday. But lower level management always had to communicate the bad news, a practice that was resented by employees.

NOISE

The **noise** surrounding a transmission channel can also affect the way in which a message is received. Noise can be defined as any interference that affects proper reception of a message. An obvious example is *actual* noise, such as the sound of a subway interfering with conversation. Other examples are the appropriateness of the channel, the reputation of the person sending the message, and other information being received at the same time.

NONVERBAL CUES

Much of what we communicate is conveyed by nonverbal means. Our words often say one thing, while our actions say another. For example, a supervisor

may tell an employee that she is interested in hearing her opinions, while at the same time she is frowning and looking out the window. The verbal message from the supervisor may be "I care," but the nonverbal message is "I'm bored." Which message will the employee pay attention to? Most likely, it will be the nonverbal, even though nonverbal cues often lead to incorrect impressions (Malandro & Barker, 1983). Nonverbal cues can be divided into three categories: body language, use of space, and use of time.

Body language The ways in which we move and position our bodies—our *body language*—communicates much to other people. For example:

- When a person's body faces the other person, it often is interpreted as a sign of liking, while a person's body turned away from another often is interpreted as a sign of dislike or lack of interest (Clore, Wiggins, & Itkin, 1975).

- Making eye contact implies interest. In a casual conversation, increased eye contact is interpreted as a sign of liking, in a bar it may be a sign of flirting, and on a football field it may be interpreted as a sign of aggression. Lack of eye contact can mean many things including disinterest, discomfort, or embarrassment (Taylor, Peplau, & Sears, 1994). A person who makes eye contact while speaking but not while listening is often perceived as being powerful or dominant.

- Raising or lowering the head or the shoulders may indicate superiority or inferiority, respectively.

- Touching someone usually indicates liking, friendship, or nurturance (S. S. Brehm & Kassin, 1996). In fact, one study has shown that a waitress who touches her customers will receive larger tips than one who does not touch (Crusco & Wetzel, 1984). Another study found that library clerks who briefly touched patrons as they were being handed books were rated by the patrons as being better employees than clerks who did not touch (J. D. Fisher, Rytting, & Heslin, 1976). Men initiate contact more often than women (Major, Schmidlin, & Williams, 1990).

Fleeting facial expressions and changes in voice pitch and eye contact can indicate that a person is lying (DePaulo, Stone, & Lassiter, 1985; Frick, 1985; Knapp, 1978). In fact, voice cues are more accurate than facial expressions when determining deception (DePaulo, Zuckerman, & Rosenthal, 1980). Thus, at times it might be advantageous to interview a job applicant or an employee by telephone rather than in person.

As you might expect, gender differences occur in the use of nonverbal cues. For example, Dolin and Booth-Butterfield (1993) found that females use nonverbal cues such as head nodding to show attention more often than do males. In social situations, females touch, smile, and make eye contact more than males (DePaulo, 1992).

Research has shown that body language can affect employee behavior. For example, Forbes and Jackson (1980) found that effective use of nonverbal cues resulted in a greater probability of being hired for a job. Similarly, Rasmussen (1984) found that the use of nonverbal cues during an interview will help if the applicant gives the correct answer to an interview question but will hurt the applicant if an incorrect answer is given.

Though body language can be a useful source of information, it is important to understand that the same nonverbal cue can mean different things in different situations and cultures. So be careful and try not to read too much into a particular nonverbal cue.

Use of space The way in which people make use of space can also provide nonverbal cues about their feelings and personalities. Dominant people or those who have authority are given more space by others and at the same time take space from others. For example, people stand farther away from such status figures as executives and police officers (and even college professors) and stand in an office doorway rather than directly entering such a person's office. These same status figures, however, often move closer as a show of power. Police officers are taught that moving in close is one method of intimidating a person.

On the other hand, status figures also increase space to establish differences between themselves and the people with whom they are dealing. A common form of this use of distance is for an executive to place a desk between herself and another person. An interesting story is told by a sports agent who was negotiating a player's contract with George Steinbrenner, owner of the New York Yankees baseball club. When the agent arrived at Steinbrenner's office, he noticed that Steinbrenner sat at one end of a long desk. At the other end was a small chair in which the agent was to sit. Recognizing the spatial arrangement to be a power play, the agent moved his chair next to Steinbrenner's. As the story goes, the Yankee owner was so rattled by this ploy that the agent was able to negotiate an excellent contract for his player client.

The following example also illustrates how the use of space can enhance a person's status by adding an image of importance. Recently, the psychology building at a university was renovated, and with efficient use of attic space, every faculty member was given an office. Students who visited during office hours had been accustomed to faculty members sharing offices. Many of these students commented on how important a psychology faculty member must be to receive his or her own office. (Of course, the faculty never told the students that all the faculty in the department had their own offices and that faculty members in other departments would also soon have their own.)

Four major spatial distance zones have been recognized and defined (E. T. A. Hall, 1963): intimacy, personal distance, social distance, and public distance.

The **intimacy zone** extends from physical contact to 18 inches away from a person and is usually reserved for close relationships such as dates, spouses, and family. When this zone is entered by strangers in such situations as crowded elevators, we generally feel uncomfortable and nervous. The **personal distance zone** ranges from 18 inches to 4 feet away from a person and is the distance usually reserved for friends and acquaintances. The **social distance zone** is from 4 to 12 feet away and is the distance typically observed when dealing with businesspeople and strangers. Finally, the **public distance zone** ranges from 12 to 25 feet away and is characteristic of such large group interactions as lectures and seminars. It is important to understand that these zones differ across cultures. For example, the personal distance zone in such countries as Iraq, Greece, and Iran is much closer than the personal distance zone used in the United States and Northern Europe.

EXHIBIT 7-6

Inflection Changes and Meaning

Inflected Sentences	Meaning
I did not say Bill stole your car.	**Someone else** said Bill stole your car.
I **did not** say Bill stole your car.	I **deny** I said Bill stole your car.
I did not **say** Bill stole your car.	I **implied** that Bill stole your car.
I did not say **Bill** stole your car.	**Someone else** stole your car.
I did not say Bill **stole** your car.	He **borrowed** your car.
I did not say Bill stole **your** car.	Bill stole **someone else's** car.
I did not say Bill stole your **car.**	Bill stole **something else** of yours.

QUICK PROJECT

Compared to others, do you need more or less personal space?

_____

_____

_____

_____

_____

The way an office is furnished also communicates a lot about that person. As mentioned earlier, certain desk placements indicate openness and power; visitors and subordinates prefer not to sit before a desk that serves as a barrier (T. R. Davis, 1984). People whose offices are untidy are perceived as being busy, while people whose offices contain plants are perceived as caring and concerned.

Use of time The way in which people make use of time is another element of nonverbal communication. If an employee is supposed to meet with a supervisor at 1:00 p.m. and the supervisor shows up at 1:10, the supervisor is communicating an attitude about the employee, the importance of the meeting, or both. Tardiness is more readily accepted from a higher status person than from a lower status person. Dean Smith, the former great basketball coach at the University of North Carolina, suspended any player who was even a minute late for a practice because he believes that tardiness is a sign of arrogance and works against the team concept.

In a similar fashion, before a meeting a supervisor sets aside 30 minutes and tells others that she is not to be disturbed because she is in conference. A definitive message thus is conveyed, one that is likely to prevent constant interruptions by telephone calls or people stopping by to say hello because they saw an open door.

PARALANGUAGE

Paralanguage involves the way in which something is said and consists of variables such as tone, tempo, volume, number and duration of pauses, and rate of speech (S. Martin, 1995). A message that is spoken quickly will be perceived differently from one that is spoken slowly. In fact, research has shown that people with fast speech rates are perceived as more intelligent, friendly, and enthusiastic (Hecht & LaFrance, 1995) than people with slow rates of speech. People who use many "uh-hums," "ers," and "ahs" are also considered less intelligent. Men with high-pitched voices are considered to be weak, while females with high-pitched voices are considered to be petite.

Simple changes in the tone used to communicate a message can change the entire meaning of the message. To demonstrate this point, consider the sentence "I didn't say Bill stole your car." At first reading, it does not seem unusual, but what does it actually mean? As Exhibit 7-6 shows, if we emphasize the first word, *I*, the implication is that *someone else* said, "Bill stole your car." But if we emphasize the word *Bill*, the meaning changes to "Someone else stole your car." And so on. Thus, a simple written message can be interpreted in seven different ways. As we can see, the message might have been better sent orally.

ARTIFACTS

A final element of nonverbal communication concerns the objects, or **artifacts**, that a person wears or with which she surrounds herself. A person who wears bright and colorful clothes is perceived differently than a person who wears such conservative colors as white or gray (D. Arthur, 1995). Similarly, the manager who places all of her awards on her office wall, the executive with a large and expensive chair, and the student who carries a briefcase rather than a book bag are all making nonverbal statements about themselves.

> **PROJECT E** *Nonverbal Communication*
> To help you apply your new knowledge of nonverbal communication, complete Project E at the end of this chapter.

AMOUNT OF INFORMATION

The amount of information contained in a message can affect the accuracy with which it is received. When a message contains more information than we can hold in memory, the information becomes leveled, sharpened, and assimilated. For example, suppose a friend told you the following message over the phone:

John Atoms worked for Mell South Corporation. He came to work on Tuesday morning wearing a brown shirt, plaid pants, white socks, and dark shoes. He leaned forward, barfed all over the floor, and then passed out. He was obviously intoxicated. He had worked for the company for 13 years, so they didn't want to fire him, but they had to do something. The company decided to suspend him for a few days and place him on probation. They were especially sensitive to his problems because he was on his eighth marriage.

What would the story sound like if you passed it on to a friend? When you **level** some of the information, unimportant details are removed. For example, information about the color of the employee's shirt and socks would probably not be passed along to the next person. When you **sharpen** the information, interesting and unusual information is kept. In the example here, the employee's "barfing" and his eight marriages would probably be the story's main focus as it is passed from you to your friend. When you **assimilate** the information, it is modified to fit your existing beliefs and knowledge. Most of us have never heard the last name Atoms, but we probably have known someone named Adams, and Mell South might be passed along as Bell South. You would probably use the word *drunk* rather than *intoxicated*.

Reactions to communication overload With many jobs, communication overload can occur when we receive more communication than we can handle. When we are overloaded, we can adapt or adjust in one of several ways to reduce the stress (J. G. Miller, 1960): omission, error, queuing, escape, using a gatekeeper, or using multiple channels.

Omission One way to manage communication overload is **omission**: a conscious decision not to process certain types of information. For example, a busy supervisor may let the phone ring without answering it so that she can finish her paperwork. Although this technique can work if the overload is temporary, it will be ineffective if the employee misses an important communication.

Error In the **error** type of response, the employee attempts to deal with every message received. But in so doing, each processed message includes reception error. The processing errors are not intentional but result from processing more than can be handled.

A good example of this is a student who has 2 hours in which to study four chapters for a test. A student using the error method would attempt to read and memorize all four chapters in 2 hours. Obviously, her test score will probably indicate that even though she did all of her reading, much of it was not remembered or remembered correctly.

The probability of error occurring can be reduced in two ways. First, the message can be made *redundant*. That is, after communicating an important message over the telephone, it is a good idea to write a memo or e-mail to the other person summarizing the major points of the conversation. Furthermore, after sending an important memo, it is wise to call the recipient to ensure that the memo was not only received but also read.

Second, error can be reduced by having the recipient *verify* the message: Ask the person to repeat the message or acknowledge that she has read and understood it. For example, after a customer has placed an order at the drive-through window of a fast-food restaurant, the employee repeats the order to the customer to make sure that it was heard correctly. (Of course, with the poor-quality intercoms used by such places, most people still cannot understand the employee.) In a second example of verification, this time verifying the receipt of a message, a single copy of a memo is sent to several different people. As shown in Exhibit 7-7, the person who heads the list reads the memo, puts her initials next to her name, and sends the memo to the next person on the list.

Queuing Another method of dealing with communication overload is **queuing**—placing the work into a

EXHIBIT 7-7

Example of a Signature Memo

DATE: June 21, 2000

TO: All Department Managers
_DS_ Donald Shula
_TL_ Thomas Landry
____ Patrick Reilly
____ William Daly
____ William Walsh

FROM: William Walsh

Attached is a copy of last month's productivity report. Please look it over carefully, initial that you have read it, and then send it to the next manager on the list.

---

queue, or waiting line. The order of the queue can be based on such variables as the message's importance, timeliness, or sender. For example, a memo sent by the company president will probably be placed near or at the beginning of the queue, as will an emergency phone message. On the other hand, a message to return the phone call of a salesperson most likely will go at the end of the queue.

With this method of handling communication overload, all of the work will usually get done. Queues are only effective, however, if the communication overload is temporary. If employees are constantly overloaded, they never reach the work at the end of the queue.

Escape If communication overload is prolonged, a common employee response is **escape,** usually through absenteeism and ultimately through resignation. This response certainly is not beneficial to an organization, but it can be beneficial to employees if it protects their mental and physical health by relieving stress.

An example of the escape response is often seen with students who withdraw from college courses. A student may enroll in six classes and realize after 2 months that she does not have enough time to do all of the reading and writing required for six classes. Rather than choosing the error or omission strategies, both of

which would result in lower grades, the student withdraws from one of her classes to reduce her overload.

Use of a gatekeeper A response to communication overload used by many executives is the use of a **gatekeeper,** a person who screens potential communication and allows only the most important to go through. Receptionists and secretaries are the most obvious examples of gatekeepers.

Use of multiple channels The final coping response to communication overload is the use of **multiple channels.** With this strategy, an organization reduces the amount of communication going to one person by directing some of it to another. For example, in a small restaurant, all of the problems that involve customers, employees, finances, and vendors are handled by the owner. But as the business grows, the owner may not be able to handle all of the communication and thus may hire others to deal with finances (a bookkeeper) and vendors (an assistant manager).

Knowing and understanding this list of responses to communication overload is important. When communication overload occurs, employees will react in ways that reduce the increased stress. Some of these strategies (omission, error, escape) result in negative consequences for the organization. Thus, the organi-

EXHIBIT 7-8

Factors Affecting the Message Received vs. the Message Interpreted

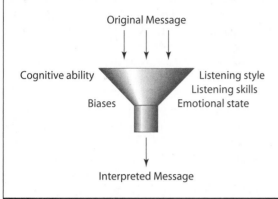

Problem Area 3: Message Received vs. Message Interpreted

Even though a person knows what she wants to say, and says it the way she wants, and even though another individual properly receives the intended message, its meaning can change depending on the way in which the receiver interprets the message that was received. As shown in Exhibit 7-8, this interpretation is affected by a variety of factors, such as listening skills, listening style, emotional state, cognitive ability, and personal biases.

LISTENING SKILLS

Listening is probably the most important communication skill for a supervisor to master. In a classic study of managers, Nichols and Stevens (1957) found that 70% of the white-collar workday is spent communicating. Of that, 9% is spent in writing, 16% is spent in reading, 30% is spent in speaking, and 45% is spent in listening. Thus, a manager spends more time in listening than in any other single activity. This is an important point for two reasons.

First, our formal education in high school and college does not prepare us for managerial communication. We are required to take English courses to improve our reading and writing and are usually required to take one speech course to improve our oral communication skills, but we spend little, if any, time learning how to listen. Thus, the amount of time spent learning about various types of communication is inversely related to the actual amount of time spent by managers on the job.

Second, listening effectiveness is poor. It has been estimated that immediately after a meeting, we retain only 50% of the material we have heard and only 25% of the material 48 hours later (Nichols & Stevens, 1957). Although much of this loss can be attributed to poor memory practices, some is the result of poor listening habits.

STYLES OF LISTENING

What can be done to increase listening effectiveness? Perhaps the most important thing we can do is to recognize that every person has a particular listening style that serves as a communication filter. Geier and Downey (1980) have developed a test, the **Attitudinal Listening Profile System**, to measure an employee's listening style. Their theory postulates six main styles of listening: leisure, inclusive, stylistic, technical, empathic, and nonconforming (LISTEN).

Leisure listening is the listening style that is practiced by "good time" people who listen only for words that indicate pleasure. For example, a student who is a leisure listener will pay attention only when

---

zation must recognize when overload occurs and aggressively adopt an acceptable strategy to deal with it.

> **PROJECT F** *Communication Overload*
> To look at how you react to communication overload, complete Project F at the end of this chapter.

the teacher is interesting and tells jokes. As an employee, she is the last one to "hear" that employees are needed to work overtime.

Inclusive listening is the style of the person who listens for the main ideas behind any communication. In an hour-long meeting full of details and facts about a decline in sales, the only information that this type of listener will "hear" is the main point that sales are down and that things had better improve. This listening style can be an advantage in allowing the listener to cut through a jungle of detail, but it can be a disadvantage when detail is important.

Stylistic listening is practiced by the person who listens to the *way* communication is spoken. Stylistic listeners will not listen unless the speaker's style is appropriate, the speaker "looks the part," or both. For example, when speaking to a stylistic listener, a lecturer on finance will find an attentive ear only if she wears a nice suit. After all, this listener reasons, if the lecturer cannot afford a nice suit, why listen to what she has to say about investing money? Similarly, if the speaker says that an event will be fun, she must *sound* as if she means it. And if an employee calls in sick to a manager who is a stylistic listener, she had better "sound" sick.

Technical listening is the style practiced by the "Jack Webb" of the listening world—"just the facts, ma'am." The technical listener hears and retains large amounts of detail, but she does not hear the *meaning* of those details. In the earlier example of the meeting in which employees are told that sales have decreased, the technical listener will hear and remember that sales last year were 12.3% higher than this year, that profits are down by 21%, and that six employees will probably be laid off—but she will miss the point that unless sales improve, she could be one of those six.

Empathic listening tunes in to the feelings of the speaker and, of the six listening types, is the most likely to pay attention to nonverbal cues. Thus, an empathic listener will listen to an employee complain about her boss and is the only one of the six types of listeners who will not only pay attention but also understand that the employee's complaints indicate true frustation and unhappiness.

Nonconforming listening attends only to information that is consistent with her way of thinking. If the nonconforming listener does not agree with a speaker, she will not listen to what the speaker says. Furthermore, the nonconforming listener will pay attention only to those people whom she considers to be strong or to have authority.

How listening styles affect communication The following example will demonstrate the importance of the six listening styles in a work setting. Suppose that an employee approaches a supervisor and tells her that she has a temperature of 106 degrees. How would each of the six listeners react?

The leisure listener would pay little attention to the employee because she does not like to hear about unpleasant things and illness certainly is not pleasant.

The inclusive listener would probably tell a story about when she had a high temperature, thinking that the topic of conversation was fever. You may have friends who often say things that are not related to your conversation; as this example points out, they are probably inclusive listeners who mistake the main points of a conversation. In this case, the employee is communicating that she does not feel well; she is not discussing "temperatures I have had."

The stylistic listener would pay attention only if the employee sounded and looked ill. You may have called an instructor or a date and tried to sound ill in order to cancel an appointment or a date. Few people actually sound ill even when they are, but we understand the importance of style in listening and behave accordingly.

The technical listener would hear every word but would not realize their meaning. That is, 10 minutes later, when another employee asked whether Sue is sick, the supervisor would respond, "She didn't say. She has a temperature of 106, but I'm not sure how she is feeling."

The nonconforming listener would pay little attention to the employee. After all, if she actually had a temperature of 106 degrees, she would be dead, and because she is not dead, she must be lying. Of course, the employee exaggerated her temperature because she was emphasizing the point that she is sick. But the nonconforming listener would not "hear" anything once she recognized that an initial statement was incorrect.

In this example, the empathic listener would be the only one who would understand the real point of the communication. The employee is mentioning her temperature because she does not feel well and wants to go home.

Understanding each of the six styles can make communication more effective in two ways. First, by becoming aware of your own style, you understand the filter that you use when listening to others. For example, a student who uses a leisure style may need to recognize that if she listens only to lectures that she finds interesting, she probably will miss a lot of important information. She might want to learn how to concentrate on lectures even when they are boring. Second, understanding the six styles can lead to better communication with others. For example, when speaking to inclusive listeners, we must either write down relevant details that we want them to remember or have them repeat the details. Otherwise, the inclusive listener will remember only the main point: "I know that there is a party tonight, but I'm not sure when or where." On the other hand, when we speak to technical listeners, it is important to tell them what the details mean. For example, if you tell a technical listener there will be a party at your house on Thursday at 8:00 p.m., you should also add that she is invited, or she will understand only that there is a party and not that she has been invited.

Of course, the million-dollar question is, "How can we tell what style of listener is listening to us?" The best way might be to test the listener on the Attitudinal Listening Profile System mentioned earlier, but this is hardly practical. The most practical method is using the person's speaking style as an indicator of listening style. If the person usually mentions how she feels about things, she is probably an empathic listener, but if she speaks with a lot of detail, she is probably a technical listener.

Someone speaking to a group, of course, must relate to all styles of listeners. The best communicators thus will have something for everyone. A good instructor will provide jokes and humorous stories for leisure listeners, use an outline format and provide main points for inclusive listeners, provide specific facts and details for technical listeners, discuss her feelings about the topic for empathic listeners, have good speaking skills and appropriate dress for stylistic listeners, and be confident and accurate for nonconforming listeners.

> **PROJECT G** *Styles of Listening*
> To determine your style of listening, complete Project G at the end of the chapter.

Tips for effective listening In addition to understanding the way in which our listening style serves as a filter, we can improve our listening effectiveness in many other ways. Perhaps the most important is to understand that we are capable of listening to 600 words per minute, yet fast speakers talk at only 100 to 150 words per minute. This gap between our listening potential and the typical speaker allows our minds to wander. Tips for effective listening include (Blodgett, 1997; Messmer, 1998):

1. Stop talking.
2. Show the speaker that you want to listen.
3. Remove distractions and clear your mind before listening.
4. Empathize with the speaker.
5. Let the other person finish speaking.
6. Don't ask excessive questions.
7. Use appropriate nonverbal cues, paralanguage, and verbals to show that you are paying attention.
8. Be silent for a few seconds after the person has finished speaking; this will encourage her to talk more.
9. Focus on what the person is saying, not your next response.
10. Don't judge; keep an open mind.
11. Try to understand what the other person means.

Golen (1990) found that bad listeners are lazy, closed-minded, opinionated, insincere, bored, and inattentive.

EMOTIONAL STATE

The interpretation of a message can certainly be affected by the receiver's emotional state (S. Martin, 1995). When we are angry, anxious, depressed, elated, or upset, we do not think as clearly as when our moods are more moderate. Think of the last time you had an argument with someone. How rational and intelligent was your conversation? After the argument was over, did both of you remember what was said in the same way?

Likewise, have you ever attended a class when your mind was somewhere else? Our guess is that neither your attention span nor your comprehension of the material was as high as normal.

COGNITIVE ABILITY

Cognitive ability is another factor than can affect the way in which a received message is interpreted. That is, a person can receive a message exactly as it was sent yet not be bright enough to understand it. For example, have you ever attended a class where you had no idea what the professor was talking about? You heard the words and saw the diagrams, but the message still made no sense. Likewise, have you ever told a great pun, only to be disappointed that the person on the receiving end of the joke did not understand it? If so, then you have firsthand experience in understanding how cognitive ability can affect the way in which information is interpreted.

BIAS

Our biases obviously affect our ability to interpret information that is received. For example, we can hate a political candidate so much that we refuse to process any of the positive information we hear about her. We do however, process every piece of information that is consistent with our opinion.

■ IMPROVING EMPLOYEE COMMUNICATION SKILLS

Organizations are always looking for employees with excellent communication skills. The difficulty in finding such employees was recently exemplified by the experience of a national insurance company. The company was having difficulty with a position that required employees to respond to customer complaints. The company had hired expensive consultants to teach its employees how to write effective letters, but performance had not improved. The company then constructed sample letters so that an employee could read a customer complaint, find a standard response form, and add a few personal lines. This also did not work. Finally, the company tried using a standardized writing test before hiring its employees. Although the test showed significant prediction for the performance of Black employees, it did not predict the performance of White employees. This case of single-group validity made the test risky to use. Thus, the question remains; How can an organization increase the communication skills of its employees?

Interpersonal Communication Skills

One of the most common methods used to increase interpersonal communication skills is the training workshop conducted by an outside consultant. Although a large number of consultants lead communication workshops, such workshops often bring only short-term improvement in skills.

An exception to this general failure to produce long-term improvements was reported by Freston and Lease (1987) from their work with Questar Corporation in Salt Lake City. As the personnel manager at Questar, Freston believed that the organization's managers were not properly trained in communication. Questar thus hired Lease as a communications consultant, and together Freston and Lease designed a new training program that included seminars on awareness, nonverbal communication, assertiveness, and listening. In addition to the seminars, Freston and Lease also used role play and group discussion. The revised training program brought more positive attitudes for supervisors, as well as increased performance quality in tasks such as performance appraisal and training.

Written Communication Skills

Attempts to improve the quality of written communication have generally taken two paths. One approach concentrates on improving the writer's skills, and the other concentrates on making material easier to read.

Improving Writing

It is difficult for an organization to overcome an employee's lack of formal training in writing (or to change bad writing habits). Several consulting firms, however, specialize in the improvement of employee writing by teaching employees the most important concepts of writing. For example, Broadbent (1997) advised that writing can be improved when writers value what they write, set personal standards and goals (e.g., a 12th-grade reading level, no grammar errors, each document will be proofread twice), and spend considerable time doing their own editing as well as getting others to edit the document. Fey (1987) stated that to improve writing, employees must learn certain basic concepts. For example, employees need to analyze their audience. If a written communication is intended for blue-collar employees, then the readability must be kept simple. If the intended audience is busy executives, the message must be kept short.

Readability

Written communication can break down when material is too difficult for many employees to read. For example, research has shown that Federal Aviation Administration (FAA) regulations are too difficult for pilots to read (Blumenfeld, 1985) and corporate annual reports are too difficult for most adults to understand (Courtis, 1995). Thus, providing employees with important material to read will be an effective communication form only if the employees can understand what is written.

To ensure that employees will be able to understand written material, several readability indices are available. When using such an index, an organization analyzes the material to be read and then compares its readability level with the typical education of the employees who will read the document. For example, if most employees have high school degrees and have not been to college, the document should be written at less than a 12th-grade level.

Each index uses a slightly different formula or method. For example, the **Fry Readability Graph** (E. Fry, 1977) uses the average number of syllables per word and the average length of sentences to determine readability. **The Flesch Index** (Flesch, 1948) uses the average sentence length and number of syllables per 100 words; the **FOG Index** (Gunning, 1964) uses the number of words per sentence and the number of 3-syllable words per 100; and the **Dale-Chall Index** (Dale & Chall, 1948) uses the number of words that are not included in a list of words known by 80% of fourth graders. As we can see from these indices, an easily read document has short sentences, uses simple rather than complicated words, and uses common rather than unusual words (Grazian, 1996). Many word-processing packages (e.g., *WordPerfect, Microsoft Word*) now contain readability indices that make it easier to determine the audience level for which the document was written.

PROJECT H *Case Study*
To apply what you have learned throughout this chapter, complete the case study found in Project H.

CHAPTER RECAP

Key points in this chapter include:

- There are three types of organizational communication: upward, downward, and horizontal.

- Upward communication moves from employees to management and uses such methods as serial communication, attitude surveys, suggestion boxes, and ombudspeople.

- Downward communication moves from management to employees and uses such methods as telephone calls, memos, voice mail, e-mail, bulletin boards, company manuals, and intranets.

- Horizontal communication is communication between people at the same level of an organization and includes rumor, the grapevine, and work groups.

- There are three main problem areas in interpersonal communication: the intended message versus the message actually sent, the message sent versus the message received, and the message received versus the message interpreted.

- A communication problem area involves the message sent versus the message received. Concerns in this problem area include the actual words used in the message, the communication channel, noise, nonverbal cues (e.g., body language, use of space, use of time), artifacts, paralanguage, and the amount of information.

- Although effective communication is essential, too much can cause communication overload. When such overload occurs, employees react by using one or more strategies including omission, error, queuing, escape, use of a gatekeeper, and use of multiple channels.

- Another communication problem area involves the message received versus the message interpreted. Problems in this area can be reduced by using more effective listening skills, understanding the six styles of listening (leisure, inclusive, stylistic, technical, empathic, and nonconforming), and considering the emotional state, cognitive ability, and personal biases of the sender and receiver.

- Written communication can be improved by learning better writing skills and by writing organizational documents at a reading level that matches the reading level of most employees.

Critical Thinking Questions

1. Why do people hate to communicate bad news?
2. When is e-mail an inappropriate method of communication?
3. What is the best way to stop a rumor?
4. Which is most important: nonverbal cues, paralanguage, or the actual words chosen to communicate?
5. Can people be taught to be effective listeners?

WEB SITES

For further information, log on to the following web sites.
www.presentations.com/deliver
Advice about how to make public presentations.
www.innovis.com/pages/a_and_t.html
Contains articles and tips about interpersonal communication.
www.sentex.net/~mmcadams/spelling.html
If you want your ego deflated, take this online spelling test. Site also has links to other spelling sites.
www.ecglink.com
Provides tips on a variety of communication areas.

KEY TERMS

Artifacts The objects people surround themselves with (e.g., clothes, jewelry, office decorations, cars) that communicate information about the person.
Assimilated A description of a message in which the information has been modified to fit the existing beliefs and knowledge of the person sending the message before it is passed on to another person.
Attitude survey A form of upward communication in which a survey is conducted to determine employee attitudes about an organization.
Attitudinal Listening Profile System A test developed by Geier and Downey that measures individual listening styles.
Bulletin board A method of downward communication in which informal or relatively unimportant written information is posted in a public place.
Channel The medium by which a communication is transmitted.
Cluster A pattern of grapevine communication in which a message is passed to a select group of people who each in turn pass the message to a few select others.
Company manual Also called a *policy manual*, a book containing formal company rules and regulations.
Complaint box A form of upward communication in which employees are asked to place their complaints in a box.

Dale-Chall Index A method of determining the readability level of written material by looking at the number of words not in a list of commonly known words.

Dead-enders Employees who receive much grapevine information but who seldom pass it on to others.

Downward communication Communication within an organization from management to employees.

Empathic listening The listening style of a person who listens for the feelings of the speaker.

Error A type of response to communication overload that involves processing all information but processing some of it incorrectly.

Escape A response to communication overload in which the employee leaves the organization to reduce the stress.

Flesch Index A method of determining the readability level of written material by analyzing average sentence length and the number of syllables per 100 words.

FOG Index A method of determining the readability level of written material by analyzing sentence length and the number of 3-syllable words.

Fry Readability Graph A method of determining the readability level of written material by analyzing sentence length and the average number of syllables per word.

Gatekeeper A person who screens potential communication for someone else and allows only the most important information to pass through.

Gossip A pattern of grapevine communication in which a message is passed to only a select group of individuals.

Grapevine An unofficial, informal communication network.

Horizontal communication Communication between employees at the same level in an organization.

Inclusive listening The listening style of a person who listens only for the main points of a communication.

Interpersonal communication Communication between two individuals.

Intimacy zone A distance zone within 18 inches of a person in which only people with a close relationship are allowed to enter.

Intranet A computer-based employee communication network used exclusively by one organization.

Isolate An employee who receives less than half of all grapevine information.

Leisure listening The listening style of a person who listens only for interesting information.

Leveled A description of a message from which unimportant information details have been removed before the message is passed from one person to another.

Liaison A person who acts as an intermediary between employees and management; or the type of employee who both sends and receives most grapevine information.

Multiple channels A strategy for coping with communication overload in which an organization reduces the amount of communication going to one person by directing some of it to another person.

MUM (minimize unpleasant messages) effect The idea that people prefer not to pass on unpleasant information with the result that important information is not always communicated.

Noise Any variable concerning or affecting the channel that interferes with the proper reception of a message.

Nonconforming listening The listening style of a person who listens only to information that is consistent with his or her way of thinking.

Ombudsperson A person who investigates employees' complaints and solves problems.

Omission A response to communication overload that involves the conscious decision not to process certain types of information.

Paralanguage Communication inferred from the tone, tempo, volume, and rate of speech.

Personal distance zone A distance zone from 18 inches to 4 feet from a person that is usually reserved for friends and acquaintances.

Probability A pattern of grapevine communication in which a message is passed randomly among all employees.

Public distance zone A distance zone greater than 12 feet from a person that is typical of the interpersonal space allowed for social interactions such as large group lectures.

Queuing A method of coping with communication overload that involves organizing work into the order in which it will be handled.

Rumor Poorly substantiated information that is passed along the grapevine.

Serial communication Communication passed consecutively from one person to another.

Sharpened A description of a message in which interesting and unusual information has been kept in the message when it is passed from one person to another.

Single strand A pattern of grapevine communication in which a message is passed in a chainlike fashion from one person to the next person until the chain is broken.

Social distance zone An interpersonal distance zone from 4 to 12 feet from a person that is typically used for business and for interacting with strangers.

Stylistic listening The listening style of a person who listens to the way in which words are spoken.

Suggestion box A form of upward communication in which employees are asked to place their suggestions in a box.

Technical listening The listening style of a person who listens for facts and details.

Union steward An employee who serves as a liaison between unionized employees and management.

Upward communication Communication within an organization from employees up to management.

PRACTICE EXAM

1. A person thinking about what she wants to say is an example of:
   a. transmission
   b. channel
   c. encoding
   d. decoding

2. Listening most involves the _____ aspect of a message.
   a. transmission
   b. channel
   c. encoding
   d. decoding

3. A variable surrounding a communication channel that interferes with the proper reception of the message is called:
   a. noise
   b. interference
   c. horizontal decay
   d. the MUM effect

4. The grapevine is an example of _____ communication.
   a. upward
   b. downward
   c. interpersonal
   d. horizontal

5. Communication from a union steward to management would be an example of _____ communication.
   a. upward
   b. downward
   c. interpersonal
   d. horizontal

6. When information in a message is _____, unimportant details are removed.
   a. leveled
   b. sharpened
   c. assimilated
   d. accommodated

7. The idea that most people don't like to give bad news is called the:
   a. sharpening effect
   b. MUM effect
   c. ROSE effect
   d. Fiedler effect

8. The grapevine pattern similar to the game of "telephone" is:
   a. gossip
   b. cluster
   c. single strand
   d. probability

9. _____ are people who receive grapevine information but do not pass it along to others.
   a. Dead-enders
   b. Isolates
   c. Stewards
   d. Liaisons

10. The difference between grapevine information and rumor is:
    a. speed
    b. accuracy
    c. cost
    d. all of the above

11. A method of handling communication overload in which the employee places work into a "waiting line" is called:
    a. error
    b. queuing
    c. using a gatekeeper
    d. omission

12. Managers spend about _____% of the time listening but immediately forget _____% of the material they hear.
    a. 45, 90
    b. 90, 90
    c. 90, 50
    d. 45, 50

13. The _____ listener listens mostly for the main points behind what it being said.
    a. leisure
    b. inclusive
    c. stylistic
    d. technical

14. The following are tips for effective listenings except:
    a. stop talking
    b. don't empathize with the speaker
    c. don't be overly critical
    d. ask questions

15. Which of the following is the best cue for the detection of deception?
    a. facial expression
    b. voice cues
    c. posture
    d. all of the above are equally accurate

16. Which of the following is true about the use of space? Dominant people:
    a. give more space
    b. are given less space
    c. take more and are given more space
    d. give less space but take more space

17. The _____ interpersonal distance zone ranges from 18 inches to 4 feet.
    a. public
    b. social
    c. intimacy
    d. personal

18. _____ are (is) the element(s) of nonverbal communication that involve(s) the objects that people surround themselves with.
    a. Parafacts
    b. Space
    c. Paralanguage
    d. Artifacts

19. The FOG and Dale-Chall are:
    a. methods for determining readability
    b. theories of office artifacts
    c. related to listening effectiveness
    d. measures of speech effectiveness

20. An easily read document:
    a. uses longer sentences to make it more interesting
    b. uses unusual words to improve the odds of being remembered
    c. uses simple words so that they can be understood
    d. all of the above contribute to an easily read document

ANSWERS 1 c, 2 d, 3 a, 4 d, 5 a, 6 a, 7 b, 8 c, 9 a, 10 b, 11 b, 12 d, 13 b, 14 b, 15 b, 16 d, 17 d, 18 d, 19 a, 20 c

Focused Free-Write

To get you thinking about how the material in this chapter relates to your own life, think of a situation in which you and another person did not communicate effectively. Describe what happened, and then indicate why you think the miscommunication took place.

_____

_____

_____

_____

_____

_____

_____

_____

_____

_____

_____

_____

_____

_____

_____

_____

_____

_____

_____

_____

_____

_____

PROJECT A

The MUM Effect

Describe a recent occasion in which you had bad news to give someone and did everything you could to avoid or delay giving them that news.

_____

_____

_____

_____

_____

_____

_____

_____

_____

_____

_____

_____

_____

_____

_____

_____

_____

_____

_____

_____

_____

_____

Voice Mail Problems

Think of the last time you got really annoyed with an automated voice mail system. What was so bad about it?

_____

_____

_____

_____

_____

_____

_____

_____

_____

_____

_____

_____

_____

_____

_____

_____

_____

_____

_____

_____

_____

_____

Communication Problem Area 1

Think of the last time you "spoke without thinking." What happened? What could you have done to make the situation better?

_____

_____

_____

_____

_____

_____

_____

_____

_____

_____

_____

_____

_____

_____

_____

_____

_____

_____

_____

_____

_____

_____

Gender Differences in Communication

What gender-consistent communication does your spouse, partner, or good friend use? What about yourself?

_____

_____

_____

_____

_____

_____

_____

_____

_____

_____

_____

_____

_____

_____

_____

_____

_____

_____

_____

_____

_____

_____

_____

PROJECT E

Nonverbal Communication

Much of what is communicated is communicated nonverbally through cues such as body language, use of space, use of time, paralanguage, and artifacts. The purpose of this exercise is to provide you with the opportunity to study the extent to which nonverbal cues, paralanguage, and artifacts exist in normal conversation.

Instructions Outside of class, go somewhere where people talk. It might be the cafeteria, the library, or a restaurant. Quietly observe the people who are talking, and record your observations on this form. Write down what you saw as well as the impression that you got from each of the cues.

Observation Record
Body Language

Eye Contact

_____

_____

_____

_____

Arms

_____

_____

_____

_____

Legs

_____

_____

_____

_____

Body Angles

_____

_____

_____

_____

Touching

_____

_____

_____

_____

Use of Space

(How far apart were the people?)

_____

_____

_____

_____

Paralanguage

Tempo of Speech

_____

_____

_____

_____

Volume of Speech

_____

_____

_____

Nonverbal Communication, continued

Number of Pauses

_____

_____

_____

_____

Artifacts
(How was each person dressed? What impression did this style of dress leave?)

Overall Observation

_____

_____

_____

_____

_____

_____

_____

_____

_____

_____

_____

_____

_____

_____

_____

_____

_____

Communication Overload

When employees are overloaded with communication or work, they react in a variety of ways such as error, omission, and escape. Some of these reactions are positive, whereas others are not. The purpose of this exercise is to provide you with the opportunity to examine how you react when overloaded.

Instructions Think of the last time you were highly stressed because you had many things to do but not enough time to get them done.

1. How did you react?
2. Which of the strategies discussed in your text did you use?
3. After reading Chapter 7, what would you do differently?

_____

_____

_____

_____

_____

_____

_____

_____

_____

_____

_____

_____

_____

_____

_____

_____

_____

_____

_____

Listening Styles

The text described six listening styles: leisure, inclusive, stylistic, technical, empathic, and nonconforming. To get an idea of your own style, look at the Employee Personality Inventory you took back in Chapter 1. Your scores on the five personality scales will give you a rough idea of your listening style. The EPI scales and their listening styles are as follows:

EPI Scale	Listening Style
Thinking	Inclusive
Directing	Nonconforming
Communicating	Leisure, Stylistic
Soothing	Empathic
Organizing	Technical

On the basis of your EPI scores, what type of listener are you? Do you agree?

_____

_____

_____

_____

_____

_____

_____

_____

_____

_____

_____

_____

_____

_____

_____

_____

_____

PROJECT H

Communication Case Study

Mohammed Shabib was frustrated with his inability to communicate with his female coworkers. He did everything he could to be nice, but they never seemed to like or understand him. For example, 2 weeks ago, when Mohammed arrived at work, he greeted everyone with a friendly "Hello, girls" and all he got in return were icy stares. The previous week, he told his coworkers that he would meet them for lunch around noon, and when he got back to the office at 12:15, they had already left for O'Reilly's Deli without him. Both events were bad enough, but yesterday was the final straw. Mohammed found that someone had taken down his "Baywatch Girls" poster—something he had bought to better fit into the American culture.

Is there a problem with Mohammed, or is there something wrong with his communication style? What does he need to change?

_____

_____

_____

_____

_____

_____

_____

_____

_____

_____

_____

_____

_____

_____

_____

_____

_____

Understanding Group Interaction

With few exceptions, most employee behavior takes place in groups. Firefighters work together when fighting a fire, managers make decisions in committee meetings, and bank tellers work together to deal with customers. Because employees tend to work in groups, it is important for a manager or a leader to understand group dynamics. This understanding is especially important in light of the increased use of teams by organizations (Filipczak, 1994). By the end of this chapter you will:

Understand what constitutes a group

Learn why people join groups

Know how to increase group performance

Be able to decide when groups perform better than individuals

■ DEFINITION OF A GROUP

The first place to begin our discussion of group behavior is defining what constitutes a group. For a collection of people to be called a group, the following four criteria must be met (J. R. Gordon, 1983): (1) The members of the group must see themselves as a unit; (2) the group must provide rewards to its members; (3) anything that happens to one member of the group affects every other member; and (4) the members of the group must share a common goal.

Multiple Members

Implicit in the first criterion is that the group must have multiple members. Obviously, one person does not constitute a group (even if he is a multiple personality). Therefore, at least two people are necessary to form a group. Usually we refer to 2 people as a dyad, 3 people as a triad, and 4 to 20 people as a small group (Forsyth, 1999). To be considered a group, these two or more people must also see themselves as a unit. Thus, three individuals walking down the sidewalk would be considered a group only if they knew one another and were together. Eight separate customers shopping at a store would also not be considered a group.

Group Rewards

The second group criterion is that membership must be rewarding for each individual in the group. We will discuss shortly the reasons people join groups, but for now it is important to remember that people will join or form a group only if it provides some form of reward.

To demonstrate this point, imagine four students studying for an exam. If the four study in separate places and do not share information, they are not a group. But take the same four people and put them at one desk in the library. If each person studies the book separately and never communicates with the other three, then the four are still not a group because none of the individuals is rewarded by the others. But if none of the four would have otherwise studied independently, then the four students would be considered a group because being together was rewarding. Even though they did not talk with one another during their time in the library, being together provided the structure for each of them to study.

> *Focused Free-Write*
> To get you thinking about the relevance of group dynamics, complete the Focused Free-Write found at the end of this chapter.

Corresponding Effects

The third group criterion is that an event that affects one group member affects all group members. That is, if something significant happens to one person and does not affect any of the other people gathered with him, then the collection of people cannot be considered a group. This requirement is called **corresponding effects**. For example, five bank tellers work side by side; one teller becomes ill and goes home. If the activities of the other four change as a result of the one teller leaving, the five might be considered a group. But if the activities of the four do not change after the one teller leaves, then the tellers cannot be considered a group.

Common Goals

The fourth and final criterion is that all members must have a **common goal**. In the teller example, if the goal of one of the tellers is to meet only young, single customers, while the goal of another teller is to serve as many customers as possible, the tellers are not considered to be a group because they work in different ways and for different reasons.

Why do we care if a collection of people meets the technical definition of a group? The answer lies within your ability to change employee performance. Over the course of this chapter, you will learn many factors affecting group performance. If you apply what you learn, you will be effective in changing performance only if the collection of individuals is actually a *group*.

REASONS FOR JOINING GROUPS

Affiliation

Affiliation involves our need to be with other people. Thus, one reason that people join groups is to be near and talk to other people. Research has demonstrated that our need for affiliation is very strong. Mayo (1946), for example, found that employees at a textile plant who worked separately from other employees were not as satisfied with their jobs as were employees at the same plant who had the opportunity to work with others. Likewise, Burling, Lentz, and Wilson (1956) found that turnover in a hospital could be reduced by assigning maids who had worked alone to work in teams.

Perhaps the most interesting demonstrations of the strength of the human affiliation need come from the writings of Schein (1956) and Naughton (1975). These researchers were interested in the reasons American prisoners of war (POWs) in World War II behaved so differently from those in the Korean and Vietnam conflicts. POWs in World War II made more escape attempts, suffered fewer deaths, and provided information less frequently to the enemy than did their counterparts in Korea and Vietnam.

Although the American public attributed the differences to a postwar decline in the American character (Hampton, Summer, & Webber, 1978), both Schein and Naughton pointed out the differences from the perspective of group dynamics. In World War II, the POWs were kept in groups that remained together for long periods of time. Thus, these men were able to receive emotional support from one another, they could work together to plan escapes, they were able to hear what each POW said to the enemy, and they knew about and supported a strong group norm about not talking to the enemy.

In the two Asian conflicts, the situations were entirely different. Rather than living in groups, these POWs were isolated and not allowed to communicate with one another. Naughton (1975) reports that the men were so in need of contact and communication with others that they scraped their cell walls to make noise and establish contact and informal communication with one another. This behavior is similar to that reported by hostages held in Beirut and Syria.

If people are not allowed the opportunity for affiliation, they make attempts to secure at least minimal contact. When even minimal contact is not possible, morale and perhaps even the will to live are lessened. Such is the concern about the new supermaximum prisons being built for inmates who behave violently while incarcerated. In these new prisons, inmates will spend 23 hours each day alone in un-airconditioned concrete stalls. There will be no books, magazines, or television and only minimal contact with guards (K. Johnson, 1997). During the remaining hour each day, inmates will be placed alone in an 18-foot by 20-foot cage where they can pace or toss a basketball at an iron hoop. As you might imagine, prisoners' rights advocates are concerned about the long-term effects of such isolation.

Of course, people are not equal in their desire or need to affiliate with others (Ray & Hall, 1995). For example, computer programmers have lower needs and desires to affiliate than people in many other occupations (Shneiderman, 1980). This point is especially interesting because a trend in the computer-programming industry is to place programmers and analysts into groups to debug programs and solve problems (Shneiderman, 1980). Although research is not yet available on the effects of such grouping, putting such strong individualists into groups does not sound like a promising idea. However, people with a high need for affiliation perform better in groups than alone (J. D. Klein & Pridemore, 1992).

Identification

Another reason we join groups is our desire for **identification** with some group or cause. There are many examples of this need to identify with others. In the 1960s and 1970s, young men wore their hair long; although some thought it attractive and comfortable, many others grew long hair because it helped them identify with other males of their generation and separated them from adult males of previous generations. Many of us still know someone who wears his hair long and refers to the 1960s and 1970s, thus identifying himself with an earlier period. In the 1980s and 1990s, punk and grunge styles of hair and clothes were worn by students in much the same way that long hair and tie-dyed shirts were worn by people in the 1960s. But in each case, the purpose may have been separating themselves from a more conservative majority and identifying with a more liberal or radical group.

Around your school you may notice many students wearing T-shirts with logos or messages. Students wearing *Backstreet Boys*, *Los Angeles Dodgers*, or *Sail Florida* shirts are all identifying with particular groups and thus making statements about themselves.

A study by Cialdini and his associates (Cialdini, Borden, Thorne, Walker, Freeman, & Sloane, 1976) investigated clothing as a means of identification. At several universities, Cialdini et al. observed the number of students who wore school-related clothing such as T-shirts and sweatshirts on the Monday following a school football game. They found that following a football victory, many more students wore school-related clothing than on Mondays following football losses. In a second study, Cialdini et al. also asked students who won the football game. As we might expect, when the football team won, the students answered by saying, "We won." When the team lost, the students answered by saying, "They lost." On the basis of these two studies, Cialdini called this identification process "basking in reflected glory."

Another example of the identification process comes from a major manufacturing plant in Virginia. Several months before union contract talks began, the company gave each employee several nice shirts with the company name printed on the front. The company did this because it had previously noticed that in the months before contract negotiations began, the employees began to wear more union caps and shirts. The company believed that this clothing helped increase the employees' level of identification with the union. To counter this effect, the company hoped that its shirts would influence the negotiation process. Although we cannot determine the exact effect of this strategy, that year was the only one in a decade in which union members did not strike.

Assistance

People often join groups to obtain assistance or help. For example, students having problems with an algebra class might form a study group, people wanting to lose weight might join Weight Watchers, and the elderly might live in a group retirement home.

Emotional Support

We also join groups to obtain emotional support. Alcoholics Anonymous, Gamblers Anonymous, and divorce support groups are good examples of groups that provide emotional support for their members.

Common Interests

People often join groups because they share a common interest. At school, students joining a geology club share an interest in geology, students joining a fraternity share an interest in socializing, and students joining a service club such as Circle K or Alpha Phi Omega share an interest in helping people.

It is an interesting side note that most campus clubs that are based on common academic interests, such as a psychology club or a Latin club, are usually smaller and less active than other campus groups. Apparently, college students have many needs, and common academic interests are usually not as strong as the social needs that are satisfied by the Greek organizations. For example, a service club on the Radford University campus was having diffi-

culty attracting members, so several advisors suggested that it increase its number of social activities to attract people who had both community service and social needs. This slight change in activities increased membership from 15 to 45.

Common Goals

People who join political parties are examples of people in pursuit of a common goal. These people may also share common interests, but their primary purpose is to get a particular person or members of a particular party elected to office.

Physical Proximity

One especially strong reason that a person might join a particular group, especially if the group is informal, is physical proximity (Forsyth, 1999). That is, people tend to form groups with people who either live or work nearby. For example, think of the softball teams in your town. Most teams consist of people who work or go to church together. At work, employees tend to form groups that consist of those who work in the same general area. And as we will discuss in greater detail in a later chapter, some employees seek close physical proximity to people in power, hoping they will become part of an elite group.

Assignment

In the workplace, employees are often assigned to groups rather than joining them voluntarily. For example, a new employee might be assigned to a department with five other employees, all of whom are asked to work together as a team. Other examples might include employees assigned to committees or quality improvement teams.

PROJECT A *Increasing Group Membership*
Complete Project A at the end of this chapter to help you apply the material you just learned on why people join groups.

■ FACTORS AFFECTING GROUP PERFORMANCE

Group Cohesiveness

Group cohesiveness is the extent to which group members like and trust one another. In general, the more cohesive the group, the greater its productivity (Mullen & Copper, 1994; Reizenstein & Burke, 1996), decision quality (Mullen, Anthony, Salas, & Driskell, 1994), and member satisfaction (Brawley, Carron, & Widmeyer, 1993; Deluga & Winters, 1991). This is especially true when group members agree with the goals of their group (Podsakoff, MacKenzie, & Ahearne, 1997). Research has demonstrated that cohesive work groups have better safety records (Geller, Roberts, & Gilmore, 1996), lower turnover and absenteeism (Spink & Carron, 1992), and higher job satisfaction (Zander, 1982). Furthermore, cohesive sports teams tend to win more games than do less cohesive teams (Matheson, Mathes, & Murray, 1997).

In its 1989 strike against Pittston Coal Co., the United Mine Workers union realized the importance of cohesiveness and identification needs by adopting a unique strategy. Each union member as well as family members and supportive friends wore camouflage shirts and fatigues as a sign of unity. Every time miners looked around, they saw others dressed alike. The union members thus developed a sense of unity and cohesiveness that helped them last through a lengthy strike. Groups such as the Boy Scouts and the Guardian Angels also wear uniforms to increase group cohesiveness.

But cohesiveness can also lower group performance, especially in a work setting. When employees become too cohesive, they often lose sight of organizational goals. For example, restaurant employees often put the needs of other employees above those of their customers. Similarly, police departments tend to be highly cohesive—so much so that anyone who is not a police officer is considered an outsider, which can make community relations difficult.

Although the majority of research supports the conclusion that cohesiveness results in better group performance, it is not always necessary to have cohesion to have high group performance. For example, the Oakland A's in the early 1970s and the New York Yankees in the mid-1970s were baseball teams that won championships despite constant fighting among the players.

Research has also demonstrated that employees in cohesive work groups will conform to a norm of lower production even though they are capable of higher performance (Forsyth, 1999). An excellent example of this conformity to a group norm involved the Hollywood Division of the Los Angeles Police Department in the early 1980s. Many of the division's officers and detectives were extensively involved in property crimes. They broke into various retail stores and radioed that they were responding to ringing burglar alarms. They then placed the stolen goods in their car trunks and proceeded as if they were investigating the break-ins. The officers later met at specific locations to hide and sell the stolen goods. Officers who did not participate in the crimes saw the merchandise and knew what was going on, but they did not report the offenders. Instead, they put their loyalty to their fellow officers above their loyalty to the city or the police department.

GROUP HOMOGENEITY

The homogeneity of a group is the extent to which its members are similar. A **homogeneous group** contains members who are similar in some or most ways, whereas a **heterogeneous group** contains members who are more different than alike. An important question for a leader to consider when developing a group is which composition, homogeneous or heterogeneous, will lead to the best group performance. Many research studies have sought to answer this question, but only mixed results have been found, with some studies finding homogeneous groups most effective and others finding heterogeneous groups most effective. For example, Hoffman (1959) found groups with homogeneous personalities to be superior in a laboratory task, whereas Aamodt and Kimbrough (1982) found groups with heterogeneous personalities to be superior for solving a laboratory problem. Likewise, Klein and Christiansen (1969) found heterogeneous basketball teams to be best, whereas Vander Velden (1971) found that homogeneous basketball teams performed better than heterogeneous teams.

Neufeldt, Kimbrough, and Stadelmaier (1983) sought to explain these mixed results by predicting that certain types of groups would do better with certain types of tasks. Neufeldt and his colleagues thus had homogeneous and heterogeneous groups each perform several different tasks. Though they expected the homogeneous groups to perform better on simple tasks and the heterogeneous groups to perform better on more complex tasks, Neufeldt et al. instead found that the type of task did not moderate the relationship between group composition and performance.

Aamodt, Alexander, and Kimbrough (1983) then hypothesized that previous research yielded mixed results because the compositions of the best-performing groups were actually somewhere between completely homogeneous and completely heterogeneous. These authors thus labeled them **slightly heterogeneous groups**.

To test their hypothesis, Aamodt and his colleagues separated 202 NCAA Division I basketball teams into three categories based on the racial composition of the starting five players. Heterogeneous groups were teams with three Whites and two Blacks or three Blacks and two Whites (3-2), homogeneous groups had five Blacks or five Whites (5-0), and slightly heterogeneous groups had either four Blacks and one White or four Whites and one Black (4-1). The study results supported the notion that slightly heterogeneous groups were superior—they won 60%

of their games. Both heterogeneous and homogeneous teams won about 53% of their games (all winning percentages are above 50% because Division I teams played and usually beat many non-Division I teams).

These results were later supported by a study that divided contestants on the television game show *Family Feud* into the same three groups as described above but with gender rather than race as the variable. The results indicated that the slightly heterogeneous teams won more money than the other two group types. The slightly heterogeneous families won an average of $330, heterogeneous families an average of $278, and homogeneous families an average of $254. A meta-analysis by Aamodt, Freeman, and Carneal (1992) found support for the superiority of slightly heterogeneous groups.

Thus this research appears to support the conclusion that the best working groups consist primarily of people who are similar but with a dissimilar person adding tension and a different vantage point. But it is not yet clear which variable is most important in terms of determining group composition. That is, variables in previous research have included race, gender, personality, intelligence, attitudes, and background. Thus, a group might be homogeneous in terms of race but heterogeneous in gender. More research is needed to clarify this issue. Though it appears that slightly heterogeneous groups result in the highest levels of performance, research indicates that homogeneous groups result in the greatest member satisfaction and lowest amount of turnover (Aamodt, Freeman, & Carneal, 1992; Jackson, Brett, Sessa, Cooper, Julin, & Peyronnin, 1991; Nolan, Lee, & Allen, 1997).

Though group performance is best in slightly heterogeneous groups, the group member who is "different" (e.g., the only female, the only African American) may not have the same level of satisfaction as the rest of the group members.

STABILITY OF MEMBERSHIP

The greater the **stability** of the group, the greater the cohesiveness. Thus, groups whose members remain in the group for long periods of time are more cohesive and perform better than groups that have high turnover. A good example again can be found on a college campus. At most colleges, fraternities and sororities usually are the most active organizations and have high levels of performance, while professional clubs and honorary societies such as Psi Chi and Lambda Alpha Beta tend to be the least active. Why is this? Certainly, it cannot be the abilities of the memberships—honorary societies have more intelligent members than most fraternities and sororities. Instead, the answer might be in the stabilities of the groups. Students tend to join Greek organizations in their freshman or sophomore years, while students tend to join

professional clubs in their junior year and honorary societies in their senior year, often only for their resume value. The Greek organizations thus have more stable memberships than the other organizations.

ISOLATION

Physical **isolation** is another variable that tends to increase a group's cohesiveness. Groups that are isolated or located away from other groups tend to be highly cohesive. A good example is the New River Valley branch of the AT&T Credit Union. The credit union has 15 branches, most located within a few miles of one another and within a few miles of the main branch in Winston-Salem, North Carolina. The New River Valley branch is 100 miles from the next closest branch; physically and psychologically, the branch is isolated from the main part of the organization. The New River Valley branch, however, is the only one to have no turnover in 5 years and is also the branch where the employees are most cohesive.

OUTSIDE PRESSURE

Groups who are pressured by outside forces also tend to become highly cohesive. To some degree, this response to **outside pressure** can be explained by the phenomenon of *psychological reactance* (J. W. Brehm, 1966). When we believe that someone is trying to intentionally influence us to take some particular action, we often react and do the opposite. Consider, for example, a teenaged dating couple. As the boy arrives to pick up his date, the girl's father notices the young man's beard and Harley-Davidson motorcycle and forbids his daughter to go out. Before this order, the daughter may not have been especially interested in the boy, but after being told she cannot go on the date, she reacts by liking the boy more.

An interesting example of psychological reactance comes from a study by Ruback and Juieng (1997), who observed drivers leaving their parking spots at a local mall. There were four conditions in the study. In the control condition, the researchers timed how long it took from the moment the driver opened his door to the moment he completely left the parking space when no other cars were present. In the distraction condition, they noted how much time was taken when a car drove past the parking space. In the low-intrusion condition, an experimenter pulled up next to the parking spot, indicating that he was waiting for the spot. In the high-intrusion condition, the waiting driver honked his horn. Consistent with psychological reactance, when a driver honked, it took 42.75 seconds for the parked driver to leave versus 26.47 seconds when there was no driver waiting for the spot (control) and 31.09 seconds when a car drove by (distraction).

EXHIBIT 8-1

Examples of Task Types

Task Type	Group Activity
Additive	Typing pool
	Relay race
	Bowling team
	Car washing
Disjunctive	Problem solving
	Brainstorming
	Golf tournament
Conjunctive	Assembly line
	Hiking

On a larger scale, such reactions are commonly seen in labor negotiations. Company managements and unions tend to disagree with and criticize one another. But often such criticism backfires: Attacking another group may serve to strengthen that group. In fact, if a company or group wants to increase the cohesiveness of its membership, it can artificially create pressure and attribute it to another group. This tactic involves building a *straw man*—an opponent who does not actually exist but to whom negative statements about the group can be charged.

GROUP SIZE

Groups are most cohesive and perform best when **group size** is small. Studies have shown that large groups have less coordination and lower morale (Frank & Anderson, 1971), share less information (Cruz, Boster, & Rodriguez, 1997), are less cohesive (Carron, 1990), and are more critical (Valacich, Dennis, & Nunamaker, 1992) than smaller groups. In fact, research suggests that groups perform best (Manners, 1975) and have greatest member satisfaction (R. Hackman & Vidmar, 1970) when they consist of approximately five members. Thus, a large organization probably works best when it is divided into smaller groups and committees and where work groups are limited to approximately five people.

This does not mean, however, that small groups are always best. Although small groups usually increase cohesiveness, high performance is only seen with certain types of tasks. **Additive tasks** are those for which the group's performance is equal to the sum of the performances by each group member. **Conjunctive tasks** are tasks for which the group's performance depends on the least effective group member (a chain is only as strong as its weakest link). **Disjunctive tasks** are those on which the group's performance is based on the most talented group member. Examples of the three task types are shown in Exhibit 8-1. Large groups are thought to perform best on disjunctive and additive tasks (Littlepage, 1991), whereas small groups perform best on conjunctive tasks (Frank & Anderson, 1971; Steiner, 1972).

The addition of more members has its greatest effect when a group is small. This idea was first investigated by Latane (1981) when he formulated **social impact theory**. Imagine a four-person committee studying safety problems at work. If the group is stable and cohesive, adding a fifth person may be disruptive. But in a factory of 3000 employees, the hiring of one new employee is not likely to change the complexion of the company. That is why sport experts have observed that a single great player can turn around a poor basketball team—as occurred with Bill Walton and the Portland Trailblazers, Kareem Abdul-Jabbar and the Milwaukee Bucks, and Shaquille O'Neal with the Orlando Magic—but not a football or baseball team.

More recent research indicates that groups working through a computer behave differently than groups working face to face. When computers are used, large groups appear to perform best and have the most satisfied members (Dennis, Valacich, & Nunamaker, 1990; Valachich, Dennis, & Connolly, 1994; Valacich, Dennis, & Nunamaker, 1992). Interestingly, when groups work via a computer, minority members are more likely to express opinions. However, these same minority members are more persuasive when the group meets face to face (McLeod, Baron, Marti, & Yoon, 1997). These findings are especially important in light of the increase in distance learning programs and computer conferencing.

EXHIBIT 8-2

Possible Communication Networks for Small Groups

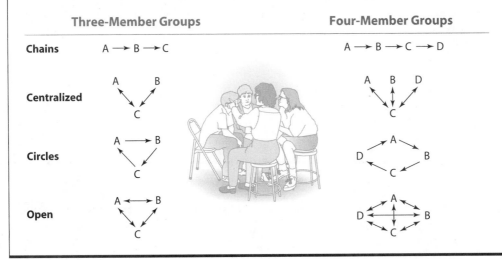

	Three-Member Groups	Four-Member Groups
Chains	A → B → C	A → B → C → D
Centralized	(A, B → C)	(A, B, D → C)
Circles	(A → B → C → A)	(A → B → C → D → A)
Open	(A ↔ B ↔ C ↔ A)	(A ↔ B ↔ C ↔ D ↔ A)

GROUP STATUS

The higher the group's status, the greater its cohesiveness. This is an important point: A group can be made more cohesive by increasing **group status**. The group does not actually have to *have* high status, but it is important that its members *believe* they have high status.

Again, look around town and notice the methods used by various groups to artificially increase their status. In our town, one civic group advertises itself as the "club of choice," while another claims to be the "club of distinction." Of course, there is little difference between the actual status and performance of most organizations, so effective leaders try to increase the cohesiveness of group members by claiming high status—and it apparently works.

One way that leaders can increase their group's status is by increasing the perception that the group is difficult to join but that, once in, members will find that the group's activities are special. In most high schools, "two-a-day" practices are typical during the week before football practice begins. During this period, each prospective team member is worked close to exhaustion. Coaches have such "hell weeks" to increase the team's status and thus its cohesion and performance. Obviously, a player cannot get into shape in a week, so the purpose of two-a-day practices is not conditioning—it is to build the status of the group members who survive the week. A similar approach is taken by the Marine Corps. By its tough basic training, the corps builds the status of its enlistees so that

Marines and non-Marines alike will believe that the corps consists of just a "few good men."

Fraternities and sororities are also notorious for hazing during their pledge weeks. Aside from the illegality and cruelty of this behavior, hazing serves the purpose of increasing the effort required for a potential member to join, thus increasing the group's cohesiveness and status. Football players, Marines, and fraternity or sorority members are not likely to quit a group that they have worked so hard to join.

Communication Structure

Another variable that affects a group's performance is its **communication structure** or network. For a group to perform successfully, good communication among members is essential. As shown in Exhibit 8-2, a variety of communication networks can be used by small groups alone; even more complex networks are possible with larger groups. Each network has its advantages and disadvantages, but the best networks depend on the situations and goals of their groups. For example, if the goal of a singles club is to allow the members to get to know one another, then a centralized structure is less conducive than a completely open one. Conversely, if the goal of a group is to solve a problem as quickly as possible, then the centralized network will be the best structure. A good leader thus carefully chooses the communication network that best facilitates the goals of his group.

Group Roles

Another factor that affects the performance of a group is the extent to which its members assume different roles. For a group to be successful, its members' roles must fall into one of three categories: task oriented, maintenance oriented, and individual (Benne & Sheets, 1948). Task-oriented roles involve behaviors such as offering new ideas, coordinating activities, and finding new information; maintenance-oriented roles involve encouraging cohesiveness and participation; and individual roles include blocking group activities, calling attention to oneself, and avoiding group interaction. Individual roles seldom result in higher group productivity.

Group members often naturally assume these roles on the basis of their individual personalities and experiences, although sometimes leaders must assign roles to certain individuals. For example, if a leader notices that every group member is filling a task-oriented role, he may either recruit a new group member or assign a current member to fill a maintenance role.

Presence of Others

SOCIAL FACILITATION AND INHIBITION

In 1898, researcher N. Triplett noticed that cyclists rode faster when competing against other cyclists than when competing against a clock. Intrigued by this observation, Triplett conducted a study in which children completed a task either alone or while competing against other children. As expected, Triplett found that children who worked against others completed their tasks faster than did children who worked alone.

Since that first study, psychologists have studied what we now call *social facilitation* and *social inhibition*. **Social facilitation** involves the positive effects of the presence of others on an individual's behavior; **social inhibition** involves the negative effects of others' presence (research examples are listed in Exhibit 8-3). Social facilitation and social inhibition can be further delineated by *audience effects* and *coaction*.

Audience effects The phenomenon of **audience effects** takes place when a group of people passively watches an individual. An example is a sporting event held in an arena.

The strength of the audience effect is a function of at least three factors. Latane (1981) hypothesized these factors to be audience size, its physical proximity to the person or group, and its status. Thus, groups are most likely to be affected by large audiences of experts who are physically close to the group (J. M. Jackson, 1986; Tanford & Penrod, 1984). Not surprisingly, the presence of an audience increases performance in extroverts but not introverts (Graydon & Murphy, 1995).

Coaction The effect on behavior when two or more people are performing the same task in the presence of one another is called **coaction**. Examples are two runners competing against each other without a crowd present or two mail clerks sorting envelopes in the same room. Shalley (1995) found that coaction decreased creativity and productivity. Two other studies provide interesting examples of coaction-influenced behavior. In the first study, Sommer, Wynes, and Brinkley (1992) found that when people shopped in groups, they spent more time in a store and purchased more goods than when alone. In the second study, de Castro and Brewer (1992) discovered that meals eaten in large groups are 75% larger than those eaten when alone.

Explaining social facilitation effects More than 200 studies of social facilitation have indicated that performance does not always increase in the presence of others. Performance will increase only when the task being performed is easy or well learned; performance will decrease when the task is difficult or not well learned (C. F. Bond & Titus, 1983; Zajonc, 1965). Social facilitation and coaction effects occur not only with humans but also with cockroaches running a maze (Zajonc, Heingartner, & Herman, 1969), chickens eating food (Keeling & Hurnik, 1996), and ants building nests (S. C. Chen, 1937). See Exhibit 8-3 for research examples.

Although researchers have not agreed on the exact reason for these findings, four explanations have each received some empirical support. The first explanation holds that the **mere presence** of others naturally produces arousal (Zajonc, 1980). This arousal or increase in energy helps an individual perform well-learned tasks but hinders him on poorly learned or unpracticed tasks.

The second explanation states that a coacting audience provides a means for **comparison**. If an individual is working on a task with another individual, he can directly compare his performance to the other person's (Seta, 1982). In some jobs, this comparison effect may increase competition and production quantity, while in other jobs, comparison effects may cause employees to slow down to be in line with the working norm.

The third explanation—**evaluation apprehension**—hypothesizes that judgment by others causes the differential effects of social facilitation (Cottrell, 1972). That is, individuals are aware that the presence of others can be rewarding (e.g., when a crowd cheers) or punishing (when a crowd boos). On well-learned tasks, the individual knows that he normally per-

EXHIBIT 8-3

Tasks Affected by Social Facilitation and Social Inhibition

Skill Level	Facilitation: Increased Performance	Inhibition: Decreased Performance
Well learned	Bicycle racing Pool shooting Simple mathematics Ant nest building Cockroaches running	
Novice		Pool shooting Learning nonsense syllables Completing a maze Complex mathematics Cockroaches running

forms well and thus expects a rewarding experience when in the presence of others. When the task is not well learned, however, the individual may believe that he will not perform well and will be embarrassed; thus he performs even worse than if he were alone.

One example of this phenomenon was seen in an experiment by Michaels, Blommel, Brocato, Linkous, and Rowe (1982). Michaels and his colleagues observed students shooting pool and found that good players increased their shot accuracy from 71% to 80% when watched by an audience, while poor players' accuracy decreased from 36% to 25% when they were watched. In another study, Thombs, Beck, and Mahoney (1993) found that high-intensity drinkers were more likely than low-intensity drinkers to drink in social situations.

The evaluation-apprehension explanation has special application to industry and training settings. Imagine a waiter who must carry five plates of food to a table. For a new waiter, this is not a well-learned task, and in the presence of others he is likely to be anxious. When the lack of practice in carrying plates is combined with a large restaurant crowd, the chance of an accident increases. So what is the solution? The waiter should practice carrying several plates before the restaurant opens.

Evaluation apprehension also occurs when performance is being monitored electronically rather than in person (Aiello & Svec, 1993). Thus, supervisors who remotely monitor employee performance over a computer must be aware of the potential effects on performance.

The fourth explanation proposes that the presence of others is **distracting** to the individual who is trying to perform a task (Sanders, 1981). On well-learned tasks, the individual is able to perform despite the distraction because the behaviors are almost automatic. On a novel or complicated task, however, the distraction caused by other people's presence keeps the individual from concentrating and learning the task. For example, Baxter, Manstead, Stradling, and Campbell (1990) found that drivers with passengers were less likely to signal than were drivers without anyone else in the car.

An example that demonstrates the effects emphasized by both the evaluation-apprehension and distraction theories is that of coaching children in sports. In a typical Little League practice, one coach must teach an 8-year-old how to bat while 10 other children stand in the field and wait for a ball to be hit to them. Each time the child at the plate fails to hit the ball, the others tease him. After a while, the children in the field are bored and begin to throw rocks and talk with one another. What is the probability of success in teaching this child to hit under these circumstances? For the coach to be successful, he must teach the child alone and away from other children.

Social facilitation effects also have been examined in the sports world by investigating the advantage that a team might have by playing its game at home. In general, having a home crowd behind a team increases the probability of its winning, especially for indoor sports (Courneya & Carron, 1992). The effect increases immediately after a crowd cheers a play or boos a referee's decision (Greer, 1983).

SOCIAL LOAFING

Whereas the social facilitation and social inhibition theory explains increases and decreases in performance when others are present and either watching the individual or working with them, the **social loafing** theory considers the effect on individual performance when people work together on a task. Social loafing was first investigated in a study by Ringleman (reported in Moede, 1927), whose subjects singly pulled as hard as possible on a rope while he measured their exerted force. Ringleman then had his subjects perform the task in pairs. He expected the force exerted by two subjects to be approximately twice that exerted by a single subject, but to his surprise he found that both subjects exerted less force than when they worked alone.

More recent research has supported the theory and has found that social loafing occurs with many tasks. For example, one study found that restaurant customers tipped about 19% of the bill when they dined alone, 16% of the bill when they dined with another person, and 13% when they dined with five others (Latane, 1981). This explains why tips, or gratuities, often are automatically added to a bill when six or more people dine at a table.

Although it is clear that social loafing occurs, especially in poor performers (Hardy & Crace, 1991), it is not clear *why* it occurs. One theory is that because group members realize their individual efforts will not be noticed, there is little chance of individual reward. A second theory, called the *free-rider theory* (Kerr & Bruun, 1983), postulates that when things are going well, a group member realizes that his effort is not necessary and thus does not work as hard as he would if he were alone. If this explanation is true, social loafing should occur only when a group project is going well.

The third theory, called the *sucker-effect theory* (Kerr, 1983), hypothesizes that social loafing occurs when a group member notices that other group members are not working hard and thus are "playing him for a sucker." To avoid this situation, the individual lowers his work performance to match those of the other members. This theory, however, does not explain the loafing of other members.

Social loafing is an important variable to keep in mind: Having employees work together on a project may not be as productive as having them work individually. Fortunately, social loafing can be reduced by identifying individual performance and providing feedback to each worker on how hard he works

when rated against some goal or standard (Williams, Harkins, & Latane, 1981) and rewarding those who achieve (George, 1995; Shepperd, 1993). Punishing social loafers has unpredictable effects—sometimes it works, sometimes it doesn't (George, 1995; J. A. Miles & Greenberg, 1993).

Individual Dominance

Another variable that can affect group performance is **individual dominance** by a leader or single group member. If the leader or group member has an accurate solution to a problem the group is trying to solve, the group will probably perform at a high level. But if the leader or group member has an inaccurate solution, he will lead the group astray, and it will perform poorly. For example, a study by LePine, Hollenbeck, Ilgen, and Hedlund (1997) found that a group of highly intelligent members will perform poorly when its leader is not very intelligent. The same relationship was found for the personality variable of conscientiousness.

Groupthink

The term **groupthink** was coined by Janis (1972) after studying the disastrous Bay of Pigs invasion of 1961. The Bay of Pigs was the Cuban landing site for 1400 Cuban exiles who sought to overthrow the government of Fidel Castro. The plan called for the U.S. Navy and Air Force to covertly protect the invasion force and its supply ships. The invaders, however, were met unexpectedly by 20,000 Cuban troops and were quickly killed or captured. The help promised by the U.S. government never appeared. Janis (1972) proposed the concept of groupthink to explain how some of the nation's brightest men could hatch such an ill-conceived plan. Individually, each of the cabinet members opposed the invasion plan, but, due to groupthink, none of the cabinet members outwardly expressed his disapproval.

With groupthink, members become so cohesive and likeminded that they make poor decisions despite contrary information that might reasonably lead them to another decision. Groupthink most often occurs when the group:

- is cohesive
- is insulated from qualified outsiders
- has an illusion of invulnerability, infallibility, or both
- believes that it is morally superior to its adversaries

- is under great pressure to conform
- has a leader who promotes a favorite solution
- has gatekeepers who keep information from other group members

Groupthink can be reduced in several ways. First, the group leader should not state his own position or beliefs until late in the decision-making process. Second, the leader should promote open discussion and encourage group members to speak. Third, a group or committee can be separated into subgroups to increase the chance of disagreement. Finally, one group member can be assigned the job of **devil's advocate**—one who questions and disagrees with the group. Though groupthink is commonly written about, a comprehensive evaluation of it by Aldag and Fuller (1993) has questioned its validity as a phenomenon as well as its negative effect.

PROJECT B *Group Performance*
To apply what you have learned about the factors affecting group productivity, complete Project B located at the end of this chapter.

■ INDIVIDUAL VS. GROUP PERFORMANCE

When several people individually work on a problem but do not interact, they are called a **nominal group**. When several individuals interact to solve a problem, they are called an **interacting group**. An important decision a leader must make is when to assign tasks to individuals, nominal groups, or interacting groups. This decision should be based on both the type of task and the outcome desired. If the *quality* of the task is most important, it should be assigned to a group or committee. Research has shown that groups generally produce higher quality results than do individuals or nominal groups (Kanekar, 1987; Lorge, Fox, Davitz, & Brenner, 1958). Group superiority in performance probably is due to the fact that a group encourages its members to work on a task more seriously, provides emotional support, and provides a broader knowledge base (Maier, 1976).

If the task involves *creating* ideas, individuals should be asked to independently create ideas and then meet as a group. Although brainstorming is a commonly used technique, it is not an effective one. In brainstorming, group members are encouraged to say aloud any and all ideas that come to mind and are not allowed to comment on the ideas until all

have been given. When research compares a brainstorming group's creativity with that of a single individual, the brainstorming group will almost always be more creative. However, when comparing the number and quality of ideas created by nominal groups to the quality and number of ideas created by an interacting group in a brainstorming session, the ideas of nominal groups are more creative and of higher quality than ideas of the interacting group (Diehl & Stroebe, 1987; Gratias & Hills, 1997; Lamm & Trommsdorff, 1973). This difference may partially be due to interacting groups setting lower goals than individuals (Larey & Paulus, 1995).

The superiority of nominal groups over interacting groups may depend on the type of task. Brophy (1996) found nominal groups to be most effective with a single brainstorming problem and interacting groups to be most effective in complex problems. Similar results were reported by Davis and Harless (1996), who found that in complex problems, interacting groups take better advantage of feedback and learning and thus outperform nominal groups.

If the task involves *taking chances* or *being risky*, then the task should be assigned to an interacting group or committee. Although showing somewhat mixed results, research has generally shown that interacting groups make more decisions that require risk than do individuals or nominal groups (Clark, 1971; D. L. Johnson & Andrews, 1971). This increased riskiness is thought in part to be due to group polarization, the tendency for group members to shift their beliefs to a more extreme version of what they already believe individually (Greenberg & Baron, 1995). In a particularly interesting piece of research, Cromwell, Marks, Olson, and Avary (1991) found that burglars committed more crimes when working as part of a group than when working alone.

An example of increased group riskiness comes from a brokerage firm that was interested in getting its brokers to make riskier but higher yielding investments. A consulting firm was asked to develop a way to select such brokers. Using its knowledge of group dynamics, the consulting firm told the brokerage company that it could obtain better results by having its brokers make investment decisions in groups rather than individually. Implementing this suggestion, the company later reported that its brokers were indeed making riskier investments.

PROJECT C *Group Process Case Study*
To use the knowledge you have learned from this chapter, complete the case study in Project C.

CHAPTER RECAP

In this chapter you learned:

- Groups consist of multiple members who perceive themselves as a unit and share a common goal or goals.

- People join groups due to a need for affiliation, to identify with success, a need for assistance or emotional support, common interests, common goals, physical proximity, or assignment.

- Factors that influence a group's success include its level of cohesiveness (the composition of its membership, the stability of the membership, group size, group status), communication structure, group roles, the presence of others, individual dominance, and groupthink.

Critical Thinking Questions

1. How can you use the knowlege of why people join groups to increase group effectiveness?

2. When are interacting groups better than nominal groups or individuals?

3. Why does the presence of others cause increased performance in some situations and decreased performance in others?

4. When can a group be too cohesive?

WEB SITES

For further information, log on to the following web sites.

www.socialpsychology.org/social.htm#group
Provides links to a variety of sites with information on groups and teams.

www.teambuildersplus.com/links.htm
Contains links to sources about teams and group dynamics.

KEY TERMS

Additive task Task for which the group's performance is equal to the sum of the performances of each individual group member.

Affiliation The need to be with other people.

Audience effect The effect on behavior when people passively watch the behavior of another person.

Coaction The effect on behavior when two or more people are performing the same task in the presence of each other.

Common goal An aim or purpose shared by members of a group.

Communication barriers Physical, cultural, and psychological obstacles that interfere with successful communication and create a source of conflict.

Communication structure The manner in which members of a group communicate with one another.

Comparison The effect when an individual working on a task compares his or her performance with the performance of another person performing the same task.

Conjunctive task Task for which the group's performance is dependent on the performance of the least effective group member.

Corresponding effects An event that affects one member of a group will affect the other group members.

Devil's advocate A group member who intentionally provides an opposing opinion to that expressed by the leader or the majority of the group.

Disjunctive task Task for which the performance of a group is based on the performance of its most talented member.

Distracting effect The idea that social inhibition occurs because the presence of others provides a distraction that interferes with concentration.

Evaluation apprehension The idea that a person performing a task becomes aroused because he or she is concerned that others are evaluating his or her performance.

Group cohesiveness The extent to which members of a group like and trust one another.

Group size The number of members in a group.

Group status The esteem in which the group is held by people not in the group.

Groupthink A state of mind in which a group is so concerned about group cohesiveness that it ignores important information.

Heterogeneous group Group whose members share few similarities.

Homogeneous group Group whose members share the same characteristics.

Identification The need to associate ourselves with the image associated with other people, groups, or objects.

Individual dominance One member of a group dominating the group.

Interacting group A collection of individuals who work together to perform a task.

Isolation The degree of physical distance of a group from other groups.

Mere presence theory The theory that states that the mere presence of others naturally produces arousal and thus may affect performance.

Nominal group A collection of individuals whose results are pooled but who never interact with one another.

Outside pressure The amount of psychological pressure placed on a group by people who are not members of the group.

Slightly heterogeneous group Group in which a few group members have different characteristics from the rest of the group.

Social facilitation The positive effects that occur when a person performs a task in the presence of others.

Social impact theory A theory that the addition of a group member has the greatest effect on group behavior when the size of the group is small.

Social inhibition The negative effects that occur when a person performs a task in the presence of others.

Social loafing The theory that individuals in a group often exert less individual effort than they would if they were not in a group.

Stability The extent to which the membership of a group remains consistent over time.

PRACTICE EXAM

1. Which of the following is not a criterion for a collection of people to be called a group?
   a. multiple members   b. corresponding effects
   c. cohesiveness   d. common goals

2. A reason that people wear shirts printed with messages and logos might be their need for:
   a. affiliation   b. identification
   c. assistance   d. common goals

3. Alcoholics Anonymous is an example of a group formed because of a need for:
   a. affiliation   b. identification
   c. emotional support   d. common goals

4. "Basking in reflected glory" is a demonstration of the need for:
   a. affiliation   b. identification
   c. assistance   d. common goals

5. The extent to which group members like and trust one another refers to:
   a. cohesiveness   b. group status
   c. social impact   d. identification

6. Which of the following is the most productive group?
   a. homogeneous
   b. heterogeneous
   c. slightly heterogeneous
   d. homogeneity is not related to productivity

7. Groups are more cohesive when they are:
   a. isolated   b. under no pressure
   c. large   d. heterogeneous

8. In general, which of the following group sizes would be best?
   a. 2   b. 5
   c. 10   d. size doesn't matter

9. An assembly line would be an example of a(n) _____ task.
   a. additive   b. conjunctive
   c. disjunctive   d. exciting

10. Social impact theory states that the addition of a member to a group would have the greatest impact when the group is:
    a. small   b. large
    c. cohesive   d. additive

11. Which of the following would not result in a situation conducive to groupthink?
    a. a cohesive group
    b. a group insulated from outsiders
    c. great group pressure to conform
    d. the group as a whole is insecure

12. Compared to individuals or nominal groups, interacting groups:
    a. have higher quality solutions
    b. are more creative
    c. are less risky
    d. all of the above

13. Social facilitation is likely to occur when performing a _____ task, and social inhibition is likely to occur when performing a _____ task.
    a. well-learned, new
    b. new, well-learned
    c. well-learned, well-learned
    d. new, new

14. An employee who notices that the group is performing well might decrease her performance. This action is called _____ and can be explained by the _____ theory.
    a. social inhibition, free rider
    b. social loafing, free rider
    c. social loafing, sucker
    d. social inhibition, sucker

15. In which of the following communication structures does each group member communicate only with a leader?
    a. chain   b. centralized
    c. circle   d. open

ANSWERS 1 c, 2 b, 3 c, 4 b, 5 a, 6 c, 7 a, 8 b, 9 b, 10 a, 11 d, 12 a, 13 a, 14 b, 15 b

Focused Free-Write

To get you thinking about the relevance of group dynamics in your own life, think
of a group that you currently belong to or recently belonged to (e.g., a committee,
club, team). Describe why you joined that group and why you think the group
performed as well or as poorly as it did.

_____

_____

_____

_____

_____

_____

_____

_____

_____

_____

_____

_____

_____

_____

_____

_____

_____

_____

_____

_____

_____

_____

Increasing Group Membership

By understanding the reasons why people join groups, a leader is better able to attract members to the group. To apply what you learned, think of a group that you belong to. Why do people join this group? On the basis of the discussion in the chapter, what could you do to attract more members?

_____

_____

_____

_____

_____

_____

_____

_____

_____

_____

_____

_____

_____

_____

_____

_____

_____

_____

_____

_____

_____

_____

PROJECT B

Group Performance

By understanding the factors that affect the performance of groups, a leader may be more able to increase the performance of any group. This exercise will provide you with an opportunity to apply this knowledge to increase the performance of a group.

Instructions Either by yourself or with a group of your classmates, think of a group that you or a classmate belongs to. Using what you have learned from your text, design a campaign that will increase the productivity of your club or group.

_____

_____

_____

_____

_____

_____

_____

_____

_____

_____

_____

_____

_____

_____

_____

_____

_____

_____

_____

Group Process Case Study

Jan Svensen is one of ten employees assigned to the Safety Committee at Taflinger Industries. The committee's purpose is to identify safety problems at the plant and make recommendations to eliminate these problems. The committee meets once a month for 2 hours and consists of one representative from each of the ten departments in the plant. The committee was first formed 2 years ago and Jan is the only remaining original member. In the past 2 years, 55 different employees have been on the committee at one time or another.

Currently, Jan is thinking of quitting the committee. She feels that the committee doesn't get anything accomplished, no one appreciates the time she has spent on the committee, and the constant arguing at committee meetings leaves her frustrated and angry. The few times the committee has actually made a recommendation, Jan was chosen to do all the work necessary to research the problem and write the formal recommendation. Of course, the other nine members' names were on the report, and they got credit for all her work!

If you were Jan's supervisor, what insight could you give her about the group's problems?

_____

_____

_____

_____

_____

_____

_____

_____

_____

_____

_____

_____

_____

_____

_____

_____

CHAPTER NINE

Getting Other People to Like Us

How People Form Impressions

Trying to Manage Impressions

Using Impression Formation to Write a Resume

Cover Letters

Chapter Recap

Key Terms

Practice Exam

Projects
Focused Free-Write

Project A: Attribution Theory

Project B: Locus of Control

Project C: Writing Resumes and Cover Letters

A teacher walks into a room and the students decide that this will be a good class. A jury gets its first look at the defendant and without hearing any testimony, the jurors all know she is guilty. A job applicant hasn't even started his interview yet the manager knows he's the right person for the job.

How did the students, the jurors, and the manager make their impressions? In this chapter, you will:

> Learn how we form impressions of others
>
> Understand the situational factors that affect our impressions of others
>
> See how people try to manage the impressions that others form of them
>
> Learn how we combine information to make judgments about others

Throughout the chapter, we will demonstrate how understanding the principles of impression formation can help when interviewing for a job. At the end of the chapter, we will demonstrate how these same principles can be used to write a resume and a cover letter.

■ HOW PEOPLE FORM IMPRESSIONS

You have only the length of the interview to get the interviewer to respond favorably to you, your skills, and your presentation of yourself. Three sets of factors come into play: those directly associated with you, those associated with the situation, and those associated with the interviewer.

Factors Associated With the Person Being Judged

ATTRACTIVENESS

One of the things we first notice about people is their physical attractiveness. Not surprisingly, research is clear that physical attractiveness is one of the most important factors that affects our impressions of others. It is the main factor in determining our initial attraction to members of the opposite sex (Green, Buchanan, & Heuer, 1984; Walster, Aronson, Abrahams, & Rottman, 1966) and an important factor in how an applicant is perceived in an employment interview, how a defendant is judged by a jury, how well a speaker is able to persuade an audience, how a student is perceived by a teacher, and how a politician is evaluated by voters. Perhaps the reason that attractiveness is such an important factor in impression formation is that we believe that "beauty is good" and that beautiful people have many positive

personality characteristics that unattractive people do not (Eagly, Ashmore, Makhijani, & Longo, 1991).

> **Focused Free-Write**
> To get you thinking about impression formation in your own life, complete the Focused Free-Write found at the end of this chapter.

Because attractiveness is important in creating a positive impression, job applicants "dress to impress," political parties choose attractive candidates to run for office (e.g., John Kennedy, Dan Quayle, Bill Clinton), and companies choose attractive people to market their products. Though attractiveness alone is not enough for a lasting positive impression, that first impression is so important that it is essential that job applicants concentrate on looking attractive. Now keep in mind that attractiveness is not the same as "good looking." Instead, attractiveness means that a person is pleasing to look at. To enhance your attractiveness in a job interview, experts recommend the following:

- Wear conservative colors (e.g., dark blue, gray, black) that don't jump out at the interviewer (e.g., lime green, plaid). If the interviewer remembered what you wore, your clothes were probably too flashy.

- Avoid wearing accessories such as flashy large earrings and brightly colored ties. No earring should be worn by males, and no applicant should wear nose rings, eye rings, or any other visible body ring.

- Hair should be worn conservatively—avoid "big hair" and colors such as purple and green. Impersonating Madonna or basketball player Dennis Rodman is not good interview strategy.

- Shoes should be well polished and conservative.

- Don't chew gum!

SIMILARITY

Do "birds of a feather flock together" or do "opposites attract"? If you answered "birds of a feather," you would be correct. In general, we form positive impressions of people who are similar to us in terms of personality, attitudes, values, and sense of humor. Unfortunately, we also form positive impressions of people who are similar to us in terms of race and gender.

Though we initially have positive impressions of people who are attractive, when it comes to dating, we eventually date people whose attractiveness levels are similar to our own. That is, at first we all want a 10, but then reality sets in and we settle for someone who is a bit more like us—if we are a 7, we date a 7, if we are a 2, we date a 2. To demonstrate how common this attractiveness matching is, think of your parents and others who have been together for years. Don't they look similar? Act similar? Even watch the same television shows? In fact, think of the last time you saw a couple whose attractiveness levels didn't match. You probably noticed the difference and may even have asked "I wonder what she sees in him?"

Is it possible for opposites to attract? Sure, but it is not as common as being attracted to someone who is similar. Thus, a key to creating a positive impression with others is to appear similar to them. In an employment interview, applicants can make themselves appear similar to the interviewer by first scanning the interview room for cues about the interviewer. Is there a plaque showing membership in the Kiwanis, Lions, or Rotary? Is there a diploma on the wall? Pictures of children on the desk? Use these cues to point out similarities. For example, you might say "I see you are in the Kiwanis Club, so was my father" or "I see you have two young children, so do I."

NONVERBAL CUES

As discussed in Chapter 7, a person's nonverbal cues play a huge role in the impressions we form of others. Though our use of nonverbal cues is often inaccurate, we use them to form such impressions as:

- If a person does not make eye contact, she must be lying.
- A person who makes eye contact is confident and truthful.
- A person who leans forward and nods her head is interested in what we are saying.
- A person who smiles a lot is a friendly person.

In an employment interview, appropriate nonverbal behaviors begin when you first meet the interviewer—stand up straight, smile, look the interviewer in the eye, and offer a firm (but not bone crushing) handshake. Once you walk into the interview room, wait to sit until either the interviewer tells you to sit or the interviewer sits down. When you sit, keep a straight posture, fold your hands on your lap, and either keep your feet on the floor or cross them at the ankles. During the interview, show the interviewer you are listening by making eye contact, leaning forward, and nodding your head.

Factors Associated With the Situation

PROXIMITY

Think about your first few days at college or on a job. Who were the first few people you met and became friends with? If you are consistent with research, the answer is the people who were physically near you—your roommate or the people you commute with, students who sat near you in class, coworkers whose desks were near yours. Two classic studies demonstrate this point. In the first, researchers (Festinger, Schachter, & Back, 1950) studied residents in an apartment complex called Westgate West. They asked each resident "Which three people in Westgate West do you see socially most often?" and found that 41% of next-door neighbors were chosen compared to only 22% of people two doors away and 10% of people several doors away. In the second study, Whyte (1956) studied the social events that occurred in a small, newly built community and kept track of the people who attended each event. Not surprisingly, the people who attended each event lived only a few doors or blocks from each other.

Our former neighborhood on Charlton Lane in Radford, Virginia is an excellent example of the powerful effect of proximity. Charlton lane is a cul-de-sac containing 14 middle-class houses. For the past 15 years, the neighbors have played poker every other Wednesday night, gone to ballgames and played golf together, helped raise each other's kids, and had neighborhood cookouts and pizza parties. Even after we moved to another town, the "Charlton Lane Crew" are still our best friends.

Why is the effect of proximity so powerful? Researchers have hypothesized two reasons: mere exposure and anticipation of interaction. The idea behind the **mere exposure effect** is that the more often we see someone or something, the more positive we become toward that person or thing. Research has shown that repeated exposure to such varied stimuli as pictures, real people, and drawings has resulted in more favorable impressions than if exposure to the stimuli is limited. The idea behind **anticipation of interaction** is that if we live or work close to somebody, the odds are greater that we will at some point interact with her than if we lived or worked far away. Because we are likely to interact with the person, we initially form a positive impression so that we don't dread the thought of meeting the person.

How can proximity be used to create a positive impression? First, try to make sure that your office or workstation is physically near the people you want to impress. That is, being next door to the boss is better than an office on a different floor. Second, be visible—eat lunch around others, study in the library rather than at home, exercise at a gym rather than at home. Third, keep the door to your office open while you work to increase your ability to see others and to be seen by them.

CLASSICAL CONDITIONING

If you were going on a first date, would you choose to take your date to a documentary on the brutality of the Pinochet regime in Chile or to a highly acclaimed comedy? If you answered the comedy, you demonstrated your awareness of the importance of classical conditioning in impression formation. That is, through **classical conditioning**, people associate us with the people we are with and the environment we are in. For example, if you attend a great party in which everyone has a good time, you become associated with that good time and thus are seen in a positive light even though you may not have done anything to make the party a success. Or think about the worst class you ever took. Did you meet someone in that class who became your friend? How about in the best class you ever had (hopefully, this class!)? When we ask our students these two questions, we find that very few students indicate that they dated someone or made a friend in the classes they hated, whereas most indicate that they dated someone or made a friend in a favorite class. Why the difference? Through classical conditioning, you became associated with the characteristics of the bad instructor and the boring topic in the one class and thus, even though you didn't teach the class, your classmates formed a worse impression of you than they would have with a better class. So, the moral of this story is to choose your classes and instructors carefully or you will never have any friends!

MISATTRIBUTION

A third situational factor that can affect our impressions of others is **misattribution**. An attribution is a reason that something occurs; a misattribution is an attribution that is not true. The idea behind misattribution is that physiologically most of our emotions are the same. That is, there is little difference physiologically between being scared and in love. How then do we know if we are scared or in love? According to the Schacter-Singer theory, when we become physiologically aroused, we subconsciously scan the environment to interpret our arousal. For example, suppose that we are physiologically aroused and look around and see a rabid dog—our brain interprets the arousal as fear. Likewise, if we look around and see an attractive member of the opposite sex, our brain interprets our arousal as love (or something related to love).

How does this apply to impression formation? Imagine that you are a patient in a hospital about to have surgery, and your doctor is an attractive member of the opposite sex. Prior to your surgery you are physiologically aroused, in reality because you are scared, but you misattribute your arousal to being attracted to your doctor. Such misattributions are common in the helping professions and are one of the reasons that doctors and therapists don't get their egos inflated when a patient or client becomes attracted to them.

Factors Associated With the Person Making the Judgment

SCHEMAS

Suppose that we told you that our neighbor had a job. Could you describe this person? Probably not. However, what if we told you that our neighbor was a plumber? Could you now make a better description? Our students usually respond to this question by saying that our neighbor is a male, wears jeans that reveal his butt when he bends over, wears a baseball cap, is overweight and has a pot belly, knows his job well but is not very worldly. How is it that you were able to describe our neighbor even though you never met this person? The answer might be in something called a **schema**.

Schemas are the way we organize material in our minds, and they are different for every person. Take for example, the organized schema represented in Exhibit 9-1. The further down we go in a schema, the more images or stereotypes that instantly come to mind. So, if we are told that a person is a personal injury attorney, our initial schema and stereotypes might cause us to initially form a negative impression (e.g., ambulance chaser) even though we have never met the person.

JUST WORLD HYPOTHESIS

Imagine that a young woman tells the police that she was raped at a party. She explains that she had been drinking and at 3:30 a.m. a man pulled her into the bedroom. The officers raise their eyebrows and ask "What were you doing at a party that late?" This all too common story is an example of how we often attribute blame to victims of crime, sickness, and natural disasters. One of the reasons for such an attribution is the **just world hypothesis**.

The just world hypothesis is an irrational belief that we live in a "just world" where good things happen to good people and bad things happen to bad people. So, if a person is raped, has a disability, or loses her keys, somehow it must have been her fault, and consequently, she must be a bad person. As a result of the just world hypothesis, we tend to form worse impressions of people who have bad things happen to them.

Why do people believe in the just world hypothesis when it is obvious that such thinking is irrational? Psychologists believe that such thinking helps us get through the day. That is, if we believe we are a good person, and we live in a just world where good things

EXHIBIT 9-1

Example of a Schema

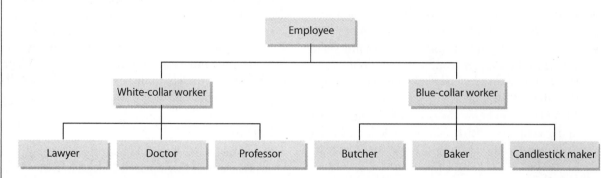

happen to good people and bad things happen to bad people, then nothing bad will happen to us. We can drive to work without worrying about getting into an accident, we can walk down a dark street and not fear getting mugged, and we can eat unhealthy food and not worry about getting cancer.

What happens then when something bad happens to us? Do we quit believing in the just world hypothesis? Unfortunately, the answer is often no. Victims of crime, accidents, and natural disasters constantly blame themselves and lament "If only I would have. . . ." As a result of such thinking, therapists often concentrate on getting victims to understand that bad things can happen to good people and then take steps to help rebuild the victim's self-esteem.

Positivity Bias

For most people, our inclination is to think positively of people when we first meet them. Perhaps the reason for this positivity bias is that if we are going to spend time with someone, we would prefer that we enjoy that time. Thus, when we first meet someone, if we assume that she is a likeable person, we can also assume that we will have a positive experience. Of course, not all people have this positivity bias. We all know people who avoid social situations because they assume that they will not enjoy socializing with others. For these people, the initial assumption is that the interaction will be negative and that people must "prove themselves" before being liked.

How Do We Weight Information?

As mentioned earlier in the chapter, when we form impressions of others, we use many types of information such as attractiveness, similarity, and nonver-

bal cues. However, not all information is weighted equally when we form impressions of others. Instead, we weight some information more heavily based on such factors as primacy, priming, relevance, negativity, and recency.

Primacy

Not too surprisingly, our first impressions of others carry more weight than subsequent impressions. For example, imagine that you meet a person at a party and your initial impression (**primacy effect**) is that the person is rude and boring. Do you talk to the person for the next 3 hours to see if your initial impression was wrong or do you walk away at the first opportunity?

Support for the importance of first impressions comes from research indicating that interviewers make a decision about an applicant in the first 5 minutes of an interview; the initial impression of a house by prospective home buyers determines their interest in a property; and people decide in the first 12 minutes of a service whether they want to join a particular church.

First impressions greatly influence interview judgments. Research indicates that information presented prior to the interview (Dougherty, Turban, & Callender, 1994) or early in the interview carries more weight than does information presented later in the interview. Furthermore, research suggests that interviewers decide about a candidate within 5 minutes after the start of a 15-minute interview (Dessler, 1984). In fact, of a group of personnel professionals, 74% said they can make a decision within the first 5 minutes of an interview (Buckley & Eder, 1989). Thus, the primacy effect may help explain why research has shown no relationship between interview length and outcome (Huegli & Tschirgia, 1975).

To form a positive first impression during an interview:

- Follow the suggestions for attractiveness presented earlier in the chapter.

- Be on time. In a study we conducted, no applicant who arrived to the interview late was hired.

- Use the suggestions for nonverbal cues presented earlier in the chapter (e.g., make eye contact, smile, have a firm handshake) when you first see the interviewer.

- Make sure you know the name of the interviewer and greet him or her by saying something such as "It is good to meet you, Mr. Anderson." People like to hear their names and it shows that not only do you have good social skills, but that you prepared for the interview.

CONTRAST EFFECTS

With the **contrast effect**, our impressions of one person may affect our impressions of the next person we encounter. For example, suppose that Bob is a moderately attractive individual. If you saw Mel Gibson and then saw Bob, the contrast effect would probably cause you to lower your opinion of Bob's attractiveness. However, if you saw Woody Allen and then saw Bob, the contrast effect would probably cause you to raise your opinion of Bob's attractiveness. Support for the contrast effect is abundant. For example, in a study of the contrast effect and ratings of attractiveness, Kenrick and Gutierres (1980) found that males who had just watched an episode of *Charlie's Angels* rated the attractiveness levels of females at a college much lower than males who had not recently seen a *Charlie's Angels* episode.

Research involving the contrast effect and interview scores showed similar results (Carlson, 1970; Wexley, Sanders, & Yukl, 1973). If a terrible applicant precedes an average applicant, the interview score for the average applicant is higher than if no applicant or a very qualified applicant had preceded her. In other words, an applicant's performance is judged in relation to the performance(s) of previous interviewees. Thus, it may be advantageous to be interviewed immediately after someone who has done poorly.

NEGATIVE-INFORMATION BIAS

Negative information apparently weighs more heavily than positive information. For example, suppose we told you that our friend has a great job, is attractive, has a great sense of humor, loves children and animals, and spent 5 years in prison, would you agree to a date? According to research, the **negative-information bias** indicates that the one piece of negative information (the prison sentence) would outweigh all the positive attributes.

Our awareness of this negative-information bias is supported by the observation that most job applicants are afraid of being honest in interviews for fear that one negative response will cost them their job opportunities. Similarly, instructors who write letters of recommendation seldom say even one negative thing out of fear that one negative comment will outweigh a page of positive comments.

PRIMING

Our impressions of others are often affected by what we hear about them prior to meeting them—that is, prior information **primes** us for what is to come. For example, imagine that your instructor will be going out of town and has arranged for a guest speaker. She tells you that the speaker is really funny and that you will really like her. After 10 minutes of talking, the guest speaker makes a joke. What is your impression? Based on research, you would probably think the speaker is funny because her one joke confirmed what you had heard about her. Now, take the same speaker and the same 10-minute talk. However, in this case, your instructor warned you that the guest speaker was "a bit dry" but really smart. Would the one joke change your opinion? Probably not.

When you were in junior high or high school, you probably used priming without knowing it. To demonstrate this point, think about a person you were interested in asking out or being asked out by. Did you tell your friends to tell that person how much fun you were? That is, did you send your friends to do some priming before you actually approached the person?

In the employment interview, we use our resume to prime the interviewer that we are highly qualified. We are also priming if we have someone in the company put in a good word for us prior to the interview.

RELEVANCE

In forming an impression of others, we place more weight on information that is relevant than we do on irrelevant information. For example, suppose that we wanted you to date a friend of ours and told you that our friend was an excellent writer. You would probably put little weight on that information because it is not relevant to going out on a date. However, if we told you our friend was attractive and had a good sense of humor, you would place more weight on that information than you would on our friend's writing ability. But, if you were a newspaper editor looking for a writer, you would hopefully place more weight on our comment about writing ability than you would on our comments on our friend's attractiveness.

UNUSUAL INFORMATION

We also place more weight on information that is unusual than we do routine information. For example, if we told you our friend likes pizza, how much attention would you pay to that comment? Probably very little. However, if we told you that our friend had ten cats, biked across the country, or liked to bungee jump, we would probably have your attention!

RECENCY

We discussed previously that first impressions are the most important (primacy). However, recent impressions carry additional weight as well. For example, suppose that your significant other gave you flowers for the first 3 months of your relationship, gave you nothing for 3 months, and then gave you flowers yesterday. Would you consider him or her to be a romantic person? Based on primacy and recency, the answer would be yes.

ATTRIBUTION

Imagine that Dave and Temeka are at a party. Dave walks by Temeka and trips over her feet. Would you attribute Dave's tripping to Dave being a klutz? Would you attribute the tripping to Temeka being a prankster who stuck out her foot? Or, would you attribute the tripping as being an accident? When we attribute the cause of a behavior to a person, we make an **internal attribution**. When we attribute the cause to such things as chance or external factors (e.g., the room was crowded), we make an **external attribution**.

If we were to make our attributions logically, we would use three factors: distinctiveness, consistency, and consensus. When we consider **distinctiveness**, we ask if the person behaves in a particular way only in a particular situation. In our example, we would ask "Does Dave always trip over *Temeka*'s feet?" When we consider **consistency**, we ask if the person always behaves that way. In our example, we would ask "Does Dave always trip over *everyone's* feet?" When we consider **consensus**, we ask if other people behave this way. In our example, we would ask "Do others always trip over Temeka's feet?"

If we have consistency, we would probably say that Dave is a klutz. If we have consensus, we would probably attribute the tripping to Temeka being a prankster. If we have distinctiveness, we would probably say that Dave and Temeka are friends and are just kidding around. If we have none of the three, we would probably make an external attribution and assume that Dave's tripping was just an accident.

A good example of attribution comes from the process we use to select students into our graduate programs. As part of the application process, students get three people to write letters of recommendation for them. Over the years, we see many letters from the same people. That is, a professor at Colorado State might recommend one or two students each year for admission into our program. Thus, we have a "history" of recommendations written by many faculty. In considering how much weight to place on the recommendation, we use distinctiveness, consensus, and consistency. If we see consistency—the faculty member always writes letters saying that this is one of her best students ever—we place little weight on the recommendation. If we see consensus—all three letters say similar things—we place more weight on the recommendation. If we see distinctiveness—the professor says goods things about some people and bad things about others—we give the recommendation the greatest amount of weight.

> **PROJECT A** *Attribution Theory*
> To practice making logical attributions, complete Project A at the end of this chapter.

Does everyone use such a logical process to make attributions? Probably not. Instead, we often commit the **fundamental attribution error**—attributing others' behavior to internal causes. For example, suppose that a friend tells you that she just failed an exam. What attributions could you make for her behavior? It could be internal—she isn't smart enough or did not study—or it could be something external—the test was tricky, the instructor is known to be a hard grader. If you are like most people, you would make the fundamental attribution error and assume that your friend wasn't smart enough or didn't study. We especially tend to make this error when the person's behavior is negative (e.g., failing a test, getting into a fight, cheating).

When it comes to making attributions about our own behavior, the tendency is the opposite. In general, we make internal attributions about our successes (I got an A on the exam because I am smart) and external attributions about our failures (I got an F on the exam because it was full of tricky questions). Individual differences in the way we make attributions about our own behavior is related to our locus of control. People who have an **internal locus of control** believe that they are responsible for their successes and failures, whereas people with an **external locus of control** believe that their behavior is the result of external circumstances outside of their control.

PROJECT B *Locus of Control*
To see if you have an internal or external locus of control,
complete the test in Project B at the end of this chapter.

TRYING TO MANAGE IMPRESSIONS

Ingratiation

One method that we use to get others to like us is to ingratiate ourselves by complimenting the other person. Though we all like to be complimented, **ingratiation** only works if the compliments are considered to be sincere. For example, we have a colleague at another university who often compliments us on our book. We were always appreciative about his compliments until we discovered that he had not actually read the book!

Self-Promotion

Whereas ingratiation is an attempt to get people to like us, self-promotion is an attempt to get others to think we are competent. Attempts at self-promotion include telling others of our accomplishments, bragging, and hanging awards and diplomas on the wall. Self-promotion works best if it is the result of another person's question. For example, if someone asks if you have traveled much, and you respond that you have been to 15 countries, the person will probably be impressed. However, if in the middle of a conversation, you blurt out that you have been to 15 countries, you would probably be perceived as a blowhard. We have two good examples of both situations.

A friend of ours has very low self-esteem. Whenever we mention something positive in our lives (e.g., we went on a trip, just finished a consulting job), our friend quickly counters with something positive that has happened to him—usually something that has nothing to do with the topic. Such attempts at self-promotion are too obvious and do not result in a positive impression. We have another friend who is just the opposite. He is the Eminent Scholar on campus and has led a fascinating life. He never brags or boasts, but when asked, he will tell you about his latest adventure, or compliment him on his tie and he will tell you the interesting story about how he bought it in Italy. The difference between the two is that one is an obvious attempt to self-promote and the other a sincere answer to a question.

Intimidation

Rather than getting people to like us, there are times when we want people to think we are powerful. For example, when disciplining an employee, trying to mold a Marine Corps recruit, or getting a person to change her mind, we need to show how powerful and in control we are. In such circumstances, we might use **intimidation** to manage the impression that others form of us. With intimidation, we might use words (e.g., I'll fire you if you don't get it done), symbols (e.g., a large desk, diplomas on the wall), or nonverbal cues (e.g., standing close to someone, constant eye contact) to show power, prestige, and control.

Exemplification

If our goal is to get people to think we are good, morally superior people, we might use the impression management technique of **exemplification**. With exemplification, we manage impressions by sacrificing, helping others, and being a martyr. With exemplification, it is important not only to do these things, but to make sure that others are aware that we are doing them.

Supplication

The opposite of intimidation is **supplication**, in which we try to give the impression that we are weak. For example, we might ask for more time on a project by telling the boss that we don't learn as quickly as others. Or we might try to gain sympathy from an angry boss by telling her that we have been sick. Essentially, we are trying to plead "poor, poor me" and hope that others will be kinder to us. A good example of this comes from a manager in a small organization. He didn't really want to do any of the clerical work (e.g., using presentation software on the computer, making photocopies) so he constantly asked for help, pleading that he could not "figure out how to make the copier work." Because everyone thought he was helpless, they did many of the tasks for him. However, one evening the manager was working late and didn't realize another employee was in the building who saw him expertly operate the copier and the computer. Needless to say his impression management tactics no longer worked!

USING IMPRESSION FORMATION TO WRITE A RESUME

The information discussed in this chapter can be used to write a resume, as a resume is essentially a written way of managing others' impressions of us. If we compare resumes written today with those written 20 years ago, we see great differences. Twenty years ago, resumes were written with the view that a resume was a *history of your life*. Thus, it included every job that was worked, every school that was attended, and such information as marital status, health, number of children, and age. Today, however, we view resumes as an *advertisement of your skills*. Thus, resumes written today will include only that information that makes us look good. Consequently, much more strategy is involved in writing a resume today than there was 20 years ago. Much of this strategy is based on the impression formation principles you learned in this chapter.

Rules for Writing Resumes

If you ask 100 people for advice about how to write a resume, you will probably get 100 different responses. With such a variety of opinions, taking advice can get confusing. In this section, we will make the case that there are only three rules for writing resumes, everything else is just personal preference.

RULE 1: RESUMES MUST BE PHYSICALLY APPEALING

Remember that physical attractiveness plays a big role in the impressions that we form of others. The same is true with a resume. If your resume looks bad, so too will be the impression formed of your skills. Physically appealing resumes:

- Use a common font (e.g., Times Roman) rather than an unusual or fancy one (e.g., Onyx, *Calgary*).
- Use a font size of 12 points (never smaller than 10 points).
- Have at least a 1-inch margin on all sides, with plenty of white space (do not pack information into the resume).
- Are printed on white (or off-white) paper with black print. White paper scans, copies, and faxes more clearly than other colors.

RULE 2: THE RESUME CANNOT CONTAIN TYPING, SPELLING, GRAMMATICAL, OR FACTUAL MISTAKES

When Walter Pierce, Jr. was a personnel officer for Norfolk-Southern Corporation, his boss received a resume from an excellent applicant for a job as a computer programmer. Even though the applicant had outstanding credentials, the personnel director would not even offer him an interview because the applicant had misspelled two words on his resume. A similar story is told by Dick Williams, the General Manager for Member One Credit Union. He once received two cover letters stapled together—both referring to the resume that wasn't there. To make matters worse, four words were misspelled. We could tell you more horror stories but the point should be clear—do not make any careless mistakes!

It is also important not to make factual mistakes. Most employers conduct background checks and will catch anything that is not true. Often, these mistakes were not made intentionally, but an employer will probably assume that any mistake in dates, titles, or degrees was made with the intent to deceive the employer.

RULE 3: RESUMES SHOULD MAKE THE APPLICANT LOOK AS QUALIFIED AS POSSIBLE—WITHOUT LYING

In determining what information should be included, follow this important rule: If including hobbies, summer jobs, and lists of courses will make you look more qualified for *this particular* job, then by all means, include them. If you attended summer school at one university, but graduated from another, listing it will only clutter your resume.

If a resume follows the above three rules—that is, it looks nice, doesn't contain mistakes, and makes the applicant look as good as possible—then it is an effective resume. Opinions to the contrary (such as "use boldface type instead of underlining" or "outline your duties instead of putting them in a paragraph") probably represent differences in individual preferences rather than any major problem with the resume.

Types of Resumes

There are three main types of resumes: chronological, functional, and psychological. As shown in Exhibit 9-2, *chronological resumes* list previous jobs in order from the most to the least recent. This type of resume is useful for applicants whose previous jobs are related to their future plans and whose work histories do not contain gaps.

The *functional resume*, as shown in Exhibit 9-3, organizes jobs based on the skills required to perform them rather than the order in which they were worked. Functional resumes are especially useful for applicants who are either changing careers or have gaps in their work histories. The problem with this type of resume is that it takes employers longer to read and comprehend than the other resume types—this problem makes functional resumes the least popular with employers (Toth, 1993).

The **psychological resume** uses all the information you just learned and is based on sound psychological theory and research. As shown in Exhibit 9-4, the psychological resume should begin with a short summary

Example of a Chronological Resume

CHRISTINE R. MILLER

812 Main Street, Gainesville, FL 32789   (904) 645-1001

Objective   Entry-level management position in financial services

Education   B.S., University of Florida, May 1995

Major: Business Administration
GPA: 3.43/4.0
Minor: Information Systems
Business-Related Courses: Accounting, Money & Banking,
Principles of Marketing, Economics, Statistics

Professional Experience   July 1999–Present
Assistant Manager, TCBY Yogurt, Gainesville, FL
    Responsible for posting daily receipts and making bank deposits. Further responsible for supervising and scheduling counter personnel, writing progress reports, and handling employee disputes.

August 1998–July 1999
Cashier/Customer Service, TCBY Yogurt, Gainesville, FL
    Responsible for assisting customers promptly and courteously, maintaining a balanced cash drawer, and cleaning work station.

May 1997–August 1998
Bank Teller, Barnett Bank, Gainesville, FL
    Responsible for assisting and advising customers with financial transactions. Cash drawer balanced 99% of the time. Received excellent performance ratings.

August 1997–May 1998
Waiter, Shakers Restaurant, Gainesville, FL
    Responsible for taking food and drink orders from customers, and serving them courteously and efficiently. Worked in a high-volume, fast-paced environment.

Activities   Member of Phi Kappa Phi Honor Society
Member of Phi Beta Lambda Business Organization
Vice President, Sigma Delta Theta Social Sorority
Member of Circle K Service Organization
Participated in intramural volleyball

EXHIBIT 9-3

Example of a Functional Resume

MATTHEW F. JOHNSON

816 Broadway Road, Lexington, KY 63189
(606) 814-7282

Career Objective   Management-level position in banking services.

Banking & Management Experience

Posted receipts and made bank deposits daily for Dunkin' Donuts coffee shop in Lexington, Kentucky, July 1998–present.

Supervised and scheduled cashier personnel for Dunkin' Donuts coffee shop in Lexington, Kentucky, July 1998–present.

Bank teller for Citizen's Fidelity Bank in Lexington, Kentucky. Maintained balanced cash drawer 99% of the time. Trained in various financial transactions of the banking field. May 1999–August 1999.

Customer Service Experience

Customer service/cashier for Dunkin' Donuts coffee shop in Lexington, Kentucky. Assisted customers with placing orders and was responsible for maintaining a balanced cash drawer.

Assisted customers promptly and courteously with financial transactions at Citizen's Fidelity Bank in Lexington, Kentucky. Received excellent performance ratings. May 1999–August 1999.

Waited on customers at El Torito Mexican Restaurant in Lexington, Kentucky. After taking customers' orders, served customers promptly and courteously. August 1997–May 1998.

Leadership Experience

Vice President of Sigma Epsilon Phi Social Fraternity. Was responsible for assisting pledges with the transition into the fraternity and for raising money for the fraternity philanthropy through various fund-raisers.

Coordinated and participated in the softball intramural team for the fraternity.

Community Service and Campus Activities

Member of Key Club Service Organization on campus.

Member of Management Association.

Member of Phi Kappa Phi Honor Society.

Education   B.A., Management, University of Kentucky, May 1999
GPA: 3.44/4.0   Minor: Information Systems
Courses: Accounting, Economics, Marketing, Money & Banking, Principles of Management

EXHIBIT 9-4

Example of a Psychological Resume

ALEXANDER G. BELL
1412 Watson Drive
Ringem, Virginia 24147
(540)555-5555
abell@runet.edu

PROFESSIONAL STRENGTHS

- Bachelor's degree in business
- Two years of supervisory and leadership experience
- Three years of customer service experience
- Skilled in using spreadsheet (Excel) and presentation (PowerPoint) software
- Conversational in Spanish
- Excellent accounting and statistical skills

EDUCATION

B.S., Business Administration (May, 2000)
Radford University, Radford, VA

Highlights:

- 3.33 GPA
- Extensive coursework in human resource management
- Minored in psychology
- President, Society for the Advancement of Management (SAM)
- Received two academic scholarships
- Worked to finance 50% of own education
- Participated in a variety of college activities, including intramurals, two professional organizations, and the college band

PART-TIME AND SUMMER EMPLOYMENT

Student Manager (August 1999–present)
Radford University Dining Services, Radford, VA

Responsible for supervising 30 students working in the dining hall. Specific responsibilities include scheduling employees, solving customer complaints, balancing the cash drawers, promoting high levels of customer service, and ensuring that health regulations were being followed.

Food Server (August 1998–May 1999)
Radford University Dining Services, Radford, VA

Responsible for serving food to students, keeping work area clean, and following health regulations.

Server (Summers 1997, 1998, 1999)
Whale's Tail Restaurant, Redondo Beach, CA

of your strengths. This section takes advantage of the impression formation principles of *priming* (preparing the reader for what is to come), *primacy* (early impressions are most important), and *short-term memory limits* (the list should not be longer than seven items).

The next section of the resume should contain information about either your education or your experience—whichever is strongest for you. The design of the education section is intended to provide an organizational framework that will make it easier for the reader to remember the contents. In deciding which information to put into these two sections, three impression-management rules should be used: relevance, unusualness, and positivity. If information is *relevant* to your desired career, include it. For example, you would mention that you have two children if you are applying for day care or elementary school teaching positions but not if you are applying for a job involving a lot of travel. How far back should you go in listing jobs? Using the principle of relevance, the answer would be far enough back to include all relevant jobs. Listing hobbies is certainly acceptable if they are relevant (Oliphant & Alexander, 1982).

Unusual information should be included when possible as people pay more attention to it than to typical information. A problem for college students is that their resumes look identical to those of their classmates. That is, most business majors take the same classes, belong to the same clubs, and have had similar part-time jobs. To stand out from other graduates, an applicant needs something unusual such as an internship, an interesting hobby, or an unusual life experience (for example, spent a year in Europe, rode a bike across the country).

Though it is advisable to have unusual information, the information must also be *positive*. It probably would not be a good idea to list unusual information such as "I've been arrested more times than anyone in my class" or "I enjoy bungee jumping without cords." The unacceptability of these two examples is obvious, and few applicants would make the mistake of actually placing such information on their resumes; however, more subtle items can have the same effect. For example, suppose you enjoy hunting and are a member of the Young Democrats on campus. Including these items might make a negative impression on Republicans and on those who oppose hunting. Only include information that most people will find positive (such as Red Cross volunteer, worked to help finance education, and so on), and avoid information that may be viewed negatively such as political affiliation, religion, and dangerous hobbies (J. J. Bonner, 1993).

Of the many positive activities and accomplishments that you could list, only list your best. Do not list everything that you have done, as research by Spock and Stevens (1985) found that it is better to list a few great things rather than a few great things and many good things. This finding is based on Anderson's (1965) averaging versus adding model of impression formation, which implies that activity quality is more important than quantity. It is not necessary nor desirable to list all of your coursework.

> **PROJECT C** *Writing Resumes*
> To help you apply what you have learned about impression formation and resume writing, complete Project C found at the end of this chapter.

■ COVER LETTERS

Cover letters tell an employer that you are enclosing your resume and would like to apply for a job. Cover letters should never be longer than one page. As shown in the sample cover letters in Exhibits 9-5 and 9-6, cover letters contain a salutation, four basic paragraphs, and a closing signature.

Salutation

If possible, get the name of the person to whom you want to direct the letter. If you aren't sure of the person's name, call the company and simply ask for the name of the person (have it spelled) to whom you should send your resume. If the first name leaves doubt about the person's gender (for example Kim, Robin, Paige), ask if the person is male or female so that you can properly address the letter to Mr. Smith or Ms. Smith. Do not refer to the person by first name (e.g., Dear Sarah). If you can't get the person's name, a safe salutation is "Dear Human Resources Director." Avoid phrases such as *Dear Sir or Madam* (unless the company is a house of ill repute) or *To Whom It May Concern* (it doesn't concern me).

Paragraphs

The opening paragraph should be one or two sentences long and communicates three pieces of information: the fact that your resume is enclosed, the name of the job you are applying for, and how you know about the job opening (such as a newspaper ad or from a friend). The second paragraph states that you are qualified for the job and provides about three reasons why. This paragraph should be only four or five sentences in length and should not rehash the content of your resume. The third paragraph explains why you are interested in the particular company to which you are applying. The final paragraph closes your letter and provides information on how you can best be reached. Though your phone number will be on your resume, this paragraph is a good place to tell the employer the best days and times to reach you.

EXHIBIT 9-5

Example of a Cover Letter

November 8, 2000

Mr. John Smith
Alco, Inc.
217 West Street
Johnson, VA 24132

Dear Mr. Smith:

Enclosed find a copy of my resume. Please consider me for the position of welder that was advertised in the Roanoke Times and World News.

For several reasons, I believe that I am qualified for your position. First, I have six years of welding experience in an industrial setting. Second, I am a very dependable worker as shown by the fact that I have missed only two days of work in the last five years. Finally, I am available to work any shift at any of your three plants.

I look forward to hearing from you. I can best be reached after 3:00 p.m. on weekdays and anytime on weekends.

Cordially,

Andrew S. Jones

Example of a Customized Cover Letter

July 15, 2000

Ms. Maria Duffie, Director
Human Resources Department
Walters Cosmetics, Inc.
69 Beall Avenue
Amityville, NY 00312

Dear Ms. Duffie:

Enclosed find a copy of my resume. Please consider me for the position of sales representative that was advertised this past Sunday in the *Washington Post*. As you can see below, I am confident that my qualifications are a good match for the requirements stated in your advertisement.

Your Requirements	My Qualifications
Bachelor's degree	B.A. in marketing from Radford University
Two years of sales experience	Five years of sales experience
History of success in sales	Received three sales awards at AT&T
Strong clerical skills	A.A.S. in secretarial science
	Three years of clerical experience
	55 words per minute typing speed

I am especially interested in working for your company because I have used your products for over ten years and thus am familiar with both your product line and the high quality of your cosmetics.

I am looking forward to hearing from you. Please feel free to call me at home after 6:00 p.m. or at work from 8:00 a.m. until 5:00 p.m. Because AT&T is downsizing, my employer will not mind your calling me at work.

Cordially,

Mable Leane

2345 Revlon Blvd.
Avon, Virginia 24132
Home: (703) 435-1122
Work: (703) 435-4343

Signature

Above your signature, use words such as *cordially* or *sincerely. Yours truly* is not advised and words such as *love, peace,* or *hugs and snuggles* are strongly discouraged. Personally sign each cover letter; and type your name, address, and phone number below your signature.

Human Resources Director Ge Ge Beall provides job applicants with the following tips about cover letters:

- Avoid sounding desperate and don't beg (I really need a job bad! Please please please hire me!).

- Avoid grammar and spelling errors. Employers view cover letters and resumes as examples of the best work applicants can produce. If your cover letter contains errors, an employer will be concerned about the quality of your regular work.

- Avoid officious words or phrases. Don't use a 25 cent word when a nickel word will do. Not only will employers be unimpressed by a large vocabulary, but applicants using big words often misuse them. As an example, one applicant tried to describe his work productivity by saying that his writings were *voluptuous* rather than *voluminous*, as we think he meant to say.

- Don't discuss personal circumstances such as "I find myself looking for a job because I am recently divorced." Employers are only interested in your qualifications.

- If possible, tailor your letter to each company. Standard cover letters are efficient but not as effective as those written specifically for each job you are applying for.

- Don't write your cover letter on the stationery of your current employer.

CHAPTER RECAP

In this chapter, you learned the following:

- We initially like people who are attractive, similar to us, and use appropriate nonverbal skills.

- Such situational factors as proximity, classical conditioning, and misattribution affect the impressions that people form of us.

- Peoples' schemas, belief in a just world, and positivity bias affect their impressions of others.

- Primacy, contrast effects, negative information, priming, relevance, unusual information, and recency are used to weight information.

- People use such techniques as ingratiation, self-promotion, intimidation, exemplification,

and supplication to manage the impressions that others form of them.

- Impression management skills can help you survive an employment interview.

- Impression management skills for writing a resume include following the three rules for writing resumes and following impression management techniques.

Critical Thinking Questions

1. What impression management techniques do you use to get others to like you?

2. If most people use impression management techniques, how do we know who the "real person" is?

3. Research says that we like attractive people and people who are similar to us. Is there anything wrong with this?

4. How can you use proximity, classical conditioning, and misattribution to ensure that you make a positive impression?

5. Why do we place so much weight on negative information?

WEB SITES

For further information, log on to the following web sites.
www.channel3000.com/employment/
Provides tips on interviewing, resume writing, and cover letter writing.
www.provenresumes.com/
Provides tips on writing the perfect resume.

KEY TERMS

Anticipation of interaction The theory that we will feel more positively about people we think we might meet than we do about people we don't anticipate meeting.

Classical conditioning A type of learning in which events that occur at the same time are associated with one another.

Contrast effect The impression or performance of one person affecting the perception of the performance of the next person.

Consensus From attribution theory: most people behaving in a similar fashion when confronted with the same situation.

Consistency From attribution theory: a person usually behaving the same way in similar situations.

Distinctiveness From attribution theory: a person behaving in a particular only way when he or she is in a particular situation.

Exemplification An impression management technique in which people try to create the impression that they are morally superior.

External attribution Attributing the cause of behavior to situational factors or to luck.

External locus of control The tendency to believe that our behavior is caused by external factors that are out of our control.

Fundamental attribution error The tendency of people to make internal attributions for the failures of others.

Ingratiation An attempt to make a good impression by saying nice things about the other person.

Internal attribution Attributing the cause of behavior to personal factors such as skill or effort.

Internal locus of control The tendency to believe that our behavior is caused by factors such as skill and effort, and thus are under our control.

Intimidation An impression management technique in which people try to create the impression that they are powerful.

Just world hypothesis The belief that we live in a just world where good things happen to good people and bad things happen to bad people.

Mere exposure effect The theory that repeated exposure to someone or something causes us to form a more positive opinion of that person or thing.

Misattribution Attributing the cause of our emotions or behavior to the wrong source.

Negative information bias The fact that negative information receives more weight than does positive information.

Primacy effect The fact that impressions formed early carry more weight than impressions formed later.

Priming Providing people with information with the hope that it will affect their impression of subsequent information.

Psychological resume A resume style that takes advantage of psychological principles pertaining to memory organization and impression formation.

Schema The way in which we cognitively organize information.

Supplication An impression management technique in which people try to create the impression that they are weak.

PRACTICE EXAM

1. Attractiveness is the *main* factor in determining:
   a. attraction to members of the opposite sex
   b. how a defendant is judged by a jury
   c. how well a speaker can persuade others
   d. how a politician is evaluated by voters

2. Which of the following is most true?
   a. Opposites attract
   b. Birds of a feather flock together
   c. Both are equally true
   d. Neither is true

3. That we like people who are physically near us demonstrates the importance of:
   a. classical conditioning b. misattribution
   c. a schema   d. proximity

4. The way we organize material in our minds is called:
   a. classical conditioning b. misattribution
   c. a schema   d. proximity

5. The belief that good things happen to good people and bad things happen to bad people is called:
   a. a schema
   b. primacy
   c. the just world hypothesis
   d. the fundamental attribution error

6. Jill didn't like Jane from the moment she met her. This is an example of:
   a. priming   b. primacy
   c. relevance   d. contrast effects

7. Gerry enjoyed hiking the local mountains until he spent the summer hiking the Alps. Now his local mountains just don't seem as good. This is an example of:
   a. priming   b. primacy
   c. relevance   d. contrast effects

8. James applied for a job with Taflinger Industries. The company didn't seem impressed that James has the city's largest stamp collection. This might be a good example of:
   a. priming   b. primacy
   c. relevance   d. contrast effects

9. Ricardo and Lucille don't get along. Ricardo and Lucille are well liked by everyone else. The principle of _____ might say that the two probably have a personality conflict.
   a. distinctiveness   b. consensus
   c. consistency   d. recency

10. A person who compliments others is probably using the impression management technique of _____.
    a. self-promotion   b. exemplification
    c. intimidation   d. ingratiation

11. A person who tries to get people to like him by helping others, is probably using the impression management technique of _____.
    a. self-promotion   b. exemplification
    c. intimidation   d. ingratiation

12. A person who tells us how great she is, is probably using the impression management technique of _____.
   a. self-promotion   b. exemplification
   c. intimidation   d. ingratiation

13. A _____ resume lists jobs in order from the most recent to the least recent.
   a. functional   b. well-written
   c. chronological   d. psychological

14. The professional strengths section of a resume takes advantage of the impression management principle of _____.
   a. relevance   b. primacy
   c. contrast effects   d. attribution

15. To make a resume attractive, you should _____.
   a. use 1-inch margins
   b. print it on white paper
   c. use a standard font
   d. all three are good ideas

ANSWERS 1 a, 2 b, 3 d, 4 c, 5 c, 6 b, 7 d, 8 c, 9 a, 10 d, 11 b, 12 a, 13 c, 14 b, 15 d

Focused Free-Write

To get you thinking about impression formation, think about the last person you met that you really liked. Describe what it was that made you like that person.

_____

_____

_____

_____

_____

_____

_____

_____

_____

_____

_____

_____

_____

_____

_____

_____

_____

_____

_____

_____

_____

Attribution Theory

To help you learn how to logically make attributions, read the three descriptions below and indicate the reason for the behavior. Remember to use consensus, consistency, and distinctiveness to reach your conclusions.

1. Gen and Mike don't get along. Mike gets along with everyone and is well liked in the organization. Gen has had many conflicts and doesn't get along with many people. To what do you attribute their conflict?

_____

_____

_____

_____

2. Bob is placing an order at the drive-through of McBurger restaurant. Al is working the drive-through and asks Bob to repeat his order because Al can't understand it. Bob gets irritated and drives away thinking "What a moron. None of the people that work at these restaurants can ever get an order correct." Is Bob's attribution correct?

_____

_____

_____

_____

3. Ariel thought the movie *Dumb and Dumber* was the funniest movie she ever saw, and told her friend Ambrose to go see the movie. Ambrose likes a good comedy but didn't think this one was very funny. He hates taking advice from Ariel because she thinks every movie is "the funniest!" To what would you attribute the differing view of the movie?

_____

_____

_____

_____

Locus of Control

To determine if you have an internal or an external locus of control, complete the inventory below.

SD=strongly disagree   D=disagree   N=neither agree nor disagree
A = agree   SA = strongly agree

	SD	D	N	A	SA
1. So much of what happens in life is luck.	1	2	3	4	5
2. I am responsible for my successes and failures.	1	2	3	4	5
3. If you work hard, you will be successful.	1	2	3	4	5
4. You have to be lucky to find a good job.	1	2	3	4	5
5. I have little influence over my life.	1	2	3	4	5
6. If you treat others right, they will treat you right.	1	2	3	4	5
7. Nothing I do seems to matter.	1	2	3	4	5
8. Skill and effort will result in good performance.	1	2	3	4	5
9. I can only blame myself when I don't do well.	1	2	3	4	5
10. I ultimately control my future.	1	2	3	4	5
11. I can change the world.	1	2	3	4	5
12. You have to play with the hand life deals you.	1	2	3	4	5
13. People who are unemployed could find a job if they wanted to.	1	2	3	4	5
14. Being careful will help reduce the chance of being a victim of crime.	1	2	3	4	5
15. If you have a bad boss, there is nothing you can do about it.	1	2	3	4	5
16. Professional actors and athletes were born with their ability.	1	2	3	4	5
17. Some people are just born lucky.	1	2	3	4	5
18. My destiny is in my own hands.	1	2	3	4	5
19. Other people control my life more than I do.	1	2	3	4	5
20. There is little you can do to keep from getting sick.	1	2	3	4	5

Writing Resumes and Cover Letters

In the last half of the chapter, you learned how to apply your knowledge of impression formation to writing a resume, writing a cover letter, and surviving the employment interview. To apply this knowledge even further, write your resume using the psychological style discussed in the text. Be sure to incorporate:

- primacy
- priming and memory organization
- relevancy
- unusualness
- negative-information bias
- short-term memory limits

CHAPTER TEN

Understanding and Applying Leadership Skills

In the first 9 chapters of this text, you learned the keys to managing yourself and working with others. Over the next 6 chapters, you will learn the keys to leading and managing others. This chapter provides an overview of leadership, and Chapters 11 through 15 provide specific leadership skills.

Even if you are not currently managing other employees, the following chapters should still be useful to you for three reasons. One, by understanding leadership and organizational behavior, you will better understand your supervisors and thus be in a position to work with them more effectively. Two, you may not manage people at work but you may be in leadership positions in your community, your church, or at home. Three, learning leadership and organizational behavior skills may help you get promoted.

By the end of the chapter, you will:

- Learn what types of people become good leaders
- Understand the importance of leaders adapting their behavior to each situation
- Know what skills are essential for effective leadership
- Learn how leaders use power and influence

■ AN INTRODUCTION TO LEADERSHIP

Many different theories about leadership have been developed over the last few decades. Although none of the theories tells the whole story about leadership, each has received at least some empirical support. Understanding the theories and research behind leadership is important because the theory that company executives believe about leadership will, for the most part, determine how an organization selects or develops its managers.

Focused Free-Write
Before reading any further, complete the Focused Free-Write at the end of this chapter, which will help you focus on the relevance of leadership in your own life.

For example, if we believe that certain people are born leaders because of their personal traits, needs, or orientation, then managers could be selected partially on the basis of their scores on certain tests. But if we believe that leadership consists of specific skills or behaviors, then theoretically we should be able to train any employee to become an outstanding leader. If we believe that good leadership is the result of an interaction between certain types of behaviors and particular aspects of the situation, then we might choose certain types of people to be leaders at any

given time, or we might teach leaders how to adapt their behavior to meet the situation.

The following pages provide brief explanations of the most popular leadership theories. When reading about each theory, think about what the theory would imply about the selection or development of leaders for an organization. In addition, think of how you manage and the type of leader you wish to be.

PROJECT A *Understanding Your Own Leadership Style*
The next several pages in the text will discuss a variety of leadership styles. Before reading any further, complete the four leadership inventories found in Project A at the end of this chapter. You will score and interpret the inventories later in the chapter.

■ PERSONAL CHARACTERISTICS ASSOCIATED WITH LEADERSHIP

In the last 100 years, many attempts have been made to identify the personal characteristics that are associated with leader emergence and leader performance.

Leader Emergence

Leader emergence is the idea that leaders possess traits or characteristics different from nonleaders. This theory would say that leaders such as Ronald Reagan, John Kennedy, Adolph Hitler, Martin Luther King, Jr., and Elizabeth Dole share traits that your neighbor or a cook at McDonald's do not. If you use your school as an example, this theory would predict that the students in your student government would be different than students who do not participate in leadership activities.

Almost 100 traits have been identified in studies as differentiating leaders from nonleaders, some of which are listed in Exhibit 10-1. Only three traits—intelligence, dominance, and masculinity (such traditionally male traits as assertiveness and decisiveness)—have been commonly found to relate to leader emergence. Even then, the relationship between these traits and leader emergence is not especially strong (Kenny & Zaccaro, 1983; Lord, De Vader, & Alliger, 1986). Thus, the preponderance of research suggests that trait theories are not good predictors of leader emergence (Fiedler, 1996). Research also indicates that males and females emerge as leaders equally often (Benjamin, 1996) and that high self-monitors (people who change their behavior on the basis of the social situation)

EXHIBIT 10-1

Important Characteristics for Effective Leadership

Personal Characteristics	Physical Characteristics
Adaptable	Athletic
Assertive	Attractive
Charismatic	
Creative	
Decisive	
Dominant	
Energetic	
Extroverted	
Friendly	
Honest	
Intelligent	
Masculine	
Outgoing	
Self-confident	
Wise	

emerge as leaders more often than low self-monitors (Buchanan & Foti, 1996; Dobbins, Long, Dedrick, & Clemons, 1990; Kent & Moss, 1990).

These confusing and somewhat contradictory findings are especially perplexing because both anecdotal evidence and research do suggest that leadership behavior has some stability (Law, 1996). To illustrate this point, think of a friend whom you consider to be a leader. In all probability, that person is a leader in many situations. That is, he might influence a group of friends about what movie to see, make decisions about what time everyone should meet for dinner, and "take charge" when playing sports. Conversely, you probably have a friend who has never assumed a leadership role in his life. Thus, it appears that some people consistently emerge as leaders in a variety of situations, whereas others who share these characteristics never emerge as leaders (Kenny & Zaccaro, 1983; Sabini, 1995).

After researching the extent to which leadership is consistent across life, Bruce (1997) suggested that the best way to select a chief executive officer (CEO) is to look for leadership qualities (e.g., risk taking, innovation, vision) and success early in a person's career. As support for his proposition, Bruce cites the following examples:

- Harry Gray, the former chair and CEO of United Technologies, demonstrated vision, risk taking, and innovation as early as the second job in his career.

- Ray Tower, former president of FMC Corp., went way beyond his job description as a salesperson in his first job to create a novel sales training program. Tower continued to push his idea despite upper management's initial lack of interest.

- Lee Iacocca, known for his heroics at Ford and Chrysler, pioneered the concept of new car financing. His idea of purchasing a 1956 Ford for monthly payments of $56 ("Buy a '56 for $56") moved his sales division from last in the country to first. What is most interesting about this success is that Iacocca didn't even have the authority to implement his plan—but he did it anyway.

Leader Performance

In contrast to leader emergence, which deals with the likelihood that a person will *become* a leader, **leader performance** involves the idea that excellent leaders possess certain characteristics that poor leaders do not. For example, an excellent leader might be intelligent, assertive, friendly, and independent, whereas a poor leader might be shy, aloof, and calm. Research on the relationship between personal characteristics and leader performance has concentrated on three areas: traits, needs, and orientation. Exhibit 10-1 lists some of the characteristics that studies have associated with effective leadership.

TRAITS

The idea that certain traits are associated with effective leadership is appealing, but in 1964, a review by Heslin and Dunphy indicated that only two traits—intelligence and interpersonal adjustment—have consistently been related to leadership performance. After 40 years of studying leadership, Fiedler (1996) concluded that there is no consistent relationship between any one trait and leadership performance. Recently, it has been proposed that good leaders need to possess only one stable trait: *adaptability* or **self-monitoring** (A. R. Cohen & Bradford, 1990; M. Foster, 1989). Thus, good leaders will constantly change their behaviors to meet the demands of the situation or the person with whom they are dealing. Support for this theory comes from a study by Caldwell and O'Reilly (1982), who found that field representatives who dealt with many different types of people were more effective if they were high self-monitors. Similar results were found by Zaccaro, Foti, and Kenny (1991).

The concept of self-monitoring focuses on what leaders *do* as opposed to what they *are*. For example, a high self-monitoring leader may possess the trait of shyness and not truly want to communicate with other people. He knows, however, that talking to others is an important part of his job, so he says hello to his employees when he arrives at work, and at least once a day stops and talks with each employee. Thus, our leader has the trait of shyness but adapts his outward behavior to appear to be outgoing and confident.

An interesting extension of the trait theory of leader performance suggests that certain traits are necessary requirements for leadership excellence but that they do not guarantee it (Simonton, 1979). Instead, leadership excellence is a function of the right person being in the right place at the right time. The fact that one person with certain traits becomes an excellent leader while another with the same traits flounders may be no more than the result of timing and chance.

For example, Lyndon Johnson and Martin Luther King, Jr. were considered successful leaders because of their strong influence on improving civil rights. But other people prior to the 1960s had the same thoughts, ambitions, and skills as King and Johnson, yet they did not become successful civil rights leaders because the time was not right.

NEEDS

A personal characteristic that has received some support pertains to a leader's **need for power, need for achievement**, and **need for affiliation**. Research by McClelland and Burnham (1976) and McClelland and Boyatzis (1982) has demonstrated that high-performance managers have a **leadership motive pattern,** which is a high need for power and a low need for affiliation. The need is not for personal power but for organizational power.

This pattern of needs is thought to be important because it implies that an effective leader should be concerned more with results than with being liked. Leaders who need to be liked by their subordinates will have a tough time making decisions. A decision to make employees work overtime, for example, may be necessary for the organization's survival but will probably be unpopular with employees. Leaders with high affiliation needs may decide that being liked is more important than being successful, causing conflict with their decision.

This theory also explains why internal promotions often do not work. Consider, for example, a person who worked for 6 years as a loan officer. He and 10 coworkers often went drinking together after work and away on weekends. But one day he was promoted to manager and then had to lead the same people with whom he had been friends. The friendships and his need to be liked hindered the new manager from giving orders and disciplining his employees. When he tried to separate himself from his friends, he was quickly thought of as "being too good for his friends"—a tough situation with no apparent solution, according to this theory.

This does not mean a leader should not be friendly and care about subordinates. But successful leaders will not place their need to be liked above the goals of the organization. President Richard Nixon was thought to have a high need for being liked. He would often make a tough decision and then apologize for it because he wanted to be liked by both the public and the press.

Needs for power, achievement, and affiliation can be measured through various psychological tests. The most commonly used is the **Thematic Apperception Test (TAT)**. The TAT is a projective test in which a person is shown a series of pictures and asked to tell a story about what is happening in each picture. The stories are then analyzed by a trained psychologist who identifies the needs themes contained in the stories. Obviously, this technique is time consuming and requires a great deal of training.

Another commonly used measure is the **Job Choice Exercise (JCE)**, developed by Stahl and Harrell (1982). With the JCE, a leader reads descriptions of jobs that involve varying degrees of power, achievement, and affiliation needs and then rates how desirable he finds each particular job. These ratings are then subjected to a complicated scoring pro-

EXHIBIT 10-2

Relationship Between Managerial Grid (MG), Theory X, and Ohio State (OS) Theories

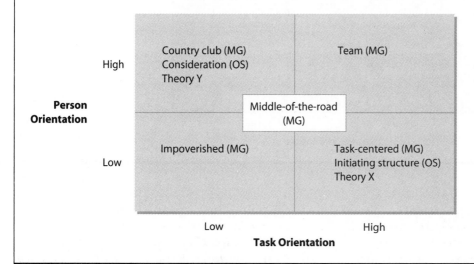

cedure that uses regression analysis to reveal scores on the three need categories.

Another method to determine leaders' needs is to examine the themes that occur in their writing and speeches. In one interesting use of this method, it was found that Presidents Franklin Roosevelt, Kennedy, and Reagan had high needs for power; Presidents Harding, Truman, and Nixon had high needs for affiliation; and Presidents Wilson, Hoover, and Carter had high needs for achievement (Winter, 1988).

TASK VS. PERSON ORIENTATION

Over the last 45 years, three major schools of thought—Ohio State Studies (Fleishman, Harris, & Burtt, 1955), Theory X (McGregor, 1960), and **Managerial Grid** (Blake & Mouton, 1984)—have postulated that differences in leader performance can be attributed to differences in the extent to which leaders are task versus person oriented. As shown in Exhibit 10-2, though the three schools of thought use different terms, they say similar things.

Person-oriented leaders (*Country Club* leaders, *Theory Y* leaders, leaders high in *consideration*) act in a warm and supportive manner and show concern for their subordinates. Person-oriented leaders believe that employees are intrinsically motivated, seek responsibility, are self-controlled, and do not necessarily dislike work. Because of these assumptions, person-oriented leaders consult their subordinates before making decisions, praise their work, ask about their families, do not look over their shoulders, and use a more hands-off approach to leadership. Under pressure, person-oriented leaders tend to become socially withdrawn (G. E. Bond, 1995).

Task-oriented leaders (*task-centered* leaders, *Theory X* leaders, leaders high in *initiating structure*) define and structure their own roles and those of their subordinates to attain the group's formal goals. Task-oriented leaders see their employees as lazy, extrinsically motivated, wanting security, undisciplined, and shirking responsibility. Because of these assumptions, task-oriented leaders tend to manage or lead by giving directives, setting goals, and making decisions without consulting their subordinates. Under pressure, task-oriented leaders become anxious, defensive, and dominant (Bond, 1995). Interestingly, task-oriented leaders tend to produce humor (e.g., tell jokes and stories) whereas person-oriented leaders tend to appreciate humor (e.g., listen to others' jokes) (Philbrick, 1989).

As shown in Exhibits 10-2 and 10-3, the best leaders (**team**) are both task and person oriented whereas the worst (**impoverished**) are neither task nor person oriented. Some leaders (**middle-of-the-road**) have moderate amounts of both orientations.

A leader's task or person orientation can be measured by several instruments, two of which are the

EXHIBIT 10-3

Consequences of Leader Orientation

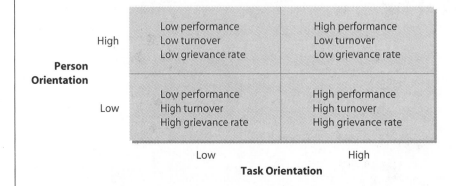

		Low	High
Person Orientation	High	Low performance Low turnover Low grievance rate	High performance Low turnover Low grievance rate
	Low	Low performance High turnover High grievance rate	High performance High turnover High grievance rate
		Low	High
		Task Orientation	

Leadership Opinion Questionnaire (LOQ) and the *Leader Behavior Description Questionnaire (LBDQ)*. The LOQ is filled out by supervisors or leaders who desire to know their own behavioral style. The LBDQ is completed by subordinates to provide a picture of how they perceive their leader's behavior. A meta-analysis by Eagly and Johnson (1990) indicated that females are more likely to have a person orientation and less likely to have a task orientation than are males.

Research on the consequences of using a task or person orientation has brought interesting findings. As shown in Exhibit 10-3, person-oriented leaders tend to have satisfied employees, whereas task-oriented leaders tend to have productive employees. Leaders scoring high in both (team leadership) have satisfied and productive employees, whereas leaders scoring low in both (impoverished leadership) tend to have unhappy and unproductive employees (Hutchison, Valentino, & Kirkner, 1998; Pool, 1997).

The above results certainly make sense, but the relationship between person and task orientation is probably more complex than was first thought. Several studies have shown that such variables as leader experience and knowledge and such external variables as time pressures and work importance tend to moderate the relationship between person-orientation scores and satisfaction and between task-orientation scores and subordinate performance.

UNSUCCESSFUL LEADERS

In a departure from research to identify characteristics of successful leaders, Hogan (1989) attempted to iden-

tify traits of unsuccessful leaders. Hogan was interested in investigating poor leaders because, according to both empirical research and anecdotal accounts, most employees report that one of the greatest sources of stress in their jobs is their supervisors' poor performance, strange behavior, or both. This finding should come as no surprise: You can probably quickly recall many examples of poor performance or strange behavior with current or former supervisors.

Lack of training On the basis of years of research, Hogan (1989) concluded that poor leader behavior has three major causes. The first is a *lack of leadership training* given to supervisors. The armed forces are among the few organizations that require supervisors to complete leadership training before taking charge of groups of people. The norm for most organizations, however, is either to promote a current employee or to hire a new employee directly into a leadership role. If training is ever provided, it is usually after the promotion and well after the supervisor has begun supervising. The serious consequences of this lack of training can best be understood if we imagine allowing doctors to perform surgery without training or allowing truck drivers to drive the highways without first learning how to drive a truck.

Cognitive deficiencies The second cause of poor leadership stems from *cognitive deficiencies*. Hogan (1989) believed that poor leaders are unable to learn from experience and are unable to think strategically (i.e., to plan ahead). They consistently make the same mistakes and do not plan ahead.

The manager of a local convenience store is an example of a person who does not learn from his mistakes. The manager did not give employees their work schedules until one or two days before they had to work. The employees complained because the hours always changed and they could not schedule their personal, family, and social lives. But the manager continued to do it his way, and most of the employees quit. Eight years later, he still does it his way, and his employees still leave at a high rate.

Personality The third, and perhaps most important, source of poor leadership behavior involves the *personality* of the leader. Hogan (1989) believed that many unsuccessful leaders are insecure and adopt one of three personality types: the paranoid/passive-aggressive, the high-likability floater, and the narcissist.

The source of insecurity for leaders who are paranoid, passive-aggressive, or both is some incident in their lives in which they felt betrayed. This *paranoid/passive-aggressive* leader has deeply rooted, but perhaps unconscious, resentment and anger. On the surface, these leaders are charming, quiet people who often compliment their subordinates and fellow workers. But they resent the successes of others and are likely to act against subordinates in a passive-aggressive manner; that is, on the surface they appear to be supportive, but at the same time they will "stab" another person in the back.

The type of leader who is insecure and seldom rocks the boat or causes trouble is known as a *high-likability floater*. This person goes along with the group, is friendly to everyone, and never challenges anyone's ideas. Thus, he travels through life with many friends and no enemies. The reason he has no enemies is because he never does anything, challenges anyone, or stands up for the rights of his employees. Such leaders will be promoted and never fired because even though they make no great performance advances, they are well liked. Their employees have high morale but show relatively low performance.

Narcissists are leaders who overcome their insecurity by overconfidence. They like to be the center of attention, promote their own accomplishments, and take most, if not all, of the credit for the successes of their group—but they avoid all blame for failure.

■ INTERACTION BETWEEN THE LEADER AND THE SITUATION

As already indicated, a leader's effectiveness often depends on the particular situation. In the past few decades, several theories have emerged that have sought to explain the situational nature of leadership.

Situational Favorability

The most well-known and controversial of the situational theories was developed by Fred Fiedler in the mid-1960s (Fiedler, 1967). Fiedler believed that an individual's leadership style is the result of a lifetime of experiences and thus is extremely difficult to change. **Fiedler's contingency model** holds that any individual's leadership style is effective only in certain situations. The way to increase leader effectiveness, then, is to help people understand their style of leadership and learn how to manipulate a situation so that the two match. To help people understand their leadership style, Fielder developed the **Least-Preferred Coworker (LPC) Scale**.

To complete the LPC Scale, leaders identify the subordinate or employee with whom they would least want to work. Leaders then rate that person on several semantic differential scales that range from *nice* to *nasty* and from *friendly* to *unfriendly*. The higher the leaders rate their least-preferred coworker, the higher the LPC score. This score is then compared to the favorableness of the situation to determine leader effectiveness. Low-scoring LPC leaders tend to be task oriented, whereas high-scoring LPC leaders tend to be more concerned with interpersonal relations (Fiedler, 1978; R. W. Rice, 1978). High-LPC leaders would fall in the same quadrant in Exhibit 10-2 as Theory Y and Consideration leaders. Low-LPC leaders would fall in the same quadrant as Theory X and Initiating Structure leaders.

The favorableness of a situation is determined by three variables. The first is **task structuredness**. Structured tasks have goals that are clearly stated and known by group members, have only a few correct solutions to a problem, and can be completed in only a few ways. The more structured the task, the more favorable the situation.

The second variable is **leader position power**. That is, the greater the position or legitimate power of the leader, the more favorable the situation. Thus, a group or organizational setting in which there is no assigned leader is not considered to be a favorable leadership situation.

The third variable is **leader-member relations**. The more that subordinates like their leader, the more favorable the situation. The leader-member relationship is considered the most important of the three variables.

As shown in Exhibit 10-4, the relationship between LPC scores and group performance is complex. Basically, low-scoring LPC leaders (those who rate their least-preferred coworker low) function best

EXHIBIT 10-4

Relationship Between LPC Scores and Group Success

	Low	Moderate	High
High LPC Score	Low performance	High performance	Low performance
Low LPC Score	High performance	Low performance	High performance

Situation Favorability

in situations that are either favorable or unfavorable, whereas high-scoring LPC leaders function best when the situation is only of moderate favorability.

In spite of psychometric problems with the LPC Scale (Kennedy, Houston, Korsgaard, & Gallo, 1987; Stewart & Latham, 1986), research generally has supported Fiedler's theory. Strube and Garcia (1981) conducted a meta-analysis of 145 independent studies that investigated Fiedler's model as well as 33 of Fiedler's own studies and concluded that the ideas were well supported by the research. C. A. Schriesheim, Tepper, and Tetrault (1994) found support for the general predictions of leader behavior but not for some of the specific predictions.

Fiedler's training program, called **Leader Match,** has also been supported by research (Strube & Garcia, 1981). This program is based on Fiedler's belief that an individual's leadership style is not easily changed. Thus, to improve their abilities, leaders learn through 4-hour workshops how to diagnose situations and then change these situations to fit their particular leadership styles (Csoka & Bons, 1978). Leader Match is probably the only training program in the country concentrating on changing the situation rather than the leader.

Organizational Climate

A more recent situational theory, known as **IMPACT theory,** was developed by Geier, Downey, and Johnson (1980) who believed that each leader has one of six behavioral styles: *Informational, Magnetic, Position, Affiliation, Coercive,* or *Tactical.* Each style is only effective in a particular situation, or in what the researchers call an *organizational climate.* As shown in Exhibit 10-5, the six styles are similar to the five

bases of power suggested several years ago by French and Raven (1959; also Raven, 1965).

INFORMATIONAL STYLE IN A CLIMATE OF IGNORANCE

The leader who has an **informational style** provides information in a climate of **ignorance,** where important information is missing from the group. For example, if a car containing four college professors and a mechanic broke down on the side of the road, who would become the leader? Almost certainly it would be the mechanic because he would have the most knowledge or information needed to solve the problem.

For many years in the U.S. Senate, Sam Nunn was one of the most powerful and respected congressional leaders. He became powerful because of his expertise in defense matters, an important area that few in Congress knew much about. Thus, Nunn used an informational style in a climate of ignorance to become a powerful leader.

MAGNETIC STYLE IN A CLIMATE OF DESPAIR

A leader with a **magnetic style** leads through energy and optimism and is effective only in a climate of **despair,** which is characterized by low morale. Ronald Reagan is perhaps the best example of a magnetic leader. As president, he was optimistic and well liked, even by people who may not have agreed with him politically. He was elected at a time when the national mood was depressed because of high inflation, high unemployment, and the Iran hostage situation. The chances of successful leadership increase in a situation

EXHIBIT 10-5

Comparison of IMPACT Styles and Bases of Power

IMPACT Style (Geier et al.)	Base of Power (French & Raven)
Informational	Expert
Magnetic	Referent
Position	Legitimate
Affiliation	
Coercive	Coercive/Reward
Tactical	

of general despair when a magnetic or charismatic individual assumes control (V. M. Latham, 1983).

POSITION STYLE IN A CLIMATE OF INSTABILITY

A person who uses the **position style** leads by virtue of the power inherent in that position. Such a person might lead through such statements as, "As your captain, I am ordering you to do it" or "Because I am your mother—that's why." Individuals who use a position style will be effective only in climates of **instability**. This style is especially effective during corporate mergers, particularly when people are not sure what actions to take. However, there are often questions about a leader's legitimate scope of power (Yukl, 1989).

AFFILIATION STYLE IN A CLIMATE OF ANXIETY

A person with an **affiliation style** leads by liking and caring about others. This style is similar to that of the person-oriented leader discussed previously. A leader using affiliation will be most effective in a climate of **anxiety** or when worry predominates. Former president Jimmy Carter provides an excellent example of the affiliation style. Carter was elected president shortly after the Watergate affair when many voters were worried that they could not trust politicians or their government. Carter campaigned successfully with statements such as "I care" and "I'm not part of that Washington crowd."

COERCIVE STYLE IN A CLIMATE OF CRISIS

A person using the **coercive style** leads by controlling reward and punishment and is most effective in a climate of **crisis**. Such a leader will often use statements such as "Do it or you're fired" or "If you can get the package there on time, I will have a little something for you." This style is typical in war. If soldiers disobey an order, an officer can have them shot. Conversely, if soldiers behave with bravery and distinction, an officer can reward them with a medal or promotion.

Support for the situational appropriateness of coercive styles of leadership was found by Mulder, de Jong, Koppelaar, and Verhage (1986) when they studied the leadership styles of bankers. Mulder and his colleagues found that in crisis situations, bankers tend to use more formal and coercive types of power than in noncrisis situations.

TACTICAL STYLE IN A CLIMATE OF DISORGANIZATION

A leader with a **tactical style** leads through the use of strategy and is most effective in a climate of **disorganization**. A good example is a class that breaks into small groups to complete an assignment. Ideally, every student knows the material well enough to complete the assignment, but normally there is a limited amount of time and too much work to do. The person who becomes the leader is the one who is best able to organize the group.

BECOMING AN EFFECTIVE LEADER ACCORDING TO IMPACT THEORY

If IMPACT theory is correct, people can become effective leaders by one of the four methods shown in Exhibit 10-6. The first is by finding a climate that is consistent with their behavioral style. This method, however, involves either a great deal of luck or a lot of patience, requiring the leader to be in the right place at the right time.

EXHIBIT 10-6

Four Leadership Strategies

- Find a climate consistent with your leadership style.
- Change your leadership style to better fit the existing climate.
- Change your followers' perception of the climate.
- Change the actual climate.

In the second method, leaders change their style to meet a particular climate (Suedfeld & Rank, 1976). That is, if the climate is one of ignorance, individuals change their behavior and use information to lead. If the climate is one of despair, individuals become more outgoing and positive. Thus, people who are willing to adapt their behavior and who have the ability to "play" each of the six leadership styles should be effective leaders.

Although there is continual debate about whether a person can be trained to be a leader, a study by Manz and Sims (1986) suggests that leaders *can indeed* be taught different styles of leadership. Manz and Sims used a behavioral modeling approach to successfully teach 40 leaders how to use positive-reward behavior, reprimand behavior, and goal-setting behavior. Thus, those who are willing to use different leadership styles can learn the necessary skills and behaviors through training programs.

The third method by which a person can become an effective leader is to change followers' perception of the climate so that the perception matches the leader's behavioral style. This tactic is common in politics, in which each candidate tries to convince the voting public that he or she is the best person for an office.

The fourth method by which a leader can become effective is by actually changing the climate itself rather than simply changing followers' perceptions of the climate. Obviously, this is difficult to do, but it is the strategy advocated in Fiedler's Leader Match training. Such a strategy is difficult but can be successful.

PROJECT B *Scoring and Interpreting Your Leadership Inventories*
Now that you have read about the different traits, orientations, and needs associated with leadership, it is time to score the inventories you took in Project A. Turn to Project B at the end of this chapter and follow the scoring and interpretation instructions.

Subordinate Ability

R. J. House (1971) believed that a leader's behavior will be accepted by subordinates only to the extent to which the behavior helps the subordinates achieve their goals. Thus, leaders will be successful only if their subordinates perceive them as working with them to meet certain goals and if those goals offer a favorable outcome for the subordinates.

Because the needs of subordinates change with each new situation, supervisors must adjust their behavior to meet the needs of their subordinates. That is, in some situations subordinates need a leader to be directive and to set goals; in others, they already know what to do and need only emotional support.

PATH-GOAL THEORY

According to House's **path-goal theory**, a leader can adopt one of four behavioral leadership styles to handle each situation: instrumental, supportive, participative, or achievement-oriented.

The **instrumental style** calls for planning, organizing, and controlling the activities of employees. The **supportive-style** leader shows concern for employees; the **participative-style** leader shares information with employees and lets them participate in decision making; and the leader who uses the **achievement-oriented style** sets challenging goals and rewards increases in performance.

Each style will only work in certain situations and depends on subordinates' abilities and the extent to which the task is structured. In general, the higher the level of subordinate ability, the less directive the leader should be. Likewise, the more unstructured the situation, the more directive the leader should be (C. A. Schriesheim & DeNisi, 1981).

R. J. House and Mitchell (1974) further advised that, to be effective, a leader should:

- Recognize the needs of subordinates and work to satisfy those needs
- Reward subordinates who reach their goals

EXHIBIT 10-7

Appropriate Situational Leadership Styles Based on Employee Ability and Willingness

	Unable	Able
Employee Willingness Level — Unwilling	Directing R1	Supporting R3
Willing	Coaching R2	Delegating R4
	Employee Ability Level	

- Help subordinates identify the best paths to take in reaching particular goals
- Clear those paths so that employees can reach their goals

Path-goal theory is intuitively appealing because it gives a manager direct advice about how to behave in certain situations. Furthermore, because it is behavior based rather than trait based, the theory could be used in training. Research thus far, however, has not supported application of this theory (Hammer & Dachler, 1975; J. F. Schriesheim & Schriesheim, 1980). Thus, if path-goal theory is to have real impact, it will need further revision.

SITUATIONAL LEADERSHIP THEORY

Another theory that focuses on the relationship between leader and follower is the **situational leadership theory** developed by Hersey and Blanchard (1988). Hersey and Blanchard postulated that a leader typically uses one of four behavioral styles: delegating, directing, supporting, or coaching. Hersey and Blanchard termed the most important follower characteristic *follower readiness*, or the ability and willingness to perform a particular task. The degree of follower readiness can be measured by either the manager's rating form or the self-rating form developed by Hersey and Blanchard. Scores from these forms place followers into one of four categories, or readiness (R) levels:

R1: Unable and unwilling or insecure

R2: Unable but willing or confident

R3: Able but unwilling or insecure

R4: Able and willing or confident

As shown in Exhibit 10-7, for R1 followers, the most effective leader behavior is the *directing approach*. That is, the leader directs the follower by telling him what to do and how to do it. A *coaching approach* should be used with R2 followers because they are willing to do the work but are not sure *how* to do it. Leaders using this approach explain and clarify how work should be done. R3 followers are given plenty of emotional support as well as opportunities for two-way communication. This approach is successful because these followers already know what to do but are not sure whether they *want* to do it. R4 followers are most productive and happy when a delegating leadership style is used. These followers are both willing and able to perform the task. Thus, the only real job for the leader is to delegate specific tasks to subordinates and then let them complete those tasks with minimal supervision or guidance.

Under this theory, effective leaders first diagnose the competency and motivation levels of employees for each goal or series of tasks and then adapt their leadership style to fit the employee's level. As the employee makes developmental progress, the leader changes his style and becomes less directive. It is important for leaders to discuss this strategy with each employee so that employees will understand why they are being treated a particular way (Blanchard, Zigarmi, & Zigarmi, 1985).

As with many theories of leadership, situational leadership theory has excellent intuitive appeal and has been successful in some organizational applications (Gumpert & Hambleton, 1979) but not others (Goodson, McGee, & Cashman, 1989; Norris & Vecchio, 1992). Unfortunately, however, until more research is available and more revisions to the theory are made, it is difficult to determine its long-term effectiveness (Nicholls, 1985).

Relationships With Subordinates

Vertical dyad linkage (VDL) theory was developed by Dansereau, Graen, and Haga (1975) and is a unique situational theory that makes good intuitive sense. The situational theories discussed earlier concentrate on interactions between leaders and situations and between leaders and employees with differing levels of ability. VDL theory, however, concentrates on the *interactions* between leaders and subordinates. These interactions are called leader-member exchanges (LMX). The theory takes its name from the relationship between two people (a *dyad*), the position of the leader above the subordinate (*vertical*), and their interrelated behavior (*linkage*).

VDL theory states that leaders develop different roles with different subordinates and thus act differently with different subordinates. Dansereau and his colleagues believed that subordinates fall into one of two groups—the *in-group* or the *out-group*.

In-group subordinates are those who have developed trusting, friendly relationships with the leader. As a result, the leader deals with in-group members by allowing them to participate in decisions and by rarely disciplining them. Out-group subordinates are treated differently from those in the in-group and are more likely to be given direct orders and to have less say about how affairs are conducted.

In general, research on VDL theory has been supportive (Gerstner & Day, 1997; Graen & Scheimann, 1978; Scandura, Graen, & Novak, 1986; Vecchio, Griffeth, & Hom, 1986; Wakabayashi & Graen, 1984). There are, however, relationships between leaders and subordinates that can be categorized into types other than in-group and out-group. Thus, further research is needed into the relationship between leaders and subordinates.

■ SPECIFIC LEADERSHIP SKILLS

Another way to think about leadership is that excellent leaders possess specific behaviors or skills that poor leaders do not. After observing thousands of leaders in a variety of situations, Yukl (1982), Carter

(1952), Hemphill and Coons (1950), and Gibbs (1969) have proposed a behavioral "theory." According to these researchers, leaders do the following:

1. Initiate ideas
2. Informally interact with subordinates
3. Stand up for and support subordinates
4. Take responsibility
5. Develop a group atmosphere
6. Organize and structure work
7. Communicate formally with subordinates
8. Reward and punish subordinates
9. Set goals
10. Make decisions
11. Train and develop employee skills
12. Solve problems
13. Generate enthusiasm

In a job analysis of first-line supervisors at the Maryland Department of Transportation, Cooper, Kaufman, and Hughes (1996) found the following skills to be essential:

■ organizing
■ analysis and decision making
■ planning
■ communication (oral and written)
■ delegation
■ work habits (high-quality work)
■ carefulness
■ interpersonal skill
■ job knowledge
■ organizational knowledge
■ toughness
■ integrity
■ development of others
■ listening

This theory is not particularly exciting and is the least described in textbooks, but it is the way that leadership is most often practiced in industry. If this theory is true, then leadership and management are something learned; if the specific behaviors and skills important for effective leadership can be identified, then almost anyone can be trained to become an effective leader. There are many examples of such training programs currently in use.

The city of San Diego has its own management academy that provides interested employees with the skills necessary to become managers. On weeknights and weekends, employees learn skills such as oral

EXHIBIT 10-8

Specific Behaviors Taught in Leadership Training Programs

Specific behavior	Corresponding chapter in this text
Communication skills	7, 13
Conflict management	6
Decision-making skills	3, 10, 13
Delegation	13
Discipline	12, 15
Ethical behavior	4
Motivation	12
Persuasion	14
Planning and organizing	3
Problem solving	
Providing performance feedback	15
Public speaking, oral communication	
Reward and punishment	12
Running a meeting	3
Soothing and supporting	7, 11
Stress management	2
Team building	8, 13
Time management	3
Training and mentoring	15
Understanding people	1, 5, 6
Writing	7

communication, report writing, decision making, conflict management, and performance appraisal. After an employee is trained and tested in each of these important skill areas, he or she receives a certificate of completion. Even though graduates of the management academy are not promised managerial positions, more often than not they are the employees who are promoted.

If you have ever attended a leadership conference, you probably have noticed that the training involved specific leadership skills such as time management, goal setting, persuasion, and communication. Such an agenda typifies the idea that leadership consists of specific and learnable skills and behaviors.

Although it is beyond the scope of this chapter to discuss each of the behaviors and skills listed in Exhibit 10-8, many are covered throughout this text. A discussion of a few additional skills follows.

Leadership Through Decision Making

Decision making is a specific behavior or skill that is important for a leader to possess. Vroom and Yetton (1973), however, pointed out that previous research has shown that only in certain situations are decisions best made by the leader; in other situations, decisions are best made with the participation of a leader's subordinates, colleagues, or both. Because of this situational aspect to decision making, Vroom and Yetton believed that leadership performance can be improved by teaching leaders to become better decision makers. To aid this process, Vroom and Yetton developed a decision tree to help leaders decide when decisions should be made alone and when they should be made with the help of others. Of course, developing a chart that would tell a leader what to do in every possible situation would be impossible. But the **Vroom-Yetton Model** does provide a flowchart that can tell a leader what *process* to go through to make a decision in a particular situation. This theory will be discussed in further detail in Chapter 13.

Leadership Through Contact: Management by Walking Around

Management by Walking Around (MBWA) is another popular specific behavioral theory. This theory holds that leaders and managers are most effective when they are out of their offices, walking around and meeting with and talking to employees and customers about their needs and progress. Many industry leaders such as the late Sam Walton of Wal-Mart have used this approach with great success. MBWA is thought to increase communication, build relationships with employees, and encourage employee participation (C. W. Miller, 1998).

In an interesting series of studies by Komaki and her associates (Komaki, 1986; Komaki, Zlotnick, & Jensen, 1986), the behavior of bank managers was observed to determine the differences between effective and ineffective managers. The results of the investigations indicated that the main difference between the two was that effective managers spent more time walking around and monitoring the behavior and performance of their employees. Empirical evidence thus seems to support the MBWA concept.

Leadership Through Power

Another strategy that leaders often use is management by power. Power is important to a leader because as it increases, so does the leader's potential to influence others. Leaders who have power are able to obtain more resources, dictate policy, and advance further in an organization than those who have little or no power.

Earlier in this chapter, French and Raven's bases of power were alluded to in terms of their relationships to Geier et al.'s IMPACT theory. These authors (French & Raven, 1959; Raven, 1992) identified five basic types of power: expert, legitimate, reward, coercive, and referent (see Exhibit 10-5).

EXPERT POWER

As mentioned earlier, in certain situations, leaders who know something useful—that is, have expert knowledge—will have power. But there are two requirements for **expert power**. First, the knowledge must be something that others in an organization need. In a university's psychology department, a researcher with an excellent grasp of statistics has

power over those who do not. Similarly, a soldier who knows how to get around the military bureaucracy has more power than those who only know how to follow established channels and procedures. Second, others must be aware that the leader knows something. Information is powerful only if other people know that the leader has it or if the leader uses it (Benzinger, 1982).

LEGITIMATE POWER

Leaders obtain **legitimate power** on the basis of their positions. For example, a sergeant has power over a corporal, a vice president has power over a supervisor, and a coach has power over players on a football team. Leaders with legitimate power are best able to get employees to comply with their orders (Rahim & Afza, 1993) but have low follower satisfaction (Rahim, 1989).

REWARD AND COERCIVE POWERS

Leaders also have power to the extent that they can reward and punish others. **Reward power** involves having control over both the obvious—salary increases, bonuses, or promotions—and the subtle—praise or more favorable work assignments.

For a leader to have **coercive power**, others must believe he is willing to use his ability to punish; he cannot maintain coercive power if employees believe he is bluffing. Punishment includes such actions as firing or not promoting and the more subtle actions of giving a cold shoulder.

REFERENT POWER

Another source of power for a leader may lie in the positive feelings that others hold for him. Leaders who are well liked can influence others even in the absence of reward and coercive power. Leaders can obtain such **referent power** by complimenting others, doing favors, and generally being friendly and supportive (Kipnis, Schmidt, & Wilkinson, 1980). Employees of leaders with referent power are most committed to their organizations and satisfied with their jobs (Rahim & Afza, 1993).

Leadership Through Vision: Transformational Leadership

Whereas most leadership theories concentrate on the short-term relationships between leaders and subordinates (Howell & Avolio, 1993), **transformational leadership** focuses on long-term goals (Bass, 1990; Howell & Avolio, 1993). Transformational leaders are often labeled as visionary, charismatic, and inspirational. They lead by developing a vision, changing organizations to fit this vision, and motivating employees to reach the vision or long-term goal. Transformational leaders are confident, have a need to influence others, and hold a strong attitude that their beliefs and ideas are correct (Bryman, 1992). They innovate, challenge the status quo, focus on people, are flexible, look to the future, carefully analyze problems, and trust their intuition (Bass, 1997; Nanus, 1992; Yukl, 1994).

A good example of a transformational leader is Herb Kelleher, the CEO who turned Southwest Airlines into one of the top airlines in the world. Kelleher is charismatic (on one occasion he settled a dispute by arm wrestling, on another he came to work dressed as Elvis), employee oriented (his employees come first, the customers second—his thinking is that happy employees will result in happy customers), visionary (his concept of a low-cost airline was designed to compete as much with ground transportation as with other airlines), and a great motivator of people.

Yukl (1994) offered the following guidelines for transformational leadership:

- Develop a clear and appealing vision.
- Develop a strategy for attaining the vision.
- Articulate and promote the vision.
- Act confident and optimistic.
- Express confidence in followers.
- Use early success in small steps to build confidence.
- Celebrate successes.
- Use dramatic, symbolic actions to emphasize key values.
- Lead by example.
- Create, modify, or eliminate such cultural forms as symbols, slogans, and ceremonies.

Some research on transformational leadership indicates that it is the most effective form of leadership, is used on every continent, and is best liked by employees (Bass, 1997). After studying a variety of successful and unsuccessful leaders, Hunt and Laing (1997) concluded that too much effort has been expended in trying to label leaders as transformational or charismatic. Instead, they proposed that excellent leadership should be defined by exemplar—that is, does a leader have characteristics similar to successful leaders and dissimilar to unsuccessful leaders? On the basis of their research, Hunt and Laing hypothesized that good leaders possess five characteristics not shared by poor leaders: vision, differentiation, values, transmission, and flaws.

VISION

Consistent with the notion of transformational leadership, goods leaders have a vision of where they want the organization to go and provide direction toward that end. Hunt and Laing (1997) found that 72% of high-performing leaders were described by their subordinates as being visionary compared to only 34% of the least successful leaders.

DIFFERENTIATION

Successful leaders are somehow different from their followers. In some cases, the difference might be one of personality, while in others it might be one of charisma, knowledge, or skill. Though successful leaders are somehow different from their followers, they are also similar enough to relate to and empathize with their followers. A good example of this point can be found in presidential elections. Candidates travel the country trying to relate to the people by wearing regional attire (e.g., cowboy hats in Texas, a John Deere cap in Iowa) but still trying to "look presidential."

VALUES

Successful leaders have strong values. For example, Wal-Mart founder Sam Walton strongly valued customer service, whereas Southwest Airlines CEO Herb Kelleher strongly values employee relations.

TRANSMISSION OF VISION AND VALUES

Successful leaders are able to communicate their vision and values to others. Thus, successful leaders tend to have good oral, written, and interpersonal skills.

FLAWS

Interestingly, successful leaders typically have a major flaw and they know it. This flaw makes the leader more human and provides a target that followers can focus on when they are upset with the leader. A look at recent presidents shows many with flaws: Nixon had his quirky mannerisms, Reagan tended to ramble and forget, and Clinton had his affairs. Our attention to these flaws often kept us from criticizing the presidents on more important problems (e.g., ethics, economy, foreign relations).

■ LEADERSHIP: WHERE ARE WE TODAY?

Most of this chapter has described leadership theories. Of course, when several theories address the same topic, the question comes to mind: "Which of the theories are true?" The answer probably is that each is somewhat true and that the best theory about leadership is some combination.

EXHIBIT 10-9

Effective Leadership: Interaction of Leader, Situation, and Follower Characteristics

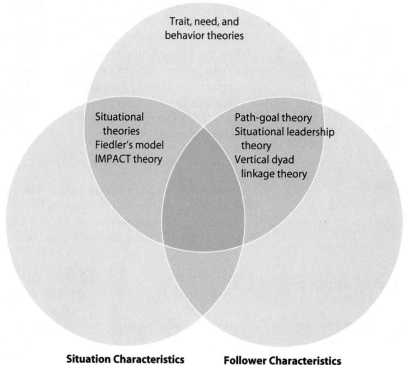

Leader Characteristics

Trait, need, and behavior theories

Situational theories
Fiedler's model
IMPACT theory

Path-goal theory
Situational leadership theory
Vertical dyad linkage theory

Situation Characteristics   **Follower Characteristics**

As Exhibit 10-9 shows, if we combine all of the theories discussed in this chapter, leadership emerges as a set of interactions: between a leader's traits and skills, between a situation's demands and characteristics, and between followers' needs and characteristics. If we begin with a leader's traits and skills, a summary of the theories would suggest that individuals would be more likely to be successful leaders if they:

- have received leadership training and mastered the skills listed back in Exhibit 10-8
- are high self-monitors
- are high in both task and person orientations
- have the leadership motive pattern (high need for power, low need for affiliation)
- are intelligent
- are emotionally stable (don't possess such problem personalities as the high-likability floater, narcissist, or passive aggressive personality)

- possess the skills and personality to be a transformational leader

If an individual has these skills and traits, their leadership performance will depend on the characteristics of the situation. Thus, as shown in Exhibit 10-10, certain people will be effective leaders in certain situations when particular types of people are followers. For example, in a structured situation in which the leader has both legitimate and referent power (highly favorable situation), a low-LPC leader will perform better than a high-LPC leader. If subordinates are unwilling and unable to perform a task, a directing leadership style will work better than a supporting style. If there is a climate of despair and the leader has referent power, a magnetic leadership style will work better than an informational style. Unfortunately, we are not yet at the stage where we can determine the exact matches that result in the best leadership for every situation. But it is probably safe to make the following assumptions.

EXHIBIT 10-10

Situational Leadership Flowchart

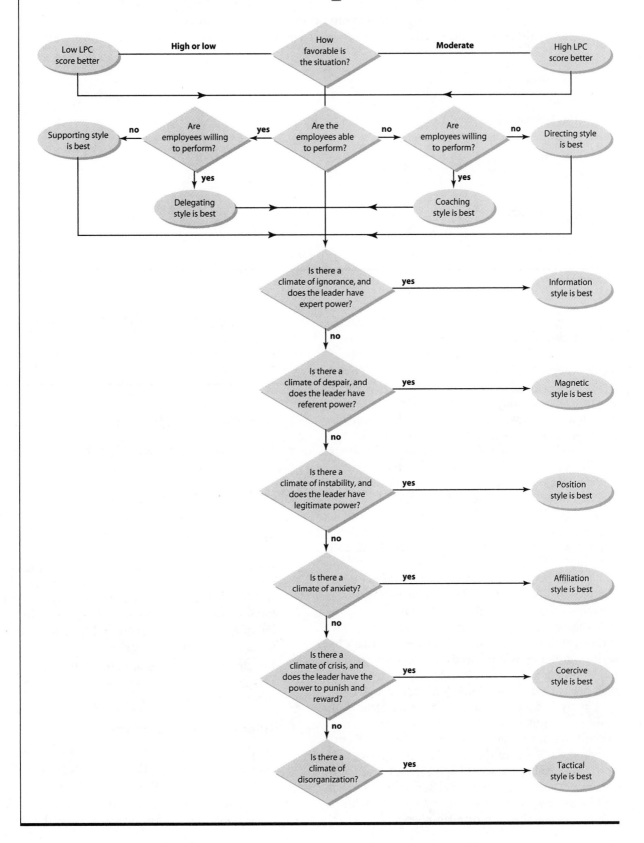

EXHIBIT 10-11

Effective Leadership Skills

Leadership Skill	Requirements of the Situation/Follower				
	Information	Direction	Empathy/Support	Motivation	Persuasion
Decision making		X			
Goal setting		X			
Persuasion	X	X		X	X
Team building			X	X	
Stress management			X		
Friendliness			X	X	
Empathy			X		
Energy				X	
Time management		X			
Technical knowledge	X				
Intelligence	X	X			

First, because different situations require different leadership styles and skills, individuals who have a wide variety of relevant skills will be best able to be effective leaders in a larger variety of situations. That is, a person who only has excellent planning skills will be an effective leader only in situations that require planning. But a leader who has excellent skills in planning, persuasion, people, goal setting, and motivation will be able to lead in many different types of situations.

The advice that follows from this assumption is obvious. As Exhibit 10-11 shows, an individual interested in becoming an effective leader should obtain as many leadership skills as possible. By attending leadership conferences, taking courses, and gaining a variety of experiences, a leader can gain most of these skills.

Second, because individuals have different needs and personalities, leaders who are able to adapt their interpersonal styles to fit the needs of followers will be better leaders than those who stick to just one behavioral style. It is much easier for a leader to adapt his style to fit the individual needs of his followers than for 30 people with different needs and styles to adapt their behavior to fit their leader's needs and style.

Finally, because a leader must use different skills in different situations and act differently with different followers, it is important that he be able to understand the needs of the situation, the follower, or both and then behave accordingly. Thus, leaders who accurately recognize situational and follower needs will be more effective than those who are unable to distinguish one situation from another.

> **PROJECT C** *Your Own Leadership Theory*
> To apply what you have learned about leadership, develop your own leadership theory by completing Project C at the end of this chapter.

CHAPTER RECAP

- Intelligence, interpersonal adjustment, self-monitoring, a leadership motive pattern (high power, low affiliation), and the combination of a task and person orientation are related to high levels of leadership performance.

- Leadership effectiveness is also a function of the interaction between the leader and the situation. Important situational aspects include situational favorability (Fiedler), organizational climate (IMPACT theory), subordinate ability (path-goal theory, situational leadership theory), and the relationship between leaders and their subordinates (vertical dyad linkage).

- Effective leaders possess specific skills, such as persuasion, motivation, and decision making, that ineffective leaders do not.

Critical Thinking Questions

1. Do those who seek leadership roles, those who emerge as leaders, and those who are successful leaders share similar traits?

2. Which of the situational theories seems to provide the best explanation for successful leadership?

3. Hogan identified three main reasons for unsuccessful leadership. Are there others that he did not mention?

4. Can effective leadership actually be taught?

5. How can a leader be more persuasive?

WEB SITES

For further information, log on to the following web sites.

www.sonic.net/~mfreeman/
Provides useful information about a variety of leadership topics.

www.perc.net/Background.HTML
Excellent site that allows you to go through a leadership simulation exercise.

www.nwlink.com/~donclark/leader/leader.html
Contains an entire leadership manual.

www.leader-values.com/
Information about leadership. Contains profiles on several great leaders.

www.epinc.com/MANAGE/MANTIPS1.HTM
Provides several lists of leadership tips.

KEY TERMS

Achievement-oriented style In path-goal theory, a leadership style in which the leader sets challenging goals and rewards achievement.

Affiliation style A leadership style in which the individual leads by caring about others and is most effective in a climate of anxiety.

Anxiety An organizational climate in which worry predominates.

Coercive power Leadership power that comes from the leader's capacity to punish others.

Coercive style A leadership style in which the individual leads by controlling reward and punishment; most effective in a climate of crisis.

Crisis A critical time or climate for an organization in which the outcome to a decision has extreme consequences.

Despair An organizational climate characterized by low morale.

Disorganization A climate in which the organization has the necessary knowledge and resources but does not know how to efficiently use the knowledge or the resources.

Expert power Power that individuals have because they have knowledge.

Fiedler's contingency model A theory of leadership that states that leadership effectiveness depends on the interaction between the leader and the situation.

Ignorance An organizational climate in which important information is not available.

IMPACT theory A theory of leadership that states that there are six styles of leadership (informational, magnetic, position, affiliation, coercive, and tactical) and that each style will be effective in only one of six organizational climates.

Impoverished leadership A style of leadership in which the leader is concerned with neither productivity nor the well-being of employees.

Informational style A style of leadership in which the leader leads through knowledge and information; most effective in a climate of ignorance.

Instability An organizational climate in which people are not sure what to do.

Instrumental style In path-goal theory, a leadership style in which the leader plans and organizes the activities of employees.

Job Choice Exercise (JCE) An objective test that is used to measure various need levels.

Leader emergence A part of trait theory that postulates that certain types of people will become leaders and certain types will not.

Leader Match A training program that teaches leaders how to change situations so that the situations are consistent with their leadership styles.

Leader-member relations The variable in Fiedler's contingency model that refers to the extent to which subordinates like a leader.

Leader performance A part of trait theory that postulates that certain types of people will be better leaders than will other types of people.

Leader position power The variable in Fiedler's contingency model that refers to the extent to which a leader, by the nature of his or her position, has the power to reward and punish subordinates.

Leadership motive pattern The name for a pattern of needs in which a leader has a high need for power and a low need for affiliation.

Least-Preferred Coworker (LPC) Scale A test used in conjunction with Fiedler's contingency model to reveal leadership style and effectiveness.

Legitimate power The power that individuals have because of their elected or appointed position.

Magnetic style A style of leadership in which the leader has influence because of his or her charismatic personality; most effective in a climate of despair.

Managerial Grid A measure of leadership that classifies a leader into one of five leadership styles.

Middle-of-the-road leadership A leadership style reflecting an approach that balances people and task orientation.

Need for achievement According to trait theory, the extent to which a person desires to be successful.

Need for affiliation According to trait theory, the extent to which a person desires to be around other people.

Need for power According to trait theory, the extent to which a person desires to be in control of other people.

Participative style In path-goal theory, a leadership style in which the leader allows employees to participate in decisions.

Path-goal theory A theory of leadership that states that leaders will be effective if their behavior helps subordinates achieve relevant goals.

Person-oriented leadership A style of leadership in which the leader is concerned about the well-being of employees but is not task oriented (Country Club, Theory Y, leaders high in consideration).

Position style A leadership style in which the leaders influence others by virtue of their appointed or elected authority; most effective in a climate of instability.

Referent power Leadership power that exists when followers can identify with a leader and the leader's goals.

Reward power Leadership power that exists to the extent that the leader has the ability and authority to provide rewards.

Self-monitoring The ability to change behavior to meet the demands of the situation or the person.

Situational leadership theory A theory of leadership that states that effective leaders must adapt their style of leadership to fit both the situation and the followers.

Supportive style In path-goal theory, a leadership style in which leaders show concern for their employees.

Tactical style A leadership style in which a person leads through organization and strategy; most effective in a climate of disorganization.

Task-oriented leadership A leadership style in which the leader is more concerned with productivity than with employee well-being (task-centered, Theory X, leaders high in initiating structure).

Task structuredness The variable in Fiedler's contingency model that refers to the extent to which tasks have clear goals and problems can be solved.

Team leadership A leadership style in which the leader is concerned with both productivity and employee well-being.

Thematic Apperception Test (TAT) A projective test that is used to measure various need levels.

Transformational leadership Visionary leadership in which the leader changes the nature and goals of an organization.

Vertical dyad linkage (VDL) theory A leadership theory that concentrates on the interaction between the leader and his or her subordinates.

Vroom-Yetton model A theory of leadership that concentrates on helping a leader choose how to make a decision.

PRACTICE EXAM

1. Which of the following traits has been consistently identified as being related to both leader emergence and leader performance?
   a. dominance
   b. intelligence
   c. sociability
   d. interpersonal adjustment

2. Which of the following is not a commonly used test to measure a leader's needs for power and affiliation?
   a. Thematic Apperception Test
   b. Job Choice Exercise
   c. Leader Descriptive Index
   d. All of the above are common measures

3. A person with the leadership motive pattern, has a:
   a. strong need for the organization to be successful
   b. strong need to be liked
   c. strong need for the organization to be successful and a low need to be liked
   d. low need for the organization to be successful and a high need to be liked

4. According to Hogan (1989), which of the following is not a major source of poor leader behavior?
   a. a lack of training
   b. a high level of self-monitoring
   c. cognitive deficiencies
   d. personality

5. A leader who resents the successes of others is an example of a:
   a. paranoid/passive-aggressive personality
   b. high-likability floater
   c. narcissist
   d. sociopathic personality

6. According to the Ohio State studies, a leader who sets goals is high in:
   a. consideration
   b. initiating structure
   c. self-monitoring
   d. emergence

7. To have both productive and happy employees, a leader should be _____ in consideration and _____ in initiating structure.

a. high / low   b. high / high
c. low / high   d. low / low

8. _____ leaders believe that employees are intrinsically lazy.
   a. Theory D   b. Theory X
   c. Theory Y   d. Theory Z

9. Leaders who adapt their behavior to the demands of the situation are:
   a. impoverished   b. low self-monitors
   c. task-centered   d. high self-monitors

10. Which of the following is not a person-oriented leader?
    a. Theory X   b. High LPC
    c. Team   d. Country Club

11. The training program for Fiedler's contingency model is called:
    a. Leader Grid   b. Managerial Grid
    c. Leader Match   d. Managerial Match

12. Which of the following styles would work best in a climate of instability?
    a. ignorance   b. coercive
    c. position   d. tactical

13. According to IMPACT theory, a person who _____ would not be a successful leader.
    a. waits until her style matches the climate
    b. adopts her style to the climate
    c. convinces her followers that the climate is consistent with her style
    d. all of the above persons would be successful

14. According to path-goal theory, which of the following leaders would set their employees' goals for them?

15. Which of the following theories concentrates on the interaction between leader and subordinates?
    a. IMPACT   b. contingency
    c. path-goal   d. vertical dyad linkage

16. Which of the following leadership theories states that a leader must adapt to both the climate and her subordinates?
    a. situational leadership theory
    b. contingency
    c. managerial grid
    d. path-goal

17. Which of the following theories involves decision making?
    a. contingency   b. Vroom-Yetton
    c. vertical dyad linkage   d. path-goal

18. In the Vroom-Yetton model, the first question that must be asked involves the:
    a. importance of the decision quality
    b. amount of leader knowledge
    c. degree of problem structure
    d. probability of decision acceptance

19. A charismatic leader has _____ power.
    a. expert   b. legitimate
    c. reward   d. referent

20. Which of the following leaders would be persuasive?
    a. a physically attractive leader
    b. a trustworthy leader
    c. a leader with a lot of relevant knowledge
    d. all of the above

ANSWERS 1 b, 2 c, 3 c, 4 b, 5 a, 6 b, 7 b, 8 b, 9 d, 10 a, 11 c, 12 c, 13 d, 14 a, 15 d, 16 a, 17 b, 18 a, 19 d, 20 d

Focused Free-Write

Think of the leader that you respect more than any other leader. This person can be an international, national, or local person. Describe what it is about this person that caused you to choose him or her.

_____

_____

_____

_____

_____

_____

_____

_____

_____

_____

_____

_____

_____

_____

_____

_____

_____

_____

_____

_____

_____

_____

Now think of the leader who is your least respected leader. Again, this person can be international, national, or local. What is it about this leader that you do not like?

_____

_____

_____

_____

_____

_____

_____

_____

_____

_____

_____

_____

_____

_____

_____

_____

_____

_____

_____

_____

_____

_____

Understanding Your Leadership Style

The following pages contain four tests of leadership styles to be discussed in this chapter. Before reading any further in the text, follow the instructions for each of the four sections below. After you have completed the tests, continue reading the chapter.

Section A

Answer true or false for the next 18 questions.

1. I find it hard to imitate the behavior of others. T F
2. At parties and social gatherings, I do not attempt to do or say things that others will like. T F
3. I can only argue for ideas that I already believe. T F
4. I can make impromptu speeches even on topics about which I have almost no information. T F
5. I guess I put on a show to impress or entertain people. T F
6. I would probably make a good actor. T F
7. In a group of people, I am rarely the center of attention. T F
8. In different situations with different people, I act like very different people. T F
9. I am not particularly good at making other people like me. T F
10. I am not always the person I appear to be. T F
11. I would not change my opinions in order to please someone else or win his or her favor. T F
12. I have considered being an entertainer. T F
13. I have never been good at games like charades or improvisational acting. T F
14. I have trouble changing my behavior to suit different people and different situations. T F
15. At a party, I let others keep the jokes and stories going. T F
16. I feel a bit awkward in company and do not show up quite as well as I should. T F
17. I can look anyone in the eye and tell a lie with a straight face (if for the right end). T F
18. I may deceive people by being friendly when I really dislike them. T F

Section B

Think of the person with whom you can work least well. He or she may be some-one you work with now or someone you knew in the past. He or she does not have to be the person you like least well, but should be the person with whom you had the most difficulty in getting a job done. Describe below how this person appears to you by placing a check in the appropriate place on the scale.

Pleasant	8	7	6	5	4	3	2	1	Unpleasant
Friendly	8	7	6	5	4	3	2	1	Unfriendly
Rejecting	1	2	3	4	5	6	7	8	Accepting
Helpful	8	7	6	5	4	3	2	1	Unhelpful
Unenthusiastic	1	2	3	4	5	6	7	8	Enthusiastic
Tense	1	2	3	4	5	6	7	8	Relaxed
Distant	1	2	3	4	5	6	7	8	Close
Cold	1	2	3	4	5	6	7	8	Warm
Cooperative	8	7	6	5	4	3	2	1	Uncooperative
Supportive	8	7	6	5	4	3	2	1	Unsupportive
Boring	1	2	3	4	5	6	7	8	Interesting
Quarrelsome	1	2	3	4	5	6	7	8	Harmonious
Self-assured	8	7	6	5	4	3	2	1	Hesitant
Efficient	8	7	6	5	4	3	2	1	Inefficient
Gloomy	1	2	3	4	5	6	7	8	Cheerful
Open	8	7	6	5	4	3	2	1	Guarded

Section C

For each statement, circle the number corresponding to the extent to which you agree.

SD=strongly disagree   D=disagree   N=neutral
A=agree   SA=strongly agree

	SD	D	N	A	SA
1. Most employees need to be told what to do.	1	2	3	4	5
2. Most employees will take advantage of a friendly supervisor.	1	2	3	4	5
3. Most decisions should be made by management rather than by employees.	1	2	3	4	5
4. When a supervisor leaves the room, employee effort goes down.	1	2	3	4	5
5. Most employees who call in sick are probably faking their illness.	1	2	3	4	5
6. The decline in productivity is mostly due to employees not caring about their work.	1	2	3	4	5
7. If welfare and work paid the same, few people would choose to work.	1	2	3	4	5

Section D

For each item below, rate the extent to which the statement is true for you. The rating is on a 5-point scale with a rating of 1 indicating that the statement is not at all true of you and a rating of 5 indicating that the statement is very true of you.

	not true at all				very true of me
1. It is important for me to accomplish many things in life.	1	2	3	4	5
2. It is important for me to have many friends.	1	2	3	4	5
3. I like to be better than others.	1	2	3	4	5
4. I feel hurt when people don't like me.	1	2	3	4	5
5. I always try to get an A in every class.	1	2	3	4	5
6. Failure greatly upsets me.	1	2	3	4	5
7. I enjoy being in charge of other people.	1	2	3	4	5
8. I hate to be alone.	1	2	3	4	5
9. Awards are important to me.	1	2	3	4	5
10. I would feel uncomfortable going to a movie alone.	1	2	3	4	5
11. I am much more of a leader than a follower.	1	2	3	4	5
12. It is important for me to be in control.	1	2	3	4	5
13. I need to have close friends.	1	2	3	4	5
14. I hate having people in charge of me.	1	2	3	4	5
15. I have high standards and goals for myself.	1	2	3	4	5

Section E

To give you an idea about your IMPACT leadership styles, go back to Project B in Chapter 1 and get your scores for the Employee Personality Inventory. Scores on these dimensions roughly correspond with the IMPACT Styles.

EPI Category	Your EPI Score	IMPACT Equivalent
Thinking	_____	Informational
Directing	_____	Position/Coercive
Communicating	_____	Magnetic
Soothing	_____	Affiliation
Organizing	_____	Tactical

Scoring and Interpreting Your Leadership Inventories

Section A

This is the Self-Monitoring Scale. To get your score:

_____ Count the number of times you chose False for Questions 1, 2, 3, 7 9, 11, 13, 14, 15, & 16

_____ Count the number of times you chose True for Questions 4, 5, 6, 8, 10, 12, 17, & 18

Add the two numbers to get your self-monitoring score: _____

Section B

This inventory is the Least Preferred Coworker (LPC) Scale. To get your score, add the numbers below each of your checkmarks. For example, your total from the two questions below would be 10 (3 + 7). Your LPC score: _____

Boring	___	___	✓	___	___	___	___	___	Interesting
	1	2	3	4	5	6	7	8	
Quarrelsome	___	___	___	___	___	___	✓	___	Harmonious
	1	2	3	4	5	6	7	8	

Section C

This inventory measures the extent to which you are a task- or person-oriented leader. To score this test, add the points from each of the numbers you circled.

Your task orientation score: _____

Section D

This inventory provides scores on need for achievement, need for affiliation, and need for power. To get your scores, add the numbers you circled for the following questions:

Need for achievement (Questions 1, 5, 6, 9, 15) _____

Need for power (Questions 3, 7, 11, 12, 14) _____

Need for affiliation (Questions 2, 4, 8, 10, 13) _____

Putting It All Together

Transfer your scores from Sections A, B, C, and D onto the chart below.

Leadership Profile

Percentile	Need for power	Need for achievement	Need for affiliation	Self-monitoring	LPC	Task orientation	Percentile
99	25	25	25	15	119	30	99
95	24	24	24	14	103	28	95
90	21	23	22	13	92	26	90
85	20		21	12	83	25	85
80	19				80	24	80
75	18	22	20	11	75		75
70		21	19	10	72	23	70
65	17				70		65
60	16		18	9	67	22	60
55		20			65	21	55
50	15	19	17	8	62		50
45				7	60	20	45
40		18	16		55		40
35			15	6	54	19	35
30	14	17	14		51	18	30
25				5	49		25
20	13	16	13		46	17	20
15	12	15	12		44	16	15
10	10	14	11	4	35	15	10
5	8	12	9	3	28	14	5

_____   _____   _____   _____   _____   _____

IMPACT Leadership Profile

Transfer your scores from Section E onto the chart below.

Percentile	Information (Thinking)	Magnetic (Communication)	Position/Coercive (Directing)	Affiliation (Soothing)	Tactical (Organizing)	Percentile
99	14	16	13	16	15	99
95	12	15	11	14	14	95
90	11	14	10	13	13	90
85	10		9	12	12	85
80	9	13	8	11	11	80
75					10	75
70		12	7	10	9	70
65						65
60	8	11		9	8	60
55			6			55
50	7	10		8	7	50
45			5			45
40		9		7		40
35	6	8			6	35
30			4	6		30
25	5	7			5	25
20		6	3	5	4	20
15		5		4		15
10	4	4	2	3	3	10
5	3	3	1	2	2	5

_____   _____   _____   _____   _____

Your Leadership Style

Are you a high or low self-monitor? _____

Are you a high- or low-LPC leader? _____

Are you a task- or person-oriented leader? _____

Do you have the leadership motive pattern? _____

What is your IMPACT style? _____

On the basis of your scores, how would you describe your leadership style? In what situations would you perform best? Worst?

_____

_____

_____

_____

_____

_____

_____

_____

_____

_____

_____

_____

_____

_____

_____

_____

_____

PROJECT C

Your Own Leadership Theory

Your text discussed a variety of leadership theories. On the basis of these theories, as well as on your own experiences, create your own leadership theory. What causes people to become leaders, and why are some leaders better than others?

_____

_____

_____

_____

_____

_____

_____

_____

_____

_____

_____

_____

_____

_____

_____

_____

_____

_____

_____

_____

Employee Satisfaction

Imagine the following situations:

- Jean Davis and Maria McDuffie have worked as customer service representatives at Fuller Technologies for the past 2 years. Jean loves her job and wants to stay with Fuller until she retires in 10 years. Maria hates her job, uses all of her available sick days, and would leave in a heartbeat if she could only find a job that paid as well.

- Rhonda Beall recently met with a career advisor to chart a new course for her life. She hates her current job and has hated every job she has ever had. She is hoping the career advisor can find "the job" for her.

- David Spoto loves his job and can't wait to get to work in the morning. He loves to work, loves his current job, and has loved every job he has ever had.

- Darnell Johnson, the HR director for Simmons Enterprises, is frustrated because his company has the highest turnover rate in the area. Even more frustrating is that employees stay with Simmons just long enough to gain experience and then leave for lower pay with Trayne Manufacturing, another local employer.

In these examples, why does Jean Davis love her job and Maria McDuffie hate the same job? Why do Rhonda Beall and David Spoto have such different attitudes about their jobs and careers? What is Trayne Manufacturing doing better than Simmons Enterprises? This chapter will help you answer these questions about **job satisfaction**—the attitude an employee has toward her job. By the end of the chapter, you will:

> Understand why an employer should even care about job satisfaction
>
> Learn the individual differences in the predisposition to be satisfied
>
> Learn ways to increase employee satisfaction
>
> Know the methods to measure employees' levels of job satisfaction
>
> Understand why employees are absent from work

Although this chapter will explore several theories that seek to explain why workers are satisfied with their jobs, none of the theories completely and accurately explains job satisfaction. However, each is valuable in that it suggests ways to increase employee satisfaction. Thus, even though a theory itself may not be completely supported by research, the resulting suggestions have generally led to increased performance or longer tenure.

Focused Free-Write
Before reading any further, complete the Focused Free-Write at the end of the chapter to get you thinking about job satisfaction in your own life

■ WHY SHOULD WE CARE ABOUT JOB SATISFACTION?

Psychologists and other human resource professionals have spent considerable time and effort to increase job satisfaction. The question is why. Of course, one reason is that we want everyone to be happy in life (even our in-laws), and anything we can do to make a person's job more satisfying contributes to that goal. However, when time and money are spent improving something, most organizations want to see a return on that investment. That is, will satisfied employees be more profitable to an organization than dissatisfied ones?

As shown in Exhibit 11-1, the answer to that question depends on the outcome we are looking at. Research has shown that job satisfaction is highly related to an employee's commitment to an organization (Tett & Meyer, 1993) but only marginally related to an employee's attendance (Hackett, 1989), tenure (Tett & Meyer, 1993), and job performance (Iaffaldano & Muchinsky, 1985). Though the relationships between job satisfaction and attendance, performance, and turnover are relatively small, it is important to note that many other factors affect work behavior. For example, a dissatisfied employee may want to quit her job, but not be able to because no other jobs are available. Likewise, a dissatisfied employee may want to miss work but realizes that she will lose pay if she does. Thus, we often find that job satisfaction is related more to a desire to quit, miss work, or reduce effort than it is to actual behaviors.

■ CAUSES OF JOB SATISFACTION

Individual Differences

Going back to our examples at the beginning of the chapter, what would explain why David Spoto loves his current job and Rhonda Beall hates hers? According to theories involving individual differences, the key is that David has been satisfied at every job he has had whereas Rhonda has never been satisfied with a job. Individual-difference theory postulates

Meta-analysis Results of the Relationship Between Job Satisfaction and Performance, Turnover, and Absenteeism

Satisfaction	Performance[a]	Turnover[b]	Absenteeism		Commitment[b]
			Frequency[c]	Duration[c]	
Facet					
Pay	.06		−.08	−.07	
Supervision	.19		−.13	−.08	
Coworkers	.12		−.07	−.07	
Work	.21		−.21	−.14	
Promotion Opportunities	.15		−.09	−.07	
Type					
Intrinsic	.23		−.25	−.01	
Extrinsic	.18		−.24	−.21	
Overall Satisfaction	.19	−.25	−.15	−.23	.70

[a] Iaffaldano and Muchinsky (1985)
[b] Tett and Meyer (1993)
[c] Hackett (1989)

that some variability in job satisfaction is due to an individual's personal tendency across situations to enjoy what she does. Thus, certain types of people will generally be satisfied and motivated regardless of the type of job they hold. This idea also makes intuitive sense. We all know people who constantly complain and whine about every job they have, and we also know people who are motivated and enthusiastic about every job or task.

For this theory to be true, job satisfaction would have to be consistent across time and situations, and research seems to support this notion. As a demonstration that job satisfaction is fairly consistent across time, significant correlations were found by Staw and Ross (1985) between the job satisfaction levels of employees in 1969 and in 1971 ($r = .33$), by Judge and Watanabe (1993) between job satisfaction levels of employees in 1972 and 1977 ($r = .37$), by Steel and Rentsch (1997) between measures of job satisfaction taken 10 years apart ($r = .37$), and by Staw, Bell, and Clausen (1986) between adolescent and adult levels of satisfaction. (See "Using This Book" in the front of the book for discussion of correlation and correlation coefficients.)

PROJECT A *Stability of Job Satisfaction*
To demonstrate the stability of job satisfaction in your own life, complete Project A at the end of this chapter.

Because there seems to be at least some consistency in job satisfaction across time and jobs, the next question concerns the types of people who seem to be consistently satisfied with their jobs. Research in this area has focused on genetic predispositions (Lykken & Tellegen, 1996), core self-evaluations (Judge, Locke, Durham, & Kluger, 1998), and life satisfaction (Tait, Padgett, & Baldwin, 1989).

GENETIC PREDISPOSITIONS

An interesting and controversial set of studies (Arvey, Bouchard, Segal, & Abraham, 1989; Keller, Bouchard, Arvey, Segal, & Dawis, 1992) suggested that job satisfaction not only may be fairly stable across jobs, but also may be genetically determined. Arvey and his colleagues arrived at this conclusion by comparing the levels of job satisfaction of 34 sets of identical twins who were separated from each other at an early age. If job satisfaction is purely environmental, there should be no significant correlation between levels of job satisfaction for identical twins who were raised in different environments and who are now working at different types of jobs. But if identical twins have similar levels of job satisfaction despite being reared apart and despite working at dissimilar jobs, then a genetic predisposition for job satisfaction is likely.

On the basis of their analysis, Arvey and his colleagues found that approximately 30% of job satisfaction appears to be explainable by genetic factors. Thus, one way to increase the overall level of job satisfaction in an organization would be to hire only those applicants who show high levels of overall job and life satisfaction. Because these findings are controversial and have received some criticism (Cropanzano & James, 1990), more research is needed before firm conclusions can be drawn.

CORE SELF-EVALUATIONS

Whether the consistency in job satisfaction is due to genetic or environmental factors, there appears to be a series of personality variables that are related to job satisfaction. That is, certain types of personalities are associated with the tendency to be satisfied or dissatisfied with one's job. Judge, Locke, Durham, and Kluger (1998) hypothesized that these personality variables are related to one another and involve people's positve outlook on life (positive affectivity), view of their self-worth (self-esteem), ability to master their environment (self-efficacy), and ability to control their environment (external vs. internal locus of control). People prone to be satisfied with their jobs have high self-esteem, high self-efficacy, high positive affectivity, and an internal locus of control. Research supporting this view has come from Judge et al. (1998), who found a significant correlation between a combination of these four variables and job satisfaction ($r = .41$) and life satisfaction ($r = .41$), and from Garske (1990), who found that employees with high self-esteem are more satisfied with their job than are employees low in self-esteem. Results consistent with the core evaluation theory were reported by Dubin and Champoux (1977), who found that some people have a job-oriented focus of life and that these people are happier in their jobs than people without this focus.

> **PROJECT B** *Core Self-Evaluation*
> To get an idea of your own predisposition to be satisfied at work, complete the inventory in Project B at the end of this chapter

LIFE SATISFACTION

Judge, Locke, Durham, and Kluger (1998), Judge and Watanabe (1993), and Tait, Padgett, and Baldwin (1989) have theorized not only that job satisfaction is consistent across time, but that the extent to which a person is satisfied with all aspects of her life (e.g., marriage, friends, job, family, geographic location) is as well. Furthermore, people who are satisfied with their jobs tend to be satisfied with life. These researchers found support for their theory, as their data indicate that job satisfaction is significantly correlated with life satisfaction. Thus, people happy in life tend to be happy in their jobs and vice versa.

In an interesting study, Judge and Watanabe (1994) found that for about two thirds of the people, high levels of life satisfaction are associated with high levels of job satisfaction. In other words, satisfaction with one's job spills over into other aspects of life, and satisfaction with other aspects of life spills over into satisfaction with one's job. For the remaining 30 or so percent of the population, either there is no relationship between life and job satisfaction or there is a negative relationship.

That life satisfaction can influence job satisfaction in the vast majority of people is an important finding. In today's business climate, managers are being asked to work miracles in making even the worst of jobs satisfying. Perhaps a more realistic approach is what we refer to as the "John Travolta Method." If you recall from those classic films *Saturday Night Fever* and *Urban Cowboy*, John Travolta had boring jobs (as a paint store employee in *Fever* and as an oil refinery worker in *Urban Cowboy*) but made his life meaningful through his dancing. Now we're not suggesting that disco and line dancing are the solutions to life's problems. Instead, we are suggesting that an employee's needs can be met in a variety of nonwork activities such as hobbies and volunteer work. A mistake that we have made for years has been to assume that a job must satisfy all of a person's needs. Instead, an organization should work toward fulfilling those needs that it can and should help employees find alternative avenues to meet their other needs. Likewise, employees who are unhappy with their jobs should find alternative ways to satisfy their needs.

An interesting study by Judge (1993) demonstrates the importance of individual differences. More than 200 nurses in a medical clinic completed a questionnaire tapping their propensity to gripe about things in everyday life and also indicating how satisfied they were with their jobs. Judge then compared the nurses' level of job satisfaction with whether or not they quit their jobs with the clinic over the next 10 months. The results of this study indicated no relationship between satisfaction and turnover for the people who griped about everything in life. For the nurses who were not chronic gripers, satisfaction was significantly correlated with turnover ($r = -.39$).

In other words, people who are unhappy in life and unhappy on their jobs will not leave their jobs because they are used to being unhappy. But for people who are normally happy in life, being unhappy at work is a reason to find another job.

> **PROJECT C** *Life Satisfaction*
> To get an idea about your own tendency to be satisfied with work and life, complete the inventory in Project C at the end of this chapter.

Discrepancy Theories

Theories in this category postulate that our satisfaction with a job is determined by the discrepancy between what we *want, value,* and *expect* and what the job actually provides (Lawler, 1973; Locke, 1969). For example, if you enjoy working with people but your job involves working with data, you are not likely to be satisfied with your job. Likewise, if you value helping others, yet your job involves selling things people don't really need, you will probably be dissatisfied with your job.

Discrepancies between what employees want and what the job gives them affect how satisfied employees will be with their jobs (Knoop, 1994; R. W. Rice, Gentile, & McFarlin, 1991). For example, imagine that Jane most values money and Akeem most values flexibility. Both are in a job that pays well but has set hours and a standard routine. Though the job and the company are the same, one employee (Jane) will be satisfied and another (Akeem) will not.

HAVE THE EMPLOYEE'S JOB EXPECTATIONS BEEN MET?

A discrepancy between what an employee expected a job to be like and the reality of the job can affect satisfaction. For example, a recruiter tells an applicant how much fun employees have at a particular company and about the unlimited potential for advancement. After 3 months on the job, however, the employee has yet to experience the fun and can't find any signs of potential advancement opportunities. Because her expectations have not been met, the employee will probably feel dissatisfied.

As you can guess from the above example, it is important that applicants be given a **realistic job preview**. Though being honest about the negative aspects of a job may reduce the applicant pool, it decreases the chances of hiring a person who will later become dissatisfied.

A good example of this comes from an employee who works for a public mental health agency. Prior to her current job, she had worked in the public sector for 10 years in a variety of administrative positions. We met her in Chapter 2 as an example of role conflict—her new boss promised policy involvement in the job interview. She was excited about this new job because of the promised opportunities for personal growth. After a year, however, it became clear that the position was clerical and had no opportunity for advancement, and that the most important decision she could make involved whether to order pizza or sandwiches for executive meetings. As you can imagine, she was deeply disappointed and angry at having been misled. Because her role as a single mother did not allow her to quit her job, she vented her dissatisfaction by buying stale doughnuts for breakfast meetings, letting the coffee get cold, and "forgetting" to bring mayonnaise for her supervisor's sandwich—behaviors that could not get her fired but allowed her in a passive-aggressive manner to maintain some form of control in her work life.

A meta-analysis by Wanous, Poland, Premack, and Davis (1992) concluded that when an employee's expectations are not met, lower job satisfaction ($r = -.39$), decreased organizational commitment ($r = -.39$), and an increased intent to leave the organization ($r = .29$) occur. These results support the importance of ensuring that applicants have realistic job expectations. Though the meta-analysis results supported the "met expectations" theory, Irving and Meyer (1994) have criticized the studies that were included in the meta-analysis. In their own study, Irving and Meyer found that an employee's experiences on the job were most related to job satisfaction and that the *difference* between their expectations and experiences was only minimally related to job satisfaction. More studies using methods similar to Irving and Meyer are needed to clarify this issue.

HAVE THE EMPLOYEE'S NEEDS, VALUES, AND WANTS BEEN MET?

A discrepancy between an employee's needs, values, and wants and what a job offers can also lead to low job satisfaction. Several theories focus on employees' needs and values: Maslow's Needs Hierarchy, ERG Theory, Two-Factor Theory, and McClelland's Needs Theory.

Maslow's needs hierarchy Perhaps the most famous theory of satisfaction and motivation was developed by Abraham Maslow (1954). Maslow believed that employees would be satisfied with their jobs at any given point in time if certain needs were met. As Exhibit 11-2 shows, Maslow believed that we have five major types of needs and that these needs are hierarchical—that is, lower-level needs must be satisfied before an employee will be concerned with the next level of needs. It is

EXHIBIT 11-2

Maslow's Hierarchy of Needs

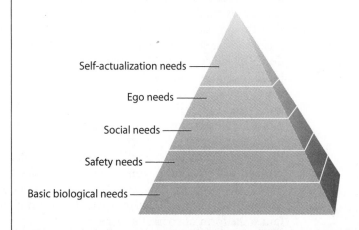

- Self-actualization needs
- Ego needs
- Social needs
- Safety needs
- Basic biological needs

helpful to look at a **hierarchy** as a staircase that is climbed one step at a time until the top is reached. The same is true of Maslow's hierarchy. Each level is taken one step at a time, and a higher level need cannot be reached until a lower level need is satisfied. Maslow's five major needs are discussed below.

Basic biological needs Maslow thought that an individual first seeks to satisfy **basic biological needs** for food, air, water, and shelter. In our case, an individual who does not have a job, is homeless, and is on the verge of starvation will be satisfied with any job as long as it provides for these basic needs. When asked how well they enjoy their job, people at this level might reply, "I can't complain, it pays the bills."

Safety needs After basic biological needs have been met, a job that merely provides food and shelter will no longer be satisfying. Employees then become concerned about meeting their **safety needs**. That is, they may work in an unsafe coal mine to earn enough money to ensure their family's survival, but once their family has food and shelter, they will remain satisfied with their jobs only if the workplace is safe.

Safety needs have been expanded to include psychological as well as physical safety. Psychological safety—often referred to as job security—can certainly affect job satisfaction. For example, public sector employees often list job security as a main benefit to their jobs—a benefit so strong that they will stay in lower paying public sector jobs rather than take higher paying, yet less secure, jobs in the private sector.

Social needs Once these first two need levels have been met, employees will remain satisfied with their jobs only when their social needs have been met. **Social needs** involve working with others, developing friendships, and feeling needed. Organizations attempt to satisfy their employees' social needs in a variety of ways. Company cafeterias provide workers the place and opportunity to socialize and meet other employees, company picnics allow families to meet one another, and company sports programs such as bowling teams and softball games provide opportunities for employees to play together in a neutral environment.

It is important that an organization make a conscious effort to satisfy these social needs when a job itself does not encourage social activity. For example, with a job such as that of a janitor or a night watchman, the employee will encounter few other people while working. Thus, the chance of making new friends is small.

A good friend of ours worked in a large public agency before becoming a writer and working out of her home. Prior to working at home, she seldom accepted invitations to attend parties or socialize. In her words "Once I get home I don't want to see another person." However, now that her only social contact during the day is a one-sided conversation with a three-legged, neurotic cat, she socializes every chance she can get.

Ego needs When social needs have been satisfied, employees concentrate next on meeting their **ego needs**. These are needs for recognition and success, and an organization can help to satisfy them through praise, awards, promotions, salary increases, and publicity. Ego needs can be satisfied in many ways. For example, former *Tonight Show* host Johnny Carson once commented that the most prestigious sign at NBC is not the salary of the television star or producer, but whether the person has his or her own parking place. Likewise, many organizations use furniture to help satisfy ego needs. The higher the employee's position, the better her office furniture. Similarly, at one engineering firm in Louisville, Kentucky, engineers are not allowed to mount their diplomas or awards on the wall until they receive their professional certification. At the university where I (Mike) work, faculty, department chairs, deans, and vice presidents are given furniture that is "commensurate with their status." Perhaps this explains the card table and folding chairs in my office!

Self-actualization needs Even when employees have friends, have earned awards, and are making a relatively high salary, they may not be completely satisfied with their jobs because their **self-actualization needs** may not have been satisfied yet. These needs are the fifth and final level of Maslow's needs hierarchy (the top level in Exhibit 11-2). Self-actualization might be best defined by the U.S. Army's recruiting slogan "Be all that you can be." An employee striving for self-actualization wants to reach her potential in every task. Thus, employees who have worked with the same machine for 20 years may become dissatisfied with their jobs. They have accomplished all that can be accomplished with that particular machine and now search for a new challenge. If none is available, they may become dissatisfied.

With some jobs, satisfying self-actualization needs is easy. For example, a college professor always has new research to conduct, new classes to teach, and new clients to help. Thus, the variety of tasks and the new problems that are encountered provide a constant challenge that can lead to higher job satisfaction.

Other jobs, however, may not satisfy self-actualization needs. A good example is an employee who welds parts on an assembly line. For 8 hours a day, 40 hours a week, she performs only one task. Boredom and the realization that the job will never change begin to set in. It is no wonder that the employee becomes dissatisfied.

Evaluation of Maslow's theory Although Maslow's needs theory makes good intuitive sense and is popular with managers and marketing analysts, and although its general components have withstood the test of time, research has generally not supported its more technical aspects (Soper, Milford, & Rosenthal, 1995; Wahba & Bridwell, 1976). Perhaps the biggest problem with the theory concerns the number of levels. Although Maslow believed there are five needs levels, research has failed to support that number and suggests there may be only two or three levels (Alderfer, 1972; Lawler & Suttle, 1972; V. F. Mitchell & Mougdill, 1976).

A second problem with the theory is that some people do not progress up the hierarchy as Maslow suggests they do. That is, most people move up from the basic biological needs level to safety needs to social needs and so on. Some people, however, have been known to skip levels. For example, bungee jumpers obviously skip the safety needs level and go straight to satisfying their ego needs. Thus, when exceptions to the hierarchical structure occur, the theory loses support.

Another problem is that the theory predicts that once the needs at one level are satisfied, the next needs level should become most important. Research, however, has shown that this does not necessarily happen (Salancik & Pfeffer, 1977).

Even if Maslow's theory has not been supported by research, it may still be useful. Some of the theory's specific assertions may not be true, but it still provides guidelines that organizations can follow to increase job satisfaction. Providing recognition, enrichment, and a safe workplace *do* increase employee satisfaction. The validity of these suggestions is probably why Maslow's theory still is widely used by human resource professionals even though it is not popular with academicians and researchers, who prefer more complicated models.

A situation at a major university provides an example of how Maslow's general principles can be used. After years of increasing enrollment and prestige, a scandal caused a rapid decline in enrollment, financial backing, and staff morale. To fix these problems, a new president was hired. His first acts were to announce a "spirit day" each Friday on which employees could dress casual, an increased emphasis on diversity issues, and his intent to start a track team. Employee satisfaction continued to drop, faculty left in great numbers, and millions of dollars were cut from the budget.

What went wrong? Among many things, the president's proposals were aimed at Maslow's levels 3 and above, whereas the employees' needs were at level 2—that is, "Will this university survive?" and "Will I still have a job next year?"

ERG Theory Because of the technical problems with Maslow's hierarchy, Alderfer (1972) developed a

EXHIBIT 11-3

ERG Theory Dimensions

| Growth needs |
| Relatedness needs |
| Existence needs |

needs theory that has only three levels. As shown in Exhibit 11-3, the three levels are existence, relatedness, and growth—hence the name **ERG Theory**. Research by Wanous and Zwany (1977) has supported Alderfer's proposed number of levels.

Other than the number of levels, the major difference between Maslow's theory and ERG theory is that Alderfer suggested that a person can skip levels. By allowing for such movement, Alderfer has removed one of the biggest problems with Maslow's theory.

Furthermore, Alderfer's theory explains why a higher level sometimes does not become more important once a lower level need has been satisfied. Alderfer believed that for jobs in many organizations, advancement to the next level is not possible because of such factors as company policy or the nature of the job. Thus, the path to the next level is blocked, and the employee becomes frustrated and places more importance on the previous level. Perhaps that is why some unions demand more money and benefits for their members rather than job enrichment. They realize that the jobs will always be tedious and that little can be done to improve them. Thus, the previous needs level becomes more important. This idea has received at least some empirical support (D. T. Hall & Nougaim, 1968; Salancik & Pfeffer, 1977).

Two-factor theory Still another needs theory, which reduces the number of levels to two, was developed by Herzberg (1966). As shown in Exhibits 11-4 and 11-5, Herzberg believed that job-related factors can be divided into two categories—motivators and hygiene factors—thus the name **two-factor theory**. **Hygiene factors** are those job-related elements that result from but do not involve the job itself. For example, pay and benefits are consequences of work but do not involve the work itself. Similarly, making new friends may result from going to work, but it is also not directly involved with the tasks and duties of the job.

Motivators are job elements that *do* concern actual tasks and duties. Examples of motivators are the level of responsibility, the amount of job control, and the interest that the work holds for the employee. Herzberg believed that hygiene factors are necessary but not sufficient for job satisfaction and motivation. That is, if a hygiene factor is not present at an adequate level (e.g., the pay is too low), the employee will be dissatisfied. But if all hygiene factors are represented adequately, the employee's level of satisfaction will only be neutral. Only the presence of both motivators and hygiene factors can bring job satisfaction and motivation.

Thus, an employee who is paid a lot of money but has no control or responsibility over her job will probably be neither satisfied nor dissatisfied. But an employee who is not paid enough *will* be dissatisfied, even though she may have tremendous control and responsibility over her job. Finally, an employee who is paid well and has control and responsibility will probably be satisfied.

Again, Herzberg's is one of those theories that makes sense but has not received strong research support. In general, researchers have criticized the theory because of the methods used to develop the two factors as well as the fact that few research studies have replicated the findings obtained by Herzberg and his colleagues (Hinrichs & Mischkind, 1967; N. King, 1970).

McClelland's needs theory The final needs theory that we will discuss was developed by McClelland (1961) and suggests that differences between individuals stem from the relationship between a job and each employee's level of satisfaction or motivation. McClelland believed that employees differ in their needs for achievement, affiliation, and power.

Employees who have a strong **need for achievement** desire jobs that are challenging and over which they have some control, whereas employees who

EXHIBIT 11-4

Examples from Herzberg's Two-Factor Theory

Hygiene Factors	Motivators
Pay	Responsibility
Security	Growth
Coworker	Challenge
Working conditions	Stimulation
Company policy	Independence
Work schedule	Variety
Supervisors	Achievement
	Control
	Interesting work

have minimal achievement needs are more satisfied when jobs involve little challenge and have a high probability of success. In contrast, employees who have a strong **need for affiliation** prefer working with and helping other people. These types of employees are found more often in people-oriented service jobs than in management or administration (R. Smither & Lindgren, 1978). Finally, employees who have a strong **need for power** have a desire to influence others rather than simply be successful.

Research has shown that employees who have a strong need for power and achievement often make the best managers (McClelland & Burnham, 1976; Stahl, 1983) and that employees who are motivated most by their affiliation needs will probably make the worst managers.

Needs for achievement, affiliation, and power are measured by one of two tests. The first and most popular is the **Thematic Apperception Test (TAT)**, discussed briefly in Chapter 10. With the TAT, an employee is shown a series of pictures and then asked to tell a story about each one. From the responses, a psychologist identifies the degree to which each theme of power, affiliation, and achievement is present in the stories.

The problem with the TAT is that it is time consuming and must be administered by a psychologist trained in its use. To avoid these problems, Stahl (1983) developed a more objective and less expensive paper-and-pencil test that measures the same three needs. Although this test has not yet become popular, research seems to indicate that it is as reliable and valid a measure as the TAT (Stahl, 1983).

QUICK PROJECT

To get an idea of what careers are a good match for your interests, go back and look at your vocational interest inventory scores from Chapter 4.

_____

_____

_____

_____

Are the Tasks Enjoyable?

Not surprisingly, research is fairly clear that employees who find their work interesting are more satisfied and motivated than are employees who do not enjoy their jobs (Gately, 1997). Interestingly, though employees rank interesting work as being the most important factor in a job, supervisors rank salary and bonus as being the most important for employees. This discrepancy is why Glanz (1997) advised employers to take innovative steps to make work more interesting.

Do Employees Enjoy Working With Their Supervisors and Coworkers?

Research indicates that people who enjoy working with their supervisors and coworkers will be more

EXHIBIT 11-5

Comparison of the Herzberg, Maslow, and ERG Theories

Maslow	ERG	Herzberg
Self-actualization	Growth	Motivators
Ego		
Social	Relatedness	Hygiene factors
Safety	Existence	
Physical		

satisfied with their jobs (Newsome & Pillari, 1992; Repetti & Cosmas, 1991). Such findings certainly make sense, as we all have had coworkers and supervisors who made our jobs unbearable and we all have had coworkers and supervisors who made our jobs fun. In a study of 500 employees at an apparel manufacturing plant, Bishop and Scott (1997) found that satisfaction with supervisors and coworkers was related to organizational and team commitment, which in turn resulted in higher productivity, lower intent to leave the organization, and a greater willingness to help.

Are Coworkers Outwardly Unhappy?

Social learning theory postulates that employees observe the levels of motivation and satisfaction of other employees and then model those levels. Thus, if an organization's older employees work hard and talk positively about their jobs and their employer, new employees will model this behavior and be both productive and satisfied. The reverse is also true: If veteran employees work slowly and complain about their jobs, so will new employees.

To test this theory, Weiss and Shaw (1979) had subjects view training videos in which assembly line workers made either positive or negative comments about their jobs. After viewing a videotape, each subject was given an opportunity to perform the job. The study found that those subjects who had seen the positive tape enjoyed the task more than did subjects who viewed the negative tape. In a similar study conducted by Mirolli, Henderson, and Hills (1998), sub-

jects performed a task with two experimenters pretending to be other subjects (these are called *confederates*). In one condition, the confederates made positive comments about the task (e.g., "Gee, this is fun"); in a second condition they made negative comments about the task (e.g., "This is boring") and in the control condition they did not make any comments. Consistent with social learning theory, actual subjects exposed to the confederates' positive comments rated the task as more enjoyable than subjects exposed to negative comments.

Though social learning theory has not yet been heavily researched, it certainly makes intuitive sense. Think of courses you have taken in which one student participated more than anyone else. After a while, the student's level of participation probably decreased to be more in line with the rest of the class. In work as in school, social pressures force a person to behave in ways that are consistent with the norm, even though the person may privately believe something different.

Are Rewards and Resources Given Equitably?

Another factor related to job satisfaction is the extent to which employees perceive that they are being treated fairly. The most well-known theory on this topic is equity theory. **Equity theory** was developed by Adams (1965) and is based on the premise that our levels of job satisfaction and motivation are related to how fairly we believe we are treated in comparison with others. If we believe we are treated unfairly, we attempt to change our beliefs or behaviors until the situation appears to be fair. Three components are involved in this perception of fairness: inputs, outputs, and input/output ratio.

Inputs are those personal elements that we put into our jobs. Obvious elements are time, effort, education, and experience. Less obvious elements include money spent on child care and distance driven to work.

Outputs are those elements that we receive from our jobs. A list of obvious outputs includes pay, benefits, challenge, and responsibility. Less obvious outputs are benefits such as friends and office furnishings.

According to the theory, employees subconsciously list all their outputs and inputs and then compute an **input/output ratio**. (Although it's called input/output ratio, the output value is divided by the input value.) By itself, this ratio is not especially useful. But employees then compute the input/output ratios for other employees and to previous work experiences and then compare them to their own. If their ratios are less favorable than those of others, they become dissatisfied and thus are motivated to make the ratios equal in one or more ways.

First, employees can seek greater outputs by such means as asking for a raise or for more responsibility. Second, employees can make the ratio more equal by reducing their inputs. Thus, they might not work as hard or might reduce their attendance.

A less practical way of equalizing the ratios would be changing the ratios of other employees. For example, employees might try to get another employee to work harder and thus increase that employee's inputs. Or they might try to reduce the outputs of another employee by withholding friendship or finding a way to reduce the other employee's bonuses. Fortunately, however, strategies to equalize input/output ratios seldom involve reducing others' outputs. Employees can also restore equity by rationalizing the input/output ratio differences, changing the person to whom they are comparing themselves, and/or leaving the organization.

In general, research has supported the idea that our job satisfaction decreases when our input/output ratios are less favorable than others'. Research on this was conducted by Lord and Hohenfeld (1979) and Hauenstein and Lord (1989) with major league baseball players. Players who either had their salary cut during their first year of free agency or had lost an arbitration case performed at lower levels the following year. Thus, players who thought that their *output* (salary) was too low responded by reducing their *inputs* (performance).

In an interesting study, O'Reilly and Puffer (1989) found that employees' satisfaction and motivation increased when coworkers received appropriate sanctions for their behavior. That is, when a high-performing group member was rewarded or a poor-performing group member was punished, the satisfaction and motivation of the group increased.

The degree of inequity that employees feel when underpaid appears to be a function of whether the employees chose the actions that resulted in underpayment (Cropanzano & Folger, 1989). That is, if employees choose to work harder than others who are paid the same, they will not feel cheated, but if they are pressured into working harder for the same pay, they will be unhappy.

An interesting prediction from this theory is a situation in which an employee's input/output ratio is *more* favorable than the ratios of others. Because the theory is based on equity, the prediction would be that the employee would still strive for equal ratios by either increasing her inputs or decreasing her outputs. In other words, she would either work harder or ask to be paid less. In fact, research has indicated that employees often do respond to being "overpaid" by working harder (Adams & Rosenbaum, 1962; Pritchard, Dunnette, & Jorgenson, 1972). But feelings of inequity caused by being "overpaid" do not last long and probably do not produce long-term changes in behavior (Carrell & Dittrich, 1978).

Research on equity has recently expanded into what researchers call **distributive justice** and **procedural justice**. Distributive justice is the perceived fairness of the actual decisions made in an organization, whereas procedural justice is the perceived fairness of the methods used to arrive at the decision. As you would expect, employees who believe that decisions were not made fairly are less satisfied with their jobs (Lowe & Vodanovich, 1995). To increase perceptions of procedural justice, organizations should be open about how decisions will be made, take time to develop fair procedures, and provide feedback to employees who might not be happy with decisions that are made (Jordan, 1997).

One of the greatest problems with equity theory is that despite its rational sense, it is difficult to implement. That is, based on equity theory, the best way to keep employees satisfied would be to treat them all fairly, which would entail paying the most to those employees who contributed the most. Although few of us would disagree with this approach, it is difficult to implement for several reasons.

The first is *practicality*. An organization certainly can control such variables as salary, hours worked, and benefits, but it cannot easily control other variables such as how far an employee lives from work or the number of friends an employee makes on the job.

The second reason that equity is difficult to achieve is that the employee's *perception* of inputs and outputs determines equity, not *actual* inputs and outputs.

For example, two students of equal ability receive the same grade on an exam. One student knows that she studied 10 hours for the exam but never saw the other student in the library. She may feel that the scores are unfair because she studied harder but received the same grade as the student whom she never saw study. Of course, the other student may have studied 20 hours while at work, but the other student would not know that. In this case, the student's perception of input level may not match reality.

Thus, it is important that employees base their judgments on factual information, which may be easier said than done. Although one way to do this would be by open and public information on salaries, many organizations keep such information confidential and even include statements in their employee manuals that forbid employees from divulging their salaries to one another. Such policies, however, encourage employees to speculate about how much other people make. This speculation usually results in employees thinking the worst and believing that others make more than they do. Thus, it is probably in the best interests of an organization to make salary and performance information available to all employees, although each employee's permission must be obtained before such information is released.

Even if an organization were able to maintain complete internal equity, employees would then compare their ratios with those of employees from other organizations. The problem with such comparisons is that an organization has little or no control over another's policies. Furthermore, perceptions of wages and benefits at other organizations most likely will be more distorted than internal perceptions. Thus, even if equity theory were completely accurate, maintaining a high level of employee satisfaction would still be difficult.

Is There a Chance for Growth and Challenge?

For many employees, job satisfaction is affected by opportunities for challenge and growth. As discussed previously, Maslow thought that the need for growth and challenge, which he labeled *self-actualization*, is only important after low-level needs (e.g., safety, social) have been met. To help satisfy employee self-actualization needs, organizations can do many things. The easiest and most common are **job rotation, job enlargement**, and **job enrichment**. With job rotation and job enlargement, an employee learns how to use several different machines or conduct several different tasks within an organization. With job rotation, the employee is given the same number of tasks to do at one time, but the tasks change from time to time. With job enlargement, an employee is given more tasks to do at one time.

A job can be enlarged in two ways: knowledge used and tasks performed. With knowledge enlargement, employees are allowed to make more complex decisions. With task enlargement, they are given more tasks of the same difficulty level to perform. As you might imagine, satisfaction increases with knowledge enlargement and decreases with task enlargement (Campion & McClelland, 1993).

Job rotation and job enlargement accomplish two main objectives. First, they challenge employees by requiring them to learn to operate several different machines or perform several different tasks. Thus, once employees have mastered one task or machine, they can work toward mastering another.

Second, job rotation helps to alleviate boredom by allowing an employee to change tasks. Thus, if an employee welds parts one day, assembles bumpers on another, and tightens screws on a third, the boredom caused by performing the same task every day should be reduced.

Perhaps an even better way to satisfy self-actualization needs is through job enrichment. The main difference between job rotation and job enrichment is that with job rotation, an employee performs different tasks, and with job enrichment, the employee assumes more responsibility over the tasks (R. Ford, 1973).

In their **job characteristics theory**, Hackman and Oldham (1975; 1976) theorized that enriched jobs are the most satisfying. Enriched jobs allow a variety of skills to be used, allow an employee to complete an entire task (e.g., process a loan application from start to finish) rather than parts of a task, involve tasks that have meaning or importance, allow employees to make decisions, and provide feedback about performance. Hackman and Oldham developed the **Job Diagnostic Survey** to measure the extent to which these characteristics are present in a given job.

If we look again at the job of college professor, job enrichment is clearly an inherent part of the job. That is, the professor decides what she will research and what she will teach in a particular course. This authority to make decisions about one's own work leads to higher job satisfaction.

With an assembly line worker, however, responsibility is something that must be added because the employee has minimal control over the way a job is done. After all, bumpers must be assembled in the same way each time and welded to the same place. So what can be done to enrich the typical factory worker's job?

One method is to give workers more responsibility over their jobs. For example, when an employee first begins working for a company, her work is checked by a quality control inspector. After the employee has been with the company long enough for the first four needs levels to be satisfied, the employee is given responsibility for checking her own quality. Likewise, more control can be given to the employee about where and when she will eat lunch, when she will take vacation time, or how fast she will accomplish her work. At one Kaiser Aluminum production plant, for example, time clocks were removed so that the workers could assume more responsibility for their performance by keeping track of their own hours.

It may seem strange to suggest that allowing an employee to make such trivial decisions as lunch times will result in higher job satisfaction. But research has shown that allowing residents in a nursing home to make such decisions resulted in lower death rates, as did allowing them to own pets (Langer & Rodin, 1976; Schulz, 1976). Thus, it is not farfetched to think that allowing control even in limited areas can increase one's level of job satisfaction.

Even when increased decision-making responsibilities are not possible, job enrichment ideas can still be implemented. For example, many organizations have or work with credit unions whose credit committees and boards of directors consist of company employees. These committees and boards provide excellent opportunities to increase employees' decision-making powers even though the decisions are not directly related to their jobs.

Another method to increase the level of job enrichment is by showing employees that their jobs have meaning and that they are meeting some worthwhile goal through their work (Hackman & Oldham, 1975). At some automobile factories, for example, this is accomplished by having employees work in teams to build cars. Instead of an employee performing a single task all day, she does several tasks, as do the other employees in her group. Thus, at the end of the day, the employee can see a completed car that she has had a major role in building.

A plant that manufactures transformers provides another example. The training department realized that even though employees spent 8 hours a day manufacturing the product, few understood what it did, who used it, and what would happen if it were not manufactured correctly. To correct this problem, the employees participated in a training session in which they were shown how the transformer was used, who used it, and the consequences that resulted from poor manufacturing.

The final method for increasing employees' self-actualization needs that we will discuss here is the use of **self-directed teams** or **quality circles**. With quality circles, employees meet as a group and make decisions about such quality-enhancing factors as the music played in the work area, the speed of the assembly line, and how to reduce waste. Quality circles are especially effective in increasing employees' job satisfaction when there is little or no chance for advancement. They allow employees to have more control and responsibility.

In an extensive review of the literature, Wagner (1994) concluded that allowing employees to participate in making decisions results in small, but significant, increases in performance and job satisfaction. J. B. Arthur (1994) found lower turnover in steel mills allowing employees to make decisions on their own than in steel mills with a more controlling style. In a more recent study, Steel and Rentsch (1998) found that job enrichment resulted in decreased absenteeism.

Though team approaches are popular, there is considerable debate about their effectiveness. Most quality improvement programs using a team approach fail to provide the desired results (Zemke, 1993). Teams will be discussed in Chapter 13.

■ INTEGRATION OF THEORIES

During this chapter, we discussed many theories of job satisfaction. The question you must be asking (other than "When does this chapter end?") is "How then do we satisfy employees?" Unfortunately, the answer to this question is complex and depends on a variety of factors. We can, however, use the theories to design an organizational climate that is more conducive to motivation and satisfaction than the typical climate.

As shown in Exhibit 11-6, individual-difference theories say that each of us brings to a job an initial tendency to be satisfied with life and its various aspects such as work. A person with a low tendency toward satisfaction might *start* a job with only 6 hypothetical satisfaction points, a person with a neutral tendency might start with 10 hypothetical points, and a person with a high tendency might bring 14.

For example, research indicates that in addition to genetics, such traits as internal locus of control (Stout, Slocum, & Cron, 1987; Surrette & Harlow, 1992), Type A behavior, patience/ tolerance (Bluen, Barling, & Burns, 1990), and social trust (Liou, Sylvia, & Brunk, 1990) are related to our tendency to be satisfied with work. Demographically, males and females are equally satisfied with work, Whites are more satisfied than Blacks, and older workers are more satisfied than younger workers (Rhodes, 1983).

Surrette and Harlow (1992) found that people will be most satisfied with a job if they had the *option to choose* that job from other alternatives rather than the

EXHIBIT 11-6

Satisfaction Flowchart

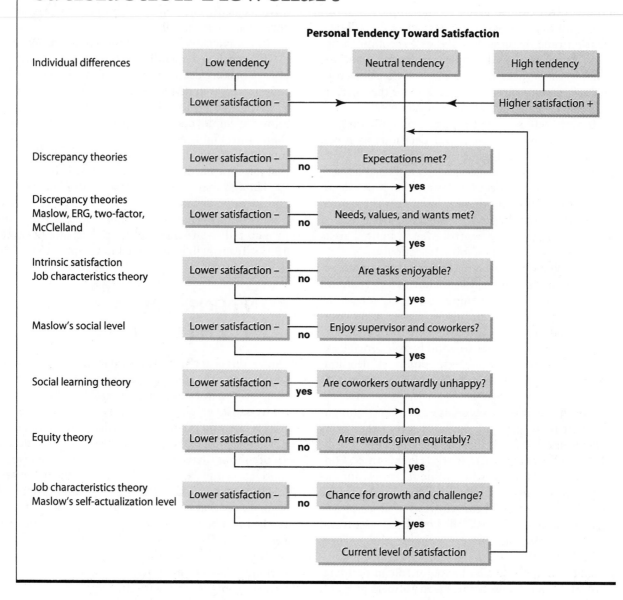

Personal Tendency Toward Satisfaction

job being their only choice. Once people are employed at a job, however, they are most satisfied when they don't have other career alternatives (Pond & Geyer, 1987).

During our years at work, certain events and conditions occur that can add to or decrease our initial level of satisfaction that was due to personal predispositions.

According to discrepancy theories (Maslow's, ERG, McClelland's, and Herzberg's), we will remain satisfied with our job if it meets our various needs, wants, expectations, and values. As we discussed previously in the chapter, individuals vary greatly on their

needs for such things as achievement, status, safety, and social contact. Thus, not every job can satisfy the needs of every employee during every period of her life. By being aware of employee needs, however, we can select the employees whose needs are consistent with the requirements and characteristics of the job.

According to the intrinsic satisfaction theory and job characteristics theory, we will be more satisfied with our jobs if the tasks themselves are enjoyable to perform. What makes a task enjoyable varies across individuals. For some, working on a computer is fun, while for others, nothing could be more boring. Many people enjoy such things as making decisions,

EXHIBIT 11-7

Simulation of Faces Scale of Job Statisfaction

Place a check under the face that expresses how you feel about your job in general.

solving conflicts, and seeing a project through from start to finish, whereas others don't.

Overall satisfaction can be affected by our satisfaction with individual facets of the job. For example, an incompetent boss, terrible coworkers, low pay, or limited opportunities for advancement can lessen overall job satisfaction. Even trivial things can lessen job satisfaction. I once worked at a job where the vending machines never worked and supplies such as paper and pens were often not available. These factors were irritants for most employees—enough so to lessen job satisfaction but certainly not enough to make any of us *dissatisfied* with the job. According to social learning theory, we will be more satisfied if our coworkers are satisfied. If everyone else is whining and complaining, it is difficult to be the only person at work who loves her job.

No matter how much we intrinsically like our work, equity theory predicts we will become dissatisfied if rewards and punishments are not given equitably. If you work harder than a coworker, yet she receives a bigger raise, you are less likely to be satisfied even though money may not be the reason you are working.

On the basis of job characteristics theory and Maslow's level of self-actualization, lack of opportunity for growth, challenge, variety, autonomy, and advancement will decrease satisfaction in many people.

The results of these factors are summed to indicate an employee's current level of satisfaction. As conditions change, so will the level of satisfaction.

PROJECT D *Case Study*

To apply what you have learned about job satisfaction, complete the case study in Project D at the end of this chapter.

■ MEASURING JOB SATISFACTION

This chapter has discussed several theories that seek to explain job satisfaction. But an important issue remains: How to determine an employee's level of job satisfaction. Generally, job satisfaction is measured in one of two ways: standard job satisfaction inventories or custom designed satisfaction inventories.

Commonly Used Standard Inventories

One of the first methods for measuring job satisfaction was developed by Kunin (1955) and is called the **Faces Scale** (a simulation is shown in Exhibit 11-7). Although the scale is easy to use, it is no longer commonly administered partly because it lacks sufficient detail and because some employees believe it is so simple that it is demeaning.

The most commonly used scale today is the **Job Descriptive Index (JDI)**. The JDI was developed by P. C. Smith, Kendall, and Hulin (1969) and consists of a series of job-related adjectives and statements that are rated by employees. The scales yield scores on five dimensions of job satisfaction: supervision, pay, promotional opportunities, coworkers, and the work itself.

A similar measure of job satisfaction is the **Minnesota Satisfaction Questionnaire (MSQ)**, which was developed by Weiss, Dawis, England, and Lofquist (1967). The MSQ contains 100 items that yield scores on 20 scales.

The fact that the JDI has 5 scales and the MSQ 20 underscores the point that job satisfaction is not easy to measure. In addition, employees' responses on the JDI are not highly correlated with their responses on the MSQ (Gillet & Schwab, 1975). Because both the JDI and the MSQ measure specific aspects of job satisfaction, Ironson, Smith, Brannick, Gibson, and Paul (1989) recently developed the **Job in General (JIG) Scale**. The JIG is useful when an organization wants to measure the overall level of job satisfaction rather than specific aspects of job satisfaction.

Nagy (1996) criticized many of the standard measures of job satisfaction because these measures ask only if employees are satisfied with a particular aspect of their job but not how important that job aspect is to them. Recall from our previous discussion on discrepancy theories that people differ about what is important to them. With this in mind, imagine that both Sally and Temea think their salaries are lower than they should be. Sally is a real social climber and thinks a person's salary is a measure of one's status in life. Temea, however, has inherited plenty of money and works because she enjoys keeping busy. Though both Sally and Temea think their pay is low, Nagy (1996) argues that only Sally would actually be dissatisfied. Thus, Nagy (1995) created the Nagy Job Satisfaction Scale, which includes two questions per facet: one asking how important the facet is to the employee and the other asking how satisfied the employee is with the facet.

Custom Designed Inventories

Though most research on job satisfaction is conducted using one or more of the previously mentioned standard inventories, most organizations tap their employees' levels of job satisfaction by using custom-designed inventories. The advantage to custom-designed inventories is the ability to ask employees questions specific to their organization. For example, a local agency recently restructured many of its jobs and wanted to tap how satisfied its employees were with the changes. To do this, a consultant designed questions that specifically tapped employees' thoughts and feelings about the new changes. Using one of the standard inventories would not have provided the needed information.

■ ABSENTEEISM

A problem faced by many organizations is employee absenteeism, as 1.5% of the workforce is absent each day (Tyler, 1997). Although 1.5% may not seem like much, absenteeism costs employers $572 per employee each year (Tyler, 1997). Understanding absenteeism is important, because it is correlated with turnover ($r = .23$) and is thought to be a warning sign of intended turnover (Mitra, Jenkins, & Gupta, 1992). However, before an organization spends time and money trying to stop absenteeism, it must first understand the theories of why people miss work. That is, punishment will reduce absenteeism only if employees make conscious decisions about attending. Likewise, wellness programs will increase attendance only if absenteeism is mostly the result of illness. Employees miss work for several reasons.

No Consequences for Attending or Missing Work

The **decision-making theory** about absenteeism essentially holds that employees make a decision each day as to whether they will or will not attend work. Although the decision-making process is not clearly understood, it probably includes weighing the consequences of going to work against the consequences of not going. For example, imagine that you have an 8:00 a.m. class and are deciding whether you will attend today. By missing class, you can sleep a few hours longer, watch the *Today Show*, and stay out of the rain. By attending class, you will get the notes that you know will be on the test but aren't in the book, get to listen to the instructor's great sense of humor, and get to sit next to the great-looking student you think is interested in you. If a good test grade and a chance at a date are most important, you will attend class. If sleep is most important, you will miss class.

On the basis of decision-making theory, attendance can be increased in several ways: rewarding attendance, disciplining absenteeism, keeping accurate attendance records, and reducing stress at work.

REWARDS FOR ATTENDING

Attendance can be increased through the use of financial incentives, time off, and recognition programs.

Financial incentives Financial incentive programs use money to reward employees for achieving certain levels of attendance. One of these programs, **well pay**, involves paying employees for their unused sick leave. For example, an employee who uses only four of her allowed six days would receive money for the other two. The amount of payment varies among organizations: Some reward the employee by paying the equivalent of daily salary while others might split the savings by paying the employee an amount equal to half her daily salary for each unused sick day.

A second method provides a financial bonus to employees who attain a certain level of attendance. With this method, an employee with perfect attendance over a year might receive a $1000 bonus, and an employee who misses 10 days receives nothing.

A meta-analysis conducted by T. L. Johnson (1990) found that well pay and financial incentives

EXHIBIT 11-8

Reducing Absenteeism: Effect of Various Methods

Methods	Number of Studies	Effect
Well pay	4	High
Flextime	10	High
Compressed work schedules	5	Medium
Discipline	12	Medium
Recognition	6	Medium
Wellness programs	6	Low
Financial incentives	7	Low
Games	6	Low

Source: Adapted from T. L. Johnson (1990). Used with permission.

showed excellent results. But the effectiveness of incentive plans is based on such factors as the size of the incentive, the nature of the incentive, and the time that elapses between attending and being rewarded.

A third financial incentive method is to use **games** to reward employees who attend work. There are many examples. One company used poker as its game, giving a playing card each day to employees who attended. At the end of the week, employees with five cards compared the value of their hands, and the winning employee would be given a prize such as dinner for two at the best restaurant in town or a gas barbecue grill. Although some studies have reported success in using such games, the meta-analysis by Johnson (1990) found that the effect for games was close to zero.

Time off Another approach is the paid-time-off program (PTO) or paid-leave bank (PLB). With this style of program, vacation, personal, holiday, and sick days are combined into one category—paid time off. For example, in a traditional system, an employee might be given 10 vacation days, 3 personal days, 5 holidays, and 10 sick days, for a total of 28 days. With a PTO, the employee might be given 23 days of paid time off with another 5 days placed into an account for a catastrophic illness. An employee who is seldom sick has more days to use for vacation and is protected in case of a long-term illness, and the organization saves money by reducing the total number of normal sick days (Markowich, 1994).

One variation of time-off programs gives unused sick time back to the employee for later use as vacation time. A neighbor of ours works for a hospital and has not missed a day of work in 5 years. As a consequence, she now has 3 months' extra vacation time, which she plans to spend with her newborn son.

Recognition programs One other way that we can make work attendance more rewarding is through recognition and praise. Formal recognition programs provide employees with such recognition as perfect attendance certificates, coffee mugs, plaques, lapel pins, and watches. In an award-winning study, Scott, Markham, and Robers (1985) directly compared recognition with other techniques such as incentives and discipline. The results of their investigation supported the effectiveness of recognition, as did Johnson's meta-analysis.

DISCIPLINE FOR NOT ATTENDING

Absenteeism can be reduced by punishing or disciplining employees who miss work. Discipline can range from giving a warning or a less popular work assignment to firing an employee. As shown in Exhibit 11-8, discipline works fairly well, especially when combined with some positive reinforcement for attending.

UNCLEAR POLICY AND POOR RECORD KEEPING

Another way to increase the negative consequences of missing work is through policy and record keeping. Most organizations measure absenteeism by counting the number of days missed, or *frequency*.

EXHIBIT 11-9

Frequency and Instance Methods of Measuring Absenteeism

Frequency Method

Patricia Austin

Days Missed:

March	4	
April	9	
May	2	
May	30	Days missed = 8
June	7	Instances = 8
July	2	
Sept	3	
Nov	24	

Instances Method

Christine Evert

Days Missed:

April	3	
April	4	
Apri	5	
July	15	Days missed = 8
July	16	Instances = 3
Dec	2	
Dec	3	
Dec	4	

Perhaps a better method would be to record the number of *instances* of absenteeism rather than the number of days. For example, instead of giving employees 12 days of sick leave, they are given 3 or 4 instances of absenteeism. Missing 1 day or 3 consecutive days each counts as one instance of absenteeism.

As shown in Exhibit 11-9, the number of days missed and the instances of absenteeism often yield different results. By decreasing the number of times that a person can miss, the odds increase that the employee will use sick leave only for actual illness. These odds can be further increased by requiring a doctor's excuse for missing a certain number of consecutive days.

Absenteeism can be decreased by setting attendance goals and providing feedback on how well the employees are reaching those goals. An interesting study by Harrison and Shaffer (1994) found that almost 90% of employees think their attendance is above average and estimate the typical absenteeism of their coworkers at a level two times higher than the actual figures. Similar results were found by Johns (1994). Thus, one reason employees miss work is that they incorrectly believe their attendance is at a higher level than their coworkers'.

Adjustment to Work Stress

Absenteeism can be reduced by removing the negative factors employees associate with going to work. One of the most important factors is *stress* . The greater the job stress, the greater the probability that most people will want to skip work. One form of stress is boredom, and it is easy to understand why a person would avoid attending a boring job or class.

Personal problems with other employees or with management constitute another reason for wanting to avoid work. If the employee feels she is not liked or will be verbally abused, it should come as no surprise that she will want to avoid dealing with her fellow employees or supervisors. Finally, employees might want to miss work to avoid physical dangers involved with work such as dealing with hazardous chemicals.

To increase attendance, then, the negative factors cited above must be eliminated. The first step in this elimination, of course, is to become aware of the negative factors that bother employees. These can be determined by asking supervisors or by distributing employee questionnaires. After the problems are known, management should work diligently to eliminate the identified problems from the workplace. Applying what you have learned in this chapter will go a long way toward reducing absenteeism.

Illness and Personal Problems

Another obvious reason why employees miss work is illness. No data are available to indicate the percentage of absenteeism in industry that results from illness, but a study conducted with college students provides some insight. Kovach, Surrette, and Whitcomb (1988) asked more than 500 general psychology students to anonymously provide the reason for each day of class they missed. Less than 30% of the missed days were the result of illness!

However strong its effect, illness is a leading cause of missed work. The question, of course, is whether illness-induced absenteeism can be reduced. The answer is not as clear as we would like, but most indications are that organizational wellness programs involving exercise, stress reduction, smoking cessation, and improved nutrition seem to help. In a meta-analysis of the small number of available studies, D. Bonner (1990) found that the effect for wellness programs in reducing absenteeism was fairly small. Results found by Erfurt, Foote, and Heirich (1992) did not support the effectiveness of wellness programs in reducing health problems.

Other sources of absenteeism are personal problems such as divorce and alcoholism. Industry, however, can reduce the effects from these factors in two ways. First, factors in the workplace that contribute to family problems and stress can be eliminated or reduced. These factors or variables include extensive employee travel, overtime, fatigue, and job-related stress. Second, some form of Employee Assistance Program (EAP) can be implemented. As mentioned in Chapter 2, EAPs use professional counselors to deal with employee problems. An employee with a problem can either choose to see a counselor on her own or be recommended by her supervisor.

The motivation for EAPs may be good, but little if any empirical evidence supports their effectiveness. Still, many organizations have used EAPs and have been quite pleased with them. Independently operated EAPs typically claim a 3-to-1 return on the dollars invested through increased productivity and reduced absenteeism and turnover.

Individual Differences

One interesting theory of absenteeism postulates that one reason people miss work is the result of a particular set of personality traits they possess. That is, certain types of people are more likely to miss work than are other types. In fact, in one study, only 25% of the employees were responsible for all of the unavoidable absenteeism (Dalton & Mesch, 1991).

Although little research has tested this theory, Kovach et al. (1988) did find that the best predictor of student attendance in general psychology courses was a compulsive, rule-oriented personality. Research by Judge, Martocchio, and Thoresen (1997) supports these findings. Judge and his colleagues found that individuals high in the personality trait of conscientiousness and low in extraversion were least likely to miss work. If more research supports this theory, then a new strategy for increasing employee attendance might be to screen out "absence prone people" during the selection stage.

Unique Events

Many times an individual will miss work because of events or conditions beyond management's control. One study estimated that 40% of absenteeism is unavoidable (Dalton & Mesch, 1991). For example, bad weather is one reason why absenteeism is higher in the Northeast than in the South. Although an organization can do little to control the weather, the accessibility of the plant or office can be considered in the decision of where to locate. In fact, better weather is one reason why many organizations have started in or moved to the so-called Sunbelt in the last two decades. Organizations could also offer some type of shuttle service for their employees to avoid not only weather problems but also mechanical failures of employees' automobiles.

Bad weather can certainly be a legitimate reason for an employee to miss work, but one study found that job satisfaction best predicted attendance on days with poor weather. That is, in good weather, most employees attended, but in inclement weather, only those employees with high job satisfaction attended. Thus, even in bad weather, the degree to which an employee likes her job will help to determine her attendance. As the late industrial psychologist Dan Johnson has asked: "How come we hear about employees not being able to get to work and students not being able to attend class because of bad weather, yet we don't ever hear about an employee or a student who can't get home because of bad weather?" It certainly makes one think!

> **PROJECT E** *Absenteeism*
> Complete Project E so that you can apply your new knowledge of the theories of absenteeism.

CHAPTER RECAP

In this chapter you learned:

- Satisfaction is moderately related to turnover and absenteeism, slightly related to performance, and very much related to organizational commitment.

- Certain types of people have a predisposition to being satisfied or dissatisfied with work and life.

- Job satisfaction can be maximized by meeting employee needs, values, and expectations and ensuring that employees are treated equitably.

- Job satisfaction is typically measured by such attitude surveys as the Faces Scale, the Job Descriptive Index (JDI), the Minnesota Satisfaction Questionnaire (MSQ), the Job in General (JIG) Scale, and the Nagy Job Satisfaction Scale.

- Absenteeism is the result of such factors as a conscious decision not to attend, adjustment to stress, illness and personal problems, individual differences, and unique events.

Critical Thinking Questions

1. Are some employees "destined" to always be dissatisfied with their jobs?
2. What do most employees value and need in a job?
3. Is it possible to treat all employees equitably?
4. What is the best way to improve employee attendance?
5. Which measure of job satisfaction is best?

WEB SITES

For further information, log on to the following web sites.
www.busreslab.com/tips/tipses.htm
Provides tips on how to measure employee satisfaction.
http://st13.yahoo.com/lib/wackenhutstore/bucks.html#Q1
An excellent example of an actual program to increase job satisfaction by showing appreciation to employees.

KEY TERMS

Basic biological needs The first step in Maslow's needs hierarchy, concerning survival needs such as the need for food, air, and water.

Decision-making theory A theory about absenteeism that holds that employees daily make a conscious decision about whether to attend work.

Distributive justice The perceived fairness of the decisions made in an organization.

Ego needs The fourth step in Maslow's hierarchy, concerning the individual's need for recognition and success.

Equity theory A theory that employees will be dissatisfied if they perceive that they are not treated fairly in relation to other employees.

ERG theory Alderfer's needs theory, which describes three levels of satisfaction: existence, relatedness, and growth.

Faces Scale A measure of job satisfaction in which raters place a mark under a facial expression that is most similar to the way they feel about their jobs.

Games An absenteeism control method in which games such as poker and bingo are used to reward employee attendance.

Hierarchy A system arranged by rank.

Hygiene factors In Herzberg's two-factor theory, job-related elements that result from but do not involve the job itself.

Input/output ratio The ratio of how much employees believe they put into their jobs to how much they believe they get from their jobs.

Inputs In equity theory, the elements that employees put into their jobs.

Job characteristics theory The theory proposed by Hackman and Oldham that suggests that certain characteristics of a job will make the job more or less satisfying, depending on the particular needs of the worker.

Job Descriptive Index (JDI) A measure of job satisfaction that yields scores on five dimensions.

Job Diagnostic Survey (JDS) A measure of the extent to which a job provides opportunities for growth, autonomy, and meaning.

Job enlargement A system in which employees are given more tasks to perform at the same time.

Job enrichment A system in which employees are given more responsibility over the tasks and decisions related to their jobs.

Job in General (JIG) Scale A measure of the overall level of job satisfaction.

Job rotation A system in which employees are given the opportunity to perform several different jobs in an organization.

Job satisfaction The attitude employees have toward their jobs.

Minnesota Satisfaction Questionnaire (MSQ) A measure of job satisfaction that yields scores on 20 dimensions.

Motivators In Herzberg's two-factor theory, elements of a job that concern the actual duties performed by the employee.

Need for achievement The extent to which a person desires to master a task.

Need for affiliation The extent to which a person desires to be around other people.

Need for power The extent to which a person desires to have influence over other people.

Outputs In equity theory, the elements that employees get from their jobs.

Procedural justice The perceived fairness of the methods used by an organization to make decisions.

Quality circles Employee groups that meet to propose changes that will improve productivity and the quality of work life.

Realistic job preview A method of recruitment in which job applicants are told both the positive and negative aspects of a job.

Safety needs The second step in Maslow's hierarchy, concerning the need for security, stability, and physical safety.

Self-actualization needs The fifth step in Maslow's hierarchy, concerning the need to realize one's potential.

Self-directed teams See quality circles.

Social learning theory A theory that employees model their levels of satisfaction and motivation from other employees.

Social needs The third step in Maslow's hierarchy concerning the need to interact with other people.

Thematic Apperception Test A projective test designed to measure various need levels.

Two-factor theory Herzberg's needs theory that postulates two factors involved in job satisfaction: hygiene factors and motivators.

Well pay A method of absenteeism control in which employees are paid for their unused sick leave.

PRACTICE EXAM

1. Job satisfaction is most related to:
   a. performance
   b. tenure
   c. absenteeism
   d. organizational commitment

2. Job satisfaction and life satisfaction are:
   a. the same
   b. positively correlated
   c. negatively correlated
   d. not correlated at all

3. About what percentage of job satisfaction is genetic?
   a. none
   b. 10%
   c. 30%
   d. 50%

4. According to _____ theory, a realistic job preview would increase job satisfaction.
   a. discrepancy
   b. equity
   c. social learning
   d. needs

5. According to Maslow's theory, the highest order need is:
   a. safety
   b. social
   c. ego
   d. self-actualization

6. Job security would fall under which of the following needs:
   a. safety
   b. social
   c. ego
   d. self-actualization

7. Which of the following is not one of the levels in ERG theory?
   a. existence
   b. ego
   c. relatedness
   d. growth

8. According to two-factor theory, which of the following is not a hygiene factor?
   a. pay
   b. responsibility
   c. benefits
   d. good coworkers

9. Which of the following needs is not part of McClelland's theory?
   a. affiliation
   b. power
   c. dominance
   d. achievement

10. Which of the following theories suggests that if our coworkers are outwardly unhappy, so too will we be unhappy?
    a. discrepancy
    b. equity
    c. social learning
    d. needs

11. According to equity theory, we will be satisfied with our job when our input/output ratio is _____ the input/output ratio of others.
    a. higher than
    b. lower than
    c. the same as
    d. the inverse of

12. According to equity theory, if an employee's input/output ratio is unfavorable, he or she might:
    a. work harder
    b. ask for a raise
    c. complain
    d. do nothing

13. Giving employees more tasks to perform at the same time is called job _____.
    a. enrichment
    b. rotation
    c. enlargement
    d. revitalization

14. The job characteristics model is mostly concerned with job _____.
    a. enrichment
    b. rotation
    c. enlargement
    d. revitalization

15. The most commonly used job satisfaction inventory is the:
    a. NSI
    b. JIG
    c. MSQ
    d. JDI

16. Which needs theory has three levels of needs and allows individuals to skip levels?
    a. Maslow's theory
    b. ERG theory
    c. two-factor theory
    d. McClelland's need theory

17. Jill wants to be promoted and influence more people. Under the McClelland theory, she seems to have a high need for:
    a. affiliation
    b. achievement
    c. power
    d. control

18. The use of well pay to reduce absenteeism is consistent with which of the following theories of absenteeism?
    a. decision making
    b. sickness and personal problems
    c. unique events
    d. individual traits

19. A snowstorm that keeps people from attending work is consistent with which of the following theories of absenteeism?
    a. decision making
    b. sickness and personal problems
    c. unique events
    d. individual traits

20. Which of the following approaches for decreasing absenteeism seems to be the least effective?
    a. games
    b. well pay
    c. wellness programs
    d. financial incentives

ANSWERS 1 d, 2 b, 3 c, 4 a, 5 d, 6 a, 7 b, 8 b, 9 c, 10 c, 11 c, 12 b, 13 c, 14 a, 15 d, 16 b, 17 c, 18 a, 19 c, 20 a

Focused Free-Write

Think of a job in which you were really unhappy. Why was it so bad?

_____

_____

_____

_____

_____

_____

_____

_____

_____

_____

_____

_____

_____

_____

_____

_____

_____

_____

_____

_____

_____

_____

_____

_____

Now think of a job in which you were very happy and satisfied. Why was it so good?

_____

_____

_____

_____

_____

_____

_____

_____

_____

_____

_____

_____

_____

_____

_____

_____

_____

_____

_____

_____

_____

_____

_____

_____

Stability of Job Satisfaction

In the space below, write down all of the jobs you have had. Then rate the extent to which you were satisfied with each of those jobs. Are your ratings consistent? Do your ratings support the idea that job satisfaction is consistent across jobs?

VD=very dissatisfied   D=dissatisfied   N=neutral   S=satisfied   VS=Very satisfied

Job	Level of Job Satisfaction				
_____	VD	D	N	S	VS
_____	VD	D	N	S	VS
_____	VD	D	N	S	VS
_____	VD	D	N	S	VS
_____	VD	D	N	S	VS
_____	VD	D	N	S	VS

Core Self-Evaluation

Circle the number corresponding to the extent to which you agree with each of the following statements.

SD=strongly disagree   D=disagree   N=neutral   A=agree   SA=strongly agree

	SD	D	N	A	SA
1. Difficult situations usually don't bother me.	1	2	3	4	5
2. I don't like a lot of things about me.	5	4	3	2	1
3. I have good ideas.	1	2	3	4	5
4. I worry a lot.	5	4	3	2	1
5. I have a low opinion of myself.	5	4	3	2	1
6. I like trying new things.	1	2	3	4	5
7. Life is fun.	1	2	3	4	5
8. If I work hard, I will be successful.	1	2	3	4	5
9. I don't seem to be able to control my life.	5	4	3	2	1
10. I am a confident person.	1	2	3	4	5
11. It seems as if my life is controlled by everyone but me.	5	4	3	2	1
12. I am not afraid to take risks.	1	2	3	4	5
13. I do most things well.	1	2	3	4	5
14. People would describe me as being anxious.	5	4	3	2	1
15. I am happy with who I am.	1	2	3	4	5
16. I handle pressure well.	1	2	3	4	5
17. I am successful at most things I try.	1	2	3	4	5
18. I am usually in a good mood.	1	2	3	4	5
19. I am a good person.	1	2	3	4	5
20. I have a lot of respect for myself.	1	2	3	4	5
21. I am as good a person as anybody.	1	2	3	4	5
22. I can overcome any obstacles in my life.	1	2	3	4	5
23. There is not much I worry about.	1	2	3	4	5
24. I am comfortable with who I am.	1	2	3	4	5
25. People who work hard will succeed.	1	2	3	4	5
26. I am responsible for my success and failure.	1	2	3	4	5
27. I get depressed a lot.	5	4	3	2	1
28. I am often nervous.	5	4	3	2	1

29. I control my own destiny.	1	2	3	4	5
30. I am a talented person.	1	2	3	4	5
31. I am a likeable person.	1	2	3	4	5
32. Others would describe me as being enthusiastic.	1	2	3	4	5
33. There are so many people I would rather be than me.	5	4	3	2	1
34. There is little I cannot accomplish if I set my mind to it.	1	2	3	4	5
35. Most of what happens in life is uncontrollable.	5	4	3	2	1
36. There is not much about my personality that I would change.	1	2	3	4	5

Scoring and Interpreting the Core Evaluation Inventory

Add the numbers associated with the answers you circled for each question.

Your total score is _____. The higher your score, the greater your predisposition to be satisfied at work and in life. The chart below will help you compare your score to those of other college students.

If Your Score Was	Your core evaluation is higher than _____ of other college students
159–180	95%
152–158	90%
145–151	80%
142–144	70%
137–141	60%
132–136	50%
129–131	40%
126–128	30%
123–125	20%
117–122	10%
36–116	5%

PROJECT C

Your Level of Life Satisfaction

Circle the number next to each question that best indicates how you currently feel.

	Not at all like me			Very much like me	
1. My life situation is better than most people's.	1	2	3	3	4
2. Most days I am very happy.	1	2	3	3	4
3. I seldom get depressed these days.	1	2	3	3	4
4. There is not much about my life that I want to change.	1	2	3	3	4
5. The world is treating me pretty well.	1	2	3	3	4
6. Things seem to be going my way.	1	2	3	3	4
7. At my current age, I am about where I want to be in life.	1	2	3	3	4
8. If I could relive the last few months, there is very little that I would change.	1	2	3	3	4
9. My thoughts are usually very positive.	1	2	3	3	4
10. I don't see how my life could get much better.	1	2	3	3	4

Scoring the Life Satisfaction Inventory

Add the numbers that you circled for each question and write that number here _____. For example, if you had circled the bold-faced numbers in the three questions below, your total would be 7 (2 + 3 + 2).

2. Most days I am very happy.	1	**2**	3	3	4
3. I seldom get depressed these days.	1	2	**3**	3	4
4. There is not much about my life that I want to change.	1	**2**	3	3	4

Interpreting the Life Satisfaction Inventory

If Your Score Was	Your level of life satisfaction is higher than_____of other college students
48–50	95%
44–47	90%
42–43	80%
40–41	70%
38–39	60%
35–37	50%
33–34	40%
31–32	30%
27–30	20%
21–26	10%
10–20	5%

Case Study

Juan Estoban was eating lunch at Anderson's Restaurant one Thursday when he noticed a help-wanted ad for the restaurant on his placemat. The ad indicated that most servers made over $10 a hour and that the restaurant atmosphere was fun, exciting, and a place to meet new friends. As a college student, Juan thought the job opportunity was perfect: The money was good, and because most of his friends were back in Arizona, the chance to have a good time and make new friends was highly appealing.

During his job interview, the restaurant manager promised Juan that he wouldn't have to work more than 20 hours a week and that he could always have one Friday or Saturday off each week. Juan accepted the job offer and began work on the following Monday.

The first week at work was spent learning the menu, restaurant rules, and serving techniques. Juan was one of five new servers, but was the only one who was also attending college. As one would expect, the second week was a bit stressful as the new servers began waiting tables. The first day was filled with mistakes, but by the end of the week the five new servers were performing like experts.

As the weeks passed, Juan began to feel stressed as he tried to balance his 15-hour courseload with the demands of his new job. Most weeks he worked 30 hours, and he had not had a Friday or Saturday night off in the past 2 months. During the next month, Juan called in sick one Friday and then again a week later on a Saturday. Juan was also feeling a financial pinch. Even though he was working more hours than he expected, his base pay and tips averaged only around $7.00 an hour. Though he liked his coworkers, Juan always seemed to be arguing with his supervisor, who Juan thought was giving the best hours to employees with less seniority than he. Even worse, the restaurant was constantly busy, and there was never any time to joke around or have fun. Juan's grades began to drop, and after failing a test in his 8:00 a.m. history class, Juan finally quit his job.

On the basis of the theories discussed in the text, what caused Juan to quit and become so dissatisfied?

_____

_____

_____

_____

_____

_____

_____

_____

_____

Absenteeism

Your text discussed several theories about absenteeism. From these theories came several suggestions for improving attendance. The purpose of this exercise is to provide you with the opportunity to apply these theories.

Instructions   You have probably noticed throughout your college career that attendance is high in some courses and low in others. You have also probably experienced a wide variety of attendance policies. For the first part of this exercise, think of the courses you have had, and write down some of the attendance policies that you have had. Indicate next to the policy whether you thought it was effective.

_____

_____

_____

_____

_____

_____

_____

_____

_____

_____

_____

_____

_____

_____

_____

_____

_____

_____

_____

For the second part of this exercise, design what you think is the ideal attendance policy for class. For every part of your plan, mention the theory or reason that supports your thinking.

_____

_____

_____

_____

_____

_____

_____

_____

_____

_____

_____

_____

_____

_____

_____

_____

_____

_____

_____

_____

_____

_____

_____

_____

CHAPTER TWELVE

Motivating Others

After an organization has selected and trained its employees, it is important and beneficial for both the organization and employees that employees be both motivated by and satisfied with their jobs. Work **motivation** is the force that drives a worker to perform well. Ability and skill determine whether a worker *can* do the job, but motivation determines whether the worker *will* do it properly. Although actually testing the relationship between motivation and performance is difficult, psychologists generally agree that increased worker motivation results in increased job performance.

In this chapter, we will explore several theories that seek to explain why workers are motivated by their jobs. None of the theories completely and accurately explains motivation, but each is valuable in that it suggests ways to increase employee performance. Thus, even though a theory itself may not be completely supported by research, the resulting suggestions have generally led to increased performance. By the end of this chapter, you will:

Know the types of people who tend to be more motivated than others

Learn how to motivate people through goal setting

Understand the importance of providing feedback

Learn how to use operant conditioning principles to motivate employees

Appreciate the importance of treating employees fairly

Learn the types of individual and organizational incentives that best motivate employees

■ WHAT MOTIVATES EMPLOYEES?

Individual Differences

Individual-difference theories postulate that some employees are more predisposed to being motivated than are others. If you remember from Chapter 11, we mentioned that such things as genetics and positive affectivity are involved in the extent to which some people tend to always be satisfied with their jobs and others always dissatisfied. The same is true for motivation. However, rather than genetics and positive affectivity, self-esteem, need for achievement, and an intrinsic motivation tendency are the individual differences most related to work motivation.

Self-Esteem

As you might recall from Chapter 11, **self-esteem** is the extent to which a person views himself as a valu-

able and worthy person. In the 1970s, Korman (1970, 1976) theorized that employees high in self-esteem will be more motivated and will perform better than employees low in self-esteem. According to Korman's **Consistency theory**, there is a positive correlation between self-esteem and performance. That is, employees who feel good about themselves are motivated to perform better at work than employees who do not feel they are valuable and worthy people. Consistency theory takes the relationship between self-esteem and motivation one step further by stating that employees with high self-esteem actually *desire* to perform at high levels and that employees with low self-esteem desire to perform at low levels. In other words, employees try to perform at levels consistent with their self-esteem level. This desire to perform at levels consistent with self-esteem is compounded by the tendency of employees with low self-esteem to underestimate their actual ability and performance (Lindeman, Sundvik, & Rouhiainen, 1995). Thus, low-self-esteem employees will desire to perform at lower levels than their actual abilities would allow.

The theory becomes somewhat complicated in that there are three types of self-esteem. **Chronic self-esteem** is a person's overall feeling about himself. **Situational self-esteem** is a person's feeling about himself in a particular situation, such as operating a machine or talking to other people. **Socially influenced self-esteem** is a person's feeling about himself on the basis of the expectations of others. All three types of self-esteem are important to job performance. For example, an employee might be low in chronic self-esteem but be very high in situational self-esteem. That is, a computer programmer might believe he is a terrible person that nobody likes (low chronic self-esteem) but feels that he can program a computer better than anyone (high situational self-esteem—also called self-efficacy).

> *Focused Free-Write*
> To get you thinking about motivation in your own life, complete the Focused Free-Write at the end of the chapter.

If consistency theory is true, we should find that employees with high self-esteem are more motivated, perform better, and rate their own performance as being higher than employees with low self-esteem. Research supports these predictions: Ilardi, Leone, Kasser, and Ryan (1993) found significant correlations between self-esteem and motivation; Lindeman et al. (1995), Levy (1993), and Farh and Dobbins (1989) reported significant relationships between self-esteem and self-ratings of performance; and

Brenden (1990) found a significant relationship between self-esteem and actual performance.

On the basis of consistency theory, we should be able to improve an employee's performance by increasing his self-esteem. Organizations can theoretically do this in three ways: self-esteem workshops, experience with success, and supervisor behavior.

Self-esteem workshops To increase self-esteem, employees can attend workshops or sensitivity groups in which they are given insights into their strengths. It is thought that these insights raise self-esteem by showing the employee that he has several strengths and is a good person. For example, in a self-esteem training program called *The Enchanted Self* (Holstein, 1997), employees try to increase their self-esteem by learning how to think positively, discovering their positive qualities that may have gone unnoticed, and sharing their positive qualities with others. More about this approach can be found on the web site at http://www.enchantedself.com.

Outdoor experiential training is another approach to increasing self-esteem (Clements, Wagner, & Roland, 1995). In training such as Outward Bound or the "ropes course," participants learn that they are emotionally and physically strong enough to be successful and meet challenges.

Experience with success With this approach, an employee is given a task so easy that he will almost certainly succeed. It is thought that this success increases self-esteem, which should increase performance, then further increase self-esteem, then further increase performance, and so on. This method is based loosely on the principle of **self-fulfilling prophecy**, which states that an individual will perform as well or as poorly as he expects to perform. In other words, if he believes he is intelligent, he should do well on tests. If he thinks he is not very smart, he should do poorly. So if an employee believes he will always fail, the only way to break the vicious cycle is to ensure that he performs well on a task.

Employees who feel they have low self-esteem can improve their self-esteem by trying new experiences. Perhaps the best approach is to take small steps toward accomplishing a goal. For example, an employee who is afraid of computers might begin by playing an easy computer game such as Solitaire to get used to the computer. When the person begins to feel more comfortable, he can move to the next stage, which might be to type and print a short memo. With each successful little step, the employee gets closer to reaching his goal of becoming proficient in using computers. Thus, rather than waiting for the organization to increase employee self-esteem, the employee can initiate the steps himself.

Supervisor behavior Another approach to increasing employee self-esteem is to train supervisors to communicate a feeling of confidence in an employee. The idea here is that if an employee feels that a manager has confidence in him, his self-esteem will increase, as will his performance. Such a process is known as the **Pygmalion effect** and has been demonstrated in situations as varied as elementary school classrooms and the military (Davir, Eden, & Banjo, 1995). The Pygmalion effect has also been portrayed in several motion pictures, including *My Fair Lady* and *Trading Places*.

The Pygmalion effect has been demonstrated repeatedly in research (e.g., Oz & Eden, 1994; Tierney, 1998). For example, Rosenthal (1994) demonstrated that our expectations of another's performance lead us to treat him differently. That is, if we think that someone will do a poor job, we will probably treat him in ways that bring that result. If a supervisor thinks an employee is intrinsically motivated, he treats the employee in a less controlling way. The result of this treatment is that the employee actually becomes more intrinsically motivated (Pelletier & Vallerand, 1996). Thus, when an employee becomes aware of others' expectations and matches his own with them, he will perform in a manner that is consistent with those expectations (Oz & Eden, 1994).

Sandler (1986) argued that our expectations are communicated to employees through such nonverbal cues as head tilting or eyebrow raising and through more overt behaviors such as providing low-expectation employees with less feedback, worse facilities, and less praise than high-expectation employees. He also stated that employees are quick to pick up on these cues. Along with Korman (1970) and Rosenthal (1994), Sandler argued that employees then adjust their behaviors to be consistent with our expectations and in a way that is self-sustaining.

Though we know that the Pygmalion effect is true, efforts to teach supervisors to communicate positive expectations have not been successful. On the basis of seven field experiments, Eden (1998) concluded that there was little support for the notion that teaching the "Pygmalion leadership style" would change the way supervisors treated their employees and thus increase employee self-esteem.

Research on self-esteem and consistency theory has brought mixed results. Laboratory studies have generally supported the theory: Subjects who were led to believe that they would perform well on a task did so, and subjects who were led to believe that they would do poorly on a task also did so (Greenhaus & Badin, 1974). The theory, however, was criticized by Dipboye (1977), who believes that factors other than self-esteem, such as the need to achieve or the need to enhance oneself, can explain the same results.

But given that consistency theory does have some reasonable research support, the next concern is how it can be used to increase employee performance. If employees do indeed respond to their managers' expectations, then it becomes reasonable to predict that managers who communicate positive and optimistic feelings to their employees will lead employees to perform at higher levels. Likewise, employees who communicate these feelings to their peers should also see better coworker performance.

> **PROJECT A** *Self-Esteem*
> To determine your level of self-esteem, complete the Radford Inventory in Project A at the end of this chapter.

NEED FOR ACHIEVEMENT

As discussed in the previous chapter on job satisfaction, employees who have a strong **need for achievement** desire and are motivated by jobs that are challenging and over which they have some control, whereas employees who have minimal achievement needs are more satisfied when jobs involve little challenge and have a high probability of success. Employees with a high need for achievement are not risk takers and tend to set goals that are challenging enough to be interesting but low enough to be attainable. Employees with a high need for achievement need recognition and want their achievements to be noticed. To find your own need for achievement level, go back to Project B in Chapter 10, and look up your score on Section D.

INTRINSIC MOTIVATION

When people are **intrinsically motivated**, they are motivated to perform well because they either enjoy performing the actual tasks or enjoy the challenge of successfully completing the task. When they are **extrinsically motivated**, they don't particularly enjoy the tasks but are motivated to perform well in order to receive some type of reward and/or avoid negative consequences (Deci & Ryan, 1985). People who are intrinsically motivated don't need external rewards such as pay or praise. In fact, being paid for something they enjoy may reduce their satisfaction and intrinsic motivation (Mossholder, 1980).

An interesting debate has arisen between researchers who believe that rewards reduce intrinsic motivation and those who don't. A meta-analysis by Cameron and Pierce (1994) concluded that research does not support the idea that rewards reduce intrinsic motivation. However, the meta-analysis has been criticized by Ryan and Deci (1996) as misrepresenting the data. Thus, it appears that this debate will continue for at least a few more years.

Individual orientations toward intrinsic and extrinsic motivation can be measured by the **Work Preference Inventory** (Amabile, Hill, Hennessey, & Tighe, 1994). The WPI yields scores on two dimensions of intrinsic motivation (enjoyment, challenge) and two dimensions of extrinsic motivation (compensation, outward orientation).

> **PROJECT B** *Work Preference Inventory*
> To determine your own level of intrinsic and extrinsic motivation, complete the WPI found in Project B at the end of this chapter. After completing this project, what do you think you can do to increase your own motivation?

Presence of Goals

To increase motivation, goal setting should be used. With **goal setting**, each employee is given a goal (or sets his own goals), which might be a particular quality level, a certain quantity of output, or a combination of the two. For goal setting to be most successful, the goals themselves should possess certain qualities.

First, they should be *concrete* and *specific* (Locke, 1996; Wood, Mento, & Locke, 1987). A goal such as "I will produce as many as I can" will not be as effective as "I will print 5000 pages in the next hour." The more specific the goal, the greater the productivity. To underscore this point, we will use an example involving pushups. If a person says that he will do as many pushups as he can, does that mean he will do as many as he can until he tires? As many as he can before he begins to sweat? As many as he did his last time? The problem with such a goal is its ambiguity and lack of specific guidelines. Setting more specific subgoals can also improve performance (Klawsky, 1990).

Second, a properly set goal is high but reasonable (Locke & Latham, 1990). If an employee regularly prints 5000 pages an hour and sets a goal of 4000 pages, performance is certainly not going to increase. Conversely, if the goal becomes 20,000 pages, it will not be effective because the employee will quickly realize that he cannot meet the goal and will quit trying.

A good example of goals set too high comes from the academic retention program at Radford University. This program is designed to help special students who are having academic trouble and whose GPAs have fallen below the minimum needed to stay in school. The program involves tutoring, study skills, and goal setting. Although it has generally been a success, many students have failed to improve their academic performances. A brief investigation revealed that the goal-setting process was one of the reasons for these failures. Students were allowed to set their own GPA goals for the semester—and students with GPAs of 1.0 were setting goals of 4.0! Obviously, none of the students was able to reach this goal. The problem typically came when students did poorly on their first test—their chance for an A in a class was gone, as was their chance for a 4.0 GPA for the semester. Because their goals could not be attained, the students felt they had failed and quit trying.

Not surprisingly, people differ in the extent to which they set high goals. Optimists tend to set higher goals than do pessimists (Ladd, Jagacinski, & Stolzenberg, 1997). Interestingly, providing encouragement (e.g., "I know you will do well") causes optimists, but not pessimists, to raise their goals (Ladd et al., 1997).

Until fairly recently, it was generally thought that a goal would lead to the greatest increase in productivity if it was set at least in part by the employee. That is, although performance would increase if the supervisor sets the employee's goal, it would increase even more if the employee participated. However, several meta-analyses have indicated that participating in goal setting does not increase performance (Mento, Steel, & Karren, 1987; Tubbs, 1986). However, as you learned back in Chapter 3 on time management, you can set your own goals and shouldn't wait for others to set them for you.

The first goal-setting study that caught the interest of industrial psychologists was conducted by G. D. Latham and Blades (1975). Their study came about because truck drivers at a logging mill were not completely filling their trucks before making deliveries. Empty space in the trucks obviously cost the company money. To increase each delivery's load, the drivers were given specific weight goals and were told that they would be neither punished for missing the goal nor rewarded for reaching it. A significant increase in the average load per delivery resulted. Although this is the most celebrated study, goal setting has been shown to be effective in a wide variety of situations.

> **PROJECT C** *Goal Setting*
> To practice goal setting, complete Project C at the
> end of this chapter.

Providing Feedback

To increase the effectiveness of goal setting, feedback should be provided to employees on their progress in reaching their goals (Locke, 1996; Locke & Latham, 1990). Feedback can include verbally telling employees how they are doing, placing a chart on a wall, or displaying a certain color of light when the employee's work pace will result in goal attainment and a different color of light when the pace is too slow to reach the goal. Feedback best increases performance when it is positive and informational rather than negative and controlling (Zhou, 1998).

An excellent example of the use of feedback comes from Domino's Pizza. Each month the average delivery and service times for each store are printed as box scores in *The Pepperoni Press*, the company's newsletter. These box scores provide each store with feedback on how it compares with other stores. This feedback is one reason why Domino's is one of the world's fastest growing fast-food outlets.

Rewarding Excellent Performance

Another set of theories hypothesizes that workers are motivated only when they are *rewarded* for their behavior. As a result, organizations offer incentives for a wide variety of employee behaviors including working overtime or on weekends, making suggestions, referring applicants, staying with the company (length-of-service awards), coming to work (attendance bonuses), not getting into accidents, and performing at a high level (Henderson, 1997).

OPERANT CONDITIONING

Operant conditioning is based on the premise that humans learn to behave in ways that result in favorable outcomes and resist behavior that results in unfavorable outcomes (Skinner, 1938, 1969). Essentially, operant conditioning principles state that employees will continue to do those behaviors for which they are reinforced and stop doing those behaviors for which they are punished. Thus, if employees are rewarded for not making errors, they are more likely to produce high-quality work. If employees are rewarded for the amount of work done, they will place less emphasis on quality and try to increase their quantity. Finally, if employees are not rewarded for any behavior, they will search for behaviors that will be rewarded. Unfortunately, these might include absenteeism (which is rewarded by going fishing) or carelessness (which is rewarded by spending more time with friends).

Although the basic principles of operant conditioning are fairly simple, additional factors can modify the effectiveness of both reward and punishment.

Timing of the consequence Research indicates that a *reinforcer* or a *punisher* is most effective if it occurs soon after the performance of the behavior. Unfortunately, if the timing of the consequence is too long, the effectiveness of operant conditioning in both training and other attempts to improve performance is hindered. For example, a restaurant employee learning how to wait on tables performs many behaviors in the course of serving a customer. A tip is usually left by the customer after the meal, which provides immediate feedback about the employee's performance. However, if the tip is small, the employee is not sure which particular behavior caused the customers' displeasure. Likewise, if the tip is large, the employee is unsure which particular behavior or behaviors initiated the large tip. Thus, the timing of the consequence by itself may not be enough.

Contingency of consequence If it is not possible to immediately reward or punish a behavior, it should at least be made clear to the employee which behaviors brought the reward or punishment. To return to our example of the waiter, if he is told the reason for the size of his tip, he will be better able to change his behavior. Have you ever given a waiter or waitress a large tip even though the service was terrible? Most of us have. When this happens, however, the waiter or waitress is reinforced for poor performance and has no incentive to improve unless poor performance has its own consequence. In a similar fashion, if the waiter has done an outstanding job but has received a small tip, the probability of his repeating his outstanding performance is reduced. Furthermore, when tips are pooled at restaurants so that each employee gets a share of all tips received, an individual employee's rewards are not as contingent on his own behavior as when tips are not pooled.

The point of these examples is that reward and punishment must be made contingent upon performance; this contingency of consequence must be clear if learning is to occur. If the reward or punishment cannot be administered immediately, the employee must be told the purpose of the consequence so that the link between behavior and outcome is clear.

Type of consequence Different types of people like different types of rewards. For example, some employees value awards and/or praise, while others value money. Thus, for a reward to be effective, it must have value to an employee. The same is true of punishment. Threatening an employee with a 3-day suspension will be effective only if he needs the money or doesn't like being off from work; yelling at an employee will be effective only if the employee does not like being yelled at; and threatening to not promote an employee will be effective only if the employee values promotions and perceives he has a reasonable chance of being promoted.

The research literature abounds with studies demonstrating the effectiveness of reinforcement and feedback. For example, Austin, Kessler, Riccobono,
and Bailey (1996) provided daily feedback and weekly monetary reinforcement to employees in a roofing crew. This intervention resulted in a 64% labor cost reduction and an 80% improvement in safety. LaFleur and Hyten (1995) used a combination of goal setting, feedback, and reinforcement to increase the quality of hotel banquet staff performance.

In an interesting use of reinforcement and feedback, Kortick and O'Brien (1996) devised the "World Series of Quality Control" at a package delivery company in New York. The 104 employees were divided into 13 teams of 8 employees each, and the teams competed against each other to have the best shipping accuracy and quantity. Performance information and team standings were posted each week with the winning team receiving pizzas. At the end of each month, the winning team received individual plaques and dinner at a local restaurant. The intervention resulted in promising increases in shipping accuracy.

Obviously, it is important to reward employees for productive work behavior. But since different employees like different types of rewards, supervisors should have access to and be trained to administer different types of reinforcers. For example, some employees can be rewarded with praise, others with awards, others with interesting work, and still others with money (Filipczak, 1993). In fact, a meta-analysis by Stajkovic and Luthans (1997) found that financial, nonfinancial, and social rewards all resulted in increased levels of performance. As a result, many organizations are offering travel awards rather than financial rewards (Poe, 1997). For example, every executive at McDonald's is allowed to nominate high-performing employees for a chance to spend a week in one of the company's condos in Hawaii, Florida, and Lake Tahoe, Nevada. At Motorola, managers can nominate employees for travel awards. Nationwide, the average value of these travel awards is $1750 (Poe, 1997).

The use of money to motivate better worker performance has again become popular (Schuster & Zingheim, 1992). As shown in Exhibit 12-1, a compensation plan should include base pay and a benefit package to provide employees with security, salary adjustments to cover such conditions as undesirable shifts and geographic areas with high costs of living, and variable pay to provide an incentive to perform better. Though incentive systems often result in higher levels of performance, when designed poorly, they can result in such negative outcomes as increased stress, decreased health, and decreased safety (Schleifer & Amick, 1989; Schleifer & Okogbaa, 1990). Incentive pay can be given for either individual performance or group performance.

Individual incentive plans Individual-based incentive plans are designed to make high levels of individual

EXHIBIT 12-1

Compensation Plan

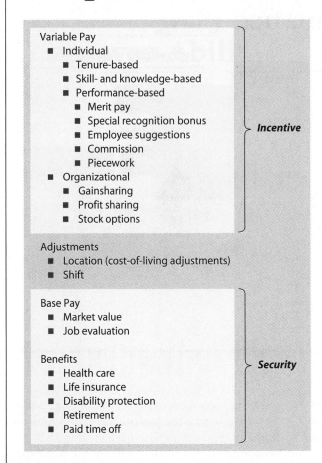

Variable Pay
- Individual
  - Tenure-based
  - Skill- and knowledge-based
  - Performance-based
    - Merit pay
    - Special recognition bonus
    - Employee suggestions
    - Commission
    - Piecework
- Organizational
  - Gainsharing
  - Profit sharing
  - Stock options

} *Incentive*

Adjustments
- Location (cost-of-living adjustments)
- Shift

Base Pay
- Market value
- Job evaluation

Benefits
- Health care
- Life insurance
- Disability protection
- Retirement
- Paid time off

} *Security*

---

performance financially worthwhile. Individual incentives help reduce such group problems as social loafing that were discussed in Chapter 8. Two main problems are associated with individual incentive plans. The first is the difficulty in measuring individual performance. Not only are objective measures difficult to find, but supervisors are reluctant to evaluate employees, especially when the outcome will determine the amount of money an employee will receive (Schuster & Zingheim, 1992).

The second problem is that individual incentive plans can foster competition among employees. Though competition is not always bad, it is seldom consistent with the recent trend toward a team approach to work. When done right, however, team environments and individual incentive programs can coexist and result in high levels of employee performance (Steers & Porter, 1991).

The two most common individual incentive plans are pay for performance and merit pay.

Pay for performance Also called *earnings-at-risk (EAR) plans*, **pay-for-performance** plans pay employees according to how much they individually produce. Simple pay-for-performance systems with which you are probably familiar include commission and piecework.

The first step in creating more complicated pay-for-performance plans is to determine the average or standard amount of production. For example, the average number of envelopes sorted by mail clerks might be 300 per hour. The next step is to determine the desired average amount of pay. We might decide that, on average, our mail clerks should earn $9 an hour. We then compute the piece rate by dividing hourly wage by number of envelopes sorted (9/300), which is .03. Thus, each correctly sorted envelope is worth 3 cents. If a mail clerk is good and sorts 400 envelopes per hour, he will make $12 per hour. If our clerk is not a good worker and can sort only 200 pieces per hour, he will make $6 per hour. To protect workers from the

EXHIBIT 12-2

Phoenix, Arizona, Hourly Rates for Pay-for-Performance Plan

Production as a % of Minimum	Quality Rating			
	1	2	3	4
101	$ 7.20	$ 7.45	$ 7.70	$ 7.95
110	$ 7.56	$ 7.81	$ 8.06	$ 8.31
121	$ 7.92	$ 8.17	$ 8.42	$ 8.67
131	$ 8.28	$ 8.53	$ 8.78	$ 9.03
141	$ 8.64	$ 8.89	$ 9.14	$ 9.39
151	$ 9.00	$ 9.25	$ 9.50	$ 9.75
161	$ 9.36	$ 9.61	$ 9.86	$10.11
171	$ 9.72	$ 9.97	$10.22	$10.47
181	$10.08	$10.33	$10.58	$10.83
191	$10.44	$10.69	$10.94	$11.19
201	$10.80	$11.05	$11.30	$11.55
211	$11.16	$11.41	$11.66	$11.91
221	$11.52	$11.77	$12.02	$12.27
231	$11.88	$12.13	$12.38	$12.63
241	$12.24	$12.49	$12.74	$12.99
251	$12.60	$12.85	$13.10	$13.35

effects of external factors, minimum wage laws ensure that even the worst employee will make enough money to survive. As suggested in Exhibit 12-1, most organizations provide a base salary to ensure that employees will have at least minimal financial security. In fact, research indicates that employees paid a flat hourly rate plus a performance bonus perform at levels equal to employees who are paid on a piece-rate plan (Dickinson & Gillette, 1993).

A good example of such a plan comes from the Superior Court Records Management Center in Phoenix, Arizona (Huish, 1997). After conducting a study that showed a negative correlation between employee salary and productivity ($r = -.49$), the Clerk of the Court decided to try a pay-for-performance system. Each employee was given a base salary of $7.20 per hour and on the basis of the quantity and quality of his work (see Exhibit 12-2), could earn incentive pay. This pay-for-performance intervention resulted in an average increase in employee pay of $2.60 per hour, a reduction in cost per unit (a unit was a court document page transferred to microfilm) of $0.39 to $0.21, and a decreased need for storage space.

Union National Bank in Little Rock, Arkansas, has had tremendous success by paying its workers for the number of customers they serve, the number of new customers gained, the amount of time taken to balance accounts at the end of the day, and so on. The bank's pay-for-performance program has resulted in the average employee making 25% more in take-home pay, and the bank itself has almost doubled its profits.

Nucor in Charlotte, North Carolina, is another company that has used a pay-for-performance plan. By paying its steelworkers for the amount of work they do, Nucor has seen productivity more than double and its workers make more than $30,000 per year while the industry average is some $27,000. Though pay-for-performance plans appear to be successful for both the employee and the employer, some research suggests that employees are not satisfied with such plans (Brown & Huber, 1992).

Merit pay The major distinction between **merit pay** and pay for performance is that merit pay systems base their incentives on performance appraisal scores rather than on such objective performance measures as sales and productivity. Thus, merit pay is a potentially good technique for jobs in which productivity is difficult to measure.

The actual link between performance appraisal scores and the amount of merit pay received by an employee varies greatly around the United States. In the state of Virginia's merit pay system, employees' performance appraisal scores at each office are ranked, and the top 30% of employees each receive a $1000 annual bonus.

In the merit pay system used by one nonprofit mental health agency, each employee's performance appraisal rating is divided by the total number of performance points possible, and this percentage is then multiplied by the maximum 3% merit increase that can be received by an employee. With this system, an employee must receive a perfect rating to receive the full 3% increase. Most employees receive between 2% and 2.5%.

The merit pay system used by a California public transit system is similar to that used by the mental health agency, with the exception that the merit increase becomes part of an employee's base salary for the next pay period. Thus, increases are perpetuated each year, unlike the mental health system's one-time reward.

Research on merit pay has brought mixed reviews. Some research has shown that employees like the idea of merit pay, but other research has found that it is not popular with all employees and that many employees do not consider the merit ratings to be fair (Hills, Scott, Markham, & Vest, 1987; Wisdom & Patzig, 1987). Employees are most satisfied with merit pay if they help develop the system (Gilchrist & White, 1990).

One of merit pay's biggest problems is that increases are based on subjective performance appraisals. Aware of this, some supervisors will inflate performance appraisal scores to increase their employees' pay and thus more positive employee feelings about the supervisors. Managers have also been known to inflate performance appraisal ratings when they believe the base salaries for certain positions are too low.

Another problem with merit pay is that its availability or amount often changes with each fiscal year. Thus, excellent performance one year might result in a large bonus, while the same performance another year might bring no bonus at all. This is especially true in the public sector. Thus, for merit pay to be successful, funding must be consistently available, and information about its availability and amount should be shared with employees (Wisdom & Patzig, 1987).

Organizational incentives The idea behind organization-based incentive plans is to get employees to participate in the success or failure of the organization (Schuster & Zingheim, 1992). Rather than encouraging individual competition, these plans reward employees for reaching group goals. The problems with group incentive plans are that they can encourage social loafing and can get so complicated that they become difficult to explain to employees.

Profit sharing Profit sharing was developed in America by Albert Gallatin way back in 1794 (Henderson, 1997). As its name implies, profit-sharing programs provide employees with a percentage of *profits* above a certain amount. For example, in addition to their base salary, employees might receive 50% of the profits a company makes above 6%. Organizations will usually not share the initial 5% or so of profits, as that money is needed for research and development and as a safety net for unprofitable years. The profits to be shared can be paid directly to employees as a bonus (cash plans) or placed into the employees' retirement fund (deferred plans). Profit sharing will only motivate employees if they understand the link between performance and profits and believe that the company has a reasonable chance of making a profit. Research indicates that profit sharing results in greater employee commitment (Fitzgibbons, 1997; Florkowski & Schuster, 1992).

Gainsharing A related plan, known as **gainsharing**, uses pay incentives based on *improvement* in organizational performance. Though the first gainsharing program was developed back in 1935 by the Nunn-Bush Shoe Company in Milwaukee, gainsharing has only become popular in the last two decades (Gowen, 1990). About 39% of large organizations have gainsharing programs. Gainsharing programs consist of two elements: a cooperative/participative management philosophy and a group-based bonus formula (Hanlon & Taylor, 1992).

The typical gainsharing program works as follows. First, the company monitors performance measures over some period of time to derive a **baseline**. Then productivity goals above the baseline are set, and the employees are told that they will receive bonuses for each period that the goal is reached. To make goal setting more effective, constant feedback is provided to employees on how current performance is in relation to the goal. At the end of each reporting period, bonuses are paid on the basis of how well the group did.

An excellent example of a successful gainsharing program can be found at the Dana Spicer Heavy Axle Division facility in Ohio (Hatcher, Ross, & Ross, 1987). Employees at the Dana plant receive a financial bonus when productivity surpasses the baseline. The gainsharing program has dramatically increased the number of employee suggestions, product quality, and productivity. Employees' bonuses average 14% above their normal pay each month, with year-end bonuses between 11% and 16%.

As another example, Southern California Edison employees agreed to surrender 5% of their base pay. In return, they were given the opportunity to earn 10% to 15% of their base pay in a gainsharing plan. In 1995 alone, this plan generated $96 million in savings—$40 million of which was passed on to the employees.

In general, gainsharing plans seem to be effective. A review of gainsharing studies indicates improvements in productivity, increased employee and union satisfaction, and declines in absenteeism (Gowen, 1990). As with any incentive plan, gainsharing is most effective when employees are formally involved in its design and operation (Bullock & Tubbs, 1990) and when there is not a long delay between performance and the financial payoff (Mawhinney & Gowen, 1990).

Stock options Though stock options represent the most complicated organizational incentive plan, they are offered by more than 10,000 organizations and involve more than 10 million employees (Bencivenga, 1997). With stock options, employees are given the opportunity to purchase stock in the future; typically at the market price on the day the options were granted. Usually stock options vest over a certain period of time and must be exercised within a maximum time frame. The idea is that as a company does well, the value of its stock increases as does the employee's profit. For example, suppose that AT&T stock is selling for $55 per share on June 1, and the company gives employees the option of purchasing the stock for $55-per-share anytime in the next 10 years. Ten years later, the stock is worth $75 per share and the employee can purchase the stock for the $55-per-share option price—a $20-per-share profit. However, if the stock had fallen from $55 to $45, the employee would not exercise his option to purchase the stock at $55 per share.

Stock options allow employees to share in the long-term success of an organization. In fact, such organizations as GTE, United Airlines, Home Depot, and Foldcraft Company report not only are their employees making good money through their stock ownership, but that organizational productivity has improved as well. At times, stock options may not be good motivators because employees have trouble understanding the concept of stock and because the incentive (profit made on the selling of stock) is psychologically well removed from day-to-day performance. However, having partial ownership in a company can increase performance. For example, in a study of hotel managers, Qian (1996) found a significant correlation between the amount of manager ownership and the hotel's profit margin.

Punishment Rather than rewarding desired behaviors, we can change employee performance by punishing undesired behaviors. That is, instead of rewarding employees who don't miss work, we punish them when they do. Instead of providing monetary incentives for high levels of performance, we suspend employees for low levels of performance. Though many psychologists advise against punishment, it is common, and managers generally believe it to be effective (Butterfield, Trevino, & Ball, 1996).

Proponents of using punishment to change employee behavior argue that if applied properly, punishment not only reduces undesired behaviors in a particular employee, but also sets an example for other employees. Opponents of punishment argue that punishment changes behavior only in the short run, does not teach an employee proper behaviors, and causes resentment. Furthermore, punishment causes employees to learn new methods to break rules, rather than teaching them not to break rules.

For punishment to be effective, an employee must understand why he is being punished and be shown alternative ways of behaving that will result in some type of desired reinforcement. The punishment must also "fit the crime" in that too severe a punishment will cause resentment and too lenient a punishment will not motivate a change in behavior. As you would imagine, punishment should usually be done in private rather than in front of other employees.

Premack Principle Another reinforcement technique stems from the **Premack Principle** (Premack, 1963), which states that reinforcement is relative and that a supervisor can reinforce an employee with something that on the surface does not appear to be a reinforcer. The best way to explain this principle is to construct a **reinforcement hierarchy** on which an employee lists his preferences for a variety of reinforcers.

As Exhibit 12-3 shows, our hypothetical employee most desires money and time off from work and least desires typesetting and cleaning the press. Our employee can enjoy and do a better job of cleaning his press if we give him money for each time he properly completes the task, but such a reward system can become expensive. Thus, according to the Premack Principle, we can get our employee to clean his press properly by allowing him to do one of the activities he likes more than cleaning. From his reinforcement hierarchy, we can see that he ranks throwing out oily rags as more enjoyable because he can take a short break by walking outdoors to the disposal area. Thus, all we need for a reward is to let him dispose of the rags.

The Premack Principle may sound silly, but think of the reinforcers you have used to reward yourself for studying. After reading a certain number of pages, you might allow yourself a trip to the water fountain. Certainly, getting a drink of water is hardly anyone's idea of a good time, but it may be more interesting than studying and so can become a reinforcer to increase studying.

EXHIBIT 12-3

The Premack Principle: Example of a Reinforcement Hierarchy

Most desired

Money
Time off from work
Lunch time
Working next to Wanda
Supervisor praise
Running the press
Getting printing plates
Throwing out oily rags
Typesetting
Cleaning the press

⎱ Reinforcers

Least desired

In high school, one of us (Mike) worked at a printing plant that produced stock reports. All entry level employees were *collators,* whose jobs were to place 500 copies of a book page on a piece of wood strapped to their necks and then walk around a room placing a piece of paper in each of 500 slots. This process was repeated about 300 times until a complete book was put together. As you can imagine, the job was extremely boring. To motivate us, our supervisor would "reward" the fastest collators by allowing them to take out the trash, to go pick up lunch (it was kind of cool ordering 100 Whoppers and 100 fries and watching the Burger King employees' expressions), or to move the paper carts from one end of the building to the other. The realization didn't hit until 10 years later that the boss was using the Premack Principle: Rewarding performance of a very boring task by allowing us to perform a less boring task.

As another example, Mike's current boss (the department chair) is a master at using the Premack Principle. Because salary raises are small in size and never a certainty, it is difficult to motivate faculty to do the "little things" by offering financial rewards. Instead, the chair rewards good departmental citizenship by giving the best faculty their most desired schedule (no 8:00 a.m.'s for me!), their favorite classes, and their favorite committee assignments. From what we have seen, these reinforcers work better than money!

Of course, the department chair is successful in using the Premack Principle because he has a good sense of every faculty member's reinforcement hierarchy. For example, Mike hates serving on committees whereas a colleague gets his entire self-worth by chairing department and university committees. So the chair reinforces the colleague by putting him on committees and reinforces Mike by giving him some data to play with. Likewise, some faculty love early morning classes whereas others would rather teach at night.

In an example from the research literature, Welsh, Bernstein, and Luthans (1992) demonstrated the effectiveness of the Premack Principle with employees at a fast-food restaurant. Employees whose errors decreased in a given day were rewarded by being allowed to work in their favorite workstation (e.g., cooking fries vs. flipping burgers). This use of the Premack Principle resulted in a decrease in employee errors.

The beauty of the Premack Principle is that you can use it to motivate yourself. For example, suppose that you need to study for a test, but hate to study. To motivate yourself, you might allow yourself to get a soda for every 100 pages you read or to "shoot a few hoops" at the end of each chapter. Likewise, if you hate to return phone calls at work, you can "reward" yourself for each call you return by typing a memo. It's not exciting but rewarding yourself with less boring tasks can motivate you to perform the more boring ones.

Even though operant conditioning and the Premack Principle have been successful in improving motivation and performance, a note of caution comes from Deci (1972), who believes that for some people and some jobs, work is intrinsically motivating. That is, people are motivated because they enjoy working, not because they are being rewarded. A reasonable body of research, much of it conducted by Deci himself, demonstrates that paying a person for the amount of work done will reduce the degree to which he enjoys performing the task. Thus, when financial incentives are no longer available, the employee will be less motivated to work than before rewards were used. As interesting as this concept sounds, some researchers (e.g., Dickinson, 1989) argue that Deci's conclusions that extrinsic rewards decrease intrinsic motivation are flawed.

> **PROJECT D** *Reinforcement Hierarchy*
> To apply the Premack Principle to your own life, complete Project D at the end of this chapter.

EXPECTANCY THEORY

An influential theory of worker motivation is **expectancy theory**, which was first proposed by Vroom (1964) and then modified by others, including Porter and Lawler (1968). This theory has three components, the definitions of which vary with each modification of the theory. The following definitions, however, are combinations of those suggested by others and make the theory easier to understand:

- **expectancy (E):** the perceived relationship between the amount of effort an employee puts in and the resulting outcome

- **instrumentality (I):** the extent to which the outcome of a worker's performance, if noticed, results in a particular consequence

- **valence (V):** the extent to which an employee values a particular consequence

To understand or predict an employee's level of motivation, these components are used in the following formula:

$$\text{motivation} = E\,(I \times V)$$

Thus, for each possible outcome of a behavior: The valence of each outcome is multiplied by the probability that it occurs at a particular performance level, and this product is multiplied by the expectancy of an employee putting in the effort to attain the necessary level of performance. Then adding these products for all the outcomes yields the total motivation for that behavior. As can be seen from this formula, the higher the score on each component, the greater the employee's motivation. To expound on this, let us examine each component in more detail.

In terms of *expectancy*, if an employee believes that no matter how hard he works, he will never reach the necessary level of performance, then his motivation will probably be low. For *instrumental-*

ity, the employee will be motivated only if his behavior results in some specific consequence. That is, if the employee works extra hours, he expects to be rewarded, or if he is inexcusably absent from work, he expects to be punished. For a behavior to have a desired consequence, two events must occur. First, the employee's behavior must be noticed. If the employee believes that he is able to attain the necessary level of performance but that his performance will not be noticed, then his level of motivation will be low. Second, noticed behavior must be rewarded. If no rewards are available, then, again, motivation will be low. As will be discussed in greater detail later in this chapter, if appropriate behavior does not have positive consequences or if inappropriate behavior does not have negative consequences, then the probability that a worker will continue undesired behaviors increases, and the probability that an employee will continue desired behaviors decreases.

For *valence*, if an employee is rewarded, the reward must be something that he values (Mobaraki, 1996). If good performance is rewarded by an award, then the employee will be motivated only if he values awards. Likewise, if we punish an employee by suspending him, then the punishment will be effective only if the employee needs the money. If he does not particularly like his job and would rather spend a few days at the lake, the suspension will obviously not be effective. In an applied study, Fox, Scott, and Donohue (1993) found that in a pay-for-performance environment, pay served as an incentive only for employees with a high monetary valence.

This theory can be used to analyze the situation experienced by one bank in Virginia. Concerned that the bank's tellers were averaging only three new Visa customers each month, the management sought to increase the number of Visa applications taken by each teller. Tellers were expected to ask each customer if he or she had a Visa card. If not, the tellers were to give him or her an application. The tellers would receive $5 extra per month each if they increased the number of new Visa customers per month to 25.

The program was a flop, much to management's surprise. Applying expectancy theory, however, we could have predicted the program's lack of success. First, let us look at the expectancy component. If the tellers currently averaged only three new Visa customers each month, they probably did not believe that, even working hard, they would be able to generate 25 new customers. Thus, the expectancy probability for the program was low.

Second, most tellers probably did not place much value on an extra $5 per month, so the valence component also was low. Thus, with two of three components having low values, the program was destined to fail from the start. The bank later reduced the monthly number of new Visa cards to 10 and increased the teller reward to $20. These simple changes brought the desired increase in new Visa customers.

In addition to predicting employee effort, expectancy theory has been applied successfully to predict speeding by drivers and cheating by students. To demonstrate this last behavior, imagine the typical examination in a typical college class.

First, look at the expectancy component. We might ask what the probability is for catching a cheater. Students who cheat most likely believe that it is very low. To determine the instrumentality component, we might ask what the probability is for some negative consequence if a cheater is caught. In many universities, this probability is low. Not only is it difficult to prove that a student cheated, but if it is the first time a student is caught, punishment usually results in no more than a few days' suspension.

Finally, we examine the valence component. Even if a student *was* caught and suspended, how terrible would that be? For many students, a few days of vacation may not seem so terrible. Thus, when combining the three components, we should not be surprised that cheating often occurs.

Expectancy theory can also be used to suggest ways to change employee motivation. As we saw with the bank, motivation was increased by making the performance standard more reasonable and increasing the value of the consequence. Similarly, if we wanted to apply the theory to decrease cheating, we would increase the probability of catching cheaters, make convicting a person who has cheated easier, and make the consequences for cheating more severe.

Although expectancy theory is an interesting and useful method of predicting and increasing employee motivation, some researchers have criticized it. The major criticism involves the components equation. As it is now written, all of the components are multiplied. Some researchers have questioned whether the addition of some components would be more appropriate than their multiplication (Schmidt, 1973). When the components are multiplied, a zero in any component results in a prediction of zero motivation, even when ratings in the other components are high.

A second criticism involves the values that are assigned to each component (Ilgen, Nebeker, & Pritchard, 1981). Research has indicated that even though valence and instrumentality can be reliably measured (T. R. Mitchell, 1974), the theory is most predictive when people behave rationally (Stahl & Harrell, 1981), which they often do not, and have an internal locus of control (Lied & Pritchard, 1976), which may not always be the case. Despite problems with the equation, however, the theory is still one of the most useful for predicting employee behavior.

Treating Employees Fairly

In Chapter 11, we discussed equity theory and concluded that employees who perceive they are being treated fairly will be more satisfied with their jobs than employees who do not perceive they are being treated fairly. The same holds true for motivation: Employees who feel they are not being treated fairly will be less motivated to perform well than will employees who feel they are being treated fairly.

If an employee believes that his input/output ratio is less favorable than the ratios of other people, he will most likely be less motivated to perform well or to do those "extra things" to help out the organization. As we saw in the research studies in Chapter 11, major league baseball players who either had their salary cut during their first year of free agency or lost an arbitration case performed at lower levels the following year. In a study of professional basketball players, Harder (1992) found that overpaid players responded by being more team oriented (e.g., passing the ball, rebounding), whereas underpaid players responded by being more selfish (e.g., taking shots). However, as mentioned in the previous chapter, employees who feel that their input/output ratios are more favorable than others will not be more motivated.

Morrison and Robinson (1997) have expanded equity theory to include promises made by an organization to an employee. That is, employees compare what the organization promised to do for them (e.g., provide a computer, support continued education) with what the organization actually did. If the organization does less than it promised, employees will be less motivated to perform well and will retaliate by doing less than they promised the organization they would do.

Exhibit 12-4 summarizes the findings of equity theory research.

> **PROJECT E** *Expectancy and Equity Theory*
> To practice using expectancy and equity theory, complete Project E at the end of this chapter.

The Motivation Level of Other Employees

As mentioned in Chapter 11 in our discussion of social learning theory, employees observe the levels of motivation and satisfaction of other employees and then model those levels. Thus, if an organization's older employees work hard and talk positively about their jobs and their employer, new employees will model this behavior and be both productive and satisfied. The reverse is also true: If veteran employees work slowly and complain about their jobs, so will new employees.

EXHIBIT 12-4

Equity Theory Research

When an employee s inputs are greater than his outputs (underpayment), he:

Works less hard (Hauenstein & Lord, 1989)

Becomes more selfish (Harder, 1992)

Has lower job satisfaction (McLoughlin, Hodgson, & McLachan, 1996)

When an employee s outputs are greater than his inputs (overpayment), he:

Is less likely to be persuaded by his underpaid peers (Stewart & Moore, 1992)

Does not feel guilty (Lapidus & Pinkerton, 1995)

Works harder (Adams & Rosenbaum, 1962; Pritchard,
    Dunnette, & Jorgenson, 1972)

Becomes more team oriented (Harder, 1992)

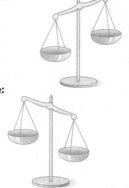

INTEGRATION OF MOTIVATION THEORIES

In this chapter we discussed many theories of work motivation. As shown in Exhibit 12-5, people come to a job with a predisposition toward motivation. That is, some people, such as those with high self-esteem, are generally more motivated than others.

From goal-setting theory, we find that employees who have, understand, and agree to goals will be more motivated than those without goals or with unclear goals. From expectancy theory and goal-setting theory, we know that the goals must be challenging but reasonable.

From operant learning and expectancy theories, it is clear that extrinsically motivated people will be more motivated if behavior results in a reward. From these same two theories plus discrepancy theory, the needs theories, and the Premack Principle, we know that the rewards must have value to the employee in order to be motivating. Because different people value different rewards, care must be taken to ensure that a variety of rewards are available.

From equity theory, we know that rewards that are valued will be motivating only if they are given in an equitable way. As discussed previously in the chapter, *perceptions* of equity are as important as the *reality* of equity.

Social learning theory tells us that if other employees are motivated, there is an increased probability that we will model their behavior and be motivated.

The results of these factors are summed to indicate an employee's current level of motivation. As conditions change, so will the motivation level.

PROJECTS F AND G *Putting It All Together*
To practice what you have learned in this chapter, complete the case study in Project F and develop your own theory in Project G.

CHAPTER RECAP

In this chapter you learned:

- Employees who have high self-esteem, a high need for achievement, and intrinsic motivation, and who are expected to perform well by others are more motivated than their low self-esteem, low-achievement need, extrinsically motivated counterparts.

- Goals are most effective if they are concrete and specific, are of high but reasonable difficulty, and are set with the input of the employee.

- Providing feedback on goal attainment and performance levels will also increase performance.

- Operant conditioning principles can be used to motivate employees.

- Employees who are treated fairly are more motivated to perform well.

- Common individual incentive plans include pay for performance and merit pay. Common organizational incentive plans include profit sharing, gainsharing, and stock options.

Critical Thinking Questions

1. Does getting paid for a task that one enjoys performing reduce intrinsic motivation?

EXHIBIT 12-5

Motivation Flowchart

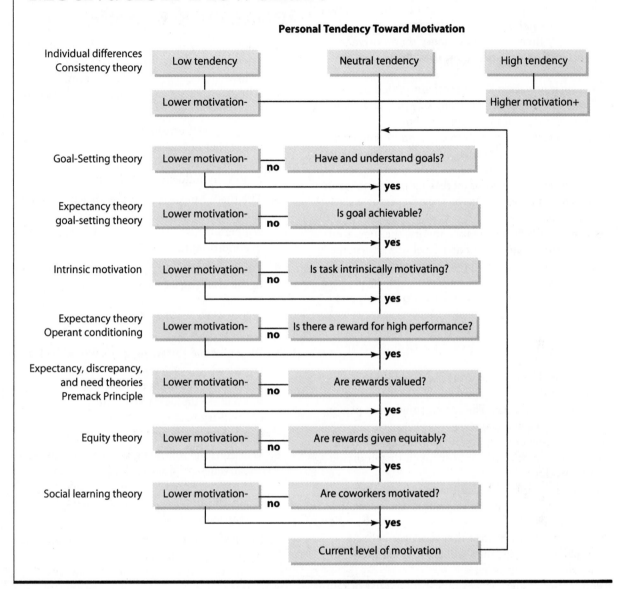

Personal Tendency Toward Motivation

2. If the right techniques are used, can everyone be motivated to perform well?

3. Which of the individual incentive plans is best?

4. What is the optimal level at which goals should be set?

5. Is the threat of punishment an effective motivator?

WEB SITES

For further information, log on to the following web sites.

www.employer-employee.com/howtomot.htm

A short article on how to motivate employees without money.

www.qualitydigest.com/jul/gainshre.html
Provides information about gainsharing plans.

KEY TERMS

Baseline The level of productivity before the implementation of a gainsharing plan.

Chronic self-esteem The positive or negative way in which a person views him- or herself as a whole.

Consistency theory Korman's theory that employees will be motivated to perform at levels consistent with their levels of self-esteem.

Expectancy In expectancy theory, the perceived probability that a particular amount of effort will result in a particular level of performance.

Expectancy theory Vroom's theory that motivation is a function of expectancy, instrumentality, and valence.

Extrinsic motivation Work motivation that arises from such nonpersonal factors as pay, coworkers, and opportunities for advancement.

Gainsharing A group incentive system in which employees are paid a bonus based on improvements in group productivity.

Goal setting A method of increasing performance in which employees are given specific performance goals to aim for.

Instrumentality In expectancy theory, the perceived probability that a particular level of performance will result in a particular consequence.

Intrinsic motivation Work motivation in the absence of such external factors as pay, promotion, and coworkers.

Merit pay An incentive plan in which employees receive pay bonuses based on performance appraisal scores.

Motivation The force that drives an employee to perform well.

Need for achievement The extent to which a person desires to be successful.

Pay for performance A system in which employees are paid on the basis of how much they individually produce.

Premack Principle The idea that reinforcement is relative both within an individual and between individuals.

Pygmalion effect The idea that if people believe something is true, they will act in a manner consistent with that belief.

Reinforcement hierarchy A rank-ordered list of reinforcers for an individual.

Self-esteem The positive or negative way in which a person views him- or herself.

Self-fulfilling prophecy The idea that people behave in ways consistent with their self-image.

Situational self-esteem The positive or negative way in which a person views him- or herself in a particular situation.

Socially influenced self-esteem The positive or negative way in which a person views him- or herself based on the expectations of others.

Valence In expectancy theory, the perceived desirability of a consequence that results from a particular level of performance.

Work Preference Inventory A measure of an individual's orientation toward intrinsic versus extrinsic motivation.

PRACTICE EXAM

1. Employees with _____ levels of self-esteem are most motivated to perform well.
   a. low
   b. medium
   c. high
   d. self-esteem is not related to motivation

2. _____ self-esteem is the way people feel about themselves.
   a. chronic
   b. situational
   c. socially influenced
   d. temporal

3. The theory most involved with self-esteem is:
   a. equity
   b. expectancy
   c. operant conditioning
   d. consistency

4. Employees with _____ need for achievement desire challenging jobs over which they have control.
   a. low
   b. medium
   c. high
   d. no

5. Which of the following goals would be least effective?
   a. I will sell 45 units per day
   b. I will do the best that I can
   c. I will try to improve by 5%
   d. all three goals would be equally effective

6. Which of the following will not increase the effectiveness of goal setting?
   a. a concrete goal
   b. a specific goal
   c. a high but reasonable goal
   d. a self-set goal

7. Rewards and punishments are most associated with _____ theory.
   a. equity
   b. expectancy
   c. operant conditioning
   d. consistency

8. Which of the following is an individual incentive plan?
   a. merit pay
   b. gainsharing
   c. stock options
   d. profit sharing

9. Which of the following incentive plans is based on *improvements* in performance?
   a. merit pay
   b. gainsharing
   c. stock options
   d. profit sharing

10. Which of the following incentive plans is most related to employee commitment?
    a. merit pay
    b. gainsharing
    c. stock options
    d. profit sharing

11. Which of the following incentive plans is most difficult for employees to understand?
    a. merit pay
    b. gainsharing
    c. stock options
    d. profit sharing

12. A reinforcement hierarchy is the basis for the _____ Principle.
    a. Vroom
    b. Skinner
    c. Porter
    d. Premack

13. Which of the following is not a component of expectancy theory?
    a. expectancy
    b. instrumentality
    c. reinforcement
    d. valence

14. Which part of expectancy theory involves the relationship between effort and the resulting outcome?
    a. expectancy
    b. instrumentality
    c. reinforcement
    d. valence

15. Our motivation is highest when our input/output ratio is _____ when compared to others.
    a. favorable
    b. not favorable
    c. the same
    d. it doesn't matter

16. The Pygmalion effect is an example of increasing self-esteem through:
    a. training seminars
    b. success on easy tasks
    c. supervisor behavior
    d. harder work

17. The self-fulfilling prophecy is best utilized through:
    a. training seminars
    b. success on easy tasks
    c. supervisor behavior
    d. harder work

18. If a supervisor didn't notice that an employee performed well, the _____ component of expectancy theory would be low.
    a. expectancy
    b. instrumentality
    c. valence
    d. equity

19. The most motivated employee would be one who is _____ in self-esteem and _____ in need for achievement.
    a. high / low
    b. low / high
    c. low / low
    d. high / high

20. A person who is motivated by the enjoyment of performing a task is high in:
    a. self-esteem
    b. need for achievement
    c. extrinsic motivation
    d. intrinsic motivation

ANSWERS 1 c, 2 a, 3 d, 4 c, 5 b, 6 d, 7 c, 8 a, 9 b, 10 d, 11 c, 12 d, 13 c, 14 a, 15 a, 16 c, 17 b, 18 b, 19 d, 20 d

Focused Free-Write

Describe a job (or a class) you have had in which you were very motivated to perform well. Why do you think you were so motivated?

_____

_____

_____

_____

_____

_____

_____

_____

_____

_____

_____

_____

_____

_____

_____

_____

_____

_____

_____

_____

_____

_____

Now describe a job (or class) in which you were not motivated to perform well. Why?

_____

_____

_____

_____

_____

_____

_____

_____

_____

_____

_____

_____

_____

_____

_____

_____

_____

_____

_____

_____

_____

_____

_____

_____

Self-Esteem

The Radford Self-Esteem Inventory

Following is a list of statements about feelings. For each statement, place an X in the appropriate column to indicate the extent to which you agree with the statement.

SD=Strongly Disagree   D=Disagree   N=Neutral   A=Agree   SA=Strongly Agree

	SD	D	N	A	SA
1. Difficult situations usually don't bother me.	1	2	3	4	5
2. I don't like a lot of things about me.	5	4	3	3	2
3. I have good ideas.	1	2	3	4	5
4. I have a low opinion of myself.	5	4	3	3	2
5. I like trying new things.	1	2	3	4	5
6. I am a confident person.	1	2	3	4	5
7. I am not afraid to take risks.	1	2	3	4	5
8. I do most things well.	1	2	3	4	5
9. I am happy with who I am.	1	2	3	4	5
10. I am a likable person.	1	2	3	4	5
11. There is not much about my personality that I would change.	1	2	3	4	5
12. I am successful at almost everything I try.	1	2	3	4	5
13. I am a good person.	1	2	3	4	5
14. I have a lot of respect for myself.	1	2	3	4	5
15. I am comfortable with who I am.	1	2	3	4	5

	SD	D	N	A	SA
16. There is little I cannot accomplish if I set my mind to it.	1	2	3	4	5
17. I am a talented person.	1	2	3	4	5
18. I can overcome any obstacles in my life.	1	2	3	4	5
19. I am as good a person as anyone.	1	2	3	4	5
20. There are so many people I would rather be than me.	1	2	3	4	5

Scoring and Interpreting the Radford Inventory

The Radford Inventory measures your level of self-esteem. To score the inventory, add the points that correspond to the choices you made for each question.

Your self-esteem score is _____. To interpret your score, look at the chart below and circle where your scores fall.

	Self-Worth
Top 20%	82–100
Next 20%	78– 81
Middle 20%	75– 77
Next 20%	68– 74
Bottom 20%	20– 67

On the basis of what you learned about consistency theory, how motivated would your self-esteem score suggest that you would be?

_____

_____

_____

_____

_____

_____

_____

_____

PROJECT B

Work Preference Inventory

Please rate each item in terms of how true it is of you. Please circle one and only one letter for each question according to the following scale:

N=Never or almost never true of you   S=Sometimes true of you
O=Often true of you   A=Always or almost always true of you

1.	I am concerned about what other people think of my work.	N	S	O	A
2.	I prefer having someone set clear goals for me in my work.	N	S	O	A
3.	The more difficult the problem, the more I enjoy trying to solve it.	N	S	O	A
4.	I am keenly aware of the goals I have for getting good grades.	N	S	O	A
5.	I want my work to provide me with opportunities to increase my knowledge and skills.	N	S	O	A
6.	To me, success means doing better than other people.	N	S	O	A
7.	I prefer to figure things out for myself.	N	S	O	A
8.	No matter what the outcome of a project, I am satisfied if I feel I gained a new experience.	N	S	O	A
9.	I dislike relatively simple, straightforward tasks.	N	S	O	A
10.	I am keenly aware of the GPA (grade point average) goals I have for myself.	N	S	O	A
11.	Curiosity is the driving force behind much of what I do.	N	S	O	A
12.	I'm less concerned with what work I do than what I get for it.	N	S	O	A
13.	I enjoy tackling problems that are completely new to me.	N	S	O	A
14.	I prefer work that stretches my abilities over work I know I can do well.	N	S	O	A
15.	I'm concerned about how other people are going to react to my ideas.	N	S	O	A
16.	I often think about grades and awards.	N	S	O	A
17.	I'm more comfortable when I can set my own goals.	N	S	O	A
18.	I believe that there is no point in doing a good job if nobody else knows about it.	N	S	O	A
19.	I am strongly motivated by the grades I can earn.	N	S	O	A
20.	It is important to me to be able to do what I enjoy most.	N	S	O	A
21.	I prefer working on projects with clearly specified procedures.	N	S	O	A
22.	As long as I can do what I enjoy, I'm not that concerned about exactly what grades or awards I earn.	N	S	O	A
23.	I enjoy doing work that is so absorbing that I forget about everything else.	N	S	O	A
24.	I am strongly motivated by the recognition I can earn from other people.	N	S	O	A
25.	I have to feel that I'm earning something for what I do.	N	S	O	A
26.	I enjoy trying to solve complex problems.	N	S	O	A
27.	It is important for me to have an outlet for self-expression.	N	S	O	A
28.	I want to find out how good I really can be at my work.	N	S	O	A
29.	I want other people to find out how good I really can be at my work.	N	S	O	A
30.	What matters most to me is enjoying what I do.	N	S	O	A

Interpreting the Work Preference Inventory

The Work Preference Inventory was developed by Dr. Teresa Amabile and measures your predisposition to be intrinsically and extrinsically motivated. To score the WPI, give yourself 1 point if you circled N, 2 points if you circled S, 3 points if you circled O, and 4 points if you circled A.

To determine your level of intrinsic motivation, add your points for Questions 3, 5, 7, 8, 9, 11, 13, 14, 17, 20, 23, 26, 27, 28, and 30: _____

To determine your level of extrinsic motivation, add your points for Questions 1, 2, 4, 6, 10, 12, 15, 16, 18, 19, 21, 24, 25, and 29: _____ On Question 22 reverse your score (A = 1, O = 2, S = 3, and N =4), and add this score to the total for the other 14 questions: _____.

To interpret your score, look at the chart below and circle where your scores fall. Are you an intrinsically or extrinsically motivated person?

	Intrinsic Motivation	Extrinsic Motivation
Top 20%	46–60	43–60
Next 20%	45–47	39–42
Middle 20%	43–44	37–38
Next 20%	40–42	35–36
Bottom 20%	15–39	15–34

On the basis of what you read in the text, what does your score on the WPI tell you about your personal tendency toward motivation?

_____

_____

_____

_____

_____

_____

_____

_____

_____

_____

Work Preference Inventory: College Student Version; Copyright 1987, Teresa M. Amabile, used with permission of the author.

PROJECT C

Goal Setting

The text discussed the value of goal setting as a way to improve employee performance. However, goal setting works in many settings outside of work. The purpose of this project is to provide you with the opportunity to use your knowledge of goal setting to set your academic and career goals.

Instructions In the space below, set goals for what you want to accomplish next semester as well as for the rest of your life. Once these goals have been set, indicate how you plan to reach these goals. For example, if you set a goal of getting a job that pays $30,000 a year, what are you going to do that will allow you to get this salary?

_____

_____

_____

_____

_____

_____

_____

_____

_____

_____

_____

_____

_____

_____

_____

_____

_____

_____

Reinforcement Hierarchy

It is often difficult to reward employees because each employee values different things in life. The purpose of this project is to give you the opportunity to create your own reinforcement hierarchy so you can then apply the Premack Principle to your own life.

Instructions Think of your current job or one that you have had recently. Once you have this job in mind, create a reinforcement hierarchy for yourself. Use the example in your text as a guide.

Most Liked

1. _____

2. _____

3. _____

4. _____

5. _____

6. _____

7. _____

8. _____

9. _____

10. _____

11. _____

12. _____

13. _____

14. _____

15. _____

Least Liked

Expectancy and Equity Theories

Think of the job that you have now or one that you recently had. If you were in charge, how would you use the expectancy and equity theories to increase employee motivation and job satisfaction?

_____

_____

_____

_____

_____

_____

_____

_____

_____

_____

_____

_____

_____

_____

_____

_____

_____

_____

_____

_____

_____

Motivation Case Study

For the past 5 months, Vacua Can, a manager at Orion Manufacturing, has come home from work depressed and angry. It seems no matter what she does, she can't motivate her employees to improve their performance. Over the past year, Vacua sent each employee to an extensive training seminar, spent money on new equipment, and transferred out the employees who lacked the ability to do their jobs. Despite these interventions, her department's performance is at the same level it was 2 years ago. Because of this performance stagnation, Vacua is worried that she will be fired.

Vacua thought that a boost in morale might increase performance so she gave each employee a 12% raise. Yet instead of morale being increased, many employees complained even louder than before.

Vacua also held a department meeting in which she gave an inspirational appeal for everyone to "work hard and do the very best job you possibly can." Her department seemed enthusiastic for a week, but productivity did not change.

Where did Vacua Can go wrong? What advice can you give her to motivate her employees?

Your Own Motivation Theory

In Chapters 11 and 12, you learned about many different theories for why employees are satisfied with their jobs and why they are motivated to perform well. Even though none of the theories has been completely supported, each of the theories has something to offer. On the basis of the various theories, as well as on your experiences, design your own theory of job motivation and satisfaction. Feel free to borrow as much as you want from each of the theories discussed in your text.

_____

_____

_____

_____

_____

_____

_____

_____

_____

_____

_____

_____

_____

_____

_____

_____

_____

_____

_____

_____

CHAPTER THIRTEEN

Developing Others: Organization Development

Managing Change

Empowering Employees

Developing Teams

Chapter Recap

Key Terms

Practice Exam

Projects

In Chapter 4, you learned that an important part of professionalism is the development of personal skills. Likewise, an important part of leading others is the development of their skills. Sometimes this is done through training and other times through organization development—the process of improving organizational performance by making organization-wide changes. Though there are many aspects to organization development, this chapter will focus on only three of the major issues: Managing change, empowering employees, and developing teams. At the end of this chapter, you will:

- Understand how and why organizations change
- Learn how to increase employee acceptance of change
- Know the importance of organizational culture
- Learn how to deal with change
- Understand when empowering employees is a good idea
- Learn the levels of employee input
- Learn what makes a group a team
- Learn how teams operate
- Understand why the team approach is not always best

■ MANAGING CHANGE

In organizations, change occurs for many reasons and takes on many forms. Some changes are due to such organization development efforts as downsizing, reorganization, or the introduction of teams. Some changes are the result of such external mandates as managed care or new governmental regulations. Still other changes occur due to new leadership or new personnel.

Sacred Cow Hunts

Perhaps the first step toward organizational change is what Kriegel and Brandt (1996) called a **sacred cow hunt.** Organizational sacred cows are practices that have been around for a long time and invisibly reduce productivity. A sacred cow hunt, then, is an organization-wide attempt to get rid of practices that serve no useful purpose. Such companies as Merck Pharmaceutical and Tractor Supply Stores have periodic sacred cow hunts in which cow bells are rung when a sacred cow is found, monthly sacred cow barbecues are held, and employees receive awards and money for finding a sacred cow. In a sacred cow hunt, an organization looks at all its practices and policies and asks such questions as:

- Why are we doing it? Does it add value, improve quality, improve service, or improve productivity?

- What if it didn't exist?
- Is it already being done by someone else?
- How and when did we start doing this?
- Can it be done better by another person, department, or company?

According to Kriegel and Brandt (1996), common types of sacred cows include the **paper cow,** the **meeting cow,** and the **speed cow.**

THE PAPER COW

Paper cows are unnecessary paperwork—usually forms and reports that cost organizations money to prepare, distribute, and read. To determine if something is a paper cow, consider the extent to which the paperwork increases efficiency, productivity, or quality. Ask if anyone actually reads the paperwork. A unique strategy tried by employees at one company was to stop sending a monthly report that had been distributed for years. The employees' thinking was that if the report was actually needed, they would receive complaints. Three months and three missing reports later, no one had complained.

A good annual practice is to review all forms and reports and determine whether they are still needed and, if they are, whether they are needed in their current format. To demonstrate the importance of this practice, review the forms used by your school or organization. How many of them are a third of a page or a quarter of a page? Probably none. There seems to be an unwritten rule that all forms must ask questions until the bottom of the page is reached. A colleague was recently preparing contracts for his graduate assistants and noticed that he was being asked questions about the university from which the students had received their undergraduate degrees, their undergraduate GPA, and their work histories. Note that these were contracts, not application forms, where this information was already contained. So, in the spirit of a good sacred cow hunt, he called the graduate college to ask why this information was necessary. Their reply? No one knew. Did anyone actually need this information? No. Will you change the form for next year? No. An example of a sacred cow hunt but no sacred cow barbecue.

PROJECT A   *Paper Cow Hunts*
To apply what you have learned about paper cow hunts, complete Project A located at the end of this chapter.

THE MEETING COW

Another area ripe for change is the number and length of meetings. Think about meetings you have attended recently. How much meeting time was spent doing business as opposed to socializing? Was the meeting really necessary? To reduce the number and length of meetings, some organizations ask the person calling the meeting to determine the cost of the meeting (e.g., 1 hour's salary of each attendee, cost of meeting room, cost of refreshments and supplies) and consider whether the cost of the meeting will exceed the potential benefits. In some of these organizations, the meeting costs are actually posted at the beginning of the meeting! Needless to say, when people are forced to consider the benefits of most meetings against their cost, most meetings will not be held.

The Speed Cow

Unnecessary deadlines are another source for potential change. Requiring work to be done "by tomorrow" is sometimes necessary. However, unnecessary deadlines cause employees to work at a faster than optimal pace, resulting in decreased quality, increased stress, and increased health problems.

In addition to sacred cow hunts, Kriegel and Brandt (1996) suggested that effective change can be encouraged by using the following strategies:

- Think like a beginner: Ask stupid questions, constantly ask why things are being done a certain way, and don't assume anything makes sense.
- Don't be complacent with something that is working well. Keep looking for ways to improve, new markets to enter, new products to introduce.
- Don't play by everyone else's rules, make your own. Domino's Pizza is a great example of this type of thinking. While all the other pizza chains competed for ways to increase the number of customers entering their restaurants, Domino's decided to change the rules and bring the restaurant to the people rather than bringing the people to the restaurant.
- Rather than penalizing mistakes, reward employees for making the attempt to change or to try something new.

Employee Acceptance of Change

Though change is often beneficial to organizations, employees are often initially reluctant to change. This reluctance is understandable, as employees are comfortable doing things the old way. They may fear that change will result in less favorable working conditions and economic outcomes than what they were used to. According to consultant William Bridges (1985), it is common for employees undergoing change to feel out of control and feel as if they are losing identity (Who am I? What am I supposed to do?), meaning (How do

I fit into the newly changed organization?), and belonging (Why do I have to work with a bunch of new people I don't even know?).

Stages of Change

Carnall (1990) suggested that employees typically go through five stages during major organizational changes: Denial, defense, discarding, adaptation, and internalization.

Stage 1: Denial During this initial stage, employees deny that any changes will actually take place, try to convince themselves that the old way is working, and create reasons why the proposed changes will never work (e.g., "We tried that before and it didn't work," "Something like that won't work in a company like ours").

Stage 2: Defense After employees begin to believe that change will actually occur, they become defensive and try to justify their positions and ways of doing things. Because the organization is changing the way in which employees perform, the employees sense an inherent criticism that they must have previously been doing things wrong.

Stage 3: Discarding At some point, employees begin to realize not only that the organization is going to change but that the employees are going to have to change as well. That is, change is inevitable, and it is in the best interest of the employee to discard the old ways and start to accept the change as the new reality.

Stage 4: Adaptation At this stage, employees test the new system, learn how it functions, and begin to make adjustments in the way they perform. Employees spend tremendous energy at this stage and can often become frustrated and angry.

Stage 5: Internalization In this final stage, employees have become immersed in the new culture, become comfortable with the new system, and accepted their new coworkers and work environment.

Important Factors

The extent to which employees readily accept and handle change is dependent on the reason behind the change, the leader making the change, and the personality of the person being changed.

The reason behind the change Employee acceptance of change is often a function of the reason behind the change. For example, employees understand (but don't necessarily like) change that is due to financial problems, external mandates, or attempts to improve the organization. Acceptance is lower when employees perceive the change to be a change in organizational philosophy, a whim on the part of the person making the change ("Hey, let's do teams"), or a change because everyone else is changing ("Everyone else has teams, so we need to create them now before we get left behind"). Employees are least likely to accept change if they don't understand or were not told the reasons behind the change.

The person making the change Another factor affecting employee acceptance of change is the person making or suggesting the change. Changes proposed by leaders who are well liked and respected and who have a history of success are more likely to be accepted than changes proposed by leaders whose motives are suspect. Here are two very different examples.

In the first example, the head of a small consulting firm decided to change the focus of her business from delivering training seminars to helping companies switch from a traditional organizational approach to a flatter, team-based approach. Though the consultant's employees were apprehensive about the change in focus, they quickly accepted the change because the consultant was well respected for her knowledge, treated her employees as family, and had on a prior occasion changed the company's focus, resulting in a 30% increase in revenue.

In the second example, due to financial and regulatory reasons, a local mental health agency was forced to move its 120 employees from their current buildings to a new location. A management committee was formed to determine the location for the new building. When the new location was announced, the employees were very upset. The new building was expensive, in a highly congested traffic area, and located far away from most of the agency's clients. The employees' unhappiness was not due to the relocation but to the choice of buildings. It just didn't make sense. That is, it didn't make sense until several of the employees realized that the new building was only 5 minutes from where each of the deciding committee members lived. We don't have to finish the story for you to understand the importance of motive.

The difference in these two stories is clear. In the first, employees quickly accepted change because they trusted the person making the change. In the second, the employees did not accept the change because the decision makers were not well respected and acted in a manner not consistent with the well-being of the majority of employees.

For organizational change of any type to work, it is essential that employees trust the organization as a whole as well as the specific individuals making the change. Viking Glass in Sioux Falls, South Dakota, realized the importance of trust when it decided to change the organization to foster more employee participation. Viking Glass spent more than a year laying the foundation to increase the extent to which its employees trusted the company. After gaining its employees' trust, the company successfully increased the level of employee empowerment (Andrews, 1994).

The person being changed As you would imagine, there is considerable variability in the way in which people instigate or react to change. **Change agents** are people who enjoy change and often make changes just for the sake of change. A change agent's motto might best be expressed as "If it ain't broke, break it." Though many people like to call themselves a change agent, it may not be such a compliment. That is, reasoned change is good, but change for the sake of change is disruptive.

Let us give you an example. When Mike was about 30, he was president of our local Kiwanis Club. Now before you get too impressed, he was asked to be president because he was the only person in the club who had not yet been president and one of only five or so members who was under the age of 60. His first act as president was to restructure all of the committees and create an impressive-looking matrix to depict these changes. When he presented this matrix at the board meeting, each member just stared at him (some were already asleep) until one person said, "Mike, you can't change committees. It's in the national bylaws." Mike's response was to say "whoops" and move on to the next topic. Though this story is not an example of good leadership skills, it is a perfect example of being a change agent. By the way, with some maturity, Mike hopes he has become a change analyst.

Change analysts are not afraid to change or make changes but want to make changes only if the changes will improve the organization. Their motto might be "If it ain't broke, leave it alone; if it's broke, fix it." Change analysts are people who constantly ask such questions as "Why are we doing this?" and "Is there a better way we could be doing this?" But in contrast to the change agent, they are not driven by a need to change constantly.

Receptive changers are people who probably will not instigate change but are willing to change. Their motto is "If it's broke, I'll help fix it." Receptive changers are essential for any major organizational change to be successful.

Reluctant changers will certainly not instigate or welcome change, but they will change if necessary. Their motto is "Are you sure it's broken?" **Change resisters** hate change, are scared by it, and will do anything they can to keep change from occurring. Their motto is "It may be broken but it's still better than the unknown."

Implementing Change

Another important factor in employee acceptance of change is the way in which the change is implemented. That is, how and when will details be communicated? How long will the implementation take? Does the organization have the right personnel for the change? What types of training needs does the organization have?

CREATING AN ATMOSPHERE FOR CHANGE

According to Denton (1996), one of the first steps in organizational change is to create the proper atmosphere for change. This process begins by creating dissatisfaction with the current system. Employees should be surveyed to determine how satisfied they are with the current system. If things go as normal, the results of the survey will indicate that many employees are unhappy with the ways things are currently done and have suggestions for improvement. By sharing these results with employees, an organization can protect itself from employees reacting to change by remembering the "good old days." Instead, employees will focus on the "bad old days" and be more willing to change.

Perhaps a good example of this comes from some friends of ours who had been dating for several years. For the last few months of their relationship, each of the two privately told us how stale their relationship had become and said that it was time for a change. "Jill" made the decision to end the relationship and told "Jack" of her decision on a Friday night. The following week, Jill was energetic and enthusiastic, talked of dating new people, and even asked if we knew any good-looking single guys. Jack, however, whined all week about how good a relationship he and Jill had and how he would never be able to find another woman he would love so much. What was the sudden difference in their attitudes? Jill kept the "bad old days" in mind when she made the decision to end the relationship, and Jack remembered only the "good old days" after the relationship ended.

Some of this pining for the good old days seems inevitable. A colleague had been complaining for years about his college president. The president eventually was fired and replaced by a new president who made many strange changes. It didn't take a year before our colleague lamented about how much he missed his former boss. It took only a few reminders of the horror stories about his previous boss to quiet this lamenting.

After creating dissatisfaction with the status quo, Denton (1996) advised organizations to work hard to reduce the fear of change by providing emotional support, allowing employees to vent and discuss their feelings, and providing employees with a safety net that allows them to make mistakes during the transition period. This fear can also be reduced by describing the benefits of the change.

COMMUNICATING DETAILS

Employees are most responsive to change when they are kept well informed. Unless there is a need for secrecy (e.g., a merger), employees should be aware of and involved in all aspects of the change from the initial planning to the final implementation. If employees are kept in the dark until the very end, they usually suspect that something bad is happening. It seems to be human nature to think the worst when we don't know something. After undergoing a major restructuring, staff at the Educational Testing Service (ETS) in Princeton, New Jersey reported that poor communication was responsible for many of the difficulties encountered in the change process (Wild, Horney, & Koonce, 1996). During their restructuring, ETS learned:

1. *Communicating change is hard work* Early in the change process, ETS thought it had done a good job in communicating the reasons for and details of their restructuring. However, a change readiness survey that ETS administered to its employees indicated that many employees didn't understand the change or were still resisting the change. The survey results told ETS that it still had a ways to go in communicating important information to its employees.

2. *Training is needed* The employees who were given the responsibility for communicating the change had not been properly trained in such areas as dealing with employee hostility and resistance.

3. *Two-way communication is essential* Employees must have the opportunity to provide feedback to the people making the changes.

4. *Honesty is the best policy* Be honest with employees and tell them information as it arises rather than waiting until all aspects of the change are completed.

TIME FRAME

Most successful organizational changes occur in a timely fashion. The longer it takes to change, the greater the opportunity for things to go wrong and the greater the chance that employees will become disillusioned. Many consultants advise that organizations should not remain in a "change mode" for longer than 2 years.

TRAINING NEEDS

After an organization has made a major change, training is often necessary. For example, if an organization changes to a new computer system, all employees working with computers will need to be trained how to use the new system. Likewise, if an organization is changing to a self-directed team environment, employees will need to be trained in such areas as goal setting, teamwork, presentation skills, and quality analysis.

PROJECT B *Accepting Change*
To apply what you have learned about acceptance of change, complete Project B located at the end of this chapter.

Organizational Culture

Another important consideration in organizational change is organizational culture, which we discussed in Chapter 4. Often referred to as corporate culture or climate, **organizational culture** is the shared values, beliefs, and traditions that exist among individuals in organizations (Nwachukwu & Vitell, 1997; Schein, 1985; Weber, 1996). This culture establishes workplace norms of appropriate behavior (what's wrong or right) and defines roles and expectations that employees and management have of each other (Nwachukwu & Vitell, 1997; Sackman, 1991; Weber, 1996). Most cultures have a subculture. For example, the environment in which you were raised is a subculture of a bigger culture—the American culture.

In organizations, each department or office can be a subculture with norms of behaviors that may be different from those of the overall organization. How each department reacts to change is a result of that subculture. Most major changes, such as changing management philosophies, will require a culture and a subculture change to support the implementation of new ideas throughout the entire organization. This is discussed in more detail later in this section.

Think of your school as an organization with its own culture and your classroom as a subculture. Your school probably has created a culture of honesty and trust where each student is expected to adhere to honor codes. To enforce or maintain that culture, it uses sanctions such as taking you before the Judicial Board if you are caught cheating or violating some other rule.

From the first day of class, norms such as good attendance and participation in class have been established that create a subculture. These norms were probably established by rules that your instructor orally communicated or were written in your class syllabus. If you know that the classroom culture is one where you are expected to discuss your reading material, you are more likely to read your text each week prior to class. Your instructor may use certain rewards (such as giving points for classroom partici-

pation) or sanctions (such as taking off points) to maintain the culture. Eventually, this culture, which includes the instructor's expectations, gets communicated to other students, who at that point decide whether they want to be members of that culture or not. In other words, if the class and expectations are too hard, students will sign up for a different class with a more compatible culture.

Culture and norms also result from observing, or modeling, the behaviors of others. Just like your individual personal cultures, which contained role models such as your parents, community leaders, and friends who significantly influenced you over the years, organizational culture also has role models who influence your work behavior and teach you norms (Nwachukwu & Vitell, 1997; Weber, 1996). Going back to the classroom example, if you observe your instructor coming in late every class or several of your classmates consistently arriving late or leaving early without negative consequences, this may begin to create a culture of irresponsibility or unaccountability. You may eventually become one of those students with poor attendance because this has become the accepted "norm." To transform that culture into one of accountability and responsibility, the leader (your instructor) needs to model appropriate behavior and to use some strategy (such as taking off points for tardiness) to maintain the better culture.

As you can see, organizational culture can aid employees in behaving optimally. However, it can also be a contributing factor in many undesirable behaviors such as unethical decision making. For example, if an organization's top management consistently engages in unethical behaviors and decision making, employees will likely learn those norms and incorporate them into their own professional value system and behave accordingly (A. Y. Chen, Sawyers, & Williams, 1997; Nwachukwu & Vitell, 1997). To change that behavior, the cultural norms that hinder change must be eliminated (e.g., unethical supervisors, positive consequences of unethical behavior such as financial rewards; Van Slyke, 1996).

As important as it is, organizational culture has traditionally been ignored during restructuring and other changes—either because there is a general belief that culture can't be changed or because many organizations do not know how to change their cultures. In fact, in a recent survey of 500 corporations, 70% stated that they did not have the knowledge to address cultural issues (Sherriton & Stern, 1997). Without such knowledge, changes in the way the company operates, and thus, the way its employees behave, will not be long-lasting. Consequently, it is important that an organization knows how to include culture in its change process.

CHANGING CULTURE

Making organizational changes doesn't necessarily mean that everything about the existing culture must change. According to one manager, "The change process includes holding on to the successful elements of the present culture and adding new elements that are important" (Laabs, 1996, p. 56). Consequently, the first step in changing culture is assessing the desired culture and comparing it with the existing one to determine what needs to change. Two additional steps are creating dissatisfaction with the current culture to create support for the new one and maintaining the new culture.

ASSESSING THE NEW CULTURE

Assessment of the new culture involves a great deal of discussion and analysis and should include the following steps (Sherriton & Stern, 1997).

Step 1: Needs assessment Because parts of the existing culture may actually support certain organizational changes, the current culture must be analyzed and compared with the desired culture to determine what might need to change. For example, if an organization wants to move from a traditional hierarchical management philosophy to a more empowering one where employees share more decision-making responsibilities, systems, procedures, and policies will have to be changed to fully support the new culture. Areas such as role expectations, job descriptions identifying the new decision-making responsibilities, accountability, rewards, and employee selection systems must be reviewed. Data for an analysis are usually collected through observations, review of existing documentation, and employee interviews and surveys that ask for potential recommendations for changes.

Step 2: Determining executive direction Management must then analyze the needs assessment to determine the decisions or actions that will reinforce the culture and to assess the feasibility of certain changes. Using the example above, if most of the supervisors and managers in an organization are unwilling to share their decision-making authority, a true empowering culture cannot be maintained. Consequently, that may be a change that will not be reinforced by the culture. According to research, it takes the whole-hearted support of top management to implement an empowering philosophy (Schuster, Morden, Baker, McKay, Dunning, & Hagan, 1997). Addressing possible obstacles to culture change during the transformation process can usually minimize unintended consequences (Gilmore, Shea, & Useem, 1997).

Step 3: Implementation considerations This step addresses how the new culture will be implemented. Will committees or ad hoc groups be set up to carry out changes or will management execute the changes? If the organization's desired culture is to allow more input by employees, employees should participate in the implementing of an empowering organization in order to support the new culture.

Step 4: Training Culture change means a change of philosophy, and that ultimately means different role expectations. As with any new skill, all organizational members must be trained in a new philosophy for the new culture to thrive and be long-lasting. Lack of training has often been the biggest barrier in organizations that have declared that their members are now empowered to share in decisions. Employees, both management and lower level, are typically not trained on what that means. As explained later in this chapter, management and employees have a different interpretation of what empowerment culture means and how to carry it out. Training can reduce such ambiguity and confusion.

Step 5: Evaluation of the new culture As with any changes, an evaluation mechanism must be established to review the new culture. Issues such as whether the change actually has occurred or whether old norms and procedures still exist should be addressed. If change has not occurred, additional strategies must be identified to establish and support the new culture.

Now that the ideal culture has been determined, the next step is implementing it. This is done by creating dissatisfaction with the existing one (Van Slyke, 1997).

Creating dissatisfaction with existing culture Just as we discussed earlier in the chapter about creating dissatisfaction with the status quo in general, to begin acceptance of a new culture, the existing culture and status quo must be "upset." This might mean communicating to employees the future impact of continuing to "do business as usual." For example, many organizations share data that show technological trends and the financial performance of the company. If employees see this information as negatively affecting either them or the organization as a whole, the necessary displeasure with the status quo can be generated and can be the catalyst for developing a new business strategy.

Another way to create dissatisfaction is to distribute attitude surveys that ask people how satisfied they are with the organization's goal and to suggest ideas for changes. The results of the survey are distributed throughout the organization so that people can see the dissatisfaction level and begin to buy into a new culture and other organizational changes.

The key at this point is to allow input from employees in the process. A successful culture transformation requires commitment from all levels of the organization. When employees have an opportunity to be an actual part of the change, they are more likely to be committed to it (Van Slyke, 1996). Once you have started the process of transformation, it is important that it be maintained.

MAINTAINING THE NEW CULTURE

If the new culture is expected to last, developing new reward systems and selection methods should occur. Rewarding current employees for successfully participating and cooperating with the new system is imperative (Hawk, 1995). These rewards can include pay for performance in jobs that have increased responsibilities due to the new culture or other changes. But they also go beyond financial rewards and can include employee recognition and meaningful work.

SELECTION OF EMPLOYEES

Future employees should be selected on the basis of how well they epitomize the new culture. For example, if the new culture is one of team decision making, new employees should have not only the ability but the willingness and personality to perform in such an environment. As current employees are replaced by the new ones, the new culture can become "frozen" into the desired system selected by the leadership (Lewin, 1951). On the other hand, continuing to hire employees who prefer a more structured management philosophy and who work better alone will eventually cause the organization to revert to its old culture.

Finally, the socialization process of new employees must reinforce the new culture. **Organizational socialization** is the process whereby new employees learn the behaviors and attitudes they need to be successful in the organization. It also helps any newcomer to the organization define her role and what is expected of her in this position (Morrison, 1993). Informal as well as formal strategies help with this process. Informal strategies of socialization include such things as hearing the same stories repeated by several different employees. For example, you have probably listened to people in the workforce talk about getting the best stories by hanging around the water cooler or the copier. Usually, stories about some "bad decision" are discussed. New employees who hear stories consistently repeated will get an understanding of the type of culture the organization is. If the discussions are negative, the new employee will begin to believe that the organization is incompetent, mistreats its employees, and/or is unethical.

There are also formal ways organizations can influence the socialization process. One way is through establishing rituals. **Rituals** are procedures in which employees participate to become "one of the gang." Activities such as annual awards banquets or staff picnics are rituals that reinforce the impression of a caring organization. Another ritual is requiring all new employees to go through a probationary period before being considered a permanent employee.

Finally, symbols that represent certain attitudes of the organization can be used. **Symbols** are a communication technique that convey a certain message to employees. For example, establishment of an on-site wellness center conveys the organization's interest in health. In addition, communication techniques such as mission and value statements can help acculturate the new person to her environment.

> **PROJECT C** *Organizational Culture*
> To apply what you have learned about organizational culture, complete Project C at the end of this chapter.

Coping With Change

Though organizational change can be traumatic for employees, it can also be exciting and full of new opportunities. Organizational change expert Price Pritchett (1993) offered the following advice to employees involved in organizational change. This advice can be communicated by management to other employees throughout the organization.

SPEED UP

It is natural for people faced with a new situation to be cautious and want to take things slowly. However, Pritchett advised employees to get involved, increase the pace of their work, and not get left behind. This advice is analogous to paddling a canoe: If you move faster than the current, you can control where you are going. Slowing down or remaining at the same speed of the current results in being swept wherever the current takes you.

TAKE THE INITIATIVE

Instead of waiting for instructions and for people to tell you what to do, chart your own course. Show initiative, try to solve problems, make suggestions. Don't be afraid to take risks, and don't be afraid to make mistakes. As hockey star Wayne Gretsky once said, "You miss 100% of the shots you don't take."

SPEND ENERGY ON SOLUTIONS

Instead of spending energy complaining and resisting change, accept change, and then spend your energy trying to solve problems and make the new system work. Take personal responsibility for fixing what doesn't work and making suggestions for ways in which the system can improve.

To remove the stress associated with change, some psychologists suggest that organizations do innovative things to make work more fun (Brotherton, 1996). For example, consultant Matt Weinstein offered the following suggestions to managers:

- Post baby pictures of managers so that employees can laugh at them and realize that the people making the change weren't always in powerful positions.

- Create a stress-free zone where employees can go to relax for a few moments. The Brookstar Corporation in Michigan went so far as to put a punching bag in a room so that employees could take out their frustration on the bag rather than on each other.

- Give employees a surprise hour off. Store managers at Crate and Barrel tell one employee each week to take an hour and have fun, go shopping, or take a nap.

- Other suggestions included holding an ugly tie contest, giving employees stuffed animals, and designing personalized fortune cookies.

Though we certainly have no scientific evidence that any of these techniques will work, the idea is that managers should realize the stress inherent in change and take creative measures to reduce that stress.

■ EMPOWERING EMPLOYEES

As discussed back in the Chapter 11, many employees are more satisfied with their jobs if they feel they have some control over what they do. As a result, many organizations are empowering employees to participate in and make decisions. As you will see in the following pages, empowering employees can range from asking employees for their opinion to giving them complete decision-making control. However, before discussing ways to empower employees—which we will refer to as ways to increase "levels of employee input"—we want to discuss why and when employees *should* be involved in decisions.

Making the Decision to Empower

FACTORS IN MAKING THE DECISION TO EMPOWER

Employees need to be involved in decisions in circumstances in which the quality of the decision is im-
portant, the decision affects employees, the supervisor doesn't have the knowledge to make the decision, and/or the employees don't trust the supervisor. As shown in Exhibit 13-1, Vroom and Yetton (1973) have developed a flowchart to help determine when employees should be involved in making decisions. The flowchart uses the following seven factors.

Importance of decision quality The first concern when making a decision is whether one decision will be better than another. For example, if a supervisor is trying to decide whether to sign a letter with blue ink or black ink, her decision probably will not make any difference to the organization. Thus, the importance of the decision quality is low, and little time or effort should be spent making it.

Leader knowledge of the problem area The second concern of decision making involves the extent to which leaders have sufficient information to make the decision alone. If they do, then consultation with others is desired only if leaders want their subordinates to feel involved. If leaders lack sufficient knowledge to make a decision, consultation is essential. For example, it would be difficult for managers to select a benefit package without first asking their employees about the type of benefits they need.

Structure of the problem The third concern is the extent to which a leader knows what information is needed and how it can be obtained—that is, the problem's structure. If the leader does not know how to obtain this information, the decision-making process will require other people, and the decision will take longer to reach.

Importance of decision acceptance The fourth decision-making concern involves the degree to which it is important that the decision be accepted by others. For example, for a supervisor to decide what hours each employee will work, it is important the employees agree with and have input into the decision-making process. However, if the supervisor is deciding what she wants for lunch, whether others agree with or have input into the decision is not important (unless, of course, the choices involve onions or garlic).

Probability of decision acceptance The fifth decision-making concern is subordinate acceptance. If the leader feels that she can make the decision herself but that acceptance of the decision is important, she must determine whether her subordinates will accept it. If the leader is popular and viewed as being competent, her subordinates will probably accept and follow the decision. But if the leader is not popular, powerful, and competent, she will probably

EXHIBIT 13-1

The Vroom-Yetton
Decision-making Flowchart

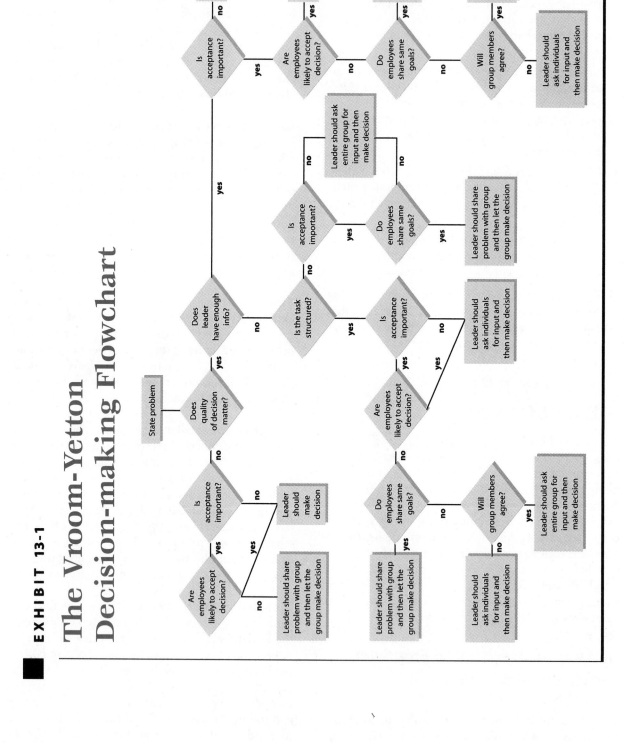

want help from subordinates and colleagues in making the decision, even though she has the ability to make the decision herself. This is why leaders often ask subordinates and colleagues for their opinions. The leader may already know what she will decide, but gaining the support of others by eliciting opinions and comments increases the chances that they will accept the decision when she announces it.

A colleague told us a story that provides a perfect example of the importance of considering the need for subordinate acceptance. At her university, the graduate college changed the way in which it administered and awarded graduate assistantships. The assistant dean was placed in charge of developing and implementing the new system. A week prior to the end of school, the new system was announced, and the graduate faculty went crazy. The awarding of the assistantships came too late to recruit students, the new application forms did not provide the information needed by departments to make decisions, and the deadlines for paperwork were convenient for the graduate college but not for the students or the departments.

What went wrong? If we look at the Vroom-Yetton model, two problems stand out. First, the assistant dean did not have the information necessary to make the decision. She had never taught a class, been a graduate student, or been involved in the financial aid process. In spite of this lack of experience and information, she chose to not consult any of the stakeholders (e.g., faculty, department chairs, graduate students) who would be affected by the decisions. Second, although acceptance of her decision was certainly important, she made no attempt to communicate the reasons for her decisions or to work with the departments to increase acceptance. Furthermore, the staff at the graduate college was viewed by faculty as incompetent, not trustworthy, and tending to make decisions beneficial to the Dean's career but not always in the best interest of the students, faculty, or university as a whole.

Subordinate trust and motivation The sixth concern of the decision-making process is the extent to which subordinates are motivated to achieve the organizational goals and thus can be trusted to make decisions that will help the organization. For example, suppose that a marketing survey indicates that a bank will attract more customers if it is open on Saturdays. If the branch manager allows her employees to decide whether the branch should be open on Saturdays, can she trust the employees to make the decision on the basis of what is best for the bank and its customers rather than what is best for the employees? If the answer is no, the branch manager will need to make the unpopular decision after receiving input from her subordinates.

Probability of subordinate conflict The final concern of the decision-making process involves the amount of conflict that is likely among the subordinates when various solutions to the problem are considered. If there are many possible solutions and the employees are likely to disagree about which is best, the leader will be served best by gathering information from employees and then, as in the previous situation, making the decision herself.

DECISION-MAKING STRATEGIES USING THE VROOM-YETTON MODEL

Answering the questions in the flowchart shown in Exhibit 13-1 will lead to one of five possible decision-making strategies: Autocratic I, Autocratic II, Consultative I, Consultative II, or Group I.

With the **Autocratic I** strategy, leaders use the available information to make the decision without consulting their subordinates. This is an effective strategy when the leader has the necessary information and when acceptance by the group either is not important or is likely to occur regardless of the decision.

With the **Autocratic II** strategy, leaders obtain the necessary information from their subordinates and then make their own decisions. The leader may or may not tell the subordinates about the nature of the problem. The purpose of this strategy is for leaders to obtain information they need to make a decision even though acceptance of the solution by the group is not important.

Leaders using the **Consultative I** strategy share the problem on an individual basis with some or all of their subordinates. After receiving their input, the leader makes a decision that may or may not be consistent with the thinking of the group. This strategy is especially useful in situations in which it is important for the group to accept the decision but in which the group members may not agree regarding the best decision.

Leaders using the **Consultative II** strategy share the problems with their subordinates as a group. After receiving the group's input, the leader makes a decision that may or may not be acceptable to the group. The main difference between this strategy and the Consultative I strategy is that with Consultative II the entire group is involved, whereas in Consultative I only a few employees are asked to provide input. This strategy is used when acceptance of the decision by the group is important and when the individual group members are likely to agree with one another about the best solution.

With the **Group I** strategy, the leader shares the problem with the group and lets the group reach a solution. The role of the leader is merely to assist in the decision-making process. This strategy is effective when group acceptance of the decision is important and when the group can be trusted to arrive at a decision that is consistent with the goals of the organization.

Although relatively little research has been conducted on the Vroom-Yetton model, the results of a few studies have been encouraging. For example, R. H. Field and House (1990) and Jago and Vroom (1977) found that managers who used the decision-making strategy recommended by the model had better quality decisions than managers who used decision-making strategies that the model would not have recommended. Similar results were found by Brown and Finstuen (1993) with military officers and Paul and Ebadi (1989) with sales managers.

PROJECT D *Vroom-Yetton Decision-Making Model*

To practice using the Vroom-Yetton model, complete Project D at the end of this chapter.

Levels of Employee Input

When employers talk about empowering employees, they seldom intend to let employees make all of the decisions affecting an organization. Instead, they most often want to give employees "more say" in day-to-day activities. Unfortunately, when employees are told that they are being empowered, they often apply a different meaning to the word than intended by the employer. In fact, one organization going through change spent 2 full weeks meeting with employees to hash out what *empowerment* should and would mean in that organization! Thus, it might be useful to set aside the word *empowerment* and talk instead of levels of employee input and control. We will provide two examples of why *levels of input* might be a better choice of terms than *empowerment*.

Several years ago, we were hired by a large poultry company to help design a system to empower their employees. In such situations, our first question is always "Why do you want to empower your employees?" In this case, the response was that they were implementing a total quality management (TQM) system and were at the stage in which they were supposed to empower employees. In other words, the organization was making a change because they thought they were "supposed to do it" rather than because something was actually going wrong. When we asked them if they *wanted* to actually empower their employees to make most of the decisions about their jobs, the company responded that it did not. When asked what they meant by *empower*, their response was that they weren't sure. So, we conducted a training workshop and discussed the concept of empowerment and the levels of employee

input discussed in the following paragraphs. At the end of the workshop, we told them to discuss what they had just learned and make a decision about what level of employee input they wanted their employees to be at. It took just a short time for the managers to reach consensus that they wanted their employees at the advisory level, that their employees already had one of the best suggestion/advisory systems in the nation, and that there was no real need to change. In other words, the organization was already empowering its employees at the optimal level for that particular industry.

The second example comes from a university setting in which a new president appointed a number of committees to study such issues as summer school and student recruitment and "empowered" these committees to make changes to improve the current system. The committees worked diligently for several months and then presented their new systems to the president. After a week of consideration, the president thanked the committees and told them that he appreciated their hard work but had decided not to follow any of their recommendations. The committee members were shocked at this response, because, to them, being told they were "empowered" meant that their decisions were final and thus would become the new policy. The president responded by saying that he had empowered them to "study" the issues and make "recommendations." His intent had never been to allow a committee to make a final decision.

As these two examples demonstrate, *empowerment* means many things to many people. Exhibit 13-2 shows the five main levels of employee input and control.

FOLLOWING

Employees at the following level have no real control over their jobs. They are given instructions about what to do, when to do it, and how it should be done. Furthermore, their work is often checked by other employees (e.g., quality control) or by their supervisor. Employees at this level can be those who are new or inexperienced to the work being performed or those with weak decision-making skills.

This level has what psychologist Rick Jacobs (1997) calls *redundant systems*. With a redundant human system, every person's work is checked by another person. In some organizations, a single piece of work might even be checked by several different people. The logic behind redundant systems is that with more than one person checking quality, there is less chance of a poor-quality product reaching a consumer. Furthermore, in many cases, an employee might not have the skill level necessary to check her own work. For example, a secretary might well be an excellent typist but might not have the grammati-

EXHIBIT 13-2

Levels of Employee Input

High level

Trust and responsibility

Absolute
Employee has sole responsibility for making decisions and is responsible for the outcomes of decisions.

Shared/Participative/Team
Employee has an equal vote in making decisions. Employee reaches consensus with others to make decisions.

Advisory
Employee makes recommendations, suggests new ideas, provides input.

Ownership of own product
Employee becomes responsible for own quality.

Following
Work is closely checked/approved by others. Employee is closely or constantly supervised.

Low level

cal skills to know if her memos contain mistakes. Even if she did have the skills, we have all missed typos because we knew what we wanted to say and thus proofread a sentence the way we meant to say it rather than the way we actually wrote it.

Though redundant systems make sense in many cases, they do have their drawbacks. The most relevant of these to this chapter is that satisfaction, motivation, and performance are often lessened when others check our work. A prime example occurs at our university: Graduate students must submit a program of studies covering the courses they intend to take during their 2 years in graduate school. The student completes the form, signs it, and then gets her advisor to sign it. The advisor must then get her department chair to sign the form, and the department chair must then get the graduate dean to sign the form. Keep in mind that because 10 of our 12 classes are required and thus standard for all graduate students, theoretically there should be little room for error.

However, as advisors, we often see mistakes made by our students, who then say that they didn't bother to read the catalogue because they knew we would find any mistakes. The problem is that we seldom read the forms because we figure if there are any mistakes, the department chair will catch them. She never reads the forms because she figures the dean will catch them. Thus, the very redundant system designed to prevent errors is actually the cause of errors!

OWNERSHIP OF OWN PRODUCT

At this level, employees are still told what to do but are solely responsible for the quality of their output. For example, an employee working on an assembly line would follow a set of procedures in assembling a product but would decide if the quality of the assembled product was good enough. Likewise, a secretary would type a report the way it was submitted but would be responsible for ensuring that there were no typographical errors.

As you can imagine, making employees responsible for their own output does a number of things. It motivates employees to check their work more carefully, provides them with a sense of ownership in their product, and provides a greater sense of autonomy and independence. In the Saturn division of General Motors, employees receive feedback on problems that drivers encounter with the cars assembled by their particular group of employees. This feedback helps employees gauge their quality control efforts—and it affects the size of their bonus.

ADVISORY

At the advisory level, employees are asked to provide feedback, suggestions, and input into a variety of organizational concerns. The key at this level is that there is no guarantee that an organization will follow the advice given by the employees; the only guarantee is that the organization will seriously consider the advice.

The idea behind this level is that employees often have the best knowledge about their jobs and that getting their input makes good business sense. As previously discussed, though employees often have the knowledge to make a decision, they are placed at an advisory level because they may not have the "motivation" to make the best decision. In such situations, an organization will ask employees for their opinions and preferences to better understand the employees' positions but will reserve the right to make the actual decision.

SHARED/PARTICIPATIVE/TEAM

The fourth level of employee input and control allows an employee to make a decision. However, this decision is made at a group level. For example, an organization might put a team together to find better ways to market its projects or to determine what type of benefits package employees will receive. This level differs from the previous level (advisory) in that only in very rare circumstances will the team's decision not be implemented. At this level, employees must not only be well trained in decision making but also be willing to take on the responsibility of making decisions.

ABSOLUTE

The final level of employee input and control gives an employee the absolute authority to make a decision on her own—no group consensus, no supervisory approval. It is important to point out that although the employee has absolute power to make a decision, she is also responsible for the consequences of that decision. So if she makes the wrong decision, she may encounter such negative consequences as being reprimanded or fired. Because of these poten-

tial consequences, many employees are leery about being given absolute power. Thus it is important in many circumstances to remove the potential for a negative sanction.

For example, Holiday Inn has empowered each of its employees to take any reasonable means necessary to satisfy a customer. This decision was made so that an unhappy guest can have her problem solved immediately rather than passed on to a manager. So if a guest complains to a housekeeper that there are not enough towels in her room, the housekeeper is empowered to deal with the situation. The housekeeper might opt to apologize or might opt to take $25 off the night's stay. Let's imagine that a particular housekeeper gives a free night's lodging to each of ten people who complained about not having enough towels. The manager thinks that these decisions were excessive and fires the housekeeper. What effect will the firing have on future employee decisions?

The idea here is that when employees are empowered to make decisions, they must first receive some training about how to make decisions. If an employee makes a bad decision, rather than punishing the employee, it is better for the organization to discuss with the employee what might have been a better decision and explain the reasons that the employee's decision was improper. Without such training and coaching, employees are not likely to enthusiastically accept their newly empowered status, especially if their new level of authority is not accompanied by an increase in pay.

Empowerment Charts

It is important to understand that organizations never have just one level of employee input and control that applies to every employee. Instead, levels will differ by employee as well as by task. For example, a bank teller might be placed at the absolute level to decide when she will take her breaks, at the advisory level when it comes to hiring new employees, and at the following level when it comes to scheduling waiving check fees. To reduce confusion, it is a good idea for organizations to develop what we call individual employee **empowerment charts.** An example of such a chart is shown in Exhibit 13-3.

In Exhibit 13-3, notice that for each task a range of control/input is allowed. For example, according to our chart, the task of opening new accounts can be performed at the following, ownership, or advisory levels. The "J" in the chart indicates that our new employee Jane is at the following level, whereas our experienced teller Emily is at the advisory level. In most organizations, a new employee would most likely be placed at the following level until she demonstrated mastery in performing the task. Indi-

EXHIBIT 13-3

Example of an Employee Empowerment Chart

Job Component	Following	Ownership	Advisory	Participative	Absolute
Job-Related Tasks					
Opening new accounts	[-----J--------------------------------E-----]				
Approving loans	[-----J--------------------------------E-----]				
Waiving check fees	[-----J--E-----]				
Scheduling Issues					
Taking breaks	[---J-E-------]				
Taking vacations	[---J-E-------]				
Scheduling hours	[---J-E-----]				
Personnel Issues					
Hiring new staff					
Innovation Issues					
Changing procedures/methods			[-----E-----]		
Developing new products			[-----E-----]		

J = Jane, E = Emily

vidual employee empowerment charts reduce confusion and provide a systematic plan for providing employees with more autonomy as their skills and experience increase.

> **PROJECT E** *Empowerment Charts*
> To practice creating an employee empowerment chart, complete Project E located at the end of this chapter.

Consequences to Empowerment

As shown in Exhibit 13-4, being at a higher level of control/input has many positive aspects. For example, research indicates that for most people, increased empowerment results in increased job satisfaction. The increased responsibility can result in higher skill levels, which in turn can result in higher pay, increased job security, and increased potential to find other employment. However, empowerment can have its downside. With increased responsibility comes increased stress. With the power to make decisions comes the risk of making bad decisions and thus being fired or denied a promotion.

One of the things that is true throughout life is that people are different and not everything affects everyone the same way. For example, imagine that we place all of the employees in a fast-food restaurant at the ab-solute level in making such decisions as when to give free drinks or a meal if the service is slow or the food is bad or when to allow customers to make substitutions. For many of these employees, this authority will be welcome as it reduces the time taken to get permission from a supervisor and provides them with a sense of power. However, for some employees, the increased stress of making decisions and being accountable far outweighs any feelings of "empowerment."

■ DEVELOPING TEAMS

Though group behavior was discussed extensively in Chapter 8, the next section of this chapter will focus on teams—a popular method of increasing employee empowerment. Though the concept of employee work teams had been around for decades (they were often called quality circles in the 1970s), the use of work teams greatly increased in the 1990s. Surveys indicate that 47% of Fortune 1000 companies use teams, and 60% plan either to start using teams or to increase their use of teams over the next few years (Bishop & Scott, 1997).

Unfortunately, this increase in the use of teams is often the result of "keeping up with the Joneses" rather than a strategically planned method of organization development. As with any type of organizational

EXHIBIT 13-4

Consequences to Empowerment

Personal

1. Increased job satisfaction for most
2. Stress
   a. Decreased stress due to greater control
   b. Increased stress due to greater responsibility

Financial

1. Bonuses
2. Pay increases

Career

1. Increased job security
2. Promotions
3. Increased marketability
4. Increased chance of being terminated

---

intervention, teams can improve performance in some, but not all, situations. Teams work best in situations in which the job requires high levels of employee interaction, a team approach will simplify the job, a team can do something an individual cannot, and there is time to create a team and properly train team members (Kriegel & Brandt, 1996).

What Is a Team?

At times, putting employees into teams fails because the team is really a group or a committee rather than a true team. Before calling a group of individuals a *team*, several factors should be considered (Donnellon, 1996).

IDENTIFICATION

Identification is the extent to which group members identify with "the team" rather than other groups. For example, suppose that a committee was created composed of one representative from each of five different departments (e.g., accounting, engineering, human resources). During the meetings, members use such statements as "Our department won't agree," "This committee just doesn't like us in engineering," or "We didn't even want to be on this committee." Notice that

the use of *we*, *our*, and *us* referred to their departments rather than the committee. According to Donnellon (1996), for the committee to be considered a team, those same words would need to refer to the committee—for example, "How can we convince the accounting department?" or "Our solution is a good one."

INTERDEPENDENCE

In a team, members need and desire the assistance, expertise, and opinions of the other members. If a team member can perform her job without the assistance of others, the group is not a team. For example, some teams (e.g., a surgical team in a hospital) have very high task **interdependence** in that what one member does greatly influences what another member does. Other teams (most committees) have low task interdependence in that each member completes a task and the separate parts are compiled at the end. Though each part is important in completing the final product, the completion of each part is not dependent on another group member. The importance of task interdependence was demonstrated by Liden, Wayne, and Bradway (1996), who found that empowerment increased the performance of teams with high task interdependence but decreased the performance of teams with low task interdependence.

POWER DIFFERENTIATION

In a team, members try to decrease **power differentiation** by treating others as equals and taking steps to ensure equality. In groups that are not teams, members challenge, correct, and interrupt each other, give orders, and use sarcasm. For example, we worked with one organization that had an "administrative team." What we discovered, however, was that one individual in that team was treated differently, had less authority, and had no voting power. Consequently, rather than being a "team," they were a "committee."

In teams, members apologize for overstepping their roles, ask indirect questions to avoid challenges, and are polite to one another (Donnellon, 1996). For example, in a team, a member might disagree with another member by saying something like "I don't know your field as well as you do, but what if we tried . . ." whereas in a nonteam, a member might disagree by saying, "That's so stupid; I'll tell you what will work."

SOCIAL DISTANCE

In a team, members try to decrease **social distance** by being casual, using nicknames, and expressing liking, empathy, and common views. Nonteam members use formal language and forms of address, excessive politeness, and impersonal conversations. For example, team members would use such phrases as "Hey, how's it going?" "Thanks, pal," and "I understand your feelings on that." Nonteam members might address another member as Mr. Jones rather than Josh or agree with someone by saying "I concur with your opinion" rather than "I'm right with you on that one."

CONFLICT MANAGEMENT TACTICS

Team members respond to conflict by collaborating, whereas nonteam members respond by forcing and accommodating (remember our discussion of these styles back in Chapter 6). In nonteams, members react to conflict by threatening, directing, or giving in. In teams, members try to understand the others' views, make attempts to compromise, and use non-threatening tones (Donnellon, 1996).

NEGOTIATION PROCESS

In teams, members negotiate in a win-win style in which the goal is for every person to come out ahead. In nonteams, members negotiate so that they win and the other members lose.

On the basis of the six factors just discussed, Donnellon (1996) used a chart to place teams into one of five categories: collaborative teams, emergent teams, adversarial teams, nominal teams, and doomed teams.

Collaborative teams and emergent teams are what we have referred to as "true teams," whereas nominal teams and doomed teams are what we have referred to as "nonteams." Adversarial teams are somewhere in between a "true team" and a "nonteam."

Though not affecting the extent to which a group is officially a "team," teams differ in two other ways. Teams differ as to their permanency. That is, some teams are designed to work together permanently, whereas others are formed to solve a particular problem and then are expected to dissolve. For example, the university appointed a task force to create a new system for students to use to evaluate faculty. Once the system was created, the team disbanded.

Teams can also differ in the proximity of their members. Members of surgical teams, baseball teams, and the cast of a Broadway play not only are task interdependent but work physically close to one another. Members of teams such as task forces and committees may well be task interdependent but may be physically located at a great distance from one another. In fact, increased computer technology has resulted in **virtual teams,** whose members use e-mail, fax machines, and computer-based video conferencing to carry out their team functions (Townsend, DeMarie, & Hendrickson, 1996).

Types of Teams

Teams come in many shapes and sizes based on the factors discussed earlier in the chapter. Because it would be impossible (and boring) to list every type of possible team, here are some examples of a few teams commonly found in organizations.

Cross-functional teams consist of representatives from various departments (functions) within an organization. For example, a team formed to reduce the time to ship a product might include members from the sales, shipping, production, and customer service departments. For cross-functional teams to be successful, it is important that they have a clear purpose, receive support from each functional area, and take steps to increase the trust levels of team members. Building trust in cross-functional teams is especially important, as members are often torn between representing the interests of their function and doing what is best for the organization as a whole.

Self-directed work teams consist of production employees and are formed to increase the quality and cost-effectiveness of a product. As shown in Exhibit 13-5, the traditional method of manufacturing a product is to have employees specialize in performing one particular task. For example, a company might have a supervisor, sorter, assembler, solderer,

EXHIBIT 13-5

Traditional vs. Team Approaches

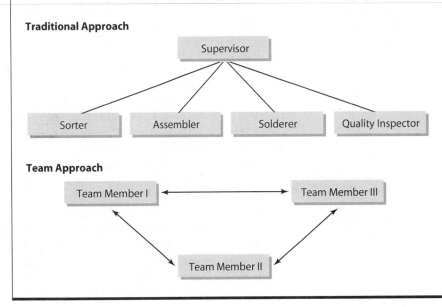

Traditional Approach

Team Approach

and quality inspector. The sorter places parts on the assembly line, the assembler puts the parts together, the solderer solders the parts, and the quality control inspector makes sure the part is properly assembled.

In a team approach, there would be no supervisor. Each of the production workers is called a "team member" and is cross-trained to perform all of the tasks. In this way, if parts are assembled faster than they can be soldered, the sorter might spend some time soldering rather than sorting or waiting. The team is responsible for checking its own quality, and one of the production workers would probably be appointed as a team leader. The use of production teams saves money by removing management layers and making the team responsible for its own production.

Customer service teams are commonly found in restaurants and retail stores. In the traditional customer service model at a restaurant, each employee is assigned specific tasks (e.g., serving, cooking, busing tables) in specific areas. With the team approach, each employee may still be assigned a primary duty and area but is expected to "do what it takes" to satisfy customers. For example, suppose that Ken is your server at a very busy restaurant. You want a new drink (milk of course), but Ken is at another table. The closest person to you is Barbie, who is busing tables. In the traditional system, a request of more milk from Barbie would result in a response such as "I only bus tables; you'll have to wait for your server." In the team approach, Barbie would

have been cross-trained in serving beverages and would be able to comply with your request.

How Teams Develop

Teams typically go through four developmental phases: forming, storming, norming, and performing. In the **forming stage,** team members get to know each other and decide what roles each member will play. At this stage, team members are on their best behavior as they try to impress and get along with the other team members. Team members are often excited about the potential to accomplish something but are also anxious about working with others in a team. During the later part of this stage, the team determines its purpose, discusses its goals, and sets rules and procedures. A meta-analysis by Salas, Mullen, Rozell, and Driskell (1997) indicated that formal team building (training on how to be a team) that focuses on role clarification will slightly improve team performance.

During the **storming stage,** the good behavior disappears. On an individual level, team members often become frustrated with their roles, show the stress of balancing their previous duties with their new team responsibilities, and question whether they have the ability to accomplish the goals set in the forming stage. Interpersonally, team members begin to disagree with one another and challenge each other's ideas. From this tension and conflict the team often gets the energy to perform well in later stages.

During the **norming stage,** the team works toward easing the tension from the storming stage. Team members begin to acknowledge the reality of the team by accepting the team leader and working directly with other team members to solve difficulties. At this point, team members have either accepted their initial roles or made adjustments to roles for which they are better suited.

In the **performing stage,** the team begins to accomplish its goals. Group members make innovative suggestions, challenge one another without defensive responses, and participate at high levels. At this stage, group members actually enjoy their team membership.

Why Teams Don't Always Work

The literature contains an abundance of advice about how to create successful teams. In a study investigating this advice, Hyatt and Ruddy (1997) found that customer service teams were most effective when they received the necessary support from management (e.g., information, technology, training); had confidence in their ability to complete their tasks; were customer oriented; exhibited an open, supportive, and professional communication style; had set appropriate goals; and followed an agreed-upon group process. Moran, Musselwhite, and Zenger (1996) have identified 12 common problems encountered by teams. The six most important are:

THE TEAM IS NOT A TEAM

Consistent with our discussion above, "teams" often aren't successful because they are teams in name only.

EXCESSIVE MEETING REQUIREMENTS

A common problem with teams is that they either meet too often or they waste time when they do meet. The key to successful team meetings is to limit the topics to be discussed and meet only when the entire team is needed to contribute. Furthermore, teams often feel the need to meet for the entire time for which a meeting is scheduled, even though the necessary business could be conducted in much less time. This tendency to stretch a meeting can reduce the motivation and enthusiasm of a team.

As an example of the tendency to meet too often, the university created several teams to address specific problems. Our team leader (committee chair) wanted us to meet every Wednesday at 2:00 until our task was completed. Because of the nature of our task, weeks might pass before we had anything new to bring to the group. Yet we still met every Wednesday. After 4 weeks, attendance at the meetings dropped to about 50%. When our angry team leader confronted our team members, she was shocked to hear such comments as "These weekly meetings are a waste of time" and "I always attend the important meetings, just not the worthless ones."

Another committee at the university demonstrated the tendency to stretch meetings. The committee contained 25 people and met one Friday a month from 3:00 to 4:30. When the Dean ran the meetings, they always ended at exactly 4:30. When the dean was out of town, the committee's vice chair (the second in command, not the person in charge of vice) would start the meetings by saying, "Let's do our business and get out of here." On these occasions, we never met past 3:45.

LACK OF EMPOWERMENT

Many teams are formed to solve problems but are not given sufficient authority to conduct their business. According to Moran et al. (1996), teams aren't empowered because managers worry that the job won't be done correctly, the teams will move too fast, and the teams will overstep their boundaries such that other parts of the organization will be affected. This last managerial concern is especially important because as teams work to solve problems, their solutions often involve many different departments. If the teams are not properly empowered, they will lack the authority to overcome the political resistance of each affected department.

Though empowerment is essential for the success of most teams, it is not uncommon for team members to reject their empowered status. After all, with the advantages of empowerment come the risks of making mistakes and getting others angry. To many employees, these risks override the benefits of empowerment.

LACK OF SKILL

It is assumed that members assigned to a team have the skills necessary to effectively carry out their assignment. Unfortunately, this is often not the case. Most commonly, team members either lack the skills needed to work in a team (e.g., communication, problem solving) or the expertise to solve the problem itself. As an example, universities typically form committees whose membership consists of representatives from various colleges (e.g., arts and sciences, education) and departments (e.g., history, psychology, economics). Such a membership strategy makes sense if the issue is one on which various departments might differ. That is, a committee asked to determine general education requirements or summer school offerings should have representatives from each department. However, a committee formed to develop fund-raising strategies would be better served with a membership of marketing and psychology faculty rather than history and music faculty.

DISTRUST OF THE TEAM PROCESS

Many teams don't succeed because management doesn't trust the concept of teams. A study by the consulting firm Zinger Miller found that in organizations in which top management was not enthusiastic about the team approach, only 49% of teams made satisfactory progress. However, in teams with supportive management, 84% of teams made satisfactory progress (Moran et al., 1996). Some of this distrust comes from managers being unwilling to give up any authority. Managers, too, need to be trained in the team process if the team concept is going to survive. Another source of this distrust is that not all work is appropriate for teams (Drexler & Forrester, 1998). That is, some tasks (e.g., typing) are better done individually and others, such as kissing, are performed better with the help of others.

UNCLEAR OBJECTIVES

Teams work best when they know why they were formed, what they are expected to accomplish (what is the team's "charge"), and when they are supposed to be finished. Though this sounds obvious, you would be surprised at how many teams aren't sure what they are supposed to do. As an example, on the university committee entitled "Committee on Student Evaluation of Faculty," we spent most of the time during our first few meetings asking such questions as "What are we supposed to do?" "Are we supposed to design a new evaluation instrument?" and "Do we make decisions or do we just make recommendations?" It took almost a month to get clarification, and during that time the committee made no progress, its members became frustrated, and attendance dropped.

> **PROJECT F** *Teams*
> To practice what you have learned about teams, complete Project F at the end of this chapter.

CHAPTER RECAP

In this chapter you learned:

- Employees react to change by going through the stages of denial, defense, discarding, adaptation, and finally internalization.

- Employees best accept change if the reason behind the change makes sense and the person making the change is trusted and respected.

- Change is best implemented by creating an atmosphere for change, communicating details, making the change over a reasonable period of time, and training employees.

- Employees can best accept change if they speed up, take initiative, and spend energy on solutions rather than complaining.

- The five levels of employee input are following, ownership of own product, advisory, shared, and absolute.

- Teams go through four developmental stages: forming, storming, norming, and performing.

- The team approach is not always best.

Critical Thinking Questions

1. Why are employees reluctant to change?

2. How important is organizational culture on organization development?

3. When organizations talk about empowering employees, what do they actually mean?

4. How do we build effective teams?

WEB SITES

For further information, log on to the following web sites.
www.ammedia.com/trainers/trainerstips.html
Contains a variety of tips for increasing employee performance.
www.workteams.unt.edu/links.htm#5
Provides links to a variety of sources on organization development.

KEY TERMS

Adaptation The fourth stage of change, in which employees try to adapt to new policies and procedures.

Autocratic I strategy Leaders use available information to make a decision without consulting their subordinates.

Autocratic II strategy Leaders obtain necessary information from their subordinates and then make their own decision.

Change agent A person who enjoys change and makes changes for the sake of change.

Change analyst A person who is not afraid of change but makes changes only when there is a compelling reason to do so.

Change resister A person who hates change and will do anything to keep change from occurring.

Consultative I strategy Leaders share the problem on an individual basis with their subordinates and then make a decision that may or may not be consistent with the thinking of the group.

Consultative II strategy Leaders share the problem with the group as a whole and then make a decision that may or may not be consistent with the thinking of the group.

Cross-functional teams A team consisting of representatives from various departments (functions) within an organization.

Defense The second stage of change, in which employees accept that change will occur but try to justify the old way of doing things.

Denial The first stage in the emotional reaction to change, in which an employee denies that an organizational change will occur.

Discarding The third stage of change, in which employees accept that change will occur and decide to discard their old ways of doing things.

Empowerment chart A chart made for each employee that shows what level of input the employee has for each task.

Forming stage The first stage of the team process, in which team members "feel out" the team concept and attempt to make a positive impression.

Group I strategy Leaders share the problem with the group and let the group reach a decision or solution.

Identification The extent to which team members identify with the team rather than their other groups.

Internalization The fifth and final stage of organizational change, in which employees become comfortable with and productive in the new system.

Interdependence The extent to which team members need and rely on other team members.

Meeting cow Unnecessary or unnecessarily long meeting.

Norming stage The third stage of the team process, in which teams establish roles and determine policies and procedures.

Organizational culture The shared values, beliefs, and traditions that exist among individuals in an organization.

Organizational socialization The process whereby new employees learn the behaviors and attitudes they need to be successful in an organization.

Paper cow Unnecessary paperwork found in organizations.

Performing stage The fourth and final stage of the team process, in which teams work toward accomplishing their goals.

Power differentiation The extent to which team members have the same level of power and respect.

Receptive changer A person who is willing to change.

Reluctant changer A person who will initially resist change but will eventually go along with change.

Rituals Procedures in which employees participate to become "one of the gang."

Sacred cow hunt The first step in organizational change in which employees look for practices and policies that waste time and are counterproductive.

Social distance The extent to which team members treat each other in a friendly, informal manner.

Speed cow The tendency for organizations to require employees to work faster and produce work sooner than needed.

Storming stage The second stage in the team process in which team members disagree and resist their team roles.

Symbols Organizational behaviors or practices that convey messages to employees.

Virtual teams Teams that communicate through e-mail rather than face to face.

PRACTICE EXAM

1. Which of the following is *not* a target of a sacred cow hunt?
   a. unnecessary paperwork
   b. short meetings
   c. too many meetings
   d. unnecessary deadlines

2. Which of the following is the *first* stage in organizational change?
   a. denial   b. defense
   c. discarding   d. adaptation

3. The motto "If it ain't broke, break it" best fits:
   a. change analysts   b. change resisters
   c. change agents   d. receptive changers

4. The motto "If it's broke, I'll help fix it" best fits:
   a. change analysts   b. change resisters
   c. change agents   d. receptive changers

5. Organizations should not be in a "change mode" any longer than:
   a. a few weeks   b. several months
   c. 2 years   d. 5 years

6. The final step in the assessment of a new organizational culture is:
   a. needs assessment
   b. evaluation of the new culture
   c. training
   d. to determine executive direction

7. An organization establishes an on-site wellness center to convey its interest in employee health. The wellness center is an example of a:
   a. symbol   b. ritual
   c. parafact   d. cash cow

8. Which of the following is *not* good advice for coping with change?
   a. Take the initiative
   b. Spend energy on solutions
   c. Speed up
   d. Slow down

9. In deciding to empower an employee, several factors must be considered. According to the Vroom-Yetton model, the *first* of these factors is:
   a. problem structure
   b. importance of decision acceptance
   c. probability of decision acceptance
   d. importance of decision quality

10. Leaders can make decisions without consulting others unless:
    a. their subordinates trust them
    b. the leader is knowledgeable
    c. the problem is unstructured
    d. the decision quality is unimportant

11. _____ leaders make decisions without consulting their subordinates.

    a. Autocratic I
    b. Autocratic II
    c. Consultative I
    d. Consultative II

12. When employees are asked to provide feedback but are not allowed to make decisions, they are at the _____ level of employee input.
    a. following
    b. advisory
    c. absolute
    d. ownership of own product

13. The use of nicknames or communicating liking occurs in the _____ team component.
    a. identification
    b. social distance
    c. interdependence
    d. power differentiation

14. A _____ team consists of representatives from various departments.
    a. virtual
    b. self-directed
    c. cross-functional
    d. customer service

15. Team members are on their best behavior during the _____ stage.
    a. forming
    b. storming
    c. norming
    d. performing

ANSWERS 1 b, 2 a, 3 c, 4 d, 5 c, 6 b, 7 a, 8 d, 9 d, 10 c, 11 a, 12 b, 13 b, 14 c, 15 a

Paper Cow Hunts

For this exercise, get several forms that you must fill out at your school. These can include such forms as applications to graduate, registration forms, and change-of-grade forms. For each of the forms, conduct a paper cow hunt—determine if the form is really needed. If it is, is all the information and are all of the signatures asked for actually necessary?

Form 1: _____

_____

_____

_____

_____

_____

_____

_____

_____

Form 2: _____

_____

_____

_____

_____

_____

_____

_____

_____

_____

Form 3: _____

_____

_____

_____

_____

_____

_____

_____

_____

Form 4: _____

_____

_____

_____

_____

_____

_____

_____

_____

Accepting Change

Think about the last major change you went through either at work or at school. How did you react to the change? What could have made your acceptance of the change better?

_____

_____

_____

_____

_____

_____

_____

_____

_____

_____

_____

_____

_____

_____

_____

_____

_____

_____

_____

_____

_____

_____

Organizational Culture

Think about either your current job or one that you held previously. How would you describe the organizational culture? What types of values, beliefs, and traditions were there? What type of climate existed? Compare this culture to that of another job. If you have not had enough work experience, think about the culture of two classes you have had or about two clubs you have belonged to.

_____

_____

_____

_____

_____

_____

_____

_____

_____

_____

_____

_____

_____

_____

_____

_____

_____

_____

_____

Vroom-Yetton Decision-Making Model

The Vroom-Yetton model shown in Exhibit 13-1 provides leaders with a system to help determine how a decision should be made. This exercise will provide you with the opportunity to use the Vroom-Yetton Model.

Below, you will find several situations that require a decision to be made. Using the chart in Exhibit 13-1, determine which of the five strategies–Autocratic I, Autocratic II, Consultative I, Consultative II, Group I—the leader should use to make the decision.

Situation A

Jonathan Hancock has been asked to set production goals for his welders and then to return a signed copy of these goals to the plant manager. Mr. Hancock has been a supervisor for 10 years. He always dreads setting goals and does not think they are useful. What strategy should he use?

_____ Autocratic I

_____ Autocratic II

_____ Consultative I

_____ Consultative II

_____ Group I

Why did you choose this strategy?

_____

_____

_____

Situation B

Krista Harrison is the branch manager for a small bank and must schedule vacations for her ten employees. The regional manager wants the vacation lists to her in the next week. What strategy should she use?

_____ Autocratic I

_____ Autocratic II

_____ Consultative I

_____ Consultative II

_____ Group I

Why did you choose this strategy?

_____

_____

_____

Situation C

Kent Clark is an optometrist and has four assistants who work for him. Dr. Clark is considering purchasing a new piece of equipment that will allow him to more accurately measure the vision needs of his patients. What decision-making strategy should he use?

_____ Autocratic I

_____ Autocratic II

_____ Consultative I

_____ Consultative II

_____ Group I

Why did you choose this strategy?

_____

_____

_____

Situation D

Debika Johnson is the vice president for Reilly College. She has been at Reilly for 6 months and must create a policy for student evaluation of faculty. That is, she needs to decide what type of evaluation instrument will be used, how often evaluations will occur, and how much weight the student evaluations should carry in the overall evaluation of a faculty member. What strategy should she use?

_____ Autocratic I

_____ Autocratic II

_____ Consultative I

_____ Consultative II

_____ Group I

Why did you choose this strategy?

_____

_____

_____

Employee Empowerment Charts

Think of your current job or a job that you recently held. Create an employee empowerment chart for that job similar to the one found in Exhibit 13-3 in this chapter.

Job Component	Following	Ownership	Advisory	Participative	Absolute
_____					
_____					
_____					
_____					
_____					
_____					
_____					
_____					
_____					

Job Component	Following	Ownership	Advisory	Participative	Absolute
_____					
_____					
_____					
_____					
_____					
_____					
_____					
_____					
_____					

Teams

Think of the last team that you were a member of. It could be a work team, an athletic team, or a team assigned to complete a group project. On the basis of what you read in the chapter:

1. Was your team actually a team?

_____

_____

_____

_____

_____

_____

_____

_____

_____

2. Did the team go through the forming, storming, norming, and performing stages?

_____

_____

_____

_____

_____

_____

_____

_____

_____

3. Was the team successful? Why or why not?

_____

_____

_____

_____

_____

_____

_____

_____

_____

Persuading and Influencing Others

An important aspect of managing others is to persuade them or influence them to behave in an appropriate manner. For example, suppose that you wanted several employees to work overtime. How would you get them to do it? What if you had a new committee and wanted employees to participate? How would you get them to join the committee? In general, we have four ways in which we can influence others: We can give orders and expect obedience, use others as an example and expect conformity, make requests and expect compliance, or use a persuasive argument and expect agreement. In this chapter, you will:

> Understand why people obey orders
>
> Learn the factors that affect the probability that we will obey an order
>
> Discover why giving orders is not always a good idea
>
> Learn the factors that determine if we will conform to the behaviors of others
>
> Determine how we can increase the likelihood of people agreeing to our requests
>
> Learn how to persuade others and change their attitudes

■ GIVING ORDERS AND EXPECTING OBEDIENCE

One way that we can influence others is to give them an order. That is, a supervisor can order an employee to work overtime, a professor can order a student to work on a project, or parents can order their child to study harder. Though giving orders can be an effective way to influence others, it has its drawbacks.

Problems With Giving Orders

BLIND OBEDIENCE

When we give orders, we expect people to obey. However, blind obedience is not always a good thing. Consider the following situations:

- As part of an ethnic cleansing program in the late 1990s, Serbian soldiers murdered civilians, raped women, and destroyed towns because they were told to do so by their leaders.

- In a real-life event made famous by the novel and television miniseries *At Mother's Request*, 17-year-old Marc Schreduer killed his grandparents because he was ordered to do so by his mother Frances Schreduer.

- Employees at several Avis Car Rental agencies knowingly broke the law and refused to rent cars to African Americans because they were ordered not to do so by their boss, who believed that "Blacks seldom return the cars they rent."

As shown in the preceding situations, when we order people to do things (as opposed to asking them), we often lose the opportunity to get feedback from the person as to whether our order is a good idea. This blind obedience and lack of feedback can result in people engaging in behavior that they know is wrong.

The study of obedience by psychologists began in the early 1960s with the classic studies by Stanley Milgram and his students (Milgram, 1963). Milgram conducted his studies to help explain the behavior of the German soldiers during World War II. Though many Americans attributed the behavior to the Germans being "terrible people," Milgram thought it might have more to do with social psychology than personality. That is, it was the setting, not the people, that caused soldiers to obey orders to kill millions of people in concentration camps.

To study the power of obedience, Milgram conducted a series of innovative experiments. Milgram ran advertisements in newspapers to recruit male subjects who were told they would be participating in a study on learning. When a subject arrived, he was joined by another "subject" who, unbeknownst to the real subject, was a confederate of Milgram pretending to be a subject. The real subject was assigned the role of "teacher" and the confederate the role of "student." The two received further instructions that the purpose of the study was to investigate the effect of punishment on learning. The teacher would read aloud pairs that the student would memorize. If the student made a mistake, the teacher would punish him by giving him increasingly severe shocks.

> **PROJECT A** *Giving Orders*
> To get you thinking about obedience, complete Project A at the end of the chapter

The student sat in a chair in one room, while the teacher sat in front of an impressive looking shock machine in another room. As shown in Exhibit 14-1, the shock machine contained a series of levers labeled with voltages ranging from "slight" to "intense" to "Danger: severe shock" to "xxx (450 volts)." In the initial study, the teacher and the student could not see each other but communicated through an intercom. Before starting the learning exercise, the experimenter gave the teacher a sample shock that, even though it was fairly painful, was labeled as a mild shock.

During the experiment, the student made several errors. After each error, the teacher was instructed to give the student a shock, which increased in voltage after each error. As the shocks became stronger, the

EXHIBIT 14-1

Pictures from the Milgram Experiment

(a)

(b)

(c)

These photographs show how intimidating—and authoritative—the Milgram experiment must have been. The first picture (a) shows the formidable-looking shock generator. The second (b) shows the role player, who pretends to be getting the electric shock, being hooked up. The third (c) shows an experimental subject (seated) and the experimenter (standing, in lab coat).

Source: Milgram, 1974, p. 25. © Copyright 1965 by Stanley Milgram. From the film *Obedience* distributed by Penn State, Media Sales.

---

student would yell in pain, pound the wall, and ask to be released from the experiment. Finally, the student quit responding. If the teacher hesitated in giving a shock, the experimenter would say "Please continue. The experiment must go on. It is necessary for you to continue." This process was completed for each of the 40 male subjects.

Milgram was shocked by how many of these 40 subjects punished another person just because they were ordered to do so (a terrible pun, but one that we couldn't resist). All 40 subjects applied very strong shocks (240 volts) and 65% applied shocks strong enough that they may have killed the student! Now it is important to point out that none of the students (the confederates) actually received any shock. They were actors who did such a good job that every teacher (the subjects) thought they were shocking the student. Many of the subjects showed outward signs of stress—sweating, stuttering, nervous laughter—

and pleaded with the experimenter to stop the experiment. In spite of these reservations, almost two thirds of the subjects gave the highest level of shock.

As the Milgram studies and many current events demonstrate, an order will often result in obedience. But is blind obedience always in the best interests of an organization?

LACK OF AUTHORITY

A second reason that giving orders is not always an effective method of influence is that we often do not have the authority or stature to give orders. For example, we can't really order our peers to do anything. Likewise, if a supervisor isn't respected by employees, they may not follow his orders. Research has shown that two factors regarding authority affect the extent to which people will obey an order: the status of the authority figure and the proximity of the authority figure.

Status of the authority figure In trying to understand why 65% of his subjects administered the potentially deadly levels of shock simply because they were "told to do so," Milgram hypothesized that people obeyed because Milgram was a well-known professor at Yale University. What percentage of the subjects would have obeyed if Milgram were a nobody? To test this idea, Milgram conducted another study in a run-down building in downtown Bridgeport, CT rather than on the Yale University campus. When the study was conducted by a well-known scholar at prestigious Yale University, 65% of the subjects obeyed orders to give the highest levels of shock. However, in the lower status study conducted in downtown Bridgeport, only 48% obeyed the order to give the highest level of shock. In a similar study, Milgram left the room and put a student in charge. Only 20% fully obeyed the low-status person in charge. Thus, obedience works best when the authority figure is well respected. How often in organizations are the leaders giving orders not well respected?

Proximity of the authority figure Other research indicates that people will obey only if the authority figure is present. In another study by Milgram, when the experimenter issued his orders by telephone rather than in person, the percentage of subjects administering the highest level shocks dropped from 65 to 25. Such results are not surprising when we think of the way children behave when their parents leave the room, what students do when the teacher is not in the classroom, and how employees break rules when the boss is away.

PSYCHOLOGICAL REACTANCE

A third problem with giving orders is **psychological reactance**—when people feel their freedom to make choices is threatened, they react by disobeying the order that threatens their freedom. For example, suppose that a 16-year-old girl has a date with a boy she is not particularly interested in, but is going out with him because she has nothing else to do on Friday night. When her parents hear that he has spiked hair and three rings in his nose, they forbid her from going with him. How do you think she would react to this order? Would she obey? Or would she become more determined to date this boy even though she really isn't interested in him? The theory of psychological reactance suggests that she would become more determined—a prediction with which most parents would agree.

A friend of ours provides an excellent example of reactance. He teaches at a university that was undergoing considerable change. As part of this change, our friend was appointed chair of a committee charged with developing a new system for student evaluation of faculty. After surveying faculty and students, the committee decided to recommend that faculty receive student evaluations every semester rather than the previous practice of every 3 years. Based on the results of the surveys, the committee expected easy approval of their recommendation. However, before the committee could make its recommendation for approval to the faculty senate, the vice president announced that faculty would be evaluated every semester and that there would be no discussion on the matter. The faculty went wild and voted to have evaluations every 3 years rather than every semester.

Why the sudden change in attitude? Probably due to psychological reactance. The faculty felt that the vice president's order took away their right to choose, so they did what comes naturally and did the opposite of what the vice president wanted. In other words, they voted against what they really wanted just to show the vice president that she could not push them around! Similar examples of reactance are found in studies of juries. When ordered by a judge to "disregard the previous testimony," jurors actually do the opposite and pay more attention to the testimony! These examples demonstrate the idea that when you think people will agree with you, ask them what they want to do, don't tell them what you want them to do.

> **PROJECT B** *Conformity*
> To get you thinking about conformity, complete Project B at the end of this chapter.

■ CONFORMITY

A second way in which people are influenced by others is **conformity**—social behavior that is the result of a norm. When we talk about conformity to our classes, we ask our students to raise their hands if they are a conformist. Though few of our students claim to be conformists, we all conform in one way or another. What kind of things did you list for Project B?

Not All Conformity Is the Same

Though we engage in many conforming behaviors, there are two main types of conformity—normative and informational. With **normative conformity**, we conform out of a concern for what others will think about us. For example, you might not wear your favorite pocket protector because you are afraid others will think you are a dork. Or, you might not talk in class because you are worried that your peers would think you are kissing up to the professor.

With **informational conformity**, we conform because we are unsure of what to do in a situation. For

EXHIBIT 14-2

Lines Used in the Asch Experiment

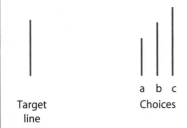

Target line

a b c
Choices

example, suppose you are attending a seminar and when you first walk into the seminar room, you notice that everyone is sitting on the right side of the room. Where would you sit? Most people respond that they would sit on the right side, not out of concern for what people would think, but instead because they assume that there is a reason that everyone is sitting on the right side (e.g., better view of the instructor, the left side is reserved for some group).

Factors Affecting Conformity

The first comprehensive studies of conformity were conducted by Solomon Asch in the 1950s. Asch had subjects sit at a table with four other subjects who, unbeknownst to the real subject, were confederates of the experimenter. The experimenter showed the five people lines similar to that depicted in Exhibit 14-2, and asked them which of the three lines on the right was closest in length to the line on the left. Though it is clear that line B is the correct answer, the first person/confederate answers line A as do each of the next three people/confederates. Now the real subject is asked for his opinion. Will he choose line B, which he thinks is correct, or does he choose line A like the other four subjects? This process is repeated a total of 12 times for each subject. Asch found that 75% of the subjects conformed at least once and 35% conformed on all 12 trials. So, even in a simple task where the answer is clear, people tend to conform. However, not everybody conformed and only 35% conformed on all 12 trials. When are we most likely to conform to the behavior of others?

TASK AMBIGUITY

In the study just described, the answer to the task was clear yet 35% conformed on all 12 trials. What if the answer was not so clear? Would even more people have conformed? The answer to this question is yes, as 80% of the subjects in one study conformed when the answer to the task was ambiguous (staring at a small light and estimating how far the light appeared to have moved), 60% conformed when the task was moderately ambiguous (counting the number of ticks on a metronome), and 37% when the talk had low ambiguity (the Asch lines).

The implication from this study is fairly clear—when we aren't sure what to do, we are more likely to conform. Thus, the first day of class for freshmen, the first day of work for a new employee, and the first day of basic training for Army recruits are likely to be full of people conforming. However, after our students, employees, and recruits get more comfortable with their social environment, we can expect conformity to drop.

THE GROUP

Group size If there had been only one confederate in the Asch study, would the conformity have been as high? What if there had been 15 instead of 4, would the amount of conformity increase? Asch repeated his experiment, varying the number of confederates from 1 to 14, and found that 2 confederates brought more conformity than 1, 3 brought more than 2, and 4 brought more than 3. Adding more than 4 confederates did not increase conformity. Other research has confirmed that in general, conformity will peak when 4 or 5 people respond the same way.

Group unanimity Conformity also drops when the group is not unanimous. For example, suppose that your teacher tells your class that he wants to keep you an extra 15 minutes today because there is so much material to cover. You are horrified because you have another class immediately after this one. The teacher asks each student if he or she minds staying and the first 15 say they don't mind. Now it comes to you. Would you speak up? According to research, you probably wouldn't. However, what if the first 6 students said they didn't mind staying, the seventh person said he did mind, and the next 8 students said they didn't mind? Would that one person who disagreed change the probability that you would conform? According to research, when even one person disagrees with the group, conformity drops by about 75%.

This finding has been cited by proponents of 12-person juries. For many types of crimes, the Supreme Court has ruled that juries, which normally have 12 jurors, can have as few as 6. Though the research shows that jury size actually has little effect on the verdict, some psychologists correctly argue that the larger juries discourage conformity. That is, suppose that the vote is 5 to 1 in a 6-person jury. Based on the research by Asch and others, we would expect that lone person to conform to the other 5 (unless, of course, you are Henry Fonda in *12 Angry Men*). However, if there were 12 jurors instead of 6, we would expect the vote to be 10 to 2. With the addition of the one nonconforming juror, we would not expect conformity to occur.

The group members Are some people more likely to conform than others? Apparently so, as research has shown that culture and gender are related to conformity. For example, cross-cultural research shows that people in individualistic societies such as the United States and Western Europe have relatively low levels of conformity whereas people from collective societies such as Norway, China, and Japan have relatively high levels of conformity. Though early research on conformity suggested that females conform more than males, more recent research suggests that the relationship between gender and conformity is more complicated than once believed. Apparently, females are a bit more likely than males to conform in public situations, but there are no conformity differences when the behavior occurs in private.

Minority Influence

Though it is true that individuals conform to group behavior, there are times when the group will conform to an individual. For example, we have all seen situations in which a group of pedestrians is waiting for the light to change from red to green so they can cross the street. Suddenly, one person crosses against the light, and at times, the rest of the pedestrians follow. Or imagine a jury in which the vote is 11 to 1 to convict. Is it possible for the one person to change the minds of the other 11? For the minority to get the majority to conform, the person in the minority must have three characteristics: status, self-confidence, and idiosyncrasy credits.

If the minority member has *status*, the group is more likely to be influenced. In our jury example, a person with high status such as a doctor, professor, or politician will have a better chance of influencing the other jury member than a person who is unemployed. For this reason, lawyers often don't select people in high-status occupations to serve on a jury. If we go back to our example of the person crossing the street, research has shown that the group is more likely to conform when a person wearing a suit crosses against the light than a person who is poorly dressed.

The person in the minority must also be *confident*. If he hems and haws about his opinion, the group is not likely to be influenced. However if the person appears confident (I am 100% sure the person is innocent!), the probability of influencing the group increases.

It is also helpful if the person in the minority has accumulated **idiosyncrasy credits**. Every time we go along with the group, we build "credits" as being a team player. The more of these credits we accumulate, the greater the chance the group will agree to what we want. For example, suppose that you go to lunch with the same five people every day. For the past 2 months, you have agreed to go to whatever restaurant one of the five suggested. Today, however, you are dying for a tofu taco and suggest that the group go to Vinny's Vegetarian Cafe. Though the group hates that kind of food, they will probably agree because you always do what they want. However, suppose that for the past 2 months you have whined and complained about every choice the group made. What is the likelihood that the group will agree to go to Vinny's? Probably pretty low.

■ COMPLIANCE

A third method that we can use to influence others is **compliance**—social behavior that is the result of a request. That is, we can ask an employee to work overtime, a citizen to vote on election day, or a group of students to read the chapter before coming to class. To increase the probability that others will comply with our request, we can use several interesting techniques.

> **PROJECT C** *Compliance*
> To get you thinking about this next section, complete Project C at the end of the chapter.

Foot-in-the-Door Technique

With the **foot-in-the-door technique**, you start by making a request so small that you know the person will say yes. You then follow that small request with the larger request in which you are really interested. For example, suppose that you wanted to borrow a quarter from a stranger. To increase the chance that the stranger will comply with your request, you first ask him what time it is (the foot-in-the-door) and then follow up by asking if you can borrow a quarter.

An abundance of research supports the effectiveness of the foot-in-the-door technique (Dillard, 1991). The first study was conducted by Freedman and Fraser (1966) who tried to get California residents to put an ugly "Drive Carefully" billboard in their front yards. In the control condition, the researchers approached residents and asked them if they would put the sign in their front yard—17% said yes. In the foot-in-the-door condition, a researcher first asked the residents to sign a petition favoring safe driving, then a few weeks later, a different researcher asked if they would put the sign in their front yard. With the foot-in-the-door technique, a whopping 55% said yes!

A similar study was conducted by Pliner, Hart, Kohl, and Saari (1974), who were trying to raise funds for the Cancer Society. When they approached people and asked them to make a small donation, 46% agreed. However, when they asked people a day earlier to wear a lapel pin in support of the Cancer Society (the foot-in-the-door), and then asked them for money, 90% agreed.

Why does this technique work? At first, psychologists thought that the foot-in-the-door caused the person to commit either to the requester or the cause. However, research has shown that the technique will work even if the person making the second request is not the same person who made the first request (Chartrand, Pinckert, & Burger, 1999), and the technique will work even if the small request was to help one cause (e.g., sign a petition for the Red Cross) and the larger request was to help another cause (e.g., donate to the March of Dimes).

Instead, the foot-in-the-door technique works because the person being asked the request undergoes a change in self-perception. That is, after complying to a small request such as signing a petition or wearing a lapel pin, the person asks himself why he did it. Why would I sign a petition for safe driving? Why would I wear a lapel pin for the Red Cross? The person's probable answer is that he did it because he is a good, caring person. So, if he thinks he is a good and caring person, and he is later asked to donate to a charity or place a large sign in his front yard, to be consistent with his self-perception as a good person, he has to comply.

Door-in-the-Face Technique

A second technique for increasing compliance is the **door-in-the-face technique**. With this technique, you begin by making a request so large that you know the person will turn you down. You then follow this large request with a smaller, much more reasonable request. In the first experimental test of this technique, Cialdini and his colleagues (1975) approached college students and asked if they would be willing to take a day to chaperon a group of juvenile delinquents who were going to the zoo—17% said yes. To increase this percentage, the researchers approached another group of college students and first asked if they would be willing to commit to spending 2 hours per week for the next 2 years working with the juvenile delinquents (door-in-the-face). After being turned down for this request, they were asked if they would be willing to take just 1 day to chaperon a group of juvenile delinquents who were going to the zoo. After turning down the experimenter for the large request, 50% said yes to the smaller request—almost a threefold increase in compliance compared to the control group!

The door-in-the face technique is a powerful technique that has been supported many times over in the scientific literature. Perhaps that is why you see it so often in life. For example:

- Nobody pays full price for a new car. The sticker price serves as an effective door-in-the-face.
- When asking for a raise, most people ask for more than they want (e.g., $1.00-an-hour increase), hoping their boss will counter with a smaller offer that is more in line with the 50-cent-an-hour raise expected by the employee.
- When teens ask their parents if they can stay out until 1:00 a.m., they know they will get turned down, but are hoping they will get the 12:00 a.m. curfew that they really want.
- At work, we tell our boss that we can get a report completed in 2 weeks, hoping the boss will agree to a 1-week deadline.

As you can see, the door-in-the-face is a powerful technique. Its power comes from something psychologists call **reciprocal concessions**. We all like to think we are good, reasonable people. Thus, if you do something for me, I will do something for you. With the door-in-the-face, the person making the request responded to being turned down by making a smaller request, in essence, making a concession and backing down. If the requester backed down by making a smaller request, what would be the right thing for you to do? Back down and make a concession as well.

This need to reciprocate is evident throughout our lives. When somebody gives us something or does a favor for us, we feel a need to do something for them. If we receive a birthday card from someone, we make sure to send them one in return. If a neighbor gives us a ride to work, we feel a need to do something for them. If a retailer gives us a free sample of food at a store, we feel the need to purchase the product.

Even-a-Penny Technique

A third method of increasing compliance is the **even-a-penny technique**. With this technique, you tell the person what you want, why you want it, and then close with a line that indicates that even a small amount of compliance would be useful. For example, in one experiment conducted by Cialdini and Schroeder (1976), researchers approached students and did one of two things. In the control condition, they told the students they were collecting money for the March of Dimes, explained what the March of Dimes did, and then asked for a contribution. In the even-a-penny technique, they did the same things but closed with the line "Even a penny will do." Twenty-nine percent of the students in the control condition donated money compared to 50% in the even-a-penny condition.

In real life, we often use this technique. When we ask for a raise we might say "Even a penny an hour more will help." When we ask an employee to work overtime we might say "Even 5 minutes extra will be helpful." When a child wants to stay up later, he might say "Come on Mom, how about 5 more minutes?"

This technique seems to work well for two reasons. First, it takes away a person's option to say no. For example, could any of the students honestly say that they didn't have 1 penny? Could an employer honestly say that he could not afford to pay the employee a penny more per hour? Could the employee honestly say that he couldn't work an extra 5 minutes? Furthermore, once we know you can't say no, could you actually give us exactly what we are asking? Could the students actually give a penny, the employer a penny-per-hour raise, the employee only 5 minutes of overtime? Not without looking bad.

The second reason the technique works is because it legitimizes small contributions. For example, suppose that you were one of the students who was approached and you had only 50 cents on you. Normally, you would feel cheap giving such a small donation so to protect your image, you would probably not donate anything. However, if you know that "even a penny would do," you would feel more comfortable donating that 50 cents.

Suggest-an-Attribution Technique

Former *Tonight Show* host Johnny Carson used to start his monologue with the expression "You are a great audience, not like last night's audience." After which, the audience would cheer loudly because they were after all, "a great audience." Similarly, the country-rock group Alabama starts each concert by telling the audience "We understand that you folks in Arkansas (or Missouri or whatever state they were in) are the rowdiest fans in America" and the crowd would then go nuts and stay loud the entire evening. Both Johnny Carson and Alabama were using a method called the **suggest-an-attribution technique.**

The suggest-an-attribution technique takes advantage of the idea that we often don't know much about ourselves or why we do what we do in life, by suggesting a reason (an attribution) for why you are going to comply with my request. In one study, teachers were having trouble getting kids to pick up their trash in the classroom. In one condition, the students were told to pick up their trash. In a second condition, the students were given a persuasive argument about why it is important to pick up their trash. In the third condition, the teacher told the students that they were his favorite class because they always picked up their trash. The next day, 25% of the students who were told to pick up their trash did so, compared to 45% who heard the persuasive argument and 80% who were told they were a responsible class.

Imagine-the-Effect Technique

A fifth compliance technique is called the **imagine-the-effect technique.** With this method, people are asked to imagine or visualize what would occur if they complied with a request. For example, in one study (Gregory, Cialdini, & Carpenter, 1982), telemarketers called people to see if they wanted to subscribe to cable television. In the control condition, they were given the normal sales pitch. In the imagine-the-effect condition, they were given the sales pitch and asked to imagine their family sitting in front of the TV watching first-run movies. In the imagine-the-effect condition, 47.4% signed up for cable TV compared to only 19.5% in the control condition.

Guilt Technique

A sixth and final compliance technique is guilt. Guilt is an effective method of obtaining compliance but not one that is recommended because it has negative side effects as people resent being made to feel guilty. However, to show you how powerful guilt can be, let's discuss two experiments. In the first study, subjects sat in a room waiting to be called for their turn to participate in the experiment. In the control condition, a confederate (a person pretending to be a subject) came out of the experimental room and told the subject that it was his turn to participate. In the guilt condition, the confederate came out, told the subject is was his turn to participate, and then whispered "you are going to take a test, all the answers

EXHIBIT 14-3

Characteristics of Persuasive People

When the message is about	The persuader should be
Something factual	Expert
	Trustworthy
	Confident
Values, opinions	Attractive
	Similar
	Charismatic
	Confident

are false." After entering the experiment room, the researcher asked the subjects if they had heard anything about the experiment—all of them said no. After completing the experiment, the researcher told the subject that he was really pressed for time and wondered if the subject could stay for a while and help score tests. In the control condition, only 2% of the subjects agreed to stay and help the experimenter. However, in the guilt condition (the subjects lied to the experimenter about hearing details about the study), 63% agreed to stay and help!

Similar results were found in a study in which shoppers were approached by a tourist who asked them to take a picture of him and his wife. As the shopper tried to take the picture, the camera wouldn't work. In the control condition, the "tourist" said "That's OK, the camera never seems to work." In the guilt condition, the tourist said "You broke my camera, it worked fine until you touched it." A few moments later, an experimenter pretending to be a shopper dropped her packages in front of the shopper. In the control condition, only 15% helped pick up the packages. However, of the subjects who were made to feel guilty about breaking the camera, 55% helped pick up the packages.

> **PROJECT D** *Compliance Revisited*
> To apply what you have learned about compliance, complete Project D at the end of this chapter.

■ PERSUASION

One skill that is commonly needed by people in organizations is the ability to persuade others. Supervisors often need to persuade upper-level managers that a new program will work; politicians need to persuade fellow politicians to vote a particular way; and public relations executives often want to persuade the public to change its perception of an organization or a product. We will only briefly discuss two important aspects of persuasion here—the communicator and the message.

Characteristics of the Persuader

Considerable research has indicated that people who are experts, trustworthy, attractive, similar, charismatic, and confident are more persuasive than people who lack these characteristics. As shown in Exhibit 14-3, some of these characteristics work best when the message involves facts (e.g., where is the best place to lay the new cable lines), whereas others work best when the message involves values and opinions (e.g., who is the best candidate).

EXPERTISE

Research has found that, in general, a leader who either has or is perceived as having **expertise** about a topic will be more persuasive than a leader who does not (Libo, 1996; Wilson & Sherrell, 1993). An excellent example of this occurred in the spring of 1999 when the United States was trying to determine what its military strategy should be in stopping the ethnic cleansing taking place in Kosovo. Senator John McCain, a former POW and decorated soldier, was instantly sought for his opinions by the media and the public, whereas President Clinton, who never served in the armed forces, was unable to persuade the American people that his strategy was best.

Thus, for leaders to persuade their followers, they must be the most knowledgeable about their common interest. In many high-technology fields, technical knowledge is an essential characteristic for a leader. If, however, those who are to be persuaded also are knowledgeable about a topic, the leader's expertise plays a smaller role.

TRUSTWORTHINESS

Another leader characteristic that is important in persuasion is *trustworthiness*. Used-car salespeople, for example, have difficulties in persuading customers to buy cars because customers do not trust them. And in many corporations, management is distrusted by its employees and thus has trouble convincing union members, especially, that the organization does not have the money available to grant raises. When being persuaded, then, people look not only at the expertise of the persuader, but also at his motives.

To improve his trustworthiness, a leader can do several things. First, he can occasionally argue against what appears to be his own self-interest. For example, he can sometimes tell his employees not to work as hard, or he can disagree with other managers. In doing so, he will not appear to be one-sided. Robert Byrd, the legendary senator for West Virginia, provides an excellent example of this tactic. Prior to the Senate impeachment trial of President Clinton, Senator Byrd, a liberal Democrat, called the impeachment charges serious and declared that he might vote for impeachment. That such a strong Democrat argued against the leader of his own party gave him great credibility, not only in the Senate, but in the public arena as well. Byrd eventually voted against the impeachment articles and was able to sway several Republicans to do so as well.

SIMILARITY

People who are perceived as being similar to their audience are more persuasive than those who are perceived as being dissimilar. This effect explains why politicians on the campaign trail wear hats and clothing representative of the local area. A close look at past presidential elections shows that the candidate who was best able to convince the American people that he was "most like the typical American," was elected.

In an organization, a leader can communicate to those he hopes to persuade not only that he is similar to them, but also that his goals are the same as theirs. For example, a manager trying to increase his department budget can explain to the vice president that his goal includes saving the company money, but to do so he needs a larger recruiting budget so that better quality employees can be hired.

ATTRACTIVENESS

Chapter 9 observed that attractive people tend to receive higher interview scores than do unattractive people. Attractiveness has the same effect with per-

suasion: Attractive people are more persuasive than unattractive people. This is why television commercials generally use attractive people and why attractive politicians are considered to be ideal candidates.

Characteristics of the Person Being Persuaded

Just as certain types of people are more persuasive, so too are certain types of people more easily persuaded. In general, people who are young, have moderate self-esteem, and are high in self-monitoring are more easily persuaded than older folks, people with high or low self-esteem, and low self-monitors.

QUICK PROJECT

How Easy Are You to Persuade?
Go back to Project B in Chapter 10. What was your self-monitoring score in Section A? Go back to Project A in Chapter 12. What was your self-esteem score? Based on these scores, how easy are you to persuade?

_____

_____

_____

_____

_____

Characteristics of the Message

In addition to the leader's personal attributes, the type of message that is presented also has a role in persuasion. Research has focused on three aspects of the message: message discrepancy, one-sided versus two-sided arguments, and the use of threats.

MESSAGE DISCREPANCY

Suppose that you are representing a group of employees in a labor negotiation. The employees currently are paid $8 per hour, but you think they deserve $10 per hour. What strategy would best achieve an increase to $10? Would it be to ask for $20 an hour and hope that management will actually give you more than $10? Or would the best strategy be honesty—that is, ask for exactly what you want—$10 per hour? Or would the best strategy be to ask for $13 an hour so that you appear reasonable but still have room to "give in" when management offers $8.50 per hour?

According to persuasion research, the third choice would be best. Ask for more than you want and then back down during negotiations (Cialdini, 1985). Asking for too much, or making an argument that is too far away from the other side's, diminishes your credibility. Asking for the amount you actually desire leaves no room for negotiation.

ONE-SIDED VS. TWO-SIDED ARGUMENTS

Another question that arises concerning the persuasive message is whether giving only one side of an argument is better than giving both sides. The answer is, "It depends." If the person being persuaded already is positive about an idea, it is usually better to argue only one side of an issue. If, however, the other person disagrees with the reasoning, it is better to argue both sides. When the other side is presented, the other person's perspective is acknowledged as legitimate and understood. But after the other side of the issue has been argued, it can be refuted, and the favored side can then be reargued. If you know that an opponent will bring up negative information about you or your position, it is better to bring it up yourself to "steal their thunder" (Williams, Bourgeois, & Croyle, 1993).

THREATS

The threat is another method of persuasion that a leader can use when appropriate. For a threat to be effective, however, the person being persuaded must actually believe that it will be carried out—that is, that the consequences of not complying *are* undesirable and inevitable (Tedeschi, Bonoma, & Schlenker, 1972).

For example, a supervisor tells an employee that he will be fired if he does not work overtime. For the threat to be effective, the employee must believe that the supervisor has both the authority and the willingness to fire him. Even then, the threat will be effective only if the employee values his job.

Threats certainly can be effective in persuasion, but they also can have negative consequences. Few people like being threatened, and many will resent the person who makes the threat. Some may even so react against the threat that they do the opposite of what the leader wants.

CHAPTER RECAP

- People will obey orders, especially when the authority figure has status.
- Problems with giving orders include blind obedience, lack of authority, and psychological reactance.
- Conformity is most likely when the situation is ambiguous, the group has about five people in it, and the group is unanimous in their opinion or behavior.
- Compliance can be increased by using the foot-in-the-door, door-in-the-face, even-a-penny, imagine-the-effect, suggest-an-attribution, or guilt techniques.
- People who are attractive, similar, trustworthy, expert, charismatic, and confident are most persuasive.
- People who are young, have moderate self-esteem, and are high in self-monitoring are most easily persuaded.

Critical Thinking Questions

1. How does one know when obedience, conformity, compliance, or persuasion is the best influence tactic?
2. What is the best compliance tactic to use?
3. Can knowledge of social influence techniques make us a better consumer?
4. Can anybody learn to be persuasive?
5. Are women easier to persuade than men?

WEB SITES

For further information, log on to the following web sites.
www.influenceatwork.com
Provides useful information about influence and persuasion in organizations.
www.socialpsychology.org/social.htm#socialinfluence
Provides links to a variety of sites with information about influence and persuasion.

KEY TERMS

Compliance Social behavior that is the result of a request.

Conformity Social behavior that is the result of a norm.

Door-in-the-face technique A compliance technique in which a very large request is followed by a smaller request.

Even-a-penny technique A compliance technique that legitimizes small contributions.

Expertise The knowledge or skill a person has about a topic that makes him or her more persuasive.

Foot-in-the-door technique A compliance technique in which a very small request is followed by a larger request.

Idiosyncrasy credits Increased minority influence that comes from usually going along with the norm.

Imagine-the-effect technique A compliance technique in which the target is asked to imagine the outcome of a request.

Informational conformity Conformity due to a lack of knowledge about how to behave.

Normative conformity Conformity out of concern for what others will think.

Psychological reactance When people feel their freedom to make choices is threatened, they react by disobeying the order that threatened that freedom.

Reciprocal concessions The psychological need to offer a concession when the other person offers us a concession.

Suggest-an-attribution technique A compliance technique in which it is subtly suggested why a person should comply.

PRACTICE EXAM

1. Social behavior that is the result of a norm is called _____.
   a. obedience
   b. conformity
   c. compliance
   d. persuasion

2. Social behavior that is the result of an order is called _____.
   a. obedience
   b. conformity
   c. compliance
   d. persuasion

3. People are most likely to obey when the person giving the order _____.
   a. is in another room
   b. uses the phone
   c. is not an authority figure
   d. has status

4. Which of the following is not a potential problem with giving orders?
   a. psychological reactance
   b. lack of authority
   c. people seldom obey orders
   d. blind obedience

5. Sarah wants to wear a dress to school but doesn't because none of the other girls wear dresses. Her behavior is an example of _____ .
   a. normative conformity
   b. informational conformity
   c. psychological reactance
   d. compliance

6. Juan notices that everyone in class has opened their books to Chapter 15 so he does so as well. His behavior is an example of _____.
   a. normative conformity
   b. informational conformity
   c. psychological reactance
   d. compliance

7. We are most likely to conform when:
   a. the size of the group is very small
   b. not everyone conforms
   c. the task is ambiguous
   d. none of the above is true

8. Which of the following is not a factor in minority influence?
   a. status
   b. attractiveness
   c. self-confidence
   d. idiosyncrasy credits

9. Which of the following is most associated with research on obedience?
   a. Asch
   b. Brooks-Cole
   c. Wadsworth
   d. Milgram

10. Fatima asks Fred if she can borrow his pen. A few minutes later, she asks if she can borrow his car for a few hours. She is probably using the technique of compliance.
    a. foot-in-the-door
    b. door-in-the-face
    c. even-a-penny
    d. suggest-an-attribution

11. Helen asks Wei-Lik if he will drive her 5 hours to pick up her car. After he says no, she asks if he will drive her to the bus station, which is 10 miles away. She is probably using the _____ technique of compliance.
    a. foot-in-the-door
    b. door-in-the-face
    c. even-a-penny
    d. suggest-an-attribution

12. Temea tells Lakisha that she is the most caring, helpful, and considerate person she has ever known. Two days later, Temea asks Lakisha if she will lend her $20. Temea is probably using the _____ technique of compliance.
    a. foot-in-the-door
    b. door-in-the-face
    c. even-a-penny
    d. suggest-an-attribution

13. Which of the following is not a factor associated with being persuasive?
    a. similarity
    b. attractiveness
    c. expertise
    d. self-monitoring

14. Which of the following is a characteristic of people who are easily persuaded?
    a. low self-monitoring
    b. being a male
    c. a moderate level of self-esteem
    d. attractiveness

15. If I am trying to persuade a hostile audience, I should:
    a. use a two-sided argument
    b. use a one-sided argument
    c. use threats
    d. use the even-a-penny technique

ANSWERS 1 b, 2 a, 3 d, 4 c, 5 a, 6 b, 7 c, 8 b, 9 d, 10 a, 11 b, 12 d, 13 d, 14 c, 15 a

Giving Orders

Think about the last few times when either you were given an order
or in which you gave an order. Describe the order. Was the order obeyed?
How did people react?

Conformity

Think about your daily life. List below the things you think you do because
you are conforming to a social norm.

1. _____
_____
_____

2. _____
_____
_____

3. _____
_____
_____

4. _____
_____
_____

5. _____
_____
_____

6. _____
_____
_____

7. _____
_____
_____

Compliance

Think about the last time someone got you to purchase something you probably didn't want. Describe the situation and the techniques that were used by the person to get you to buy the product.

_____

_____

_____

_____

_____

_____

_____

_____

_____

_____

_____

_____

_____

_____

_____

_____

_____

_____

_____

_____

_____

_____

_____

_____

PROJECT D

Compliance Revisited

Now that you have learned about compliance techniques, read the situation you described in Project C and identify the specific techniques that were used on you.

_____

_____

_____

_____

_____

_____

_____

_____

_____

_____

_____

_____

_____

_____

_____

_____

_____

_____

_____

_____

_____

_____

_____

_____

CHAPTER FIFTEEN

Communicating Expectations

Communicating Expectations Through Job Descriptions

Communicating Expectations Through Performance Appraisals

Terminating Employees

Chapter Recap

Key Terms

Practice Exam

Projects

An important rule in managing others is to ensure that they understand what is expected of them. For example, employees may not sort the mail if they don't realize it is part of their job; two employees might engage in a conflict about who has authority over a particular matter (you might remember the term "jurisdictional ambiguity" from Chapter 6); or employees might think they are doing a good job and are surprised when they are fired for poor performance. In previous chapters, you learned that goal setting is one way to communicate expectations. This chapter will focus on two additional methods: job descriptions and performance appraisal reviews. By the end of this chapter, you will:

- Learn how to write a job description
- Learn about the increased use of 360-degree feedback
- Know how to administer a performance appraisal system
- Understand the problems associated with performance ratings
- Be able to conduct a performance appraisal review
- Understand how to legally terminate an unproductive employee

■ COMMUNICATING EXPECTATIONS THROUGH JOB DESCRIPTIONS

Job descriptions provide guidelines that can be followed by employees, which can lead to greater employee performance by clearly defining the employer's expectations of the employee in a particular job. A **job description** is a relatively short summary of a job and should be about two to five pages in length. This suggested length is not really typical of most job descriptions used in industry; they tend to be only one page. But for a job description to be of any real value, it must describe a job in enough detail that decisions about activities such as selection and training can be made. Such decisions probably cannot be made if the description is written in just one page.

Though organizational psychologists believe that job descriptions should be detailed and lengthy, many supervisors resist such efforts. These supervisors worry that listing each activity will limit their ability to direct employees to perform tasks not listed on the job description. The concern is that an employee, referring to the job description as support, might respond "it's not my job." This fear, however,

can be countered with two arguments. The first is that duties can always be added to a job description and job descriptions can, and should, be updated on a regular basis. The second is to include the statement "and performs other job-related duties as assigned" to the job description. In fact, Virginia Tech has a policy stating that the university can require employees to perform any duties not on the employee's job descriptions for a period not to exceed 3 months. After 3 months, the duty must either be eliminated or permanently added to the employee's job description, at which time a review will also be made to determine if the addition is significant enough to merit a salary increase.

Job descriptions can be written in many ways, but the following format has been used successfully for many jobs and is a combination of methods used by many companies and suggested by several researchers. A job description should contain the following seven sections: job title, brief summary, work activities, tools and equipment used, work context, performance standards, and personal requirements.

Job Title and DOT Code

A job title is important for several reasons. An accurate title describes the nature of the job. When industrial psychologist David Faloona started a new job at Washington National Insurance in Chicago, his official title was Psychometric Technician. Unfortunately, none of the other workers knew what he did. To correct that problem, his title was changed to Personnel Assistant, and supervisors then began consulting with him on human resource-related problems. A job analysis conducted by your authors provides another example. After analyzing the position of *secretary* for one credit union, we found that her duties were actually those of a position that other credit unions title *loan officer*. This change in title resulted in the employee receiving a higher salary as well as vindication that she was indeed "more than a secretary."

An accurate title also aids in employee selection and recruitment. If the job title indicates the true nature of the job, potential applicants for a position will be better able to determine if their skills and experience match those required for the job. The "secretary" example above demonstrates this because secretarial applicants might not possess the lending and decision-making skills needed by a loan officer.

When conducting a job analysis, it is not unusual for an analyst to discover that some workers do not have job titles. Job titles provide workers with some form of identity. Instead of just saying that they are "workers at the foundry," people can say that they are welders or machinists. At most colleges, students receiving financial aid are called "work study students" rather than titles such as clerk, computer operator, or mail sorter. This inaccurate title causes many students to think they are supposed to study as they work rather than sort mail or operate a computer.

Job titles can also affect perceptions of the status and worth of a job. For example, job descriptions containing gender-neutral titles such as administrative assistant are evaluated as being worth more money than ones containing titles with a female sex linkage such as executive secretary (Naughton, 1988). As another example, B. N. Smith, Hornsby, Benson, and Wesolowski (1989) had subjects read identical job descriptions that differed only in the status of the title. Jobs with higher status titles were evaluated as being worth more money than jobs with lower status titles. Some authors, however, have questioned the gender effects associated with titles (Mount & Ellis, 1989; Rynes, Weber, & Milkovich, 1989).

In addition to a title, federal regulations (the Uniform Guidelines) suggest that a job description contain a code from the **Dictionary of Occupational Titles (DOT)**. The DOT is produced by the federal government and contains descriptions of thousands of jobs, each of which is accompanied by an identifying code, commonly referred to as the *DOT Code*. Use of this code makes it easier to compare jobs and summarize industry-related information such as affirmative action, safety, and career guidance reports.

Brief Summary

The summary need only be a paragraph in length but should briefly describe the nature and purpose of the job. This summary can be used in help wanted advertisements, internal job postings, and company brochures.

Work Activities

The work activities section lists the tasks and activities in which the worker is involved. These tasks and activities should be organized into meaningful categories to make the job description easier to read and understand. The category labels are also convenient to use in the brief summary. As you can see in the sample job description in Exhibit 15-1, the 72 work activities performed by the bookkeeper are divided into seven main areas: accounting, clerical, teller, share draft, collections, payroll, and financial operations.

Much has been written about the proper way to write a task statement, but one should not get too bogged down worrying about format. Instead, the task statements in this section should be short and written at a level that can be read and understood by a person with the same reading ability as the typical job incumbent. The statement should make sense by itself. That is, "makes photocopies" does not provide as much detail as "makes photocopies of transactions for credit union members," which indicates what types of materials are photocopied and for whom they are copied. It also has been suggested that for those activities that involve decision making, the level of authority be indicated. This level lets incumbents know which decisions they are allowed to make on their own and which ones they need approval from a higher level (Degner, 1995).

Tools and Equipment Used

A section should be included that lists all the tools, equipment, and software programs used to perform the work activities in the previous section. Even though tools and equipment may have been mentioned in the activities section, placing them in a separate section makes their identification simpler. Information in this section is primarily used for employee selection and training. That is, applicants can be asked if they can operate an adding machine, a computer, and a credit history machine.

Work Context

This section should describe the environment in which the employee works and should mention stress level, work schedule, physical demands, level of responsibility, temperature, number of coworkers, degree of danger, and any other relevant information. This information is especially important in providing applicants with disabilities with information they can use to determine their ability to perform a job under a particular set of circumstances.

Performance Standards

The job description should outline standards of performance. This section contains a relatively brief description of how an employee's performance is evaluated and what work standards are expected of the employee.

Personal Requirements

The personal requirements section contains what are commonly called **job specifications**. These are the knowledge, skills, abilities, and other (KSAOs) characteristics (such as interest, personality, training) that are necessary to be successful on the job. Job specifications are determined by deciding what types of KSAOs are needed to perform the tasks identified in

EXHIBIT 15-1

Example of a Job Description

Bookkeeper
Radford Pipe Shop Employee's
Federal Credit Union
Job Summary Under the general supervision of the office manager, the Bookkeeper is responsible for all of the accounting duties of the office. Specifically, the Bookkeeper is responsible for: keeping all financial records accurate and up to date; processing loans; and preparing and posting statements, reports, and bonds.

Work Activities The work activities of the Bookkeeper are divided into seven main functional areas:

Accounting Activities

- Prepares quarterly income statement
- Maintains and posts all transactions in general ledger book
- Pays credit union bills
- Prepares statistical reports
- Updates undivided earnings account
- Prepares and files tax returns and statements
- Completes IRA forms and reports in cooperation with CUNA
- Annually computes Cumis Bond
- Balances journal and cash records

Clerical Activities

- Looks up members' account information when requested
- Answers phone
- Makes copies of transactions for members
- Drafts statements of account to members
- Types certificates of deposit
- Makes copies of letters that are sent to members
- Picks up, sorts, and disperses credit union mail
- Folds monthly and quarterly statements and places into envelopes to be mailed to members
- Processes and mails savings and share draft statements
- Sorts checks or copies of checks in numerical order
- Orders supplies
- Types reports and minutes from board meetings
- Maintains and updates files for members
- Prepares, types, and files correspondence
- Enters change-of-address information into the computer

Teller Activities

- Enrolls new members and opens and closes accounts
- Reconciles accounts
- Issues money orders and traveler's checks
- Conducts history of accounts
- Processes and issues receipts for transactions
- Asks for identification if person making transaction is not known
- Daily enters transaction totals onto a list sent to the bank
- Orders new or replacement checks for members
- Prints and issues checks
- Makes proper referrals

Share Draft Activities

- Deducts fee from member's account when a share is returned
- Processes statements for share draft accounts
- Issues stop payments and sends copy of form to member
- Deducts fee in form of an overdraft when more than three transfers have occurred for any one member in a month
- Checks and records share drafts or additions from previous day
- Receives share draft totals for each member from CUNA data
- Decides on an individual basis whether overdrafts will be covered by credit union
- Determines if overdrafts on account have been paid
- Checks to see if share drafts have cleared
- Telephones Chase-Manhattan Bank when a member does not have enough money to cover a share draft

Collections Activities

- Holds money from member's check in order to meet loan payments
- Decides if a member who has a delinquent loan will be able to take money out of account
- Locates and communicates with members having delinquent loans
- Completes garnishee form to send to courts on delinquent loans
- Resubmits garnishee form once every 3 months until delinquent loan has been paid in full by member
- Makes collection on delinquent loans
- Checks on previous member's address and current job to see if loan payments can be made

- Determines number and length of time of delinquent loans
- Sends judgment form to court, which sends it to delinquent member
- If a member is delinquent, finds out if he or she is sick or on vacation

Payroll and Data-Processing Activities

- Checks and verifies payroll run for all necessary deductions
- Reads and interprets computer printouts
- Computes and subtracts deductions from payroll
- Sets up and changes deduction amounts for payroll savings plan
- Runs payroll on computer
- Annually sends out backup disk to outside vendor who transfers information to a magnetic tape that is sent to the IRS
- Computes payroll
- Runs daily trial balances and transaction registers
- Loads paper into printer
- Makes backup copies of all daily computer transactions
- Runs quarterly and/or monthly statements on computer

Financial Operations Activities

- Scans business/financial environment to identify potential threats and opportunities
- Makes recommendations to the board regarding investments
- Invests all excess money into accounts that will earn interest
- Computes profits and amounts to be used for investments
- Prepares statements of financial condition and federal operating fee report
- Obtains enough funds for day-to-day operation of branch
- Notifies and makes available investment funds to the NCUA

Equipment and Software Programs Used The Bookkeeper uses the following equipment and software:

- Calculator

- Personal computer with accounting software
- Word-processing software (Microsoft Word)
- Spreadsheet software (Microsoft Excel)
- Typewriter
- Computer printer
- Credit history machine
- Motor vehicle
- Photocopy machine
- Folding machine
- Microfiche reader
- Safe
- Telephone
- Security check writer

Job Context The Bookkeeper spends the majority of time making entries in and balancing journals and ledgers. The work day is spent in a climate-controlled office with four coworkers. Physical demands are minimal and sitting is required for most of the day. Stress is moderate.

Work Performance To receive an excellent performance appraisal, the Bookkeeper should:

- Maintain neat and accurate records
- Meet all deadlines
- Maintain an orderly office
- Make sure all ledgers and journals balance
- Perform duties of other jobs when the need arises

Job Qualifications Upon hire, the Bookkeeper must:

- Have a basic knowledge of math and English
- Understand financial documents
- Be able to make limited financial decisions
- Have completed advanced coursework in accounting and finance
- Have had training in data processing

After hire, the Bookkeeper must:

- Learn general office procedures
- Learn credit union style accounting procedures and regulations
- Learn how to complete the various forms

the job analysis. These KSAOs can be determined through a combination of logic, research, and use of specific job analysis techniques similar to those used in developing performance appraisal systems. The personal requirements section should be divided into two subsections. The first contains KSAOs that an employee must have at time of hiring. The second subsection contains the KSAOs that are an important part of the job but which can be obtained after being hired. The first set of KSAOs are used for employee selection and the second for training purposes (Wooten, 1993).

Once job descriptions are written, it is essential that supervisors discuss the job descriptions with their employees. The job descriptions will then provide concrete information about what is expected of each employee.

PROJECTS A AND B

To apply what you have learned in the preceding pages, complete Projects A and B at the end of this chapter. Project A gives you a chance to critique a job description, and Project B provides you with the opportunity to write your own job description.

■ COMMUNICATING EXPECTATIONS THROUGH PERFORMANCE APPRAISALS

Have you ever received a grade that you did not think was fair? Perhaps you had an 89.6 and the instructor would not "round up" to an A, or the test contained questions that had nothing to do with the class. If so, you were probably upset with the way in which your instructor appraised your performance. In this section of the chapter, we will discuss the process of evaluating and appraising employee performance.

Reasons for Evaluating Employee Performance

COMPENSATION

The difference in compensation between two individuals within the same job is a function of both tenure and job performance. That is, it would not seem fair to pay a poor-performing employee the same amount as an excellently-performing one. Thus, one important reason for evaluating employee performance is to provide a fair basis on which to determine an employee's salary.

PROMOTIONS

Another reason for evaluating performance is to determine which employees will be promoted. Although it would seem only fair to promote the best employee, this often does not occur. For example, the policy in some organizations is to promote employees with the most seniority. This is especially true of organizations whose employees belong to unions. Even though promoting employees on the basis of performance or tenure seems fair, it may not always be smart. The best employee at one level is not al-

ways the best at the next level. Promoting the best or most senior employee often results in the so-called **Peter Principle**—the promotion of employees until they reach their level of incompetence. If performance evaluations are used to promote employees, care should be taken to ensure that the employee is evaluated well on the job dimensions that are similar to the new position's dimensions.

For example, the five important job dimensions of a salesperson might be sales, communication skills, accuracy of paperwork, client rapport, and responsibility. The four important job dimensions of sales manager would be communication skills, accuracy of paperwork, motivational ability, and employee rapport. The salesperson with the highest scores on the overlapping dimensions, which in this case are communication skills and accuracy of paperwork, should be the one promoted. Sales volume might not even be used as a factor in promotion.

EMPLOYEE TRAINING AND FEEDBACK

By far, the most important use of performance evaluation is to improve employee performance by providing them feedback about what they are doing right and wrong. Even though employee training should be an ongoing process, the semiannual performance appraisal review is an excellent time to meet with employees to discuss their strengths and weaknesses. But more important, it is the time to determine how weaknesses can be corrected. This process is thoroughly discussed later in the chapter.

Another use of performance appraisal data is in training-needs analysis. If many employees score poorly on a performance appraisal dimension, an increase or change in training is probably necessary for all employees. If only a few employees have low scores, training at an individual level is indicated. Thus, performance appraisal can provide useful information about an organization's strengths and weaknesses.

The Performance Appraisal Process

DECIDING WHO WILL EVALUATE PERFORMANCE

Traditionally, employee performance has been evaluated solely by supervisors. Recently, however, organizations have realized that supervisors see only certain aspects of an employee's behavior. For example, as shown in Exhibit 15-2, a branch manager might observe only 30% of a teller's work behavior; the rest is observed by customers, peers, and support staff in other parts of the bank. Furthermore, the teller might behave very differently around her supervisor than around other people. Consequently, to obtain an ac-

EXHIBIT 15-2

Who Observes Employee Performance?

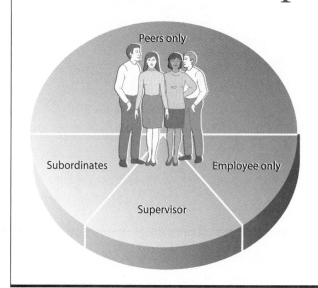

curate view of the teller's performance, these other sources should provide feedback. The buzzword for using multiple sources to appraise performance is **360-degree feedback**, a process used by more than 13% of United States organizations (Gruner, 1997). Sources of relevant information about employee performance include supervisors, peers, subordinates, customers, and self-appraisal. As shown in Exhibit 15-3, there is often little agreement in the way two supervisors evaluate an employee or a supervisor and a peer might rate an employee. Interestingly, supervisors whose self-ratings agree with others' ratings tend to be better performers than supervisors whose self-ratings are not consistent with others' (Witt, 1996).

Supervisors By far the most common type of performance appraisal is the supervisor rating. Supervisors are best able to evaluate the extent to which an employee contributes to the overall success of the organization. Though supervisors may not see every minute of an employee's behavior, they do see the end result. A supervisor may not actually see a teller sign up customers for Visa cards but will review the daily sales totals. Likewise, a professor does not see a student actually research and write a paper but infers the levels of these behaviors by viewing the results—the finished term paper.

Peers Whereas supervisors see the *results* of an employee's efforts, peers often see the actual *behavior*.

Peer ratings usually come from employees who work directly with an employee; a bank teller could be rated by other bank tellers. However, other employees in the organization, those who often come in contact with the employee, can also provide useful information. For example, our teller could be rated by employees from the loan support or Visa Card departments.

Research has shown that peer ratings are fairly reliable only when the peers who make the ratings are similar to and well acquainted with the employees being rated (Mumford, 1983). Most important, peer ratings have been successful in predicting the future success of promoted employees as they correlate highly with supervisor ratings (Cederbloom, 1989). But even though peer ratings appear promising, few organizations use them. One reason could be that peer ratings are lenient when used for evaluation purposes but not when they are used only to provide feedback (Farh, Cannella, & Bedeian, 1991).

Research suggests certain employees are more lenient in their peer ratings than are other employees. Saavedra and Kwun (1993) found that high performers evaluate their peers more strictly than do low performers. This difference in ratings is probably because employees compare others to themselves. Thus, the average employee does not appear impressive to a high performer but may to a less-productive employee. Though peers may provide a unique view of performance, employees tend to react worse to negative feedback from peers than they do to feedback

EXHIBIT 15-3

Correlations Between Raters

Agreement Between	Correlation
Two supervisors	.50
Two peers	.37
Two subordinates	.30
Supervisors and peers	.34
Supervisor and subordinates	.22
Supervisor and self	.22
Peers and subordinates	.22
Peers and self	.19

Source: Conway & Huffcutt, 1997

from experts (Albright & Levy, 1995). Employees who score high in self-esteem, high in self-monitoring, and low in individualism react most favorably to peer ratings (Long, Long, & Dobbins, 1998).

Subordinates Subordinate feedback (also called upward feedback) is an important component of 360-degree feedback because subordinates can provide a very different view of a supervisor's behavior (Whetstone, 1994). However, with the exception of students rating teachers, formal methods are neither common nor well regarded by managers (McEvoy, 1990).

Subordinate ratings can be difficult to obtain because employees fear a backlash if they unfavorably rate their supervisor, especially when a supervisor has only one or two subordinates. For example, when the supervisors at one mental health facility gave poor performance ratings to their boss, each was "called on the carpet" for having the audacity to rate the boss poorly. After such a browbeating, what do you think is the probability the subordinates will be honest again in the future? However, subordinates' feedback can be encouraged if supervisors appear open to employee comments (Baumgartner, 1994) and if the ratings are made anonymously (Antonioni, 1994).

Interestingly, subordinate ratings correlate highly with upper-management ratings of supervisors' performance (Furnham & Stringfield, 1994; Riggio & Cole, 1992). Research indicates that subordinate feedback can increase managerial performance, especially that of poorly performing managers (Reilly, Smither, & Vasilopoulous, 1996; Walker, 1997). This increase in performance is especially true for areas targeted for improvement (Clarke, Miklos, & Rogers, 1996).

Customers Though it would be unlikely that an organization would ask customers to fill out a performance appraisal instrument on an employee, organizations do value customer feedback. Informally, customers provide feedback on employee performance by filing complaints or complimenting a manager about one of her employees. Formally, customers provide feedback by completing evaluation cards such as that shown in Exhibit 15-4.

Organizations also seek customer feedback in the form of *secret shoppers*—current customers who have been enlisted by a company to periodically evaluate the service they receive. In exchange for their ratings, secret shoppers get a few dollars and a free meal. For years, we have been "employed" by a national marketing company to eat at local restaurants and secretly complete a rating of the quality of food and service. The compensation is only $4 per visit plus reimbursement for the meal, but it is a fun experience. We only wish they would have granted our request for sunglasses and trench coats!

Self-appraisal Allowing employees to evaluate their own behavior and performance is a technique used by about 12% of organizations. Research on self-appraisal, however, has found what we might expect to find: Employee self-appraisals tend to suffer from leniency (Meyer, 1980) and correlate moderately (.29) with actual performance (Mabe & West, 1982) and poorly with subordinate ratings (London & Wohlers, 1991). However, when evaluations are made with clear rating standards and social comparison information, agreement is increased between self- and supervisor ratings (Keeping & Sulsky, 1996; Schrader & Steiner, 1996).

EXHIBIT 15-4

Customer Evaluation Card

McBurger Queen Restaurants

Dear Customer:

We value your business and strive to make each of your visits a dining pleasure. To help us reach our goal, we would appreciate your completing this card and placing it in our suggestion box on your way out.

1. Was your food cooked properly?   Y   N
2. Was your server friendly?   Y   N
3. Was your server efficient?   Y   N
4. Do you plan to return?   Y   N
5. Who was your server? _____

Comments: _____

_____

_____

_____

_____

The leniency found in the self-ratings of U.S. workers may not generalize to other countries. Farh, Dobbins, and Cheng (1991) found that the self-ratings of Taiwanese workers suffered from modesty rather than leniency. However, Furnham and Stringfield (1994) and Yu and Murphy (1993) found leniency in the self-ratings of Mainland Chinese employees. Further research is still needed to investigate potential cultural differences in self-ratings.

Self-appraisals of performance appear to be most accurate when the purpose of the self-appraisal is for either research or use in performance appraisal interviews rather than for such administrative purposes as raises or promotions; employees understand the performance appraisal system; and employees believe an objective record of their performance is available with which the supervisor can compare the self-appraisal.

PROJECT C *360-Degree Feedback*
To think more about who should evaluate performance, complete Project C at the end of this chapter.

DEVELOPING A METHOD TO EVALUATE PERFORMANCE

The choice of the criteria and method used to measure the criteria are important. An excellent example of this importance comes from a study of the relationship between age and job performance. Using meta-analysis, Waldman and Avolio (1986) found a correlation of .27 between age and objective measures of job performance for 13 studies covering 40 separate samples. The correlation between age and supervisor ratings, however, was −.14. Thus, using the latter ratings would lead to the conclusion that older workers are not as good as younger workers. But using actual performance as the criterion leads to the opposite conclusion: Older workers performed better than younger workers. This difference in correlations demonstrates how inaccurate stereotypes about older workers deny them the rewards (e.g., raises, promotions) that their performance suggests they should receive.

Human resource professionals have spent considerable effort in developing different methods for

EXHIBIT 15-5

Examples of a Trait-Focused Evaluation System

Please rate the employee on the extent to which he/she is:	Low				High
Friendly	1	2	3	4	5
Dependable	1	2	3	4	5
Creative	1	2	3	4	5
Trustworthy	1	2	3	4	5
Reliable	1	2	3	4	5
Cooperative	1	2	3	4	5
Assertive	1	2	3	4	5

evaluating performance because each has its advantages and disadvantages. The human resource professional must choose the method that is most appropriate for the organization's needs. However, prior to developing the actual performance appraisal instrument, two important decisions must be made: the focus of the performance appraisal instrument and the type of rating scale that will be used. A performance appraisal instrument can focus on traits, behaviors, or results.

Trait-focused performance appraisal systems As shown in Exhibit 15-5, a trait-focused system concentrates on employees' attributes such as their dependability, assertiveness, and friendliness. Though commonly used, trait-focused performance appraisal instruments are not a good idea because they provide poor feedback and thus will not result in employee development and growth. For example, think of a performance review meeting in which the supervisor tells an employee that she received low ratings on responsibility and friendliness. Because traits are personal, the employee is likely to become defensive. Furthermore, the employee will want specific examples the supervisor may not have available. The only developmental advice the supervisor can offer would be to "be more responsible and friendly." Such advice is not specific enough for the employee to change her behavior.

Behavior-focused performance appraisal systems Whereas trait-focused instruments concentrate on who an employee *is*, behavior-focused instruments focus on what an employee *does*. That is, instead of rating bank tellers on their friendliness, supervisors using a behavior-focused instrument would rate the tellers on such specific behaviors as "Properly greets each customer," "Knows customers' names," and "Thanks customer after each transaction." The obvious advantage to a behavior-focused system is the increased amount of specific feedback that can be given to each employee. Further, the focus on behavior rather than traits not only reduces employee defensiveness but reduces legal problems. There are several methods for rating behavior.

Result-focused performance appraisal systems Result-focused systems concentrate on what employees *accomplished* as a result of what they did. Result-focused systems are tempting because they evaluate employees on their contribution to the bottom-line: Did their behavior on the job result in a tangible outcome for the organization (Planchy & Planchy, 1993)?

A problem with result-focused systems is that employees can do everything asked of them by an organization and still not get the desired results due to factors outside their control—thereby **contaminating** the data on which the results are based. In banking, tellers might not be successful in getting customers to sign up for Visa Cards because the bank's interest rate is not competitive. In law enforcement, police officers might not write many traffic citations because they patrol an area in which there are few cars. In retail, salespeople have poor sales because of their geographic location. For example, two salespersons work in different locations. Mary Anderson sells an average of 120 air conditioners per month, while Tamika Johnson averages 93. Is this criterion free from contamination? Definitely not.

The number of sales are based not only on the skills of the salesperson, but also on such factors as the number of stores in the sales territory, the average temperature in the territory, and the relations between the previous salesperson and the store owners. Thus, if we used only the number of sales, Mary Anderson would be considered our top salesperson. But if we take into account that sales are contaminated by the number of stores in the territory, we see that Mary Anderson sold 120 air conditioners in 50 possible stores, while Tamika Johnson sold 93 air conditioners in 10 stores. Thus, Mary Anderson sold an average of 2.4 air conditioners per store in an area with an average temperature of 93 degrees; Tamika Johnson sold an average of 9.3 air conditioners per store in an area with an average temperature of 80 degrees. By considering the potential areas of contamination, a different picture emerges of relative performance. As this example clearly shows, factors other than actual performance can affect criteria. Therefore, it is essential to identify as many sources of contamination as possible and to determine ways to adjust performance ratings to account for these contamination sources. It is nice to use objective data, but caution should be used in interpreting these data—contrary to popular belief, statistics can lie!

Result-focused systems use what is commonly called *objective* or *hard* criteria. Common types of hard criteria are quantity of work, quality of work, attendance, and safety.

Quantity of work Evaluation of a worker's performance in terms of **quantity** is obtained by simply counting the number of relevant job behaviors that take place. For example, we might judge a salesperson's performance by the number of units she sells, an assembly-line worker's performance by the number of bumpers she welds, or a police officer's performance by the number of arrests she makes. Even Oprah Winfrey is evaluated on the number of viewers who watch her show.

Although quantity measures appear to be objective measures of performance, they often are misleading. From our discussion of contamination, it should be readily apparent that many factors determine quantity of work other than an employee's ability and performance. Furthermore, for many people's jobs it might not be practical or possible to measure quantity. Computer programmers, doctors, and firefighters are examples.

Quality of work Another method to evaluate performance is by measuring the **quality** of the work that is done. Quality is usually measured in terms of **errors**, which are defined as deviations from a standard. Thus, to obtain a measure of quality, there must be a standard against which to compare an employee's work. For example, a seamstress's work quality

would be judged by how it compares to a "model" shirt; a secretary's work quality would be judged by the number of typos (the standards being correctly spelled words); and a cook's quality might be judged by how her food resembled a standard as measured by size, temperature, and ingredient amounts.

Kentucky Fried Chicken, for example, evaluates the quality of its franchises' food by undercover inspectors. These inspectors purchase food, drive down the road, and after parking, use a thermometer to see whether the food has been served at a standard acceptable temperature and also a scale to determine whether the weight of the mashed potatoes is within the acceptable range.

Note that the definition of an error is *any* deviation from a standard. Thus, errors can even be work quality that is higher than a standard. Why is this an error? Suppose a company manufactures shirts that are sold for $15. To keep down the manufacturing costs of its shirts, the company probably uses cheaper material and has its workers spend less time per shirt than does a company that manufactures $100 shirts. Thus, if an employee sews a shirt with 15 stitches per inch instead of the standard 10, the company will lose money because of higher quality!

When Mike was working his way through school, he held a summer job at an amusement park. The job involved wearing a pink and purple uniform and cooking prefabricated pizza. The standard for the large pepperoni pizza was 2 handfuls of cheese and 15 pieces of pepperoni. Now all pizza lovers recognize this to be a barren pizza. The cooks thus tried to increase the pizza quality by tripling the number of pepperoni pieces. The management quickly explained to the young "gourmet chefs" that exceeding the standards was considered poor work performance and that employees who did so would be fired.

A similar situation developed at a factory that produced parts for telephones. Most of the employees were older and took great pride in their work quality and in the fact that their parts had the lowest percentage of errors in the company. They were told, however, that their quality was too high and that the parts were lasting so long that the company was not getting much repeat business. Quality errors can occur in many strange ways!

Attendance A common method for objectively measuring one aspect of an employee's performance is by looking at attendance. Attendance can be separated into three distinct criteria: absenteeism, tardiness, and tenure. Both absenteeism and tardiness have obvious implications for the performance appraisal process. The weight that each has in the overall evaluation of the employee largely depends on the nature of the job.

EXHIBIT 15-6

Examples of Three Scales to Measure Behavior

Comparison to Other Employees

Refers to customers by name

_____ Much better than other tellers

_____ Better than other tellers

_____ The same as other tellers

_____ Worse than other tellers

_____ Much worse than other tellers

Frequency

Refers to customers by name

_____ Always

_____ Almost always

_____ Often

_____ Seldom

_____ Never

Extent to Which Organizational Expectations Are Met

Greatly exceeds expectations

_____ Exceeds expectations

_____ Meets expectations

_____ Falls slightly below expectations

_____ Falls well below expectations

Tenure as a criterion, however, is used mostly for research purposes when evaluating the success of selection decisions. For example, in a job such as cook at McDonald's, there is probably little difference in the quantity and quality of hamburgers or French fries that are cooked. But an employee might be considered a "success" if she stays with the company for at least 4 months and "unsuccessful" if she leaves before that time. In fact, the importance of tenure can be demonstrated by noting that several major fast-food restaurants and convenience stores have established bonus systems to reward long-tenure employees—that is, those who have worked for the company at least 6 months. For each hour the employee works, the company places a specified amount of money into an account that can be used by the employee to pay such education expenses as books and tuition.

Safety Another method used to evaluate the success of an employee is safety. Obviously, employees who

follow safety rules and who have no occupational accidents do not cost an organization as much money as those who break rules, equipment, and possibly their own bodies. As with tenure, safety is usually used for research purposes, but it also can be used for employment decisions such as promotions and bonuses.

SCALE USED TO RATE PERFORMANCE

Based on the discussion in the preceding pages, it is clear that most performance-appraisal instruments will focus on behavior. The next issue is what scale will be used to rate the performance on these behaviors. As shown in Exhibit 15-6, employees can be rated in three ways: how they compared to other employees, the frequency with which they performed certain behaviors, or the extent to which the behaviors met the expectations of the employer.

Comparisons to other employees To reduce leniency, employees can be compared with one another

EXHIBIT 15-7

Ranking Method of Evaluating Performance

	Dimension			
Employee	**Knowledge**	**Dependability**	**Quality**	**Total**
Clark	1	1	1	1.00
Bailey	2	3	2	2.33
Darden	3	2	3	2.67
Shapiro	4	5	4	4.33
Cochran	5	4	5	4.67

instead of rated individually on a scale. The easiest and most common of these methods is the **rank order**. In this approach, employees are ranked in order by their judged performance for each relevant dimension. As Exhibit 15-7 shows, the ranks are then averaged across each dimension to yield an overall rank.

Rank orders are easily used with only a few employees to rank, but they become difficult to use with larger numbers. Ranking the top few and bottom few employees is relatively easy, but deciding which 2 of 50 employees should be placed at the 30th and 31st ranks is more difficult.

A second type of employee comparison system is called the **forced-distribution** method. With this method, a predetermined percentage of employees are placed into one of the five categories shown in Exhibit 15-8. This system is much easier to use than rank order, but it also has a drawback. To use the method, you must assume that employee performance is normally distributed, that is, that certain percentages of employees are poor, average, and excellent. Employee performance probably is not normally distributed—there probably are few terrible employees because they either were never hired or were quickly fired. Likewise, truly excellent employees probably have been promoted. Thus, employee performance is distributed in a nonnormal fashion.

Another way to look at this concept is by examining the grades given in a class. When students ask an instructor to "curve" a test, technically they are asking her to force their grades into a normal curve—that is, there will be approximately 10% As and 10% Fs. (Of course, what these students are really often asking for is extra points.)

Suppose that you are at the bottom of your class, yet you still have a 75% average on class exams. Do you deserve an F? What if you are the last person in the D category, and a student withdraws from the class with 2 weeks to go. To keep the distribution normal, you are given an F. Do you consider this fair?

Perhaps the greatest problem with all of the employee-comparison methods is that they do not provide information about how well an employee is actually doing. For example, even though every employee at a production plant might be doing an excellent job, someone has to be at the bottom. Thus, it might appear that one worker is doing a poor job (because she is last), when in fact she, and every other employee, is doing well.

Frequency of desired behaviors As shown in Exhibit 15-6, behaviors can be rated based on the frequency they occur. For example, we expect our production workers to follow safety guidelines. As part of our performance appraisal system, supervisors are asked to decide whether their employees *always, almost always, often, seldom,* or *never* follow the rules. As you can imagine, it is often difficult for a supervisor to distinguish between levels such as *almost always* and *often*.

Extent to which organizational expectations are met As shown back in Exhibit 15-6, perhaps the best approach is to rate employees on the extent to which their behavior meets the expectations of the organization. Such an approach allows for high levels of feedback and can be applied to most types of employee behavior. Some behaviors, however, are not suitable for such a scale. Take for example the expectation that a police officer always wear her seat belt. If she wears it all the time, she has *met* expectations (a rating of 3): there is no way to get a higher rating

EXHIBIT 15-8

Forced-Distribution Method of Performance Appraisal

Spelling	Tilly Stone	Griffith Hannah Basinger Close	Moore Hunt	Ryan
10% Terrible	20% Poor	40% Average	20% Good	10% Excellent

because one cannot wear a seat belt more often than always and thus cannot ever exceed expectations.

EVALUATION OF PERFORMANCE APPRAISAL METHODS

Though many of the behavioral methods yield similar results, the same is not true when comparing subjective and objective ratings. A meta-analysis by Bommer, Johnson, Rich, Podsakoff, and Mackenzie (1995) indicated that objective and subjective results are only slightly correlated ($r = .39$). Interestingly, there was a stronger relationship between objective and subjective ratings of quantity ($r = .38$) than between objective and subjective ratings of quality ($r = .24$).

From a legal perspective, courts are more interested in the due process afforded by a performance appraisal system than its technical aspects. After reviewing 295 circuit court decisions regarding performance appraisal, Werner and Bolino (1997) concluded that performance appraisal systems are most likely to survive a legal challenge if they are based on a job analysis, raters receive training and written instructions, employees are allowed to review the results, and ratings from multiple raters are consistent.

A COMBINATION METHOD

As discussed above, a performance appraisal instrument should be behaviorally focused and rated based on the extent to which the employee's behavior met the expectations of the employer. The format shown in Exhibit 15-9 represents a combination of the methods previously discussed in this chapter and meets the criteria of being behavior-focused and expectation-based.

A performance appraisal instrument such as that depicted in Exhibit 15-9 is constructed by taking the task statements from a detailed job description (e.g., "Types correspondence") and converting them into behavioral performance statements representing the level at which the behavior is expected to be performed (e.g., "correspondence is typed accurately and does not contain spelling or grammatical errors").

Using the Appraisal System to Evaluate Performance

DOCUMENTING BEHAVIOR

After the actual performance appraisal instrument has been created, the next step is to develop a system so that supervisors can document employees' behaviors as they occur. Such documentation is usually a written log consisting of **critical incidents**—formal accounts of excellent and poor employee performance that were observed by the supervisor. Documentation is important for four reasons. First, documentation forces a supervisor to focus on employee behaviors rather than traits and provides behavioral examples to use when reviewing performance ratings with employees.

Second, documentation helps supervisors recall behaviors when they are evaluating performance. As shown in Exhibit 15-10, without documentation, instead of recalling all of an employee's behavior or at least a representative sample of behavior, supervisors tend to recall only a small percentage of an employee's actual behavior. Supervisors tend to remember the following:

- *First impressions* Research from many areas of psychology indicates that we remember our first impression of someone (primacy effect) more than we remember later behaviors. Consequently, supervisors recall behaviors consistent with their first impression of an employee, even though those first behaviors may not have been representative of the employee's typical performance.

EXHIBIT 15-9

Example of a New Behavioral Format

Use of Weapons and Vehicle

Definition of Dimension

This dimension considers the possession and application of knowledge and skills required in the use of firearms and vehicle. This includes maintaining current skills, knowledge level, and certification(s). This also includes applying new knowledge or techniques to work activities. Equipment would include, but is not limited to, vehicles, batons/ASP, and OC spray.

A dimension rating of "3" indicates that there were no problems in this area during the performance rating period or that a minor problem was offset by other outstanding behavior. Ratings of "4" or "5" indicate the officer was especially adept at vehicle pursuits, marksmanship, and use of force (e.g., using the better of two appropriate alternatives) and/or acquired new knowledge above that expected of the typical patrol officer.

Behavioral Elements

Behaviors that can meet or exceed expectations

_____ Effectively handled vehicle in pursuit or emergency response situations

_____ Demonstrated marksmanship above minimum requirements

Behaviors that can only meet expectations

_____ Weapons ratings are current and meet minimum requirements

_____ Weapons were carried in an appropriate manner

Behaviors falling below expectations

_____ Applied force when use of force was not justified

_____ When force was justified, did not use appropriate type and/or amount

_____ Vehicle was not operated in a safe manner or in accordance with Department policy

_____ When weapons were used, reports were filed late and/or contained inaccurate information

_____ Carried a weapon not issued and/or approved by the Department

Dimension Rating

_____ 5   Performance could not realistically be better than that exhibited by this officer

_____ 4   Officer's use of weapons and vehicle went beyond expectations

_____ 3   Officer met expectations

_____ 2   Minor problems occurred in this area

_____ 1   Serious problems occurred; officer needs immediate and extensive improvement

Comments

_____

_____

_____

_____

_____

EXHIBIT 15-10

Information Loss in the Performance Appraisal Process

- *Recent behaviors* In addition to first impressions, supervisors tend to recall the most recent behavior that occurred during the evaluation period.

- *Unusual or extreme behaviors* Supervisors tend to remember unusual behaviors more than they remember common behaviors. For example, if an average-performing police officer captures an important criminal, the officer's performance evaluations are likely to be inappropriately high. Likewise, a good officer who makes a terrible mistake is likely to receive inappropriately low ratings.

- *Behavior consistent with the supervisor's opinion* Once we form an opinion of someone, we tend to look for behaviors that confirm that opinion. If a supervisor likes an employee, she will probably only recall behaviors consistent with that opinion. The opposite would be true for a super-

visor who dislikes an employee. Once you get on someone's bad side, it is hard to get off.

Third, documentation provides examples to use when reviewing performance ratings with employees. Instead of telling an employee that she is constantly getting into arguments with customers, a supervisor can use documented critical incidents to show the employee the specific incidents and behaviors that were problematic.

Fourth, documentation helps an organization defend against legal actions taken against it by an employee who was terminated or denied a raise or promotion. As will be discussed later in this chapter, the courts closely examine the accuracy of the performance ratings upon which personnel decisions are based. Judges and juries are not likely to accept a supervisor's rating as proof of poor performance. Instead, they want to see proof of the behaviors that caused the supervisor to rate the employee poorly. Without documentation, employers will seldom win lawsuits filed against them (Rosen, 1992). The courts' need for documentation is supported by research indicating that when evaluators must justify their performance ratings, their ratings are more accurate (Mero & Motowidlo, 1995).

To use critical incidents to document performance, a supervisor maintains a log of all the critical behaviors she observes her employees performing. These behaviors are then used during the performance appraisal review process to assign a rating for each employee. The log refreshes the supervisor's memory of her employees' performance and also provides justification for each performance rating. The use of log books to record behaviors not only provides an excellent source of documentation but also results in more accurate performance appraisals. This is especially true if the logs are organized by employee rather than maintained as only a random collection of incidents observed on the job (DeNisi & Peters, 1996).

APPRAISING PERFORMANCE

Obtaining and reviewing objective data When it is time to appraise an employee's performance, a supervisor should first obtain and review the objective data that are relevant to an employee's behavior. For example, a police sergeant might review the numbers of tickets an officer wrote, arrests made, and citizen complaints received. A production supervisor might review the number of days employees were absent, number of units they produced, and the tons of material that they wasted. These data, when combined with critical-incident logs, provide a solid basis on which to rate an employee. As mentioned earlier in the chapter, when reviewing objective data, it is essential that potential sources of contamination (e.g., shift, equipment, training, coworkers, geographic area) be considered.

Reading critical incident logs After obtaining objective data, the supervisor should go back and read all of the critical incidents written for an employee. Reading these incidents should reduce the primacy, recency, and attention to unusual information errors.

Completing the rating form Once critical incident logs have been read and objective data reviewed, the supervisor is ready to assign performance appraisal ratings. While making these ratings, the supervisor must be careful not to make common rating errors involving distribution, halo, proximity, and contrast.

Distribution errors A common type of error in evaluating employee performance involves the distribution of ratings on a rating scale; such errors are known as **distribution errors**. One kind of distribution error is called **leniency error** because certain raters tend to rate every employee at the upper end of the scale, regardless of the actual performance of the employee. A related error is **central-tendency error**, which results in a supervisor rating every employee in the middle of the scale. Still another error, **strictness error**, rates every employee at the low end of the scale.

These types of errors pose problems for an organization because two employees doing equal work will receive different ratings if one employee is supervised by a lenient rater and another by a strict rater. This problem can be eliminated partly by having several people rate each employee, although this is not often feasible, especially in small branch offices with only one manager or supervisor.

Halo errors A **halo error** occurs when a rater allows either a single attribute or an overall impression of an individual to affect the ratings that she makes on each relevant job dimension. For example, a teacher might think that a student is highly articulate. Because of that, the teacher might rate the student as being intelligent and industrious when, in fact, the student's grades are below average. In this case, the instructor has allowed the student's articulateness to cloud her judgment of the student's other abilities. Halo effects occur especially when the rater has little knowledge of the job and is less familiar with the person being rated (Kozlowski, Kirsch, & Chao, 1986).

Usually, halo error is statistically determined by correlating the ratings for each dimension with those for the other dimensions. If they are highly correlated, halo error is often said to have occurred. But several industrial psychologists have argued that many times consistent ratings across several dimensions indicate not error but actual employee performance. Thus a teacher who is rated highly in classroom teaching, ability to work with students, knowledge, and fairness of grading actually may excel in those things. But proponents of the halo-error explanation would argue that the instructor is friendly and so well liked by her students that she receives high ratings on the other dimensions when, in fact, she may not have shown a high level of knowledge in her subject matter.

Halo errors may or may not be a serious problem (Balzer & Sulsky, 1992), but they can be reduced by having supervisors rate each trait at separate times. That is, the supervisor might rate the employee on attendance one day and then rate her on dependability the next day (W. H. Cooper, 1981). Of course, in reality, such a practice is seldom possible. Examples of halo, leniency, and strictness errors are shown in Exhibit 15-11.

EXHIBIT 15-11

Examples of Rating Errors

Leniency Error

Norm Nixon
Cooperation 1 2 3 4 ⑤
Knowledge 1 2 3 4 ⑤
Leadership 1 2 3 4 ⑤

Walt Davis
Cooperation 1 2 3 4 ⑤
Knowledge 1 2 3 4 ⑤
Leadership 1 2 3 4 ⑤

Earvin Johnson
Cooperation 1 2 3 4 ⑤
Knowledge 1 2 3 4 ⑤
Leadership 1 2 3 4 ⑤

John Lucas
Cooperation 1 2 3 4 ⑤
Knowledge 1 2 3 4 ⑤
Leadership 1 2 3 4 ⑤

Strictness Error

Norm Nixon
Cooperation ① 2 3 4 5
Knowledge ① 2 3 4 5
Leadership ① 2 3 4 5

Walt Davis
Cooperation ① 2 3 4 5
Knowledge ① 2 3 4 5
Leadership ① 2 3 4 5

Earvin Johnson
Cooperation ① 2 3 4 5
Knowledge ① 2 3 4 5
Leadership ① 2 3 4 5

John Lucas
Cooperation ① 2 3 4 5
Knowledge ① 2 3 4 5
Leadership ① 2 3 4 5

Halo Error

Norm Nixon
Cooperation 1 2 3 4 ⑤
Knowledge 1 2 3 4 ⑤
Leadership 1 2 3 4 ⑤

Walt Davis
Cooperation 1 2 ③ 4 5
Knowledge 1 2 ③ 4 5
Leadership 1 2 ③ 4 5

Earvin Johnson
Cooperation 1 2 3 4 ⑤
Knowledge 1 2 3 4 ⑤
Leadership 1 2 3 4 ⑤

John Lucas
Cooperation ① 2 3 4 5
Knowledge ① 2 3 4 5
Leadership ① 2 3 4 5

Proximity errors Proximity errors occur when a rating made on one dimension affects the rating made on the dimension that immediately follows it on the rating scale. The difference between this error and halo error is in the cause of the error and the number of dimensions that are affected. With halo error, all dimensions are affected by an overall impression of the employee. With proximity error, only the dimensions physically located nearest a particular dimension on the rating scale are affected; the reason for the effect, in fact, *is* the close physical proximity of the dimension rather than an overall impression.

Contrast errors The performance rating one person receives can be influenced by the performance of a previously evaluated person (Bravo & Kravitz, 1996). For example, a bank manager has six employees who are evaluated twice a year—on February 5 and again on August 5. The manager makes the evaluations in alphabetical order, starting with Joan Carr and then going to Donna Chan. Joan Carr is the best employee the bank has ever had, and she receives the highest possible rating on each dimension. After evaluating Carr, the manager then evaluates Chan. When compared to Carr, Chan is not nearly as effective an employee. Thus, Chan receives lower ratings than she might normally receive simply because she has been evaluated immediately after Carr. Her performance has been contrasted to Carr's performance rather than to some objective standard.

Such **contrast errors** can also occur between separate performance evaluations of the same person. That is, the ratings received on one performance appraisal will affect the ratings made on an appraisal 6 months later. For example, an employee's performance during the first 6 months of the year is "excellent," and she receives outstanding performance ratings. For some reason, the employee's actual behavior in the next 6 months is only "good." What type of performance ratings will she receive? Based on the results of a study by K. R. Murphy, Gannett, Herr, and Chen (1986), the answer probably is that her ratings will be less than "good." In contrast to her initial excellent performance, the employee's subsequent performance (which may indeed have been "good") appeared to be lower than it actually was.

Contrast effects occur only when the person making the evaluation actually sees the employee perform (Smither, Reilly, & Buda, 1988) and rates the employee (Summer and Knight, 1996) during both rating periods. Even if a new supervisor reads that an employee's previous evaluations were excellent but she observes poor performance by the employee, she will probably continue to give excellent ratings— even though the employee's performance deteriorated. Smither and his colleagues call this rating error **assimilation**.

> **PROJECT D** *Rating Errors*
> To get a better feel for rating errors, complete Project D at the end of this chapter.

LOW RELIABILITY ACROSS RATERS

As shown back in Exhibit 15-3, two people rating the same employee seldom agree with one another (Conway & Huffcut, 1997; Viswesvaran, Ones, & Schmidt, 1996). This lack of reliability has three major reasons. First, raters often commit the rating errors (e.g., halo, leniency) previously discussed. Thus, if one rater engages in halo error and another in contrast error, it is not surprising that their ratings of the same employee would be different.

Second, raters often have very different standards and ideas about the ideal employee. For example, we recently conducted a performance appraisal workshop for a police department. After viewing a video clip of an officer handling a disturbance call, one sergeant rated the officer's performance as excellent and another rated the officer's performance as terrible.

When asked about their different ratings, the one sergeant indicated that he thought officers should be aggressive and take command of a situation whereas the other sergeant thought officers should be more citizen-oriented. Thus, the same employee behavior elicited two very different ratings because each sergeant had a different "prototype" of the ideal cop.

Third, as mentioned earlier in the chapter, two different raters may actually see very different behaviors by the same employee. For example, a desk sergeant might see more administrative and paperwork-related behaviors whereas a field sergeant may see more law enforcement-related behaviors. Thus, different ratings by the two sergeants may simply reflect the fact that each has observed the officer perform in very different situations.

One way to reduce the number of rating errors and increase reliability is to train the people who will be making the performance evaluations. Research has indicated that training supervisors to become aware of the various rating errors and how to avoid them often increases accuracy (Smither, Barry, & Reilly, 1989), reduces leniency and halo errors (Bernardin & Buckley, 1981), increases the validity of tests validated against the ratings (Pursell, Dossett, & Latham, 1980), and increases employee satisfaction with the ratings (Ivancevich, 1982). This is especially true when the training technique uses discussion, practice in rating, and feedback about rating accuracy rather than lecture (D. E. Smith, 1986). These training effects, however, are short-lived (Noble, 1997) unless additional training and feedback are provided.

SAMPLING PROBLEMS

Recency effect Performance appraisals are typically conducted once or twice a year. The evaluation is designed to cover all of the behaviors that have taken place during the previous 6 months to a year. Research has demonstrated, however, that recent behaviors are given more weight in the performance evaluation than behaviors that occurred during the first few months of the evaluation period. This **recency effect** penalizes workers who performed well during most of the period but tailed off toward the end, and it rewards workers who save their best work until just before the evaluation. It seems that students are well aware of the recency effect when they argue that the high score on their final exam should carry more weight than the lower scores on previous exams!

Infrequent observation As shown back in Exhibit 15-2, another problem that affects performance appraisals is that many managers or supervisors do not have the opportunity to observe a representative sample of employee behavior. **Infrequent observation** occurs for two reasons. First, managers are often so busy with their own work that they often have no time to "walk the floor" and observe their employees' behavior. Instead, they make inferences based on completed work or employee personality traits. A good example involves a teacher who completes a reference form for a student. Reference forms commonly ask about characteristics such as the applicant's ability to cooperate or to get along with others. The teacher must base her evaluation on the term papers that she has seen and the student's test grades. Rarely does she have the opportunity to watch the student "get along with" or "cooperate with others." Instead, she surmises that because a group project was turned in on time and received an excellent grade, the student must have cooperated and gotten along well with other group members.

Employees often act differently around a supervisor than around other workers, which is the second reason why managers usually do not make accurate observations. When the supervisor is absent, an employee may break rules, show up late, or work slowly. But when the boss is around, the employee becomes a model worker. In the eyes of the supervisor, the employee is doing an excellent job; the other workers, however, know better.

COGNITIVE PROCESSING OF OBSERVED BEHAVIOR

Observation of behavior As Exhibits 15-12 and 15-13 show, just because an employee's behavior is observed does not guarantee that it will be properly remembered or recalled during the performance appraisal review. In fact, research (W. H. Cooper, 1981) indicates that raters recall those behaviors that are consistent with their general impression of an employee (a halo). And the greater the time interval between the actual behavior and the performance rating, the greater the probability that halo errors (Nathan & Lord, 1983) and distortion errors (Murphy, Martin, & Garcia, 1982) occur.

Emotional state The amount of stress under which a supervisor operates also affects her performance ratings. Srinivas and Motowidlo (1987) found that raters who were placed in a stressful situation produced ratings with more errors than did raters who were not under stress. This finding is important because performance evaluations are often conducted hurriedly as supervisors evaluate employee performance so that they can return to their "real" work. Methods for reducing this problem will be discussed later in this chapter.

Raters who like the person being rated may be more lenient (Varma, DeNisi, & Peters, 1996) and less accurate in rating employees than are raters who neither like nor dislike their employees (Cardy & Dobbins, 1986). But this does not mean that a person who is liked will always receive higher ratings than someone who is disliked. The rater may overcompensate in an effort to be "fair." The rater's feelings, or **affect**, toward an employee may interfere with the cognitive processing of actual performance information.

Bias Research has also indicated that **racial bias** exists in performance evaluations. Kraiger and Ford (1985) conducted a meta-analysis of 74 studies and found that White raters gave higher performance ratings to White employees and that Black raters gave higher ratings to Black employees. Interestingly, this bias occurred only with studies involving real organizations—laboratory research seldom reveals racial bias in rating.

Communicating Appraisal Results to Employees

As was stated in the beginning of this chapter, perhaps the most important use of performance evaluation data is to provide feedback to employees and assess their strengths and weaknesses so that further training can be implemented. Although this feedback and training should be an ongoing process, the semiannual **performance appraisal review** might be the best time to formally discuss employee performance. Furthermore, holding a formal review interview places the organization on better legal ground in the event of a lawsuit (H. S. Field & Holley, 1982).

Normally, in most organizations a supervisor spends a few minutes with employees every 6 months to *tell* them about the scores they received during the most recent evaluation period. This process is probably the norm because most managers do not like to judge others, and this dislike prompts them to complete the evaluation process as quickly as possible.

Furthermore, seldom does evaluating employees benefit the supervisor. The best scenario is to hear no complaints and the worst scenario is a lawsuit. In fact, one study demonstrated that dissatisfaction and a decrease in organizational commitment occurs even when an employee receives an evaluation that is "satisfactory" but not "outstanding" (Pearce & Porter, 1986). Finally, in the "tell and sell" approach to performance appraisal interviews, a supervisor "tells" an employee everything she has done poorly and then "sells" her on the ways in which she can improve. This method, however, accomplishes little.

Research suggests that certain techniques can be used to make the performance appraisal interview more effective: time, scheduling, and preparation.

EXHIBIT 15-12

Factors Affecting Information Loss

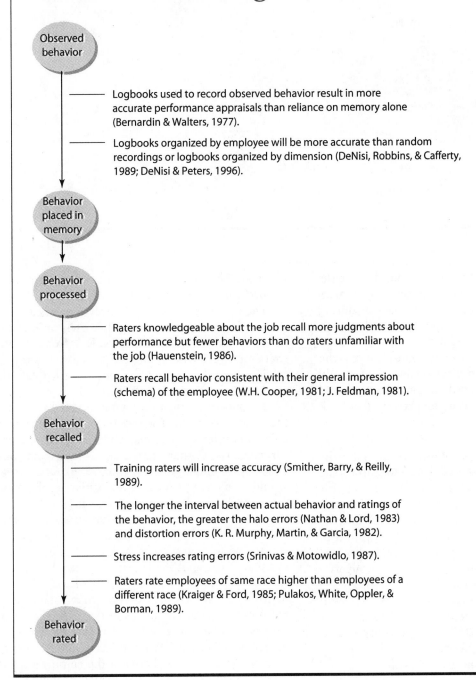

Observed behavior

——— Logbooks used to record observed behavior result in more accurate performance appraisals than reliance on memory alone (Bernardin & Walters, 1977).

——— Logbooks organized by employee will be more accurate than random recordings or logbooks organized by dimension (DeNisi, Robbins, & Cafferty, 1989; DeNisi & Peters, 1996).

Behavior placed in memory

Behavior processed

——— Raters knowledgeable about the job recall more judgments about performance but fewer behaviors than do raters unfamiliar with the job (Hauenstein, 1986).

——— Raters recall behavior consistent with their general impression (schema) of the employee (W.H. Cooper, 1981; J. Feldman, 1981).

Behavior recalled

——— Training raters will increase accuracy (Smither, Barry, & Reilly, 1989).

——— The longer the interval between actual behavior and ratings of the behavior, the greater the halo errors (Nathan & Lord, 1983) and distortion errors (K. R. Murphy, Martin, & Garcia, 1982).

——— Stress increases rating errors (Srinivas & Motowidlo, 1987).

——— Raters rate employees of same race higher than employees of a different race (Kraiger & Ford, 1985; Pulakos, White, Oppler, & Borman, 1989).

Behavior rated

PRIOR TO THE INTERVIEW

Allocating time Both the supervisor and the employee must have time to prepare for the review interview. Both should be allowed at least 1 hour to prepare before an interview and at least 1 hour for the interview itself.

Scheduling the interview The interview location should be in a neutral place that ensures privacy and allows the supervisor and employee to face one another without a desk between them as a communication barrier. Performance appraisal review interviews should be scheduled at least once every 6 months for most employees and more often for new employees.

EXHIBIT 15-13

Factors Affecting Performance

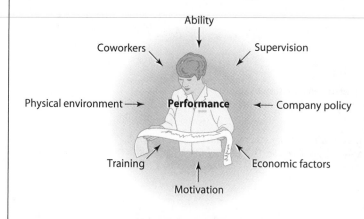

Review interviews are commonly scheduled 6 months after an employee begins working for the organization. If this date comes at a bad time (such as during the Christmas season, a busy time for retail stores), the interview should be scheduled for a more convenient time. It is important to note that although the *formal* performance appraisal review occurs only once or twice a year, informal progress checks should be held throughout the year to provide feedback (Rhoads, 1997).

Preparing for the interview While preparing for the interview, the supervisor should review the ratings she has assigned to the employee and the reasons for those ratings. This step is important because the quality of feedback given to employees will affect their satisfaction with the entire performance appraisal process (Mount, 1983). Furthermore, employees perceive and react to the amount of time that a supervisor prepares for the interview (P. King, 1984).

Meanwhile, the employee should rate her own performance using the same format as the supervisor (Laumeyer & Beebe, 1988). The employee also should write down specific reasons and examples that support the ratings she gives herself.

DURING THE INTERVIEW

At the outset of the interview, the supervisor should communicate the following: (1) the role of performance appraisal—that making decisions about salary increases and terminations is not its only purpose; (2) how the performance appraisal was conducted; and (3) how the evaluation process was accomplished. It is advisable that the supervisor also communicate her own feelings about the importance of the performance appraisal process.

The review process is probably best begun with the employee communicating her own ratings and her justification for those ratings. Research indicates that employees who are actively involved in the interview from the start will be more satisfied with the results (Burke, Weitzel, & Weir, 1978).

The supervisor then communicates her ratings and the reasons for them. The supervisor should limit this communication to statements about behavior and performance rather than traits that are or are not possessed by the employee (D. Arthur, 1996). Of course, it would be nice to provide only positive feedback because employees then are more satisfied with their reviews and often develop negative attitudes toward management if feedback is negative. But few employees are perfect, and some negative feedback is inevitable. Because of this, positive feedback generally should be given first because employees will likely try to avoid negative feedback in order to maintain a positive self-image. Furthermore, supervisors tend to avoid negative feedback in an effort to reduce the chance of interpersonal conflict (Waung & Highhouse, 1997). Any major differences between the employee's self-ratings and those given by the supervisor should be discussed until both understand the differences.

The next step is perhaps the most important. Because few employees receive perfect evaluations, it is essential to discuss the reasons why an employee's performance is not considered to be perfect. The employee may lack some knowledge as to how to perform the job properly, may have been assigned too many duties, or may have outside problems that affect her work performance.

The supervisor's acknowledgment that there may be external reasons for an employee's poor performance can increase the employee's satisfaction with the review and allow her to perceive the feedback and evaluation as accurate and helpful. In addition, it will help the employee understand and appreciate the supervisor's perceptions. Feedback should be candid, specific, and behavioral rather than personal (Hequet, 1994). Awareness and acknowledgment of external factors for performance is especially important because we have a tendency, called the fundamental attribution error (see Chapter 9), to attribute others' failure or poor performance to personal rather than situational factors.

Once the problems have been identified, the next and most difficult task is to find solutions to the problems. What can the supervisor do to help? What can the organization do? What can the employee do? The idea here is that solutions to the problems result from joint effort. Too often, we attribute poor performance as being solely the fault of the employee, when, in fact, performance is affected by many factors (see Exhibit 15-13).

At the conclusion of the interview, goals should be mutually set for future performance and behavior, and both supervisor and employee should understand how these goals will be met. Goals and goal setting were thoroughly discussed in Chapters 3 and 12. For now, however, we should remember that goals should be concrete, reasonable, and set by both employee and supervisor.

PROJECT E *Performance Appraisal Reviews*
To practice conducting a performance appraisal review interview, complete Project E at the end of this chapter.

■ TERMINATING EMPLOYEES

The primary use of performance appraisal results is to provide feedback to employees about their behavior, and the results are also used to make positive personnel decisions such as raises and promotions. Unfortunately, there are times when managers have to terminate an employee's employment, and performance appraisal results are used then as well. Over the next few pages, we will discuss the legal aspects of terminating an employee.

Employment-at-Will Doctrine

There is a big difference between terminating an employee in the public sector versus the private sector. In the private sector, the **employment-at-will doctrine** in most states allows employers freedom to fire an employee without a reason—*at will*. The idea behind employment at will is that because employees are free to quit their jobs at will, so too are organizations free to terminate an employee at will (Ballam, 1995). This doctrine has some limitations:

- *State law* Some states such as California and New York have laws that an employee can only be fired for cause—breaking a rule or an inability to perform.

- *Provisions of federal or state law* Employees cannot be fired for reasons protected by federal or state law. For example, an employer cannot fire an employee because she is female, pregnant, nonwhite, or over the age of 40.

- *Public policy/interest* Employers cannot terminate an employee for exercising a legal duty such as jury duty or refusing to violate the law or professional ethics. For example, a large savings and loan institution ordered one of its appraisers to appraise homes higher than their actual value so that its customers could qualify to finance property. Citing federal regulations and professional ethics against inflating property values, the employee refused the company order. After being terminated, the employee successfully filed a lawsuit (one of over 200 filed by employees against this institution) claiming that he had been fired for refusing to violate the law and the ethical standards of his profession.

- *Contracts* Obviously, if an individual employee has a signed employment contract stipulating a particular period of employment, an organization cannot fire the employee without cause. Likewise, unions enter into collective bargaining agreements (contracts) with employers that also limit or negate employment at will.

- *Implied contracts* Employment at will is nullified if an employer implies that an employee "has a job for life" or can be fired only for certain reasons. For example, if an interviewer tells an applicant "at this company, all you have to do is keep your nose clean to keep your job," the employer will not be able to terminate the employee for minor rules infractions or for poor performance.

- *Covenants of good faith and fair dealing* Though employers are generally free to hire and fire at will, the courts have ruled that employers must still act in good faith and deal fairly with an employee. These rulings have been based on an item in the Uniform Commercial Code stating "Every contract . . . imposes an obligation of good faith in its performance or enforcement" and the fact that courts consider employment decisions to be a form of a contract.

EXHIBIT 15-14

Sample Employment-at-Will Statement

I understand that, if employed, I have the right to end my employment with Taflinger Industries. Likewise, I understand that my employment with Taflinger Industries is not for any definite period of time, and Taflinger Industries has the right to terminate my employment with or without cause and with or without notice. I understand that no representative of Taflinger Industries is authorized to imply any contract for permanent employment.

To protect their right to use a policy of employment at will, most organizations include **employment-at-will statements,** such as that shown in Exhibit 15-14, in their job applications and employee handbooks. These statements usually hold up in court (Jenner, 1994) and employees seem to not challenge them (Hilgert, 1991).

Legal Reasons for Terminating Employees

In situations not covered by employment at will, there are only three reasons that an employee can be legally terminated: violation of company rules, inability to perform, or an economically caused reduction in force (layoffs).

VIOLATION OF COMPANY RULES

Courts consider five factors in determining the legality of a decision to terminate an employee for violating company rules. The first factor is that a rule against a particular behavior must actually exist. Though this may seem obvious, organizations often have unwritten rules governing employee behavior. These unwritten rules, however, will not hold up in court. For example, a manufacturer fired an employee for wearing a gun under his jacket at work. The employee successfully appealed on the grounds that even though common sense would say that guns should not be brought to work, the company did not have a written rule against it.

If a rule exists, a company must prove that the employee knew the rule. Rules can be communicated orally during employee orientation and staff meetings and in writing in the handbooks, newsletters, bulletin boards, and paycheck stuffers. Rules communicated in handbooks are the most legally defen-sible. To prove that an employee knew a rule, organizations require employees to sign statements that they received information about the rule, read the rule, and understand the rule.

The third factor is the ability of the employer to prove that an employee actually violated the rule. Proof is accomplished through such means as witnesses, video recordings, and job samples. Human resource professionals almost have to be detectives because proving rule violations is often not easy. For example, two supervisors saw an employee stagger into work and could clearly smell alcohol on her breath. She was terminated for violating the company rule against drinking. During her appeal of the termination, she claimed that she staggered because she had the flu and what the supervisors smelled was cough syrup rather than alcohol. The employee won the appeal. As a result of this case, the company now has an on-site nurse and Breathalyzer tests are administered to employees suspected of using alcohol at work.

The fourth factor considered by the courts is the extent to which the rule has been equally enforced. That is, if other employees violated the rule but were not terminated, terminating an employee for a particular rule violation may not be legal. This factor poses a dilemma for many organizations. Because courts look at consistency, lawyers advise organizations to fire any employee who violates a rule. To not fire a rule breaker sets a precedent making termination of future rule breakers more difficult. There are many times when a good employee breaks a rule, a situation that normally would result in termination. However, because the employee is highly valued, the organization does not want to fire the employee.

Such a situation occurred at a bank. In violation of a bank rule, a teller did not ask for the ID of a customer who cashed what turned out to be a forged check. The bank was torn as to what it should do.

Because the employee was one of their best tellers, the bank did not want to fire her. However, not firing her in this case would increase the chance of losing a future lawsuit if the bank terminated another employee for doing the same thing. The bank's unusual decision was to terminate the employee, but it called a competitor, told it of the situation, and asked if it would hire her—which it did.

The fifth and final factor is the extent to which the punishment fits the crime. Employees in their probationary period (usually their first 6 months) can be immediately fired for a rule infraction. For more tenured employees, however, the organization must make a reasonable attempt to change the person's behavior through **progressive discipline** (Falcone, 1997). The longer an employee has been with an organization, the greater the number of steps that must be taken to correct her behavior. Discipline can begin with something simple such as counseling or an oral warning, progress to a written warning or probation, and end with steps such as reductions in pay, demotions, or termination.

For violations of some rules, progressive discipline is not always necessary. It is probably safe to say that an employer can terminate an employee who steals money or shoots someone at work.

INABILITY TO PERFORM

Employees can also be terminated for an inability to perform the job. To do so though, an organization will need to prove that the employee could not perform the job and that progressive discipline was taken to give the employee an opportunity to improve. For an employer to survive a court challenge to terminating a poor performing employee, it must first demonstrate that a reasonable standard of performance was communicated to the employee. The organization must next demonstrate a documented failure to meet the standard. Such documentation can include critical incident logs and work samples (e.g., poorly typed letters for a secretary, improperly hemmed pants for a tailor).

A properly designed performance appraisal system is the key to legally terminating an employee. Legal performance appraisal systems (M. L. Smith, 1993):

- Are based on a job analysis.
- Have concrete, relevant standards that have been communicated to employees.
- Involve multiple behavioral measures of performance.
- Include several raters, each of whom has received training.
- Are standardized and formal.
- Provide the opportunity for an employee to appeal.

REDUCTION IN FORCE (LAYOFF)

Employees can be terminated if it is in the best economic interests of a organization to do so. Reductions in force, more commonly called layoffs, have been used by the vast majority of Fortune 500 companies in the past decade (Byrne, 1994). In cases of large layoffs or plant closings, the Worker Adjustment and Retraining Notification Act (WARN) requires that organizations provide workers with at least 60 days notice. Though layoffs are designed to save money, research indicates that not only do force reductions have a devastating effect on employees (Leana & Feldman, 1992), but they often do not result in the desired financial savings (Byrne, 1994).

The Termination Meeting

PRIOR TO THE MEETING

Once a decision has been made to terminate an employee, Connolly (1986) advises that certain steps should be taken to prepare for the meeting in which the decision will be communicated to the employee. The first step is to ensure that the legal process has been followed. For example, if an organization is about to terminate an employee for a rule violation, it must be sure that a rule actually existed, that the employee knew the rule, the organization has proof that the rule was violated, progressive discipline was used, and the rule was applied equally to all employees. An important responsibility for human resource professionals is to ensure that a termination decision is legally defensible.

The next step is to determine how much help, if any, the organization wants to offer the employee. Forms of help can include references, severance pay, and outplacement assistance. Usually, greater levels of help are given to employees who sign agreements to not sue the organization.

The final step is to schedule an appropriate place and time for the meeting to occur. The meeting should be held in a neutral, private location (DuBose, 1994). To avoid potential damage caused by a hostile reaction to the termination decision, the meeting should not be held in a supervisor's office. Rather than late on Friday afternoon, as is traditional, the meeting should take place on a Monday or Tuesday so that the employee has an opportunity to seek advice and the organization has a chance to talk to its employees (Scrivner, 1995). When a termination is made on a Friday afternoon, the employee is unable to contact sources of help over the weekend. Likewise, the terminated employee has all weekend to get on the phone to tell her side of the story to other employees while the organization must wait until Monday to refute the gossip.

DURING THE MEETING

During the meeting, the supervisor should get to the point about terminating the employee. The employee usually knows why she has been called in, and there is no reason to prolong the agony. The supervisor should rationally state the reasons for the decision, express gratitude for the employee's efforts (if sincere), and offer whatever assistance the organization intends to provide. Administrative duties such as obtaining copies of keys and completing paperwork are then performed. Finally, the employee is asked to gather personal belongings and is escorted out the door.

We realize the advice in the above paragraph sounds cold. However, terminating an employee is a difficult task, and little can be done to make it pleasant. If you have ever ended a romantic relationship, you will understand the feelings that go into terminating an employee. It is an emotional time, and the key is to be brief and professional (Pollan & Levine, 1994).

AFTER THE MEETING

Once the meeting is over, the natural reaction of the supervisor is to feel guilty. To relieve some of this guilt, a supervisor should review the facts—she gave the employee every chance to improve, but the employee chose not to. A human resource professional for Valleydale Foods tells employees "Through your behavior, you fired yourself. I'm just completing the paperwork."

When an employee is fired, other employees will be tense. Consequently, it is important to be honest with the other employees about what happened (Marchetti, 1997); at the same time, negative statements about the terminated employee's character must be avoided.

CHAPTER RECAP

In this chapter you learned that:

- Job descriptions are important and should contain detailed information about a job.
- The use of 360-degree feedback is increasing.
- There are five steps in creating a performance appraisal system: (1) determine the reasons for performance evaluation; (2) create an instrument to evaluate performance; (3) explain the system to those who will use it; (4) evaluate employee performance; and (5) review the results of the evaluation with the employee.
- Common rating errors such as leniency, central tendency, strictness, halo, proximity, contrast, recency, and infrequent observation of behavior hinder the accuracy of performance appraisal results.

- Important factors in the success of this discussion include scheduling the review to eliminate or minimize interruptions, letting the employee discuss her feelings and thoughts, and mutually setting goals for improvements in future performance.
- In organizations not subject to employment at will, employees can only be terminated for violating a company rule, inability to perform, or as part of a force reduction.

Critical Thinking Questions

1. Why are job descriptions so important?

2. How should a job description be written?

3. What is the most important purpose for performance appraisal?

4. What problems might result from using 360-degree feedback?

5. What is the best way to communicate performance appraisal results to employees?

6. Is the employment-at-will doctrine a good idea?

WEB SITES

For further information, log on to the following web sites.

www.mapnp.org/library/staffing/specify/job_desc.htm
Provides links to hundreds of sources about writing job descriptions.

www.work911.com/performance/art.htm
Provides links to sources about conducting performance appraisals.

KEY TERMS

Affect Feelings or emotion.

Assimilation A type of rating error in which raters base their rating of an employee during one rating period on the ratings that they gave the employee in a previous rating period.

Central-tendency error A type of rating error in which a rater consistently rates all employees in the middle of the scale, regardless of their actual levels of performance.

Contamination The condition in which a criterion score is affected by things other than those under the control of the employee.

Contrast error A type of rating error in which the rating of the performance level of one employee affects the ratings given to the next employee being rated.

Critical incidents A method of performance appraisal in which the supervisor records employee behaviors that were observed on the job and rates the employee on the basis of that record.

Dictionary of Occupational Titles (DOT) A document produced by the federal government that contains thousands of job descriptions.

Distribution errors Rating errors in which a rater will use only a certain part of a rating scale when evaluating employee performance.

Employment-at-will doctrine The opinion of courts in most states that employers have the right to hire and fire an employee at will and without any specific cause.

Employment-at-will statements Statements in employment applications and company manuals reaffirming an organization's right to hire and fire at will.

Errors Deviations from a standard of quality.

Forced distribution A performance appraisal method in which a predetermined percentage of employees are placed into a number of performance categories.

Halo error A type of rating error that occurs when raters allow either a single attribute or an overall impression of an individual to affect the ratings that they make on each relevant job dimension.

Infrequent observation The idea that supervisors do not see most of an employee's behavior.

Job description A 2–5 page formal summary of a job.

Job specifications The knowledge, skills, abilities, and other characteristics (KSAOs) needed to perform a job.

Leniency error A type of rating error in which a rater consistently gives all employees high ratings, regardless of their performance levels.

Performance appraisal review A meeting between a supervisor and a subordinate for the purpose of discussing performance appraisal results.

Peter Principle The idea that organizations tend to promote good employees until they reach the level at which they are not competent.

Progressive discipline Providing employees with punishments of increasing severity in order to change behavior.

Proximity error A type of rating error in which a rating made on one dimension influences the rating made on the dimension that immediately follows it on the rating scale.

Quality A type of objective criterion used to measure job performance by comparing a job behavior with a standard.

Quantity A type of objective criterion used to measure job performance by counting the number of relevant job behaviors that occur.

Racial bias The tendency to give members of a particular race lower evaluation ratings than are justified by their actual performance or to give members of one race lower ratings than members of another race.

Rank order A method of performance appraisal in which employees are ranked in order from best to worst.

Recency effect The tendency for supervisors to recall and place more weight on recent behaviors when they evaluate performance.

Strictness error A type of rating error in which a rater consistently gives all employees low ratings, regardless of their actual levels of performance.

360-degree feedback A performance appraisal system in which feedback is obtained from multiple sources such as supervisors, subordinates, and peers.

PRACTICE EXAM

1. The first step in the performance appraisal process is to:
   a. identify relevant criteria
   b. determine the reasons for conducting a performance appraisal
   c. choose methods for measuring the criteria
   d. explain the system to both supervisors and employees

2. The performance review interview should start with:
   a. the employee communicating her own ratings
   b. the supervisor communicating her ratings
   c. negative feedback
   d. positive feedback

3. The most important use for performance evaluation is:
   a. promotions and salary increases
   b. compensation
   c. needs assessment and evaluation
   d. training and feedback

4. A job analysis will help determine if a criterion is:
   a. reliable
   b. congruent with organizational needs
   c. relevant
   d. free from contamination

5. The _____ code should be placed beneath the title on a job description.
   a. FJA   b. Morse
   c. DOT   d. CIT

6. Which of the following is **not** an example of an objective criterion?
   a. quantity of work   b. quality of work
   c. attendance   d. all of the above are objective measures

7. Quality of work is measured by _____ which are deviations from _____.

a. errors, standards   b. errors, norms

c. standards, errors   d. standards, norms

8. Which of the following measures of attendance would *not* be appropriate for a performance appraisal system designed for the purpose of salary increases?

    a. absenteeism   b. tenure

    c. tardiness   d. all of the above would be appropriate

9. The most common type of performance appraisal is(are):

    a. supervisor ratings   b. quantity measures

    c. quality measures   d. attendance measures

10. With _____, a predetermined percentage of employees are placed into rating categories.

    a. graphic rating scales   b. rank order

    c. paired comparisons   d. forced distribution

11. Job specifications are placed in the _____ section of a job description.

    a. brief summary

    b. work context

    c. performance standards

    d. personal requirements

12. Raters commit the _____ error when they allow an overall impression to affect ratings made on each dimension.

a. leniency   b. central-tendency

c. strictness   d. halo

13. Which of the following is *not* true about peer ratings?

    a. They can predict the success of promoted employees

    b. They are most reliable when the peer is similar to the person being rated

    c. They are commonly used by organizations

    d. They are highly correlated with supervisor ratings

14. Self-appraisals of performance are:

    a. best used for performance appraisal review purposes

    b. commonly used

    c. correlated highly with actual performance

    d. not subject to leniency

15. A rater who rates every employee as average is probably committing the _____ error.

    a. leniency

    b. central-tendency

    c. strictness

    d. halo

Critiquing a Job Description

The purpose of this exercise is to familiarize you with the correct form for the various parts of a job description. On the next two pages, you will find a job description that contains several errors. See if you can identify the errors.

_____

_____

_____

_____

_____

_____

_____

_____

_____

_____

_____

_____

_____

_____

_____

_____

_____

_____

_____

_____

_____

_____

_____

_____

Restaurant Associate
Nora's Scarf 'n Barf Restaurant

Job Summary

The Restaurant Associate is responsible for performing a variety of tasks involved in the preparation and sales of food. Duties include preparing food, cooking food, taking customer orders, and cleaning the restaurant.

Work Activities

Food Preparation

- Removes buns from boxes and places on food preparation table
- Takes meat and chicken from the freezer and places on table to thaw
- Takes condiments from the refrigerator and places them on food preparation table
- Inspects meat and chicken to make sure they are safe to eat
- Handles problems

Cooking

- Places fries and breaded fish patties into vat and removes when high-pitched alarm goes off
- Cooks hamburgers, chicken, and hot dogs on the grill
- Puts grilled food onto bun and adds requested condiments

Cleaning

- Wipes counter and tables as needed
- Cleans the grill at the end of each shift
- Changes cooking oil when the bottom of the vat can't be seen or after several customer complaints
- Uses RK-9 to clean tables after manager indicates a 10-6 has occurred
- Mops
- Cleans cooking utensils at end of shift
- Sweeps and cleans parking lot area

Tools and Equipment Used

- Deep-fat fryer
- Grill
- Cleaning materials (e.g., mop, rags, cleanser)
- Cash register
- Common cooking utensils (e.g., spatulas, tongs)

Materials and Substances Exposed To

- RK-9
- Wesson cooking oil
- Meat, poultry, chicken, fish, potatoes, bread
- Drano

Job Context

The Restaurant Associate works an 8-hour shift, 5 days per week. The actual days and times worked vary based on a rotating schedule. Psychological stress is high when the restaurant is busy or customers get angry. Physical stress is moderate as the Restaurant Associate spends all 8 hours standing, with extensive bending and leaning. At times, crates weighing 80 pounds must be lifted.

Performance Appraisal

The Restaurant Associate is evaluated each month on the standard Scarf 'n Barf performance appraisal instrument. Bonuses can be earned by having few customer complaints, no shrinkage, and no citations for health or safety violations.

Personal Requirements

Upon Hire

- Ability to count change back to customers
- No mental or physical problems
- Must be bondable
- Excellent communication skills
- Be flexible

After Hire

- Knowledge of restaurant menu and recipes
- Knowledge of restaurant policies

Writing a Job Description

You have learned how to write a job description. This exercise gives you a chance to apply that knowledge. To complete this exercise:

1. Pair up with another person in your class.
2. Take turns interviewing each other about jobs that each of you currently has or had at one time.
3. Use the information from the interviews to write a job description similar to that found in your text.
4. You will probably want to type your job description so that it looks professional.

Notes:

_____

_____

_____

_____

_____

_____

_____

_____

_____

_____

_____

_____

_____

_____

_____

_____

_____

360-Degree Feedback

The practice of 360-degree feedback—having a variety of sources evaluate an employee's performance—is increasingly popular. Imagine that you have been asked to design a 360-degree-feedback system for servers (waiters, waitresses) in a restaurant. In the space below, indicate what sources you would use to evaluate performance and what percentage of the server's overall evaluation should come from each source.

Rating Source   **Percentage**

_____   _____

_____   _____

_____   _____

_____   _____

_____   _____

_____   _____

_____   _____

_____   _____

Comments

_____

_____

_____

_____

_____

_____

_____

_____

Rating Errors

Think of four instructors that you had in the last year. Write their names in the places below and then rate each instructor on the five dimensions.

Instructor A: _____

Knowledge of subject	1	2	3	4	5
Fairness of grades	1	2	3	4	5
Organization	1	2	3	4	5
Speaking skills	1	2	3	4	5
Interest in students	1	2	3	4	5

Instructor B: _____

Knowledge of subject	1	2	3	4	5
Fairness of grades	1	2	3	4	5
Organization	1	2	3	4	5
Speaking skills	1	2	3	4	5
Interest in students	1	2	3	4	5

Instructor C: _____

Knowledge of subject	1	2	3	4	5
Fairness of grades	1	2	3	4	5
Organization	1	2	3	4	5
Speaking skills	1	2	3	4	5
Interest in students	1	2	3	4	5

Instructor D: _____

Knowledge of subject	1	2	3	4	5
Fairness of grades	1	2	3	4	5
Organization	1	2	3	4	5
Speaking skills	1	2	3	4	5
Interest in students	1	2	3	4	5

Once you have finished, look at the pattern of ratings that you made. Did your ratings suffer from any of the rating errors discussed in the text?

_____

_____

_____

_____

_____

_____

_____

_____

_____

_____

_____

_____

_____

_____

_____

_____

_____

_____

_____

_____

_____

_____

PROJECT E

Performance Appraisal Interviews

The most important aspect of the performance appraisal system is the feedback that it provides an employee. This feedback, which should improve employee performance, is usually given during the performance appraisal review. This exercise provides you with an opportunity to conduct a performance appraisal review.

Instructions First, think of the important dimensions for a server at a restaurant. Second, think of the last waiter or waitress who served you at a restaurant. Once you have this person in mind, use a 5-point scale to rate the server on the dimensions that you identified. Write down comments about specific good and bad behaviors that you saw this server perform.

Dimension	Rating	Comments
_____	_____	_____
_____	_____	_____
_____	_____	_____
_____	_____	_____
_____	_____	_____
_____	_____	_____
_____	_____	_____
_____	_____	_____
_____	_____	_____

Pair up with another member of your class and pretend that you are the restaurant owner and the student is actually your server. Using the knowledge that you obtained from your text, conduct the performance appraisal interview with your classmate posing as the server. When you have completed your interview, switch roles and let your classmate conduct his or her interview with you.

What did you do in the performance appraisal interview? How did the "server" react to what you did and said? What could you do to improve the review?

_____

_____

_____

_____

_____

_____

_____

_____

_____

_____

_____

_____

_____

_____

_____

_____

_____

_____

_____

_____

_____

_____

_____

References

Aamodt, M. G., Freeman, D. M., & Carneal, D. H. (1992). *Effects of group homogeneity on group performance: Two studies and a meta-analysis.* Paper presented at the annual meeting of the Virginia Psychological Association, Roanoke, VA.

Aamodt, M. G., & Kimbrough, W. W. (1982). Effect of group heterogeneity on quality of task solutions. *Psychological Reports, 50*(1), 171–174.

Aamodt, M. G., Alexander, C. J., & Kimbrough, W. W. (1983). A preliminary investigation of the relationship between team racial heterogeneity and team performance in college basketball. *Journal of Sports Sciences, 1,* 131–133.

Abramis, D. J. (1994). Work role ambiguity, job satisfaction, and job performance: Meta-analysis and review. *Psychological Reports, 75,* 1411–1433.

Adams, J. S. (1965). Inequity in social change. In L. Berkowitz (Ed.), *Advances in experimental social psychology* (Vol. 2), (pp. 267–299). New York: Academic Press.

Adams, J. S., & Rosenbaum, W. B. (1962). The relationship of worker productivity to cognitive dissonance about wage inequities. *Journal of Applied Psychology, 46,* 161–164.

Aiello, J. R., & Svec, C. M. (1993). Computer monitoring of work performance: Extending the social facilitation framework to electronic presence. *Journal of Applied Social Psychology, 23*(7), 537–548.

Albright, M. D., & Levy, P. E. (1995). The effects of source credibility and performance rating discrepancy on reactions to multiple raters. *Journal of Applied Social Psychology, 25*(7), 577–600.

Aldag, R. J., & Fuller, S. R. (1993). Beyond fiasco: A reappraisal of the groupthink phenomenon and a new model of group decision processes. *Psychological Bulletin, 13*(3), 533–552.

Alderfer, C. P. (1972). *Existence, relatedness, and growth: Human needs in organizational settings.* New York: Free Press.

Alessandra, T. & Hunsaker, P. (1993). *Communicating at work.* New York: Simon & Schuster.

Allport, G. W. (1961). *Pattern and growth in personality.* New York: Holt, Rinehart & Winston.

Amabile, T. M., Hill, K. G., Hennessey, B. A., & Tighe, E. M. (1994). The Work Preference Inventory: Assessing intrinsic and extrinsic motivational orientations.

Journal of Personality and Social Psychology, 66(5), 950–967.

Ambraziejus, A. (1992). *Managing Time.* Stamford, CT: Long Meadow Press.

Anderson, N. H. (1965). Adding versus averaging as a stimulus combination rule in impression formation. *Journal of Experimental Psychology, 70,* 394–400.

Andrews, G. (1994). Mistrust, the hidden obstacle to empowerment. *HR Magazine, 39*(9), 66–70.

Antonioni, D. (1994). The effects of feedback accountability on upward appraisal ratings. *Personnel Psychology, 47*(2), 349–356.

Armour, S. (1998, February 15). Workers fear genetic discrimination. *USA Today,* B-4.

Arthur, D. (1995). The importance of body language. *HR Focus, 72*(6), 22–23.

Arthur, D. (1996). Performance appraisals: Face-to-face with the employee. *HR Focus, 73*(3), 17–18.

Arthur, J. B. (1994). Effects of human resource systems on manufacturing performance and turnover. *Academy of Management Journal, 37*(3), 670–687.

Arvey, R. D., Bouchard, T. J., Segal, N. L., & Abraham, L. M. (1989). Job satisfaction: Environmental and genetic components. *Journal of Applied Psychology, 74,* 187–192.

Asch, S. (1951). Effects of group pressure upon the modification and distortion of judgement. In M. H. Guetzkow (Ed.), *Groups, leadership and men* (pp. 117–190). Pittsburgh: Carnegie.

Austin, J., Kessler, M. L., Riccobono, J. E., & Bailey, J. S. (1996). Using feedback and reinforcement to improve the performance and safety of a roofing crew. *Journal of Organizational Behavior Management, 16*(2), 49–75.

Azar, B. (1999). New pieces filling in addiction puzzle. *Monitor, 30*(1), 1.

Ballam, D. A. (1995). The traditional view on the origins of the employment-at-will doctrine: Myth or reality. *American Business Law Journal, 33*(1), 1–50.

Balzer, W. K., & Sulsky, L. M. (1992). Halo and performance appraisal research: A critical examination. *Journal of Applied Psychology, 77*(6), 971–986.

Barton, M. (1993). National origin discrimination claims rising. *HR News, 12,* 5.

Bass, B. M. (1990). *Bass & Stogdill's handbook of leadership: Theory, research, and application* (3rd ed.). New York: Free Press.

Bass, B. M. (1997). Does the transactional-transformational leadership paradigm transcend organizational and national boundaries? *American Psychologist, 52*(2), 130–139.

Baumgartner, J. (1994). Give it to me straight. *Training & Development Journal, 48*(6), 49–51.

Baxter, J. S., Manstead, A. S., Stradling, S. G., & Campbell, K. A. (1990). Social facilitation and driving behavior. *British Journal of Psychology, 81*(3), 351–360.

Beehr, T. A. (1996). *Basic organizational psychology.* Boston: Allyn & Bacon.

Bencivenga, D. (1997). Employee-owners help bolster the bottom line. *HR Magazine, 42*(2), 78–83.

Benjamin, A. J. (1996). *Evaluation of leader emergence in a leaderless group discussion.* Unpublished master's thesis, University of California at Fullerton.

Benne, K. D., & Sheets, P. (1948). Functional roles of group members. *Journal of Social Issues, 4*(2), 41–49.

Benzinger, K. (1982, May–June). The powerful woman. *Hospital Forum*, pp. 15–20.

Berk, R. (1997, September). *The 7 humorous habits of highly effective professors (plus 3 bonus habits).* Invited address presented to the Mid-Atlantic Personnel Assessment Consortium Fall Conference, Baltimore, MD.

Bernardin, H. J., & Beatty, R. W. (1984). *Performance appraisal: Assessing human behavior at work.* Boston: Kent.

Bernardin, H. J., & Buckley, M. R. (1981). Strategies in rater training. *Academy of Management Review, 6,* 205–242.

Bernardin, H. J., & Walters, C. S. (1977). Effects of rater training and diary-keeping on psychometric error in ratings. *Journal of Applied Psychology, 62,* 64–69.

Bernstein, A. J., & Rozen, S. C. (1992). *Neanderthals at work.* New York: Ballantine Press.

Biegeleisen, J. I. (1994). *Make your job interview a success* (4th ed). Englewood Cliffs, NJ: Prentice Hall.

Bird, F. B. (1996). *The muted conscience: Moral silence and the practice of ethics in business.* Westport, CT: Quorum Books.

Bishop, J. W., & Scott, K. D. (1997). How commitment affects team performance. *HR Magazine, 42*(2), 107–111.

Blake, R. R., & Mouton, J. S. (1984). *The managerial grid III.* Houston: Gulf.

Blanchard, K. H., Zigarmi, P., & Zigarmi, D. (1985). *Leadership and the one minute manager.* New York: William Morrow.

Blaun, R. (1996). How to eat smart. *Psychology Today, 29*(3), 34–44.

Blodgett, P. C. (1997). Six ways to be a better listener. *Training & Development, 51*(7), 11–12.

Bluen, S. D., Barling, J., & Burns, W. (1990). Predicting sales performance, job satisfaction, and depression using the Achievement Strivings and Impatience-Irritability dimensions of Type A behavior. *Journal of Applied Psychology, 75,* 212–216.

Blumenfeld, W. S. (1985). Appropriateness of readability of a Federal Aviation Agency regulation, a flight crew manual, and a company pilot labor agreement for an airline's pilots. *Perceptual and Motor Skills, 61,* 1189–1190.

Bommer, W. H., Johnson, J. L., Rich, G. A., Podsakoff, P. M., & Mackenzie, S. B. (1995). On the interchangeability of objective and subjective measures of employee performance: A meta-analysis. *Personnel Psychology, 48*(3), 587–605.

Bond, C. F., & Titus, L. J. (1983). Social facilitation: A meta-analysis of 241 studies. *Psychological Bulletin, 94,* 265–292.

Bond, G. E. (1995). *Leadership behavior: How personality, stress, and gender affect leader behavior.* Unpublished doctoral dissertation, University of Washington.

Bonner, D. (1990). Effectiveness of wellness programs in industry. *Applied H.R.M. Research, 1*(2), 32–37.

Bonner, J. J. (1993). *Measurement of resume content preference.* Unpublished master's thesis, Radford University, Radford, VA.

Bouchard, T. J. (1994). Genes, environment, and personality. *Science, 254,* 1700–1701.

Bramson, R. (1981). *Coping with difficult people.* New York: Anchor.

Branch, S. (1997). So much work, so little time. *Fortune, 135*(2), 115–117.

Brandon, M. C. (1997). From the three B's to the high C's: The history of employee communication. *Communication World, 14*(5), 18–21.

Brass, D. J., Butterfield, K. D., & Skaggs, B. C. (1998). Relationships and unethical behavior: A social network perspective. *Academy of Management Review, 23*(1), 14–31.

Bravo, I. M., & Kravitz, D. A. (1996). Context effects in performance appraisals: Influence of target value, context polarity, and individual differences. *Journal of Applied Social Psychology, 26*(19), 1681–1701.

Brawley, L. R., Carron, A. V., & Widmeyer, W. N. (1993). The influence of the group and its cohesiveness on perceptions of group goal-related variables. *Journal of Sport and Exercise Psychology, 15*(3), 245–260.

Brehm, J. W. (1966). *A theory of psychological reactance.* New York: Academic Press.

Brehm, S. S., & Kassin, S. M. (1996). *Social psychology* (3rd ed.). Boston: Houghton Mifflin.

Brenden, N. R. (1990). *Self-esteem in the training and performance of village health workers.* Unpublished doctoral dissertation, Yeshiva University.

Bretz, R. D., & Judge, T. A. (1994). Person-organization fit and the theory of work adjustment: Implications for satisfaction, tenure, and career success. *Journal of Vocational Behavior, 44*(1), 32–54.

Bretz, R. D., & Thomas, S. L. (1992). Perceived equity, motivation, and final offer arbitration. *Journal of Applied Psychology, 77*(3), 280–287.

Bridges, W. (1985). How to manage organizational transition. *Training, 22*(9), 28–32.

Brinkman, R., & Kirschner, R. (1994). *Dealing with people you can't stand.* New York: McGraw-Hill.

Broadbent, B. (1997). Writing for the 90's. *Training & Development, 51*(3), 11–12.

Brody, R. (1982). *Problem-solving.* New York: Human Science Press.

Brophy, D. R. (1996). *Matching individual and group creativity to different types of problems*. Poster presented at the 11th annual conference of the Society for Industrial and Organizational Psychology, San Diego, CA.

Brotherton, P. (1996). The company that plays together . . . *HR Magazine, 41*(12), 76–82.

Brown, K. A., & Huber, V. L. (1992). Lowering floors and raising ceilings: A longitudinal assessment of the effects of an earnings-at-risk plan on pay performance. *Personnel Psychology, 45*(2), 279–311.

Brown, W. F., & Finstuen, K. (1993). The use of participation in decision making: A consideration of the Vroom-Yetton and Vroom-Jago normative models. *Journal of Behavioral Decision Making, 6*(3), 207–219.

Bruce, H. J. (1997). Looking for a CEO? Look for early career signs of "leadership without portfolio." *Directors & Boards, 21*(2), 20–21.

Bruno, J. E. (1996). Time perceptions and time allocation preferences among adolescent boys and girls. *Adolescence, 31*(121), 109–127.

Bryman, A. (1992). *Charisma & leadership*. Newbury Park, CA: Sage.

Buchanan, L., & Foti, R. J. (1996). *Emergent female leaders: Effects of self-monitoring, priming, and task characteristics*. Poster presented at the 11th annual conference of the Society for Industrial and Organizational Psychology, San Diego, CA.

Buckley, M. R., & Eder, R. W. (1989). The first impression. *Personnel Administrator, 34*(5), 72–74.

Bullock, R. J., & Tubbs, M. E. (1990). A case meta-analysis of gainsharing plans as organization development interventions. *Journal of Applied Behavioral Science, 26*(3), 383–404.

Burke, R. J., Weitzel, W., & Weir, T. (1978). Characteristics of effective employee performance review and development interviews. *Personnel Psychology, 31*, 903–919.

Burling, T., Lentz, E., & Wilson, R. (1956). *To give and take in hospitals*. New York: Putnam.

Butterfield, K. D., Trevino, L. K., & Ball, G. A. (1996). Punishment from the manager's perspective: A grounded investigation and inductive model. *Academy of Management Journal, 39*(6), 1479–1512.

Byrne, J. A. (1994, May 9). The pain of downsizing. *Business Week*, 60–69.

Caldwell, D. F., & O'Reilly, C. A. (1982). Boundary spanning and individual performance: The impact of self-monitoring. *Journal of Applied Psychology, 67*, 124–127.

Cameron, J., & Pierce, W. D. (1994). Reinforcement, reward, and intrinsic motivation: A meta-analysis. *Review of Educational Research, 64*(3), 363–423.

Campion, M. A., & McClelland, C. L. (1993). Follow-up and extension of the interdisciplinary costs and benefits of enlarged jobs. *Journal of Applied Psychology, 78*(3), 339–351.

Cardy, R. L., & Dobbins, G. H. (1986). Affect and appraisal accuracy: Liking as an integral dimension in evaluating performance. *Journal of Applied Psychology, 71*, 672–678.

Carlson, R. E. (1970). Effects of applicant sample on ratings of valid information in an employment setting. *Journal of Applied Psychology, 54*, 217–222.

Carnall, C. A. (1990). *Managing change in organizations*. New York: Prentice Hall.

Carpi, J. (1996, January/February). Stress: It's worse than you think. *Psychology Today*, 34–42.

Carrell, M. R., & Dittrich, J. E. (1978). Equity theory: The recent literature, methodological considerations, and new directions. *Academy of Management Review, 3*, 202–210.

Carron, A. V. (1990). Group size in sport and physical activity: Social psychological and performance consequences. *International Journal of Sport Psychology, 21*(4), 286–304.

Carter, J. H. (1952). Military leadership. *Military Review, 32*, 14–18.

Cederbloom, D. (1989). Peer and supervisor evaluations: An underused promotion method used for law enforcement. *Proceedings of the 13th Annual Meeting of the International Personnel Management Association Assessment Council*.

Chartrand, T., Pinckert, S., & Burger, J. M. (1999). When manipulation backfires: The effects of time delay and requester on the foot-in-the-door technique. *Journal of Applied Social Psychology, 29*(1), 211–221.

Chen, A. Y., Sawyers, R. B., & Williams, P. F. (1997). Reinforcing ethical decision making through corporate culture. *Journal of Business Ethics, 16*, 855–865.

Chen, S. C. (1937). Social modification of the activity of ants in nest-building. *Physiological Zoology, 10*, 420–436.

Chong, J. (1998). Crime indicators for alcohol and drug abuse. *Criminal Justice and Behavior, 25*(3), 283–305.

Chowdhary, V. (1993). Self-perceived somatotypes and clothing-related behavior of older men and women. *Perceptual and Motor Skills, 77*(1), 307–323.

Chubb, R. (1995). Humor: A valuable laugh skill. *Journal of Child and Youth Care, 10*(3), 61–66.

Cialdini, R. B. (1985). *Influence: Science and practice*. Glenview, IL: Scott, Foresman.

Cialdini, R. B., Borden, R., Thorne, A., Walker, M., Freeman, S., & Sloane, L. T. (1976). Basking in reflected glory: Three (football) field studies. *Journal of Personality and Social Psychology, 34*, 366–375.

Cialdini, R. B., & Schroeder, D. A. (1976). Increasing compliance by legitimizing paltry contributions: When even a penny helps. *Journal of Personality and Social Psychology, 34*, 599–604.

Cialdini, R. B., Vincent, J. E., Lewis, S. K., Catalan, J., Wheeler, D., & Darby, B. L. (1975). Reciprocal concessions procedure for inducing compliance: The door-in-the-face technique. *Journal of Personality and Social Psychology, 31*, 206–215.

Clark, R. D. (1971). Group-induced shift toward risk: A critical appraisal. *Psychological Bulletin, 76*, 251–271.

Clarke, D. L., Miklos, S. M., & Rogers, V. M. (1996). *Upward appraisal: Does it make a difference?* Paper presented at the 11th annual meeting of the Society for Industrial and Organizational Psychology, San Diego, CA.

Clements, C., Wagner, R. J., & Roland, C. C. (1995). The ins and outs of experiential training. *Training & Development, 49*(2), 52–56.

Clore, G. L., Wiggins, N. H., & Itkin, S. (1975). Gain and loss in attraction: Attributions from nonverbal behavior. *Journal of Personality and Social Psychology, 31,* 706–712.

Cohen, A. (September 1972). *The role of psychology in improving worker safety and health under the Worker Safety and Health Act.* Paper presented at the annual meeting of the American Psychological Association, Honolulu, HI.

Cohen, A. R., & Bradford, D. L. (1990). *Influence without authority.* New York: John Wiley.

Cohen, D. (1997). *Cohen Conflict Response Inventory.* Washington, DC: author.

Cohen, S. (1998). Knowledge management's killer app: Here's how an intranet can wire employees to information and knowledge without fragmenting a company's culture. *Training & Development, 52*(1), 50–56.

Coleman, F. T. (1998, November). Workplace dispute arbitration: An idea whose time has come. *HR News,* 17.

Connolly, P. M. (1986). Clearing the deadwood. *Training & Development Journal, 40*(1), 58–60.

Conrad, C., & Sinclair-James, L. (1995.) Institutional pressures, cultural constraints, and communication in community mediation organizations. In A. M. Nicotera (Ed.), *Conflict and organizations.* Albany, NY: State University of New York Press.

Conway, J. M., & Huffcutt, A. I. (1997). Psychometric properties of multisource performance ratings: A meta-analysis of subordinate, supervisor, peer, and self-ratings. *Human Performance, 10*(4), 331–360.

Cooper, M., Kaufman, G., & Hughes, W. (1996). Measuring supervisory potential. *IPMA News,* December, pp. 8–9.

Cooper, W. H. (1981). Ubiquitous halo. *Psychological Bulletin, 90,* 218–244.

Cordes, C. L., & Dougherty, T. W. (1993). Review and integration of research on job burnout. *Academy of Management Review, 18*(4), 621–656.

Cottrell, N. B. (1972). Social facilitation. In C. G. McClintock (Ed.), *Experimental Social Psychology* (pp. 185–236). New York: Holt, Rinehart & Winston.

Courneya, K. S., & Carron, A. V. (1992). The home advantage in sport competitions: A literature review. *Journal of Sport and Exercise Psychology, 14*(1), 13–27.

Courtis, J. K. (1995). Readability of annual reports: Western versus Asian evidence. *Accounting, Auditing and Accountability, 8*(2), 4–17.

Covey, S. R. (1989). *The seven habits of highly effective people.* New York: Simon & Schuster.

Crane, S. (1994). *What do I do now? Making sense of today's changing world.* Irvine, CA: Vista Press.

Cromwell, P. F., Marks, A., Olson, J. N., & Avary, D. W. (1991). Group effects on decision-making by burglars. *Psychological Reports, 69*(2), 579–588.

Cropanzano, R., & Folger, R. (1989). Referent cognitions and task decision autonomy: Beyond equity theory. *Journal of Applied Psychology, 74,* 293–299.

Cropanzano, R., & James, K. (1990). Some methodological considerations for the behavioral genetic analysis of work attitudes. *Journal of Applied Psychology, 75,* 433–439.

Crusco, A. H., & Wetzel, C. G. (1984). The Midas touch: The effects of interpersonal touch on restaurant tipping. *Personality and Social Psychology Bulletin, 10,* 512–517.

Cruz, M. G., Boster, F. J., & Rodriguez, J. I. (1997). The impact of group size and proportion of shared information on the exchange and integration of information in groups. *Communication Research, 24*(3), 291–312.

Csoka, L. S., & Bons, P. M. (1978). Manipulating the situation to fit the leader's style: Two validation studies of Leader Match. *Journal of Applied Psychology, 63,* 295–300.

Dale, E., & Chall, J. S. (1948). A formula for predicting readability. *Educational Research Bulletin, 27,* 37–54.

Daley, A. J., & Parfitt, G. (1996). Good health—Is it worth it? Mood states, physical well-being, job satisfaction and absenteeism in members and non-members of a British corporate health and fitness club. *Journal of Occupational and Organizational Psychology, 69,* 121–134.

Dalton, D. R., & Mesch, D. J. (1991). On the extent and reduction of avoidable absenteeism: An assessment of absence policy provisions. *Journal of Applied Psychology, 76*(6), 810–817.

Dansereau, F., Graen, G., & Haga, W. J. (1975). *A vertical dyad linkage approach to leadership within the formal organization.* Unpublished report, State University of New York, Buffalo.

Davidson, J. (1997). *The Complete Idiot's Guide to Managing Stress.* New York: Simon & Schuster Macmillan Company.

Davir, T., Eden, D., & Banjo, M. L. (1995). Self-fulfilling prophecy and gender: Can women be Pygmalion and Galatea? *Journal of Applied Psychology, 80*(2), 253–270.

Davis, D. D., & Harless, D. W. (1996). Group v. individual performance in a price-searching experiment. *Organizational Behavior and Human Decision Processes, 66*(2), 215–227.

Davis, K. (1953). Management communication and the grapevine. *Harvard Business Review, 31*(5), 43–59.

Davis, M. G., Lundman, R. J., & Martinez, R. (1991). Private corporate justice: Store policy, shoplifters, and civil recovery. *Social Problems, 38*(3), 395–411.

Davis, T. R. (1984). The influence of the physical environment in offices. *Academy of Management Review, 9,* 271–283.

de Castro, J. M., & Brewer, E. M. (1992). The amount eaten in meals by humans is a power function of the number of people present. *Physiology and Behavior, 51*(1), 121–125.

Deci, E. L. (1972). The effects of contingent and noncontingent rewards and controls on intrinsic motivation. *Organizational Behavior and Human Performance, 8,* 217–229.

Deci, E. L., & Ryan, R. M. (1985). *Intrinsic motivation and selfdetermination in human behavior.* New York: Plenum.

Degner, J. (1995). Writing job descriptions that work. *Credit Union Executive, 35*(6), 13–17.

Deluga, R. J., & Winters, J. J. (1991). Why the aggravation? Reasons students become resident assistants. *Journal of College Student Development, 32*(6), 546–552.

Dempcy, M. H., & Tihista, R. (1996). *Dear job stressed*. Palo Alto, CA: Davies-Black Publishing.

DeNisi, A. S., & Peters, L. H. (1996). Organization of information in memory and the performance appraisal process: Evidence from the field. *Journal of Applied Psychology, 81*(6), 717–737.

DeNisi, A. S., Robbins, T., & Cafferty, T. P. (1989). Organization of information used for performance appraisals: Role of diary-keeping. *Journal of Applied Psychology, 74*, 124–129.

Dennis, A. R., Valacich, J. S., & Nunamaker, J. F. (1990). An experimental investigation of the effects of group size in an electronic meeting environment. *IEEE Transactions on Systems, Man, and Cybernetics, 20*(5), 1049–1057.

Denton, D. K. (1996). 9 ways to create an atmosphere for change. *HR Magazine, 41*(10), 76–81.

DePaulo, B. M. (1992). Nonverbal behavior and self-presentation. *Psychological Bulletin, 111*, 203–243.

DePaulo, B. M., Stone, J. L., & Lassiter, G. D. (1985). Deceiving and detecting deceit. In B. R. Schlenker (Ed.), *The self and social life* (pp. 323–370). New York: McGraw-Hill.

DePaulo, B. M., Zuckerman, M., & Rosenthal, A. R. (1980). Detecting deception: Modality effects. In L. Wheeler (Ed.), *The review of personality and social psychology*. Beverly Hills, CA: Sage.

Dessler, G. (1984). *Personnel management*. Reston, VA: Reston.

Deutsch, M. (1973). *The resolution of conflict*. New Haven, CT: Yale University Press.

Deutsch, M. (1994). Constructive conflict resolutions: Principles, training, and research. *Journal of Social Issues, 1*, 13–32.

Dickinson, A. M. (1989). The detrimental effects of extrinsic reinforcement on intrinsic motivation. *Behavior Analyst, 12*(1), 1–15.

Dickinson, A. M., & Gillette, K. L. (1993). A comparison of the effects of two individual monetary incentive systems on productivity and piece rate pay versus base pay plus incentives. *Journal of Organizational Behavior Management, 14*(1), 63–82.

Diehl, M., & Stroebe, W. (1987). Productivity loss in brainstorming groups: Toward the solution of a riddle. *Journal of Personality and Social Psychology, 53*, 497–509.

Dietz, P. E. (1994). *Overview of workplace violence*. Seminar presented to the Society for Human Resource Management, Roanoke, VA.

Digh, P. (1998, September/October). Race matters. *MOSAICS: SHRM Focuses on Workplace Diversity, 4*(5), 1–4.

Dillard, J. P. (1991). The current status of research on sequential-request compliance. *Personality and Social Psychology Bulletin, 17*(3), 283–288.

Dipboye, R. L. (1977). A critical review of Korman's self-consistency theory of work motivation and occupational choice. *Organizational Behavior and Human Performance, 18*, 108–126.

Dobbins, G. H., Long, W. S., Dedrick, E. J., & Clemons, T. C. (1990). The role of self-monitoring and gender on leader emergence: A laboratory and field study. *Journal of Management, 16*(3), 609–618.

Dolin, D. J., & Booth-Butterfield, M. (1993). Reach out and touch someone: Analysis of nonverbal comforting responses. *Communication Quarterly, 41*(4), 383–393.

Donnellon, A. (1996). *Team talk: The power of language in team dynamics*. Boston: Harvard Business School Press.

Donnellon, A., & Kolb, D. (1994). Constructive for whom? The fate of diversity disputes in organizations. *Journal of Social Issues, 1*, 139–155.

Donnerstein, E., & Wilson, D. W. (1976). Effects of noise and perceived control on ongoing and subsequent aggressive behavior. *Journal of Personality and Social Psychology, 34*, 774–781.

Dougherty, T. W., Turban, D. B., & Callender, J. C. (1994). Confirming first impressions in the employment interview: A field study of interviewer behavior. *Journal of Applied Psychology, 79*(5), 659–665.

Drexler, A. B., & Forrester, R. (1998). Teamwork—not necessarily the answer. *HR Magazine, 43*(1), 55–58.

Duane, M. J. (1989). Sex differences in conflict management. *Psychological Reports, 65*(3, pt. 1), 1033–1034.

Dubin, R., & Champoux, J. E. (1977). Central life theory and job satisfaction. *Organizational Behavior and Human Performance, 18*, 366–377.

DuBose, C. (1994). Breaking the bad news. *HR MAGAZINE, 39*(4), 62–64.

Eagly, A. H., & Johnson, B. T. (1990). Gender and leadership style: A meta-analysis. *Psychological Bulletin, 108*(2), 233–256.

Eden, D. (1998). *Implanting Pygmalion leadership style through training: Seven true field experiments*. Paper presented at the annual meeting of the Society for Industrial and Organizational Psychology, Dallas, TX.

Eggert, M. (1992). *The perfect interview*. New York: Random House.

Elias, M. (1997, May). Mood a stroke risk factor: Depression may be prelude. *USA Today*, p. A1.

Erfurt, J. C., Foote, A., & Heirich, M. A. (1992). The cost-effectiveness of worksite wellness programs for hypertension control, weight loss, smoking cessation, and exercise. *Personnel Psychology, 45*(1), 5–28.

Evans, G. W., Hygge, S., & Bullinger, M. (1995). Chronic noise and psychological stress. *Psychological Science, 6*(6), 333–338.

Eysenck, H. J. (1964). Crime and personality (1st ed.). London: Methuen.

Falcone, P. (1997). The fundamentals of progressive discipline. *HR Magazine, 42*(2), 90–94.

Farh, J., Cannella, A. A., & Bedeian, A. G. (1991). Peer ratings: The impact of purpose on rating quality and user acceptance. *Group and Organization Studies, 16*(4), 367–386.

Farh, J., & Dobbins, G. H. (1989). Effects of self-esteem on leniency bias in self-reports of performance: A structural equation model analysis. *Personnel Psychology, 42*(4), 835–850.

Farh, J., Dobbins, G. A., & Cheng, B. S. (1991). Cultural relativity in action: A comparison of self-ratings made by Chinese and U.S. workers. *Personnel Psychology, 44*(1), 129–147.

Feldman, J. (1981). Beyond attribution theory: Cognitive processes in performance appraisal. *Journal of Applied Psychology, 66,* 127–148.

Feldman, R. S. (1998). *Social psychology.* Englewood Cliffs, NJ: Prentice Hall.

Ferrari, J. R. (1991). Compulsive procrastination: Some self-reported characteristics. *Psychological Reports, 68,* 455–458.

Ferrell, O. C., & Gardiner, G. (1991). In pursuit of ethics: Tough choices of the workplace. Springfield, IL: Smith Collins.

Festinger, L., Schachter, S., & Back, K. (1950). Social pressures in informal groups: A study of human factors in housing. New York: Harper.

Fey, C. (1987). Engineering good writing. *Training, 24*(3), 49–54.

Fiedler, F. (1967). *A theory of leadership effectiveness.* New York: McGraw-Hill.

Fiedler, F. (1978). Recent developments in research on the contingency model. In L. Berkowitz (Ed.), *Group processes* (pp. 207–223). New York: Academic Press.

Fiedler, F. (1996). Research on leadership selection and training: One view of the future. *Administrative Science Quarterly, 41*(2), 241–250.

Field, H. S., & Holley, W. H. (1982). The relationship of performance appraisal system characteristics to verdicts in selected employment discrimination cases. *Academy of Management Journal, 25,* 392–406.

Field, R. H., & House, R. J. (1990). A test of the Vroom-Yetton model using manager and subordinate reports. *Journal of Applied Psychology, 75*(3), 362–266.

Filipczak, B. (1993). Why no one likes your incentive program. *Training, 30*(5), 19–25.

Filipczak, B. (1994). 1994 industry report. *Training, 31*(10), 29–64.

Finch, L. (1987). *Telephone courtesy and customer service.* Los Altos, CA: Crisp Publications.

Fisher, J. D., Rytting, M., & Heslin, R. (1976). Hands touching hands: Affective and evaluative effects of an interpersonal touch. *Sociometry, 39,* 416–421.

Fisher, R. (1994). Generic principles for resolving intergroup conflict. *The Society for the Psychological Study of Social Issues,* 47–63.

Fisher, R., & Ury, W. (1991). *Getting to yes* (2nd ed.). New York: Penguin Books.

Fiske, S. T. (1998, July/August). Interpersonal power: New principles of stereotypes and stereotyping. *Psychological Science Agenda, 11*(4), 9–11.

Fitzgibbons, A. (1997). Employees' perceived importance of profit sharing plays a role in profit sharing's organizational impact. *Proceedings of the 18th Annual Graduate Conference in Industrial/Organizational Psychology and Organizational Behavior, 18,* 43–44.

Fleishman, E. A., Harris, E. F., & Burtt, H. E. (1955). *Leadership and supervision in industry.* Columbus, OH: Ohio State University Press.

Flesch, R. (1948). A new readability yardstick. *Journal of Applied Psychology, 32,* 221–233.

Flores, F. (1992). Team building and leadership. *Supervisory Management, 43,* 8–9.

Florkowski, G. W., & Schuster, M. H. (1992). Support for profit sharing and organizational commitment: A path analysis. *Human Relations, 45*(5), 507–523.

Forbes, R. J., & Jackson, P. R. (1980). Nonverbal behaviour and the outcome of selection interviews. *Journal of Occupational Psychology, 53,* 65–72.

Ford, R. (1973). Job enrichment lessons at AT&T. *Harvard Business Review, 73,* 96–106.

Ford, R. C., & Richardson, W. D. (1994). Ethical decision-making: A review of the empirical literature. *Journal of Business Ethics, 13,* 205–221.

Forsyth, D. R. (1999). *Group dynamics* (3rd ed.). Pacific Grove, CA: Brooks/Cole.

Foster, M. (1989). *Relationship between self-monitoring, personality and supervisor performance.* Unpublished master's thesis, University of Georgia.

Foster, R. S., Aamodt, M. G., Bodenmiller, J. A., Rodgers, J. G., Kovach, R. C., & Bryan, D. A. (1988). Effect of menu sign position on customer ordering times and number of food-ordering errors. *Environment and Behavior, 20*(2), 200–210.

Fowler, J. (1991). *How to get the job you want in tough times.* Los Angeles: RGA Publishing Group.

Fox, J. B., Scott, K. D., & Donohue, J. M. (1993). An investigation into pay valence and performance in a pay-for-performance field setting. *Journal of Organizational Behavior, 14,* 687–693.

Frank, F., & Anderson, L. R. (1971). Effects of task and group size upon group productivity and member satisfaction. *Sociometry, 34,* 135–149.

Franz, C., & Jin, K. (1995, May). The structure of group conflict in a collaborative work group during information systems development. *Journal of Applied Communication Research, 23*(2), 108–127.

Freedman, J. L., & Fraser, S. L. (1966). Compliance without pressure: The foot-in-the-door technique. *Journal of Personality and Social Psychology, 4,* 195–202.

French, J. R. P., & Raven, B. H. (1959). The bases of social power. In D. Cartwright (Ed.), *Studies in social power* (pp. 150–167). Ann Arbor: University of Michigan Press.

Frese, M., & Semmer, N. (1986). Shiftwork, stress, and psychosomatic complaints: A comparison between workers in different shift work schedules, non-shiftworkers, and former shift workers. *Ergonomics, 29,* 99–114.

Freston, N. P., & Lease, J. E. (1987). Communication skills training for selected supervisors. *Training and Development Journal, 41*(7), 67–70.

Frick, R. W. (1985). Communicating emotion: The role of prosodic features. *Psychological Bulletin, 97,* 412–429.

Frone, M. R., Russell, M., & Cooper, M. L. (1995). Job stressors, job involvement and employee health: A test of identity theory. *Journal of Occupational and Organizational Psychology, 68,* 1–11.

Fry, E. (1977). Fry's Readability Graph: Clarifications, validity, and extension to level 17. *Journal of Reading, 21,* 243–252.

Fulger, R. (1977). Which costs less—the phone or the letter? *Management World, 6,* 13–14.

Furnham, A., & Stringfield, P. (1994). Congruence of self and subordinate ratings of managerial practices as a correlate of superior evaluation. *Journal of Occupational and Organizational Psychology, 67*(1), 57–67.

Gardenswartz, L., & Rowe, A . (1998, September/October). Diversity Q&A: How can we energize our organization's diversity council? *MOSAICS: SHRM Focuses on Workplace Diversity, 4*(5), 3–7.

Gardenswartz, L., & Rowe, A. (1999, January/February). Diversity Q&A: "How do we handle jokes being told in our workplace that violate our diversity policy?" *MOSAICS: SHRM Focuses on Workplace Diversity, 5*(1), 3.

Garske, G. G. (1990). The relationship of self-esteem to levels of job satisfaction of vocational rehabilitation professionals. *Journal of Applied Rehabilitation Counseling, 27*(2), 19–22.

Gately, R. F. (1997, March). Why motivation is free. *IPMA News,* p. 14.

Gebhardt, D. L., & Crump, C. E. (1990). Employee fitness and wellness programs in the workplace. *American Psychologist, 45*(2), 262–272.

Geier, J. G., & Downey, D. E. (1980). *Attitudinal Listening Profile System.* Minneapolis, MN: Performax Systems International.

Geier, J. G., Downey, D. E., & Johnson, J. B. (1980). *Climate impact profile.* Minneapolis, MN: Performax Systems International.

Geller, E. S., Roberts, D. S., & Gilmore, M. R. (1996). Predicting propensity to actively care for occupational safety. *Journal of Safety Research, 27*(1), 1–8.

George, J. M. (1995). Asymmetrical effects of rewards and punishments: The case of social loafing. *Journal of Occupational and Organizational Psychology, 68*(4), 327–338.

Gerstner, C. R., & Day, D. V. (1997). Meta-analytic review of leader-member exchange theory: Correlates and construct issues. *Journal of Applied Psychology, 82*(6), 827–844.

Gibbs, C. A. (1969). Leadership. In G. Lindzey & E. Aronson (Eds.), *Handbook of social psychology* (pp. 205–282). Reading, MA: Addison-Wesley.

Gilchrist, J. A., & White, K. D. (1990). Policy development and satisfaction with merit pay: A field study in a university setting. *College Student Journal, 24*(3), 249–254.

Gillet, B., & Schwab, D. P. (1975). Convergent and discriminant validities of corresponding Job Descriptive Index and Minnesota Satisfaction Questionnaire scales. *Journal of Applied Psychology, 60,* 313–317.

Gilmore, T. N., Shea, G. P., & Useem, M. (1997). Side effects of corporate cultural transformations. *Journal of Applied Behavioral Science, 33*(2), 174–189.

Glanz, B. A. (1997, March). Spread contagious enthusiasm. *IPMA News,* pp. 13–14.

Glass, L. (1995). *Toxic people.* New York: Simon & Schuster.

Goleman, D. (1998). *Working with Emotional Intelligence.* New York: Bantam Books.

Golen, S. (1990). A factor analysis of barriers to effective listening. *Journal of Business Communication, 27,* 25–36.

Goodson, J. R., McGee, G. W., & Cashman, J. F. (1989). Situational leadership theory: A test of leadership prescriptions. *Group and Organization Studies, 14*(4), 446–461.

Gordon, J. R. (1983). *A diagnostic approach to organizational behavior.* Boston: Allyn & Bacon.

Gottesman, I. I. (1991). *Schizophrenia genesis: The origins of madness.* New York: W. H. Freeman.

Gottlieb, J. A., & Sanzgiri, J. (1996). Towards an ethical dimension of decision making in organizations. *Journal of Business Ethics, 15,* 1275–1285.

Gowen, C. R. (1990). Gainsharing programs: An overview of history and research. *Journal of Organizational Behavior Management, 11*(2), 77–99.

Graen, G., & Scheimann, W. (1978). Leader member agreement: A vertical dyad linkage approach. *Journal of Applied Psychology, 63,* 206–212.

Graham, J. P. (1991). Disgruntled employees—ticking time bombs? *Security Management,* 83–85.

Gratias, M. B., & Hills, D. A. (1997). *Social loafing in individuals versus groups: Assessing quantity, quality, and creativity.* Poster presented at the 12th annual conference of the Society for Industrial and Organizational Psychology, St. Louis, MO.

Gray, P. M. (1997). How to become intranet savvy. *HR Magazine, 42*(12), 66–71.

Graydon, J., & Murphy, T. (1995). The effect of personality on social facilitation whilst performing a sports related task. *Personality and Individual Differences, 19*(2), 265–267.

Grazian, F. (1996). Frequently asked questions about readability. *Public Relations Quarterly, 41*(3), 19–20.

Green, S. K., Buchanan, D. R., & Heuer, S. K. (1984). Winners, losers, and choosers: A field investigation of dating initiation. *Personality and Social Psychology Bulletin, 10*(4), 502–511.

Greenberg, J., & Baron, R. A. (1995). *Behavior in organizations* (5th ed.). Englewood Cliffs, NJ: Prentice Hall.

Greenhaus, J. H., & Badin, I. J. (1974). Self-esteem, performance, and satisfaction: Some tests of a theory. *Journal of Applied Psychology, 59,* 722–726.

Greer, D. L. (1983). Spectator booing and the home advantage: A study of social influence in the basketball arena. *Social Psychology Quarterly, 46,* 252–261.

Gregory, W. L., Cialdini, R. B., & Carpenter, K. M. (1982). Self-relevant scenarios as mediators of likelihood estimates and compliance: Does imagining make it so? *Journal of Personality and Social Psychology, 43*(1), 89–99.

Griffin, E., & Sparks, G. G. (1990). Friends forever: A longitudinal exploration of intimacy in same-sex friends and platonic pairs. *Journal of Social and Personal Relationships, 7,* 29–46.

Gruner, S. (1997). Feedback from everyone: Are 360-degree performance reviews a silly fad—or a smart management tool? *Inc., 19*(2), 102–103.

Gumpert, R. A., & Hambleton, R. K. (1979). Situational leadership: How Xerox managers fine-tune managerial styles to employee maturity and task needs. *Management Review,12,* 9.

Gundry, L. K., & Rousseau, D. M. (1994). Critical incidents in communicating culture to newcomers: The meaning is in the message. *Human Relations, 47*(9), 1063–1088.

Gunning, R. (1964). *How to take the FOG out of writing.* Chicago: Dartnell Corp.

Guppy, A., & Rick, J. (1996). The influences of gender and grade on perceived work stress and job satisfaction in white collar employees. *Work and Stress, 10*(2), 154–164.

Guy, M. E. (1990). *Ethical decision-making in everyday work situations.* Westport, CT: Greenwood Press.

Hackett, R. D. (1989). Work attitudes and employee absenteeism: A synthesis of the literature. *Journal of Occupational Psychology, 62*(3), 235–248.

Hackett, R. D., & Bycio, P. (1996). An evaluation of employee absenteeism as a coping mechanism among hospital nurses. *Journal of Occupational and Organi-zational Psychology, 69*(4), 327–338.

Hackman, J. R., & Oldham, G. R. (1975). Development of the job diagnostic survey. *Journal of Applied Psychology, 60,* 159–170.

Hackman, J. R., & Oldham, G. R. (1976). Motivation through the design of work: Test of a theory. *Organizational Behavior and Human Performance, 16,* 250–279.

Hackman, R., & Vidmar, N. (1970). Effects of size and task type on group performance and member reactions. *Sociometry, 33,* 37–54.

Hall, D. T., & Nougaim, K. E. (1968). An examination of Maslow's need hierarchy in an organizational setting. *Organizational Behavior and Human Performance, 3,* 12–35.

Hall, E. T. A. (1963). A system for the notation of prox-emic behavior. *American Anthropologist, 65,* 1003–1026.

Hammer, T. H., & Dachler, H. P. (1975). A test of some assumptions underlying the path goal model of supervision: Some suggested conceptual modifications. *Organizational Behavior and Human Performance, 14,* 60–75.

Hammond, K. H. (1996, June 10). The issue is employment, not employability. *Business Week, 64.*

Hampton, D. R., Summer, C. E., & Webber, R. A. (1978). *Organizational behavior and the practice of management.* Glenview, IL: Scott, Foresman.

Hanlon, S. C., & Taylor, R. R. (1992). How does gain-sharing work? Some preliminary answers following application in a service organization. *Applied H.R.M. Research, 3*(2), 73–91.

Harder, J. W. (1992). Play for pay: Effects of inequity in a pay-for-performance context. *Administrative Science Quarterly, 37,* 321–335.

Hardy, C. J., & Crace, R. K. (1991). The effects of task structure and teammate competence on social loafing. *Journal of Sport and Exercise Psychology, 13*(4), 372–381.

Harrison, D. A., & Shaffer, M. A. (1994). Comparative examinations of self-reports and perceived absenteeism norms: Wading through Lake Wobegon. *Journal of Applied Psychology, 79*(2), 240–256.

Hatcher, L., Ross, T. L., & Ross, R. A. (1987). Gain-sharing: Living up to its name. *Personnel Administrator, 32*(6), 154–164.

Hauenstein, N. M. A. (1986). *A process approach to ratings: The effects of ability and level of processing on encoding, retrieval, and rating outcomes.* Unpublished doctoral dissertation, University of Akron, Akron, OH.

Hauenstein, N. M. A., & Lord, R. G. (1989). The effects of final-offer arbitration on the performance of major league baseball players: A test of equity theory. *Human Performance, 2*(3), 147–165.

Hawk, E. J. (1995, April). Culture and rewards. *Personnel Journal,* pp. 30–37.

Healey, J. F. (1998). *Race, Ethnicity, Gender, and Class* (2nd ed.). Thousand Oaks, CA: Pine Forge Press.

Heaney, C. A., & Clemans, J. (1995). Occupational stress, physician-excused absences, and absences not excused by a physician. *American Journal of Health Promotion, 10*(2), 117–124.

Heath, C. (1996). Do people prefer to pass along good or bad news? Valence and relevance of news as predictors of transmission propensity. *Organizational Behavior and Human Decision Processes, 68*(2), 79–94.

Hecht, M. A., & LaFrance, M. (1995). How (fast) can I help you? Tone of voice and telephone operator efficiency in interactions. *Journal of Applied Social Psychology, 25*(23), 2086–2098.

Hemphill, J. K., & Coons, A. E. (1950). *Leader behavior description.* Columbus, OH: Personnel Research Board, Ohio State University.

Henderson, R. I. (1997). *Compensation management: Rewarding performance.* Englewood Cliffs, NJ: Prentice Hall.

Hequet, M. (1994). Giving good feedback. *Training, 31*(9), 72–77.

Hersey, P., & Blanchard, K. H. (1988). *Management of organizational behavior* (5th ed.). Englewood Cliffs, NJ: Prentice Hall.

Herzberg, F. (1966). *Work and the nature of man.* Cleveland: World.

Heslin, R., & Dunphy, D. (1964). Three dimensions of member satisfaction in small groups. *Human Relations, 17,* 99–112.

Hilgert, R. L. (1991). Employees protected by at-will statements. *HR Magazine, 36*(3), 57–59.

Hills, F. S., Scott, K. D., Markham, S. E., & Vest, M. J. (1987). Merit pay: Just or unjust desserts. *Personnel Administrator, 32*(9), 53–59.

Hinrichs, J. R., & Mischkind, L. A. (1967). Empirical and theoretical limitations of the two-factor hypothesis of job satisfaction. *Journal of Applied Psychology, 51,* 191–200.

Hoffman, L. R. (1959). Homogeneity of member personality and its effect on group problem solving. *Journal of Abnormal and Social Psychology, 58,* 27–32.

Hogan, R. (1989, June). *The darker side of charisma.* Paper presented at 13th annual meeting of International Personnel Management Association Assessment Council, Orlando, FL.

Holstein, B. B. (1997). *The enchanted self.* Amsterdam: Harwood Academic Publishers.

House, B. (1997). Cop an attitude for effective employee communication. *Communication World, 14*(4), 30–31.

House, R. J. (1971). A path-goal theory of leader effectiveness. *Administrative Science Quarterly, 9,* 321–332.

House, R. J., & Mitchell, T. R. (1974, Autumn). Path-goal theory of leadership. *Journal of Contemporary Business, 3,* 81–98.

Howell, J. M., & Avolio, B. J. (1993). Transformational leadership, transactional leadership, locus of control, and support of innovation: Key predictors of consolidated-business-unit performance. *Journal of Applied Psychology, 78*(6), 891–902.

Huegli, J. M., & Tschirgia, H. D. (1975). Monitoring the employment interview. *Journal of College Placement, 39,* 37–39.

Huijbregts, P., Feskens, E., Rasanen, L., Fidanza, F., Alberti-Fidanza, A., Nissinen, A., Giampoli, S., & Kromhout, D. (1998). Dietary patterns and cognitive function in elderly men in Finland, Italy, and the Netherlands. *European Journal of Clinical Nutrition, 52*(11), 826–831.

Huish, G. B. (1997, August). Piece-rate pay plan in clerk's office motivates quantum leap in quality productivity. *IPMA News,* pp. 22–27.

Hunt, J. W., & Laing, B. (1997). Leadership: The role of the exemplar. *Business Strategy Review, 8*(1), 31–42.

Hutchison, S., Valentino, K. E., & Kirkner, S. L. (1998). What works for the gander does not work as well for the goose: The effects of leader behavior. *Journal of Applied Social Psychology, 28*(2), 171–182.

Hyatt, D. E., & Ruddy, T. M. (1997). An examination of the relationship between work group characteristics and performance: Once more into the breach. *Personnel Psychology, 50*(3), 533–585.

Iaffaldano, M. T., & Muchinsky, P. M. (1985). Job satisfaction and job performance: A metaanalysis. *Psychological Bulletin, 97,* 251–273.

Ilardi, B. C., Leone, D., Kasser, T., & Ryan, R. M. (1993). Employee and supervisor ratings of motivation: Main effects and discrepancies associated with job satisfaction and adjustment in a factory setting. *Journal of Applied Social Psychology, 23*(21), 1789–1805.

Ilgen, D. R., Nebeker, D. M., & Pritchard, R. D. (1981). Expectancy theory measures: An empirical comparison in an experimental simulation. *Organizational Behavior and Human Performance, 28,* 189–223.

Ironson, G. H., Smith, P. C., Brannick, M. T., Gibson, W. M., & Paul, K. B. (1989). Construction of a job in general scale: A comparison of global, composite, and specific measures. *Journal of Applied Psychology, 74,* 193–200.

Irving, G. P., & Meyer, J. P. (1994). Reexamination of the met-expectations hypothesis: A longitudinal analysis. *Journal of Applied Psychology, 79*(6), 937–949.

Ivancevich, J. M. (1982). Subordinates' reactions to performance appraisal interviews: A test of feedback and goal-setting techniques. *Journal of Applied Psychology, 67,* 581–587.

Jackson, J. M. (1986). In search of social impact theory: Comment on Mullen. *Journal of Personality and Social Psychology, 50,* 511–513.

Jackson, S. E., Brett, J. F., Sessa, V. T., Cooper, D. M., Julin, J. A., & Peyronnin, K. (1991). Some differences make a difference: Individual dissimilarity and group homogeneity as correlates of recruitment, promotions, and turnover. *Journal of Applied Psychology, 76*(5), 675–689.

Jacobs, R. (1997). *Organizational effectiveness: Downsizing, one of many alternatives.* Keynote address presented at the 18th annual Graduate Student Conference in Industrial Organizational Psychology and Organizational Behavior, Roanoke, VA.

Jago, A. G., & Vroom, V. H. (1977). Hierarchical level and leadership style. *Organizational Behavior and Human Performance, 18,* 131–145.

Jamal, M. (1981). Shiftwork related to job attitudes, social participation, and withdrawal behavior: a study of nurses and industrial workers. *Personnel Psychology, 34,* 535–547.

Janik, J., & Hagness, W. (1994). *Firing under fire.* Paper presented at the 23rd annual meeting of the Society for Police and Criminal Psychology, Madison, WI.

Janis, I. L. (1972). *Victims of groupthink.* New York: Houghton Mifflin.

Jenner, L. (1994). Employment-at-will liability: How protected are you? *HR Focus, 71*(3), 11.

Jockin, V., McGue, M., & Lykken, D. T. (1996). Personality and divorce: A genetic analysis. *Journal of Personality and Social Psychology, 71,* 288–299.

Johns, G. (1994). Absenteeism estimates by employees and managers: Divergent perspectives and self-serving perceptions. *Journal of Applied Psychology, 79*(2), 229–239.

Johnson, D. L., & Andrews, I. R. (1971). The risky-shift hypothesis tested with consumer products as stimuli. *Journal of Personality and Social Psychology, 30,* 382–385.

Johnson, J. L., & Bloom, A. M. (1995). An analysis of the contribution of the five factors of personality to variance in academic procrastination. *Personality and Individual Differences, 18,* 127–133.

Johnson, K. (1997, August 4). New prisons isolate worst inmates. *USA Today,* pp. A1–A2.

Johnson, T. L. (1990). A meta-analytic review of absenteeism control methods. *Applied H.R.M. Research, 1*(1), 23–26.

Jordan, K. (1997). Play fair and square when hiring from within. *HR Magazine, 42*(1), 49–51.

Judge, T. A. (1993). Does affective disposition moderate the relationship between job satisfaction and voluntary turnover? *Journal of Applied Psychology, 78*(3), 395–401.

Judge, T. A., Locke, E. A., Durham, C. C., & Kluger, A. N. (1998). Dispositional effects on job and life satisfaction: The role of core evaluations. *Journal of Applied Psychology, 83*(1), 17–34.

Judge, T. A., Martocchio, J. J., & Thoresen, C. J. (1997). Five-factor model of personality and employee absence. *Journal of Applied Psychology, 82*(5), 745–755.

Judge, T. A., & Watanabe, S. (1993). Another look at the job satisfaction-life satisfaction relationship. *Journal of Applied Psychology, 78*(6), 939–948.

Judge, T. A., & Watanabe, S. (1994). Individual differences in the nature of the relationship between job and life-satisfaction. *Journal of Occupational and Organizational Psychology, 67,* 101–107.

Kanekar, S. (1987). Individual versus group performance: A selective review of experimental studies. *Irish Journal of Psychology, 8*(1), 9–19.

Keeling, L. J., & Hurnik, F. (1996). Social facilitation acts more on the appetite than the consummatory phase of feeding behavior in domestic fowl. *Animal Behavior, 52*(1), 11–15.

Keeping, L. M., & Sulsky, L. M. (1996). *Examining the quality of self-ratings of performance.* Poster presented at the 11th annual meeting of the Society for Industrial and Organizational Psychology, San Diego, CA.

Keller, L. M., Bouchard, T. J., Arvey, R. D., Segal, N. L., & Dawis, R. V. (1992). Work values: Genetic and environmental influences. *Journal of Applied Psychology, 77*(1), 79–88.

Kennedy, J. K., Houston, J. M., Korsgaard, M. A., & Gallo, D. D. (1987). Construct space of the Least Preferred Coworker (LPC) Scale. *Educational and Psychological Measurement, 47*(3), 807–814.

Kenny, D. A., & Zaccaro, S. J. (1983). An estimate of variance due to traits in leadership. *Journal of Applied Psychology, 68,* 678–685.

Kenrick, D. T., & Guitierres, S. E. (1980). Contrast effects and judgments of physical attractiveness: When beauty becomes a social problem. *Journal of Personality and Social Psychology, 38*(1), 131–140.

Kent, R. L., & Moss, S. E. (1990). Self-monitoring as a predictor of leader emergence. *Psychological Reports, 66*(3), 875–881.

Kerr, N. L. (1983). Motivation loss in small groups: A social dilemma analysis. *Journal of Personality and Social Psychology, 45,* 819–828.

Kerr, N. L., & Bruun, S. E. (1983). Dependability of member effort and group motivation loss: Free-rider effects. *Journal of Personality and Social Psychology, 44,* 78–94.

King, N. (1970). Clarification and evaluation of the two-factor theory of job satisfaction. *Psychological Bulletin, 74*(1), 18–31.

King, P. (1984). *Performance planning and appraisal.* New York: McGraw-Hill.

Kipnis, D., Schmidt, S., & Wilkinson, I. (1980). Intra-organizational influence tactics: Exploration in getting one's way. *Journal of Applied Psychology, 65,* 440–452.

Kirkwood, C. (1993). *Your services are no longer required.* New York: Penguin Group.

Klawsky, J. D. (1990). The effect of subgoals on commitment and task performance. *Proceedings of the 11th Annual Graduate Conference in Industrial/ Organizational Psychology and Organizational Behavior.*

Klein, J. D., & Pridemore, D. R. (1992). Effects of cooperative learning and need for affiliation on performance, time on task, and satisfaction. *Educational Technology Research and Development, 40*(4), 39–47.

Klein, M., & Christiansen, G. (1969). Group composition, group structure, and group effectiveness of basketball teams. In J. W. Loy & G. S. Kenyon (Eds.), *Sport, culture, and society* (pp. 397–428). Toronto: Macmillan.

Knapp, M. L. (1978). *Nonverbal communication in human interaction.* New York: Holt, Rinehart & Winston.

Knoop, R. (1994). The relationship between importance and achievement of work values and job satisfaction. *Perceptual and Motor Skills, 79*(1), 595–605.

Knowdell, R. L. (1996). *Building a career development program.* Palo Alto, CA: Davies-Black Publishing.

Komaki, J. L. (1986). Toward effective supervision: An operant analysis and comparison of managers at work. *Journal of Applied Psychology, 71,* 270–279.

Komaki, J. L., Zlotnick, S., & Jensen, M. (1986). Development of an operant-based taxonomy and observational index of supervisory behavior. *Journal of Applied Psychology, 71,* 260–269.

Korabik, K., Barel, G. L., & Watson, C. (1993). Managers' conflict-management style and leadership effectiveness: the moderating effects of gender. *Sex Roles, 29*(5–6), 405–420.

Korman, A. K. (1970). Toward a hypothesis of work behavior. *Journal of Applied Psychology, 54,* 31–41.

Korman, A. K. (1976). Hypothesis of work behavior revisited and an extension. *Academy of Management Review, 1,* 50–63.

Kortick, S. A., & O'Brien, R. M. (1996). The world series of quality control: A case study in the package delivery industry. *Journal of Organizational Behavior Management, 16*(2), 77–93.

Kovach, R., Surrette, M. A., & Whitcomb, A. J. (1988, January). *Contextual, student, and instructor factors involved in college student absenteeism.* Paper presented at the 10th annual National Institute on the Teaching of Psychology, St. Petersburg, FL.

Kozlowski, S. W., Kirsch, M. P., & Chao, G. T. (1986). Job knowledge, ratee familiarity, conceptual similarity and halo error: An exploration. *Journal of Applied Psychology, 71,* 45–49.

Kraiger, K., & Ford, J. K. (1985). A meta-analysis of ratee race effects. *Journal of Applied Psychology, 70,* 56–65.

Kressel, K., Frontera, E., Forlenza, S., Butler, F., & Fish, L. (1994). The settlement-orientation vs. problem-solving style in custody mediation. Special Issue: Constructive conflict management: An answer to critical social problems? *Journal of Social Issues, 40*(1), 67–84.

Kriegel, R., & Brandt, D. (1996). *Sacred cows make the best burgers.* New York: Warner.

Kunin, T. (1955). The construction of a new type of attitude measure. *Personnel Psychology, 8,* 65–78.

Laabs, J. J. (1996, July). Expert advice on how to move forward with change. *Personnel Journal,* pp. 54–63.

Ladd, D., Jagacinski, C., & Stolzenberg, K. (1997). Differences in goal level set for optimists and defensive pessimists under conditions of encouragement. *Proceedings of the 18th Annual Graduate Conference in*

Industrial/Organizational Psychology and Organizational Behavior, 18, 85–86.

Ladio, J. (1996). A primer on in-house message networks. *HR Magazine, 41*(11), 84–91.

LaFleur, T., & Hyten, C. (1995). Improving the quality of hotel banquet staff performance. *Journal of Organizational Behavior Management, 15*(1), 69–93.

Laing, M. (1993). Gossip: Does it play a role in the socialization of nurses? *Journal of Nursing Scholarship, 25*(1), 37–41.

Lakein, A. (1973/1996). *How to get control of your time and your life.* New York: New American Library.

Lamm, H., & Trommsdorff, G. (1973). Group versus individual performance on tasks requiring ideational proficiency (brainstorming): A review. *European Journal of Social Psychology, 3,* 361–388.

Lang, S. S. (1997). Childhood sexual abuse affects relationships in adulthood. *Human Ecology Forum, 25*(2), 3.

Langer, E. J., & Rodin, J. (1976). The effects of choice and enhanced personal responsibility for the aged: A field experiment in an institutional setting. *Journal of Personality and Social Psychology, 34,* 191–198.

Lapidus, R. S., & Pinkerton, L. (1995). Customer complaint situations: An equity theory perspective. *Psychology and Marketing, 12*(2), 105–122.

Larey, T. S., & Paulus, P. B. (1995). Social comparison and goal setting in brainstorming groups. *Journal of Applied Social Psychology, 25*(18), 1579–1596.

Latane, B. (1981). The psychology of social impact. *American Psychologist, 36,* 343–356.

Latham, G. P., & Blades, J. J. (1975). The practical significance of Locke's theory of goal setting. *Journal of Applied Psychology, 60,* 122–124.

Latham, V. M. (1983). Charismatic leadership: A review and proposed model. *Proceedings of the 4th Annual Graduate Conference in Industrial/Organizational Psychology and Organizational Behavior.*

Laumeyer, J., & Beebe, T. (1988). Employees and their appraisals. *Personnel Administrator, 33*(12), 76–80.

Law, J. R. (1996). *Rising to the occasion: Foundations, processes, and outcomes of emergent leadership.* Unpublished doctoral dissertation, University of Texas at Austin.

Lawler, E. E. (1973). *Motivation in work organizations.* Belmont, CA: Brooks/Cole.

Lawler, E. E., & Suttle, J. L. (1972). A causal correlational test of the need hierarchy concept. *Organizational Behavior and Human Performance, 7,* 265–287.

Lawson, R., & Shen, Z. (1998). *Organizational behavior.* New York: Oxford University Press.

Leana, C. R., & Feldman, D. C. (1992). *Coping with job loss.* New York: Lexington.

LePine, J. A., Hollenbeck, J. R., Ilgen, D. R., & Hedlund, J. (1997). Effects of individual differences on the performance of hierarchical decision-making teams: Much more than *g. Journal of Applied Psychology, 82*(5), 803–811.

Levy, P. E. (1993). Self-appraisal and attributions: A test of a model. *Journal of Management, 19*(1), 51–62.

Lewin, K. (1951). *Field theory in social science.* New York: Harper & Row.

Libo, G. M. (1996). *The use and effectiveness of influence tactics in hospital-manager-physician relationships.* Unpublished doctoral dissertation, New Mexico State University.

Liden, R. C., Wayne, S. J., & Bradway, L. (1996). Connections make the difference. *HR Magazine, 41*(2), 73–79.

Lied, T. L., & Pritchard, R. D. (1976). Relationship between personality variables and components of the expectancy-valence model. *Journal of Applied Psychology, 61,* 463–467.

Lindeman, M., Sundvik, L., & Rouhiainen, P. (1995). Under- or overestimation of self? Person variables and self-assessment accuracy in work settings. *Journal of Social Behavior and Personality, 10*(1), 123–134.

Liou, K. T., Sylvia, R. D., & Brunk, G. (1990). Nonwork factors and job satisfaction revisited. *Human Relations, 43,* 77–86.

Littlepage, G. E. (1991). Effects of group size and task characteristics on group performance: A test of Steiner's model. *Personality and Social Psychology Bulletin, 17*(4), 449–456.

Locke, E. A. (1969). What is job satisfaction? *Organizational Behavior and Human Performance, 4,* 309–336.

Locke, E. A. (1996). Motivation through conscious goal setting. *Applied and Preventative Psychology, 5,* 117–124.

Locke, E. A., & Latham, G. P. (1990). *A theory of goal setting and task performance.* Englewood Cliffs, NJ: Prentice Hall.

London, M. & Wohlers, A. J. (1991). Agreement between subordinate and self-ratings in upward feedback. *Personnel Psychology, 44,* 375–390.

Long, W. W., Long, E. J., & Dobbins, G. H. (1998). Correlates of satisfaction with a peer evaluation system: Investigation of performance levels and individual differences. *Journal of Business and Psychology, 12*(33), 299–317.

Lord, R. G., De Vader, C. L., & Alliger, G. M. (1986). A metaanalysis of the relation between personality traits and leadership perceptions: An application of validity generalization procedures. *Journal of Applied Psychology, 71,* 402–410.

Lord, R. G., & Hohenfeld, J. A. (1979). Longitudinal field assessment of equity effects in the performance of major league baseball players. *Journal of Applied Psychology, 64,* 19–26.

Lorge, I., Fox, D., Davitz, J., & Brenner, M. (1958). A survey of studies contrasting the quality of group performance versus individual performance. *Psychological Bulletin, 55,* 337–372.

Lovelace, K., & Rosen, B. (1996). Differences in achieving person-organization fit among diverse groups of managers. *Journal of Management, 22*(5), 703–722.

Lovenheim, P. (1996). *How to mediate your dispute.* Berkeley, CA: Nolo Press.

Lowe, R. H., & Vodanovich, S. J. (1995). A field study of distributive and procedural justice as predictors of satisfaction and organizational commitment. *Journal of Business and Psychology, 10*(1), 99–114.

Lowman, R. L. (1998). *The ethical practice of psychology in organizations*. Washington, DC: American Psychological Association.

Lulofs, R. S. (1994). *Conflict from theory to action*. Scottsdale, AZ: Gorsuch Scarisbrick, Publishers.

Lykken, D. T., & Tellegen, A. (1996). Happiness is a stochastic phenomenon. *Psychological Science, 7(3),* 186–189.

Mabe, P. A., & West, S. G. (1982). Validity of self-evaluation of ability: A review and meta-analysis. *Journal of Applied Psychology, 67,* 280–296.

Macan, T. H. (1994). Time management: Test of a process model. *Journal of Applied Psychology, 79(3),* 381–391.

MacKenzie, R. A. (1972). *The time trap: How to get more done in less time*. New York: McGraw-Hill.

Maier, N. R. F. (1976). *The appraisal interview*. La Jolla, CA: University Associates.

Major, B., Schmidlin, A. M., & Williams, L. (1990). General patterns in social touch: The impact of setting and age. *Journal of Personality and Social Psychology, 58,* 634–643.

Malandro, L. A., & Barker, L. L. (1983). *Nonverbal communication*. Reading, MA: Addison-Wesley.

Manners, G. E. (1975). Another look at group size, group problem solving, and member consensus. *Academy of Management Journal, 18,* 715–724.

Mantell, M. & Albrecht, S. (1994). *Ticking bombs: Defusing violence in the workplace*. New York: Business & Irwin.

Manz, C. C., & Sims, H. P. (1986). Beyond limitation: Complex behavioral and affective linkages resulting from exposure to leadership training models. *Journal of Applied Psychology, 71,* 571–578.

Marchetti, M. (1997). The fine art of firing. *Sales and Marketing Management, 149(4),* 6–7.

Markowich, M. (1994). Reengineering sick pay. *HR Focus, 71(4),* 12–13.

Martin, G. E., & Bergmann. T. J. (1996, December). The dynamics of behavioural response to conflict in the workplace. *Journal of Occupational and Organizational Psychology, 69(4),* 377–388.

Martin, S. (1995). The role of nonverbal communication in quality improvement. *National Productivity Review, 15(1),* 27–39.

Maslow, A. H. (1954). *Motivation and personality*. New York: Harper & Row.

Massey, M. (1975). *What you are is what you were when*. Farmington Hills, MI: CBS Fox Video.

Masters, F. W., & Graves, D. C. (1967). The Quasimodo complex. *British Journal of Plastic Surgery, 20,* 204–209.

Matheson, H., Mathes, S., & Murray, M. (1997). The effect of winning and losing on female interactive and coactive team cohesion. *Journal of Sport Behavior, 20(3),* 284–298.

Mawhinney, T. C., & Gowen, C. R. (1990). Gainsharing and the law of effect as the matching law: A theoretical framework. *Journal of Organizational Behavior Management, 11(2),* 61–75.

Mayo, E. (1946). *The human problems of an industrial civilization*. Cambridge, MA: Harvard University Press.

McCann, N., & Lester, D. (1996). Smoking and stress: Cigarettes and marijuana. *Psychological Reports, 79(2),* 366.

McClelland, D. C. (1961). *The achieving society*. Princeton, NJ: Van Nostrand.

McClelland, D. C., & Boyatzis, R. E. (1982). Leadership motive pattern and long-term success in management. *Journal of Applied Psychology, 67,* 737–743.

McClelland, D. C., & Burnham, D. H. (1976). Power is the great motivator. *Harvard Business Review, 54(2),* 102–104.

McEvoy, G. M. (1990). Public sector managers' reactions to appraisals by subordinates. *Public Personnel Management, 19(2),* 201–212.

McGregor, D. (1960). *The human side of enterprise*. New York: McGraw-Hill.

McLeod, P. L., Baron, R. S., Marti, M. W., & Yoon, K. (1997). The eyes have it: Minority influence in face-to-face and computer-mediated group discussion. *Journal of Applied Psychology, 82(5),* 706–718.

McWhirter, B. T. (1998). Personality characteristics of competitive and recreational cyclists. *Journal of Sport Behavior, 21(4)* 408–416.

Meier, P. (1993). *Don't let jerks get the best of you*. Nashville, TN: Thomas Nelson Publishers.

Mento, A. J., Steel, R. P., & Karren, R. J. (1987). A meta-analytic study of the effects of goal setting on task performance: 1966–1984. *Organizational Behavior and Human Decision Processes, 39,* 52–83.

Mero, N. P., & Motowidlo, S. J. (1995). Effects of rater accountability on the accuracy and the favorability of performance ratings. *Journal of Applied Psychology, 80(4),* 517–524.

Messmer, M. (1998). Improving your listening skills. *Management Accounting, 79(9),* 14.

Meyer, H. H. (1980). Selfappraisal of job performance. *Personnel Psychology, 33,* 291–296.

Michaels, J. W., Blommel, J. M., Brocato, R. M., Linkous, R. A., & Rowe, J. S. (1982). Social facilitation and inhibition in a natural setting. *Replications in Social Psychology, 2,* 21–24.

Miles, D. R., & Carey, G. (1997). Genetic and environmental architecture of human aggression. *Journal of Personality and Social Psychology, 72,* 207–217.

Miles, E. W., Patrick, S. L., & King, W. C. (1996). Job level as a systematic variable in predicting the relationship between supervisory communication and job satisfaction. *Journal of Occupational and Organizational Psychology, 69(3),* 277–292.

Miles, J. A., & Greenberg, J. (1993). Using punishment threats to attenuate social loafing effects among swimmers. *Organizational Behavior and Human Decision Processes, 56(2),* 246–265.

Milgram, S. (1963). Behavioral study of obedience. *Journal of Abnormal and Social Psychology, 67,* 371–378.

Miller, C. W. (1998, January 18). Managers benefit from walking around, talking with workers. *The Roanoke Times,* p. B2.

Miller, J. G. (1960). Information input, overload, and psychopathology. *American Journal of Psychiatry, 116,* 695–704.

Mirolli, K., Henderson, P., & Hills, D. (1998). *Coworkers' influence on job satisfaction*. Paper presented at the 19th annual Graduate Student Conference in Industrial/Organizational Psychology and Organizational Behavior, San Diego, CA.

Mishra, J. (1990). Managing the grapevine. *Public Personnel Management, 19*(2), 213–226.

Mitchell, T. R. (1974). Expectancy models of job satisfaction, occupational preference, and effort: A theoretical, methodological, and empirical approach. *Psychological Bulletin, 81*, 1053–1077.

Mitchell, V. F., & Mougdill, P. (1976). Measurement of Maslow's need hierarchy. *Organizational Behavior and Human Performance, 16*, 334–349.

Mitra, A., Jenkins, G. D., & Gupta, N. (1992). A meta-analytic review of the relationship between absence and turnover. *Journal of Applied Psychology, 77*(6), 879–889.

Mobaraki, G. R. (1996). *A study to determine effective means to motivate employees*. Unpublished doctoral dissertation, Walden University.

Moede, W. (1927). Die Richtlinien der Leistungs-Psychologie. *Industrielle Pscyhotechnik, 4*, 193–207.

Monroe, C., Borzi, M. G., & DiSalvo, V. S. (1989). Difficult subordinate's conflict. *Southern Communication Journal, 54*, 311–329.

Moore, C. W. (1987). *The mediation process*. San Francisco: Jossey-Bass.

Moores, J. (1990). A meta-analytic review of the effects of compressed work schedules. *Applied H.R.M. Research, 1*(1), 12–18.

Moran, L., Musselwhite, E., & Zenger, J. H. (1996). *Keeping teams on track*. Chicago: Irwin.

Morehouse, R. L. (1997, November). Three keys to becoming a leader. *HR Magazine*.

Morrison, E. W. (1993). Newcomer information seeking: Exploring types, modes, sources, and outcomes. *Academy of Management Journal, 36*(3), 557–589.

Morrison, E. W., & Robinson, S. L. (1997). When employees feel betrayed: A model of how psychological contract violation develops. *Academy of Management Review, 22*(1), 226–256.

Mossholder, K. W. (1980). Effects of externally mediated goal setting on intrinsic motivation: A laboratory experiment. *Journal of Applied Psychology, 65*(2), 202–210.

Moulton, D. A. (1994). *Effects of organizational policies and training on sexual harassment*. Unpublished master's thesis, Radford University, Radford, VA.

Mount, M. K. (1983). Comparisons of managerial and employee satisfaction with a performance appraisal system. *Personnel Psychology, 36*, 99–110.

Mount, M. K., & Ellis, R. A. (1989). Sources of bias in job evaluation: A review and critique of research. *Journal of Social Issues, 45*(4), 153–167.

Mulder, M., de Jong, R. D., Koppelaar, L., & Verhage, J. (1986). Power, situation, and leaders' effectiveness: An organizational field study. *Journal of Applied Psychology, 71*, 566–570.

Mullen, B., Anthony, T., Salas, E., & Driskell, J. E. (1994). Group cohesiveness and quality of decision making: An integration of the groupthink hypothesis. *Small Group Research, 25*(2), 189–204.

Mullen, B., & Copper, C. (1994). The relation between group cohesiveness and performance: An integration. *Psychological Bulletin, 115*(2), 210–227.

Mumford, M. D. (1983). Social comparison theory and the evaluation of peer evaluations: A review and some applied implications. *Personnel Psychology, 36*, 867–881.

Murphy, K. R., Gannett, B. A., Herr, B. M., & Chen, J. A. (1986). Effects of subsequent performance on evaluations of previous performance. *Journal of Applied Psychology, 71*, 427–431.

Murphy, K. R., Martin, C., & Garcia, M. (1982). Do behavioral observation scales measure observation? *Journal of Applied Psychology, 67*, 562–567.

Murphy, S. T., Monahan, J. L., & Miller, L. C. (1998). Inference under the influence: The impact of alcohol and inhibition conflict on women's sexual decision making. *Personality and Social Psychology Bulletin, 24*(5), 517–529.

Nagy, M. S. (1995). *An integrated model of job satisfaction*. Unpublished doctoral dissertation, Louisiana State University.

Nagy, M. S. (1996, April). What to do when you are dissatisfied with job satisfaction scales: A better way to measure job satisfaction. *Assessment Council News*, pp. 5–10.

Nanus, R. (1992). *Visionary leadership*. San Francisco: Jossey-Bass.

Nash, L. L. (1993). *Good intentions aside*. Boston: Harvard Business School Press.

Nathan, B., & Lord, R. (1983). Cognitive categorization and dimensional schemata: A process approach to the study of halo in performance ratings. *Journal of Applied Psychology, 68*, 102–114.

Naughton, R. J. (1975). Motivational factors of American prisoners of war in Vietnam. *Naval War College Review, 27*(4), 2–14.

Naughton, T. J. (1988). Effect of female-linked job titles on job evaluation ratings. *Journal of Management, 14*(4), 567–578.

Neubauer, P. J. (1992). The impact of stress, hardiness, home and work environment on job satisfaction, illness, and absenteeism in critical care nurses. *Medical Psychotherapy, 5*, 109–122.

Neufeldt, D., Kimbrough, W. W., & Stadelmaier, M. F. (1983, April). *Relationship between group composition and task type on group problem solving ability*. Paper presented at the 11th annual Graduate Student Conference in Personality and Social Psychology, Norman, OK.

Newsome, M., & Pillari, V. (1992). Job satisfaction and the worker-supervisor relationship. *The Clinical Supervisor, 9*(2), 119–129.

Nicholls, J. R. (1985). A new approach to situational leadership. *Leadership and Organization Development Journal, 6*(4), 27.

Nichols, R. G., & Stevens, L. A. (1957). *Are you listening?* New York: McGraw-Hill.

Nicholson, N., Jackson, P., & Howes, G. (1978). Shift-work and absence: A study of temporal trends. *Journal of Occupational Psychology, 51*, 127–137.

Nicotera, A. M. (1995). *Conflict and organizations*. Albany, NY: State University of New York Press.

Noble, S. A. (1997). *Effects of a time delay on frame-of-reference training*. Poster presented at the 12th annual conference of the Society for Industrial and Organizational Psychology, St. Louis, MO.

Nolan, J., Lee, K., & Allen, N. (1997). *Work group heterogeneity, performance, and turnover: Some meta-analytic findings*. Poster presented at the 12th annual conference of the Society for Industrial and Organizational Psychology, St. Louis, MO.

Norris, W. R., & Vecchio, R. P. (1992). Situational leadership theory: A replication. *Group and Organization Management, 17*(3), 331–342.

Nwachukwu, S. L., & Vitell, S. J. (1997). The influence of corporate culture on managerial ethical judgments. *Journal of Business Ethics, 16*, 757–776.

Occupational Outlook Handbook (1995). Washington, DC: U.S. Department of Labor.

Offerman, L. R. & Gowing, M. K. (1990). Organizations of the future: Changes and challenges. *American Psychologist, 45*(2), 95–108.

Oliphant, V. N., & Alexander, E. R. (1982). Reactions to resumes as a function of resume determinateness, applicant characteristics, and sex of raters. *Personnel Psychology, 35*, 829–842.

O'Reilly, C. A., & Puffer, S. M. (1989). The impact of rewards and punishments in a social context: A laboratory and field experiment. *Journal of Occupational Psychology, 62*(1), 41–53.

Ornish, D. (1984). *Stress, diet, and your health*. New York: Signet.

Overman, S. (1994). Teams score on the bottom line. *HR Magazine, 39*(5), 82–84.

Oz, S., & Eden, D. (1994). Restraining the Golem: Boosting performance by changing the interpretation of low scores. *Journal of Applied Psychology, 79*(5), 744–754.

Packard, M. (1997). Getting vocal about voice mail and automated phone systems. *RV Business, 48*(1), 29.

Parker, P. A., & Kulik, J. A. (1995). Burnout, self- and supervisor-related job performance, and absenteeism among nurses. *Journal of Behavioral Medicine, 18*(6), 581–599.

Parrott, A. C. (1995). Smoking cessation leads to reduced stress, but why? *International Journal of the Addictions, 30*(11), 1509.

Paul, R. J., & Ebadi, Y. M. (1989). Leadership decision making in a service organization: A field test of the Vroom-Yetton model. *Journal of Occupational Psychology, 62*(3), 201–211.

Pearce, J. L., & Porter, L. W. (1986). Employee responses to formal performance appraisal feedback. *Journal of Applied Psychology, 71*, 211–218.

Pelletier, L. G., & Vallerand, R. J. (1996). Supervisors' beliefs and subordinates' intrinsic motivation: A behavioral confirmation analysis. *Journal of Personality and Social Psychology, 71*(2), 331–340.

Peterson, K. S. (1997, November 3). Interracial dating is no big deal for teens. *USA Today*, A-10.

Philbrick, K. D. (1989). *The use of humor and effective leadership styles*. Unpublished doctoral dissertation, University of Florida.

Pingitore, R., Dugoni, B. L., Tindale, R. S., & Spring, B. (1994). Bias against overweight job applicants in a simulated employment interview. *Journal of Applied Psychology, 79*(6), 909–917.

Pinkley, R., & Northcraft, G. (1994). Conflict frames of reference: Implications for dispute processes and outcomes. *Academy of Management, 37*(1), 193–205.

Planchy, R. J., & Planchy, S. J. (1993). Focus on results, not behavior. *Personnel Journal, 72*(3), 28–30.

Pliner, P., Hart, H., Kohl, J., & Saari, D. (1974). Compliance without pressure: Some further data on the foot-in-the-door technique. *Journal of Experimental Social Psychology, 10*, 17–22.

Plomin, R. (1994). Nature, nurture, and development. In R. J. Sternberg (Ed.), *Encyclopedia of human intelligence*. New York: Macmillan.

Podsakoff, P. M., MacKenzie, S. B., & Ahearne, M. (1997). Moderating effects of goal acceptance on the relationship between group cohesiveness and productivity. *Journal of Applied Psychology, 82*(6), 974–983.

Poe, A. C. (1997). Productivity via paradise. *HR Magazine, 42*(10), 91–94.

Pollan, S. M., & Levine, M. (1994). Firing an employee. *Working Woman, 19*(8), 55.

Pollitt, E. (1995). Does breakfast make a difference in school? *Journal of the American Dietetic Association, 95*(10), 1134–1139.

Pond, S. B., & Geyer, P. D. (1987). Employee age as a moderator or the relationship between perceived work alternatives and job satisfaction. *Journal of Applied Psychology, 72*, 552–557.

Pool, S. W. (1997). The relationship of job satisfaction with substitutes of leadership, leadership behavior, and work motivation. *Journal of Psychology, 131*(3), 271–283.

Porter, L. W., & Lawler, E. E. (1968). *Managerial attitudes and performance*. Homewood, IL: Dorsey.

Pospisil, V. (1997). Keep it simple: Automated answering. *Industry Week, 246*(12), 8.

Premack, D. (1963). Prediction of the comparative reinforcement values of running and drinking. *Science, 139*, 1062–1063.

Pritchard, R. D., Dunnette, M. D., & Jorgenson, D. (1972). Effects of perceptions of equity on worker motivation and satisfaction. *Journal of Applied Psychology, 56*(1), 75–94.

Pritchett, P. (1993). *Culture shift: The employee handbook for changing corporate culture*. Dallas: Pritchett & Associates.

Pritchett, P., & Pound, R. (1995). *The stress of organizational change*. Dallas, TX: Pritchett & Associates.

Pulakos, E. D., White, L. A., Oppler, S. H., & Borman, W. C. (1989). Examination of race and sex effects on performance ratings. *Journal of Applied Psychology, 74*, 770–780.

Pursell, E. D., Dossett, D. L., & Latham, G. P. (1980). Obtaining valid predictors by minimizing rating errors in the criterion. *Personnel Psychology, 33*, 91–96.

Qian, Y. J. (1996). *Managers' stock ownership and performance in lodging industry*. Unpublished master's thesis, University of Nevada at Las Vegas.

Quinn, J. F., & Petrick, J. A. (1993). Emerging strategic human resource challenges in managing accent discrimination and ethnic diversity. *Applied H.R.M. Research, 4*(2), 79–93.

Rahim, M. A. (1989). Relationships of leader power to compliance and satisfaction with supervision: Evidence from a national sample of managers. *Journal of Management,15*(4), 545–556.

Rahim, M. A., & Afza, M. (1993). Leader power, commitment, satisfaction, compliance, and propensity to leave a job among U.S. accountants. *Journal of Social Psychology, 133*(5), 611–625.

Rahim, M. A., & Bonoma, T. V. (1979). Managing organizational conflict. A model for diagnosis and intervention. *Psychological Reports, 44*, 1323–1344.

Rahim, M. A., Garrett, J. E., & Buntzman, G. F. (1992). Ethics of managing interpersonal conflict in organizations. *Journal of Business Ethics, 11*, 423–432.

Rahim, M. A., & Psenicka, C. (1996). A structural equations model of stress, locus of control, social support, psychiatric symptoms, and propensity to leave a job. *The Journal of Social Psychology, 136*(1), 69–84.

Raine, A. (1993). *The psychopathology of crime*. San Diego, CA: Academic Press.

Rasmussen, K. G. (1984). Nonverbal behavior, verbal behavior, resume credentials, and selection interview outcomes. *Journal of Applied Psychology, 69*, 551–556.

Raven, B. H. (1965). Social influence and power. In I. D. Steiner & M. Fishbein (Eds.), *Current studies in social psychology* (pp. 371–382). New York: Holt, Rinehart & Winston.

Raven, B. H. (1992). A power/interaction model of interpersonal influence: French and Raven thirty years later. *Journal of Social Behavior and Personality, 7*(2), 217–244.

Ray, J. J., & Hall, G. P. (1995). Need for affiliation and group identification. *Journal of Social Psychology, 135*(4), 519–521.

Raynes, B. L. (1997a). *Predicting difficult employees: The relationship between vocational interests, self-esteem, and problem communication styles*. Unpublished master's thesis, Radford University, Radford, VA.

Raynes, B. L. (1997b). Screening for difficult people. *Assessment Council News, 10*, 8–11.

Reilly, R. R., Smither, J. W., & Vasilopoulous, N. L. (1996). A longitudinal study of upward feedback. *Personnel Psychology, 49*(3), 599–612.

Reizenstein, R. M., & Burke, M. J. (1996). *Another look at relationships between group cohesion and group performance*. Poster presented at the 11th annual conference of the Society for Industrial and Organizational Psychology, San Diego, CA.

Repetti, R. L., & Cosmas, K. A. (1991). The quality of the social environment at work and job satisfaction. *Journal of Applied Social Psychology, 21*(10), 840–854.

Repetti, R. L., & Wood, J. (1997). Effects of daily stress at work on mothers' interactions with preschoolers. *Journal of Family Psychology, 11*(1), 90–108.

Reynolds, L. (1997). Fighting domestic violence in the workplace. *HR Focus, 74*(11), 8–9.

Rhoads, C. (1997). A year-round schedule said to take sting out of performance reviews. *American Banker, 162*(28), 6.

Rhodes, S. R. (1983). Age-related differences in work attitudes and behavior: A review and conceptual analysis. *Psychological Bulletin, 93*, 328–367.

Rice, R. E. (1993). Media appropriateness: Using social presence theory to compare traditional and new organizational media. *Human Communication Research, 19*(4), 451–484.

Rice, R. W. (1978). Psychometric properties of the esteem for Least Preferred Coworker (LPC) Scale. *Academy of Management Review, 3*, 106–118.

Rice, R. W., Gentile, D. A., & McFarlin, D. B. (1991). Facet importance and job satisfaction. *Journal of Applied Psychology, 76*(1), 31–39.

Rifkind, L. J., & Harper, L. F. (1994). Conflict management strategies for the equal opportunity difficult person in the sexually harassing workplace. *Public Personnel Management, 23*(3), 487–500.

Riggio, R. E., & Cole, E. J. (1992). Agreement between subordinate and superior ratings of supervisory performance and effects on self and subordinate satisfaction. *Journal of Occupational and Organizational Psychology, 65*, 137–158.

Robbins, S. P. (1998). *Organizational behavior* (7th ed.). Englewood Cliffs, NJ: Prentice Hall.

Romanov, K., Appelberg, K., Honkasalo, M., & Koskenvuo, M. (1996). Recent interpersonal conflict at work and psychiatric morbidity: A prospective study of 15,530 employees aged 24–64. *Journal of Psychosomatic Research, 40*(2), 169–176.

Rosen, D. J. (1992). Appraisal can make or break your court case. *Personnel Journal, 71*(11), 113–116.

Rosen, S., & Tesser, A. (1970). Reluctance to communicate undesirable information: The MUM effect. *Sociometry, 33*, 253–263.

Rosenthal, R. (1994). Interpersonal expectancy effects: A 30 year perspective. *Current Directions in Psychological Science, 3*(6), 176–179.

Ross, W. R., & Wieland, C . (1996). Effectiveness of interpersonal trust and time pressure on managerial mediation strategy in a simulated organizational dispute. *Journal of Applied Psychology, 81*(3), 228–248.

Rothstein, M. A., Craver, C. B., Schroeder, E. P., Shoben, E. W., & VanderVelde, L. S. (1994). *Employment law*. St. Paul, MN: West Publishing Company.

Ruback, R. B., & Juieng, D. (1997). Territorial defense in parking lots: Retaliation against waiting drivers. *Journal of Applied Social Psychology, 27*(9), 821–834.

Rushton, J. P. (1995). Construct validity, censorship, and the genetics of race. *American Psychologist, 50*(1), 40–41.

Ryan, R. M., & Deci, E. L. (1996). When paradigms clash: Comments on Cameron and Pierce's claim that rewards do not undermine intrinsic motivation. *Review of Educational Research, 66*(1), 33–38.

Rynes, S. L., Weber, C. L., & Milkovich, G. T. (1989). Effects of market survey rates, job evaluation, and job gender on job pay. *Journal of Applied Psychology, 74*(1), 114–123.

Saavedra, R., & Kwun, S. K. (1993). Peer evaluation in self-managing work groups. *Journal of Applied Psychology, 78*(3), 450–462.

Sabath, A. M. (1993). *Business etiquette in brief*. New York: Adams Media Corporation.

Sabini, J. (1995). *Social psychology* (2nd ed.). New York: Norton.

Sackman, S. (1991). Uncovering culture in organizations. *Journal of Applied Behavioral Science, 27*(3), 294–315.

Sahl, R. J. (1996). Using tailored employee attitude surveys to measure HR's effectiveness. *Employment Relations Today, 23*(3), 55–63.

Salancik, G., & Pfeffer, J. (1977). An examination of needsatisfaction models of job satisfaction and job attitudes. *Administrative Science Quarterly, 22*, 427–456.

Salas, E., Mullen, B., Rozell, D., & Driskell, J. E. (1997). *The effects of team building on performance: An integration.* Poster presented at the 12th annual conference of the Society for Industrial and Organizational Psychology, St. Louis, MO.

Sanders, G. S. (1981). Driven by distraction: An integrative review of social facilitation theory and research. *Journal of Experimental Social Psychology, 17*, 227–251.

Sandler, L. (1986). Self-fulfilling prophecy: Better management by magic. *Training, 23*, 60–64.

Scandura, T. A., Graen, G. B., & Novak, M. A. (1986). When managers decide not to decide autocratically: An investigation of leader-member exchange and decision influence. *Journal of Applied Psychology, 71*, 579–584.

Schaubroeck, J., Ganster, D. C., & Kemmerer, B. E. (1994). Job complexity, Type A behavior, and cardiovascular disorder: A prospective study. *Academy of Management Journal, 37*(2), 426–439.

Schein, E. (1956). The Chinese indoctrination program for prisoners of war. *Psychiatry, 19*, 149–177.

Schein, E. H. (1985). *Organizational culture and leadership: A dynamic view*. San Francisco: Jossey-Bass.

Schleifer, L. M., & Amick, B. C. (1989). System response time and method of pay: Stress effects in computer-based tasks. *International Journal of Human Computer Interaction, 1*(1), 23–39.

Schleifer, L. M., & Okogbaa, O. G. (1990). System response time and method of pay: Cardiovascular stress effects in computer-based tasks. *Ergonomics, 33*(12), 1495–1509.

Schmidt, F. L. (1973). Implications of a measurement problem for expectancy theory research. *Organizational Behavior and Human Performance, 10*, 243–251.

Schoenthaler, S. J. (1982). The effect of sugar on the treatment and control of anti-social behavior: A double-blind study of an incarcerated juvenile population. *International Journal of Biosocial Research, 3*(1), 1–9

Scholtes, P., Joiner, B., & Streibel, B. (1996). *The team handbook* (2nd ed.). Madison, WI: Joiner Associates.

Schor, J. (1991). *The overworked American*. New York: Basic Books.

Schrader, B. W., & Steiner, D. D. (1996). Common comparison standards: An approach to improving agreement between self and supervisory performance ratings. *Journal of Applied Psychology, 81*(6), 813–820.

Schriesheim, C. A., & DeNisi, A. S. (1981). Task dimensions as moderators of the effects of instrumental leadership: A two-sample replicated test of path-goal leadership theory. *Journal of Applied Psychology, 66*, 589–597.

Schriesheim, C. A., Tepper, B. J., & Tetrault, L. A. (1994). Least Preferred Coworker score, situational control, and leadership effectiveness: A meta-analysis of contingency model performance predictions. *Journal of Applied Psychology, 79*(4), 561–573.

Schriesheim, J. F., & Schriesheim, C. A. (1980). A test of the path-goal theory of leadership and some suggested directions for future research. *Personnel Psychology, 33*, 349–370.

Schulz, R. (1976). Effects of control and predictability on the physical and psychological well-being of the institutionalized aged. *Journal of Personality and Social Psychology, 33*, 563–573.

Schuster, F. E., Mordern, D. L., Baker, T. E., McKay, I. S., Dunning, K. E., & Hagan, C. M. (1997). Management practice, organization climate, and performance: An exploratory study. *Journal of Applied Behavioral Science, 33*(2), 209–226.

Schuster, J. R., & Zingheim, P. K. (1992). *The new pay*. New York: Lexington.

Scott, K. D., Markham, S. E., & Robers, R. W. (1985). Rewarding good attendance: A comparative study of positive ways to reduce absenteeism. *Personnel Administrator, 30*, 72–75.

Scrivner, T. W. (1995). The art of employment termination. *Credit Union Executive, 35*(6), 18–21.

Sears, D. (1988). Symbolic racism. In P. Katz & D. Taylor (Eds.), *Eliminating Racism: Profiles in Controversy* (pp. 53–84). New York: Plenum.

Sessa, V. I. (1994). Can conflict improve team effectiveness? *Issues & Observations, 14*(4), 1–5.

Seta, J. J. (1982). The impact of comparison processes on coactor's task performance. *Journal of Personality and Social Psychology, 42*, 281–291.

Shalley, C. E. (1995). Effects of coaction, expected evaluation, and goal setting on creativity and productivity. *Academy of Management Journal, 38*(2), 483–503.

Shepperd, J. A. (1993). Productivity loss in performance groups: A motivation analysis. *Psychological Bulletin, 113*(1), 67–81.

Sherif, M. (1961). *Intergroup conflict and cooperation: The Robbers Cave experiment*. Norman, OK: University Book Exchange.

Sherman, A., Bohlander, G. W., & Snell, S. (1998). *Managing human resources* (11th ed.). Cincinnati, OH: South-Western Publishing.

Sherriton, J., & Stern, J. (1997). HR's role in culture change. *HR Focus, 74*(4), 27.

Shneiderman, B. (1980). *Software psychology.* Cambridge, MA: Winthrop.

Simon, T. R., Richardson, J. L., Dent, C. W., Chou, C. P., & Flay, B. R. (1998). Prospective psychosocial, interpersonal, and behavioral predictors of handgun carrying among adolescents. *The American Journal of Public Health, 88*(6), 960–964.

Simonton, D. K. (1979). Multiple discovery and invention: Zeitgeist, genius, or chance? *Journal of Personality and Social Psychology, 37,* 1603–1616 .

Skinner, B. F. (1938). *The behavior of organizations.* New York: Appleton.

Skinner, B. F. (1969). *Contingencies of reinforcement.* New York: Appleton-Century-Crofts.

Slage, J. K. (1997). Attack on violence. *Industry Week, 246*(4), 15–17.

Smith, B. N., Hornsby, J. S., Benson, P. G., & Wesolowski, M. (1989). What is in a name: The impact of job titles on job evaluation results. *Journal of Business and Psychology, 3*(3), 341–351.

Smith, D. (1998). New emphasis on ethics. *Blue Ridge Business Journal, 10*(5), 1 & 6–10.

Smith, D. E. (1986). Training programs for performance appraisal: A review. *Academy of Management Review, 11,* 22–40.

Smith, E. R. & Mackie, D. M. (1995). *Social psychology.* New York: Worth.

Smith, M. L. (1993). Defensible performance appraisals. *Journal of Management in Engineering, 9*(2), 128–135.

Smith, P. C., Kendall, L. M., & Hulin, C. L. (1969). *The measurement of satisfaction in work and retirement.* Chicago: Rand McNally.

Smither, J. W., Barry, S. R., & Reilly, R. R. (1989). An investigation of the validity of expert true score estimates in appraisal research. *Journal of Applied Psychology, 74,* 143–151.

Smither, J. W., Reilly, R. R., & Buda, R. (1988). Effect of prior performance information on ratings of recent performance: Contrast versus assimilation revisited. *Journal of Applied Psychology, 73,* 487–496.

Smither, R., & Lindgren, H. C. (1978). Salary, age, sex, and need for achievement in bank employees. *Psychological Reports, 42,* 334.

Snyderman, M., & Rothman, S. (1987). Survey of expert opinion on intelligence and aptitude testing. *American Psychologist, 42,* 137–144.

Sommer, R., Wynes, M., & Brinkley, G. (1992). Social facilitation effects in shopping behavior. *Environment and Behavior, 24*(3), 285–297.

Soper, B., Milford, G. E., & Rosenthal, G. T. (1995). Belief when evidence does not support theory. *Psychology and Marketing, 12*(5), 415–422.

Spink, K. S., & Carron, A. V. (1992). Group cohesion and adherence in exercise classes. *Journal of Sport and Exercise Psychology, 14*(1), 78–86.

Spock, G., & Stevens, S. (1985). A test of Anderson's averaging versus adding model on resume evaluations. *Proceedings of the 6th Annual Graduate Conference in Industrial/Organizational Psychology and Organizational Behavior,* pp. 95–96.

Srinivas, S., & Motowidlo, S. J. (1987). Effects of rater's stress on the dispersion and favorability of performance ratings. *Journal of Applied Psychology, 72,* 247–251.

Stahl, M. J. (1983). Achievement, power, and managerial motivation: Selecting managerial talent with the job choice exercise. *Personnel Psychology, 36,* 775–789.

Stahl, M. J., & Harrell, A. M. (1981). Modeling effort decisions with behavioral decision theory: Toward an individual differences model of expectancy theory. *Organizational Behavior and Human Performance, 27,* 303–325.

Stahl, M. J., & Harrell, A. M. (1982). Evolution and validation of a behavioral decision theory measurement approach to achievement, power, and affiliation. *Journal of Applied Psychology, 67,* 744–751.

Stajkovic, A. D., & Luthans, F. (1997). A meta-analysis of the effects of organizational behavior modification on task performance, 1975–95. *Academy of Management Journal, 40*(5), 1122–1149.

Stanten, M. (May 1997). Fit tips: Smart talk for active living. *Prevention Magazine,* p. 69.

Staw, B. M., Bell, N. E., & Clausen, J. A. (1986). The dispositional approach to job attitudes: A lifetime longitudinal test. *Administrative Science Quarterly, 31,* 56–77.

Staw, B. M., & Ross, J. (1985). Stability in the midst of change: A dispositional approach to job attitudes. *Journal of Applied Psychology, 70,* 469–480.

Steel, R. P., & Rentsch, J. R. (1997). The dispositional model of job attitudes revisited: Findings of a 10-year study. *Journal of Applied Psychology, 82*(6), 873–879.

Steel, R. P., & Rentsch, J. R. (1998). *Using job design as absence control policy: Short- and long-term payoffs.* Paper presented at the Academy of Management meeting, San Diego, CA.

Steers, R. M., & Porter, L. W. (1991). *Motivation and work behavior* (4th ed.). New York: McGraw-Hill.

Steiner, I. D. (1972). *Group process and productivity.* New York: Academic Press.

Stewart, D. W., & Latham, D. R. (1986). On some psychometric properties of Fiedler's contingency model of leadership. *Small Group Behavior, 17*(1), 83–94.

Stewart, P. A., & Moore, J. C. (1992). Wage disparities and performance expectations. *Social Psychology Quarterly, 55*(1), 78–85.

Stout, S. K., Slocum, J. W., & Cron, W. L. (1987). Career transitions of superiors and subordinates. *Journal of Vocational Behavior, 30,* 124–137.

Strube, M. J., & Garcia, J. E. (1981). A meta-analytic investigation of Fiedler's contingency model of leadership effectiveness. *Psychological Bulletin, 90,* 307–321.

Suedfeld, P., & Rank, A. D. (1976). Revolutionary leaders: Long-term success as a function of changes in conceptual complexity. *Journal of Personality and Social Psychology, 34,* 169–178.

Summer, H. C., & Knight, P. A. (1996). Assimilation and contrast effects in performance ratings: Effects of rating the previous performance on rating subsequent performance. *Journal of Applied Psychology, 81*(4), 436–442.

Surrette, M. A., & Harlow, L. L. (1992). Level of satisfaction and commitment to a decisional choice as mediated by locus of control. *Applied H.R.M. Research, 3*(2), 92–113.

Sutton, H. W., & Porter, L. W. (1968). A study of the grapevine in a governmental organization. *Personnel Psychology, 21,* 223–230.

Tait, M., Padgett, M. Y., & Baldwin, T. T. (1989). Job and life satisfaction: A reexamination of the strength of the relationship and gender effects as a function of the date of the study. *Journal of Applied Psychology, 74,* 502–507.

Tanford, S., & Penrod, S. (1984). Social influence model: A formal integration of research on majority and minority influence processes. *Psychological Bulletin, 95,* 189–225.

Tannen, D. (1986). *That's not what I meant!* New York: Ballantine.

Tannen, D. (1990). *You just don't understand: Women and men in conversation.* New York: Ballantine.

Tannen, D. (1994). *Talking 9 to 5.* New York: Morrow.

Tannen, D. (1998). *The Argument Culture: Moving from debate to dialogue.* New York: Random House.

Taylor, S. E., Peplau, L. A., & Sears, D. D. (1994). *Social psychology* (8th ed.). Englewood Cliffs, NJ: Prentice Hall.

Tedeschi, J. T., Bonoma, T. V., & Schlenker, B. R. (1972). Influence, decision, and compliance. In J. T. Tedeschi (Ed.), *The social influence process* (pp. 346–418). Chicago: AldineAtherton.

Tett, R. P., & Meyer, J. P. (1993). Job satisfaction, organizational commitment, turnover intention, and turnover: Path analyses based on meta-analytic findings. *Personnel Psychology, 46*(2), 259–293.

Thomas, K. W. (1970). Conflict and conflict management. In M. D. Dunnette (Ed.), *Handbook of industrial and organizational psychology.* Chicago: Rand McNally.

Thombs, D. L., Beck, K. H., & Mahoney, C. A. (1993). Effects of social context and gender on drinking patterns of young adults. *Journal of Counseling Psychology, 40*(1), 115–119.

Thompson, K. M. (1990). Refacing inmates: A critical appraisal of plastic surgery programs in prison. *Criminal Justice and Behavior, 17*(4), 448–466.

Thompson, R. W. (1997, November). Internet, e-mail seen as enhancing productivity. *HR News,* p. 7.

Thornburg, L. (1993). When violence hits business. *HR Magazine, 38*(7), 40–45.

Thornburg, L. (1994). Change comes slowly. *HR Magazine, 39*(2), 46–49.

Tierney, P. (1998). *The role of the Pygmalion effect in employee creativity.* Poster presented at the annual meeting of the Society for Industrial and Organizational Psychology, Dallas, TX.

Timm, P. (1992). *51 ways to save your job.* Hawthorne, NJ: Career Press.

Tonowksi, R. F. (1993, September). Assessing a violent situation: Violence and personnel assessment practices in the U.S. Postal Service. *IPMA News,* pp. 3–5.

Torgersen, S. (1983). Genetic factors in anxiety disorders. *Archives of General Psychiatry, 40,* 1085–1089.

Toth, C. (1993). Effect of resume format on applicant selection for a job interview. *Applied H.R.M. Research, 4*(2), 115–125.

Townsend, A. M., DeMarie, S. M., & Hendrickson, A. R. (1996). Are you ready for virtual teams? *HR Magazine, 41*(9), 123–126.

Trenn, K. (1993, December). Third of survey respondents report violent episodes. *HR News,* pp. 2–4.

Tubbs, M. E. (1986). Goal setting: A meta-analytic examination of the empirical evidence. *Journal of Applied Psychology, 71,* 474–483.

Tucker, J. (1993). Everyday forms of employee resistance. *Sociological Forum, 8*(1), 25–45.

Turner, J. T. (1994). *Violence in the workplace: First line of defense.* Paper presented at the 23rd annual meeting of the Society of Police and Criminal Psychology, Madison, WI.

Tyler, K. (1997). Dependability can be a rewarding experience. *HR MAGAZINE, 42*(12), 57–61.

Ury, W. (1993). *Getting past no.* New York: Bantam Books.

Valacich, J. S., Dennis, A. R., & Connolly, T. (1994). Idea generation in computer-based groups: A new ending to an old story. *Organizational Behavior and Human Decision Processes, 57*(3), 448–467.

Valacich, J. S., Dennis, A. R., & Nunamaker, J. F. (1992). Group size and anonymity effects on computer-mediated idea generation. *Small Group Research, 23*(1), 49–73.

Valacich, J. S., Parantia, D., George, J. F., & Nunamaker, J. F. (1993). Communication concurrency and the new media: A new dimension for media richness. *Communication Research, 20*(2), 249–276.

Vander Velden, L. (1971). *Relationships among member, team, and situational variables and basketball team success.* Unpublished doctoral dissertation, University of Wisconsin, Madison.

Van Slyke, E. J. (1996). Busting the bureaucracy. *HR Focus, 73*(7), 15–16.

Van Slyke, E. J. (1997). Facilitating productive conflict. *HR Focus, 74*(4), 17.

Varma, A., DeNisi, A. S., & Peters, L. H. (1996). Interpersonal affect and performance appraisal: A field study. *Personnel Psychology, 49*(2), 341–360.

Vecchio, R. P., Griffeth, R. W., & Hom, P. W. (1986). The predictive utility of the vertical dyad linkage approach. *Journal of Social Psychology, 126*(5), 617–625.

Viswesvaran, C., Ones, D. S., & Schmidt, F. L. (1996). Comparative analysis of the reliability of job performance ratings. *Journal of Applied Psychology, 81*(5), 557–574.

Vodanovich, S. J., & Seib, H. M. (1997). Relationship between time structure and procrastination. *Psychological Reports, 80,* 211–215.

Volker, K. D. (1993). *Obesity and perceived interview performance.* Unpublished master's thesis, Radford University, Radford, VA.

Vroom, V., & Yetton, P. W. (1973). *Leadership and decision making.* Pittsburgh, PA: University of Pittsburgh Press.

Vroom, V. H. (1964). *Work and motivation.* New York: John Wiley.

Waddell, J. R. (1996). You'll never believe what I heard. *Supervision, 57*(8), 18–20.

Wagley, C. & Harris, M. (1958) *Minorities in the new world: Six case studies.* New York: Columbia University Press.

Wagner, J. A. (1994). Participation effects on performance and satisfaction: A reconsideration of research evidence. *Academy of Management Review, 19*(2), 312–330.

Wahba, M. A., & Bridwell, L. T. (1976). Maslow reconsidered: A review of research on the need of hierarchy theory. *Organizational Behavior and Human Performance, 15*, 212–240.

Wakabayashi, M., & Graen, G. B. (1984). The Japanese career progress study: A seven-year follow-up. *Journal of Applied Psychology, 69*, 603–614.

Waldman, D. A., & Avolio, B. J. (1986). A meta-analysis of age differences in job performance. *Journal of Applied Psychology, 71*, 33–38.

Walker, A. G. (1997). *Upward feedback: Incremental improvement in managers' performance over five years.* Poster presented at the 12th annual conference of the Society for Industrial and Organizational Psychology, St. Louis, MO.

Walling, A. D. (1997). Iron supplementation and cognitive performance. *American Family Physician, 55*(3), 941–942.

Walster, E., Aronson, E., Abrahams, D., & Rottman, L. (1966). On increasing the persuasiveness of a low prestige communicator. *Journal of Experimental Social Psychology, 2*, 325–342.

Walton, E. (1961). How efficient is the grapevine? *Personnel, 28*, 45–49.

Wanous, J. P., Poland, T. D., Premack, S. L., & Davis, K. S. (1992). The effects of met expectations on newcomer attitudes and behavior: A review and meta-analysis. *Journal of Applied Psychology, 77*(3), 288–297.

Wanous, J. P., & Zwany, A. (1977). A cross-sectional test of need hierarchy theory. *Organizational Behavior and Human Performance, 18*, 78–97.

Watson, C. (1994). Gender differences in negotiating behavior and outcomes: Fact or artifact? In A. Taylor & J. B. Miller (Eds.), *Conflict and gender.* Cresskill, NJ: Hampton Press.

Waung, M., & Highhouse, S. (1997). *Feedback inflation: Empathic buffering or fear of conflict?* Poster presented at the 12th annual conference of the Society for Industrial and Organizational Psychology, St. Louis, MO.

Weber, Y. (1996). Corporate cultural fit and performance in mergers and acquisitions. *Human Relations, 49*(9), 1181–1203.

Weiss, H. M., Dawis, R. V., England, G. W., & Lofquist, L. H. (1967). *Manual for the Minnesota Satisfaction Questionnaire.* Minneapolis: University of Minnesota, Industrial Relations Center.

Weiss, H. M., & Shaw, J. B. (1979). Social influences on judgments about tasks. *Organizational Behavior and Human Performance, 24*, 126–140.

Welsh, D. H., Bernstein, D. J., & Luthans, F. (1992). Application of the Premack Principle of reinforcement to the quality performance of service employees. *Journal of Organizational Behavior Management, 13*(1), 9–32.

Werner, J. M., & Bolino, M. C. (1997). Explaining U.S. Courts of Appeals decisions involving performance appraisal: Accuracy, fairness, and validation. *Personnel Psychology, 50*(1), 1–24.

Wexley, K. N., Sanders, R. E., & Yukl, G. A. (1973). Training interviewers to eliminate contrast effects in employment interviews. *Journal of Applied Psychology, 57*, 233–236.

Whetstone, T. S. (1994). Subordinates evaluate supervisory and administrative performance. *Police Chief, 61*(6), 57–62.

Whyte, W. F. (1956). Problems of industrial sociology. *Social Problems, 4*, 148–160.

Widom, C. S. (1989). Does violence beget violence? A critical examination of the literature. *Psychological Bulletin, 106*(1), 3–28.

Wild, C., Horney, N., & Koonce, R. (1996). Cascading communications creates momentum for change. *HR Magazine, 41*(12), 94–100.

Williams, K. D., Bourgeois, M. J., & Croyle, R. T. (1993). The effects of stealing thunder in criminal and civil trials. *Law and Human Behavior, 17*(6), 597–609.

Williams, K. D., Harkins, S., & Latane, B. (1981). Identifiability as a deterrent to social loafing: Two cheering experiments. *Journal of Personality and Social Psychology, 40*, 303–311.

Williamson, A. M., Gower, C. G. I., & Clarke, B. C. (1994). Changing the hours of shift work: A comparison of 8- and 12-hour shift rosters in a group of computer operators. *Ergonomics, 37*(2), 287–298.

Wilson, E. J., & Sherrell, D. L. (1993). Source effects in communication and persuasion research: A meta-analysis of effect size. *Journal of the Academy of Marketing Science, 21*(2), 101–112.

Winter, D. G. (1988). What makes Jesse run? *Psychology Today, 22*(6), 20–24.

Wisdom, B., & Patzig, D. (1987). Does your organization have the right climate for merit? *Public Personnel Management, 16*, 127–133.

Wisinski, J. (1993). What to do about conflicts? *Supervisory Management, 40*(3), 11.

Witt, L. A. (1996). *Listen up! Your upward feedback results are speaking.* Poster presented at the 11th annual conference of the Society for Industrial and Organizational Psychology, San Diego, CA.

Wolkinson, B. W., & Block, R. N. (1996). *Employment law.* Cambridge, MA: Blackwell Publishers.

Wood, R. F., Mento, A. J., & Locke, E. A. (1987). Task complexity as a moderator of goal effects: A meta-analysis. *Journal of Applied Psychology, 72*, 416–425.

Wooten, W. (1993). Using knowledge, skill and ability (KSA) data to identify career pathing opportunities: An application of job analysis to internal manpower planning. *Public Personnel Management, 22*(4), 551–563.

Young, T. J., & French, L. A. (1998). Body mass indexes and historical ratings of U.S. Presidents. *Perceptual and Motor Skills, 86*(3), 965–966.

Yu, J., & Murphy, K. (1993) Modesty bias in self-ratings or performance: A test of the cultural relating hypothesis. *Personnel Psychology, 46*(2), 357–363.

Yukl, G. A. (1982, April). *Innovations in research on leader behavior.* Paper presented at the annual meeting of the Eastern Academy of Management, Baltimore, MD.

Yukl, G. A. (1989). *Leadership in organizations.* Englewood Cliffs, NJ: Prentice Hall.

Yukl, G. A. (1994). *Leadership in organizations.* (3rd ed.) Englewood Cliffs, NJ: Prentice Hall.

Zaccaro, S. J., Foti, R. J., & Kenny, D. A. (1991). Self-monitoring and trait-based variance in leadership: An investigation of leader flexibility across multiple group situations. *Journal of Applied Psychology, 76*(2), 308–315.

Zajonc, R. B. (1965). Social facilitation. *Science, 149,* 269–274.

Zajonc, R. B. (1980). Compressence. In P. B. Paulus (Ed.), *Psychology of group influence.* Hillsdale, NJ: Lawrence Erlbaum.

Zajonc, R. B., Heingartner, A., & Herman, E. M. (1969). Social enhancement and impairment of performance in the cockroach. *Journal of Personality and Social Psychology, 13,* 83–92.

Zander, A. (1982). *Making groups effective.* San Francisco: Jossey-Bass.

Zaremba, A. (1988). Working with the organizational grapevine. *Personnel Journal, 67*(6), 38–42.

Zemke, R. (1993). Rethinking the rush to team-up. *Training, 30*(11), 55–61.

Zhou, J. (1998). Feedback valence, feedback style, task autonomy, and achievement orientation: Interactive effects on creative performance. *Journal of Applied Psychology, 83*(2), 261–276.

Zunker, V. G. (1990). *Career counseling. Applied concepts of life planning* (3rd ed.) Pacific Grove, CA: Brooks/Cole.

Name Index

A

Aamodt, M. G., 6, 109, 257–258
Abraham, L. M., 337
Abrahams, D., 276
Abramis, D. J., 33
Adams, J. C., 344
Adams, J. S., 345, 382
Afza, M., 314
Ahearne, M., 257
Aiello, J. R., 262
Albrecht, S., 37, 42
Albright, M. D., 463
Aldag, R. J., 264
Alderfer, C. P., 341
Alessandra, T., 89, 91
Alexander, C. A., 6
Alexander, C. J., 257
Alexander, E. R., 287
Allen, N., 258
Allen, Woody, 280
Alliger, G. M., 302
Allport, Gordon, 12
Amabile, T, M., 372
Ambraziejus, A., 56, 58
Amick, B. C., 374
Anderson, L. R., 259
Anderson, N. H., 287
Andrews, G., 406
Andrews, I. R., 264
Anthony, T., 257
Antonioni, D., 464
Appelberg, K., 34
Armour, S., 138
Aronson, E., 276
Arthur, D., 223, 478
Arthur, J. B., 347
Arvey, R. D., 337–338
Asch, S., 441–442
Ashmore, R. D., 276
Austin, J., 374
Avary, D. W., 264
Avolio, B. J., 314, 465
Azar, B., 4

B

Back, K., 277
Badin, I. J., 371
Bailey, J. S., 374
Baker, T. E., 409
Baldwin, T. T., 337–338
Ball, G. A., 378
Ballam, D. A., 479
Balzer, W. K., 473
Banjo, M. L., 371
Barel, G. L., 178
Barker, L. L., 220
Barling, J., 347
Baron, R. A., 264
Baron, R. S., 259
Barry, S. R., 475
Barton, M., 136
Bass, B. M., 314–315
Baumgartner, J., 464
Baxter, J. S., 262
Beall, Ge Ge, 290
Beatty, R. W., 463
Beck, K. H., 262
Bedeian, A. G., 463
Beebe, T., 478
Beehr, T., 28
Bell, N. E., 337
Benjamin, A. J., 302
Benne, K. D., 261
Benson, P. G., 459
Benzinger, K., 314
Bergmann, T. J., 177
Berk, R., 38
Bernardin, H. J., 463, 475
Bernstein, A. J., 174
Bernstein, D. J., 379
Biegeleisen, J. I., 91–92
Bird, F. B., 99, 102
Bishop, J. W., 344, 417
Blades, J. J., 373
Blake, R. R., 305
Blanchard, K. H., 311
Blaun, R., 5

Block, R. N., 91
Blodgett, P. C., 227
Blommel, J. M., 262
Bloom, A. M., 58
Bluen, S. D., 347
Blumenfeld, W. S., 228
Bodenmiller, J. A., 218
Bohlander, G. W., 145
Bolino, M. C., 470
Bommer, W. H., 470
Bond, C. F., 262
Bond, G. E., 305
Bonner, D., 353
Bonner, J. J., 287
Bonoma, T. V., 178, 447
Bons, P. M., 308
Booth-Butterfield, M., 221
Borden, R. , 255
Borzi, M. G., 174
Boster, F. J., 259
Bouchard, T. J., 4, 337
Bourgeois, M. J., 447
Boyatzis, R. E., 304
Bradford, D. L., 304
Bradway, L., 418
Bramson, R., 174
Branch, S., 56, 62, 66
Brandon, M. C., 213
Brandt, D., 404–405, 418
Brannick, M. T., 350
Brass, D. J., 100
Bravo, I. M., 473–474
Brawley, L. R., 257
Brehm, J. W., 258
Brehm, S. S., 221
Brenden, N. R., 371
Brenner, M., 264
Brett, J. F., 258
Bretz, R. D., 33, 180
Brewer, E. M., 262
Bridges, W., 405
Bridwell, L. T., 341
Brinkley, G., 262
Brinkman, R., 174

Broadbent, B., 228
Brocato, R. M., 262
Brody, R., 184
Brophy, D. R., 264
Brotherton, P., 411
Brown, K. A., 376
Brown, W. F., 414
Bruce, H. J., 303
Brunk, G., 347
Bruno, J. E., 64
Bruun, S. E., 263
Bryan, D. A., 218
Bryman, A., 315
Buchanan, D. R., 276
Buchanan, L., 303
Buckley, M. R., 279
Buckley, R. W., 475
Buda, R., 475
Bullinger, M., 34
Bullock, R. J., 378
Buntzman, G. F., 171
Burger, J. M., 443
Burke, M. J., 256
Burling, T., 255
Burnham, D. H., 304
Burnham, D. H., 343
Burns, W., 347
Burtt, H., 305
Butler, F., 180
Butterfield, K. D., 100, 378
Bycio, P., 37
Byrd, Robert, 446
Byrne, J. A., 481

C

Caldwell, D. F., 304
Callender, J. C., 279
Cameron, J., 372
Campbell, K. A., 262
Campion, M. A., 346
Cannella, A. A., 463
Cardy, R. L., 476
Carey, G., 4
Carlson, R. E., 280
Carnall, C. A., 405
Carneal, D. H., 258
Carpenter, K. M., 444
Carpi, J., 30, 35, 38
Carrell, M. R., 345
Carron, A. V., 257, 259, 263
Carson, Johnny, 341, 444
Carter, J. H., 312
Carter, Jimmy, 305, 309
Cashman, J. F., 312
Castro, Fidel, 263
Cederbloom, D., 463
Chall, J. S., 228
Champoux, J. E., 338
Chao, G. T., 473
Chartrand, T., 443

Chen, A. Y., 100, 408
Chen, J. A., 475
Chen, S. C., 262
Cheng, B. S., 465
Chong, J., 12
Chou, C. P., 12
Chowdhary, J., 6
Christiansen, G., 257
Chubb, R., 38
Cialdini, R. B., 255–256, 443–444, 447
Clark, R. D., 264
Clarke, B. C., 130
Clausen, J. A., 337
Clemans, J., 36, 38
Clements, C., 371
Clemons, T. C., 303
Clinton, Bill, 135, 138, 276, 315, 445–446
Clore, G. L., 220
Cohen, A., 34
Cohen, A. R., 304
Cohen, D., 178, 195
Cohen, S., 215
Cole, E. J., 464
Coleman, F. T., 180
Connolly, P. M., 481
Connolly, T., 259
Conrad, C., 177
Conway, J. M., 464, 475
Coons, A. E., 312
Cooper, D. M., 258
Cooper, M., 312
Cooper, M. L., 33
Cooper, W. H., 473, 476
Copper, C., 256
Cordes, C. L., 32–33, 36
Cosmas, K. A., 344
Cottrell, N. B., 262
Courneya, K. S., 263
Courtis, J. K., 228
Covey, S., 57
Crace, R. K., 263
Crane, S., 89
Craver, C. B., 91
Cromwell, P. F., 264
Cron, W. L., 347
Cropanzano, R., 338, 345
Croyle, R. T., 447
Crump, C. E., 38
Crusco, A. H., 221
Cruz, M. G., 259
Csoka, L. S., 308

D

Dachler, H. P., 311
Dale, E., 228
Daley, A. J., 38
Dalton, D. R., 353
Dansereau, F., 312
Davidson, J., 28, 39

Davir, T., 371
Davis, M. G., 6
Davis, D. D., 264
Davis, K., 215
Davis, K. S., 339
Davis, T. R., 222
Davitz, J., 264
Dawis, R. V., 337, 349
Day, D. V., 312
de Castro, J. M., 262
de Jong, R. D., 309
De Vader, C. L., 302
Deci, E. L., 372, 379–380
Dedrick, E. J., 303
Degner, J., 459
Deluga, R. J., 257
DeMarie, S. M., 419
Dempcy, M. H., 30
DeNisi, A. S., 310, 473, 476
Dennis, A. R., 259
Dent, C. W., 12
Denton, D. K., 407
DePaulo, B. M., 221
Dessler, G.,, 279
Deutsch, M., 177, 186
Dickinson, A. M., 376, 380
Diehl, M., 264
Dietz, P. E., 41–42
Digh, P., 143,145
Dillard, J. P., 443
Dipboye, R L., 371
DiSalvo, V. S., 174
Dittrick, J. E., 345
Dobbins, G. H., 303, 370, 463, 465, 476
Dole, Elizabeth, 302
Dolin, D. J., 221
Donnellon, A., 177, 418–419
Donnerstein, E., 34
Donohue, J. M., 380
Dossett, D. L., 475
Dougherty, T. W., 32–33, 36, 279
Downey, D. E., 225, 308
Drexler, A. B., 422
Driskell, J. E., 257, 420
Duane, M. J., 178
Dubin, R., 338
DuBose, C., 481
Dugoni, B. L., 6
Dunnette, M. D., 345, 382
Dunning, F. E., 409
Dunphy, D., 304
Durham, C. C., 337–338

E

Eagly, A. H., 276, 306
Ebadi, Y. M., 414
Eden, D., 371
Eder, R. W., 279
Eggert, M., 91

Lofquest, L. H., 349
London, M., 464
Long, E. J., 463
Long, W. S., 303
Long, W. W., 463
Longo, L. C., 276
Lord, R. G., 302, 345, 382, 476
Lorge, I., 264
Lovelace, K., 33
Lovenheim, P., 180
Lowe, R. H., 345
Lowman, R. L., 86, 94, 101
Lulofs, R. S., 168, 184
Luthans, F., 374, 379
Lykken, D. T., 4, 337

M

Mabe, P. A., 464
Macan, T. H., 56, 64, 66
MacKenzie, R. A., 68
MacKenzie, S. B., 257, 470
Mackie, D. M., 173
Mahoney, C. A., 262
Maier, N. R. F., 264
Major, B., 221
Makhijani, M. G., 276
Malandro, L. A., 220
Manners, G. E., 259
Manstead, A. S., 262
Mantell, M., 37, 42
Manz, C. C., 310
Marchetti, M., 482
Markham, S. E., 351, 377
Marks, A., 264
Marti, M. W., 259
Martin, C., 476
Martin, G. E., 177
Martin, S., 96, 222, 227
Martocchio, J. J., 353
Maslow, A. H., 339–342, 348–349
Massey, Morris, 6, 8, 9
Masters, F. W., 6
Matheson, H., 257
Mawhinney, T. C., 378
Mayo, E., 255
McCain, John, 445
McCann, N., 39
McClelland, C. L., 346
McClelland, D. C., 304, 342–343
McEvoy, G. M., 464
McFarlin, D. B., 339
McGee, G. W., 312
McGregor, D., 305
McGue, M., 4
McKay, I. S., 409
McLeod, P. L., 259
McWhirter, B. T., 6
Meier, P., 174
Mento, A. J., 372–373
Mero, N. P., 473
Mesch, D. J., 353

Messmer, M., 227
Meyer, H. H., 464
Meyer, J. P., 336, 339
Michaels, J. W., 262
Miles, D. R., 4
Miles, E. W., 212
Miles, J. A., 263
Milford, G. E., 341
Milgram, S., 438–440
Milkovich, G. T., 459
Miller, C. W., 314
Miller, J. G., 223
Miller, S. T., 12
Mirolli, K., 344
Mischkind, L. A., 342
Mishra, J., 217
Mitchell, T. R., 310, 381
Mitchell, V. F., 341
Mitra, A., 36, 350
Mobaraki, G. R., 380
Moede, W., 263
Monahan, J. L, 12
Monroe, C., 174
Moore, C. W., 184
Moore, J. C., 382
Moore, Joe, 136
Moores, J., 130
Moran, L., 421–422
Morden, D. L., 409
Morrison, E. W., 381, 410
Moss, S. E., 303
Mossholder, K. W., 372
Motowidlo, S. J., 473, 476
Mougdill, P., 341
Moulton, D. A., 94
Mount, M. K., 459, 478
Mouton, J. S., 305
Muchnisky, P. M., 336
Mulder, M., 309
Mullen, B., 256–257, 420
Mumford, M. D., 463
Murphy, K. R., 465, 475–476
Murphy, S. T., 12
Murphy, T., 261
Murray, M., 257
Musselwhite, E., 421

N

Nagy, M. S., 350
Nanus, R., 315
Nash, L L., 98
Nathan, B., 476
Naughton, R. J., 255
Naughton, T. J., 459
Nebeker, D. M., 381
Neubauer, P. J., 36
Neufeldt, D., 257
Newsome, M., 344
Nicholls, J. R., 312
Nichols, R. G., 225
Nicholson, N, 34

Nicotera, A. M., 183
Nixon, Richard, 315
Noble, S. A., 475
Nolan, J., 258
Norris, W. R., 312
Northcraft, G., 186
Nougaim, K. E., 342
Novak, M. A., 312
Nunamaker, J. F., 212, 259
Nunn, Sam, 308
Nwachukwu, S. L., 100–101, 408

O

O'Brien, R. M., 374
Offerman, L. R., 34
Okogbaa, O. G., 374
Oldham, G. R., 346
Oldham, G. R., 347
Oliphant, V. N., 287
Olson, J. N., 264
Ones, D. S., 475
O'Reilly, C. A., 304, 345
Ornish, D., 30, 38
Overman, S., 217
Oz, S., 371

P

Packard, M., 214
Padgett, M. Y., 337–338
Parantia, D., 212
Parfitt, G., 38
Parker, P. A., 36
Parkinson, C. N., 61
Parrott, A.C., 39
Patrick, S. L., 212
Patzig, D., 377
Paul, K. B., 350
Paul, R. J., 414
Paulus, P. B., 264
Pearce, J. L., 476
Pelletier, L. G., 371
Pemack, D., 378–379
Penrod, S., 261
Peplau, L. A., 220
Pesci, Joe, 131
Peters, L. H., 473, 476
Peterson, K. S., 138
Petrick, J. A., 136
Peyronin, K., 258
Pfeffer, J., 341–342
Philbrick, K. D., 305
Pierce, W. D., 283, 372
Pillari, V., 344
Pinckert, S., 443
Pingitore, R., 6
Pinkerton, L., 382
Pinkley, R., 185
Planchy, R. J., 466
Planchy, S. J., 466
Pliner, P., 443
Plomin, R., 4

Podsakoff, P. M., 257, 470
Poe, A. C., 374
Poland, T. D., 339
Pollan, S. M., 482
Pollitt, E., 5
Pond, S. B., 348
Pool, S. W., 306
Porter, L .W., 215, 375, 380, 476
Pospisil, V., 214
Pound, R., 40
Premack, S. L., 339
Pridemore, D. R., 255
Pritchard, R. D., 345, 381, 382
Pritchett, P., 40, 410
Psenicka, C., 33
Puffer, S. M., 345
Pursell, E. D., 475

Q

Qian, Y. J., 378
Quayle, Dan, 276
Quinn, J. F., 136

R

Rabasca, L., 339
Rahim, M. A., 33, 171, 178, 314
Raine, A., 4
Rank, A. D., 310
Rasmussen, K. G., 221
Raven, B. H., 308, 314
Ray, J. J., 255
Raynes, B., 174
Reagan, Ronald W., 302, 305, 308, 315
Reilly, R. R., 464, 475
Reizenstein, R. M., 256
Rentsch, J. P., 337
Repetti, R. L., 35, 344
Reynolds, L., 41
Rhoads, C., 478
Riccobono, J. E., 374
Rice, R. E., 214, 307
Rice, R. W., 339
Rich, G. A., 470
Richardson, J. L, 12
Richardson, W. C., 102
Richardson, W. D., 99
Rick, J., 30
Rifkind, L. J., 174
Riggio, R. E., 464
Robbins, S. P., 36, 64, 98
Robers, R. W., 351
Roberts, D. S., 257
Robinson, S. L., 381
Rodin, J., 347
Rodriguez, J. I., 259
Rogers, J. G., 218
Roland, C. C., 371
Romanov, K., 34
Roosevelt, Franklin, 305
Rosen, B., 33

Rosen, D. J., 472
Rosen, S., 212
Rosenbaum, W. B., 345, 382
Rosenthal, A. R., 221
Rosenthal, G. T., 341
Rosenthal, R., 371
Ross, J., 337
Ross, R. A., 377
Ross, T. L., 377
Ross, W. R., 180, 184
Rothman, S., 4
Rothstein, M. A., 91
Rouhiainen, P., 370
Rousseau, D. M., 100
Rowe, A., 145
Rowe, J. S., 262
Rozell, D., 420
Rozen, S. C., 174
Ruback, R. B., 258
Ruddy, T. M., 421
Rushton, J. P., 135
Russell, M., 33
Ryan, R. M., 370, 372
Rynes, S. L., 459
Rytting, M., 221

S

Saari, D., 443
Saavedra, R., 463
Sabini, J., 303
Sackman, S., 408
Sahl, R. J., 213
Salancik, G., 341–342
Salas, E., 257, 420
Saldivar, Efren, 97
Sanders, G. S., 262
Sanders, R. E., 280
Sandler, L., 371
Sanzgiri, J., 100
Sawyers, R. B., 100, 408
Scandura, T. A., 312
Schachter, S., 277
Schaubroeck, J., 29
Scheimann, W., 312
Schein, E. H., 255, 408
Schleifer, L. M., 374
Schlenker, B. R., 447
Schmidlin, A. M., 221
Schmidt, F. L., 381, 475
Schmidt, S., 314
Schneiderman, B., 255
Schoenthaler, S. J., 5
Scholtes, P., 171–172
Schor, J., 61
Schrader, B. W., 464
Schriesheim, C. A., 308, 310–311
Schriesheim, J. F., 311
Schroeder, D. A., 444
Schroeder, E. P., 91
Schulz, R., 347
Schuster, F. E., 409

Schuster, J. R., 374–375, 377
Schuster, M. H., 377
Schwab, D. P., 350
Scott, K. D., 344
Scott, K. D., 351, 377, 380, 417
Scrivner, T. W., 481
Sears, D. D., 220
Sears, D. O., 138
Segal, N. L., 337
Seib, H. M., 59
Semmer, N., 34
Sessa, V. I., 168
Sessa, V. T., 258
Seta, J. J., 262
Shaffer, M. A., 352
Shalley, C. E., 261
Shaw, J. B., 344
Shea, G. P., 409
Sheets, P., 261
Sheldon, William, 6
Shen, Z., 168, 177
Shepperd, J. A., 263
Sherif, M., 132
Sherman, A., 145
Sherrell, D. L., 445
Sherriton, J., 101, 408
Shoben, E. W., 91
Simon, T. R., 12
Sims, H. P., 310
Sinclair-James, L., 177
Skaggs, B. C., 100
Skinner, B. F., 373
Slage, J. K, 41
Sloane, L. T., 255
Slocum, J. W., 347
Smith, B. V., 459
Smith, D., 97
Smith, D. E., 475
Smith, E. R., 173
Smith, M. L., 481
Smith, P. C., 349–350
Smither, J. W., 464, 475
Smither, R., 343
Snell, S., 145
Snyderman, M., 4
Sommer, R., 262
Soper, B., 341
Sparks, G. G., 132
Spink, K. S., 257
Spock, G., 287
Spring, B., 6
Srinivas, S., 476
Stadelmaier, M. F., 257
Stahl, M. J., 304, 343, 381
Stajkovic, A. D., 374
Stanten, M., 38
Staw, B. W., 337
Steel, R. P., 373
Steele, R. P., 337
Steers, R. M., 375
Steiner, D. D., 464

Subject Index

A

Aamodt Vocational Interest Survey, 87
Absenteeism, 36–37, 350–354
  decision-making theory, 350, 354
  discipline, 351
  individual differences, 353
  policy and record keeping, 351–352
  rewards for attending, 350–351
  stress, 352–353
  unique events, 353
Accommodating style, 178, 188
Accountability, 186
Achievement-oriented style, 310, 319
Action-step planning, 65–66, 71, 88
Active listening, 183, 188
Adaptability, 304
Adaptation, 405, 422
Additive tasks, 259, 265
Adverse impact, 143, 147
Affect, 476, 482
Affective evaluation, 130
Affiliation, 255, 265
Affiliation style, 309, 319
Affirmative action, 139–141, 147
Age, 136–137
Age Discrimination in Employment Act, 137, 147
Aggression, 4, 5
Agreeableness, 12
Alcohol, 12, 37
Americans with Disabilities Act, 137, 147
Analysis, 170
Anger, 12
Angry customers, 175–176
Anticipation of interaction, 277, 290
Anxiety, 309, 319
Anxiety disorders, 4
Appearance, 91–92
Arbitration, 179–180, 188
Arousal levels, 4,5
Artifacts, 223, 229
Assertiveness, 60–61, 65, 71

Assignment to groups, 256
Assimilating information, 223, 229
Assistance, 256
At Mother's Request, 438
AT&T, 86
Attendance, 467
Attitude survey, 213, 229
Attitudes, 130, 133, 147, 168
Attitudinal Listening Profile System, 225, 229
Attitudinal time-wasters, 57, 71
Attractiveness, 5–6, 276, 283, 446
  impression formation, 276
  personality, 5–6
  persuasion, 446
  resume writing, 283
Attribution, 281
Audience effects, 261, 265
Autocratic I, 413, 422
Autocratic II, 413, 422
Averaging versus adding, 287
Avis Car Rental, 438
Avoidance, 59–60, 65, 71
Avoiding style, 178, 188

B

Basking in reflected glory, 256
Bay of Pigs , 263
Behavioral time-wasters, 57–58, 71
Berserkers, 42
BFOQ, 143, 147
Bias and communication, 227
Bias in performance appraisal, 476
Big 5, 12, 14
Biological needs, 340, 354
Birth order, 8
Blamer, 175–176
Blood sugar, 5
Body language, 220–221
Body type, 6
Brain abnormalities, 4
Bulletin board, 214, 229
Burnout, 36, 43
Business etiquette, 93–94

C

California Personality Inventory, 13
Calm questioning technique, 146
Cardinal traits, 13, 14
Career planning, 86–90, 103
Census, 135
Central traits, 12, 14
Central-tendency error, 473, 482
Change, 404–411
  coping with change, 410–411
  employee acceptance of change, 405–406
  implementing change, 407–408
  organizational culture, 408–410
  sacred cow hunts, 404–405
Change agents, 406, 422
Change analysts, 406, 422
Change resisters, 406, 422
Charlie's Angels, 280
Child, 175–176
Childhood trauma, 8
Chronic self-esteem, 370, 383
Chronological resume, 283–284
Chrysler, 303
Civil Rights Act, 135, 147
Classical conditioning, 277–278, 290
Clinical Assessment Questionnaire, 13
Closure questions, 184
Coaching approach to leadership, 311
Coaction, 261–262, 265
Code of ethics, 100–103
Coercive power, 314, 319
Coercive style, 309, 319
Cognitive ability (also see intelligence),
  communication, 227
  decision-making, 12
  leadership, 306–307
Cognitive evaluation, 130
Cognitive reasoning, 12
Cohen Conflict Response Inventory, 178, 195–197
Cold conflict, 168, 188

Inquiring silence, 184
Instability, 309, 319
Instant gratification, 58, 71
Instrumental style, 310, 319
Instrumentality, 380–381, 384
Intelligence (*also see* cognitive
    ability), 4, 302, 304
Interacting group, 264, 265
Interdependence, 168, 418, 423
Intergroup competition, 132
Internal attribution, 281, 291
Internal customers, 176, 189
Internal locus of control, 281, 291
Internal timekeepers, 30–31, 43
Internalization, 405, 423
Interpersonal adjustment, 304
Interpersonal conflict, 172, 189
Interviews, 276–277, 280
Intimidation, 282, 291
Intranets, 215, 230
Intrinsic motivation, 372, 379–380,
    384
Introversion, 5
Isolates, 216, 230
Isolation, 258, 265

J

Job characteristics theory, 346–347,
    354
Job Choice Exercise (JCE), 304, 319
Job descriptions, 458–462, 483
    example, 460–461
    importance, 458
    parts, 458–462
Job Descriptive Index, 349, 354
Job enlargement, 346, 354
Job enrichment, 346, 354
Job in General Scale , 350, 354
Job rotation, 346, 354
Job satisfaction, 4, 335–350
    consequences, 336
    discrepancy theories, 339–343
    equity, 344–346
    individual differences, 336–339
    integration of theories, 347–349
    job characteristics, 346–347
    measuring job satisfaction,
        349–350
    social learning, 344
Job specifications, 459–460, 483
Jurisdictional ambiguity, 173, 189
Just world hypothesis, 278, 291

K

Know-it-all, 174–175, 186
Knowledge, 88–90

L

Laughter, 38
Law abiders, 134, 147

Leader Behavior Description
    Questionnaire, 306
Leader emergence, 302–303, 319
Leader match, 308, 310, 319
Leader performance, 303–315, 319
Leader position power, 307, 319
Leader-member exchange, 312, 319
Leader-member relations, 307–308,
    319
Leadership, 301–320
    decision-making, 313–314
    integration of theories, 315–317
    leader emergence, 302–303, 319
    leader performance, 303–315, 319
    needs, 304–305
    organizational climate, 308–310
    power, 314
    situational factors, 307–312
    skills, 312–318
    subordinate ability, 310–312
    task vs. person orientation,
        305–306
    traits, 304
    transformational leadership,
        314–315
    unsuccessful leadership, 306–307
Leadership Opinion Questionnaire,
    306
Leading questions, 184
Learned behavior, 132
Learning, 172
Least-Preferred Coworker Scale,
    307–308, 319
Legitimate power, 314, 319
Leisure listening, 225, 230
Leniency error, 473, 483
Lethal Weapon 4, 131
Leveling information, 223, 230
Liaisons, 213, 216, 230
Life satisfaction, 338
Listening, 225–227
Love, 12

M

Magnetic style, 308, 319
Management by walking around, 314
Managerial Grid, 305, 319
Maslow's need hierarchy, 339–341
Maybe person, 174–175, 186
McClelland's needs theory, 342–343
Mediation, 180–182, 189
Meeting cows, 404–405, 423
Meetings, 62–65, 421
Member One Credit Union, 283
Memos, 213
Mere exposure, 277, 291
Mere presence, 262, 265
Meridian Insurance, 217
Merit pay, 376–377, 384
Mesomorphs, 6,14
Middle-of-the-road leaders, 305, 319

Millon Clinical Multiaxial Inventory,
    13
Minnesota Multiphasic Personality
    Inventory, 13
Minnesota Satisfaction
    Questionnaire, 349–350, 355
Minority groups, 130–131
Misattribution, 278, 291
Moral development, 98–99, 103
Motivation, 370–384
    expectancy theory, 380–381
    feedback, 373
    goal setting, 372–373
    individual differences, 370–372
    integration of theories, 382–383
    rewards, 373–380
    self-esteem, 370–372
    social learning, 381
Motivators, 342–343, 355
Multiple channels, 224, 230
MUM effect, 212, 230
Murphy's Law, 61
My Fair Lady, 371

N

NAACP, 176
Nagy Satisfaction Scale, 350
Narcissists, 307
National origin, 136
Neanderthals, 174–175
Need for achievement, 304, 319,
    342–343, 355, 372, 384
Need for affiliation, 304, 319, 343,
    355
Need for power, 304, 320, 343, 355
Needs, 304, 339–340
Needs assessment, 409
Negative information bias, 280, 291
Negotiation, 181–182, 419
Negotiation model, 182
Neurons, 4,14
Neuroticism, 12
Neurotransmitter, 4,14
Noise, 220, 230
Nominal group, 264, 266
Nonconforming listening, 226, 230
Nonverbal cues, 220–221, 277
Norfolk-Southern Corporation, 283
Normative conformity, 440, 448
Norming stage, 421, 423
Nothing person, 174–175, 186
Nucor, 376
Nunn-Bush Shoe Company, 377

O

Obedience, 438–440
    blind obedience, 438–439
    lack of authority, 439–440
    psychological reactance, 440
Occupational Outlook Handbook, 87
Occupational stressors, 32–33